ADOLESCENT LITERACIES

Also from Kathleen A. Hinchman

Best Practices in Adolescent Literacy Instruction, Second Edition
Edited by Kathleen A. Hinchman and Heather K. Sheridan-Thomas

Tutoring Adolescent Literacy Learners
Kelly Chandler-Olcott and Kathleen A. Hinchman

ADOLESCENT LITERACIES

A Handbook of Practice-Based Research

Edited by
Kathleen A. Hinchman
Deborah A. Appleman

Foreword by Donna E. Alvermann

THE GUILFORD PRESS
New York   London

Copyright © 2017 The Guilford Press
A Division of Guilford Publications, Inc.
370 Seventh Avenue, Suite 1200, New York, NY 10001
www.guilford.com

All rights reserved

No part of this book may be reproduced, translated, stored in a retrieval system, or transmitted, in any form or by any means, electronic, mechanical, photocopying, microfilming, recording, or otherwise, without written permission from the publisher.

Printed in the United States of America

This book is printed on acid-free paper.

Last digit is print number: 9   8   7   6   5   4   3   2   1

Library of Congress Cataloging-in-Publication Data is available from the publisher.

ISBN 978-1-4625-2767-0 (hardcover)

About the Editors

Kathleen A. Hinchman, PhD, is Professor in the Reading and Language Arts Center and Associate Dean for Academic Affairs in the School of Education at Syracuse University. A former middle school teacher, Dr. Hinchman teaches literacy methods courses and seminars. She is coeditor of the *Journal of Adolescent and Adult Literacy* and has authored or edited several books, including *Best Practices in Adolescent Literacy Instruction, Second Edition*, with Heather K. Sheridan-Thomas, and *Reconceptualizing the Literacies in Adolescents' Lives, Third Edition,* with Donna E. Alvermann. Her current scholarship explores policy implications of literacy-related secondary school reform and the use of formative design to explore alternative methods of adolescent literacy instruction.

Deborah A. Appleman, PhD, is the Hollis L. Caswell Professor and Chair of Educational Studies and Director of the Summer Writing Program at Carleton College in Northfield, Minnesota. Her recent research has focused on teaching college-level language and literature courses at the Minnesota Correctional Facility–Stillwater. A former high school English teacher, Dr. Appleman is the author of *Critical Encounters in Secondary English, Third Edition* (winner of the CEE Richard Meade Award from the National Council of Teachers of English), and coauthor of *Teaching Literature to Adolescents, Third Edition,* among other books on adolescent literacy.

Contributors

Ursula S. Aldana, PhD, School of Education, University of San Francisco, San Francisco, California

Deborah A. Appleman, PhD, Educational Studies Department, Carleton College, Northfield, Minnesota

Richard Beach, PhD, Department of Curriculum and Instruction, University of Minnesota, Minneapolis, Minnesota

Mollie V. Blackburn, PhD, Department of Teaching and Learning, College of Education and Human Ecology, The Ohio State University, Columbus, Ohio

David Bloome, PhD, Department of Teaching and Learning, College of Education and Human Ecology, The Ohio State University, Columbus, Ohio

Stergios Botzakis, PhD, Department of Theory and Practice in Teacher Education, University of Tennessee, Knoxville, Knoxville, Tennessee

Eileen Buescher, MS, Department of Teaching and Learning, College of Education and Human Ecology, The Ohio State University, Columbus, Ohio

Tanja Burkhard, MA, Department of Teaching and Learning, College of Education and Human Ecology, The Ohio State University, Columbus, Ohio

Jill Castek, PhD, Department of Teaching, Learning, and Sociocultural Studies, College of Education, The University of Arizona, Tucson, Arizona

Amy Koehler Catterson, MA, Graduate School of Education, University of California, Berkeley, Berkeley, California

Samantha Caughlan, PhD, Research Images, LLC, Lansing, Michigan

Kelly Chandler-Olcott, EdD, Reading and Language Arts Center, School of Education, Syracuse University, Syracuse, New York

Catherine Compton-Lilly, PhD, Department of Curriculum and Instruction, University of Wisconsin–Madison, Madison, Wisconsin

Michelle Duffy, PhD, School of Education, Virginia Commonwealth University, Richmond, Virginia

Zhihui Fang, PhD, School of Teaching and Learning, University of Florida, Gainesville, Florida

Bob Fecho, PhD, Teachers College, Columbia University, New York, New York

Jill Fitzgerald, PhD, School of Education, University of North Carolina at Chapel Hill, Chapel Hill, North Carolina

Sharon Fransen, MS, College of Education, Temple University, Philadelphia, Pennsylvania

Antero Garcia, PhD, Department of English, Colorado State University, Fort Collins, Colorado

Carolyn Giroux, MA, School of Education, University of Michigan, Ann Arbor, Michigan

Brent Goff, MS, Department of Teaching and Learning, College of Education and Human Ecology, The Ohio State University, Columbus, Ohio

Steve Graham, EdD, Mary Lou Fulton Teachers College, Arizona State University, Tempe, Arizona

Michael F. Graves, PhD, Department of Curriculum and Instruction (Emeritus), University of Minnesota, Minneapolis, Minnesota

Cynthia Greenleaf, PhD, WestEd, Oakland, California

Seung Yon Ha, MS, Department of Teaching and Learning, College of Education and Human Ecology, The Ohio State University, Columbus, Ohio

Marcelle Haddix, PhD, Reading and Language Arts Center, School of Education, Syracuse University, Syracuse, New York

Jim Harmon, MEd, Education Consultant, Lakewood, Ohio

Kathleen A. Hinchman, PhD, Reading and Language Arts Center, School of Education, Syracuse University, Syracuse, New York

Alan Hirvela, MS, Department of Teaching and Learning, College of Education and Human Ecology, The Ohio State University, Columbus, Ohio

Gay Ivey, PhD, Department of Teacher Education, University of Wisconsin–Madison, Madison, Wisconsin

Robert T. Jiménez, PhD, Department of Teaching and Learning, Vanderbilt University, Nashville, Tennessee

Mary Juzwik, PhD, Department of Teacher Education, Michigan State University, East Lansing, Michigan

Amir Kalan, MS, Department of Curriculum, Teaching and Learning, Ontario Institute for Studies in Education, University of Toronto, Toronto, Ontario, Canada

Christopher Keyes, PhD, Department of Teacher Education, Shippensburg University, Shippensburg, Pennsylvania

Min-Young Kim, MS, Department of Teaching and Learning, College of Education and Human Ecology, The Ohio State University, Columbus, Ohio

Valerie Kinloch, PhD, Department of Teaching and Learning, College of Education and Human Ecology, The Ohio State University, Columbus, Ohio

Steven J. Landry, MEd, Department of Language and Literacy Education, University of Georgia, Athens, Georgia

Tzu-Jung Lin, MS, Department of Teaching and Learning, College of Education and Human Ecology, The Ohio State University, Columbus, Ohio

David E. Low, PhD, Department of Literacy, Bilingual, and Special Education, California State University, Fresno, Fresno, California

Kati Macaluso, MEd, Alliance for Catholic Education, University of Notre Dame, Notre Dame, Indiana

Mike Macaluso, MEd, Alliance for Catholic Education, University of Notre Dame, Notre Dame, Indiana

Danny C. Martinez, PhD, School of Education, University of California, Davis, Davis, California

Cori McKenzie, MA, Department of Teacher Education, Michigan State University, East Lansing, Michigan

Elizabeth Birr Moje, PhD, School of Education, University of Michigan, Ann Arbor, Michigan

Nick Muehling, MA, School of Education, University of Michigan, Ann Arbor, Michigan

George E. Newell, PhD, Department of Teaching and Learning, College of Education and Human Ecology, The Ohio State University, Columbus, Ohio

David G. O'Brien, PhD, Department of Curriculum and Instruction, University of Minnesota, Minneapolis, Minnesota

Lisa Ortmann, PhD, Department of Curriculum and Instruction, Western Illinois University, Macomb, Illinois

P. David Pearson, PhD, Graduate School of Education, University of California, Berkeley, Berkeley, California

Carlotta Penn, MA, Department of Teaching and Learning, College of Education and Human Ecology, The Ohio State University, Columbus, Ohio

Natasha Perez, MA, Department of Teacher Education, Michigan State University, East Lansing, Michigan

Detra Price-Dennis, PhD, Department of Curriculum and Teaching, Teachers College, Columbia University, New York, New York

Kelly Puzio, PhD, Department of Teaching and Learning, Washington State University, Pullman, Washington

Joanna M. Robertson, PhD, Department of Education, Old Dominion University, Norfolk, Virginia

Amy Rouse, PhD, Department of Teaching and Learning, Southern Methodist University, Dallas, Texas

SangHee Ryu, MS, Department of Teaching and Learning, College of Education and Human Ecology, The Ohio State University, Columbus, Ohio

Rachelle Savitz, MS, Department of Theory and Practice in Teacher Education, University of Tennessee, Knoxville, Knoxville, Tennessee

Ryan Schey, MEd, Department of Teaching and Learning, College of Education and Human Ecology, The Ohio State University, Columbus, Ohio

John Scott, MA, Berkeley Center for New Media, University of California, Berkeley, Berkeley, California

Robert Simon, PhD, Department of Curriculum, Teaching and Learning, Ontario Institute for Studies in Education, University of Toronto, Toronto, Ontario, Canada

Peter Smagorinsky, PhD, Department of Language and Literacy Education, University of Georgia, Athens, Georgia

Amanda Smith, BA, Department of Teacher Education, Michigan State University, East Lansing, Michigan

Michael W. Smith, PhD, College of Education, Temple University, Philadelphia, Pennsylvania

Laurel Taylor, MEd, T. C. Williams High School, Alexandria City Public Schools, Alexandria, Virginia

Sheila W. Valencia, PhD, College of Education, University of Washington, Seattle, Washington

Jennifer Lynn VanDerHeide, PhD, Department of Teacher Education, Michigan State University, East Lansing, Michigan

Larkin Weyand, MFA, Department of Teaching and Learning, College of Education and Human Ecology, The Ohio State University, Columbus, Ohio

Jennifer J. Whitley, MAT, Department of Language and Literacy Education, University of Georgia, Athens, Georgia

Jeffrey D. Wilhelm, PhD, Department of English, Boise State University, Boise, Idaho

Kelly Wissman, PhD, School of Education, University at Albany, State University of New York, Albany, New York

Kristien Zenkov, PhD, College of Education and Human Development, George Mason University, Fairfax, Virginia

Foreword

Sometimes a book makes its debut at the most auspicious moment. In this instance, it's *Adolescent Literacies: A Handbook of Practice-Based Research*. Not a day too soon, in my view. With debates gathering momentum once again around the future of teacher education—often without adequate representation from the target audience—a volume such as this one assumes added significance, if for no other reason than its unique approach to putting research and practice in touch with each other.

The phrase "organically produced" comes to mind when I think of practice-based research. For if, by chance or design, the living matter of classrooms that animates most literacy research produces new insights for classroom teachers, then the inquiry process has come full circle. A compendium such as this one readily suggests that practice-based research is comparable to a nonlinear system of moving parts—organs, if you will.

In addition to benefiting from the editors' superb accomplishments in orchestrating a volume in which the voices of teachers, learners, and researchers mingle, readers are treated to major updates on numerous and multifaceted issues that encompass adolescent literacy. For instance, the chapter authors confidently present accessible research findings that address the concerns of literacy educators responsible for college and university graduate-level classes, professional growth workshops and seminars, policy roundtables (including school boards and legislative colloquia), broadcast news media, and the ever-growing community of web and cable commentators.

Even undergraduates at various stages in their certification or licensure program stand to benefit from interacting with the content presented here, provided their instructors use appropriate scaffolding and draw attention to the implications section for each chapter. This high praise is not to imply that *Adolescent Literacies: A Handbook of Practice-Based Research* is easy reading. It's not. But the *Handbook*'s approach to practice-based research provides a fairly firm footing for individuals in their preprofessional years.

Whatever one's entry level, the *Handbook* is likely to appeal most to readers who can think critically, and for themselves. I say this because the chapter authors are unrelenting in their efforts to demonstrate how literacies matter in studies of youth identity and young people's literacy practices in formal and informal learning contexts, especially in relation to the texts they choose and the pedagogical implications that ensue. Sometimes a chapter's findings may support, but at other times ruffle or challenge, what readers bring to this text. This is as it should be. When we find ourselves grappling with the unknown or unexpected, this is likely a time when we're experiencing a high in professional learning.

And just when we think we've figured out the ideologies and practices driving the editors and authors of this book, we encounter a chapter that convinces us otherwise. For me, as a first-time reader of *Adolescent Literacies: A Handbook of Practice-Based Research,* those encounters were the most meaningful and memorable. They were also sobering in that I learned the value of holding certain predispositions and biases at bay until the outcomes were revealed. Surprises aside, it was the reflecting I did that proved most helpful in the end. For when I stepped back and let a chapter's findings sink in, it was then that I realized just how much the field of literacy education has changed since I first tested the waters more than three decades ago.

As a field, we tend to conduct our research with passion, especially when we're focused on practice-based research—something that is organic to most of us in literacy education. Be it inquiry couched in one theory or another, or in mixed methods, quantitative, qualitative, or a hybrid methodology, we ask questions in search of answers that hold promise for addressing any number of the most pressing issues in our field. But it's a busy world in which we live—one that I characterize as filled with potential connectors and connections that all too often go unexplored. Or at least not as fully explored as I would like or think possible. For instance, I wonder how far the ideas that engaged me in *Adolescent Literacies: A Handbook of Practice-Based Research* will travel. Is there an action plan for moving practice-based research and policy ever closer in contact with what young people value and find useful about their own literacies? If so, who is responsible for shouldering that responsibility and with what leadership skills in hand? If not— and here I find my dogged optimism pushing back from even asking the question—what are we to make of the long hours, hard work, and prized insights to be gained from practice-based research?

Any initiative as large and comprehensive as the *Handbook* has proven to be is worth touting far and wide. I agreed to write the Foreword because I was convinced the people involved would have something to say that I could wrap my head around. They did, and within chapters of reasonable word length and structure. Organic to the core, *Adolescent Literacies: A Handbook of Practice-Based Research* is here for taking up, wondering about, coming to grips with, and implementing—each in our own way.

Onward.

DONNA E. ALVERMANN, PhD
University of Georgia

Introduction

The State of Practice-Based Research in Adolescent Literacies

KATHLEEN A. HINCHMAN and DEBORAH A. APPLEMAN

Let's face it. Literacy research handbooks like this one all too often gather dust in academic libraries or provide resume fodder for chapter authors. The literature reviews they include can seem precious when they represent only some ideas for helping kids develop literacy, skewed to particular perspectives rather than the wide-ranging practical needs that we witness in our schools and communities. When we, Kathy and Deborah, approached one another about compiling this text, we discussed the need for a more comprehensive approach. We also talked about how we have learned our most important lessons about what to do from our work with adolescents engaging in literacy practices in and out of school, and from teachers and researchers who work with them in these contexts. We were motivated to gather into a single source insights from a wide range of well-respected literacy researchers who do this kind of work.

The purpose of *Adolescent Literacies: A Handbook of Practice-Based Research* is to provide a compendium of useful, practice-based research about adolescent literacies. Its chapters review inquiry that delineates the literacy accomplishments of adolescents, as well as their challenges. Its authors synthesize research that is situated in a variety of settings, texts, and literacy tasks. They use their findings to argue for instruction and professional development that acknowledge the expertise of youth to enhance their reading, viewing, and composing, and, as a result, the opportunities that are available to them.

BACKGROUND

We are former secondary school literacy teachers who locate ourselves as practice-based researchers and teacher educators. Our work is generated from interactions with adolescents in and outside school, often designed, shaped, and implemented alongside full-time secondary school educators. Grounding our research in practice yields the kinds of insights we find most engaging and significant. Facilitating adolescents' literacy development represents, after all, a careful balance of explicit literacy instruction and situated literacy practice. This means offering ideas to enhance literacy practice that respect youth, and that youth, in turn, see as relevant and useful for addressing both their daily needs and aspirations. Such instruction means understanding situated practice, an understanding that is derived from research that grows from practice.

Why practice-based research? This term has been prevalent in medical research for quite some time. In medicine, practice-based research often occurs in networks that test laboratory applications in day-to-day medical practice in concert with the work of laboratory scientists. Interestingly, even though practice-based medical research generates worries that practitioners and patients might alter behaviors when they know they are part of research projects, studies suggest that such bias does not necessarily occur, due at least in part to the collaborative nature of the work (Beasley, 2000; Eraut, 2004; Fernald, Coombs, DeAlleaume, West, & Parnes, 2012).

Educational research has been dominated by the idea that theory should drive research, and research should drive practice. In this spirit, the What Works Clearinghouse (*ies.ed.gov/ncee/wwc*), sponsored by the U.S. Department of Education, is among the organizations that gauge the quality and therefore the significance of research designs, populations, and methods to discern instructional approaches with maximum applications. We are among those who advocate attending to these instructional practices.

Yet we and other literacy researchers have long understood that the relationships among theory, research, and practice are more complex than linearly causal. We recognize that effective use of any literacy practice or instructional approach involves situating them in specific contexts that vary from conditions of the original research (Brandt & Clinton, 2002). Scholars with understanding of these complexities have most recently developed approaches to participatory action and teacher research (Cochran-Smith & Lytle, 1990; Goswami & Stillman, 1987); qualitative research into sociolinguistic and sociocultural aspects of literacies, identities, and classroom interactions (e.g., Heath, 1983; Street, 1984); critical analyses of social constructions circulating among literacies, identities, and classroom interactions (e.g., Cammarota & Fine, 2008; Freire, 1970; Haddix, 2015); and single-subject and formative design experiments exploring key features of best-practice implementation (e.g., Duke & Mallette, 2011; Reinking & Bradley, 2008).

Such practice-based research is inquiry that explores how individuals engage in literacy practices and instruction in particular contexts. A relatively new term for educational research, it embraces a well-accepted set of premises: Practice-based research values such situation-dependent aspects of literacy enactments as identities, purposes, actions, and discourses in relation to one another. Like our medical research colleagues, those who operate from this perspective value situating research in the material and social reality of individuals' day-to-day lives. This research is conducted with the realization that no other study of literacies or literacy instruction can be applied to any specific context, because contextual features cannot ever perfectly align. In some cases, the particulars of a specific situation or context do not align at all, such as when research about first-grade phonemic awareness instruction is applied to seventh graders, when research on comprehension for seventh graders who struggle in this area is applied to instruction for all seventh graders, or when research on fifth-grade composition instruction is applied to 12th graders.

To state the obvious, when research is inappropriately applied, it does not work, and practitioners and adolescents make that abundantly clear. Unfortunately, researchers have not always listened to their concerns. Increasingly, however, research across methodological paradigms is grounded in the acknowledgment that adolescents are authors of their own literacy narratives, and experienced practitioners are often the most expert when it comes to supporting and expanding those narratives. Teachers, adolescents, and their families generate counternarratives about literacy that refute conventional wisdom, reflecting instead lived experience of today's enormous global demographic shifts. Researchers who were once privileged as the purveyors of new knowledge now seek to collaborate with those who possess this local knowledge as they construct new knowledge and new insights. In other words, important new understandings about literacy and literacy instruction are as likely to be generated in classrooms, extracurricular programs, homes, and social media as in university laboratories.

We share the urgency that school reformers feel about the many structural impediments to adolescent literacy, and we agree with many of their critiques of current school practices. We share their commitment to improve the literacy opportunities of all students. Where we diverge from some is our belief that a single, flat test score cannot represent all that young people know and can do. We worry about the effect that the increased emphasis on standardization of curriculum, instruction, and method will have on an increasingly diverse adolescent population. We fear that blanket endorsement and narrow, assessment-driven readings of the Common Core State Standards will not serve adolescents well. We believe that what is needed are more complex ways to respect and enhance the literacies students bring with them to school, in ways that honor and build from their knowledges, without constructing them as deficient. We privilege positive pedagogies and productive classroom practices to help students add to their literacies and opportunities.

Thus, practice-based research, as we use the term here, is any qualitative, quantitative, interpretive, or mixed-method research that is situated in adolescents' in-school or out-of-school, personal, civic, or academic literacy practices. It includes researching in collaboration with adolescents to better understand their literacy practices, as well as with communities of teachers to test instructional ideas in teacher–researcher collaborations and formative design studies. It involves researching our own teaching practices, too, in classrooms and in out-of-school contexts as well.

THE PURPOSE OF THIS VOLUME

We realized that there was no compilation of practice-based research as we have just defined it, that is, work with an array of designs situated in the day-to-day contexts of adolescents' lives. We decided to develop a volume that would do just that—a volume to review and provide examples of research that share what practice-based research has shown about how literacies are situated in adolescents' evolving identities, about the contexts within which adolescents locate the literacies in their lives, about the multiple texts of literacies, and about what we have come to identify as effective classroom literacy instructional practices. Our authors are well respected in the field of literacy research for work that explores these important ideas—sometimes by collaborating in classrooms, sometimes by coteaching, and sometimes by working with adolescents both in and out of school.

For far too long, our research has too narrowly defined adolescent literacy as school-sponsored, school-located performances of traditional reading and writing tasks designed by classroom teachers to fulfill specific curricular objectives. Often, these acts of literacy are judged and measured by decontextualized standardized tests. With the scholars whose work we present here, we believe that adolescents perform literacy in a wide variety of contexts, in dramatically varying modes, for multiple purposes, and with different audiences in mind.

In addition to changes in focus, epistemology, and methodology, this *Handbook* also considers the effects of shifting educational policy on literacy instruction. Recent policy reforms have meant that much of our knowledge about adolescent literacy has been overlooked in the flurry of policy development and implementation. These initiatives often require frequent measurement of a narrow band of specific literacy skills thought to be needed for college and career readiness. Yet little about these reforms addresses what research tells us about adolescents' interests, identities, and skills, or about the situated nature of literacy. In response, researchers, teachers, and adolescents have been collaborating to generate new knowledge that integrates what we know from extensive existing research to address continuously evolving standards.

The suite of practice-based research in this text is meant to be useful to youth, teachers, and others who want to understand how classrooms can work, if they are constructed in a way that begins with the reality of classroom lives. Together, the chapters in this text contribute to changing the language of reform to the language of practice. We shift focus from testing and remediation to an emphasis on what actually happens in classrooms. This research then loops through classroom practice and back into research in a dynamic and nonhierarchical exploration.

By offering such a varied array of performances, we hope to help deepen our collective understanding of all that constitutes practice-based research on adolescent literacies. We hope that this deepened, more nuanced, and complicated conceptualization of adolescent literacy will help us resist, for the sake of adolescents and their teachers, today's ever-increasing emphasis on standardization, both in terms of instruction and assessment.

CURRENT THEMES IN RESEARCH ON ADOLESCENT LITERACIES

The chapters in this volume represent some of the most current and important work on practice-based research on adolescent literacy. In addition to the importance and implications of each individual study, the studies also collectively herald the current state of practice-based research in adolescent literacy. Through these considerations of contemporary research studies, we have been able to identify some major important trends, trends that not only reflect current best practice in practice-based literacy research but also point to future directions.

Although the chapters in this volume vary considerably in content, context, and methodology, there are several themes that reflect current research in adolescent literacies, themes that these chapters both underscore and strengthen. First, there has been a paradigm shift in the way expertise is located in the field. In the past, the relationship between theory and practice assumed a vertical, hierarchical structure, one that presupposed that the experts are the university researchers, who "deliver" knowledge to classroom practitioners. In recent years, our field has shifted to a more horizontal structure, one in which researchers and classroom-based practitioners are equal partners as they co-construct new insights about adolescent literacies based on joint inquiry.

In addition to a shift in structure, our gaze has shifted, too, from the often confining contexts of secondary classrooms to a dazzling variety of spaces in which adolescent literacies, broadly construed, may be observed. These spaces, where adolescents are when they are not with us, include neighborhood hangouts, community centers, after-school gatherings, cafés, and other social spaces. We have come to realize (and shame on us for taking so long) that often the most interesting literacy performances are those that occur out of school.

In addition to the acknowledgment of out-of-school literacies, another current theme to emerge from this spate of research is the multimodal nature of literacy that adolescents use to communicate in today's society. In order to capture adolescent literacies fully, we need to be mindful of all these platforms. These include social media, such as Facebook and Twitter, smartphones and other personal devices, and digital recording platforms, such as Snapchat and Vine.

In many ways, the state of adolescent literacy research reflects the state of the contemporary adolescent landscape. The work in this volume reflects the changing nature of adolescence itself. These changes are significantly marked by changes in demographics, changes in the kinds of schools adolescents attend, changes in the kinds of platforms available for adolescents to perform literacy, even changes in how contemporary society both defines and regards adolescence itself.

One significant trend that characterizes most of the fine work in this volume is definitionally central to practice-based research. This is the changing relationship between the individual researched and the researcher. As we have already mentioned, researchers have deliberately shifted their relationship and stance to those who are at the heart of the research. The former hierarchical vertical structures have been dismantled in favor of more democratic horizontal structures. For example, classroom teachers who were once the object of study are now coinvestigators (e.g., Kristien Zenkov, Bob Fecho, Rob Simon, and Amir Kalan). In addition to the classroom practitioners, adolescents themselves are frequently coparticipants in the research (e.g., Valerie Kinloch and Kelly K. Wissman). This shift in perspective is not merely a methodological one; it is a fundamental shift in the way research, both classroom and university based, regards the centrality of adolescents in their own literacy learning.

Another important theme that springs from many of the studies is the emphasis on the ways in which literacy helps adolescents discover and perform identity. This issue of adolescent identity construction transcends and, in fact, replaces the mere consideration of skills acquisition. Several of the studies explore the ways in which adolescent literacy performances help adolescents shape and in some cases transform their evolving identities, both in and out of school. Those performances also contribute to our growing understanding of the complex nature of adolescence itself in the 21st century.

The subject of New Literacies is clearly a thread that redefines the current state of practice-based research. These multimodal literacies are also shaped by, and in turn shape, a consideration of the ways in which technology transforms both how adolescents perform literacy and how their teachers teach it. This focus gives rise to considerations of multimodality, as we explore the different kinds of literacies, and the multiple platforms across which students express themselves. This area of research in many ways will continue to reshape and define the state of literacy research for decades to come.

Finally, and importantly, many of the researchers featured here (e.g., Kelly Chandler-Olcott, Mollie V. Blackburn, Marcelle Haddix, Catherine Compton-Lilly, and Peter Smagorinsky) critique the ongoing standardization of schooling. They criticize the persistent efforts to standardize what adolescents do and learn in school and how their teachers approach literacy lessons. These researchers struggle with the irony that just as our field has finally begun to acknowledge the diversities and pluralities of adolescent literacy learners and their needs, literacy teachers are faced with an increasingly urgent mandate for the standardization of instruction, including the Common Core State Standards.

INTRODUCTION TO THE PARTS

In each part of this book you will find some chapters that give us an overview of the topic itself, and review relevant and recent studies. In other cases, the chapters focus primarily on an individual study, offering rich detail of a specific site of inquiry. As editors, we embrace this variety of examples of practice-based research and hope that you, the reader, find it both useful and interesting. Each chapter is an individual mosaic tile, and although the tiles may vary, together they create a vibrant and more complete picture of practice-based research.

The text offers findings from several categories of adolescent research. Part I explores adolescent identities and literacy. Part II describes contexts of adolescent literacy practices. Part III focuses on the multiple texts of adolescent literacy. Part IV outlines pedagogical approaches to support adolescent literacies. In the Foreword, Donna E. Alvermann situates our volume in today's contentious times. She notes how practice-based research underscores just how much our field has changed since she and we became literacy educators.

PART I: ADOLESCENT LITERACIES AND IDENTITIES

Our *Handbook* opens with a collection of chapters on "Adolescent Literacies and Identities." We begin the *Handbook* with this section for several reasons. With the scholars who are represented in Part I, we believe that a central thrust of contemporary work on adolescent literacies explores the complex and interrelated relationship between adolescent literacies and identity. Rather than focusing on the acquisition of a set of academic skills, the scholars here consider the ways in which literacies are defined and shaped by the nature of adolescence itself. In turn, the narratives of adolescents are under constant revision and are reshaped as new literacies are learned or adopted.

Chapter 1, "Navigating Cultures and Identities to Learn Literacies for Life: Rethinking Adolescent Literacy Teaching in a Post-Core World," by Elizabeth Birr Moje, Carolyn Giroux, and Nick Muehling, provides an insightful overview of how literacies help adolescents navigate cultures and power both in and out of school. In Chapter 2, "Youth, Popular Culture, and the Media: Examining Race, Class, Gender, Sexuality, and Social Histories," Marcelle Haddix, Antero Garcia, and Detra Price-Dennis also consider the intersection of popular culture and adolescent literacies as they explore the ways in which various frames of identity inform adolescent literacy performances. Applying one of those dimensions of identity, sexual identity, in Chapter 3, "Adolescent Literacies beyond Heterosexual Hegemony," Mollie V. Blackburn and Ryan Schey use queer theory to help us move beyond heterosexist binary frames.

Critical race theory helps frame Valerie Kinloch, Tanja Burkhard, and Carlotta Penn's powerful Chapter 4, "Beyond School: Examining the Out-of-School Literacies and Counternarratives of Adolescent Learners." Through case study and literature review, Kinloch and her colleagues offer powerful counternarratives on the lived realities of Black adolescents in and out of school. Linguistic identity and its role in shaping adolescent literacy in bilingual youth is deftly explored in Chapter 5, "Emergent Bilingual Youth in U.S. Secondary Schools," by Danny C. Martinez and Ursula S. Aldana, who offer an increasingly critical perspective on adolescent identity and literacy performance. Disability, a dimension of adolescent identity that is often ignored in literacy scholarship, is thoughtfully and thoroughly explicated by Kelly Chandler-Olcott, Michelle Duffy, and Joanna M. Robertson in Chapter 6, "What Research Says (and Doesn't Say) about Literacy for Youth with Disabilities." Finally, Catherine Compton-Lilly deepens our understanding of the role of family and community in shaping and informing adolescent identities in her insightful Chapter 7, "The Development of Literate Identities and Practices across a Decade: Families, Friends, and Schools."

PART II: LOCATING ADOLESCENT LITERACIES

The second part of the *Handbook*, "Locating Adolescent Literacies," broadens the lens of inquiry from the adolescents themselves to the multivaried contexts in which they find themselves. These chapters interrogate the dimensions of those contexts and the complex constellation of factors that adolescents navigate as they develop a wide range of multimodal literacies. These chapters insightfully explore those contexts, with some focusing on school and others focusing on the myriad out-of-school contexts in which adolescent literacies are performed.

Part II begins with a thorough overview by Mary Juzwik and her colleagues. In Chapter 8, "Constructing Literacies in Secondary English Language Arts Curriculum: Discourses, Histories, Ethics," they offer a useful perspective that deepens our understanding of where the field has been and where it is going. From this airplane view, Kristien Zenkov, Laurel Taylor, and Jim Harmon, in Chapter 9, "Diverse Youth, New Teachers, and 'Picturing' Literacy: Using Photovoice to 'Partner' Our Way to Adolescents' Perspectives on Literacy," bring us to the ground level of practice with a particular pedagogical approach, photovoice.

In the more philosophical and general Chapter 10, "The Power of Fostering Pleasure in Reading," Michael W. Smith, Jeffrey D. Wilhelm, and Sharon Fransen argue that regardless of pedagogical approach and learning context, more emphasis should be paid to helping adolescents experience pleasure as they read. They underscore the theme of new literacies and an ever-changing adolescent landscape. In Chapter 11, "Disciplinary Literacy: A Multidisciplinary Synthesis," David G. O'Brien and Lisa Ortmann focus on the ways in which new literacies can shape and enhance content-area learning. Peter Smagorinsky, in the moving and provocative Chapter 12, "Misfits in School Literacy: Whom Are U.S. Schools Designed to Serve?," examines the ways in which the contexts of school work against many adolescents. Finally, Bob Fecho, Jennifer J. Whitley, and Steven J. Landry in Chapter 13, "Avoiding the Cheapest Room in the House: Dialoguing through

Fear of Dialogical Practice," invite us to consider the importance of dialogical practice as we reframe and revise our literacy practices with adolescents in school.

PART III: ADOLESCENT LITERACIES AND MULTIPLE TEXTS

The third part of the *Handbook,* "Adolescent Literacies and Multiple Texts," identifies the multiple, multimodal texts that mediate adolescents' literacies, including their reading, writing, and viewing. These chapters share considerable detail from the research of both the authors and others about the texts adolescents use and generate. We learn about texts whose utility is questioned by the adolescents and sometimes their teachers, texts that resonate with utility for adolescents and their teachers, texts that are more valued in school than out of school and vice versa, and texts that should be valued but are not.

Cynthia Greenleaf and Sheila W. Valencia lead off the section with Chapter 14, "Missing in Action: Learning from Texts in Subject-Matter Classrooms." This chapter is filled with nuanced insights about the current nominal use of disciplinary texts in schools, along with descriptions of the realities associated with teaching around the texts regardless of what school districts and state education departments claim about what is going on in classrooms. They conclude with a discussion of what to do next to facilitate change in the current state of affairs, as well as ideas about how to do this.

Kelly Wissman shares her own research into an important alternative to current use of texts in schools in Chapter 15, " 'No More Paperwork!': Student Perspectives on Multimodal Composing in Response to Literature." Wissman extends Rosenblatt's reader response theory to describe how young people use multimodal composing in a reading support class to respond to a novel with the software program Comic Life. In Chapter 16, "Let's Translate!: Teaching Literary Concepts with English Language Learners," Kelly Puzio, Christopher Keyes, and Robert T. Jiménez describe how they designed research to honor adolescents' translingual practices by engaging them in collaborative translation to interpret and critique meanings of texts. They note that this approach taps into local knowledge that bilingual students bring to schools to collaborate to understand key textual concepts, fostering several important language strategies as students focus on discussion of the text.

"Acquiring Processes for Responding to and Creating Multimodal Digital Productions" is the focus of Richard Beach, Jill Castek, and John Scott in Chapter 17. These authors describe how multimodal virtual and real representations can be used to express or critique ideas, identity, and agency, even as they mediate social and rhetorical events. In their overview in Chapter 18, "Adolescents Reading Graphic Novels and Comics: What We Know from Research," Stergios Botzakis, Rachelle Savitz, and David E. Low note that affinity with the visual and textual media we often call "comics"—including the now-popular graphic novel form—reveals much about their readers' identities and motivations. They argue that this form offers many unique and appealing affordances for youths' meaning making and challenges educators to find increasing uses for them in schools.

Zhihui Fang, in Chapter 19, "Academic Language and Subject-Area Learning," presents an in-depth overview including attention to the lexical, grammatical, and discursive patterns valued within and across disciplines as grist for explicit instructional attention, recommending language-based pedagogy as an effective way to promote added dimensions of disciplinary learning. Wrapping up the discussion of texts is Gay Ivey's Chapter 20, "Young Adult Literature and Classroom-Based Research," in which she notes a relative shortage of practice-based research on what happens as a result of adolescents' reading of young adult literature that matters to them.

PART IV: PEDAGOGIES OF ADOLESCENT LITERACIES

Our move to include our collection of practice-based research in the fourth and final part of this handbook, "Pedagogies of Adolescent Literacies," is deliberate. With other sections prioritizing youths' literacies, locations, and texts, we are now ready to share practice-based research that explores how literacies are and could be situated in schools. These chapters add significant detail about existing pedagogies, as well as substantive direction for situating reading, writing, and viewing instruction for all learners in classrooms and communities.

Noting that college-bound English language learners report feeling unprepared for college writing, Jill Fitzgerald, in Chapter 21, "How Practice-Based Research Informs Adolescent English Language Learners' Composing and Compositions," leads off Part IV with a review organized to reflect the processes and sociocultural transactions of English language learners in practice-based research. Chapter 22, "Teaching and Learning Literary Argumentation in High School English Language Arts Classrooms," by George E. Newell, David Bloome, and their collaborators from the Argumentative Writing Project, calls into question narrow ways in which literary argumentation is traditionally viewed, arguing instead that how students read and understand text is shaped by teachers' willingness to invite discussion of warrants and evidence. In Chapter 23, "Adolescent Literacy and Collaborative Inquiry," Robert Simon and Amir Kalan demonstrate practice-based research that shows how collaborative inquiry can be key to integrating others' research results in local contexts in ways that respect and matter to all constituents. Michael F. Graves, in Chapter 24, "Scaffolding Adolescents' Reading of Challenging Text: In Search of Balance," cites practice-based research to call for an alternative model to enrich youths' efforts to read and interpret complex text.

In Chapter 25, "Teaching Writing to Adolescents: The Use of Evidence-Based Practices," Amy Rouse and Steve Graham summarize evidence-based practices for developing both the explicit instruction and situated practice in their writing instruction. In Chapter 26, "A Close Reading of Close Reading: What Does the Research Tell Us about How to Promote the Thoughtful Interrogation of Text?," Amy Koehler Catterson and P. David Pearson broaden our understanding of practice-based research on close reading both in and out of school.

FINAL THOUGHTS

As the chapters in this volume attest, the field of adolescent literacy has never been filled with more dynamic, innovative, and critical work. The research of scholars we have been privileged to bring together in this volume may vary in focus, context, methodology, guiding questions, and analysis. But they all share the goal of helping adolescents achieve the kinds of literacies they need to thrive both in and out of school.

Additionally, this collected work animates the paradigmatic shift of knowledge construction we described earlier in this Introduction, in which adolescents and their teachers are at the center of inquiry, where they belong. They are our fellow researchers and collaborators, not merely the objects of analysis or passive recipients, for better or worse, of university-based research. Our focus on practice-based research has, we hope, included the perspectives and expertise of classroom teachers, as well as the varied contexts, talents, and, in some cases, the voices and work of the adolescents themselves.

Compiling this volume has confirmed for both of us what we have long believed: As adolescent literacy scholars, our work has never been more important or more urgent. As adolescents face an increasingly complex and challenging world filled with heretofore unimaginable digital and global dimensions, we hope that our combined efforts will help improve our understanding of what they need to navigate these complexities. That is the true purpose of this volume, and we hope that you will find both confirmation of the work you have already done and inspiration for the work you will continue to do. This text is dedicated to your efforts.

REFERENCES

Beasley, J. W. (2000). Practice-based research in the United States. *Primary Health Care Research and Development, 1,* 135–137.

Brandt, D., & Clinton, K. (2002). Limits of the local: Expanding perspectives on literacy as social practice. *Journal of Literacy Research, 34,* 337–356.

Cammarota, J., & Fine, M. (2008). *Revolutionizing education: Youth participatory action research in motion.* New York: Routledge.

Cochran-Smith, M., & Lytle, S. (1990). Research on teaching and teacher research: The issues that divide. *Educational Research, 19*(2), 2–11.

Duke, N., & Mallette, M. (Eds.). (2011). *Literacy research methodologies* (2nd ed.). New York: Guilford Press.

Eraut, M. (2004). Practice-based evidence. In G. Thomas & G. Pring (Eds.), *Evidence-based practice in education* (pp. 91–101). London: Open University Press.

Fernald, D. H., Coombs, L., DeAlleaume, L., West, D., & Parnes, B. (2012). An assessment of the Hawthorne effect in practice-based research. *Journal of the American Board of Family Medicine, 25,* 83–86.

Freire, P. (1970). *Pedagogy of the oppressed.* New York: Bloomsbury.

Goswami, D., & Stillman, P. (1987). *Reclaiming the classroom: Teacher research as an agency for change.* Upper Montclair, NJ: Boynton Cook.

Haddix, M. (2015). *Cultivating racial and linguistic diversity in literacy teacher education: Teachers like me.* New York: Routledge.

Heath, S. B. (1983). *Ways with words: Language, life and work in communities and classrooms.* Cambridge, UK: Cambridge University Press.

Reinking, D., & Bradley, B. (2008). *Formative design and experiments: Approaches to language and literacy research.* New York: Teachers College Press.

Street, B. (1984). *Literacy in theory and practice.* Cambridge, UK: Cambridge University Press.

Contents

Foreword DONNA E. ALVERMANN	xi
Introduction: The State of Practice-Based Research in Adolescent Literacies KATHLEEN A. HINCHMAN and DEBORAH A. APPLEMAN	xiii

PART I. ADOLESCENT LITERACIES AND IDENTITIES

1. Navigating Cultures and Identities to Learn Literacies for Life: Rethinking Adolescent Literacy Teaching in a Post-Core World ELIZABETH BIRR MOJE, CAROLYN GIROUX, and NICK MUEHLING	3
2. Youth, Popular Culture, and the Media: Examining Race, Class, Gender, Sexuality, and Social Histories MARCELLE HADDIX, ANTERO GARCIA, and DETRA PRICE-DENNIS	21
3. Adolescent Literacies beyond Heterosexual Hegemony MOLLIE V. BLACKBURN and RYAN SCHEY	38
4. Beyond School: Examining the Out-of-School Literacies and Counternarratives of Adolescent Learners VALERIE KINLOCH, TANJA BURKHARD, and CARLOTTA PENN	61
5. Emergent Bilingual Youth in U.S. Secondary Schools DANNY C. MARTINEZ and URSULA S. ALDANA	78
6. What Research Says (and Doesn't Say) about Literacy for Youth with Disabilities KELLY CHANDLER-OLCOTT, MICHELLE DUFFY, and JOANNA M. ROBERTSON	93
7. The Development of Literate Identities and Practices across a Decade: Families, Friends, and Schools CATHERINE COMPTON-LILLY	110

PART II. LOCATING ADOLESCENT LITERACIES

8. Constructing Literacies in Secondary English Language Arts Curriculum: 129
Discourses, Histories, Ethics
MARY JUZWIK, JENNIFER LYNN VANDERHEIDE, KATI MACALUSO, AMANDA SMITH,
NATASHA PEREZ, SAMANTHA CAUGHLAN, MIKE MACALUSO, and CORI MCKENZIE

9. Diverse Youth, New Teachers, and "Picturing" Literacy: Using Photovoice 148
to "Partner" Our Way to Adolescents' Perspectives on Literacy
KRISTIEN ZENKOV, LAUREL TAYLOR, and JIM HARMON

10. The Power of Fostering Pleasure in Reading 169
MICHAEL W. SMITH, JEFFREY D. WILHELM, and SHARON FRANSEN

11. Disciplinary Literacy: A Multidisciplinary Synthesis 182
DAVID G. O'BRIEN and LISA ORTMANN

12. Misfits in School Literacy: Whom Are U.S. Schools Designed to Serve? 199
PETER SMAGORINSKY

13. Avoiding the Cheapest Room in the House: Dialoguing through Fear 215
of Dialogical Practice
BOB FECHO, JENNIFER J. WHITLEY, and STEVEN J. LANDRY

PART III. ADOLESCENT LITERACIES AND MULTIPLE TEXTS

14. Missing in Action: Learning from Texts in Subject-Matter Classrooms 235
CYNTHIA GREENLEAF and SHEILA W. VALENCIA

15. "No More Paperwork!": Student Perspectives on Multimodal Composing 257
in Response to Literature
KELLY WISSMAN

16. Let's Translate!: Teaching Literary Concepts with English Language Learners 276
KELLY PUZIO, CHRISTOPHER KEYES, and ROBERT T. JIMÉNEZ

17. Acquiring Processes for Responding to and Creating Multimodal 292
Digital Productions
RICHARD BEACH, JILL CASTEK, and JOHN SCOTT

18. Adolescents Reading Graphic Novels and Comics: 310
What We Know from Research
STERGIOS BOTZAKIS, RACHELLE SAVITZ, and DAVID E. LOW

19. Academic Language and Subject-Area Learning 323
ZHIHUI FANG

20. Young Adult Literature and Classroom-Based Research 341
GAY IVEY

PART IV. PEDAGOGIES OF ADOLESCENT LITERACIES

21. How Practice-Based Research Informs Adolescent English Language 357
Learners' Composing and Compositions
JILL FITZGERALD

22. Teaching and Learning Literary Argumentation in High School 379
English Language Arts Classrooms
GEORGE E. NEWELL, DAVID BLOOME, and THE ARGUMENTATIVE WRITING PROJECT

23. Adolescent Literacy and Collaborative Inquiry 398
ROBERT SIMON and AMIR KALAN

24. Scaffolding Adolescents' Reading of Challenging Text: In Search of Balance 421
MICHAEL F. GRAVES

25. Teaching Writing to Adolescents: The Use of Evidence-Based Practices 443
AMY ROUSE and STEVE GRAHAM

26. A Close Reading of Close Reading: What Does the Research Tell Us 457
about How to Promote the Thoughtful Interrogation of Text?
AMY KOEHLER CATTERSON and P. DAVID PEARSON

Author Index 477

Subject Index 493

PART I
ADOLESCENT LITERACIES AND IDENTITIES

CHAPTER 1

Navigating Cultures and Identities to Learn Literacies for Life
Rethinking Adolescent Literacy Teaching in a Post-Core World

Elizabeth Birr Moje, Carolyn Giroux,
and Nick Muehling

There was a time when those who studied adolescent literacy had to work hard to make an argument for attention to the literacy development and learning of youth past age 10. Adolescent literacy researchers and educators argued for specific ways of reading and writing in "content areas." We claimed that literacy development continues throughout one's life as one enters new and different domains. We wrote about the need to keep learning new ways of reading and writing to participate in a global society. We wrote about the need for critical literacy in an age of information or access to knowledge in a fast capitalist economy. We argued for access and opportunity for those who had not achieved reading proficiency at an early age.

Those days are over. Now the argument is simple: Calls for attention to adolescent literacy teaching across the curriculum rest their legitimacy on the need to meet the Common Core State Standards (CCSS; National Governors Association & Council of Chief State School Officers [NGA & CCSSO], 2010) and, more recently, on the Next Generation Science Standards (Next Generation Science Standards Lead States, 2013) and the College, Career, and Civic (C3) Life Framework (National Council for the Social Studies, 2013). Indeed, so commonplace is this call to the Common Core and other standards[1] that many readers are likely now to skip reading the CCSS-driven arguments of researchers and go straight to the particulars of whatever study or program the authors

---
[1] Although all standards are increasingly called upon to justify attention to adolescent and disciplinary literacy teaching, for simplicity's sake we use the "the Core" to refer to standards documents, and more generally to the standards movement. The Core launched this movement, so it seems fitting to attribute the current status of adolescent and disciplinary literacy teaching to it.

are addressing. To be fair, the CCSS embed many of the learning demands implicated by our prior arguments in calls for close reading (to build critical literacy) or for developing skills in evidence-based argument (to allow for the careful exchange and evaluation of information). The premise is that if teachers hew to these standards, then students will learn all they need to learn to succeed in college and careers.

One wonders, however, is this as good as it gets? That is, do the CCSS provide all the warrant needed for educators, policymakers, parents, and researchers to care about the literacy learning and development of youth? Despite the claim that the Core will help develop in students the abilities to "understand other perspectives and cultures" (NGA & CCSSO, 2010), the CCSS, in fact, do not attend explicitly to the social, emotional, or cultural development of young people, nor do the standards call for attention to adolescent students' personal, social, and cultural connections to or purposes for the texts they read or write. What is our evidence that advancing the skills outlined in the standards is enough to meet the needs of young people in our society, especially the future society whose values and needed skills we cannot predict? In particular, world events of the early 21st century should ask us whether teaching youth to read complex texts closely or to offer evidence-based arguments will meet the needs of a fractured world filled with injustice and violence.

Lest we appear to be "Core-bashing," we want to underscore that we think the CCSS have made an important impact on education reform, particularly secondary education reform, by drawing attention to the role of language and literacy skill development in all curricular areas. We also respect the demand for developing sophisticated reading and writing practices among all youth, across all domains. What concerns us, however, is how the CCSS have been taken up; they were intended to be a set of goals for expanding and enhancing student learning, but have instead become the end in themselves for many educators. Teachers are exhorted to engage in close reading for the sake of close reading; they are being told to make sure that students can produce evidence-based arguments without a reason to argue and without attention to many other reasons and genres people write to and for audiences. Students are not learning to think, read, and communicate when the goal is to achieve the Core, particularly when students' social, cultural, and emotional needs, interests, and demands are left out of the equation. Without attention to the complex intersection of students' backgrounds and interests with the goals of reading, writing, and communicating complex texts with and across multiple audiences, the goals of the Core feel empty.

To counter this trend, we offer a "post-Core" view, one that recognizes the value of the skills laid out in the CCSS and moves those forward to help students learn literacies for life. To be clear, by "post-Core" we do not mean to suggest an "anti-Core" view, but one that expands the standards and equips teachers to help young people achieve not only the standards, but also literacy skills that will allow them to live satisfying lives and work together to rebuild a troubled world. Thus, in this review, we use research from cultural studies of youth and disciplinary literacy to show that adolescent literacy scholars and practitioners should not just engage in literacy instruction so that we can achieve a set of national standards, but instead that fluency with and the ability to navigate across domain-specific literacy and cultural practices is critical to educate young people for life.

By focusing on literacy "for life" we want to suggest that youth should learn literacy in a way that helps them not only in passing state tests or college entrance exams, but also in managing their personal lives; serving others in the community; making reasoned familial, social, and political decisions; or taking action to end injustices in the world. We use research studies to show that thinking about literacy for life—rather than for national standards movements—can carry youth forward to be informed adult citizens.

The research we present makes clear that to do that kind of literacy learning for life, adolescent literacy development needs to be about more than learning words, or even the ways with language, of a discipline or domain. Because learning is always situated in and mediated by social and cultural practices, individual learners bring social and cultural practices to their learning in the disciplines. Moreover, the disciplines are themselves cultures, with their own ways with words. Rather than assuming that we should treat youths' ethnically mediated literacy practices as "cultural" but treat disciplinary literacy practices as somehow natural, true, or objective, we argue that all of the different language and literacy practices youth engage on a daily basis are embedded in particular cultures. Thus, any teaching of literacy requires the practice of teaching youth to navigate among and across the many different cultural groups (i.e., disciplines) they experience every day in school and among and across those groups and the groups in which they hold membership outside of the classroom and outside school.

In what follows, we offer brief reviews of research on how young people navigate the world in many different ways and how those navigations implicate a different kind of literacy learning—and teaching—than is demanded by most standards documents. We knit these research findings and theories together in a way that illustrates the power of navigating across social and cultural identities, discourses, cultures, and relationships, and that makes the lack of attention to the social and cultural dimensions of disciplinary literacy learning in various standards documents inexcusable. These areas include (1) navigating identities; (2) navigating home, youth, and school cultures; and (3) navigating networks and relationships of power and privilege. Although we divide these studies into the three categories named here for the purposes of highlighting particular dimensions (identity, culture, and power), identities, cultures, and power relations are always intertwined in the lived world, especially in regard to the ways they shape literacy practices. As a result, the sections may appear a bit imbalanced in treatment, with the third category being the briefest, largely because all of the studies speak to issues of power and privilege.

NAVIGATING IDENTITIES

The identities that youth bring to and enact in school are central to their reading and writing practices (Moje & Luke, 2009). Numerous studies have shown the impact that identities can have on youth reading and writing practices in and out of school. Here we offer two exemplars of this work focused on youth identities as readers and writers.

In a case study of three teachers and three students that the teachers had marked as "struggling," Hall (2010) found that students purposely disengaged from classroom instruction designed to teach aspects of reading because by participating they would take on the identity of "bad reader." Through separate interviews with teachers and students and observations of their interactions in whole-class observations, Hall documented teachers' definitions of what it meant to behave like a good reader; she also noted through observation of instruction that the teachers were more likely to engage with students who fit their definitions of "good reader." Conversely, students were aware that displaying some of the behavior of good readers, such as asking questions and participating in group discussion, would position them as bad readers because through this kind of participation they would show that they needed help. As a result, they refrained from this kind of participation in class even though it could help them to develop their skill in reading. This study suggested that the ways teachers position students either inadvertently or purposefully as good or bad readers can have a direct effect on the students' participation in class and development in reading.

The title of a recent study, "Feeling Like I'm Slow Because I'm in This Class" (Learned, 2014), poignantly captured the ways that reading identities shape and are shaped by reading experiences. Youth of different achievement levels and different race and class backgrounds were positioned and positioned themselves as readers in the various contexts they traversed in a typical high school day, from literacy "remediation" classes to English language arts, to social studies, and to mathematics. Learned observed the youth as they interacted with teachers and other adolescents across those varied high school classrooms, interviewed focal students, and administered a range of reading assessments. She documented what, why, and how these youth read, with a focus on analyzing why and when they read the way they did; how they saw themselves as readers, learners, and human beings; and how their teachers saw them, which was often in ways that did not align with observed and measured skills. Learned's research showed clearly how identities as readers (or not) were constructed in the spaces of school, how those reading identities shaped future possibilities for youth, and how teachers might learn from and about students' identities in ways that could reposition and reshape young people's reading achievement. Of particular importance, students' race, social class, and gender intersected with determinations of reading ability on the basis of test scores and those qualities of difference shaped teachers' interactions with students. This study offers a powerful example of the intersection of identities and contexts or cultures. The contexts of learning—including the relationships, interactions, and power relations of those spaces—shaped how young people in this study were seen and saw themselves as readers and as learners.

NAVIGATING AMONG HOME, YOUTH, AND DISCIPLINARY CONTEXTS AND CULTURES

In this section, we draw attention to the ways that the different contexts and cultures young people move through on a daily basis shape how they engage with literacy. Within the category of context and culture we examine several important constructs, including discourses, funds of knowledge, and linguistic codes.

Understanding and Using Differences between Home and School Discourses

Researchers have documented differences between home and school discourses, that is, ways that people use language and other communication cues, in many communities over the past 40 years of work on the social and cultural contexts of learning. In work in reservation schools and homes, for example, Philips (1972) documented that cultural participation structures governed how students were viewed by teachers and the amount of student participation. Similarly, Heath's (1983) study of the language practices of two communities—one mainly White; the other mainly Black; both working class—in the

Caroline Piedmont demonstrated that rich traditions of oral and written language were not recognized or valued in the White, middle-class schools the children of those communities attended (Heath, 1982a, 1982b).

Heath's work is often taken up as an explanation for different ways with words shaped by race and socioeconomic status. Less often acknowledged is the important work Heath did with teachers and parents to build practices for helping children learn to navigate the language and literacy differences between their home and school lives. Heath engaged teachers, parents, and students in community-based science learning projects that expanded the discursive repertoires of all involved, suggesting the power of teacher–parent partnerships in working toward achieving the standards laid out in the current Core documents. Teachers in Heath's study learned to understand, respect, and incorporate a range of language practices in their instruction; parents learned the expectations for school language; and the children learned new practices.

Others have written about building hybrid or syncretic practices that not only employ but also bridge and critique different discourses. Gutiérrez and her colleagues have offered richly detailed accounts of teachers helping children and youth learn to merge official classroom scripts with their "counterscripts" drawn from their own lived experiences (Gutiérrez & Rogoff, 2003; Gutiérrez, Rymes, & Larson, 1995). These teachers actively listened for students' underground, whispered talk and employed it as a tool for helping students learn other ways with words, both from the disciplinary domains of school and from the lives of others in the classroom.

In relation to science learning, many scholars have studied the ways that young people's cultural and linguistic practices shape the sense they make of classroom science. The Chèche Konnen team at TERC (Technology Education Research Center; e.g., Warren, Ballenger, Ogonowski, Rosebery, & Hudicourt-Barnes, 2001) offered a range of inquiry-based curricular tools designed to help teachers help students navigate the differences in discourse from everyday home discourses to those of school science. Much of the Chèche Konnen work has been conducted at the elementary level, but the principles of practice are similar whether supporting children's or adolescents' navigations across discourse and language communities. Indeed, attention to the multiple discourse communities of adolescents seems critical if educators hope to help them achieve the specialized reading, writing, and communication skills outlined in the various standards. Adolescents have much to learn about transferring their language and literacy skills across many domains, and they have much to offer from their home, youth, and popular cultural experiences as springboards for instruction, if we listen closely.

In contrast to studies that leverage youths' everyday cultural discourses, Ives (2011) focused on the home and everyday discourses that are available in the classroom and not used (see also Moje et al., 2004). These "foolbirds" are discourses and literacies of students that they learn to hide from their teacher in order to follow the norms of classroom routine, classroom discourse patterns, and the expectations of the teacher. Ives documented that home discourses and literacies are present in the classroom, but students learned to camouflage and silence these discourses because they believed it was necessary to position themselves as good students. For example, in a lesson on metaphor, one student, Jamal, engaged in metaphorical wordplay with his friends in his group of desks. When the teacher asked him to define the difference between a simile and metaphor, Jamal could not provide the right answer. The teacher scolded him for not listening to her, but Jamal was listening and interacting with the material. He simply could not provide the answer in the discourse that the teacher recognized as correct. His fluency with figurative speech could not be a starting point to learn about navigating between language play with friends and English language arts content because he chose to hide his language play, keeping his voice low with friends and not realizing that an example of this language play might serve to answer part of the question his teacher asked.

Instead of focusing on the cultural practices of a specific group, some researchers have attended simply to everyday ways of thinking and doing to teach students to navigate between everyday and disciplinary ways with words. In a study of two high school English language arts (ELA) classrooms, Levine (2014) showed how teachers supported students to use out-of-school interpretive practices as a bridge to interpreting literature in disciplinary ways (Lee, 1993, 2007). In Levine's affective heuristic students were asked to

1. Draw on their everyday affect-based interpretative practices to identify language in a literary text that they feel is particularly affect-laden.
2. Ascribe valence (a range of positive and/or negative values) to that language.
3. Explain or justify their ascriptions. (Levine, 2014, p. 284)

For example, a student reading the final line of Morrison's *The Bluest Eye* would read about a girl searching "among the garbage and the sunflowers of [a] town" and would first identify the word "sunflowers" as a word that evokes emotion. After identifying that this word evokes a positive emotion, in the third step of the heuristic, students would connect "sunflowers" to concepts of beauty and hope (Levine, 2014, p. 284). As students worked through canonical text, they were coached to use the everyday reasoning that they already possessed to craft their own literary interpretations. At the end of the unit, students who were exposed to this heuristic were more likely to make interpretive statements about literature than students engaged in more traditional methods of literary interpretation.

A study of middle school science students (Bricker & Bell, 2011) similarly shows how and why everyday argumentative reasoning can be used teach students to make scientific arguments. Recognizing that students routinely make judgments and arguments as they navigate their out-of-school world, Bricker and Bell designed a 3-year ethnography involving 128 middle school students. They found that when students described "argument" within the context of their daily lives, their definition was more nuanced than the conventional idea of an argument as a fight.

What's more, they found that students attended to evidence and were able to link evidence to claims using a variety of linguistic markers. Most important, Bricker and Bell (2011) discussed the necessity of distinguishing between argument as weighing evidence and argument as verbal dispute. They also provided guidelines to make classroom debates "identity safe," that is, to treat multiple points of view as worthy of intellectual pursuit. Their final recommendation was to teach the practices of the scientific disciplines so students can take on the argumentative practices of the larger community of scientists while still in school. Bricker and Bell acknowledged the power differentials in the formal language and literacy practices of the science disciplines. They argued that navigation between everyday argumentation and argumentation as it exists in the discipline of sciences should be taught to children "in hopes that the sciences become more democratic and representative" (Bricker & Bell, 2011, p. 130).

Across a number of studies, Moje and colleagues (2004) make a case for helping youth navigate across the multitude of cultural groups they experience in daily life and the disciplinary cultures in which they are expected participate in secondary school and beyond. This long-term study followed youth outside school to examine how they engaged with the world outside school. The young people they studied engaged in many different activities that demanded skills often necessary in scientific practice (e.g., searching for objects in the park to hypothesize where they came from and what purpose they originally served; writing letters to protest a policy made by the school system).

A second study led by Moje (Moje, Overby, Tysvaer, & Morris, 2008) showed that 86% of a sample of over 800 young people in one urban community reported writing outside school. However, this kind of writing not only did not help them in school but it also was correlated to negative achievement in their languages arts classes. The authors hypothesized that the nature of the writing—journal entries, song lyrics, and poetry—did not prepare them for the writing they were asked to do in their language arts courses. The gap between the two types of writing was not mediated by their teachers, perhaps because the teachers did not realize what their students were doing outside of school or perhaps because they felt the stress of needing to prepare students for the only kind of writing valued on the state tests. Whatever the reasons, the students' writing scores (and their writing on samples the authors assessed independently) remained low over the 5-year period of the study.

In a related study, Stockdill and Moje (2013) interviewed a subsample ($n = 26$) of the same large group of students. They found that the youth read and wrote many different texts with themes that could easily be tied to history and social science learning (e.g., war, immigration, poverty, violence, and struggle). In most cases, however, these youth left those texts at the classroom door and reported an extreme distaste for studying social studies in school (i.e., it was routinely reported as students' least favorite class).

Finally, Moje and Speyer (2014) reported on a design-based research study of a unit on the history of U.S. immigration law that they cotaught in the same community, illustrating the many spaces in which students could insert their cultural experiences, concerns, and questions given an imminent immigration protest planned in the predominantly Latin@/o community. To avoid overlooking student input, as had occurred in other such studies, the unit design made space for students to draw from cultural texts and experiences as they read the different immigration laws enacted in the United States over time. To support students in reading those primary sources and connecting the historical laws to current experiences, the teachers engaged in whole-class close reading activities in which teachers scaffolded students' reading by attending to particular words and phrases, explicitly asked students whether the texts reminded them of anything in their own lives, and led students to note the differences in text. Thus, the teachers not only recognized students' experiences but also used the knowledge and discourses youth brought to the classroom to build a deeper understanding of U.S. immigration law.

Building on this idea of instructional designs that seek and make use of students' cultural experiences, practices, and ways with words, Athanases and de Oliveria (2014) showed that the practice of being a culturally relevant teacher goes beyond mere knowledge of student's cultural background. Helping students become prepared "for life" necessitates a connection with the larger disciplinary culture. Students cannot be prepared for life in a classroom where their home cultures are not a consideration in lesson planning. Nor can they be prepared for life in a classroom where a teacher incorporates their cultures into instruction that lacks a disciplinary frame. In their study of two novice (less than 3 years' experience) teachers' scaffolding in an urban Latin@/o community, the teacher who used scaffolding to support student text engagement without a disciplinary literacy frame struggled to understand the purpose of her scaffolds. Although committed to social justice and willing to design instruction that would support students, she acknowledged that her scaffolds resulted in students merely mimicking her own process of thinking through text. Worse yet, when she pulled away the scaffolds at what she thought was an age-appropriate point ("juniors don't need sentence starters"), she was frustrated with her students' lack of independent skill. The other teacher, however, who employed scaffolding techniques within a disciplinary frame, was able to use scaffolding to support students to do their own thinking by providing texts for an activity and encouraging students to make and support their own claims. Although the teacher thought that the students were not prepared to be independent without her scaffolding, her scaffolding in connection with disciplinary inquiry was more effective in engaging students beyond the basic literacy practices.

In short, a long tradition of practice-based research has demonstrated that home, youth, and disciplinary discourses are often different in kind, and also in the nature and amount of discourse between peers and older authority figures. That same research, however, has often demonstrated the ways that teachers can draw from and expand on the discourse practices in young people's home lives to expand their repertoires. Perhaps most important, teachers can recognize that discursive difference does not equal cognitive (or discursive) deficit. Teachers can also recognize that their discourse practices are socially and culturally mediated, including those most valued in schools. We need to consider the cultural or social mediators of students' speaking, reading, writing, and listening and then seek out and enact strategies to support them in learning the language and literacy practices exhorted by the Core—without devaluing their home, community, and youth cultural practices.

Incorporating Funds of Knowledge

Closely related to the work on home and school discourse differences is another form of navigating among home, youth, and school cultures. This work involves incorporating the various funds of knowledge (Moll & Gonzalez, 1994; Moll & Greenberg, 1990) available to students in their everyday lives into classroom instruction. Here is it critical that we distinguish between knowledge itself and the funds of knowledge youth have available in their everyday lives. In a funds of knowledge framework, the funds themselves are as important as—if not more important than—the knowledge itself. People learn new knowledge in social networks, communities, and relationships. Time and time again, youth literacy researchers have documented the power of the network, community, or relationship to engage youth in literacy practices (Moll, Veléz-Ibañéz, & Greenberg, 1989). As Moje et al. (2008) documented, an analysis of thousands of youth describing their reasons for reading and writing showed that reading and writing practices played important roles within their social networks and funds of knowledge; their motivation to engage with certain texts stemmed largely from the contexts—or funds—in which the texts were embedded. Thus, becoming aware of and, when appropriate, employing, youths' funds can both motivate and scaffold their reading and writing. There are many different kinds of funds, three of which we highlight here because of recent research on these funds: transnational communities, out-of-school reading groups, and religious groups.

Transnational Communities as Funds

In a study of a classroom multimodal writing project, Honeyford (2014) documented that as English learners in the class created presentations to prepare for the literacy demands of joining a mainstream class, they also were able to write their own narratives, many of which provided counternarratives to the larger immigrant experience. In particular, the visuals in the multimodal project helped students to position and reposition themselves in their communities, affording students the agency to define their own identity in school spaces. Lam (2009; Lam & Rosario-Ramos, 2009) found that students who were learning English as an additional language also used social media as a way to communicate with other youth. These youth used instant messaging, chatrooms, e-mail, and other social media in both their newly acquired language and their first languages, using the sites to work on their language and also to connect with others who accepted and supported them (see also Black, 2006; McLean, 2010). In many of these studies, both the transnational and digital communities were important funds for youth not only to feel connected but also to learn new language while maintaining their first languages.

Out-of-School Reading and Writing Groups as Funds

One important fund of knowledge for teachers wishing to enhance students' reading and writing engagement and skill is out-of-school reading and writing groups. Many teachers appear to assume that young people do not read or write outside of schools, but a number of studies contest this assumption. For example, Alvermann, Young, Green, and Wisenbaker (1999) offer an analysis of what drew young people to—and kept them in—an out-of-school book discussion group. Simply put, they appreciated not only the opportunity to choose texts they wanted to read but also the freedom to explore the books as they chose. Worth noting was that they did not go their own ways or deviate radically from the texts in their discussions. They managed to read closely without an adult telling them how, when, why, and what to read. Equally important, they drew from and connected to their own experiences. As other scholars have suggested, it is impossible to read a text closely without connecting the ideas of a text to one's own experiences and to other texts (Hartman, 1995).

In a study with Latin@ youth in a large urban area, Moje, Peek-Brown, Sutherland, Marx, Blumenfeld, et al. (2004) drew attention to the young men's participation in Lowrider car and bike clubs.[2] The Lowrider clubs were particularly significant funds of knowledge because they were spaces in which older men—fathers, brothers, uncles, and others—engaged with the younger men around a shared interest. Club activities included reading *Lowrider* magazine (and, to a lesser extent at the time of the study, the Lowrider website) and trading information gleaned from the site as a resource for working on the cars. This fund was particularly powerful for the young men in the study because it

---

[2]Latin@s in the study also talked about Lowriders and reported sometimes reading the magazine, but this particular group—or fund—was male-dominated in this setting.

brought together gendered relationships, ethnic cultural symbols and practices, and the reading of complex texts about automotive concepts and information. These and other community-based funds, and the knowledge and skills they produce, could be called upon in both social and natural science teaching as a way of connecting and extending students' disciplinary learning. They could also be used to raise questions about the values and assumptions embedded in social and natural scientific thinking (Moje, Collazo, Carrillo, & Marx, 2001).

An analysis of literature discussion groups in an LGBTQQ (lesbian, gay, bisexual, transgender, queer, questioning) youth center demonstrated the complicated nature of such groups as funds of knowledge, illustrating both the possibilities and limitations of out-of-school reading groups (Blackburn & Clark, 2011). In this study, the students in the reading group worked through many canonical (and noncanonical) works in a queer-friendly environment. Analysis of the discourse showed that group members supported and challenged each other as they explored complex issues but their discourse also constrained some aspects of the conversation. For example, students were more likely to question heteronormativity in the text but at other times, they reinforced dichotomies, for example, between masculine and feminine gay men. Although overall this study shows the possibility of drawing on these funds to promote text-based discussion, teachers need also to be cautious because discussion of text in a supportive environment for LGBTQQ youth is not enough. Attention to discourse is essential if teachers wish to build both safe and brave spaces for all students to discuss sexual identities in school settings.

Studies of youth writing outside of school also show clearly that many young people learn from and teach others about written language through out-of-school funds for writing and using digital social media. Ingalls (2005) examined college-age youths' engagements in spoken word poetry, comparing their experiences with the writing experiences they had in introductory college writing courses. Ingalls found that although both contexts had strict norms for writing, the college writing courses contained (Bowden, 1993) students' writing in ways that also constrained the students, whereas the spoken word contexts, or containers, seemed to generate new ideas and new ways of writing and performing. Some of the differences were a matter of youth having choice in the spoken word funds, but Ingalls also documented the power of the social interaction, which produced a reason to communicate, in the spoken word spaces.

A study of young people writing fanfiction on line (Shultz, 2009) yielded similar findings, documenting that college writers engaged in fanfiction, despite tightly established norms and rules for both content and language use, because the fanfic writing funds offered student writers a community who would weigh in on both the language and the content of the stories they wrote. Notably, even when "beta readers" (i.e., online readers akin to editors or even teachers who comment on and edit drafts) critiqued the fanfic products, writers maintained their enthusiasm, suggesting that young people will write and revise when they have something to say and an audience who cares to read it.

For teachers, this work can serve as a reminder that youth who might appear to be struggling with school writing may be embedded in and connected to funds of knowledge—such as spoken word poetry groups, fanfiction sites, or other social media—outside of school that could be productively engaged to support students' learning. In addition, teachers need to be reminded to ask themselves what skills youth might possess within out-of-school contexts but not know how to transfer to school learning. Finally, given findings that out-of-school writing can actually detract from in-school writing achievement, teachers should consider what they can do to explicitly teach the different epistemologies and assumptions of various types of school-based writing.

Religious Communities as Funds

Of increasing interest over the last few decades are youth religious literacies and the funds of knowledge that shape them. This interest was perhaps first spurred by Heath's (1983) finding that the interpretive and critical reading practices of children in the White, working-class community of her study were shaped by the ways of reading in their church communities. Or perhaps a recognition that religious communities produce cultural values and norms, and thus shape youth literacy practices, prompted this turn to religious funds. Whatever the reason, a number of youth researchers have investigated what religious funds mean for young people's literacies in and out of school. At least three recent studies offer important considerations for classroom teachers.

Sarroub's (2002) study of young women who not only practiced the tenets of Islam, but also followed the dress codes by wearing the *hijab,* showed ways in which these young women often found themselves "in between" multiple cultures. This was especially demonstrated as they tried to navigate what Islam deems appropriate for women's interactions with men and what their teachers wanted them to do in classroom discussions and activities.

Likewise, a study of two groups of religious youth—one Methodist and the other Mormon—documented both similarities and differences in their text reading practices (Rackley, 2014). Navigating the demands of interpretive work, in particular, was challenging for the students who followed Mormon traditions, not because the work was cognitively challenging, but because interpretation—especially critical interpretation—was not promoted in church-based reading activities. Like Heath's students whose families practiced fundamentalist religions, critique and interpretation were discouraged in church reading.

Finally, a study of Catholic and Protestant youth in a public school classroom (Skerrett, 2014) showed that students were able to recruit their religious funds of knowledge, discourse, and literacies to understand secular literature. Equally important, however, the teacher's attention to multiliteracies and discussion of multiple ways to make meaning of text allowed students to use religious knowledge to interpret literature and engage in academic writing. For example, one student learned to write memoir by explaining the religious significance and impact of her grandmother's life. Other students were able to use religious frames to recognize and interpret symbols in classroom text, such as an image of a poor man stretching out his arms as reminiscent of Jesus on the cross. The teacher, who did not share the students' faith, supported students to by emphasizing their shared human empathy, voicing a simple, "It's OK," when she saw disagreement among student ideas and her own. Following the teacher's example, students learned to ask questions about different perspectives, and look for commonalities across experience as a way to maintain their classroom community. This study shows that attention to the funds, knowledges, and discourses the students possessed, and to multiple ways of interpreting and generating text, allowed the teacher to recruit religious literacies without privileging any one religious culture. Equally important, her use of multiple texts and her drawing out of multiple perspectives also prepared students to go beyond these literacies and acquire other ways of engaging with various academic texts.

Code Switching and Code Breaking

Complementary to findings about the differences among home, school, and youth cultures and discourses is a robust set of studies that make a case for thinking of the movements across spaces as a matter of knowing where, when, and how to use the linguistic and other "codes" valued in one culture or another. Much of the work that focuses on code switching and code breaking revolves around teachers (and others, including youth themselves) using everyday linguistic codes to teach academic linguistic codes. The work is distinct from simply recognizing that discourses and literacies might differ or that students have important funds that can be brought to the classroom. This code-switching work makes the power of the codes central. Lisa Delpit (1988) wrote, for example, about a teaching colleague who helped her students understand how to code-switch by using the metaphor of a picnic versus a formal dinner party. Her goal was to convey the idea that both settings are important and valuable, but that the location, the food one serves, the plates one uses, and even one's behavior are likely to shift from one setting to another. She likened those differences in dining practices to the different ways her students might need to talk, read, or write in different contexts.

Cross and Strauss (2003) offer an analysis of the kind of code switching older adolescents engage in at elite postsecondary institutions as they move across contexts of their everyday lives. Recognizing the threat of stereotype (Steele & Aronson, 1995) in certain contexts, these high-achieving young people knew to change their language practices much as the teacher Delpit described taught young children. Code switching, thus, can be a form of teaching youth to navigate different contexts. However, the teaching of multiple codes is always a risky business, requiring careful attention to validating the different codes for their usefulness so that one is not seen as inherently more powerful than another, but instead is understood to be powerful in context and because of the unequal power relations in social interaction (Alim, 2007). In other words, students can learn that certain codes are useful not only because they are efficient (as in technical language of the disciplines) or evocative (as in the language and discourse practices of the arts), but also because someone in power has determined one code to be more appropriate than another. Students can also be taught to challenge the codes of power (Delpit, 1988). In support of such work in disciplinary literacy teaching, Moje (2015) recommends a heuristic in which examining and evaluating words, and ways with words, for their usefulness and power in different contexts are critical components of instruction that helps youth learn to navigate multiple disciplinary and life domains.

Leveraging Resources of the African American Verbal Tradition in Writing

The African American Verbal Tradition (AVT) is a rich source of language that teachers can leverage in order to teach academic writing (Lee, 1993, 2007). In fact, students who use African American discourse styles score higher on national assessments of writing (Smitherman, 1993). Since the Students' Right to Their Own Language resolution (endorsed by the Conference on College Composition and Communication, 1974), both researchers and practitioners have worked to develop curriculum that allows students to use their home language in academic environments. Although this work has yet to focus on the middle and high schools, there is a lot to be learned from first-year college-writing instruction that is applicable within the K–12 context. One of these studies (Williams,

2013) introduced African American English rhetorical patterns, narrativizing and signifying, to two cohorts of first-year college-writing students with varying levels of familiarity with African American English rhetoric. Through lectures, activities, and writing workshops, students improved their own academic writing by integrating these rhetorical features.

Perryman-Clark's (2013) study of three students in an Afrocentric first-year writing course also shows that African American English speakers demonstrated sophisticated knowledge of audience and purpose and critical awareness of language when allowed to code-switch in their writing. However, she also questions why African American rhetoric is seen as strength while African American phonology and syntax are seen as error. Taken together, these two studies of first-year writing courses not only document the power of allowing code switching in writing but also highlight the need for teachers to foster a critical viewpoint when teaching and leveraging code-switching practices so students can value and assert their home language in a variety of academic contexts.

Leveraging Resources of Bilingual and Bidialectal Students

In line with Gutiérrez's (2008) work in sociocritical literacy, Alim (2007) designed a unit of study in which students take on the work of linguists and ethnographers in the "third space" of the classroom, an environment that for many marginalized linguistic groups can be a battleground between their home language and the hegemony of Standard English. In the first two stages of the project, students increase their metalinguistic knowledge by investigating their own language use and the language of their peers, families, and communities. At the third stage of the project students discuss the relationship between language and power. In this stage students use examples from interviews with community members to illustrate how language can be used to marginalize and disempower those that do not speak the standard dialect. Alim's work illustrates that code-switching pedagogies do not support students unless they teach students to navigate and transform the contexts that marginalize their home language.

NAVIGATING NETWORKS AND RELATIONSHIPS OF POWER

In this section, we explore the dilemma between teaching students to navigate so that they can participate in dominant power structures/relations (Delpit, 1988; Hirsch, Kett, & Trefil, 1987) and teaching students to navigate in a way that teaches skills for speaking back to or resisting the dominant (Freire, 1970; Freire & Macedo, 1987). Assisting students with understanding and living within this tension empowers students to live as informed citizens beyond their years of schooling and encourages them to participate in the further labor needed for equity and justice in our current global context, where the lack of equity and justice is maddening.

This is work that can have social and political impact on a grand scale. However, it begins with the difficult work of teaching navigation in individual classrooms. Delpit (1988) makes a strong theoretical case for giving students access to the culture of power that is in operation in every classroom. In classrooms, the rules of written and oral discourse, personal interaction, and dress are reflective of the rules of those who have power outside of the classroom. However, these rules are often invisible. Students should, therefore, be explicitly taught the rules of the culture of power, not to abandon their own cultures, but so they might be empowered through having access to their home and youth cultures together with the cultures of power. The goal is to enable full student participation in multiple cultures, multiple worlds, and multiple domains of life.

Full participation in cultures of power is more than a matter of learning unwritten rules and discourse patterns, however. Hirsch et al. (1987) argued that a body of general cultural knowledge is also necessary. The point is not the piling up of facts in the heads of individual students. Instead, Hirsch et al. asserted that all communities are founded on shared knowledge. Consequently, "Only by piling up specific, communally shared information can children learn to participate in complex cooperative activities with other members of their community" (p. xv). From their perspective, such information is the necessary background information, and is alluded to and referenced in the discourse of the culture of power. Having the knowledge is one of the keys to gaining access to dominant discourse and culture. However, gaining the knowledge of the culture of power has its risks. First, who decides what gets counted in a list of powerful cultural texts? How might teachers help students access power without giving up their existing cultural and language practices? How do we add to students' discourses, knowledge, and literacies without subtracting from the practices students already possess and value (Valenzuela, 1999)?

Teaching students the unwritten rules, discourse patterns, and knowledge of the culture of power is going to have little impact if students see no reason and have no interest in navigating power and relationships. Learning to navigate networks and relationships of power must be an act of hope and vision for students. Gutiérrez (2008) shows how powerful this can be in her work with the Migrant Summer Leadership Institute, a summer educational program for the children of migrant workers. These students were taught to place themselves socially and historically as individuals and as members of a group. This work gave students a sense of inequality in the past and the present as power structures were illuminated. Students then found methods of empowerment for the future. In the vignettes Gutiérrez offers, empowerment came from the understanding that higher education was a realistic possibility and a way to gain individual power and affect social change. In only 4 weeks, students increased access to the culture of power and dominant discourse, while also developing hope and vision for social change.

Finally, Hull and Stornaiuolo's (2014) account of a 3-year design research study with high school-age youth from the United States, India, South Africa, and Norway illustrates the way that power flows through seemingly simple academic tasks such as learning to write argument (a significant demand across the standards documents). The young people in this study used multimodal tools embedded in diverse social networks to engage audiences in understanding others across social networks and power differentials. Of particular importance, the youth composed multimodal products so that they could engage and collaborate, rather than persuade and dominate. Such moves changed the typical workings of power in traditional views of writing and rhetoric, in which the goal is to argue, or to persuade a reader to change perspective. Interestingly, students did change their perspectives, but they did so as they sought to understand, rather than to persuade, which seems at odds with the current standards focus on evidence-based argument.

Equally at odds with the standards is the underscoring of communication in this cosmopolitan (Hull & Stornaiuolo, 2014) view of composition. Although evidence-based argument is a form of communication, it is often framed in terms of parts of a rubric, such as "claim, evidence, and reasoning" (Moje, Ciechanowski, et al., 2004). When students struggle to address one of these rubric parts, it is often because they fail to recognize that they are writing for a disciplinary or other community, and they fail to understand the power of the other and of the argument they hope to make. By contrast, composing in a cosmopolitan world is all about communication across networks and relationships of power. It is also all about trying to understand.

IMPLICATIONS FOR ADOLESCENT LITERACY TEACHING IN A POST-CORE WORLD

The first implication for literacy teaching in a post-Core world is the need for teachers, school leaders, and policymakers to recognize that even seemingly struggling students can possess a repertoire of literacy practices, are familiar with multiple discourses, and have access to background knowledge that is as deep and rich as the multiple worlds and social networks they inhabit. If the various standards are to be a framework for planning meaningful instruction, then students must learn to navigate and transform their own worlds rather than learning skills in isolation. And for students to learn to navigate and transform their own worlds, the standards need to be applied to the real, lived experiences of students rather than asking students to leave their knowledge and identities behind to learn disconnected academic literacy skills.

Second, it is important to acknowledge that whether a student recruits this knowledge to apply within the classroom depends heavily on teachers and learning contexts. As our review illustrates, students make choices not to use or to disguise literacy practices and change their behavior to adapt to what the teacher deems valuable; therefore, teachers need to actively invoke and leverage home, youth, or community literacy skills and practices and help students see how these skills and practices can be employed both to learn and to critique new skills and practices. Such teachers need to include multiple literacy practices and be aware that students can take on multiple identities. The work cited in our review lays out examples of what it looks like to teach students to navigate these multiple discourse communities inside classrooms (see especially Alim, 2007; Alvermann et al., 1999; Gutiérrez, 2008; Levine, 2014; Moje & Speyer, 2014). The work is respectful of students' experiences, even as it is intentional about expanding those experiences.

Finally, if the CCSS, or any other standards, are to be relevant to and made use of in the real, lived experiences of youth, then it is necessary to discuss the relationship between literacy and power that exists in and across cultural groups. Teachers can help students build the skills to navigate across and into more powerful discourse communities by teaching the codes of power and giving students the tools to critique and even change these powerful codes and cultures. Without a conversation about discourse and power that attends to students' cultural backgrounds, however, the standards are not just disconnected from students' lives but also are in danger of reproducing inequalities. Although many see the establishment of standards as a way to equalize the playing field for all, achieving standards that do not attend to the power differentials in society and in students' lives will not ensure that students are equipped to grapple with and redress those imbalances. When teachers help students to navigate among multiple discourse communities and cultures, they can then begin a discussion of the power relationships that students encounter in this navigation. In so doing, they will teach students to identify and work against inequality in their own lives and in the world. We can teach them literacy for life.

REFERENCES

Alim, S. (2007). Critical hip-hop language pedagogies: Combat, consciousness, and the cultural politics of communication. *Journal of Language, Identity, and Education, 6*(2), 161–176.

Alvermann, D. E., Young, J. P., Green, C., & Wisenbaker, J. M. (1999). Adolescents' perceptions and negotiations of literacy practices in after-school read and talk clubs. *American Educational Research Journal, 36*(2), 221–264.

Athanases, S. Z., & de Oliveria, L. C. (2014). Scaffolding versus routine support for Latina/o youth in an urban school: Tensions building toward disciplinary literacy. *Journal of Literacy Research, 46*(2), 263–299.

Black, R. W. (2006). Language, culture, and identity in online fanfiction. *E-Learning, 3*(2), 170–184.

Blackburn, M., & Clark, C. (2011). Analyzing talk in a long-term literature discussion group: Ways of operating within LGBT-inclusive and queer discourses. *Reading Research Quarterly, 46*(3), 222–248.

Bowden, D. (1993). The limits of containment: Text-as-container in composition studies. *College Composition and Communication, 44*(3), 364–379.

Bricker, L. A., & Bell, P. (2011). Argumentation and reasoning in life and in school: Implications for the design of school science learning environments. In M. S. Khine (Ed.), *Perspectives on scientific argumentation: Theory, practice, and research* (pp. 117–134). New York: Springer.

Conference on College Composition and Communication. (1974). *Students right to their own language.* Urbana, IL: National Council of Teachers of English.

Cross, W., & Strauss, L. (2003, June). *Transacting Black identity in everyday life.* Presented at the William T. Grant Faculty Scholars Retreat, Charlottesville, VA.

Delpit, L. D. (1988). The silenced dialogue: Pedagogy and power in educating other people's children. *Harvard Educational Review, 58,* 280–298.

Freire, P. (1970). *Pedagogy of the oppressed.* New York: Continuum.

Freire, P., & Macedo, D. (1987). *Literacy: Reading the word and the world.* Westport, CT: Bergin & Garvey.

Gutiérrez, K. D. (2008). Developing a sociocritical literacy in third space. *Reading Research Quarterly, 43,* 148–164.

Gutiérrez, K. D., & Rogoff, B. (2003). Cultural ways of learning: Individual traits or repertoires of practice. *Educational Researcher, 32*(5), 19–25.

Gutiérrez, K. D., Rymes, B., & Larson, J. (1995). Script, counterscript, and underlife in the classroom: James Brown versus Brown v. Board of Education. *Harvard Educational Review, 65,* 445–471.

Hall, L. A. (2010). The negative consequences of becoming a good reader: Identity theory as a lens for understanding struggling readers, teachers, and reading instruction. *Teachers College Record, 112*(7), 1792–1829.

Hartman, D. K. (1995). Eight readers reading: The intertextual links of proficient readers reading multiple passages. *Reading Research Quarterly, 30,* 520–561.

Heath, S. B. (1982a). Questioning at home and at school: A comparative study. In G. Spindler (Ed.), *Doing the ethnography of schooling.* New York: Holt, Rinehart & Winston.

Heath, S. B. (1982b). What no bedtime story means: Narrative skills at home and school. *Language in Society, 11*(1), 49–76.

Heath, S. B. (1983). *Ways with words: Language, life, and work in communities and classrooms.* Cambridge, UK: Cambridge University Press.

Hirsch, E. D., Kett, J. F., & Trefil, J. S. (1987). *Cultural literacy: What every American needs to know.* Boston: Houghton Mifflin.

Honeyford, M. A. (2014). From Aquí and Allá: Symbolic convergence in the multimodal literacy practices of adolescent immigrant students. *Journal of Literacy Research, 46*(2), 194–233.

Hull, G. A., & Stornaiuolo, A. (2014). Cosmopolitan literacies, social networks, and "proper distance": Striving to understand in a global world. *Curriculum Inquiry, 44,* 15–44.

Ingalls, R. L. (2005). *Taking a page from their books: Negotiating containment and resuscitating rhetoric in writing across academic and spoken-word genres.* Doctoral dissertation, University of Michigan, Ann Arbor.

Ives, D. (2011). Spotting foolbirds: Literacies hiding in plain sight in an urban English language arts classroom. *Journal of Literacy Research, 43*(3), 250–274.

Lam, W. S. E. (2009). Multiliteracies on instant messaging in negotiating local, translocal, and transnational affiliations: A case of an adolescent immigrant. *Reading Research Quarterly, 44*(4), 377–397.

Lam, W. S. E., & Rosario-Ramos, E. (2009). Multilingual literacies in transnational digitally mediated contexts: An exploratory study of immigrant teens in the United States. *Language and Education, 23*(2), 171–190.

Learned, J. E. (2014). *"Feeling like I'm slow because I'm in this class": Secondary school contexts and the identification and construction of struggling readers.* Doctoral dissertation, University of Michigan, Ann Arbor, MI. Retrieved from *http://hdl.handle.net/2027.42/108819 http://mirlyn.lib.umich.edu/record/013578462.*

Lee, C. D. (1993). *Signifying as a scaffold for literary interpretation: The pedagogical implications of an African American discourse genre* (NCTE Research Report No. 26). Urbana, IL: National Council of Teachers of English.

Lee, C. D. (2007). *Culture, literacy, and learning: Taking bloom in the midst of the whirlwind.* New York: Teachers College Press.

Levine, S. (2014). Making interpretation visible with an affect-based strategy. *Reading Research Quarterly, 49*(3), 283–303.

McLean, C. A. (2010). A space called home: An immigrant adolescent's digital literacy practices. *Journal of Adolescent and Adult Literacy, 54*(1), 13–22.

Moje, E., & Luke, A. (2009). Literacy and identity: Examining the metaphors in history and contemporary research. *Reading Research Quarterly, 44,* 415–437.

Moje, E. B. (2015). Doing and teaching disciplinary literacy with adolescent learners: A social and cultural enterprise. *Harvard Educational Review, 85,* 254–278.

Moje, E. B., Ciechanowski, K. M., Kramer, K. E., Ellis, L. M., Carrillo, R., & Collazo, T. (2004). Working toward third space in content area literacy: An examination of everyday funds of knowledge and discourse. *Reading Research Quarterly, 39*(1), 38–71.

Moje, E. B., Collazo, T., Carrillo, R., & Marx, R. W. (2001). "Maestro, what is 'quality'?": Language, literacy, and discourse in project-based science. *Journal of Research in Science Teaching, 38*(4), 469–496.

Moje, E. B., Overby, M., Tysvaer, N., & Morris, K. (2008). The complex world of adolescent literacy: Myths, motivations, and mysteries. *Harvard Educational Review, 78,* 107–154.

Moje, E. B., Peek-Brown, D., Sutherland, L. M., Marx, R. W., Blumenfeld, P., & Krajcik, J. (2004). Explaining explanations: Developing scientific literacy in middle-school project-based science reforms. In D. Strickland & D. E. Alvermann (Eds.), *Bridging the gap: Improving literacy learning for preadolescent and adolescent learners in grades 4–12* (pp. 227–251). New York: Carnegie Corporation.

Moje, E. B., & Speyer, J. (2014). Reading challenging texts in high school: How teachers can scaffold and build close reading for real purposes in the subject areas. In K. Hinchman & H. Sheridan-Thomas (Eds.), *Best practices in adolescent literacy instruction* (2nd ed., pp. 207–231). New York: Guilford Press.

Moll, L. C., & Gonzalez, N. (1994). Critical issues: Lessons from research with language-minority children. *Journal of Reading Behavior, 26*(4), 439–456.

Moll, L. C., & Greenberg, J. (1990). Creating zones of possibilities: Combining social contexts for instruction. In L. C. Moll (Ed.), *Vygotsky and education* (pp. 319–348). New York: Cambridge University Press.

Moll, L. C., Veléz-Ibañéz, C., & Greenberg, J. (1989). *Year one progress report: Community knowledge and classroom practice: Combining resources for literacy instruction* (IARP Subcontract No. L-10). Tucson: University of Arizona.

National Council for the Social Studies. (2013). *The college, career, and civic life (C3) framework for social studies state standards: Guidance for enhancing the rigor of K–12 civics, economics, geography, and history*. Silver Springs, MD: Author.

National Governors' Association Center for Best Practices & Council of Chief State School Officers (NGO & CCSSO). (2010). *Common Core State Standards for English language arts and literacy, history/social studies, science, and technical subjects*. Washington, DC: Authors.

Next Generation Science Standards Lead States. (2013). Next generation science standards: For states, by states. Retrieved from *www.nextgenscience.org/next-generation-science-standards*.

Perryman-Clark, S. M. (2013). *Afrocentric teacher-research: Rethinking appropriateness and inclusion*. New York: Peter Lang.

Philips, S. U. (1972). Participant structure and communicative competence: Warm Springs children in community and classroom. In C. Cazden, D. Hymes, & W. J. John (Eds.), *Functions of language in the classroom* (pp. 370–394). New York: Teachers College Press.

Rackley, E. R. (2014). Scripture-based discourses of Latter-Day Saint and Methodist youths. *Reading Research Quarterly, 49*(4), 417–435.

Sarroub, L. (2002). In-betweeness: Religion and conflicting visions of literacy. *Reading Research Quarterly, 37*(2), 130–148.

Shultz, S. (2009, March). *Legitimizing and marginalizing: How the Internet has shaped responses to online fan communities and practices*. Paper presented at the Conference on College Composition and Communication, San Francisco, CA.

Skerrett, A. (2014). Religious literacies in a secular literacy classroom. *Reading Research Quarterly, 49*, 233–250.

Smitherman, G. (1993). *"The blacker the berry, the sweeter the juice": African American student writers and the national assessment of educational progress* (ERIC No. 366944). Urbana, IL: ERIC Clearinghouse for English Language Arts.

Steele, C. M., & Aronson, J. (1995). Stereotype threat and the intellectual test performance of African Americans. *Journal of Personal Social Psychology, 69*(5), 797–811.

Stockdill, D., & Moje, E. B. (2013). Adolescents as readers of social studies: Examining the relationship between students' everyday and social studies literacies and learning. *Berkeley Review of Education, 4*, 35–68.

Valenzuela, A. (1999). *Subtractive schooling: U.S.–Mexican youth and the politics of caring*. Albany: State University of New York Press.

Warren, B., Ballenger, C., Ogonowski, M., Rosebery, A., & Hudicourt-Barnes, J. (2001). Rethinking diversity in learning science: The logic of everyday languages. *Journal of Research in Science Teaching, 38*, 1–24.

Williams, B. J. (2013). *Students "write" to their own language: Teaching the African American verbal tradition as a rhetorically effective writing skill*. Unpublished doctoral dissertation, Michigan State University, East Lansing, MI.

CHAPTER 2

Youth, Popular Culture, and the Media
Examining Race, Class, Gender, Sexuality, and Social Histories

MARCELLE HADDIX, ANTERO GARCIA, and DETRA PRICE-DENNIS

In this chapter, we review practice-based research literature that provides insights and perspectives on how best to situate the lived experiences of today's youth in the literacy classroom. This is particularly important to consider and forefront in our educational agendas given that we are living in an era in which young people are leading social change and writing social history. As we write this chapter, young people across the United States, from Ferguson to Baltimore to New York City, are organizing and protesting against the persistent violence inflicted on working-class communities of color through police brutality, economic inequities, and educational inequalities. Today's youth literacy practices are anchored in deeply personal and political causes. What is popular to young people is not about what is trendy or "hot," but instead about what is relevant, significant, and necessary in transforming life outcomes. The youth are making a mark on the world and proving that the revolution will be led by the young people.

Their voices and stories are also being broadcast and tweeted through social media, television, film, and other mainstream media. What it means to be a young person growing up in the 21st century is quite different from the experiences of many teachers and educators who were raised and educated during the 20th century, a time before the onset of digital and online technology and social media networks. The most popular media were print newspapers and television news shows. Still today, literature curricula largely consists of texts written pre-2000 with themes and ideas that reflect a different time period. Disciplinary content is being taught using outdated examples and materials and antiquated pedagogical strategies. If schools are to meet the changing demands and needs of today's youth generation, curricula and instructional practices must reflect and represent who young people are today and the tools, skills and information they will need to be successful in the future.

This review is guided by the following questions: What are best practices for centering the lives of young people in the classroom? How do we support their literacy practices and honor the diverse histories that they represent? We consider the myriad ways that literacy educators are working to make education relevant for young people today. It is essential that we answer the questions, often asked of us by our students: Why does this matter? Why is this important? Young people want to see themselves reflected in their education, and they want to know that their time spent in educational spaces is purposeful, productive, and worthwhile.

The chapter is organized in three main sections: (1) youth and popular culture; (2) youth, media, and digital technology; and (3) intersections of youth identities. The chapter is centered on the role of texts, tools, and intersections in shaping the literacy classroom. In the first section, we define popular culture, and specifically popular youth culture, then discuss particular kinds of popular culture texts and productions, such as young adult (YA) literature and hip-hop culture. We also explore practice-based research literature on the ways that young people are self-authoring popular texts through fan fiction, the arts, media and other multimodal compositions. In the second section, we look more closely at the kinds of tools that young people are using both in school and in out-of-school spaces. We consider what it means to be a native 21st-century digital technologies and literacies user and how this youth identity can inform teachers' instructional practices and choices.

In the final section, we highlight the importance of honoring the intersecting identities that young people embody and embrace through their literacy practices and how we, as literacy educators, might learn from their identity constructions as we think about our curricular and instructional choices. We challenge the implementation of culturally relevant pedagogy as a set of tools or methods and strategies, and instead look toward more nuanced and complicated attendance to the raced, gendered, classed, and other cultural understandings that young people take up. The National Council of Teachers of English/International Reading Association (NCTE/IRA; NCTE, 2012) standards recognize that "students participate as knowledgeable, reflective, creative, and critical members of a variety of literacy communities" and they "use spoken, written, and visual language to accomplish their own purposes (e.g., for learning, enjoyment, persuasion, and the exchange of information)." We look explicitly at how their participation in these literacy communities for their own purposes is shaped by their understandings of who they are and how literacy educators can leverage their identity constructions in the classroom. Their self-definitions and declarations become the starting point for promising literacy instruction.

YOUTH AND POPULAR CULTURE

What is "popular culture"? Particularly in researching the literacies of young people in the 21st century, popular culture bleeds digitally into academic, digital, and civic spaces in ways that are "connected" (Ito et al., 2013). At the same time, to better understand what can be read as *popular culture* for young people, a critical understanding of the term and its origins is important.

Heron-Hruby and Alvermann (2009) describe popular culture as "a complex system involving interplay among people, texts, and technologies" (p. 211). Their definition is broad enough to encompass both print media and digital, "participatory culture" (Jenkins, 2008). At the same time, by looking at the convergence of people and products, Heron-Hruby and Alvermann (2009) remind literacy scholars that popular culture is entrenched in the ideologies, identities, and concerns of the people producing, consuming, and exchanging ideas within society. More importantly, Heron-Hruby and Alvermann remind us that popular culture is a contested space of clashing ideologies; that is, what makes something popular and to whom is largely dependent on socially constructed hegemony. What is popular for a society's dominant group may not be the case for minority groups. The music, film, and online media that are construed as popular today ebb and flow with each generation. Yet decisions about popularity are not made at the individual level; they are conglomerations of repeated sounds, images, ideas. This is often driven by a corporate culture industry. And while digital technologies have partially disrupted some of the effectiveness of large industry conglomerates to drive definitions of popularity and adolescence, trends of what remains popular, consumptive media are still defined by record labels, corporate advertisements between do-it-yourself (DIY) YouTube videos, and Hollywood.

In addition to offering a critical understanding of how popular youth culture is a systematic construction that reaches far beyond individuals' personal tastes, we also must understand that this culture plays a significant role in shaping *who* students are perceived to be. And just as we earlier asked, "What is popular culture?," now we must ask two equally crucial questions for conscious literacies research in the 21st century: For whom is this culture? And who is represented? While literacy research has looked at how popular YA literature can help reflect identities and experiences of teens (Carroll, 1999), these identities tie specifically to themes of crises and health, or are relegated to looking at ethnic portrayals of youth in literature (Bishop, 2007; Sims, 1982). Looking at the covers of YA novels, the posters of the latest Hollywood blockbusters, and the images pasted to articles (both in print and on popular online media), "popular" can be often distilled to key cultural designators: White, thin, able-bodied, heterosexual, wealthy. Furthermore, popular images of people of color or of varied sexuality often reinforce dominant stereotypes. As we'll explore below, even the smattering of YA literature about nondominant groups can be seen as essentializing texts that reify stereotypes for mainstream readers.

Reading these dominant images manifested via the culture industry, the kinds of literacy practices of youth around popular culture today begin to become clear. The increasing fluidity and variability of modes of new media discourse (Kress, 2003) only heighten the need for students not simply to develop a media literacy (Baker, 2012; Hobbs, 2011; Schiebe & Rogow, 2012) but to incorporate more fully a critical media literacy lens that explores counterhegemonic readings of popular culture (Kellner, 1995; Share, 2008). Furthermore, in today's digital age, critical media literacy is not only about deciphering and critiquing popular culture but also actively constructing it (Garcia, Seglem, & Share, 2013; Jocson, 2014).

It is also important to note that the "youth" aspect of exploring youth popular culture is largely a modern conception that emerged in the years following World War II (Hine, 2000; Savage, 2007). Years following global conflict and industrialized innovation left youth with time, resources, and common experiences to shape a youth culture. It is in this context that familiar themes of rebellion, dissatisfaction, and personal exploration of aspects of identities such as class, gender, and sexuality emerged.

Petrone, Sarigianides, and Lewis (2015) suggest analyzing the representations of adolescents and teenagers through a youth lens, that is, with an analytic approach that seeks first to understand the ways that young people are reading their world. Such suggestions point to new ways literacy scholars will further take up a reading of popular culture within the lives of young people.

Below we look at genres of popular culture that have resonated within literacies research. In particular, we consider the role of YA literature and the increasingly globalized rise in hip-hop in youth culture as areas that have been significantly explored in both online and nondigital contexts. We follow this exploration of popular genres with a look at forms of 21st century literacies production that have been described in recent scholarship as an illustration of the forms of popular culture being generated within schools and informal learning environments.

YA Literature and Hip-Hop as Youth Culture

Following the previously mentioned rise of a teenage demographic, books written for and about teenage life have been largely a development of the 20th century, flourishing into a lucrative Hollywood market in the early years of the 21st century. Particularly rising in readership and reception in the 1960s and 1970s, YA literature has spoken to themes of adolescence in ways that continue to resonate with readers today. Topics such as angst, uncertainty, loss, longing, and desire made authors like Judy Blume, S. E. Hinton, and Robert Cormier perpetually familiar names for generations. And while these topics of YA literature continue to be mined by new authors and consumed by new readers, we want to highlight the voices too frequently missing in YA literature and how literacies research has taken up these spaces. In particular, the role of multicultural literature in the development of adolescents' identities has been seen as "transformative" (Haddix & Price-Dennis, 2013); youths' ability to see themselves within the texts that are written for them has become a crucial aspect of how YA literature is framed in English classrooms and as tools for preservice teacher development (Glenn, 2012).

At the same time, we've found the authors and choices of kinds of multicultural texts limiting. A multicultural canon (Garcia, 2013) of a small smattering of recurring authors (e.g., Walter Dean Myers, Sharon Draper, Sandra Cisneros, Sherman Alexie, and Gary Soto) means young people's exposure to protagonists of color in popular YA literature is limited. In a newspaper column, Corbin (2008), suggested that rather than simply mirroring lived experiences of Black males, the work of Walter Dean Myers "has been single-handedly responsible for educating suburban and private school kids about the lives of those who attend segregated city schools." Such anecdotal concerns, too, mirror the challenging ways that dominant ideologies refuse to see characters of color within the racialized lens an author may intend. In looking at racist vitriol toward the character Rue *in The Hunger Games*, our own scholarship (Garcia & Haddix, 2014, 2015) points to the invisibility of race even when racial markers are described by an author. Again, literacy scholarship within YA literature looks at positive aspects of the role of multicultural literature but does not always consider the scope of such texts as larger "learning ecologies" (Brown, 2000) on which social discourse ensues.

At the same time, literacies studies have only begun to explore the general "convergence" (Jenkins, 2008) of YA literature and the lucrative Hollywood film industry in the 21st century. In the post-Harry Potter world of book serializations transforming into blockbuster film franchises, the trend in YA literature is action-packed yarns that spill across trilogies (or longer) and are ripe for Hollywood adaptation. In this sense, we are reminded again to question who deems something popular and in what context. When the stakes of book publishing are aligned with larger filmgoing audiences, the literacy needs, civic identities, and identity conceptions that are taken up by teen readers become secondary concerns for publishers. Though tremendous literacy scholarship has taken up YA literature as a source for adolescent literacy development, it is largely done so with the recognition that such a genre is constant under flux and beyond the influence of educators.

Perhaps to a lesser degree than YA literature, the role of hip-hop—as both a music genre and a cultural practice—has become a central factor in how popular culture is understood by literacy research. Though the incorporation of rap lyrics into classrooms may be the most obvious avenue of the inclusion of hip-hop in formal literacy development, the role of hip-hop in shaping youth identity practices has also been a particularly important component of literacy scholarship (Sarkar & Allen, 2007). Furthermore, the linguistic practices of hip-hop in global contexts, popular rhetoric, and the lives of youth are also spaces for significant research (Alim, Baugh, & Bucholtz, 2011).

Looking at both YA literature and hip-hop as spaces of popular culture investigated by literacies research, we see a growing trend in these and other parts of popular culture in terms of how such media are leveraged for youth literacy development. In particular, a broad umbrella of literacy research has focused on harnessing popular culture as a means of youth self-exploration. From unpacking lived experiences to better question the world vis-à-vis autoethnography (Camangian, 2010) to looking at popular media depictions of sexual activity (Yang, 2014), popular culture as a literacy tool for academic, cultural, social, and emotional learning is a growing space of literacy research. Furthermore, the space of youth culture is particularly relevant in understanding how youths' literate lives are conceptualized. In constructing spaces in which students are empowered to engage in social justice and transformative dialogue, the environment of student literacies is just as key as the content of their popular culture (Gutiérrez, 2008).

Scholars have explored popular culture for unpacking representations of gender (Muhammad, 2015), race (Rubenstein-Avila, 2007), sexuality (Blackburn, 2014; Miller, 2014), and the intersection *across* these various aspects of identity (Haddix, 2012). In doing so, literacy research prods at the purposes of popular culture in young people's literate lives and how we conceptualize ourselves in adolescent contexts.

Forms of Popular Culture Literacy Production

Similar to harnessing popular culture as a means for self-exploration, we also want to address the various forms of writing and media production studied by literacy scholars within academic settings. Mirroring larger cultural trends in the 21st century, youth popular culture is increasingly more and more digitally mediated and performed in online spaces such as social networks. As a result, the genres of literacies performances are ones that are dispersed and often focus increasingly on the productive rather than consumptive elements of texts. For example, Black's (2009) research with English language learners within fanfiction communities—online communities where writers remix characters, places, or plots from existing narratives to tell new, original stories—emphasizes how the development of academic proficiencies does not have to omit any attention to the ways that students engage with digital technologies and popular media. In fact, her work illustrates how English language learners' participation in fanfiction communities becomes a pathway for their effective participation in an increasingly globalized and technology-oriented society as they are learning, creating, and communicating with other youth across the globe. Their identity as English language learners does not position them in a deficit way in fanfiction communities; instead, their knowledge and experience with popular media is celebrated and viewed as a strength.

In much the same way, being a language learner should not prohibit or deny student access to disciplinary content learning in the classroom space, particularly, as argued in Black's (2009) research, literacy learning that is grounded in 21st-century digital technologies and popular culture. Roozen (2009), too, explores the interplay of students' vernacular literacies in fanfiction communities out of school with disciplinary engagement in school. A potential implication, Roozen argues, of youths' out-of-school literacy practices for 21st-century classrooms is for teachers to find ways to incorporate, or "repurpose," youths' vernacular literacies to help students make sense of and engage with disciplinary literate activities. Engagement in out-of-school literacy practices such as fanfiction communities again becomes a pathway to in-school learning. Other studies have shown how educators incorporate the use of digital tools such as video (Jocson, 2014) and other composing tools (Kesler, Tinio, & Nolan, 2014) to employ critical literacy frameworks, encouraging students to question popular culture media and to then author and produce their own multimodal narratives and media. Students use digital tools to make deliberate authorial choices to create counternarratives to dominant media representations of youth culture.

YOUTH, MEDIA, AND 21ST-CENTURY LITERACIES

What it means to be a young person today is quite different from what it was just a few decades ago. Young people are understanding and communicating their lives through new forms of literacy production. Their accessibility to and ability to use digital tools to connect, to gather information, and to tell stories easily moves beyond the purview of schools and the classroom. Furthermore, the media are no longer dominated by mainstream journalists and the images and messages they convey. Dominant narrative representations about today's youth by mainstream media sources are challenged by the fast-pace production and publication of stories by youth about youth through the use of 21st-century digital tools (i.e., smartphones, tablets, computers) and social media platforms (i.e., Twitter, Instagram).

NCTE's (2013) definition of 21st-century literacies recognizes that "as society and technology change, so does literacy" and as such, youth must develop proficiency and competency in their use of digital tools. What constitutes a digital tool is ever-growing and changing, as new technologies are developing each day. While schools are challenged to keep up with the ongoing list of new technologies, youth are often the first to know of new developments in digital technologies because of their out-of-school literacy practices and engagements. Teachers can use digital tools as entry points to bringing critical literacy into the classroom (Avila & Moore, 2012). Employing digital tools within a critical literacy framework can challenge the move toward standardization movements and instead encourage students and teachers' creativity and individualization.

Both composing and comprehending processes are mediated through the use of 21st-century digital tools both out of school (Brass, 2008) and in school (Redmond & Maya, 2014). While much of today's youth communication takes place outside of school, the use of digital tools has tremendous potential to facilitate authentic learning and promote 21st-century skills inside our classrooms. Moreover, the educational scene of the 21st century necessitates new literacy abilities that require effective uses of digital tools for full participation. Literacy in the digital world demands that young people develop a range of reading and writing skills, including the abilities to access, analyze, evaluate, and communicate effectively using printed, visual, oral, and blended formats (Hobbs, 2011). Through the integration of critical media literacy and creative production experiences, we can shape our curricula to address evolving conceptions of literacy, meet Common Core State Standards, and foster 21st-century skills.

Literacy scholars have considered how new literacies pedagogies invite marginalized youth into the classroom space and can promote educational equity (Choudhury & Share, 2012; Ertl & Helling, 2011; Parker, 2013; Warschauer, Matuchniak, Pinkard, & Gadsden, 2010). Research on youth's digital literacy practices challenges old conceptions of a digital divide and the idea that certain groups lack access to technology and instead aims to unpack and complicate the ways that youth use technology based on race, gender, and class (Haddix & Sealey-Ruiz, 2012; Stewart, 2014; Warschauer et al., 2010). In case studies of the social networking literacy practices of four Latin@ immigrant youth, Stewart (2014) discusses how they are literate in a number of ways, including ways that are not privileged by schools, highlighting the disconnect that can occur between school, home, and their postsecondary lives. Incorporating the use of digital tools to create multimedia projects, as in Choudhury and Share's (2012) study of a first-year teacher's journey to implement a critical media literacy approach, allowed students to connect back to the issues relevant in their communities, while at the same time building self-esteem. And, although not the focus of their research study, the authors found that there were also increases in English proficiency on standardized tests. More important, however, was students' increased engagement with literacy learning on school-based tasks and expectations. The purpose of their literacy engagement was not just to perform well on tests; students were also able to see real connections and relevance to their communities and in their lives.

New literacies pedagogies also require that both students and teachers broaden their notions of what constitutes literacy and literacy learning. Inviting the use of digital tools into classroom spaces can only happen when such tools are viewed as legitimate, valued, and necessary resources for optimal literacy learning. By taking the time to implement technologies in classrooms, teachers are able to expand their pedagogy and the definition of literacy, and to approach literacy from a place of multiplicity (Labbo & Place, 2010). Ertl and Helling (2011) raised awareness about gender stereotypes in the context of digital literacy, which suggests that boys are more interested in computer hardware and programming, while girls are more interested in software and Internet applications. They instead advocate for critical media literacy approaches that allow for and encourage youth to rescript their gender representations and to closely examine their own self-concepts related to digital technologies and use. Students can do such rescripting, rewriting, and reimagining through their own media productions.

Parker (2013) explores what can happen when students take on the identity of filmmakers in an examination of social factors that impact the lives of U.S. Latin@

immigrants. Parker writes about "their roles as media makers, analyzing how media creations can add to and potentially challenge the sociopolitical logic" (p. 669). In this work, students were able to broaden their understanding and notions of literacy. Furthermore, the opportunity to engage through filmmaking allowed the emergence of these particular students' voices and helped them to flourish. The author applies the borderlands concept to the school, writing about how the students crossed traditional boundaries set by schools to deal with complex subjects and to conduct difficult interviews with adults in their filmmaking project.

In response to literature, and in support of their comprehension processes, teachers' incorporation of digital media production (Redmond & Maya, 2014) and digital storytelling (Tobin, 2012) not only facilitate students' development of oral language and multimedia communication skills but also provide for greater literary connection to texts. Teachers use digital tools to engage students in multimedia character analyses (Redmond & Maya, 2014), in multimodal and multimedia approaches to literature circles (Tobin, 2012), and in the creation of digital comics and other forms of digital storytelling to make meaning of fiction and nonfiction texts (Wissman & Costello, 2014). In Wissman and Costello's study of eighth graders participating in a reading support class as they read *The Outsiders* (Hinton, 1967), they expected students to talk about the appeal of using new technologies and digital literacies in school when asked to speak about their experiences creating a digital comic to represent a scene from the text. Instead, they found that many students described their learning in language more closely aligned with the arts, self-expression, and literary response. Students spoke enthusiastically about the opportunity to be creative, to use their imaginations, and to share their own perspectives on the novel. The use of digital tools was a conduit for this, but the emphasis was on the forms of creative expression that were facilitated through these new literacy pedagogies. Starting with the premise that "students are legitimate authorities on issues of teaching and learning" (Cook-Sather, 2006, p. 345) and on their own literate lives, the authors contend that rich descriptions of students' creative processes, products, and perspectives have implications for integrating the digital arts into classrooms. Instead of implementing digital tools for the sake of keeping up with changing technologies, it is important that instructional goals and objectives remain attuned to the arts, aesthetics, and literacies (Vasudevan, 2010) and to transactional theories of response to literature (Rosenblatt, 1982).

The use of digital tools require that teachers rethink their role as teachers and their thinking about literacy instruction (Roach & Beck, 2012). In fact, digital technologies are a powerful tool for instigating the shifting of instructional ideologies and philosophies. Wickens, Manderino, and Glover (2015) describe one teacher's "efforts to bridge digital literacies with disciplinary literacy" and shows "how classroom blogging activities can facilitate the development of disciplinary thinking and reasoning" (p. 24). The teacher uses *kidblog.org* and integrated the blog created through this website into her English language arts (ELA) and social studies curricula. They found that the blog platform increased both the quantity and depth of student writing and changed the kinds of teacher–student interactions that were possible. Blogging as a new instructional technology led to a shift in the teacher's instruction and thinking about what counts as literacy. Sometimes teachers who are novices at using digital technology can learn about new literacies pedagogies while implementing its use.

In considering popular culture and the role of media in the classroom space, the use of digital tools and new literacies can be a way for teachers to support students in their own identity constructions and in the telling of their own stories. McGinnis, Goodstein-Stolzenberg, and Costa Saliani (2007) reviewed three case studies of transnational youth (youth who hold affinity ties and/or affiliations to two or more countries) who present their identities, maintain social relations, and create transnational communities through digital spaces and online communication. They used digital tools, such as social networking sites, blog spaces, and online websites, to reflect multiple identifications and negotiate their various social locations, specifically those based on gender, race, and ethnicity. They found that youth utilize such spaces to maintain international relationships, to articulate and respond to global politics, and to express pride in their cultural heritage. In addition to engaging in digital literacies, such spaces allowed them to draw on multiple languages and to use multimodal forms to enact their identities. Through the use of 21st-century literacies, digital tools, and social media, teachers can leverage students' perspectives and their abilities to think and communicate critically about issues important to them and to their communities.

INTERSECTIONS OF RACE, CLASS, GENDER, SEXUALITY, AND SOCIAL HISTORIES IN YOUTH MEDIA AND POP CULTURE

In this final section, we review approaches that create critical spaces in which young people examine the intersections of race, class, gender, sexuality, and other social histories and identities in youth media and popular culture. We look more closely at the role of identities in literacy practices and, by extension, literacy instruction. One of our aims in this final section is to disrupt the deficit framing of youth literacy users, and the devaluing and undermining of their literacy practices. We also want to avoid limited and narrow representations of their multiple and complex identities by reviewing the literature in categories organized by identity markers. In this way, intersectionality demands that voices be heard and lives be acknowledged (Dill & Zambrana, 2009). We cross identity borders in efforts to address the importance of creating classroom spaces that uphold a fuller vision of the identities, histories, and experiences of the youth, and honor the intersections of those identities. In other words, understanding one's racial identity requires situating race within the context of gender, sexuality, class, and other lived experiences and cultural ways of knowing. Every two Black young persons are not the same, and what it means to be queer for one person might mean something completely different for another. As we reconsider the literacy research on 21st-century youth, popular culture, media, tools, and texts discussed in the previous sections, we make an explicit turn toward centering the self-identifications of the young people with whom we work and identifying those pedagogical approaches that encourage us to do so.

There exists a long line of research that advocates culturally relevant (Ladson-Billings, 1995), responsive (Gay, 2000), affirming (Nieto & Bode, 2011), and sustaining (Paris, 2012) pedagogies, as well as critiques of how these theories have been misinterpreted and misused (Ladson-Billings, 2014; Paris & Alim, 2014). These approaches risk doing harm when not connected to 21st-century youth culture and ever-shifting global identities, because they then become mere checklists and scripted curricula disconnected from youths' lived realities. As stated earlier, what it means to be a young person today and in this moment is distinct from what this meant 20 years ago and even 20 months ago. What is important and relevant to young people is rapidly shifting, and as literacy educators, we must stay tuned in to these shifts that are digitally mediated and socially networked. Appropriating pedagogical approaches introduced 20 years ago within a particular context is not sufficient when addressing the demands and interests of young people in our classrooms today. So, the question becomes, what does it mean to be culturally relevant and responsive in a 21st-century digital world? What are the links between engaging culturally relevant pedagogical approaches and bringing popular culture into the classroom?

Centering Youth Cultures and Identities First

The acts of teaching and learning are largely about establishing relationships and building trust. Optimal learning can take place in school spaces when students and teachers feel valued, respected, seen, and heard. Culturally relevant pedagogy then becomes more than teaching that incorporates elements of youth culture or popular culture and is about "seeing" and "knowing" the students in authentic, concrete ways. As discussed earlier, Camangian (2010) describes how the use of autoethnography in a high school classroom led to the creation of a more caring and humanized learning space. The act of caring is a pedagogical objective requiring that teachers value students' cultural experiences and associate youth culture with positive impacts on student effort, increased engagement with course content, and improved academic achievement. Camangian also discusses how taking a sociocritical literacy stance can maximize students' abilities to read, write, think, and communicate by drawing from their funds of knowledge (Moll, Amanti, Neff, & Gonzalez, 1992). By taking this stance, teachers also encourage students to interrogate their multiple identities and the social conditions that define their worldviews. Additionally, the creation of autoethnographies provided students with a space to make sense of their experiences while beginning to understand how it shaped their identities. Students began to value learning from one another's lived experiences, to understand one another across differences, and to unify at personal, cultural, and community levels. Hearing other youths' perspectives provided students with multiple lenses through which to view their community realities and allowed them to recognize common social oppression and marginalization.

Ultimately, Camangian (2010) presented an approach to literacy instruction that puts students first and that begins with a critical interrogation of both teachers and students about their social locations and histories. In creating classroom spaces that operate on a caring and humanizing premise, teachers listen to the voices of their students. Duncan-Andrade (2004) disrupts a simplistic, additive approach to incorporating popular culture into the classroom by seeking the perspectives of young people. Youth are seen as knowledge producers with critical perspectives that are invaluable to instructional planning. He interviewed students who articulated their dissatisfaction with current teaching practices around the use of popular culture. He drew upon their voiced experiences to argue for a more culturally relevant curriculum that uses popular films and music as legitimate academic texts, envisioning a new kind of multicultural curriculum. He saw that while the aims of and the value of popular culture in education might appear progressive and student centered, a paradoxical outcome is that incorporating popular culture can readily become a process of consumption and not production or individual and collective interpretation. Furthermore, when popular culture texts were viewed as rewards and positioned opposite the mainstream texts that were viewed as the norm, students were denied the opportunity to see their engagement with popular culture and media as a legitimate form of literacy development. Duncan-Andrade argues for the use of a "culture as additive" model of education, insisting that it allows teachers to employ an ethic of authentic caring through the creation of a classroom culture that draws from the cultural sensibilities of young people. Similarly, Reyes (2009) writes about how this is possible in a biology club when she describes how a Latin@ high school student was able to reflect her multiple identities, especially her religious identity, in a science scrapbook. When the student was "outed" as being religious in her classroom, she chose to create a scrapbook that documented her experiences in the biology club. The scrapbook included religious drawings and Spanish-language poetry, and contained letters and notes to friends that mention religion and spirituality both in English and Spanish. Reyes uses the example of the student's creation of the scrapbook to argue that innovative texts may allow students to reflect their changing, culture-embedded identities.

Presuming Competence in and out of School Spaces

A prevalent theme within the research literature is the false binaries created around youths' literacy practices in school versus out-of-school spaces (Hull & Shultz, 2001). An example is when a teacher is surprised to learn about the myriad ways his or her student engages in literacy practices in out-of-school spaces in comparison to that student's literacy performance in school. There exists an assumption that if a student does not display literacy proficiencies on school-sanctioned tasks, he or she is somehow not literate. This deficit perspective and framing then positions the student's out-of-school literacy practices as exceptional and encourages the teacher's disbelief. Furthermore, the use of popular culture to engage the student is viewed as a hoax and is situated oppositionally to the real tasks at hand—standardized testing and traditional, mainstream curriculum. What might happen if we presume literacy competence for those students most at risk for being seen and understood from deficit perspectives—students of color, students with disabilities, and English language learners, for example? What if we begin to see their literacy engagements with popular culture as the norm and not as the exception?

For example, there exists widespread (mis)belief that hip-hop culture is one way that educators risk dumbing down the curriculum to engage urban youth, particular youth of color from working-class backgrounds. Instead, engaging hip-hop culture in the literacy curriculum is one way to centralize students' lives and maximize possibilities for learning (Alim et al., 2011; Sakar & Allen, 2007). Hip-hop culture is instead positioned as a strength and not as a deficit. Alim et al. (2011) discuss the idea of "ill-literacies," the hybrid, transcultural linguistic and literacy practices of hip-hop youth in local and global contexts. The term *ill-literacy* refers to schools' misreading of the cultural gap as an achievement gap, and in particular, limiting and prescribing limits to the intellectual possibilities of youths' use of and identification with nonstandard language varieties as opposed to standard forms. Alim et al. provide several examples of these global ill-literacies to demonstrate the expansive nature of hip-hop language and to signal the need for schools to adopt new definitions of language to prioritize youth identities. Within hip-hop cultural spaces, youth identities are viewed from a dominant perspective, and engagement with hip-hop culture provides for youth an opportunity to participate in the creation of the cultural and linguistic diversity around them. Global ill-literacies, Alim et al., argue, make the politics of literacy explicit by framing literacy as a contested site of unequal power relationships, and they call for a student-centered pedagogical practice requiring a revolutionary focus on intimacy, the creation of safe space for students, the view that literacy is liberatory, and a willingness to engage conflict. As discussed earlier, engaging hip-hop pedagogy in the classroom can be a move toward these goals and the development of students' critical literacy awareness and meta-literacy. This is one way that out-of-school literacies achieve presumed competence and are viewed as funds of knowledge for students' in-school learning.

There is also a fear that the curriculum is somehow not rigorous enough if it engages popular culture or students' outside interests. Centering students' identities, experiences, and interests does not have to replace the use of critical pedagogies, theories, and literacies. Several literacy scholars have examined the use of critical literacy (Johnson & Vasudevan, 2012; Luke, 2000), sociocritical literacy (Gutiérrez, 2008), and critical media literacy as frameworks for supporting young people's critical engagements with texts and as a tool for young people to resist and challenge misrepresentations of their identities. Gutiérrez (2008) discusses how *sociocritical literacy*—a historicizing literacy that privileges and is contingent on students' sociohistorical lives, both proximally and distally—can create third spaces that reorganize everyday concepts into scientific or school-based concepts. In third spaces, students begin to reconceive who they are and what they might be able to accomplish academically. Moje et al. (2004) ask the questions: What are the different funds of knowledge and discourses that may shape students' reading, writing, and talking about texts in their science classrooms? And, when and how, if at all, do students bring these knowledges and discourses to bear on school learning? In their ethnographic study with Latino middle school students working with popular culture in the science curriculum, Moje and her colleagues found that the third space mediated students drawing on both their strong sense of ethnic identity and popular culture texts to make connections with the science curriculum.

In out-of-school and "other" spaces (Wissman, 2011), youth writers presume writing competence, and their writing practices extend well beyond the expectations of school. Their critical encounters with popular culture texts, media, and in digital spaces, cultivate the creation of multimodal expressions and genres that disrupt the dichotomous positioning of out-of-school literacy practices to those in schools. Their youth literacies can be a bridge to the other kinds of writing that they are expected to complete in school. Acknowledging that writing happens beyond school walls also challenges a deficit framing of their writing proficiencies and capacities. Writing can be conceptualized as a thread that crosses in-school and out-of-school settings, and that relationships exist between these writing practices (Haddix, 2012; Muhammad, 2012; Schultz, 2002; Wissman, 2011; Yi, 2010).

Acknowledgement of out-of-school writing can help students develop a writer identity and it can help teachers understand their students as writers. Haddix (2012) found that the African American male students participating in her summer writing institute began to take on a writing identity and to see school as a place where they belonged, that is, where their identities and backgrounds where legitimated, valued, and welcomed. Wissman (2011) examined the literacy practices that emerged in an in-school elective course centered in the literacy tradition of African American women. She considered it an "other space," in which there is no mandated curriculum or standardized test pressures. Instead, the space is informed by an understanding of the connections among literacies, lived experiences, and identities. In this class, students created a writing community and read, discussed, and wrote about being young women. Students took up opportunities to pursue literacy work and crafted the space to meet their own purposes. They explored the sociopolitical and embodied nature of literacies, pursued self-definition, and made meaning within a community. In a summer writing institute for Black adolescent female writers, Muhammad (2012) found that writing was a key literacy practice for Black adolescent girls to make meaning of their identities. Within the summer writing institute, there were opportunities for the female writers to discuss their writing and to exert selfhood, an outcome that was not often achieved on in-school writing assignments. Muhammad's work offers concrete strategies for how this identity work can happen in school spaces and stresses the point that in-school writing must not be devoid of an awareness and appreciation of student' interests and expressions of their selves.

Disrupting (Mis)representations of Youth Identities and Youth Culture

Teachers can employ a critical literacy approach to support students' unpacking and deconstructing of media representations of youth culture and identities. A critical literacy approach can also move teachers toward a broader understanding and empathy toward youths' ways of knowing and being. Ultimately, much of this work is about seeing and hearing students' lived and embodied experiences, and making connections to their literacy learning and practices (Johnson & Vasudevan, 2012). Johnson and Vasudevan offer an expanded definition of critical literacy that draws attention to what counts as popular culture texts and that is inclusive of youth's physical bodies, gestures, dress, and performances. Youths' literacy performances and embodied experiences can push back against dominant misrepresentations of who they are and how they envision and imagine themselves.

By exploring youth literacy performances from a critical literacy perspective, teachers can also work with youth to make explicit and unpack dominant discourses about race, class, gender, and sexuality. Using queer theory, critical feminism, critical race theory, and New Literacy studies, Blackburn (2003) explores the literacy practices of queer youth in a Speaker's Bureau in an LGBTQ (lesbian, gay, bisexual, transgender, queer) youth center. In the Speaker's Bureau, the youth were charged with the facilitation of an outreach program and became activists through their work. Though they worked to disrupt heterosexism and homophobia in their outreach work, their reading, writing, and composing while doing so reified unequal power dynamics within the center. Blackburn's work has illuminated the complexities and nuanced nature of a critical literacy approach that requires teachers and students to read beyond the text and to attend directly to social issues, injustices, and power dynamics. Teachers can create spaces for young people who want to take a social justice stance against stigmatizing media representations and work against racist, sexist, classist, and homophobia ideologies and practices through their multimodal composing and critical encounters with popular culture texts (Guzzetti & Gamboa, 2004; Kelly, 2006).

INVITING IN WHAT'S "POPULAR" IN STUDENTS' LIVES

Our goal in this chapter has been to consider the myriad ways that popular culture is understood in the lives of young people—both within and beyond school spaces—and how educators might leverage popular youth culture connections in order to (1) honor their cultural and personal expressions of selfhood and (2) support their literacy practices that aim to disrupt and dismantle media misrepresentations of race, class, gender, and sexuality. What is "popular" extends well beyond a notion of what's trendy, in vogue, or adorned by the newest celebrity frenzy. Instead, the conceptions of "popular," "culture," and "text" are intrinsically linked to students' understandings of themselves, their histories, and their lived experiences. These conceptions are also connected to young people's sense of agency and activism, and their desire to be civically engaged with real issues in the world. They are using 21st-century digital technologies to voice and communicate their ideas and narratives, as well as to participate in global conversations.

How students engage with and create popular culture texts does not have to be relegated to outside the classroom. Furthermore, it is damaging and counterproductive to maintain false binaries between in- and out-of-school literacy practices and performances. Instead, literacy educators must have at the forefront not only a desire and a primary objective to acknowledge and celebrate the social histories of their students but also to be explicit about the ways that their literacy performances and engagements can prepare them for postsecondary life. Young people want to see and understand the relevance of literacy tasks beyond the passing of standardized tests. Reading and writing popular culture and engaging with 21st-century literacies are not trivial undertakings. In fact, these youth literacy performances exemplify reading and being in the world.

REFERENCES

Alim, H. S., Baugh, J., & Bucholtz, M. (2011). Global Ill-literacies: Hip hop cultures, youth identities, and the politics of literacy. *Review of Research in Education, 35*, 120–146.

Avila, J., & Moore, M. (2012). Critical literacy, digital literacies and a Common Core state standards: A workable union? *Theory Into Practice, 51*, 27–33.

Baker, F. W. (2012). *Media literacy in the K–12 classroom.* Eugene, OR: International Society for Technology in Education.

Bishop, R. S. (2007). *Free within ourselves: The development of African American children's literature.* Portsmouth, NH: Heinemann.

Black, R. W. (2009). English-language learners, fan communities, and 21st-century skills. *Journal of Adolescent and Adult Literacy, 52*(8), 688–697.

Blackburn, M. (2003). Exploring literacy performances and power dynamics at the loft: "Queer youth reading the world and the word." *Research in the Teaching of English, 37*, 467–490.

Blackburn, M. (2014). Humanizing research with LGBTQ youth through dialogic communication, consciousness raising, and action. In D. Paris & M. T. Winn (Eds.), *Humanizing research: Decolonizing qualitative inquiry with youth and communities* (pp. 43–57). Thousand Oaks, CA: Sage.

Brass, J. J. (2008). Local knowledge and digital movie composing in an after-school literacy program. *Journal of Adolescent and Adult Literacy, 51*(6), 464–473.

Brown, J. S. (2000, March/April). Growing up digital: How the web changes work, education, and the ways people learn. *Change,* pp. 10–20.

Camangian, P. (2010). Starting with self: Teaching autoethnography to foster critically caring literacies. *Research in the Teaching of English, 45*(2), 179–204.

Carroll, P. S. (Ed.). (1999). *Using literature to help troubled teenagers cope with societal issues.* Westport, CT: Greenwood Press.

Choudhury, M., & Share, J. (2012). Critical media literacy: A pedagogy for new literacies and urban youth. *Voices from the Middle, 19*(4), 39–44.

Cook-Sather, A. (2006). "Change based on what students say": Preparing teachers for a more paradoxical model of leadership. *International Journal of Leadership in Education, 9,* 345–358.

Corbin, M. (2008). The invisibles: Young adult fiction has yet to hear the voices of young, urban, and black readers. Retrieved November 17, 2012, from *www2.citypaper.com/special/story.asp?id=16744*.

Dill, B. T., & Zambrana, R. E. (2009). *Emerging intersections: Race, class, and gender in theory, policy, and practice.* New Brunswick, NJ: Rutgers University Press.

Duncan-Andrade, J. M. R. (2004). Your best friend or your worst enemy: Youth popular culture, pedagogy, and curriculum in urban classrooms. *Review of Education, Pedagogy, and Cultural Studies, 26*(4), 313–337.

Ertl, B., & Helling, K. (2011). Promoting gender equality in digital literacy. *Journal Educational Computing Research, 45*(4), 477–503.

Garcia, A. (2013). *Critical foundations in young adult literature: Challenging genres.* Rotterdam, The Netherlands: Sense.

Garcia, A., & Haddix, M. (2014). The revolution starts with Rue: Online fandom and the racial politics of *The Hunger Games.* In S. P. Connors (Ed.), *The politics of Panem: Challenging genres* (pp. 213–217). Rotterdam, The Netherlands: Sense.

Garcia, A., & Haddix, M. (2015). Reading YA with "Dark Brown Skin": Race, community, and Rue's uprising. *The ALAN Review, 42*(2), 37–44.

Garcia, A., Seglem, R., & Share, J. (2013). Transforming teaching and learning through critical media literacy pedagogy. *Learning Landscapes, 6*(2), 109–123.

Gay, G. (2000). *Culturally responsive teaching: Theory, research, and practice.* New York: Teachers College Press.

Glenn, W. J. (2012). Developing understandings of race: Preservice teachers' counter-narrative (re)constructions of people of color in young adult literature. *English Education, 4,* 326–353.

Gutiérrez, K. D. (2008). Developing a sociocritical literacy in the third space. *Reading Research Quarterly, 43*(2), 148–164.

Guzzetti, B. J., & Gamboa, M. (2004). Zines for social justice: Adolescent girls writing on their own. *Reading Research Quarterly, 39*(4), 408–436.

Haddix, M. (2012). Reclaiming and rebuilding the writer identities of Black adolescent males. In D. E. Alvermann & K. A. Hinchman (Eds.), *Reconceptualizing the literacies in adolescents' lives: Bridging the everyday/academic divide* (3rd ed., pp. 112–131). New York: Routledge.

Haddix, M., & Price-Dennis, D. (2013). Urban fiction and multicultural literature as transformative tools for preparing English teachers for diverse classrooms. *English Education, 45*(3), 247–283.

Haddix, M., & Sealey-Ruiz, Y. (2012). Cultivating digital and popular literacies as empowering and emancipatory acts among urban youth. *Journal of Adolescent and Adult Literacy, 56*(3), 189–192.

Heron-Hruby, A., & Alvermann, D. E. (2009). Implications of adolescents' popular culture use for school literacy. In K. D. Wood & W. E. Blanton (Eds.), *Literacy instruction for adolescents: Research-based practice* (pp. 210–224). New York: Guilford Press.

Hine, T. (2000). *The rise and fall of the American teenager: A new history of the American adolescent experience.* New York: Harper Perennial.

Hinton, S. E. (1967). *The outsiders.* New York: Viking Penguin.

Hobbs, R. (2011). *Digital and media literacy: Connecting culture and classroom.* Thousand Oaks, CA: Corwin.

Hull, G., & Schultz, K. (2001). Literacy and learning out of school: A review of theory and research. *Review of Educational Research, 71*(4), 575–611.

Ito, M., Gutierrez, K., Livingstone, S., Penuel, B., Rhodes, J., Salen, K., et al. (2013). *Connected learning: An agenda for research and design.* Irvine, CA: Digital Media and Learning Research Hub.

Jenkins, H. (2008). *Convergence culture: Where old and new media collide*. New York: New York University Press.

Jocson, K. (2014). Critical media ethnography: Youth media research. In D. Paris & M. T. Winn (Eds.), *Humanizing research: Decolonizing qualitative inquiry with youth and communities* (pp. 105–123). Thousand Oaks, CA: Sage.

Johnson, E., & Vasudevan, L. (2012). Seeing and hearing students' lived and embodied critical literacy practices. *Theory Into Practice, 51*(1), 34–41.

Kellner, D. (1995). *Media culture: Cultural studies, identity and politics between the modern and the postmodern*. London: Routledge.

Kelly, D. M. (2006). Frame work: Helping youth counter their misrepresentations in media. *Canadian Journal of Education, 29*(1), 27–48.

Kesler, T., Tinio, P. P. L., & Nolan, B. T. (2014). What's our position?: A critical media literacy study of popular culture websites with eighth-grade special education students. *Reading and Writing Quarterly, 32*, 1–26.

Kress, G. (2003). *Literacy in the new media age*. New York: Routledge.

Labbo, L., & Place, K. (2010). Fresh perspectives on new literacies and technology integration. *Voices in the Middle, 17*, 9–18.

Ladson-Billings, G. (1995). Toward a theory of culturally relevant pedagogy. *American Educational Research Journal, 32*(3), 465–491.

Ladson-Billings, G. (2014). Culturally relevant pedagogy 2.0: a.k.a. the remix. *Harvard Educational Review, 84*, 74–84.

Luke, A. (2000). Critical literacy in Australia: A matter of context and standpoint. *Journal of Adolescent and Adult Literacy, 43*(5), 448–461.

McGinnis, T., Goodstein-Stolzenberg, A., & Costa Saliani, E. (2007). "indnpride": Online spaces of transnational youth as sites of creative and sophisticated literacy and identity work. *Linguistics and Education, 18*, 283–304.

Miller, s. j. (2014). Hungry like the wolf: Gender non-conformity in YAL. In C. Hill (Ed.), *The critical merits of young adult literature: Coming of age* (pp. 55–72). New York: Routledge.

Moje, E. B., McIntosh Ciechanowski, K., Kramer, K., Ellis, L., Carrillo, R., & Collazo, T. (2004). Working toward third space in content area literacy: An examination of everyday funds of knowledge and discourse. *Reading Research Quarterly, 39*(1), 38–70.

Moll, L. C., Amanti, C., Neff, D., & Gonzalez, N. (1992). Funds of knowledge for teaching: Using a qualitative approach to connect homes and classrooms. *Theory Into Practice, 31*(2), 132–141.

Muhammad, G. E. (2012). Creating spaces for Black adolescent girls to "write it out!" *Journal of Adolescent and Adult Literacy, 56*(3), 203–211.

Muhammad, G. E. (2015). In search for a full vision: Writing representations of African American adolescent girls. *Research in the Teaching of English, 49*(3), 224–247.

National Council of Teachers of English. (2013). The NCTE definition of 21st century literacies. Retrieved from *www.ncte.org/positions/statements/21stcentdefinition*.

Nieto, S., & Bode, P. (2011). *Affirming diversity: The sociopolitical context of multicultural education* (6th ed.). Boston: Pearson.

Paris, D. (2012). Culturally sustaining pedagogy: A needed change in stance, terminology, and practice. *Educational Researcher, 41*(3), 93–97.

Paris, D., & Alim, H. S. (2014). What are we seeking to sustain with culturally sustaining pedagogy?: A loving critique forward. *Harvard Educational Review, 84*, 85–100, 134, 136–137.

Parker, J. (2013). Critical literacy and the ethical responsibilities of the student media production. *Journal of Adolescent and Adult Literacy, 56*(8), 668–676.

Petrone, R., Sarigianides, S. T., & Lewis, M. A. (2015). The youth lens: Analyzing adolescence/ts in literary texts. *Journal of Literacy Research, 46*(4), 506–533.

Redmond, T., & Maya, M. (2014). Multimedia character analysis: How digital production fosters twenty-first century literacy. *Voices from the Middle, 22*(1), 63–69.

Reyes, C. C. (2009). El libro de recuerdos [book of memories]: A Latina student's exploration of self and religion in public school. *Research in the Teaching of English, 43*(3), 263–285.

Roach, A., & Beck, J. (2012). Before coffee, facebook: New literacy learning for 21st century teachers. *Language Arts, 89*(4), 244–255.

Roozen, K. (2009). "Fan fic-ing" English studies: A case study exploring the interplay of vernacular literacies and disciplinary engagement. *Research in the Teaching of English, 44*(2), 136–169.

Rosenblatt, L. (1982). The literary transaction: Evocation and response. *Theory Into Practice, 21*(4), 268–277.

Rubenstein-Avila, E. (2007). Examining representations of young adult female protagonists through a critical race feminism. *Changing English, 14,* 363–374.

Sarkar, M., & Allen, D. (2007). Hybrid identities in Quebec hip-hop: Language, territory, and ethnicity in the mix. *Journal of Language, Identity, and Education, 6*(2), 117–130.

Savage, J. (2007). *The prehistory of youth culture, 1875–1945.* New York: Penguin Books.

Scheibe, C., & Rogow, F. (2012). *The teacher's guide to media literacy: Critical thinking in a multimedia world.* Thousand Oaks, CA: Corwin.

Schultz, K. (2002). Looking across space and time: Reconceptualizing literacy learning in and out of school. *Research in the Teaching of English, 36,* 356–390.

Share, J. (2008). *Media literacy is elementary: Teaching youth to critically read and create media.* New York: Peter Lang.

Sims, R. (1982). *Shadow and substance: Afro-American experience in contemporary children's fiction.* Urbana, IL: National Council of Teachers of English.

Stewart, M. A. (2014). Social networking, workplace, and entertainment literacies: The out-of-school literate lives of newcomer Latina/o adolescents. *Reading Research Quarterly, 49*(4), 365–369.

Tobin, M. (2012). Digital storytelling: Reinventing literature circles. *Voices from the Middle, 20*(2), 40–48.

Vasudevan, L. (2010). Education remix: New media, literacies, and emerging digital geographies. *Digital Culture and Education, 2*(1), 62–82.

Warschauer, M., Matuchniak, T., Pinkard, N., & Gadsden, V. (2010). New technology and digital worlds: Analyzing evidence of equity in access, use, and outcomes. *Review of Research in Education, 34,* 179–225.

Wickens, C. M., Manderino, M., & Glover, E. A. (2015). Developing disciplinary literacy through classroom blogging. *Voices from the Middle, 22*(3), 24–32.

Wissman, K., & Costello, S. (2014). Creating digital comics in response to literature: Aesthetics, aesthetic transactions, and meaning making. *Language Arts, 92*(2), 103–117.

Wissman, K. K. (2011). "Rise up!": Literacies, lived experiences, and identities within an in-school "other space." *Research in the Teaching of English, 45*(4), 405–438.

Yang, H. C. (2014). Teaching sexual matters in Taiwan: The analytical framework for popular culture and youth sexuality education. *Asia Pacific Journal of Education, 34*(1), 49–64.

Yi, Y. (2010). Adolescent multilingual writers' transitions across in- and out-of-school writing contexts. *Journal of Second Language Writing, 19*(1), 17–32.

CHAPTER 3

Adolescent Literacies beyond Heterosexual Hegemony

MOLLIE V. BLACKBURN and RYAN SCHEY

This chapter reviews current literature in the fields of education and literacy with particular attention to sexual identities and gender expressions beyond what Atkinson and DePalma (2009) call heterosexual hegemony. We draw on sociocultural notions of literacy, or, in Street's (1999) terms, the *ideological model of literacy*. This model recognizes literacy, that is, reading and writing, as social practices, in that literacy is "always practiced in social contexts" (p. 37), including but not limited to schools. As such, literacy "varies with social context and is not the same, uniform thing in each case" (p. 37). That is to say, just as writing a text or email to a friend is different work than writing an argumentative essay for a teacher, so too is writing an argumentative essay for the same teacher in the same class about an issue in which one is deeply invested different than one that is not. The work, the writing, is simply qualitatively different, both across contexts and within any given context. Therefore, in order to study literacy, one must examine literacy events, which are "observable behaviors around literacy" (p. 38), to develop an understanding of literacy practices, which focus on "cultural practices with which uses of reading and/or writing are associated in given contexts" (p. 38). In order to study texting among adolescents, we must not only study one or more texts but also the young people writing, sending, receiving, reading, and responding to them, as well as the spaces they inhabit as they do so. According to Hornberger (2000), examining literacy events in relation to literacy practices invites an understanding of "the more ideological aspects" of literacy, such as "underlying norms, values, and conventions" (p. 60). In other words, literacy events are occasions, such as texting someone, while literacy practices are series of occasions in which the sociocultural values reflected in these occasions are made visible.

To conceptualize sexual identity and gender expression, we turn to Butler's (1990) critique of the heterosexual matrix, in which sexuality and gender are socially and culturally constructed as dichotomous; that is, there are boys/men who are masculine and as such desire girls/women who are feminine. The notion of masculine girls/women or feminine boys/men is impermissible in the heterosexual matrix. Moreover, the notion that boys/men might desire each other, rather than girls/women, or vice versa, is also impermissible. Such notions of gender (and sex) are understood by some people as natural, just the way things are, but they also constrain people; think here of a feminine boy who likes other boys. The constraints come with consequences; that boy is called names such as "faggot" and is slammed into lockers at school. He is, in very material ways, punished for his performance of gender; he is oppressed, pushed out. As such, the "natural" order of gender (and sex) is maintained; the heterosexual matrix is maintained. Thus, Butler argues, dichotomous notions of gender are insidious cultural fictions that work to control people, forcing them into the confines of the heterosexual matrix, which ensures privileges for straight men in particular.

Atkinson and DePalma (2009), however, drawing on later work by Butler, argue that "through naming and believing the heterosexual matrix and identifying evidence of its operation, we reify, reinforce and reinscribe it, even as we attempt to subvert, unsettle or deconstruct it" (p. 17). In other words, they say, "our critique [of the heterosexual matrix] actually generates heteronormativity by consent" (p. 19). For example, by conjuring the image of the effeminate boy shoved up against a locker, we remind people of the dangers of breaking with heteronormativity; in a sense, we scare people into conforming. Atkinson and DePalma, then, offer an alternative: "*heterosexual hegemony,* which they define as a "collective process, that . . . requires constant construction" (p. 18). Heterosexual hegemony provokes but also depends on "consensual heteronormativity" (p. 18). We must "disorganise" (p. 18) consensual heteronormativity, according to Atkinson and DePalma, in order to disrupt heterosexual hegemony. We need to attend to the guy who did the slamming, the shoving; we need to unpack his need to assert his heteronormativity, his masculinity, so violently, to reveal his fears. We also need to attend to the slammed, the shoved guy not only at the locker but when he is holding hands with his boyfriend and when he is vogueing with his friends. We must refuse to consent to heterosexual hegemony, to heteronormativity. So, when we say that we are focusing on sexual identities and gender expressions beyond heterosexual hegemony, we mean that we are paying particular attention to people who claim lesbian, gay, bisexual, asexual, queer, and questioning sexual identities and trans, intersex, queer, and questioning gender expressions. We are thus working to disrupt or, in Atkinson and DePalma's words, disorganize consensual heteronormativity.

METHODS OF IDENTIFYING AND ANALYZING STUDIES

For our purpose in this chapter, we limit our attention to contexts designed to be educational, even if outside of schools. In these contexts, we focus on literacy, which means leaving out studies that focus on literature in isolation from readers and writers. Also, when turning to schools, we focus on middle and high school students, although we also give a brief nod to elementary school students, which means that we exclude college and university-based studies, including those focused on teacher preparation. Even when we turn away from schools to afterschool clubs and out-of-school groups, we limit our scope to those groups that serve school-age youth.

As we studied this body of literature, we were struck by the importance of the paradigmatic grounding used in each of the pieces, the difference contexts made in the studies, the difference age made in the studies, and the ways that identities were taken up by the various authors. These concepts organize the chapter. For each of these concepts, we sorted the literature into various categories, which morphed throughout our analytic processes but landed, ultimately, into what are the subcategories of this chapter. We discuss each of these next.

PARADIGMATIC GROUNDINGS

We found that the paradigmatic grounding of a study impacted the nature of the literacy events and practices that were accessible, or inaccessible, to youth. By *paradigmatic grounding,* we mean the way in which the researcher and/or research participants articulate or articulated, whether implicitly or explicitly, their relationship with LGBT[1] (lesbian, gay, bisexual, and transgender) studies and queer theory.

As discussed by Lovaas, Elia, and Yep (2006), the fields of LGBT studies and queer theory are, in many ways, overlapping. They both use qualitative approaches in order to research sexuality and gender. They also intertwine scholarly and activist work in that they seek to "liberate sexual and gender 'minorities' from oppressive forms of heteronormativity" (p. 6). But so, too, are they distinctive. For one thing, each has a different conceptualization of sexuality and gender. Scholars in LGBT studies tend to understand sexuality and gender as stable, whereas queer theorists aim to "continuously destabilize and deconstruct the notion of fixed sexual and gender identities" (p. 6). Additionally, there is a difference in theoretical approach. LGBT studies embrace a modernist approach in which "history is seen as a linear process of progressive development" (p. 4), which undergirds the "logic of much of the 'coming-out' literature" (p. 5). Queer theory, on the other hand, " 'is really poststructuralism (and postmoderninsm) applied to sexualities and genders' " (Plummer, 2003, cited by Lovaas et al., 2006, p. 5).

While Lovaas et al. (2006) consolidate major trends in the two fields, they also caution against furthering any scholarly divides by separating them in analysis. We share their concern, since we understand the fields as not neatly distinct but as mutually influential. We believe that both paradigms have something to offer in terms of making the world a better place, particularly for those who claim lesbian, gay, bisexual, asexual, queer, and questioning sexual identities and trans, intersex, queer, and questioning gender expressions. As such, it will not do to drop one for the other. Instead, we agree that they should "coexist in an ongoing productive tension" in which neither holds or pursues "theoretical hegemony" (pp. 4–5). We seek to work this tension productively.

LGBT Studies

The literacy events and practices documented in studies that we identified as being paradigmatically grounded in LGBT studies (Athanases, 1996; Blazar, 2009; Epstein, 2000; Greenbaum, 1994; Halverson, 2007; Hamilton; 1998; Hoffman, 1993; Reese, 1998; Ryan, 2011; Schall & Kaufmann, 2003; Vetter, 2010; Whelan, 2006) were distinctive in two ways. One way centers around the notion of an essential identity; the other centers

---
[1] Here, we use LGBT in reference to a paradigm that is distinct from queer theory.

around the notion of a linear development model. Assuming an essential identity model means understanding that someone simply is lesbian, for example; she either knows it or must discover it. It is a truth that exists whether or not she has come to know it. Assuming a developmental model means understanding, for example, that a person must go through a series of steps to become gay. Whether that person is gay from the start is irrelevant, but he will endure a series of processes to become gay, and then, that's it. He is gay. (For more on this distinction, particularly in the context of young adult literature, see Blackburn, Clark, & Nemeth, 2015). In some literacy events, the understanding of an essential sexual or gender identity is conveyed in the focal text or texts. For example, Blazar (2009) read *Angels in America* with his high school seniors. He describes the playwright as "unapologetic about gay identity" and the characters in these ways:

> Louis Ironson, a 20-something gay Jew working in New York City . . . Joseph Pitt, a Mormon and repressed homosexual . . . Roy Cohn, the New York lawyer who was lead counsel for Senator Joseph McCarthy during his House Un-American Activities Committee hearings and a closeted homosexual who died of AIDS in 1986. (p. 78)

In introducing the playwright and characters in such terms, Blazar conveys that being gay is a core part of one's identity, whether or not one chooses to acknowledge it. Furthermore, he even suggests that choosing not to acknowledge one's gay identities can have detrimental, even fatal, consequences. As an essential part of one's identity, sexuality, then, is stable.

In other literacy events, this understanding of identity as essential and stable is represented through talk about the text. For example, when 10th-grade students in an ethnic literature course discuss McNaught's "Dear Anita: Late Night Thoughts of an Irish Catholic Homosexual," they discuss whether being homosexual is a choice (Athanases, 1996). One student, Richard, asks the question, and several students join him in suggesting that the homosexual narrator of the text could have "chosen to stay with women" (p. 242). Ultimately, that being homosexual is a choice is identified as a myth, and this myth is refuted by an articulation that being homosexual is an orientation, which is "often constitutional" (p. 239). As such, sexual identity is constructed through talk as a stable identity that is an essential part of someone's being rather than something that could be chosen or rejected or changing over time.

An understanding of development as linear is sometimes embodied by a character in a text that is central to a particular literacy event. In fact, the coming-out narrative is quite common in LGBTQQ (lesbian, gay, bisexual, transgender, queer, and questioning)-themed literature, particularly young adult literature, which already tends to focus on coming-of-age narratives, which neatly align with coming-out narratives. For example, Vetter (2010) points readers toward Howe's *Totally Joe*, which she describes as a novel about a "boy in middle school who comes to grips with his sexuality as he realizes he is gay" (p. 107). In defining this book as such, the value of the coming-out narrative, in which one neatly develops from identifying as straight to identifying as lesbian, gay, or bisexual is underscored. The notion of a more variable or fluid sexual identity is not invited.

Other times, an understanding of development as linear is embodied by readers in a literacy event. Rather than this being a development from a straight to a lesbian, gay, or bisexual identity, though, it is a development from a homophobic to an ally identity. For example, Hoffman (1993) had high school students journal throughout their reading of *Torch Song Trilogy*. He found that the "journals were full of indications that reading the play has changed students' perceptions and attitudes" (p. 57). To illustrate this point, he quoted one student extensively, concluding with "'By reading this book I was exposed to a homosexual and realized that they are people too. They think, feel, and love'" (p. 58). Although some scholars claimed less significant gains (e.g., Epstein, 2000) than others (e.g., Schall & Kauffman, 2003), all of them asserted that reading and discussing LGBTQQ-themed texts with their students, across age levels, moved them away from being homophobes and toward being allies. This seems to be a driving force behind the work of the literacy events and practices documented in scholarship grounded in LGBT studies.

Queer Analyses of LGBT Work

In a second group of studies (Blackburn & Smith, 2010; Helmer, 2015; Martino, 2009; Moita-Lopes, 2006), the literacy events and practices are paradigmatically grounded in LGBT studies yet analyzed by scholars through a queer theory lens. A queer theory lens is much like a poststructural lens, in that it attends to multiple, variable, and fluid notions of identity, but with particular attention to sexual and gender identities beyond heterosexual hegemony. By framing sexual and gender identities with heterosexual hegemony, queer theory acknowledges and strives to disrupt institutional power dynamics. Scholars who analyze through this lens view work grounded in LGBT studies as emphasizing an individual's linear development, whether a gay or lesbian character realizing a true identity or readers moving from homophobe to ally identities. They argue that such literacy practices obscure the construction of normality and thus reify rather than interrogate a homosexual–heterosexual binary. We understand this critique as aligned with queer theory's poststructural underpinnings that destabilize and deconstruct. For example, Martino (2009) analyzed a school board-initiated theater event designed to address homophobia through the inclusion of a gay character in the plot. However, instead of interrupting homophobia, the play provided a platform for its rehearsal as the audience displayed hegemonic masculinity and disregarded the gay character. Martino asserted that the frame for reading focused on the moral responsibility of bystanders to intervene, a view located in a developmental identity model. Thus, literacy practices reified rather than challenged heteronormativity because they concealed rather than foregrounded power structures and assumed linear rather than fluid identities.

These scholars also illustrate that readers in literacy events shaped by LGBT studies resisted fluidity in or suspension of identity categories. For example, Helmer (2015) argued that youth in a high school gay and lesbian literature course resisted reading characters, such as Molly in *Rubyfruit Jungle,* as experiencing fluidity. They instead asserted in classroom discussion that she struggled to accept her essential lesbian identity. Thus, scholars who used queer theory to analyze literacy events and practices grounded in LGBT studies revealed that an exclusive reliance on developmental identity models offered opportunities for rehearsals of homophobia. Additionally, since such literacy practices foregrounded the individual and obscured considerations of social structures, they not only risked reifying heteronormativity and cisnormativity but in their rejection of fluidity also risked reifying homonormativity.

Queer Pedagogy

The literacy events and practices in a third group of studies (Allan, Atkinson, Brace, DePalma, & Hemingway, 2008; Atkinson & DePalma, 2009; DePalma, 2013; Gonzales, 2010; Kenney, 2010; Ryan, Patraw, & Bednar, 2013; Sieben & Wallowitz, 2009; Smith, 2008) were shaped by the scholars' and/or participants' paradigmatic grounding in queer theory. These, however, contained an unnamed tension. While participants in literacy events used queer reading strategies to disrupt heteronormative social structures, they simultaneously relied upon essentialist or developmental notions of identities rather than fluid ones. At times, they also excluded representations of LGBTIAQQ (lesbian, gay, bisexual, transgender, intersex, asexual, queer, and questioning) people.[2] In this way, we did not find in our review of the literature a queer analysis of queer work; vestiges of LGBT studies and/or heteronormativity always remained.

For example, Ryan et al. (2013) explored Bednar teaching elementary students about transgender and gender-nonconforming people. Reading strategies were grounded in Bednar's "sense that different kinds of oppression and marginalization were interrelated" (p. 95). Following queer theory, she attempted to deessentialize identities by using curriculum to "disrupt the links between biological/chromosomal sex, gender identity, and gender expression" (p. 88). However, at times, participants reproduced essentialism. For example, as classroom participants discussed "a wide range of paths that a [transgender] person might take to transition" (p. 96), she characterized these as a linear process "that meant moving toward living authentically as 'who they feel they really are'" (p. 96). Thus, there was an unnamed tension between LGBT studies and queer theory in literacy events as participants explored the social production of normality yet sometimes constructed essentialist identities.

At times, teachers drew upon queer theory to trouble the construction of normality but did not include representations of LGBTIAQQ communities in literacy events (e.g., Sieben & Wallowitz, 2009; Smith, 2008). For example, Smith used a young adult novel, *Montana 1948*. She explained how her high school students used queer theory to analyze the characters' experience of social norms around marriage and heterosexual activity, even in the absence of LGBTIAQQ characters.

Critical/Queer Tension

The literacy events and practices in a fourth group (Blackburn, 2002/2003, 2003a, 2005a, 2005b, 2007; Blackburn & Clark, 2011a; de Castell & Jenson, 2007) were shaped by the critical activist scholars' explicit navigation of critical and queer paradigms. Much of this work was done by one of us, Mollie. For example, Mollie (Blackburn, 2002/2003, 2003a) studied critical literacy practices in a youth center run by and for queer youth. She recognized that queer theory argues for the suspension of identity categories "in an effort to work against the oppression that comes with being named, labeled, and tagged"

---

[2] You will notice that the acronym we use varies throughout this chapter. We always strive to be simultaneously inclusive and honest. This means, when we write about people in communities beyond heterosexual hegemony, we use LGBTIAQQ. When we write about people being represented in literature and/or studies, we use LGBTQQ, since intersex and asexual characters and people have not traditionally been included (for an exception, see *Beyond Magenta*). Unless we write about the absence, then, we are inclusive. There are other times when we use the acronym used by the scholarship being represented.

(Blackburn, 2003a, p. 472). On the other hand, critical feminism and critical race theory argue that failing to name such categories ignores people's lived experiences. She resolved this tension by naming macro-level identity categories, while also describing multiple facets of participants' identities using their own words. Such critical/queer tensions impacted literacy events and practices in two ways.

First, these critical activist scholars developed a greater reflexive awareness of power imbalances in relation to fluid identities. For example, Mollie (Blackburn, 2003a) studied the literacy practices of the Speaker's Bureau, a group of youth employed by a queer youth center to participate in speaking and educational activism events outside of the center. Her study revealed that the youth challenged power dynamics such as heteronormativity outside of the center, yet at times reinforced them within the center. The youth thus fluidly moved among different identities during different literacy events, at times occupying counterhegemonic positions and at other times, hegemonic ones.

Second, these scholars' attention to the tensions between critical and queer theories led them to broaden the range of literacy practices available to youth. For example, de Castell and Jenson (2007) collaborated with "street-involved 'queer and questioning' youth" (p. 131) using video ethnography to understand the conditions and needs of the youth and to advocate for improved support systems for them. They argued that such a shift in literacy practices "helped [the youth] access and develop more powerful cognitive, social and political analyses than any amount of the kinds of essentially passive, logocentric ventriloquations of teacher-approved discourses" (p. 149). In this way, a broad conception of literacy practices was not only a shift in research emphasis but also one reflecting the political commitments of the work, commitments that foregrounded the everyday potential to disrupt hegemony and to position LGBTIAQQ youth as agents and experts.

The varying relationships among LGBT studies, queer theory, and critical theory in the existing literature have implications for our understandings of literacy and adolescents, particularly those who embody sexual identities and gender expressions beyond heterosexual hegemony. For example, literacy events paradigmatically grounded in LGBT studies have sanctioned visible representations of LGBTQQ people but often have made invisible the role of social structures in producing and regulating stable notions of normality. On the other hand, teachers drawing upon queer pedagogy at times focused so heavily on making visible marginalizing social structures and sanctioning the interrogation of these structures that they excluded representations of LGBTIAQQ people. Thus, we resist any impulse to drop one paradigm for another and argue instead that a productive blending of paradigmatic affordances can have the greatest possibilities for disrupting homophobia, transphobia, heteronormativity, cisnormativity, and homonormativity.

CONTEXTS

In addition to a study's paradigmatic grounding, we found in our review of the literature that contextual characteristics influenced the literacy events and practices available, and not available, to youth. Contexts, such as classroom instructional spaces, afterschool or extracurricular noninstructional spaces, queer youth centers, city streets, and homes, shaped literacy events and practices in four ways: psychosocial priorities, interpretive authority and purpose, positioning of students, and reading over writing. Below, we first discuss in-school contexts, then out-of-school contexts.

Schools

In school literacy events, the psychosocial priorities of adults tended to dominate. That is to say, educators reported feelings of fear and/or perceptions of risk associated with broaching topics of sexual identity and/or gender expression. These adults' perceptions limited literacy events in various ways, frequently deemphasizing, if not erasing, considerations of youths' psychosocial priorities. For example, Schall and Kaufmann (2003) investigated curricular representations of lesbian and gay people in an upper elementary school classroom. Because of anxieties, the teacher circumscribed literacy events in several ways. First, students could opt out of reading texts featuring lesbian and gay people. Second, in order to allow students to explore their ideas honestly, the adults in the classroom did not challenge students' responses. Instead, they ratified students' comments, even when they were homophobic and/or factually inaccurate. Third, when students asked questions about lesbian and gay experiences, adults did not provide information. As such, adult psychosocial priorities significantly impacted students' engagement with representations of LGBTIAQQ people.

Educators experienced fear as originating from different sources. They commonly felt personal risk in the form of losing their job, especially if they were early career teachers or new hires in a district (e.g., Sieben & Wallowitz, 2009). Some worried that controversy would originate from complaints stemming from parents/families (e.g., DePalma, 2013) or communities (e.g., Blazar, 2009). Some located a vague sense of threat that someone might endanger them without specifying an origin (e.g., Gonzales, 2010). Others were concerned about a lack of administrative support in the form of criticism and/or censure (e.g., Kenney, 2010). It is notable that educators were influenced by such feelings even when explicit legal mandates were in place supporting curricular inclusion (e.g., Moita-Lopes, 2006). While, overwhelmingly, educators named fear, only one (Kenney, 2010) discussed materializations of such anxieties. Kenney, an out lesbian who taught English language arts at a high school, experienced two occurrences of negative parental reactions. For instance, one student unenrolled in the school, reportedly because of the parent's disagreement with the "lifestyle choices of some of the teachers" (p. 60). While Kenney wrote that she felt lucky that her school administration supported her decisions, she wished that she didn't have to feel lucky. While Kenney's experiences were undoubtedly serious, there were not other reported instances. In contrast, others (e.g., DePalma, 2013; Greenbaum, 1994; Ryan et al., 2013; Schall & Kauffman, 2003; Sieben & Wallowitz, 2009; Vetter, 2010) named positive responses from students, families, and/or communities for inclusion of sexual identities and/or gender expressions beyond heterosexual hegemony in literacy events.

School literacy practices were commonly defined by instructional purposes where educators didactically mediated youth interpretive practices (see also Clark & Blackburn, 2009). Specifically, teachers shaped meaning-making activities toward explications of anti-homophobic and pro-tolerance stances. Some attempted to do so merely by displaying LGBTQQ people (e.g., Gonzales, 2010; Helmer, 2015; Hoffman, 1993; Martino, 2009; Schall & Kauffman, 2003). Others attempted to include representations and then mediate students' discussion in order to trouble talk that reflected homophobia and transphobia and/or heteronormativity and cisnormativity (e.g., Allan et al., 2008; Atkinson & DePalma, 2009; Athanases, 1996; Blazar, 2009; DePalma, 2013; Greenbaum, 1994; Hamilton, 1998; Kenney, 2010; Reese, 1998; Ryan et al., 2013). Still others did not include representations of LGBTIAQQ people but discussed sexual identity and/or gender expression during instructional times (e.g., Sieben & Wallowitz, 2009; Smith, 2008; Vetter, 2010).

As Mollie noted in her work with Caroline Clark (Clark & Blackburn, 2009), literacy events and practices in schools offer readers limited positions due to the context created by the teacher, text, and/or institution. Since their review, unfortunately, we have found a similar trend. The literacy events and practices occurring in the school-based studies primarily positioned representations of LGBTQQ people as windows (Bishop, 1990; Botelho & Rudman, 2009) for youth to look through to understand experiences different from their own. In doing so, literacy events made available straight and cisgender positions to youth, thus reifying heteronormativity and cisnormativity.

In contrast to the trend identified (Clark & Blackburn, 2009), there have been a few examples (Blackburn, 2002/2003; Gonzales, 2010; Kenney, 2010; Schey & Uppstrom, 2010; Vetter, 2010) that included school-based instances of LGBTQQ youth using literacy events and practices as mirrors, that is, as a way "to see themselves reflected so as to affirm who they and their communities are" (Botelho & Rudman, 2009, p. 1). In Gonzales's high school class, for example, a student rewrote a scene from *Romeo and Juliet,* such that it included same-sex couples.

Literacy events and practices in schools tended to foreground reading over writing. Even in the case of Hoffman (1993), in which high school students journaled about *Torch Song Trilogy,* the reading practices circumscribed students' choice and authority, and positioned them as passive, whereas the writing practices became a vehicle for the empathic promise of texts as windows. In Hoffman's words, "I asked students to keep journals . . . to focus on the way the students reacted to reading about homosexuality and what changes, if any, the play wrought on their understanding of the world beyond school" (p. 56).

Out of Schools

The studies that were conducted outside of schools stood in sharp contrast to the trend of fear and perceived risk in schools. Instead, youths' needs, desires, and experiences were the primary decision-making considerations shaping literacy events. This trend paralleled the displacement of adult didactic purposes by youth-centered interpretive purposes. For example, Mollie (Blackburn, 2002/2003, 2005a, 2005b, 2005c) discussed a literacy group called Story Time that met weekly at the Attic, a youth-led queer youth center in Philadelphia. She explained that the youth requested that Story Time be specifically a recreational instead of a support group, since several support groups already existed at the center. Thus, the purpose of the group itself was controlled by youths' perspectives. Additionally, at each meeting, the youth democratically chose the activities and texts for that session. Meetings opened with the opportunity for youth to share texts they had created or brought. If no one decided to share, they would then select texts from choices Mollie had brought. In summary, youths' psychosocial priorities and interpretive purposes, rather than adults', shaped literacy events in this outside-of-school context.

In studies that occurred outside of schools, youth were overwhelmingly positioned as LGBTQQ and not exclusively straight and, therefore, used literacy events and practices as mirrors, which makes sense considering that most of them took place in contexts designed to cater to LGBTQQ youth, such as youth centers and an LGBTQ youth theater company. Some of the out-of-school literacy events featured more complex explorations of reader positioning. Mollie's (Blackburn, 2002/2003, 2003a, 2005a, 2005b, 2005c) study of the Attic, for example, considered power dynamics, because men had more power than women, and lesbian and gay youth had more power than trans youth in the literacy practices of the youth center. So, Mollie pointed to complex relationships between literacy practices and LGBTQ youth that troubled a homogenous (and potentially homonormative) notion of mirrors.

Literacy events in out-of-school contexts contained greater balance and reciprocity among reading and writing or, more broadly, reception and production practices, than those in schools. Halverson (2007), for example, documented the dramaturgical process a theater company designed for LGBTIAQQ youth in which adolescents "told each other the stories of their lives, adapted those stories into scripted scenes, and performed these scenes for . . . Chicago theatergoers" (p. 153). Thus, the youth collaborated together in a recursive process involving reception and production practices in order to represent their lives and experiences to others. Overall, adults in these studies tended to position LGBTQQ youth agentically, reinforcing their tendency to foreground youths' desires and needs, their interpretive authority, and fluid subject positions.

Overall, in- and out-of-school contexts made a world of difference in terms of psychosocial needs, interpretive purposes, positioning of students, and reading and writing. More specifically, adults' priorities and purposes dominated in school, and those of youth dominate outside of school. Moreover, studies we reviewed that took place in schools attended to students as straight and mostly homophobic, whereas those outside of schools attended to students as embodying sexual identities and gender expressions beyond heterosexual hegemony. And in terms of literacy, reading was emphasized above writing in schools but they were understood in relationship not only to each other but also to the identities of the adolescent readers and writers in out-of-school contexts.

AGE

The majority of literacy scholarship focused on youth and sexual identities and gender expressions beyond heterosexual hegemony attends to young people in high schools and middle schools or people of that age. Although less of it focuses on elementary school students, there is some scholarship in this area. Below, we foreground scholarship on adolescents but reference scholarship on younger children, because it offers insights through contrast about the importance of engaging in collections of LGBTQ-themed texts and considering the consequences when these engagements are adult-defined or youth-defined. Studying this body of literature through the lens of age also makes apparent the importance of multiple perspectives, youth agency, and the risks they take in asserting it, particularly in schools.

Texts in Isolation versus Collections

By far, the most documented and analyzed way that adults engage teens with LGBTQQ-themed topics via literacy events and practices is by focusing on single texts. Athanases (1996), for example, studied 10th graders' responses to "Dear Anita: Late Night

Thoughts of an Irish Catholic Homosexual" in a unit on short stories; Blazar (2009) looked at seniors reading *Angels in America;* Hoffman (1993) examined high school students discussing Fierstein's *Torch Song Trilogy;* Gonzales (2010) and Kenney (2010) read "A Letter to Harvey Milk" with high school students; and Martino (2009) offered a queer critique of a performance of a play with a gay character. In middle schools, both Hamilton (1998) and Reese (1998) engaged students with the novel *Jack,* and Reese also read *The Arizona Kid* with his students.

Another way that adults engaged teens with single texts was by looking for gay subtexts in books regularly read in schools, whether those subtexts are more prominent, as in *Cat on a Hot Tin Roof* and *The Color Purple* (Greenbaum, 1994), or more discrete, as in *Catcher in the Rye* (Reese, 1998). A final way that adults engaged teens with single texts was by using strategies grounded in queer theory to interpret texts that are not LGBTQQ-themed. Smith (2008), for example, worked with high school students to conduct a queer reading of *Montana 1948*.

When high school and middle school students are asked to study a particular text, the text itself can obstruct the attention paid to LGBTQQ people. So, for example, Hoffman (1993) selected *Torch Song Trilogy* for his creative writing class because of its "innovative structure" (p. 56). He states, "It was the play's structural uniqueness that led me to think that students in creative writing could benefit from studying it" (p. 56). And, accordingly, the "bulk of [students' journal] entries were direct responses to the text—character analyses, expressions of confusion about the structure of several scenes, delight at the sheer entertainment the play offered" (p. 56). That is, focusing on the text gave students one way of not talking about the gay-themed content in the play.

A less frequently studied way that teens engage with LGBTQQ-themed topics via literacy events and practices is by focusing on collections of texts. Helmer (2015) studied a trimester-long high school English class entitled Gay and Lesbian Literature, in which students read novels including *Rubyfruit Jungle* and *The Hours*. Mostly, though, teen engagement with collections of texts happened in out-of-school contexts such as LGBTQQ youth centers (Blackburn, 2002/2003, 2005a, 2005b, 2005c; Blackburn & Clark, 2011a; Clark & Blackburn, 2009) and programs (Halverson, 2007) and city streets (de Castell & Jenson, 2007). There are several advantages of this approach. One is that the named focus is LGBTQQ content; as such, this content is not easily concealed. Another is that multiple texts offer readers opportunities to learn about the wide range of diversity among the experiences of LGBTIAQQ people, as captured in these texts. Ryan, the second author of this chapter (not to be confused with Caitlin Ryan, who is cited throughout this chapter), in his work with Ariel Uppstrom (Schey & Upstrom, 2010) accomplished this by reading an anthology of short stories with LGBT themes, *Am I Blue?*, with students in a Gay–Straight Alliance extracurricular club.

This is in stark contrast to the ways that elementary school-age youth tended to engage in collections of texts rather than singular ones (Epstein, 2000; Ryan et al., 2013; Schall & Kauffmann, 2003). Schall and Kauffmann, for example, report a deliberate effort by Kauffmann to integrate a collection of texts that represent gay and lesbian, although primarily gay, people into a unit in her class of fourth and fifth graders. Bednar, as documented by Ryan, engaged her third- and fourth-grade students in a collection of texts that represent a range of gender expressions; among these were *The Other Side,* a video entitled *Tomboy, Totally Joe, My Princess Boy,* and *10,000 Dresses*. In doing so, she provoked a series of conversations that worked to trouble gender rules and regulations (Ryan et al., 2013). As with older readers, this approach allows young readers to experience multiple perspectives.

Unfortunately, though, this approach sometimes had the consequence of distracting readers from the queer content. For example, in Kauffman's class (Schall & Kauffman, 2003), students were studying a unit entitled "Survival through Imagination" (p. 37), so if students did not want to take up lesbian and gay themed texts, they could, alternatively, "return to their focused text sets" (p. 42). Now, we should say that Schall and Kauffman gave very good reasons for giving students the option of reading the gay- and lesbian-themed books or not, and we respect their decision, but it is a decision with consequences. That is, the unit could, if students so desired, block out the attention paid to gay and lesbian people. This was not the case, however, when the collections for younger readers were explicitly named as being LGBTQ-themed (i.e., Ryan et al., 2013). This is brought to the fore in The No Outsiders Project (Allan et al., 2008), where a teacher–researcher read a gay-themed text, *King and King,* in conjunction with a straight but feminist-themed book, *The Paper Bag Princess,* but presented that book in such a way that fostered a queer reading of it. In doing so, the "teacher–researcher challenged taken-for-granted heterosexuality" (p. 318).

Adult-Initiated and Youth-Initiated Texts

In all of the previous accounts of teens (and younger children) engaging in LGBTQQ-themed literature in literacy events and practices, adults initiated and/or facilitated readers' engagement. There are few exceptions. One is Moita-Lopes's (2006) study of gay-themed discourses among 12- to 14-year-olds in a school in Brazil. He did not find that youth initiated their own engagement with such literature in literacy events and practices, unfortunately. Rather, he documented an adult, a teacher in this case, preventing such engagement. In this study, a fifth-grade teacher in a school in Rio de Janeiro, Brazil, squelched a conversation about gay people that some of the students were having, even though the state-published educational guideline "calls for anti-homophobic education" (p. 32). So, this teacher mediated the event, but she did not initiate or facilitate it; rather, she suppressed it.

There are accounts, though, in which teens had opportunities to select LGBTQ-themed texts (Blackburn, 2002/2003, 2005c; Blackburn & Clark, 2011a; Clark & Blackburn, 2009; Vetter, 2010; Whelan, 2006) and create their own such texts (Blackburn, 2002/2003, 2003a, 2005a; deCastell & Jenson, 2007; Halverson, 2007; Vetter, 2010). Whelan (2006) offers several brief anecdotal accounts of adolescents engaging with LGBTQQ-themed literature independently, for example, and Vetter (2010) documented a teen selecting and creating LGBTQQ-themed texts for her multigenre research project for her high school English class. This approach allows for a focus on queer content, invites readers and writers to define and include their own perspectives, and provides them with opportunities to engage in literacy events and practices on their own terms. However, in contexts where there is significant homophobia and transphobia, such as schools (Vetter, 2010) and city streets (de Castell & Jenson, 2007), youth mediation of LGBTQQ-themed literacy events and practices puts them at increased risk. This is documented in elementary school classrooms as well (Ryan, 2011), when a girl in kindergarten shared a family time line that she created. Although this student had two moms, she did not make that explicit on her time line or in her sharing of it, until a classmate directly asked about her two moms. As such, the text was "mediated entirely by [the student] herself, in front of her entire class, and therefore require[d] social risk" (p. 105). Such risk was eliminated with another young person documented by Ryan, but in this case, the risk was eliminated by the lack of opportunity for students to make connections between their schooling and their lives outside of schools.

At home, though, young people with lesbian parents could assert their agency by initiating and generating LGBTQQ-themed texts without incurring such social risk. Ryan (2012) documented home-based literacy events and practices of children of lesbian-headed households and documented their reading and writing books containing LGBTQQ people and families, mothers' day cards for more than one parent, a father's day card written to "donor dad," modified baby books to align with their families' terms, and signs made for pride parades and pro-gay buttons, among other texts and literacy events. Here, we see elementary-age readers and writers enjoying the multiple perspectives, including their own, of collections of texts; the focus on LGBTQ-themed texts; and the opportunities to initiate and generate literacy events and practices without the risks associated with more explicitly homophobic environments, such as schools.

Multiple Perspectives, Agency, and Risk

Clustering this body of literature by age of readers and writers also brought to the fore issues of multiple perspectives, agency, and risk. In terms of multiple perspectives, although younger children seem less likely to be introduced to texts that invite them to explore LGBTQQ-themed topics, when they are, they are more likely to be introduced to a variety of texts that allow for multiple representations of what it might be like to be in and/or among LGBTQQ communities. In fact, almost entirely, when adolescents engage with such texts in schools, the texts stand in isolation, with the exception being documented by Helmer (2015). Adolescents are more likely to encounter multiple perspectives about LGBTQQ people, though, when engaging in literacy events and practices outside of school.

Related to the issue of multiple perspectives is the importance of youth having opportunities to select and generate LGBTIAQQ-themed texts. That is to say, it matters which among the multiple perspectives is their own. We do not, however, see this regularly documented. When we do, it is not limited by age. The students of Gonzales (2010), for example, performed a queer adaptation of *Romeo and Juliet,* and Vetter (2010) documented a student including lesbian themes in her multigenre paper. Similarly, Mollie's earlier work shows that Justine (Blackburn, 2002/2003) and Kira (Blackburn, 2003b) create texts that offer their perspectives both in and out of school. These were high school students, but we also see a kindergartner share a family time line, which prompted a classmate to ask about her two moms and therefore imposed a lesbian theme on a text that was not necessarily designed as such. When young people selected and generated texts, they offered their perspectives and therefore asserted their agency with respect to identities beyond heterosexual hegemony.

In doing so, though, they took risks. That is, by choosing or creating texts with LGBTQQ themes, students across grade levels risk being stigmatized. That is, they may be understood as being one of those stigmatized identities just because they choose to read or write about them. This, as Ryan's (2012) study shows, might demand that the young person mediate challenging dynamics. This risk can be alleviated by adult facilitators, including but not limited to teachers, choosing LGBTQ-themed texts and/or assigning writing that explores LGBTIAQQ themes. Moreover, they can facilitate the discussions of such texts. In other words, it is important that adults engage young people in LGBTIAQQ-themed texts. That said, it is also important that youth have opportunities to engage themselves and one another in these texts. When young people do this, adults are called on to create contexts in which LGBTIAQQ identities are less stigmatized.

IDENTITIES

Educational literacy scholarship focused on youth and sexual identities and gender expressions beyond heterosexual hegemony pays, by far, more attention to gay and lesbian identities, in that order, than to trans and bisexual identities, again, in that order. It pays no attention to intersex and asexual identities, as far as we know. Moreover, it too often neglects to attend to the multiple identities that intersect with sexuality and gender. This neglect impacts or, more specifically, limits our understandings in the field of literacy education. We discuss these issues next, beginning first with trans, bisexual, and intersex identities, then moving to intersectional identities.

Trans, Bisexual, Intersex, and Asexual Identities

Some scholars in this field use the acronym or some version of it, the word *queer* (e.g., Helmer, 2015), and/or the word *sexuality* (e.g., Epstein, 2000), each of which conveys a particular paradigmatic approach but really only attends to gays (e.g., Moita-Lopes, 2006) and/or lesbians (e.g., Blackburn, 2002/2003) in any depth. We get the sense that the effort here is to be inclusive of all multiple, variable, and possible sexual identities, and perhaps gender expressions that might be represented in the scope of the authors' consideration. We respect this intent, indeed, have been among those using this approach. But we worry about this approach concealing the relative lack of attention paid to trans, bisexual, intersex, and asexual readers, writers, and characters.

In contrast, some scholars name their focus from the onset and maintain it throughout the article or chapter. Athanases (1996), Blazar (2009), and Hoffman (1993) use the name *gay* in the titles of these pieces and maintain that focus throughout them, as does Reese (1998), using, instead, the word *homosexuality*. Similarly, in Mollie's earlier work, she identifies her focal participant as lesbian, among a series of derivatives of this, early in the article and focuses solely on this young person (2003a). Greenbaum (1994), Ryan (2011), and Schall and Kauffmann (2003) use the name *gay and lesbian,* or vice versa, in the titles of these pieces and maintain this focus throughout, although Ryan (2011) really focuses on lesbians in this piece. Our point here, though, is that initially we found this a bit off-putting, as if these scholars, and again, we are pointing our fingers at ourselves along with our colleagues, were failing to be inclusive of people who are marginalized within LGBTIAQQ communities, particularly those who are trans, intersexual, and asexual. Upon closer analysis, though, we acknowledge the importance of making explicit and visible the parameters of the work that is and is not being done.

We found uniquely promising the scholars who name and focus on issues pertinent to trans people. Consider, for example, the Ryan et al. (2013) work in which Ryan documented Bednar's teaching third- and fourth-grade students about gender diversity and gender nonconformity through the reading and discussion of age-appropriate literature. They report on using Woodson's *The Other Side,* in which race is central, to talk about "social rules . . . that shape our behavior" (p. 90), including but not limited to those pertinent to gender expression. They also examine the use of *Totally Joe* to talk about how gender expression and sexual identity get tied up together. Finally, they study Bednar's reading of *10,000 Dresses* to facilitate a discussion about the differences between being transgender and gender nonconforming. Here we see an acknowledgment of sexual identities, as well as other intersecting identities, but with a real focus on trans identities.

Some scholars use some version of the LGBTIAQQ acronym and talks across it in broad, general terms (e.g., Blackburn, 2005c), which is less helpful, but others use the acronym generally, then hone in on one participant, character, or issue in order to explore a particular identity in more depth (Blackburn, 2003b, 2005b; Blackburn & Smith, 2010). Halverson (2007), for example, reports on a group of adolescents, among whom at least one identifies as lesbian, gay, bisexual, and/or transgender. Adele is one of the two in the group who identifies as bisexual. Halverson documented this group, taking up Adele's story entitled "Being Bisexual in a Gay/Straight World" by adapting and performing it. In this biographical story, Adele "draws a remarkable parallel between the documented way in which bisexual identity is often relegated to a non-identity and Adele's feeling that her own story was similarly relegated" (p. 161) in this youth group. Here we see real attention being paid to marginalized identities without isolating the people who claim them from larger LGBTIAQQ communities.

Another issue that comes up when considering who gets named and who actually gets attention in this scholarship is what happens when scholars use the word *queer.* As we mentioned earlier, there are times when queer gets named but the focus is mostly limited to gay and lesbian people (Helmer, 2015). There are other times when *queer* gets named and, more appropriately, sexual identities and gender expressions that are beyond heterosexual hegemony are central, as in de Castell and Jenson's (2007) study of street-involved queer youth. But there are also times when *queer* gets used to talk about sexuality in broader terms, including heterosexuality, emphasizing the disruption of normality in such ways that identities beyond heterosexual hegemony essentially fade into invisibility (e.g., Smith, 2008). We point this out not as a way of saying we do not think that using one word or term over another makes this work any better or worse, but to say that our efforts as scholars and educators to include diversity, including but not limited to sexual and gender diversity, require breadth and depth but not, in any case, superficiality.

Intersectional Identities

We found some literacy scholarship focused on youth and sexual identities and gender expressions beyond heterosexual hegemony that attended to multiple identities that intersect with sexuality and gender. However, we certainly recognize that not all of the scholarship we reviewed did so. We speak first to those that do and finally to those that do not. Of course, the scholarship does not fall neatly into these two camps, and we talk about those studies as well, in between.

The scholars who make intersectional identities central to their understandings of literacy events and practices are particularly compelling, whether those identities are race, class, nationality, religion, and language, among others, and whether the person embodying those identities is a reader and a writer or a character (Athanases, 1996; Blackburn,

2002/2003, 2003a, 2003b; Blazar, 2009; de Castell & Jenson, 2007; Hoffman, 1993; Ryan, 2011, 2012; Kenney, 2010; Moita-Lopes, 2006; Vetter, 2010). The Athanases (1996) article, for example, attends to students' multiple and intersecting identities, as well as those of the central character in the memoir they read and discussed together. With respect to the students, Athanases describes "community influences" (p. 235) in this way: "It was an African American neighborhood, with a lot of Baptist churches. Another significant population at the school was Chinese Americans. Their neighborhood had a prominent Catholic church. He notes that "religion plays a central role in the lives" (p. 236) of the students in the study. He goes on to describe their likely exposure to gay and lesbian people, in both positive and negative terms. With respect to the character, the teacher "began with a discussion of McNaught's Irish heritage and Catholic upbringing; specifically, she asked how these might have shaped his attitudes and sense of self, particularly given the view of homosexuality on Catholicism" (p. 241). In other words, Athanases offers a nuanced analysis of intersecting identities of both readers and writers, as well as characters.

We were surprised to find, though, that some scholars engaged instersectionality from a deficit perspective. Blazar (2009), for example, talks about how his students were "mostly Roman Catholic immigrants or children of immigrants from the Dominican Republic and are not widely knowledgeable about gayness. They might use derogatory language like *maricón* (the Spanish equivalent of *faggot*) without necessarily understanding the meaning and repercussion" (p. 77). In other words, he attends to religious, national, and linguistic identities but ties them to a homophobic perspective, albeit one grounded more in ignorance than in hatred. Hoffman (1993), however, describes his students as "one-hundred percent ghetto population," "two-thirds . . . minorities," and then states, "It is hard to imagine a more homophobic group, convinced as they are that gay males and lesbians are diseased creatures, sub-human and destined for hell" (p. 56). In other words, acknowledging intersectionality is important work to do, but it must be done with understanding and compassion rather than condemnation.

There are other ways that intersectionality gets taken up in peripheral ways. For example, Martino (2009) articulates an understanding of the importance of intersectionality, but his analysis is solidly centered around the interrogation of heterosexuality. Epstein (2000), on the other hand, integrates identities beyond sexual and gender identities into her analysis of literacy events and practices, but in ways that suggest various identities are parallel rather than intersecting. However, much of the scholarship in this field (Blackburn, 2005a, 2003b; Blackburn & Clark, 2011; Halverson, 2007; Reese, 1998; Ryan et al., 2013; Schall & Kauffmann, 2003) represents identities besides sexuality and gender expression, mostly in words but sometimes in images (Whelan, 2006), but does not explore them in ways that convey their pertinence to literacy events or practices. Still other scholars (Allan et al., 2008; Atkinson & DePalma, 2009; Clark & Blackburn, 2009; DePalma, 2013; Gonzales, 2007; Greenbaum, 1994; Hamilton, 1998) do not name identities other than sexual and gender identities.

Studying this body of literature with respect to how identities are named, described, and considered brought to the fore issues of inclusivity and precision, and complexity and compassion. We value efforts to be as inclusive as is honestly possible. Although our understandings of inclusivity and precision developed from our looking for representations of trans, bisexual, intersex, and asexual identities, and our understandings of complexity and compassion developed from our examination of intersectionality, the implications stretch across these concepts. That is to say, whether we are considering sexual identities and gender expressions or the many identities that intersect with those, we, as scholars and educators, should strive toward honest inclusivity and compassionate complexity as we understand participants, students, and even characters.

IMPLICATIONS

Our analysis of literature in the fields of education and literacy, with particular attention to sexual identities and gender expressions beyond heterosexual hegemony, leads us to consider both curricular and pedagogical implications. We discuss each next, then reflect on the significance of risk, agency, and compassion with respect to both curriculum and pedagogy.

Curriculum

Multiple and varied representations of LGBTIAQQ people must be included in curricula so that young people come to understand any single experience or representation as neither monolithic nor any single group as homogenous and undifferentiated. Multiple and variable representations can offer diverse youth opportunities to see people like themselves, or families like their own, reflected in the curriculum, while providing opportunities for other young people to develop new understandings and empathy. To this end, adolescents must have opportunities, like younger children, to engage with collections of LGBTIAQQ-themed texts in schools rather than only doing so in isolated ways, if at all. In addition, inclusive representations should be distributed throughout the curriculum rather than concentrated in a single unit or moment during the school year.

Moreover, multiple and varied representations invite explorations of intersecting identities. Sexual identities and gender expressions cannot and should not be decontextualized or isolated from their sociohistorical contexts and communities. So, curricular representations of LGBTIAQQ people must attend to a variety of dimensions of difference, such as race, class, religion, disability, linguistic diversity, nationality, and indigeneity. Such an approach enables teachers and students to explore how these dimensions of identity mutually shape and constitute one another, helping to dehomogenize understandings of LGBTIQQ experiences.

Multiple and varied representations must include different notions of identity and the self. Texts with different paradigmatic groundings, whatever their relationships to LGBT studies and queer theory, can offer readers different understandings of what identity is and how they can participate in their own identity work. Representations grounded in essentialist and developmental notions of the self can provide youth with resources, such as stability and coherence, for navigating their own experiences and communities. Representations grounded in poststructural and/or queer notions of the self can disrupt such static notions, offering different resources to youth, such as fluidity and multiplicity. In this way, no single paradigm is afforded theoretical or practical hegemony, but instead the pragmatic affordances of each become available in literacy events and practices.

Diverse representations must also consider sexual identities and gender expressions in ways that are both inclusive and precise. Here, we value efforts to be as inclusive as is honestly possible. So when we advocate for representations of LGBTIAQQ people, we argue for the inclusion of representations of LGBTIAQQ people, in other words, for a broad and inclusive variety of people and experiences with respect to sexual identities and gender expressions beyond heterosexual hegemony. This idea has larger implications. When literacy educators and scholars use the term LGBTIAQQ, or some variation of it, they should be certain that their work includes people who represent each part of the acronym used. In other words, they should not use LGBTIAQQ to talk about gay men, for example. Doing so gives the false impression that women and bisexual, trans, intersex, asexual, queer, and questioning people are being taken up in ways that matter in the educational work when they are not actually included or represented. This use of the acronym conceals the shortcomings of literacy educators' and scholars' work, making them harder to correct. As we have shown, various versions of the acronym are used, but regardless of the acronym used, the point is the same: Be as inclusive as possible while still being honest about the parameters of the work being done. There is something to be said for precision. If you are only going to read stories with lesbian and gay characters, for example, say that. This lets others know what to expect, whether they may see some part of themselves represented or not. It may feel bad, like you are excluding bisexual, trans, intersex, asexual, queer, and questioning characters. If so, do not correct this by using the full acronym; that is still exclusion. Correct it, instead, with inclusion, that is by bringing in representations of bisexual, trans, intersex, asexual, queer, and questioning people. We advocate for breadth and depth, and we advocate against superficiality, both with respect to curricular inclusion specifically and to scholarship and advocacy generally.

Curricular choices must consider both reading and writing about sexual identities and gender expressions beyond heterosexual hegemony. Both of these offer youth different affordances around developing understandings, empathy, and identities. Neither should be given primacy, especially to the exclusion of the other. Instead, both can be productively employed to inform and develop each other as youth both learn and produce knowledge in literacy events and practices.

Pedagogy

While the curricular approaches we outlined earlier are necessary, they are not sufficient, as demonstrated by the studies we reviewed. So, curricular inclusion must be accompanied by meaning-making approaches grounded in critical and queer theories. These approaches make inequitable power relations visible and interrogate social structures. They analyze the ways that ideas of normality and abnormality are socially constructed and challenge these ideas not only by expanding the definitions of the categories but also by questioning the taken-for-granted binaries necessary for these categories to exist and enable oppression. Of course, such approaches extend and complicate multiple and varied curricular representations, particularly those that examine intersectionality and multiple notions of the self (i.e., essentialist, developmental, and poststructural). Queer meaning-making approaches sanction stances that challenge power relations in productive and agentic ways. We again emphasize the value of recursivity over time in reading LGBTIQQ-inclusive texts in queer ways, because disrupting inequitable power relations "requires not only momentary subversion, but persistence" (Atkinson & DePalma, 2009, p. 23).

We recognize the didactic nature of teachers selecting particular texts and guiding particular analyses of them. We understand that schools are designed to be places of learning and that educators must play a mediating role by, for example, providing information or cultivating youths' reading strategies. However, we are concerned that foregrounding, much less exclusively relying upon, adults' didactic purposes and analytic authority can be problematic. For example, despite well-meaning intentions, we are worried that such approaches can reinscribe what Freire (1970/2006) terms the banking model, or what others have discussed as a deficit model of education. In such configurations, students are not given space for their own values, nor are their intellectual and affective ends validated, much less used as resources. Moreover, such didacticism and singular authority can reify monolithic and absolute versions of truth.

We advocate for additional meaning-making approaches to be incorporated into literacy events and practices by opening up interpretive authority and purposes to include those of youth. There must be greater balance and nuance in creating classroom communities in which both the didactic and exploratory exist. Educators' goals and institutional agendas should not push out youths' perspectives. Youth and adults bring a variety of knowledges and resources to literacy events, which means that no single person can or should be positioned as expert, nor should anyone be positioned as wholly ignorant and empty. Instead, the resources of all participants should be acknowledged and drawn upon in order to enrich knowledge production and circulation. In this way, literacy practices within schools can be a negotiated collaboration rather than an imposition. These collaborations enrich curricula that include reading and writing, so that youth not only learn and produce knowledge but they also have a say in what types of knowledge they learn and produce.

Just as students and teachers must be invited to positions of both teaching and learning, so must they be invited to a variety of positions related to sexual identities and gender expressions. It cannot be assumed that everyone will be straight, cisgender, homophobic, and/or transphobic. Instead, there must be the possibility for a variety of identifications and understandings with respect to sexuality and gender. And no individual should be assumed to have a fixed or consistent position in regard to the ranges of identifications and understandings. Nor should it be assumed that there is an inevitable link between any identification or understanding or perspective. In this type of context, youth can take up moral stances of empathy and political alliance, possibilities complimented by expanded interpretive authorities and purposes.

We value such efforts to engage with complexity around identities, including, but not limited to, sexual identities and gender expression. This means attending to race, ethnicity, class, religion, disability, linguistic diversity, nationality, and indigeneity, among other dimensions of social differences. This requires serious attention to nuance, and such attention must be paired with compassion. In other words, to attend to, say, students' ethnicity as a way to make sweeping generalizations about their stances on any issues, including those about sexual identities and gender expressions, is simplistic and inappropriate. This is not to say that an individual's religion, for example, may not foster that person's homophobia. It certainly may, and that is an appropriate thing to acknowledge and explore, but this can be accomplished with compassion, that is, with complexity and kindness.

Mutual Risk, Shared Agency, and Compassion

In the reviewed literature, adult fears dominated the shape of literacy events in schools. The privileging of adult interpretive authority in the form of didactic purposes augmented these problems (see also Clark & Blackburn, 2009). The high stakes that educators experienced were increased because they positioned themselves as the only responsible persons rather than sharing the agency and risk, a tendency that heightened rather than mitigated the challenges they perceived. Undoubtedly, it is clear from both the literature we reviewed and other studies exploring pre- and inservice educators' dispositions (e.g., Clark, 2010; Thein, 2013) that the feelings of fear and risk are real for educators. We do not dispute this finding or attempt to dismiss the significance of such anxieties. We also understand that schools can be places where adults, like youth, are frequently regulated through power relations.

However, based on the lack of materialization of these fears in the studies we reviewed, we must push back against the use of fear and perceived risk as a rationale for excluding curricular representations of LGBTIAQQ experiences and queer reading practices from pedagogical approaches. Adults' psychosocial priorities cannot continue to dominate school literacy events and practices, especially to such a degree that they exclude youths' needs, desires, and values. With respect to risk and vulnerability, literacy educators and scholars cannot continue to consider only teachers' experiences but must broadly ask who is at risk in what ways in relation to which decisions. After all, for over a decade the Gay, Lesbian, and Straight Education Network (GLSEN) has been documenting the ways in which schools are often unsafe for LGBT youth (e.g., Kosciw, Greytak, Palmer, & Boesen, 2014), a perspective that must be in considered alongside adults' fears. Moreover, youth face specific vulnerabilities in literacy events. By choosing or creating texts with LGBTIAQQ themes, they risk being stigmatized. That is, they may be understood as being one of those stigmatized identities just because they choose to read or write about them.

So we advocate that adults and youth involved in these choices mutually recognize risk and share agency. To work against oppression and to advocate for justice in schools is a collective process involving all community members and not merely adults. However, anytime people experience vulnerability and risk, those involved must use compassion and mutual consideration to navigate the situation. Sharing agency and risk among youth and adults in this way is humanizing and pragmatic, because it acknowledges the complexities of relationships and safety while also refusing to accept and maintain the status quo of heteronormativity and cisnormativity specifically and oppression generally.

CONCLUSION

Our analysis of literature in the fields of education and literacy with particular attention to sexual identities and gender expressions beyond heterosexual hegemony leads us to argue that as literacy educators and scholars, we must make LGBTIAQQ people visible and sanctioned, as well as the social structures that define what is normal, or abnormal, with particular respect to sexual identities and gender expressions. Not only must these structures be made visible, they must also be interrogated, not once, but over time and with persistence, to use Atkinson and DePalma's (2009) words. We must allow youths' psychosocial priorities to put our own in perspective so that we might forge ahead in our efforts to improve our understandings and the material experiences of LGBTIAQQ youth. We must allow youths' interpretations to trump our own didactic purposes. We must understand youth as multiple, variable, and fluid, in terms of not only their sexual identities and gender expressions but also their stances toward that which is beyond heterosexual hegemony. We must provide and document opportunities for youth not only to read about sexual identities and gender expressions beyond heterosexual hegemony but also to write about them. We must provide young people with multiple perspectives of the experiences of sexual identities and gender expressions beyond heterosexual hegemony, not only in terms of race, class, nationality, religion, language, indigeneity, and more, but also in terms of how one experiences and embodies sexual identities and gender expressions. We must allow youth to assert their agency in adding to these many perspectives. We must recognize the risks youth take by exploring sexual identities and gender expressions beyond heterosexual hegemony and work diligently to create contexts in which those risks are minimized, if not eliminated. We must be inclusive but honest. If there are people who are being excluded, it is our responsibility to acknowledge and work to correct this. We must understand the complexity of intersecting identities with compassion and kindness. It is with such attention to the invisible, unsanctioned, and uninterrogated, to multiple perspectives, youth agency, and risk, and to inclusivity, precision, complexity, and compassion that we must move forward in our efforts to teach and learn about adolescent literacies in ways that honor sexual identities and gender expression beyond heterosexual hegemony.

REFERENCES

Allan, A., Atkinson, E., Brace, E., DePalma, R., & Hemingway, J. (2008). Speaking the unspeakable in forbidden places: Addressing lesbian, gay, bisexual and transgender equality in the primary school. *Sex Education, 8*(3), 315–328.

Athanases, S. Z. (1996). A gay-themed lesson in an ethnic literature curriculum: Tenth graders' responses to "Dear Anita." *Harvard Educational Review, 66*(2), 231–256.

Atkinson, E., & DePalma, R. (2009). Un-believing the matrix: Queering consenual heteronormativity. *Gender and Education, 21*(1), 17–29.

Bishop, R. S. (1990). Mirrors, windows, and sliding glass doors. *Perspectives: Choosing and Using Books for the Classroom, 6*(3), ix–xi.

Blackburn, M. V. (2002/2003). Disrupting the (hetero)normative: Exploring literacy performances and identity work with queer youth. *Journal of Adolescent and Adult Literacy, 46*(4), 312–324.

Blackburn, M. V. (2003a). Exploring literacy performances and power dynamics at The Loft: Queer youth reading the world and the word. *Research in the Teaching of English, 37*, 467–490.

Blackburn, M. V. (2003b). Losing, finding, and making space for activism through literacy performances and identity work. *Penn GSE Perspectives on Urban Education, 2*(1). Retrieved from www.urbanedjournal.org/articles/article0008.html.

Blackburn, M. V. (2005a). Agency in borderland discourses: Examining language use in a community center with Black queer youth. *Teachers College Record, 107*(1), 89–113.

Blackburn, M. V. (2005b). Disrupting dichotomies for social change: A review of, critique of, and complement to current educational literacy scholarship on gender. *Research in the Teaching of English, 39*(4), 398–416.

Blackburn, M. V. (2005c). Co-constructing space for literacy and identity work with LGBTQ youth. *Afterschool Matters, 4*, 17–23.

Blackburn, M. V. (2007). The experiencing, negotiation, breaking, and remaking of gender rules and regulations by queer youth. *Journal of Gay and Lesbian Issues in Education, 4*(2), 33–54.

Blackburn, M. V., & Clark, C. T. (2011). Analyzing talk in a long-term literature discussion group: Ways of operating within LGBT-inclusive and queer discourses. *Reading Research Quarterly, 46*(3), 222–248.

Blackburn, M. V., Clark, C. T., & Nemeth, N. A. (2015). Examining queer elements and ideologies in LGBT-themed literature: What queer literature can offer young adult readers. *Journal of Literacy Research, 47*(1), 11–48.

Blackburn, M. V., & Smith, J. M. (2010). Moving beyond the inclusion of LGBT-themed literature in English language arts classrooms: Interrogating heteronormativity and exploring intersectionality. *Journal of Adolescent and Adult Literacy, 53*(8), 625–634.

Blazar, D. (2009). Self-discovery through character connections: Opening up to gayness in *Angels in America*. *English Journal, 98*(4), 77–84.

Botelho, M. J., & Rudman, M. K. (2009). *Critical multicultural analysis of children's literature: Mirrors, windows, and doors*. New York: Routledge.

Butler, J. (1990). *Gender trouble: Feminism and the subversion of identity*. New York: Routledge.

Clark, C. T. (2010). Preparing LGBTQ-allies and combating homophobia in a US teacher education program. *Teaching and Teacher Education, 26*(3), 704–713.

Clark, C. T., & Blackburn, M. V. (2009). Reading LGBT-themed literature with young people: What's possible? *English Journal, 98*(4), 25–32.

de Castell, S., & Jenson, J. (2007). No place like home: Sexuality, community, and identity among street-involved queer and questioning youth. In M. V. Blackburn & C. T. Clark (Eds.), *Literacy research for political action and social change* (pp. 131–152). New York: Peter Lang.

DePalma, R. (2013). Choosing to lose our gender expertise: Queering sex/gender in school settings. *Sex Education: Sexuality, Society and Learning, 13*(1), 1–15.

Epstein, D. (2000). Sexualities and education: Catch 28. *Sexualities, 3*(4), 387–394.

Freire, P. (2006). *Pedagogy of the oppressed* (30th anniversary ed.). New York: Continuum International Publishing Group. (Original work published 1970)

Gonzales, J. (2010). Risk and threat in critical inquiry: Vacancies, violations, and vacuums. In M. V. Blackburn, C. T. Clark, L. M. Kenney, & J. M. Smith (Eds.), *Acting out!: Combating homophobia through teacher activism* (pp. 74–87). New York: Teachers College Press.

Greenbaum, V. (1994). Literature out of the closet: Bringing gay and lesbian texts and subtexts out in high school English. *English Journal, 83*(5), 71–74.

Halverson, E. R. (2007). Listening to the voices of queer youth: The dramaturgical process as identity exploration. In M. V. Blackburn & C. T. Clark (Eds.), *Literacy research for political action and social change* (pp. 153–175). New York: Peter Lang.

Hamilton, G. (1998). Reading *Jack*. *English Education, 30*(1), 24–39.

Helmer, K. (2015). *Reading queerly in the high school classroom: Exploring a gay and lesbian literature course*. Unpublished doctoral dissertation, University of Massachusetts, Amherst, MA.

Hoffman, M. (1993). Teaching "Torch Song": Gay literature in the classroom. *English Journal, 82*(5), 55–58.

Hornberger, N. H. (2000). Multilingual literacies, literacy practices, and the continua of biliteracy. In M. Martin-Jones & K. Jones (Eds.), *Multilingual literacies: Reading and writing different worlds* (pp. 353–367). Philadelphia: John Mengamins.

Kenney, L. M. (2010). Being out and reading queer-inclusive texts in a high school English classroom. In M. V. Blackburn, C. T. Clark, L. M. Kenney, & J. M. Smith (Eds.), *Acting out!: Combating homophobia through teacher activism* (pp. 56–73). New York: Teachers College Press.

Kosciw, J. G., Greytak, E. A., Palmer, N. A., & Boesen, M. J. (2014). *The 2013 National School Climate Survey: The experiences of lesbian, gay, bisexual and transgender youth in our nation's schools*. New York: Gay, Lesbian, and Straight Education Network.

Lovaas, K. E., Elia, J. P., & Yep, G. A. (2006). Shifting ground(s): Surveying the contested terrain and LGBT studies and queer theory. In K. E. Lovaas, J. P. Elia, & G. A. Yep (Eds.), *LGBT studies and queer theory: New conflicts, collaborations, and contested terrain* (pp. 1–18). New York: Harrington Park Press.

Martino, W. (2009). Literacy issues and GLBTQ youth: Queer interventions in English education. In L. Christenbury, R. Bomer, & P. Smagorinsky (Eds.), *Handbook of adolescent literacy research* (pp. 386–399). New York: Guildford Press.

Moita-Lopes, L. P. (2006). Queering literacy teaching: Analyzing gay-themed discourses in a fifth-grade class in Brazil. *Journal of Language, Identity, and Education, 5*(1), 31–50.

Reese, J. (1998). Teaching tolerance through literature: Dealing with issues of homosexuality in English class. *International Schools Journal, 17*(2), 35–40.

Ryan, C. L. (2011). Talking, reading, and writing about lesbian and gay families in classrooms: The Consequences of different pedagogical approaches. In C. Compton-Lilly & S. Greene (Eds.), *Bedtime stories and book reports: Connecting parent involvement and family literacy* (pp. 96–107). New York: Teachers College Press.

Ryan, C. L. (2012, April). *Recognizing the language and literacy resources of young children with lesbian mothers*. Paper presented at the American Educational Research Association's annual meeting, Vancouver, BC.

Ryan, C. L., Patraw, J. M., & Bednar, M. (2013). Discussing princess boys and pregnant men: Teaching about gender diversity and transgender experiences within an elementary school curriculum. *Journal of LGBT Youth, 10*(1–2), 83–105.

Schall, J., & Kauffmann, G. (2003). Exploring literature with gay and lesbian characters in the elementary school. *Journal of Children's Literature, 29*(1), 36–45.

Schey, R., & Uppstrom, A. (2010). Activist work as entry-year teachers: What we've learned. In M. V. Blackburn, C. T. Clark, L. M. Kenney, & J. M. Smith (Eds.), *Acting out!: Combating homophobia through teacher activism* (pp. 88–102). New York: Teachers College Press.

Sieben, N., & Wallowitz, L. (2009). "Watch what you teach": A first year teacher refuses to play it safe. *English Journal, 98*(4), 44–49.

Smith, J. M. (2008). *Montana 1948*: Crossing boundaries with queer theory. In A. O. Soter, M. Faust, & T. M. Rogers (Eds.), *Interpretive play: Using critical perspectives to teach young adult literature* (pp. 161–174). Norwood, MA: Christopher-Gordon.

Street, B. V. (1999). The meanings of literacy. In D. A. Wagner, R. L. Venezky, & B. V. Street (Eds.), *Literacy: An international handbook*. Boulder, CO: Westview Press.

Thein, A. H. (2013). Language arts teachers' resistance to teaching LGBT literature and issues. *Language Arts, 90*(3), 169–180.

Vetter, A. M. (2010). "Cause I'm a G": Identity work of a lesbian teen in language arts. *Journal of Adolescent and Adult Literacy, 54*(2), 98–108.

Whelan, D. L. (2006, January). Out and ignored: Why are so many school libraries reluctant to embrace gay teens? *School Library Journal*, pp. 46–50.

Yep, G. A., Lovaas, K. E., & Elia, J. P. (2003). Introduction: Queering communication: Starting the conversation. In G. A. Yep, K. E. Lovaas, & J. P. Elia (Eds.), *Queer theory and communication: From disciplining queers to queering the discipline(s)* (pp. 1–10). New York: Harrington Press.

CHAPTER 4

Beyond School

Examining the Out-of-School Literacies and Counternarratives of Adolescent Learners

VALERIE KINLOCH, TANJA BURKHARD, and CARLOTTA PENN

Rendell is a Black adolescent male who graduated from Truth High School, a midsize urban public school located in the U.S. Midwest. According to recent statistics, 81.5% of the students at the school identify as Black, 11.5% identify as White, 5% as Hispanic, 1% as Asian, and of the total percentage of enrolled students, approximately 20% use mobility devices. Within the school district—the largest in the entire state—there are approximately 51,000 students across a total of 109 schools. More than 74% of the student body belongs to non-White racial groups, and of those, 56% identify as Black. The non-White population in the district also includes students of Somali descent, as the city is home to the second largest Somali community in the United States. The English language learning (ELL) needs of Somali and other non-native English speakers are paramount in the district: 13.2% of the student population has limited English proficiency, and more than 100 languages are spoken by students (Dixon, 2016).

While the district's demographic data reveal a racially and ethnically diverse student population, the data do not reflect some of the "deeply rooted sociological distances" (Cushman, 1996, p. 8) between the location of and the work occurring in schools and its local communities. For instance, Truth High School, with its high enrollment of Black students, is located in a long-standing and predominately White residential community on the city's north side. The community consists of moderate-size single-family homes, apartment complexes, churches, a park, and popular chain restaurants. The location of the school in relation to the surrounding community is important to note here, because some of the students, as Rendell describes, "don't live right around here in this neighborhood. . . . It brings distance between us and them [residents]. If we stop assuming negativity about each other, we'd like do the impossible, create something new." Rendell continues, "'Cause see, I be wondering why schools don't let us work out there. We gotta stay inside all day, sit at desks, staring at the board doing busy work. That's learning?"

Rendell's sentiments about students "doing busy work" connect to a point made by Mariana, an 18-year-old Latin@ who was a student in Valerie's high school English class in the U.S. Northeast. During a session with high school students and preservice teacher education candidates, Mariana recalled how some of her teachers would "just go and give us textbooks as the work and they don't do no work with you [students] . . . and you don't learn nothing" (Kinloch, 2012, p. 18). To reiterate Rendell's question, "That's learning?" Similarly, Rendell's thoughts about students not being encouraged to imagine what is possible and work in the community reiterate Cushman's (1996) observation of the distances between universities and communities. She asserts that this distance "seems to be a primary factor in prohibiting scholars from approaching people outside the university." In fact, according to Cushman, "Everyday, we reproduce this distance so long as a select few gain entrance to universities, so long as we differentiate between experts and novices, and so long as we value certain types of knowledge" (pp. 10–11). Relatedly, Rendell's sentiments also reflect a widespread dilemma about the limitations of educational opportunities. As Nixon and Comber (2011) contend, "Even when new initiatives and innovations claim to be new or promise opportunities for change, schools by their very nature sometimes limit what is possible, stripping the practices to simulations and reducing meaningful tasks to skeletal approximations of what they might have been" (p. 261). Unfortunately, the previous assertions—"limiting what is possible" and "reducing meaningful tasks"—ring true for too many K–12 students attending urban public schools in the United States. On a more local level, this is often the case at Truth High School and throughout the district, especially when "the force of school time and space, as business-as-usual, can make routine and constrain even the potentially exciting" (p. 261; see also Comber & Nixon, 2005).

This was the situation for Rendell until he entered Truth High School and walked into Ms. Washington's ninth-grade English language arts class. According to Rendell, "That did it for me, being in her class, I got to work in the community. I started imagining things I thought was impossible. I started learning." As a student in Ms. Washington's class and throughout his entire tenure at Truth High School, Rendell actively participated in community-based social justice projects in the community. In fact, he partnered with Ms. Washington and a group of racially and linguistically diverse peers at the school to design a community fruit and vegetable garden and to install a wheelchair-accessible cement paver into the garden. Over time, he donated fresh fruits and vegetables from the garden to local residents and to food pantries, visited assisted living facilities, and engaged in reading and writing activities about identity, justice, ability, literacy, and human rights. He also presented reports on the work at local meetings and national conferences. In many ways, Rendell was able to engage in the work because Ms. Washington, a Black woman with more than 17 years of teaching experience in urban public schools, understands the importance of students working and learning beyond schools. That is, she recognizes the need for teachers to learn about and work with students in ways that "connect home to school, community to classroom, and learning to engagement" (Kinloch, Nemeth, & Patterson, 2015, p. 40).

SO, WHAT NOW?: AN OVERVIEW OF THE CHAPTER

What, then, can the example of Rendell teach us about the valuable role of young people developing their literacies (and being supported to do so) in out-of-school contexts?

Additionally, what does it mean to move beyond school, and why is it important to do so? What does the scholarship on out-of-school literacies indicate about young people's experiences with imagining "the impossible" and creating "something new?" As Rendell and other young people move beyond school, how are they being supported—by teachers, researchers, families, and/or community groups—to cultivate their literacies and chart their own trajectories? In other words, what are young people doing, particularly Black adolescents, beyond schools, and what theoretical and praxis-oriented lessons can teachers, teacher-educators, and literacy researchers learn from them?

Throughout this chapter, we selectively reference the out-of-school practices of Rendell as a way to highlight important insights from scholarship on literacies beyond schools. To begin, we first discuss an ideological view of literacy, which focuses on the multiplicity of literacy across various contexts. Then, we survey related literature, relevant research, and praxis-driven approaches that honor the out-of-school literacies of adolescent learners. Because we are aware that current literature on adolescents' out-of-school literacies does not readily address their counternarrative productions, we then highlight examples of how young people can rely on literacy to critique racialized encounters and produce counternarratives to mainstream assumptions about who they are and what they can or cannot do. This discussion, framed by critical race theory, points to larger lessons that teachers, teacher-educators, and literacy researchers should consider when working with adolescent learners, generally, and Black adolescents, particularly, beyond the context of schools. Doing so might lead to Rendell's desire for us all to "create something new."

ADOLESCENT LITERACIES IN OUT-OF-SCHOOL CONTEXTS

The contemporary context and ongoing climate of racism in the United States, including its horrid outgrowths—such as police brutality, the mass incarceration of Black men and other people of color, increasing educational disparities, and rising economic and social inequities—raise questions about how youth of color, with an added focus on Black adolescents, interact with and make sense of the world around them. Of course, this type of sense-making about the world and its current contexts occurs inside and outside schools, and has important implications for teaching, learning, and community engagement (Chang, 2015; Haddix, 2015; Moss, 1994). The question of how young people understand their social contexts, among others, also drives the push of contemporary literacy research to acknowledge that schools are microcosms of society and are largely shaped by power struggles. Thus, schools are not the only places in which young people engage in learning and develop their literacy practices (Kinloch, 2010; Mahiri, 2004; Skerrett & Bomer, 2011; Vasudevan & Campano, 2009). With this view, we understand that the literacy practices of young people should not be viewed as a monolithic set of skills to be acquired. Instead, literacy as a social practice is attentive to power, contexts, and, according to Hull and Schultz (2001), "the interplay between the meanings of local events and a structural analysis of broader cultural and political institutions and practices" (p. 585).

Literacies and Ideological Perspectives

For Street (1984, 1995, 2003), this view of literacy represents an ideological perspective, which stipulates that literacy is not a set of skills, but is instead "embedded in socially constructed epistemological principles" (2003, p. 77) and is shaped by the social contexts in which it is constructed. An ideological view of literacy challenges the autonomous model, which presents literacy as neutral, universal, and value-free. According to de Ünlüsoy, de Haan, Leseman, and van Kruistum (2010), "Shifting the focus of literacy engagement from a perspective on individual skills to one that conceives of literacy as a social practice entails the recognition of the existence of multiple literacies" (p. 743). They go on to assert that acknowledging multiple literacies "var[ies] according to their sociocultural meanings and the time and space where they are practiced" (p. 743). Their argument reiterates Street's (2003) belief that "the ways in which people address reading and writing are themselves rooted in conceptions of knowledge, identity, and being" (pp. 77–78).

Similarly, Alvermann (2009) notes that there exist numerous literacies that take different forms depending on the various modalities (e.g., images, printed texts, sounds) that are used to communicate meaning and make sense of the world. What counts as literacy, then, becomes a political question that is deeply embedded in the social contexts and the power differentials in which the practice of literacy occurs (Gallego & Hollingsworth, 2000). In addition to the question of what counts as literacy, the question of whose knowledges, texts, and sites of knowledge production are valued must be accounted for by educational and literacy research that seeks to find ways to diffuse the power structure inherent in the processes of teaching and learning inside and outside schools (Moore & Readence, 2001). Kinloch (2011, 2015a) argues that the focus of literacy research has shifted in recent years from a traditional view of schools as the most important sites in which literacy is practiced and explored, to a more contemporary understanding of the sites beyond schools where young people engage in literacy (e.g., churches, community centers, homes, public demonstrations, online, nonschool peer groups; see Blommaert, 2008; Hamilton, 2012; Napoli, 2013).

The shift to an ideological model also requires a rejection of deficit narratives directed toward adolescents, especially those of color, who have been largely positioned as *at risk, remedial,* or *struggling learners.* Researchers who employ a sociocultural perspective have long called for the consideration of students' funds of knowledge (Moll, Amanti, Neff, & Gonzalez, 1992; Marshall & Toohey, 2010) as one specific way to understand better the diverse experiences and knowledge base, and the cultural, literacy, and linguistic practices students bring into schools from their familial communities. Funds of knowledge, for Moll et al. (1992), are "historically accumulated and culturally developed bodies of knowledge and skills essential for household or individual functioning and well-being" (p. 133; see also Orellana & Eksner, 2006). These funds should be valued outside and inside schools, especially if literacy practitioners and researchers are to better understand who adolescents are and what their experiences entail beyond schools. This is also important if we want to learn about how adolescents engage in literacy practices in a variety of contexts, and how these engagements can be mobilized in classroom and community spaces.

Literacies Beyond Schools

Advances in technology and digital communication have produced new literacies that require flexibility and adaptability, and have also created spaces in which young people develop new methods of expression and consumption that are not often valued in schools. As Hull and Schultz (2001) contend, while it is neither necessary nor productive to dichotomize in-school and out-of-school literacy learning, a singular focus on literacy in schools disallows opportunities for learning about adolescent identities, activities, and funds of knowledge. In order to create spaces inside schools in which students' out-of-school literacy practices are valued, educators should first interrogate the values that drive their literacy-based approaches (e.g., pedagogical decisions, curricular planning, academic engagement with students). There is, in fact, a wealth of current research on adolescents' literacy engagements beyond schools. For instance, Paris and Kirkland (2011) show the artistry and creativity of youth who engage in literacy practices in nonschool digital spaces. They argue for the "opening up [of] digital spaces" and the "extending [of] a hand into youth spaces and into communities of color" (p. 190). In so doing, literacy teachers and researchers might come to better understand how "young people enact vernacular literacies across multiple borderlands at once—the borderlands at the edge of the oral and the written as well as those at the boundary of the digital and embodied" (p. 178). Teachers and researchers could also recognize how the existing literacies that adolescents are taking up outside schools impact their sense of agency and levels of commitment to complete a variety of educational and extracurricular tasks (Alvermann, 2009; Alvermann & Hinchman, 2012; Hull & Schultz, 2001).

Related to Paris and Kirkland's (2011) focus on the ways adolescents perform literacies within "multiple borderlands" is Ginwright's (2010) study of Black adolescents, activism, and healing in urban communities. Ginwright focuses on the "multiple borderlands" that exist between the communities of West and East Oakland, California. He makes the case for engaging in a dialogic process of "radical healing" and political activism on three specific levels—the individual, the community, and the broader social or societal level—in order to maintain and/or restore hope within the lives of Black youth. His attention to trauma, violence, and loss allows him to argue for social justice relationships grounded in "trust, dependence, and mutual expectations" that establish "hope, political consciousness, and the willingness to act on behalf of the common good" (p. 56). The literacy stories of Marcus, Vince, Tre, and other Black adolescents speak to the importance of engaging young people in examining their identities and cultures in community spaces.

Ginwright is not alone in emphasizing the literacy and social justice interests of Black adolescents during nonschool time. Kirkland's (2013) study of the literacies of six Black adolescent males highlights the significance of knowing more about the social worlds of young people who daily fight against systemic forms of injustice, structural racism, and marginalization. By employing an "I–us" reflexive approach to learn about the six adolescents, Kirkland emphasizes how the literacies of young people are not confined to, do not begin within, and do not end in schools. To make this point, he asserts, "Like their lives, the young men's literacies were hybrid and dialogic in nature, constitutive of the situations of the multiple spaces they traversed in our time together" (p. 8). Thus, the literacy experiences of adolescents, as with all people, are not relegated to a single place, a single experience, or a "single story—of literate beings" (p. 136). Instead, their experiences beyond schools and our documentation of them can create "a new and needed narrative" about issues related to "what it means to be literate in the 21st century—a question that yields greater importance especially in a world that constructs too many young Black men as the opposite" (p. 138; see also Fergus, Noguera, & Martin, 2014).

Insofar as urban adolescent engagement with diverse meaning-making activities—from spoken-word poetry performances, gender identity, and gender borders, to Latin@

Lowrider culture, and the connections among literacy, language, and sports—Mahiri's (2004) research serves as a strong example. In fact, Mahiri makes the case that attention to the literacies of urban youth can produce stronger understandings of who they are, how and why they engage in meaning- and sense-making activities, and how literacy teachers and researchers can rely on their out-of-school experiences to inform pedagogical practices (see also Knobel & Lankshear, 2003; Morrell, 2008).

Undoubtedly, adolescents engage in literacy practices within local communities that are not often acknowledged within the contexts of schools. These practices are heavily embedded in cultural, linguistic, intellectual, and community traditions that affirm their identities, agency, and critical consciousness (Heath & McLaughlin, 1993; Kinloch & San Pedro, 2014; Vasudevan, 2006). They also point, again, to the value of understanding young people's funds of knowledge. On this latter point, Wiltse (2015), in her research with Aboriginal teachers and adolescents in Canada, highlights the negative consequences that result when young peoples' funds of knowledge are devalued. Wiltse places attention on how one student—who was disinterested in writing prompts and completing writing tasks—reacted with excitement when given an opportunity to produce texts on topics previously deemed inappropriate by a teacher who did not share his same cultural background. She concludes that there is a disjuncture between students' home and school lives and literacy expectations.

The findings of Wiltse (2015) speak to those of McTavish (2014), who, in working with younger students, surmises that "many educators are beginning to consider that these future out-of-school contexts will indeed require not only the use of conventional print literacies but also new multiliteracies to access and construct information within private and public economic sectors, and within local and global corporate worlds" (p. 339). Based on this assertion, the various nonschool contexts that shape the literacy experiences of adolescents must be taken into account in the study and teaching of literacy, especially by all who are committed to teaching in equitable and just ways.

Since racism within schools and inside communities continues to affect the lives of adolescents of color in the United States, generally, and Black youth, particularly, studying the intersections of adolescent literacy and racial identity is an important, albeit highly underexplored, task. Studies focused on the out-of-school literacy practices of adolescents of color often respond to existing deficit narratives about youth (Ginwright, Noguera, & Cammarota, 2006; Kinloch, 2015b; Paris & Winn, 2014). For adolescents who are culturally and racially "Othered," and whose experiences are visibly marked by racism, this kind of disjuncture can add to their further internalization of deficit narratives that position them as struggling and/or at risk. A focus on literacies, then, is inextricably connected to students' identities, and requires teachers and researchers to work at better understanding "when, where, how, and why youth practice literacy" (Paris & Kirkland, 2011, p. 178) in relation to out-of-school time and space. The impact of time and space on the out-of-school literacy practices and identities of adolescents has become a central point of analysis for many researchers. Moje (2000), for example, argues that many young people engage in literacy practices to define or redefine their identities. Therefore, the physical, digital, and imagined nonschool spaces in which youth engage in literacy are linked to the ways they construct their identities.

Young people who repeatedly receive the message that they are struggling readers and/or incapable writers based on restrictive school-sanctioned evaluation measures might more readily grapple with seeing themselves as writers, poets, or intellectuals outside schools. As Williams (2005) notes, there is a disconnect between students seeing themselves as proficient literacy learners in their familial communities, and these same students who come to school and "move from thinking of themselves as competent and confident writers and readers to thinking of themselves as struggling students confronting literacies that don't seem relevant to their lives" (p. 704). To counter the internalization of deficit narratives about their capabilities, Haddix (2012) posits that young people can be encouraged to develop more fully their literate identities if they are a part of supportive writing communities. She notes that in these out-of-school communities, students, such as the Black adolescent males in her study, can be inspired to produce powerful counterstories to narratives of failure and disengagement that pervade much of educational research. In fact, they can "reclaim their literate identities" in the world (p. 129).

The significance of creating supportive literacy learning communities beyond schools points to the need to reshape conversations about adolescent learners, especially Black youth, who attend U.S. public schools. As relevant literature indicates (Muhammad, 2015; Wissman & Vasudevan, 2012), adolescents should be encouraged to see themselves as agentive, capable beings who can learn to resist and counter deficit narratives about their cultures, identities, and literacies. For this to happen, literacy practitioners and researchers would do well to take up Paulo Freire's (1971) insistence to not " 'integrate' [students] into the structure of oppression, but to transform that structure so that they can become 'beings for themselves' " (p. 55). In other words, we have a responsibility to recognize and value the funds of knowledge and out-of-school literacies adolescents bring with them from their nonschool communities.

Therefore, we need to encourage adolescents to rely on their out-of-school literacies for a variety of reasons, which includes understanding their levels of agency and resilience, interrogating systems of oppression, and producing counternarratives that contest deficit perspectives. Similarly, we must learn more about the out-of-school literacy practices of adolescents in order to better understand why, where, and how young people engage in literacy, and how their identities and activities are impacted by their engagements. Doing so can reveal important insights for designing interactive instructional and curricular approaches, and for connecting adolescent literacies across community and school contexts.

CRITICAL RACE THEORY AND COUNTERNARRATIVES

Why are the out-of-school literacies of adolescents, especially Black youth, important to recognize and study? How can critical race theory (CRT), as an intellectual tradition, contribute to expansive understandings of the nonschool literacies of adolescents and the need to support their production of counternarratives to negative assumptions that circulate about them? To think through these questions, we turn to CRT, which contends that racism remains the "central ideological underpinning of American society" (Crenshaw, 1988, p. 1331). CRT also insists that we examine and change relationships among race, power, privilege, and justice. This is ever so important to do because, as Berry and Stovall (2013) argue, "In the US, we continue to assess and evaluate people by the color of their skin" (p. 594) in ways that intensely disadvantage Black people, including Black adolescents.

In the 1970s, CRT was shaped by critical legal theorists, feminists, civil rights scholars, and other intellectuals who sought to affirm and respond to the long tradition of Black people in America decrying and resisting racism. According to CRT, racism is normal, structural, and ingrained in the fabric of U.S. cultures. Legal scholar Derrick Bell (1992), esteemed forefather of CRT, argued that "racial equality is, in fact, not a realistic goal" (p. 363). However, he also insisted that the "continued struggle can bring about unexpected benefits and gains that in themselves justify continued endeavor" (p. 378). In the following sections, we contend that CRT affords a unique opportunity to examine the nonschool literacies and counternarratives of Black youth in ways that draw attention to the presence of racism and injustice in various sociopolitical contexts.

Counternarratives

According to critical race theorists, counternarrative is a "method of telling the stories of those people whose experiences are not often told," in order to "shatter complacency, challenge the dominant discourse on race, and further the struggle for racial reform" (Solózarno & Yosso, 2002, p. 32). In educational research, counternarratives are told as personal stories, other people's stories, or composite stories, which bring together data and life experiences to emphasize a particular racialized phenomenon. Solózarno and Yosso argue that the critical race methodology of counternarrative in education must center race at all junctures of the research process, while demonstrating how race intersects with gender, class, and other facets of identity to impact experiences for students of color. In telling new stories about Black adolescent identities and experiences, scholars must reject narratives of cultural deficit that have been used to talk about Black youth. However, while recasting master narratives of Black inferiority is important, counternarratives need not necessarily be constructed in response to dominant stories. On their own, counternarratives can "help strengthen traditions of social, political, and cultural survival and resistance" (p. 32).

Additionally, legal scholar Charles Lawrence (1995) notes that narrative is a form of knowledge and data that has "revolutionary implications" (p. 347). In our estimation, stories that highlight Black youth achievement and resistance to systemic racism, especially in nonschool contexts (O'Connor, 1997; Stern, 1996), are invaluable to the revolutionary work of countering widespread assumptions about Black adolescent deviance (Moje, 2000; Sutherland, 2005). These stories also contribute to reconstructing our society based on the principles of social justice. As we recognize Black adolescents as leaders, intellectuals, and vessels of unlimited possibilities beyond schools, we can engage their power and potential for achievement across a variety of educational, social, familial, and political contexts. In other words, counternarratives of Black youth that highlight their excellence can lay the groundwork for a needed shift in perspective on the part of school administrators, teachers, security personnel, and community members who might not readily draw on or recognize the nonschool literacies and lives of adolescents. This is important to do because, according to Rendell, "They need to know us, see what we already know how to do. We doin' all this already when we ain't in school." Rendell's sentiments point to the reality that Black adolescents are engaging in rich literacy activities beyond schools. However, it is important to recognize that young people do not demonstrate potential in their communities only to become different persons, void of talent, once they enter schools.

Counternarratives highlight positive representations of Black adolescents and their academic achievement. For example, in Allen's (2015) study of Black adolescent males and their deftness in negotiating systemic racism and inequity, he notes that the counternarratives of "academically successful Black males" reveal that their parents' high expectations, along with an "understanding of the purpose of school, particularly the personal, social, and work preparation benefits" (p. 217) positively impacted their drive to succeed. While the families understood that structural racism created barriers to opportunities, access, and ultimately success, the Black adolescent males demonstrated agency to overcome. One adolescent shared, "I agree with that you have to work harder than most people, although it's not fair, it's the reality" (p. 219).

Another example of Black youth overcoming racial barriers to success centers on students at an elite, predominantly White, private school. In her study, DeCuir-Gunby (2007) examined how schooling environments impact adolescent identity development and academic and social success. The counternarratives of the adolescents revealed their desire to take advantage of the promises of meritocracy on the one hand, and their awareness that race and class made accessing opportunities (steeped in White privilege) more difficult on the other hand. DeCuir-Gunby concludes, "There is a need for better mechanisms for African American students to take advantage of the opportunities . . . and maintain their connection to the African American community, while challenging racial and class norms" (p. 33). To develop such mechanisms, it is important that the school and nonschool experiences of Black adolescents are sought out, listened to, and documented. As Williams and Portman (2014) suggest, Black adolescents have important insights to offer about their educational needs; however, there has been insufficient research into their perspectives. To address this relative absence, Williams and Portman gathered the counternarratives of five Black adolescents who graduated from schools on the South Side of Chicago, and they gained the following insights into students' beliefs about what supported their success: "Shared responsibility for educational outcomes, being a part of the solution, parental involvement by any means, natural support systems, school counselors as change agents, and community collaboration to raise a scholar" (p. 20).

Finally, counternarratives can also suggest new possibilities for Black youths' engagement in communities and schools. As indicated earlier, counternarratives by Black people are important, because "our stories have, for the most part, not been told or recorded in the [dominant] literature" (Lawrence, 1995, p. 344). In fact, the stories told for and about Black adolescents are typically steeped in negativity. Berry and Stovall (2013) write about a "curriculum of tragedy" that defines life in the United States for many Black males. They ask, "What knowledge is most worth knowing" (p. 588) about Black adolescent males? To address this question, they analyze the tragic killing of Trayvon Martin, a Black youth who was murdered in his father's neighborhood by a White adult male. Berry and Stovall suggest that the master narrative that Black boys have an "inclination towards incarceration over the ability to make informed decisions about their lives" (p. 589) leads to tragic encounters for them. They write, "If George Zimmerman . . . knew what was most worth knowing about young men of color, Trayvon Benjamin Martin might be alive today" (p. 596).

Berry and Stovall (2013) continue their argument by insisting that critical race scholars are duty-bound to promote social justice through research, and that counternarratives serve as an important strategy for such promotion. They offer a counterstory about Trayvon Martin that maintains the reality of racism while revising the "end," such that

Martin survives the encounter. Finally, they suggest that educators and researchers must engage in critical pedagogies that acknowledge, honor, and center the perspectives of people of color, as well as the realities of race and racism that shape the daily lives of all people in the United States.

Relatedly, it is Lawrence (1995) who asserts, "The ability to produce text, to stand in the position of subject and tell one's own story, is central to one's humanity and one's freedom" (p. 349). Lawrence's sentiments parallel those of hooks (1990), who, on writing about violence within the academy, states the following:

> No need to hear your voice when I can talk about you better than you can speak about yourself. No need to hear your voice. Only tell me about your pain. I want to know your story. And then I will tell it back to you in a new way. Tell it back to you in such a way that it has become mine, my own. Re-writing you I write myself anew. I am still author, authority. I am still colonizer, the speaking subject and you are now at the center of my talk. (p. 343)

We agree with the arguments of both Lawrence and hooks, and argue that the counternarratives of Black adolescents have the power and potential to revolutionize how Black youth see themselves in relation to the larger society. This is also the case for how educators might more productively, positively, and powerfully (re)engage with the lives and literacies of Black adolescents outside and inside schools. Doing so might demonstrate a collective commitment to shape a world wherein freedom and justice are realities.

Counternarratives and Black Adolescents Beyond Schools

In her last will and testament, educator and rights leader Mary McLeod Bethune (1955) wrote, "We have a powerful potential in our youth, and we must have the courage to change old ideas and practices so that we may direct their power toward good ends." Bethune dedicated her life to supporting education for Black people in the United States, and her full testament expresses hope for young Black people to maintain a "thirst for education." Although much of academic research focuses on Black adolescent underachievement, Black youth *do* demonstrate their literacy potential and power inside schools. Equally relevant, however, is the inspiring literacy and community-based, social justice work Rendell references at the beginning of this chapter, which happens beyond school. Rendell is not the only Black adolescent who is engaging in nonschool work. Consider Amiya Alexander, a Black female who, at 9 years of age, wanted to own a pink school bus dance studio. With her mother's help, she started the Amiya Mobile Dance Studio. Now a teenager, Alexander is a dancer, entrepreneur, and activist. Also, there is Asean Johnson, who, when he was only 9 years old, famously spoke out against school closings at a 2013 rally in Chicago, Illinois. In his criticism of Mayor Rahm Emanuel, Johnson stated, "You should be investing in these schools, not closing them. You should be supporting these schools, not closing them." Today, Johnson remains active in the community as a member of the Chicago Student Union. In addition to these powerful examples of Black adolescent achievement, other young people across the United States are also demonstrating leadership and a commitment to literacy within their families and nonschool communities every day.

Despite their demonstrated capacity to excel in the arts, business, and philanthropy, and although they play central roles in shaping vibrant community cultures, Black adolescents are routinely regarded with racial contempt. As Harper (2009) contends, "The typical Black boy in a K–12 educational setting is taught almost exclusively by White women who combine an insufficient anticipation for his academic achievement with high expectations for disruptive behavior, intellectual stupidity, and a dispassion for learning" (p. 697). The case of Kayleb Moon-Robinson is illustrative. At age 11, a police officer slammed, handcuffed, and removed the autistic child from school because he failed to comply with a rule that he wait for other students to leave class (Perry, 2015). Similarly, in 2015, a Black teenager in Louisiana was arrested at school for throwing skittles at fellow students on a school bus. While the aforementioned examples involve Black adolescent males, and while a plethora of academic research focuses on Black boys in education (Harper, 2009; Caton, 2012; Berry & Stovall, 2013), schooling atmospheres are equally hostile for Black girls (Evans-Winters, 2011; Evans-Winters & Love, 2015; Winn, 2011; Womack, 2013). In 2012, police handcuffed 6-year-old Salecia Johnson for reportedly throwing a tantrum and damaging school property (Campbell, 2012). In a less violent example, Vanessa VanDyke was in middle school when school administrators threatened to expel her if she did not cut her Afro, which they labeled a "distraction" (Chaiyabhat, 2013).

Unfortunately, out-of-school spaces are no less threatening for Black youth who regularly suffer from physical and deadly force, especially from police authorities. For example, in 2014, a White police officer in the state of Ohio shot 12-year-old Tamir Rice dead within seconds of approaching him. Rice was playing with a toy gun in a public park. In another example, Texas police officers attacked theretofore peacefully socializing Black teenagers at a pool party following a complaint issued by White neighbors who did not think they belonged in the neighborhood. During the chaotic encounter, a White officer violently handcuffed 15-year-old Dajerria Becton, who was unarmed, after she failed to disperse from the area without complaint. Other officers drew their guns on unarmed Black adolescents who attempted to help Becton (Orphanides, 2015). Such instances of abuse involving White adults and Black youth in public spaces are overabundant and often go unpunished.

In fact, the negative racial lens through which educators, police officers, and community members too often view Black youth results in the overrepresentation of Black adolescents in special education courses (Hopkins, 1997; Kearns, Ford, & Linney, 2005). It also leads to higher rates of suspension and dropout from school (Majors & Billson, 1992; Noguera, 2008; Schott Foundation for Public Education, 2010, 2015) and increasing rates of Black youth confinement to juvenile detention centers (O'Cummings, Bardack, & Gonsoulin, 2010). This is the case even in light of the argument that Black youth are not more likely than White youth to engage in deviant or criminal behaviors when one considers "income, neighborhood cohesion and environment, and law enforcement practices" (Haggerty, Skinner, McGlynn-Wright, Catalano, & Crutchfield, 2013, p. 145; see also Crutchfield, Skinner, Haggerty, McGlynn, & Catalano, 2009). The unreasonable numbers of Black youth under academic distress, detention, and threat of death result *not* from their lack of intellect, talent, or composure, but from mainstream society's refusal to either acknowledge Black adolescents' humanity or nurture their developing identities. This rejection of Black humanity is grounded in a larger master narrative, according to Thomas Jefferson (1801), who is widely revered as a founding father of the United States, that "blacks ... are inferior to the whites in the endowments both of body and mind (p. 150). It is important for literacy practitioners and researchers to interrogate and teach against such beliefs in ways that build on the strength, brilliance, and power of Black lives.

THE IMPORTANCE OF FOCUSING ON LITERACIES BEYOND SCHOOLS

The previous examples are steeped in a larger history of racism and violence that continues to be perpetuated against Black people in the United States, with an added focus on Black youth and youth of color. The examples are also reflective of the need for ongoing studies that emphasize how an ideological model of literacy is beneficial for understanding adolescent literacies, identities, and counternarratives outside schools. This is particularly important if literacy research is to better understand the various sociopolitical contexts adolescents navigate (e.g., homes, community sites, online, schools, the larger society) and their reasons, desires, and ways of doing so. Additionally, a focus on contexts, and how contexts are shaped by racism and other forms of hegemonic oppressions, can make visible the rich and nuanced out-of-school literacy practices of adolescents that often go unexamined in academic settings.

As our review of literature and featured examples indicate, many adolescents thrive intellectually and creatively despite dominant narratives about their disengagement, failure, and lack of academic acuity. Because we owe adolescents our best efforts, we should heed Ladson-Billings's (2006) call to reframe narratives of failure into narratives of debt that are marked by "the cumulative effect of poor education, poor housing, poor health care, and poor government services" (p. 10). This work requires that we "deploy our knowledge, skills, and expertise to alleviate ... suffering" (p. 10), and to create more equitable learning environments in which adolescents such as 18-year-old Rendell are able to feel that they are learning and making valuable contributions inside and outside schools. To achieve this, teachers, researchers, administrators, and students should collectively explore what counts as learning and as literacy. Then, they must determine critical and positive ways to capitalize on these understandings in order to reframe deficit perspectives and produce counternarratives about the literacy experiences of youth.

But this is not just about research. It is also about praxis. How can teachers work with students, as 18-year-old Mariana suggests, so that together, students and teachers can learn in ways that are valuable, relevant, and inspiring to their lives beyond school? We do not mean to suggest here that all teachers' instructional methods are limited to textbook assignments and "busy work." In fact, we acknowledge the humanizing engagements of teachers across the country who know that "the stakes are high, for our students, our communities, and our world" (Freire, 1998, p. 90). We also recognize that Mariana's and Rendell's sentiments are indicative of a ubiquitous school culture focused on standardized testing and discipline, as opposed to education as the practice of freedom (hooks, 1994). We believe it is necessary to imagine how school-based learning might look if teachers regularly worked with students, keeping busy not with testing drills, worksheets, and board-based lectures, but with the kind of critical community-to-classroom work that so inspired Rendell and that continues to inspire many other adolescents.

Finally, we contend that school administrators, policymakers, teachers, and researchers must begin to ask adolescents what matters to them, and then incorporate these important perspectives into the overall design of schools and curricula. Young people like Asean and Amiya demonstrate the power and potential of Black adolescents engaging in work that matters beyond chalkboards, textbooks, worksheets, and schools. In fact, their stories indicate that Black adolescents are ready to teach, learn, and work in their communities in ways that have the potential to lead to social justice. As educators, we must be willing to listen to, learn from, and work with young people. We must be prepared to seek out, document, and carefully consider the counternarratives that Black adolescents produce daily. We must be ready to learn about how they live, the literacies they practice, and the work they do beyond school.

REFERENCES

Allen, Q. (2015). "I'm trying to get my A": Black male achievers talk about race, school, and achievement. *Urban Review, 47,* 209–231.

Alvermann, D. E. (2009). Sociocultural constructions of adolescence and young people's literacies. In L. Christenbury, R. Bomer, & P. Smagorinsky (Eds.), *Handbook of adolescent literacy research* (pp. 14–28). New York: Guilford Press.

Alvermann, D. E., & Hinchman, K. A. (Eds.). (2012). *Reconceptualizing the literacies in adolescents' lives: Bridging the everyday/academic divide.* New York: Routledge.

Bell, D. A. (1992). Racial realism (racial equality for Afro-Americans). *Connecticut Law Review,* 24(2), 363–379.

Berry, T., & Stovall, D. (2013). Trayvon Martin and the curriculum of tragedy: Critical race lessons for education. *Race and Ethnicity in Education,* 16(4), 587–602.

Bethune, M. (1955). Dr. Bethune's last will and testament. Retrieved from *www.cookman.edu/about_bcu/history/lastwill_testament.html.*

Blommaert, J. (2008). *Grassroots literacy: Writing, identity and voice in Central Africa.* London: Routledge.

Campbell, A. (2012, April 17). Police handcuff six-year-old student in Georgia. Retrieved from *www.cnn.com/2012/04/17/justice/georgia-student-handcuffed.*

Caton, M. (2012). Black male perspectives on their educational experiences in high school. *Urban Education,* 47(6), 1055–1085.

Chaiyabhat, S. (2013, December 24). Update: African American girl won't face expulsion over "natural hair." Retrieved from *www.clickorlando.com/news/africanamerican-girl-faces-expulsion-over-natural-hair/23159400.*

Chang, B. (2015). In the service of self-determination: Teacher education, service-learning, and community reorganizing. *Theory Into Practice,* 54(1), 29–38.

Comber, B., & Nixon, H. (2005). Children re-read and re-write their neighbourhoods: Critical literacies and identity work. In J. Evans (Ed.), *Literacy moves on: Using popular culture, new technologies and critical literacy in the primary classroom* (pp. 127–148). Portsmouth, NH: Heinemann.

Crenshaw, K. W. (1988). Race, reform, and retrenchment: Transformation and legitimation in antidiscrimination law. *Harvard Law Review,* 101(7), 1331–1387.

Crutchfield, R. D., Skinner, M. L., Haggerty, K. P., McGlynn, A., & Catalano, R. F. (2009). Racial disparities in early criminal justice involvement. *Race and Social Problems, 1,* 218–230.

Cushman, E. (1996). The rhetorician as an agent of social change. *College Composition and Communication,* 47(1), 7–28.

DeCuir-Gunby, J. T. (2007). Negotiating identity in a bubble: A critical race analysis of African

American high school students' experiences in an elite, independent school. *Equity and Excellence in Education, 40*(1), 26–35.

de Ünlüsoy, A., de Haan, M., Leseman, P. M., & van Kruistum, C. (2010). Gender differences in adolescents out-of-school literacy practices: A multifaceted approach. *Computers and Education, 55*(2), 742–751.

Dixon, K. (2016). *The contested space of STEM–Art integration: Cultural humility and collaborative interdisciplinarity.* Unpublished doctoral dissertation, Ohio State University, Columbus, OH.

Evans-Winters, V. (2011). *Teaching Black girls: Resiliency in urban classrooms* (3rd ed.). New York: Peter Lang.

Evans-Winters, V., & Love, B. (Eds.). (2015). *Black feminism in education: Black women speak back, up, and out.* New York: Peter Lang.

Fergus, E., Noguera, P., & Martin, M. (2014). *Schooling for resilience: Improving the life trajectory of Black and Latino Boys.* Cambridge, MA: Harvard Education Press.

Freire, P. (1971). *Pedagogy of the oppressed.* New York: Herder & Herder.

Freire, P. (1998). *Teachers as cultural workers: Letters to those who dare teach.* Boulder, CO: Westview Press.

Gallego, M. A., & Hollingsworth, S. (Eds.). (2000). *What counts as literacy?: Challenging the school standard.* New York: Teachers College Press.

Ginwright, S. A. (2010). *Black youth rising: Activism and radical healing in urban America.* New York: Teachers College Press.

Ginwright, S. A., Noguera, P., & Cammarota, J. (Eds.). (2006). *Beyond resistance!: Youth activism and community change: New democratic possibilities for practice and policy for America's youth.* New York: Routledge.

Haddix, M. (2012). Reclaiming and rebuilding the writer identities of Black adolescent males. In D. Alvermann & K. Hinchman (Eds.), *Reconceptualizing the literacies in adolescents' lives: Bridging the everyday/academic divide* (pp. 112–131). New York: Routledge.

Haddix, M. (2015). Preparing community-engaged teachers. *Theory Into Practice, 54*(1), 63–70.

Haggerty, K. P., Skinner, M. L., McGlynn-Wright, A., Catalano, R. F., & Crutchfield, R. D. (2013). Parent and peer predictors of violent behavior of Black and White teens. *Violence and Victims, 28*(1), 145–160.

Hamilton, M. (2012). *Literacy and the politics of representation.* London: Routledge.

Harper, S. R. (2009). Niggers no more: A critical race counternarrative on Black male student achievement at predominantly White colleges and universities. *International Journal of Qualitative Studies in Education, 22*(6), 697–712.

Heath, S. B., & McLaughlin, M. W. (1993). *Identity and inner-city youth: Beyond ethnicity and gender.* New York: Teachers College Press.

hooks, B. (1990). Marginality as a site of resistance. In R. Ferguson, M. Gever, T. T. Minh-ha, & C. West (Eds.), *Out there: Marginalization and contemporary cultures* (pp. 241–243). Cambridge, MA: MIT Press.

hooks, B. (1994). *Teaching to transgress: Education as the practice of freedom.* London: Routledge.

Hopkins, R. (1997). *Educating Black males: Critical lessons in schooling, community, and power.* Albany: State University Press of New York.

Hull, G., & Schultz, K. (2001). Literacy and learning out of school: A review of theory and research. *Review of Educational Research, 71*(4), 575–611.

Jefferson, T. (1801). *Notes on the state of Virginia: With an appendix.* Newark, DE: Pennington & Gould.

Johnson, A. (2013). Amazing 9 year old Asean Johnson brings the crowd to their feet at Chicago school closings rally. *The Video Catalyst Project* (YouTube Video). Retrieved from *www.youtube.com/watch?v=oue9hiom7xu.*

Kearns, T., Ford, L., & Linney, J. A. (2005). African American student representation in special education programs. *Journal of Negro Education, 74*(4), 297–310.

Kinloch, V. (2010) *Harlem on our minds: Place, race, and the literacies of urban youth.* New York: Teachers College Press.

Kinloch, V. (Ed.). (2011). *Urban literacies: Critical perspectives on language, learning, and community.* New York: Teachers College Press.

Kinloch, V. (2012). *Crossing boundaries—Teaching and learning with urban youth.* New York: Teachers College Press.

Kinloch, V. (2015a). "Languaging their lives," places of engagement, and collaborations with urban youth. In C. Gerstl-Pepin & C. Reyes (Eds.), *Reclaiming the public dialogue in education: Putting the public in public intellectual* (pp. 17–30). New York: Peter Lang.

Kinloch, V. (2015b). Urban literacies. In J. Rowsell & K. Pahl (Eds.), *Routledge handbook of literacy studies* (pp. 140–156). London: Routledge.

Kinloch, V., Nemeth, E., & Patterson, A. (2015). Reframing service-learning as learning and participation with urban youth. *Theory Into Practice 54*(1), 39–46.

Kinloch, V., & San Pedro, T. (2014). The space between listening and storying: Foundations for Projects in Humanization. In D. Paris & M. T. Winn (Eds.), *Humanizing research: Decolonizing qualitative inquiry with youth and communities* (pp. 21–42). New York: Sage.

Kirkland, D. (2013). *A search past silence: The literacy of young Black men.* New York: Teachers College Press.

Knobel, M., & Lankshear, C. (2003). Researching young children's out-of-school literacy practices. In N. Hall, J. Larson, & J. Marsh (Eds.), *Handbook of early childhood literacy* (pp. 51–65). London: Sage.

Ladson-Billings, G. (2006). From the achievement gap to the education debt: Understanding achievement in U.S. schools. *Educational Researcher, 35*, 3–12.

Lawrence, C. (1995). The word and the river: Pedagogy as scholarship as struggle. In K. Crenshaw (Ed.), *Critical race theory: The key writings that formed the movement* (pp. 336–351). New York: New Press.

Mahiri, J. (Ed.). (2004). *What they don't learn in school: Literacy in the lives of urban youth.* New York: Peter Lang.

Majors, R., & Billson, J. M. (1992). *Cool pose: The dilemmas of Black manhood in America.* New York: Touchstone.

Marshall, E., & Toohey, K. (2010). Representing family: Community funds of knowledge, bilingualism, and multimodality. *Harvard Education Review, 80*(2), 221–241.

McTavish, M. (2014). "I'll do it my way!": A young child's appropriation and recontextualizing of school literacy practices in out-of-school spaces. *Journal of Early Childhood Literacy, 14*, 319–344.

Moje, E. B. (2000). "To be part of the story": The literacy practices of gangsta adolescents. *Teachers College Record, 102*(3), 651–690.

Moje, E. B., & O'Brien, D. G. (2001). *Constructions of literacy: Studies of teaching and learning in and out of secondary schools.* Mahwah, NJ: Erlbaum.

Moll, L. C., Amanti, C., Neff, D., & Gonzalez, N. (1992). Funds of knowledge for teaching: Using a qualitative approach to connect homes and classrooms. *Theory Into Practice, 31*(2), 132–141.

Moore, D. W., & Readence, J. E. (2001). Situating secondary school literacy research. In E. B. Moje & D. G. O'Brien (Eds.), *Constructions of literacy: Studies of teaching and learning in and out of secondary schools* (pp. 3–24). Mahwah, NJ: Erlbaum.

Morrell, E. (2008). *Critical literacy and urban youth: Pedagogies of access, dissent, and liberation.* New York: Routledge.

Moss, B. (Ed.). (1994). *Literacy across communities.* Cresskill, NJ: Hampton Press.

Muhammad, G. (2015). "Inducing colored sisters of other places to imitate their example":

Connecting historic literary societies to a contemporary writing group. *English Education* 47(3), 276–299.

Napoli, M. (2013). Girls around the globe as advocates for political, cultural, and social literacy at home. In E. O'Quinn (Ed.), *Girls' literacy experiences in and out of school: Learning and composing gendered identities*. New York: Routledge.

Nixon, H., & Comber, B. (2011). Redesigning school spaces: Creating possibilities for learning. In J. Sefton-Green, P. Thomson, K. Jones, & L. Bresler (Eds.), *The Routledge international handbook of creative learning* (pp. 253–263). Chicago: Routledge.

Noguera, P. A. (2008). What discipline is for: Connecting students to the benefits of learning. In M. Pollock (Ed.), *Everyday antiracism: Getting real about race in schools* (pp. 132–137). New York: New Press.

O'Connor, C. (1997). Dispositions toward collective struggle and educational resilience in the inner city: A case analysis of six African-American high school students. *American Educational Research Journal, 34,* 593–629.

O'Cummings, M., Bardack, S., & Gonsoulin, S. (2010). *Issue Brief: The importance of literacy for youth involved in the juvenile justice system*. Washington, DC: National Evaluation and Technical Assistance Center for the Education of Children and Youth Who Are Neglected, Delinquent, or At Risk (NDTAC).

Orellana, M. F., & Eksner, H. J. (2006). Power in cultural modeling: Building on the bilingual language practices of immigrant youth in Germany and the United States. In C. Fairbanks, J. Worthy, B. Maloch, J. Hoffman, & D. Schaller (Eds.), *National Reading Conference yearbook* (pp. 224–234). Austin: University of Texas.

Orphanides, A. (2015). The dehumanization of Black children: Tamir Rice, Kalief Browder, and Dajerria Becton. Retrieved from *www.huffingtonpost.com/alexandros-orphanides/the-dehumanization-of-black-children_b_7581404.html*.

Paris, D., & Kirkland, D. E. (2011). "The consciousness of the verbal artist": Understanding vernacular literacies in digital and embodied spaces. In V. Kinloch (Ed.), *Urban literacies: Critical perspectives on language, learning, and community* (pp. 177–194). New York: Teachers College Press.

Paris, D., & Winn, M. T. (Eds.). (2014). *Humanizing research: Decolonizing qualitative inquiry with youth and communities*. Los Angeles: Sage.

Perry, D. M. (2015, April 22). The corrosive cult of compliance in our schools. Retrieved from *http://america.aljazeera.com/opinions/2015/4/the-corrosive-cult-of-compliance-in-our-schools.html*.

Schott Foundation for Public Education. (2010). Yes we can: The Schott 50 state report on public education and black males. Retrieved from *http://schottfoundation.org/publications/schott-2010-black-male-report.pdf*.

Schott Foundation for Public Education. (2015). Black lives matter: The Schott 50 state report on public education and Black males. Retrieved from *http://blackboysreport.org*.

Skerrett, A., & Bomer, R. (2011). Borderzones in adolescents' literacy practices: Connecting out-of-school literacies to the reading curriculum. *Urban Education, 46*(6), 1256–1279.

Solórzano, D. G., & Yosso, T. J. (2002). Critical race methodology: Counter-storytelling as an analytical framework for education research. *Qualitative Inquiry, 8*(1), 23–44.

Stern, D. (1996). The uptown guide to the life of youth. In W. Ayers & P. Ford (Eds.), *City kids, city teachers: Reports from the front row* (pp. 66–78). New York: New Press.

Street, B. (2003). What's "new" in New Literacy studies?: Critical approaches to literacy in theory and practice. *Current Issues in Comparative Education, 5*(2), 77–91.

Street, B. V. (1984). *Literacy in theory and practice*. Cambridge, MA: Cambridge University Press.

Street, B. V. (1995). *Social literacies: Critical approaches to literacy in development, ethnography, and education*. London: Longman.

Sutherland, L. A. (2005). Black adolescent girls' use of literacy practices to negotiate boundaries of ascribed identity. *Journal of Literacy Research, 37*(3), 365–406.

Vasudevan, L. (2006). Making known differently: Engaging visual modalities as spaces to author new selves. Retrieved from *www.wwwords.co.uk/elea/content/pdfs/3/issue3_2.asp*.

Vasudevan, L., & Campano, G. (2009). The social production of adolescent risk and the promise of adolescent literacies. *Review of Research in Education, 33,* 310–353.

Williams, B. T. (2005). Leading double lives: Literacy and technology in and out of school. *Journal of Adolescent and Adult Literacy, 48*(8), 702–706.

Williams, J. M., & Portman, T. A. A. (2014). "No one ever asked me": Urban African American students' perceptions of educational resilience. *Journal of Multicultural Counseling and Development, 42*(1), 13–30.

Wiltse, L. (2015). Not just "sunny days": Aboriginal students connect out-of-school literacy resources with school literacy practices. *Literacy, 49,* 60–68.

Winn, M. T. (2011). *Girl time: Literacy, justice, and school-to-prison pipeline.* New York: Teachers College Press.

Wissman, K., & Vasudevan, L. (2012). Re-writing the stock stories of urban adolescents: Autobiography as a social and performative practice at the intersections of identities. In D. E. Alvermann & K. A. Hinchman (Eds.), *Reconceptualizing the literacies in adolescents' lives: Bridging the everyday/academic divide* (pp. 160–180). New York: Routledge.

Womack, E. (2013). *Uncovering the literate lives of Black female adolescents.* Unpublished doctoral dissertation, The Ohio State University, Columbus, OH.

CHAPTER 5

Emergent Bilingual Youth in U.S. Secondary Schools

DANNY C. MARTINEZ and URSULA S. ALDANA

A FOCUS ON SECONDARY EMERGENT BILINGUAL YOUTH

As former secondary teachers who worked primarily in bilingual and multilingual contexts, we approach this review with a clear sense of urgency and purpose toward working for a better understanding of how secondary school teachers can foster expansive learning environments for emergent bilinguals in which bi- and multilingualism and bilteracy[1] are normative outcomes. *Emergent bilinguals* (Garcia & Kleifgen, 2010a) are students for whom English, or the language of schooling, differs from the familial and community languages used across their daily communicative experiences. In the United States, emergent bilinguals in secondary schools are immigrants, children of immigrants, or indigenous peoples adding English, the dominant language, to their already rich repertoire of languages (Menken, 2013). Emergent bilinguals "continue to function in their home language, as well as in English—their new language and that of schools" (Garcia & Kleifgen, 2010b, p. 2).

The term *emergent bilingual* shifts educators away from both naturalizing English monolingualism and making monolingualism a goal in instruction for emergent bilinguals. Currently, educational policies and the labels used to identify emergent bilinguals implicitly perpetuate the eradication of home and community languages for nondominant groups. Instead, an emergent bilingual perspective treats the languages available to bi- and multilinguals as resources for learning, and as normative features of living in our increasingly diverse country, characterized by an increase in culturally and linguistically diverse contexts.

---

[1] *Bilteracy* is defined as "any and all instances in which communication occurs in two or more languages in or around writing" (Hornberger, 1990, p. 213).

Reyes (2012), in her own review of biliteracy among children and youth, argues that the

> concept of emergent bilingualism recognizes the ongoing nature of bilingual development and its potential to develop to include various degrees of biliteracy. Rather than emphasizing the lack of English competence as the earlier coined terms do, emergent bilingualism emphasizes the abilities in both languages that a child can leverage to gain bilingual and bilinguistic fluency. (p. 309)

Since the offering of this term by Ofelia Garcia and her colleagues, it has garnered attention and uptake for its dynamic approach to viewing and treating students in U.S. schools whose primary language differs from the English expected in schools.

The label *emergent bilingual* stands in contrast to those used by state and federal policies such as English language learners (ELLs), or limited English proficient (LEP). Garcia and Kleifgen (2010a) believe "the use of [emergent bilinguals] allows us to imagine a different scenario. Instead of being regarded as 'limited' in some way or as mere 'learners of English,' ... students are seen instead for their potential to become bilingual" (p. 3). Building on the work of Moll (2006), Orellana and Gutiérrez (2006) ask,

> Why do we categorize some students as English Learners and not others if we are all learning English every day? More perniciously, why did the field for so many years use the term "LEP"("Limited English Proficient")? Who, from a linguistic and social perspective, is more limited: those who are monolingual English Learners or speakers of other languages who are also English Learners? (p. 119)

While attempts in the field to shift the discourse on emergent bilinguals have been encouraging, ideologies perpetuated by policies must be examined to understand the elusive pressure that challenges such calls.

POLICY LANDSCAPE FOR EMERGENT BILINGUALS

The first step toward providing emergent bilinguals with instructional services came from Title VI of the Civil Rights Act in 1964, which prohibited schools engaging in discriminatory practices from receiving federal monies. Specifically, the act stated, "No person in the United States shall, on the ground of race, color, or national origin, be excluded from participation in, be denied the benefits of, or be subjected to discrimination under any program or activity receiving Federal financial assistance" (U.S. Congress, 1964). While the Civil Rights Act was a milestone in the journey toward educational equity, explicit attention to the language needs of emergent bilinguals did not appear as policy until the 1968 addition of Title VII, known as the Bilingual Education Act, to the Elementary and Secondary Educational Act (ESEA) initially authorized in 1965. While the Bilingual Education Act was the first federal education policy explicitly targeting emergent bilinguals, the act was "nonspecific about its goals—whether the bilingual instruction was to help students maintain their primary language or simply to move as rapidly into English as possible" (Gándara & Aldana, 2014, p. 741). The Bilingual Education Act would undergo several reauthorizations, in 1974, 1984, and 1994, with each iteration of the bill requiring that more instruction be provided solely in English, and even less attention to having bilingualism as an outcome, a sign of the narrowing support for bilingual education and the emerging English only, anti-immigrant sentiment that began in the 1980s that has had continued support since (Gutiérrez, Asato, Santos, & Gotanda, 2002).

In addition to federal educational policies, legal battles such as the *Lau v. Nichols* (U.S. Supreme Court, 1974) decision played into the national conversation surrounding bilingual education and the education of emergent bilinguals. The efforts of Chinese American parents were central to establishing bilingual education as a right for emergent bilinguals. These parents, in a lawsuit against the San Francisco Unified School District, argued that their children received a less than equitable education based on their inability to access instruction provided only in English. *Lau v. Nichols* was a landmark decision guaranteeing students whose primary language was not English the same access to education as their monolingual English-speaking counterparts.

While the case was foundational, it did not provide schools with "remedies" for instructing emergent bilinguals to become proficient in English, nor did it make clear that bilingualism would be an outcome of instruction. In an attempt to provide some direction, the Lau Remedies, introduced in 1975, merely outlined for schools how to categorize and instruct emergent bilinguals, and required bilingual instruction in the elementary grades, and English as a Second Language programs in the secondary grades. Explicit guidelines for instructing emergent bilinguals and backing from the federal government were never provided; therefore, the Lau Remedies were dismissed under the Reagan administration in 1981 (Garcia & Kleifgen, 2010b). Despite this, schools were still charged with supporting the needs of emergent bilinguals. However, full support for bilingual education programs were slowly in decline in the late 1970s and early 1980s, with English-only movements emerging and federal support for primary language maintenance waning (see Gándara & Gomez, 2009).

In the 1990s legal protections for bilingual education came under further attack in California (the state with the highest number of emergent bilinguals), Arizona, and Massachusetts, as Ron Unz, a Silicon Valley entrepreneur, funded state-level propositions asking voters to decide the fate of bilingual programs that he declared unsuccessful and fiscally draining. In California, the first of these measures came to light under Proposition 227, also known as the "English for the Children Initiative." In 1997, voters passed the initiative that ended bilingual instruction and replaced it with "structured emergent" instruction in English-only classrooms that were to last only 1 year. While a waiver process allowed parents to opt their children out of structured emergent programs, the process was burdensome and confusing. Access and support for parents varied across the state depending on the local support for bilingualism. Gándara and Gomez (2009) reported that after the passage of Proposition 227, bilingual instruction in California dropped from approximately 30% to less than 6%. In 2000, Ron Unz was successful in Arizona under Proposition 203, which implemented an even more restrictive environment for emergent bilinguals, with an even more complex waiver program. Unz's final campaign was in 2002, in Massachusetts, where he successfully persuaded a majority of voters to pass Question 2, which replaced "transitional bilingual programs" with structured English immersion programs.

Despite the political context, educators throughout the United States are increasingly teaching in classrooms where linguistic diversity is on the rise, and where emergent bilinguals are attending schools in greater numbers, so that they and their families are changing the demographic landscape (Gándara & Contreras, 2009). The reauthorization of ESEA in 2001, known as No Child Left Behind (NCLB; 2001), made all public schools accountable for the academic growth of all emergent bilinguals for federal accountability purposes. This is a shift from previous practices in which emergent bilinguals might be encouraged to wave out of assessments. With NCLB, attention was placed on several subgroups of students, including emergent bilinguals (referred to as ELLs in NCLB), as one of several groups for whom schools had to demonstrate growth in order to meet federal accountability benchmarks. According to researchers and practitioners, ESEA's attention to emergent bilinguals was only *one* step in the right direction, since "(1) The law fostered greater inclusion of ELs [English learners] in standards-based instruction, assessment, and accountability, and (2) it brought wider attention of policymakers and educators to ELs' language and academic needs" (Hopkins, Thompson, Linquanti, Hakuta, & August, 2013, p.101). However, these same scholars have criticized the lack of attention to assessments, teacher preparation, and teacher capacity building for emergent bilinguals, despite this added attention (Hopkins et al., 2013).

DEMOGRAPHICS OF EMERGENT BILINGUALS IN THE UNITED STATES

As of the 2012–2013 academic year, 9.2%, or an estimated 4.4 million U.S. public school students, were classified as "ELLs" (National Center for Education Statistics [NCES], 2014). States with the highest percentage of emergent bilinguals are Alaska, California, Colorado, Hawaii, Nevada, New Mexico, Oregon, Texas, and the District of Columbia, with California hosting the majority of emergent bilinguals, at 22.8% (NCES, 2014). The fastest growing percentages of emergent bilinguals are in newer destination states, such as South Carolina, Kentucky, Nevada, Delaware, Arkansas, Kansas, Mississippi, Alabama, Virginia, and North Carolina (Horsford & Sampson, 2013). Unlike states with a long history of emergent bilinguals, new destination states are struggling to create policies and dedicate funding to provide teachers with the most effective ways of instructing their emergent bilinguals (Horsford & Sampson, 2013). Across the country, as demographics shift and students attending public schools are increasingly bilingual and multilingual, educators must invest in understanding students' home language practices and engage in complex discussions around the creation of robust instructional practices for emergent bilinguals.

Emergent bilinguals are a diverse group of students whose family migration patterns differ, spurred by a range of social and political experiences. They speak over 400 different languages: 71% of "ELLs" speak Spanish as their primary language, 4% speak Chinese, and 3% speak Vietnamese (the largest three percentages for languages spoken). We know that approximately 66% of emergent bilinguals come from low-income households. The majority of emergent bilinguals were born in the United States, some of whom are second or third generation (Schonewise & Klingner, 2012).

In general, educational contexts fail to respond to the linguistic complexity and dexterity demonstrated by these youth. In a southern California sample, emergent bilingual students educated as English monolinguals or in deficit-oriented language programs had a 66% greater chance of dropping out of high school than students who have been educated toward biliteracy (Rumbaut, 2014).

At the secondary level, emergent bilingual youth also include newcomers (immigrant students who typically enter school at the middle or high school level). For newcomers, the schooling context is particularly reductive in nature given that most of these students are placed in English-only classrooms, with little opportunity to become bilingual and develop bilteracy skills. Not surprisingly, newcomers at the secondary level find themselves more likely to drop out of school. In 2009, 43% of foreign-born Mexicans between ages 16 and 19 left high schools before graduating, three times the rate of U.S.-born Mexican students (Oropesa & Landale, 2009).

Overall, schools characterize emergent bilinguals who can speak, listen, write, and read in two languages at varying levels, as having an absence of literacy in the language of schooling (Garcia & Kleifgen, 2010b). As a matter of policy and practice, emergent bilinguals are often referred to as "English learners" reifying a deficit lens focused on developing literacy in English only. This is particularly problematic given the growing body of research in the area of *translanguaging* that promotes the "multiple discursive practices in which bilinguals engage in order to make sense of their bilingual worlds" (Garcia, 2009, p. 45). In order to best serve emergent bilinguals, schools will need not only to address the complexity of language variation occurring in classrooms but also engage in teaching practices that leverage the linguistic skills these students bring in an effort to improve their schooling experience.

METHODS

To begin our review of the literature, we decided to limit our search to the last 10 years (2005–2015) of research published in peer-reviewed journals. In order to garner the same results from our searches, each author entered our designated key words using the advanced search option on the Education Resource Information Center (ERIC) database. We began with our topic of "adolescent literacy" to capture empirical work with youth in the area of literacy. We also included "secondary students" to limit our search to research within the middle and high school grades. Finally, we used a third field in our search, which changed three times, to capture the varying terms used to define the group of students who were learning English in U.S. public schools—terms such as "English language learners" (the category most used by researchers given the use of this term by NCLB, and consequently departments of education, districts, and schools); "emergent bilingual" (since we are approaching this review with a call and preference for the additive features of this term); and finally "bilingual education" or "bilingualism." We also used the term "limited English proficient"; however, this term did not yield enough results for this review, perhaps because limited English proficient has been replaced by "English language learner" within the last decade. We gathered a total of 26 articles that met our requirements.

After reading our initial 26 articles, the authors consulted one another and decided to conduct another search, adding the term "translanguaging" to capture the empirical work of scholars who are calling for a more expansive approach to thinking about the language practices of emergent bilinguals. This search yielded a total of eight additional articles that met our review requirements. We read the collection of articles, with each author writing up a précis for half of the articles. When we met to discuss themes that emerged, we decided it would benefit our review to include a set of studies that may not have focused on "ELLs" or "emergent bilinguals" explicitly. But, these studies examined the language and literacy practices of youth formerly categorized as ELLs, and those of youth who were still on the trajectory toward becoming bilingual and multilingual speakers.

The review that follows is organized by studies that take on a "language as a right" (Ruiz, 1995) orientation to language and literacy instruction. While these studies may not introduce an intervention that might be followed by an assessment, they mostly focus on examining the language and literacy practices for the sake of understanding how to build on and leverage youths' linguistic funds of knowledge for academic development. Next we considered a dynamic bilingualism/emergent bilingual pedagogy/translanguaging pedagogy that captures a newer approach to instruction that recognizes languages are dynamic and unbounded, and hybridity is a normative way of languaging in our increasingly diverse global contexts. We also examined scholarship that is redefining academic language and literacy instruction and research for emergent bilinguals in our schools, articles that we believed would add informative resources to our review.

ASSETS-BASED PEDAGOGIES

A review of the recent literature on bilingual education in the secondary classroom demonstrates a gradual ideological shift in the educational landscape. An increasing number of researchers have begun to approach student multilingual abilities not as problems, but rather as a linguistic and academic resource in the classroom (Ruiz, 1995). These studies highlight a shift towards an assets-based approach to learning, in which students' primary languages are seen as a tool for meaning making in the classroom and instrumental to their interrogation of written, visual, and spoken texts in the classroom.

A central part of this research focuses on how teachers understand and view their role in working with emergent bilingual youth. In today's educational landscape, that means teachers should understand that saturating classrooms with cultural and linguistic tools that support learning allows emergent bilinguals to access content knowledge for completing tasks (Gutiérrez, 2008). In a study of teacher candidates enrolled in a single-subject credentialing program, the majority of teacher candidates demonstrated a limited knowledge of how primary language may be used as a scaffold, particularly in the area of assessment (Elsbree, Hernandez, & Daoud, 2014). Given that the study was located in a region where emergent bilinguals make up close to 70% of students, the authors argue that educating emergent bilinguals is more than just giving them access to the curriculum. A teacher might cite the use of a student's primary language as a scaffold, but there needs to be increasing attention on why or how the primary language of students might be utilized in ways to help students engage in the literacy practices in the classroom.

Emergent bilingual youth at the secondary level face the dual task of not only learning how to effectively use Academic English as the language of school, but they are also asked to make sense of content knowledge that often is written in the language of the discipline. Teachers might expect emergent bilingual youth to jump from emergent understandings of content-area knowledge to presenting this information, without the necessary space to engage in meaning making. A sociocultural approach to learning asks teachers first to foster a language of ideas, in which students can use their linguistic resources to make meaning (Bunch, 2006). Drawing on their research with bilingual math and science teachers of Latin@ emergent bilingual youth, Hopkins, Martinez-Wenzl, Aldana, and Gándara (2013), found that teachers drew on youths' bilingual skills, specifically their knowledge of cognates.

> drawing on their bilingual skills and knowledge of cognates. For example, they often read English texts aloud by simultaneously translating them to Spanish. Rather than doing the "double work" of translating English academic material into Spanish internally as in their other classes, students translated out loud and brought the "double work" directly into the classroom space. (p. 291)

In this example, the teachers demonstrated a language as asset approach by allowing emergent bilingual students to use their first language (L1) in a public classroom space. Students reiterated how the use of their primary language not only allowed them to make sense of the content being presented in math and science courses but also positively affected their academic identity, giving them the confidence to continue in school. The connection between language and an increased sense of belonging in school cannot be understated. "In order to promote both language learning and access to subject area content, therefore, continuing efforts are needed to envision classrooms in which students can be included in, rather than excluded from, opportunities to participate in as wide a range of English for academic purposes as possible" (Bunch, 2006, p. 299). Furthermore, once students engaged in the meaning-making process, they can better negotiate meaning and language that will be presented in the "language of display" or the decontextualized language required of students in academic contexts (Bunch, 2006).

Dual language schools throughout the United States use assets-based pedagogies that run counter to reductionist English-only practices, and aim to develop students as biliterate (Alfaro, Duran, Hunt, & Aragon, 2014). However, dual language schools generally adopt the elementary or K–8 model; similarly, much of the research that demonstrates a linguistic assets-based approach to learning has focused on the primary level (Morales & Aldana, 2010). For emergent bilinguals at the secondary level, the educational experience does not develop "the academic literacy they need to succeed. It appears that they are not receiving adequate instruction designed to support their emerging bilingualism" (Schonewise & Klingner, 2012, p. 55). In fact, emergent bilinguals at the high school level have less access to rigorous course work because of the "ELL" designation (Callahan, Wilkinson, & Muller, 2010). However, in a national study of International Baccaureate (IB) high schools, Aldana and Mayer (2014) demonstrated how the incorporation of the IB program allowed teachers to enact an assets-based approach to emergent bilinguals:

> The IB program at these schools seemed to give license to teachers to move beyond a deficit orientation of Spanish heritage students and instead challenge these students academically. Spanish teachers across the eight schools spoke highly of their Spanish heritage language students and pointed to the rigorous work they often asked of these students. And despite the move towards this level of rigor, allowing Spanish heritage students to use their entire language repertoire was an important scaffold that seemed to be missing before the establishment of the IB programs. (p. 277)

Similar to the dual language model of schools, these schools are made up of educators who validate students' emergent bilingual status within the classroom by incorporating their linguistic practices as a means to engage students in the curriculum and school with the added goal of bilteracy. The use of a second language and curricular rigor central to the IB program not only provided students with access to challenging content but also facilitated meaning making for students. Unfortunately, the number of dual language and bilinguals programs has been in decline since the passage of NCLB (Menken & Solorza, 2012), and, as a result, emergent bilinguals cannot rely on formal language programs as the only pathway toward bilteracy.

DYNAMIC BILINGUALISM, AND EXPANDING LANGUAGE AND LITERACY PRACTICES FOR TEACHERS

Given that most emergent bilinguals find themselves in standard programs of study with little emphasis on bilteracy, it is critical that emergent bilinguals be met with secondary teachers who can employ "an ecological model that sees the bilteracy process as part of the natural development of young emergent bilinguals" (Reyes, 2012, p. 316). Given the abundance of reductionist approaches to language often enacted by policies and educators, emergent bilinguals face impediments to their learning process. Even in foreign/dual language program models, the practice of separating language is in contrast to the literature that demonstrates emergent bilinguals engage in dynamic bilingualism, in which both languages are not treated as separate entities. Rather, "dynamic bilingualism suggests that the language practices of all bilinguals are complex and inter-related; they do not emerge in a linear way (Garcia & Sylvan, 2011, p. 388). This process is what Garcia (2009) has extended and identified as *translanguaging,* the process through which bi- and multilinguals "engage in complex discursive practices in order to 'make sense' of, and communicate in, multilingual classrooms" (Garcia & Sylvan, 2011, p. 389).

Using these frameworks, in their study of the International Network for Public Schools (INPS), Garcia and Sylvan (2011) critique programmatic and theoretical constructs utilized by most teaching credential programs that have yet to present newer theories, such as translanguaging and dynamic bilingualism. In an effort to shift educators' approaches to literacy, their work provides a framework for the new multilingual–multicultural classroom and calls for a plurality of language practices centered on individual student experiences. They explain, "Schools that respond to this more dynamic model of bilingualism/multilingualism adopt a dynamic plurilingual approach with translanguaging as an important strategy so that students and teachers can make sense of learning moment by moment" (p. 308). In order for emergent bilinguals to engage in meaning making and authentic learning, the authors highlight the role of "individual students' linguistic practices" as the "moving force" in learning and ask teachers to note how these individual practices make up a plurality (Garcia & Sylvan, 2011). Garcia and Sylvan further describe the structures, pedagogies, and language practices within the INPS in an effort to demonstrate how singular student learning experiences can be served in multilingual classrooms.

In his study, Faltis (2013) argues that traditional theories of knowledge especially in the L1 and second language (L2) acquisition frameworks offer a limited perception of what education could look like for teachers of emergent bilinguals. Faltis stresses the importance of language learning rooted in social and local contexts, and calls for teacher education programs to prepare teachers with the newest and emerging language scholarship in mind.

> What this new sociocultural and socio-cognitive research and theoretical perspectives are saying is that teachers and the teacher educators who prepare them need to learn how to plan challenging classroom experiences that develop content and language over time (Schleppegrell & O'Hallaron, 2011), with the understanding that language English learners use to communicate thoughts and ideas will be flawed, and that students rely on and use their L1, their L1/L2, and their developing L2 for a range of purposes within academic contexts. (Faltis, 2013, p. 25)

Faltis argues that teacher-educators must understand notions of dynamic bilingualism as a naturalized process in being bilingual and multilingual. This task is difficult, because teachers' language ideologies, or their ideas and beliefs, might mediate their treatment of emergent bilinguals and their language practices.

For example, in an ethnographic study employing discourse analytic methods, Gallo, Link, Allard, Wortham, and Mortimer (2014) unearthed the language ideologies of students and teachers in two distinct schools located in what they call a New Latino Diaspora town, a region considered a new destination for Latin@ immigrants. This study highlights the varying language ideologies that can exist in one region where bilingualism was promoted in the elementary schools, while secondary educators viewed bilingualism and emergent bilinguals through deficit-oriented perspectives. This study makes clear how students' and teachers' language ideologies can mediate notions of "belonging." The authors indicate that subtractive language ideologies still existed at both sites, and draw on Garcia's (2009) claim that dynamic bilingualism and translanguaging practices should be encouraged to promote the idea among emergent bilinguals and their teachers that linguistic fluidity, translanguaging, is an acceptable mode of meaning making. Teachers should incorporate dynamic bilingualism and translanguaging approaches into pedagogical approaches to literacy and "academic" English discussions for emergent bilinguals.

RETHINKING ACADEMIC LANGUAGE FOR EMERGENT BILINGUALS

In much of the scholarship reviewed, an emphasis and overall unexplored expectation is placed on emergent bilinguals to become proficient in supposed academic varieties of English. While becoming proficient in the language and literacy activities valued in schools is an understandable goal, the overemphasis on acquiring academic language supersedes the ability of "ELLs" to become bi- or multilingual and biliterate. Few scholars have grappled with this idea, and even fewer have proposed ways in which we must rethink what counts as academic language in the classrooms of our emergent bilinguals, and the ways in which we must organize pedagogical practices in ways that both promote the addition of "academic" varieties of English and specialized content-specific language, *and* sustain the language practices that are valuable to emergent bilinguals across their everyday linguistic and literate lives.

Bunch (2006) problematizes traditional notions of academic language, first by disrupting the dichotomy created by scholars who contrast academic language with all other forms of linguistic communication. Bunch begins with the question, "How did students use language to engage in academic tasks?" in order to capture the variety of ways students use language to "get things done." In his examination of a seventh-grade "mainstream" social studies class, Bunch documented the process by which "language-minority" youth, in this case, students formerly labeled ELLs, engaged in meaning making when provided the opportunity to talk with their peers about a specific task. He argues that these youth often have limited opportunities to engage in talk given the overemphasis on teacher-led instruction. After providing students with directed opportunities to discuss a task, he documented the ways in which the discourses of these youth shifted in the preparation of a final presentation during a lesson using primary documents.

Bunch (2014) categorized the meaning making discourses in which these youth engaged as the *language of ideas* and the *language of display*. The language of ideas included "any and all" linguistic resources used by a student to complete an academic task. This was an important finding given that English often becomes a prerequisite for learning in classrooms. Yet these students made sense of the task using hybrid forms of language, including Spanish–English code switching. What followed, according to Bunch, was the language of display, which "refers to the evolving oral and written texts students develop, either individually or as a group, to present to particular academic audiences" (p. 74). The shift from the language of ideas to the language of display showcases the metalinguistic awareness youth displayed in order to respond to the audiences to which they were speaking. This approach to Academic English highlighted the process through which emergent bilinguals make meaning to perform an academic task, rather than an explicit focus on the form of their meaning making.

Enright (2011) continues this line of reasoning around Academic English, arguing that definitions of academic language and literacy vary depending on the approach researchers recruit, with some taking on traditional, somewhat narrow definitions, while others expand what counts as academic language in which youth engage in content-area classrooms. Enright herself defines academic literacy "as the skills and strategies used by young people engaged in academic work that involves reading, writing, and other formal school sanctioned modes of representation" (p. 86). In her definition of academic literacy, Enright moves away from traditional notions of academic literacy by accounting for the discursive and semiotic language and literacy tools that emergent bilinguals use to engage a text. While Bunch (2006, 2014) and Enright (2011) work to expand notions of academic language, teachers of emergent bilinguals are still charged with socializing their students with Academic English, to perform on academic assessments in Academic English. They provide an outlook to academic language that works to expand previous "traditional" (Enright, 2011) notions of academic language that are narrow in scope.

SOCIOCULTURAL TRADITION OF LEVERAGING

A tradition of scholars steeped in the Vygotskian tradition of learning and development have taken up a sociocultural approach with emergent bilingual and other linguistically minoritized youth, again, often students formerly labeled ELLs. As mentioned previously, in these approaches, there is an attempt to leverage the home and community language and literacy practices of youth, with the goal of using these skills to build academic language and literacy development (see Hull & Schultz, 2001, for review; Orellana, Martinez, Lee,

& Montaño, 2012). A sociocultural approach to language and literacy instruction treats human diversity as a resource (Cole, 1996; Hull & Schultz, 2001); therefore, any attempt to develop academic language and literacy is never a reductive practice. Below we review a few studies that were not part of our initial ERIC search. These studies target those secondary students who were former ELL students, or students for whom standard varieties of English are not spoken in the home. Therefore, these studies position the languages and literacies that are available to nondominant youth as a resource for learning that can be exploited for academic development in classrooms.

Based on more than 10 years of ethnographic research on child and youth language brokers (Orellana, 2009), Orellana and colleagues sought to use the language-brokering skills of Latin@ children of immigrants to engage in markedly similar academic tasks, such as paraphrasing and summarizing texts in classrooms (Orellana & Reynolds, 2008), and preparing written and spoken persuasive arguments (Martinez, Orellana, Pacheco, & Carbone, 2008; Orellana et al., 2012). Across this work, Orellana and colleagues found that Latin@ middle school youth had the ability to recognize metalinguistically the various ways in which they used language across settings and interlocutors. In Orellana's practice-oriented research (Martinez et al., 2008; Orellana et al., 2012; Orellana & Reynolds, 2008), youth participants found that the translating and interpreting activities they engaged in with their parents and other adults in their communities could serve a purpose in their classroom activities. This approach highlights learning that honors and values both horizontal and vertical forms of learning (Gutiérrez, 2008), learning that extends far beyond formal classroom settings, into the everyday learning environments of youth.

For example, in one study, Orellana and Reynolds (2008) highlighted how the home and community language-brokering skills of Latin@ youth mapped onto the summarizing and paraphrasing tasks asked of them in schools. Therefore, they worked with teachers to leverage these skills onto subject-specific domains, in the cultural modeling tradition pioneered by Carol Lee (2007). In two separate studies (Martinez et al., 2008; Orellana et al., 2012) in collaboration with two bilingual Latin@ teachers, Latin@ middle school youth were asked to write and present persuasive arguments to varied "professional audiences," in addition to a more personal audience of their choice. Doing so allowed students to develop a metalinguistic awareness about how they use language with diverse audiences. As an extension, Orellana and her colleagues (2012), worked with these same youth to document their linguistic repertoires for via the creation of short films. Overall, the work by Orellana and colleagues has highlighted how youth themselves demonstrated metalinguistic awareness about their own language practices, and how they can serve as resources for learning while navigating schooling tasks.

Gutiérrez and colleagues over the years have also contributed to our knowledge about creating robust learning environments for emergent bilinguals. Gutiérrez was foundational in acknowledging how *hybridity*, the various forms of language and literacy used by nondominant groups, can serve as tools for learning and development in learning ecologies. Notions of hybridity for learning moved the field to consider how Latin@ children, youth, and their teachers might engage in classroom discourse practices that draw on the full linguistic toolkits available in classrooms by drawing on moments in which students' language practices interact with teacher discourse practices, moments referred to as "third spaces" (Gutiérrez, 2008).

Similarly, Gutiérrez (2008) highlights the ways in which the language and literacy practices of Latin@ migrant students can be leveraged to produced syncretic texts that are hybrid in nature. That is, instead of organizing activities that limit students to using only one form of language and literacy, students are welcomed to integrate their hybrid language practices to produce texts that use both English and Spanish in ways that communicate nuanced meaning to their texts. These texts constitute what Gutiérrez calls *sociocritical literacies* that do not privilege dominant schooling practices, but rather language and literacy practices that are socioculturally meaningful in the lives of students, including emergent bilinguals. Gutiérrez's work has highlighted the need for reorganizing instructional practices in ways that saturate learning environments with cultural and linguistically meaningful tools and artifacts. Gutiérrez and Vossoughi (2010) argue for social design experiments that centralize equity and collaboration with youth and other stakeholders to organize learning that is expansive. That is, learning is organized in ways that consider school knowledge, in addition to knowledge and learning beyond the classroom walls and into the everyday lives of youth.

FUTURE DIRECTIONS

Scholarship that examines the classroom experiences of adolescent emergent bilinguals, while somewhat limited, is emerging as scholars point to the need for additional research that seeks to understand the everyday lives of emergent bilinguals in our public school classrooms (Menken, 2013). We believe this is a crucial call, because we are still wrestling to consider the practices that are most effective for teaching emergent bilingual youth, the experiences of emergent bilinguals, and the ways in which their translanguaging practices can serve as a rich resource for learning in our increasingly diverse classrooms.

An important area to consider as we examine the lives of emergent bilingual youth are the ways in which these youth are living in *contact zones* (Pratt, 1991) where they are coming together with diverse youth who are also speakers of languages other than dominant varieties of English. For example, Paris (2011) examines how Latin@ and Pacific Islander youth in northern California, some of whom were emergent bilinguals, were speakers of Black Languages (BL), representative of their diverse schooling and community contexts where BL was prominent. Martinez's (2015, 2016) work documents the corrective feedback practices deployed by teachers of emergent bilinguals when they engage in Black Language practices in official classroom spaces. Paris (2011) and Martinez (2015, 2016) point to the need for more studies that (1) document the peer language socialization practices (Goodwin & Kyratzis, 2011) of emergent bilinguals as they engage in communication with an increasingly diverse peers, (2) examine emergent bilinguals at varying levels and how teachers are treating their translanguaging practices in official classrooms spaces, and (3) expand, in collaboration with teachers, what counts as language for our linguistically agile emergent bilinguals.

This points to the need for additional work that examines the language ideologies of emergent bilinguals, their teachers, and the policies that mediate their instructional decisions. Flores and Rosa (2015) argue that future research should not simply consider the language ideologies of the "speaker" in the speaker–hearer dyad. Rather, they recommend research that probes the language ideologies of the hearer who makes decisions about a speaker based on his or her utterances. This is particularly needed, because the hearer often racializes the utterances of a speaker. Further research on language ideologies must interrogate how teachers as "hearers" are making sense of their emergent bilingual students. It is still important to consider those ideologies of emergent bilinguals themselves in ways that explore meanings behind certain beliefs.

Particularly, scholarship that takes on expansive perspectives on language, literacy, and learning, such as the few reviewed earlier, are limited. More studies are needed to understand fully the varied experiences of such a dynamic group. Already, from this review, we can see how this research is geographically isolated to California and New York areas. Given the reach of Latin@s across the United States, it is imperative that new research examined the particular experiences of emergent bilinguals in these new spaces previously described as the Latino diaspora. Additionally, while Latin@ youth represent the majority of emergent bilinguals in the country, even fewer studies exist that trace the experiences of non-Latin@ emergent bilinguals.

REFERENCES

Aldana, U. S., & Mayer, A. (2014). The International Baccalaureate: A college preparatory pathway for heritage language speakers and immigrant youth. In R. Callahan & P. Gándara (Eds.), *The bilingual advantage: Language, literacy and the U.S. Labor Market* (pp. 263–287). Bristol, CT: Multilingual Matters.

Alfaro, C., Duran, R., Hunt, A., & Aragon, M. A. (2014). Steps toward unifying dual language programs, Common Core State Standards, and critical pedagogy: *Oportunidades, estrategias y retos*. Retrieved from *http://amaejournal.utsa.edu/index.php/amae/article/view/194*.

Bunch, G. C. (2006). "Academic English" in the 7th grade: Broadening the lens, expanding access. *Journal of English for Academic Purposes, 5*(4), 284–301.

Bunch, G. C. (2014). The language of ideas and the language of display: Reconceptualizing "academic language" in linguistically diverse classrooms. *International Multilingual Research Journal, 8*(1), 70–86.

Callahan, R., Wilkinson, L., & Muller, C. (2010). Academic achievement and course taking among language minority youth in schools: Effects of ESL placement. *Educational Evaluation and Policy Analysis, 32*(1), 84–117.

Cole, M. (1996). *Cultural psychology: A once and future discipline.* Cambridge, MA: Belknap Press of Harvard University Press.

Elsbree, A. R., Hernandez, A., & Daoud, A. (2014). Equitable instruction for secondary Latino English learners: Examining critical principles of differentiation in lesson design. Retrieved from *http://amaejournal.utsa.edu/index.php/amae/article/view/193*.

Enright, K. A. (2011). Language and literacy for a new mainstream. *American Educational Research Journal, 48*(1), 80–118.

Faltis, C. (2013). Language, language development and teaching English to emergent bilingual users: Challenging the common knowledge theory in teacher education and K–12 school settings. *Association of Mexican American Educators, 7*(2), 18–29.

Flores, N., & Rosa, J. (2015). Undoing appropriateness: Raciolinguistic ideologies and language diversity in education. *Harvard Educational Review, 85*(2), 149–171.

Gallo, S., Link, H., Allard, E., Wortham, S., & Mortimer, K. (2014). Conflicting ideologies of Mexican immigrant English across levels of schooling. *International Multilingual Research Journal, 8*(2), 124–140.

Gándara, P. C., & Aldana, U. S. (2014). Who's segregated now?: Latinos, language, and the future of integrated schools. *Educational Administration Quarterly, 50*(5), 735–748.

Gándara, P. C., & Contreras, F. (2009). *The Latino education crisis: The consequences of failed social policies.* Cambridge, MA: Harvard University Press.

Gándara, P. C., & Gómez, M. C. (2009). Language policy in education. In G. Sykes, B. Schneider, & D. N. Plank (Eds.), *Handbook of education policy research* (pp. 581–595). New York: Routledge.

Garcia, O. (2009). *Bilingual education in the 21st century: A global perspective.* Malden, MA: Wiley-Blackwell.

Garcia, O., & Kleifgen, J. A. (2010a). Bilingualism for equity and excellence in minority education: The United States. In K. Van den Branden, P. Van Avermaet, & M. Van Houtte (Eds.), *Equity and excellence in education* (pp. 166–189). New York: Routledge.

Garcia, O., & Kleifgen, J. A. (2010b). *Educating emergent bilinguals: Policies, programs, and practices for English language learners.* New York: Teachers College Press.

Garcia, O., & Sylvan, C. (2011). Pedagogies and practices in multilingual classrooms: Singularities in pluralities. *Modern Language Journal, 95*(3), 385–400.

Goodwin, M. H., & Kyratzis, A. (2011). Peer language socialization In A. Duranti, E. Ochs, & B. B. Schieffelin (Eds.), *The handbook of language socialization* (pp. 365–390). Oxford, UK: Blackwell.

Gutiérrez, K. D. (2008). Developing a sociocritical literacy in the third space. *Reading Research Quarterly, 43*(2), 148–164.

Gutiérrez, K. D., Asato, J., Santos, M., & Gotanda, N. (2002). Backlash pedagogy: Language and culture and the politics of reform. *Review of Education, Pedagogy, and Cultural Studies, 24*(4), 335–351.

Gutiérrez, K. D., & Vossoughi, S. (2010). Lifting off the ground to return anew: Mediated praxis, transformative learning, and social design experiments. *Journal of Teacher Education, 61*(1–2), 100–117.

Hopkins, M., Martinez-Wenzl, M., Aldana, U. S., & Gándara, P. (2013). Cultivating capital: Latino newcomer young men in a U.S. urban high school. *Anthropology and Education Quarterly, 44*(3), 286–303.

Hopkins, M., Thompson, K. D., Linquanti, R., Hakuta, K., & August, D. (2013). Fully accounting for English learner performance: A key issue in ESEA reauthorization. *Educational Researcher, 42*(2), 101–108.

Hornberger, N. H. (1990). Creating successful learning contexts for bilingual literacy. *Teachers College Record, 92*(2), 212–229.

Horsford, S. D., & Sampson, C. (2013). High-ELL-growth states: Expanding funding equity and opportunity for English language learners. Retrieved from *http://vue.annenberginstitute.org/issues/37*.

Hull, G. A., & Schultz, K. (2001). Literacy and learning out of school: A review of theory and research. *Review of Educational Research, 71*(4), 575–611.

Lee, C. D. (2007). *Culture, literacy, and learning: Taking bloom in the midst of the whirlwind.* New York: Teachers College Press.

Martinez, D. C. (2012). *Expanding linguistic repertoires: An ethnography of Black and Latina/o youth communication in urban English language arts classrooms.* Unpublished doctoral dissertation, University of California, Los Angeles, CA.

Martinez, D. C. (2015). Black and Latina/o youth communicative repertoires in urban English language arts classrooms. In E. Morrell & L. Scherff (Eds.), *New directions in teaching English: Reimagining teaching, teacher education, and research* (pp. 59–79). New York: Roman & Littlefield.

Martinez, D. C. (2016). Emerging critical meta-awareness among Black and Latina/o youth during corrective feedback practices in urban English Language Arts classrooms. *Urban Education.*

Martínez, R. A., Orellana, M. F., Pacheco, M., & Carbone, P. (2008). Found in translation: Connecting translating experiences to academic writing. *Language Arts, 85*(6), 421–431.

Menken, K. (2013). Emergent bilingual students in secondary school: Along the academic language and literacy continuum. *Language Teaching, 46*(4), 438–476.

Menken, K., & Solorza, C. (2012). No child left bilingual: Accountability and the elimination of bilingual education programs in New York City schools. *Educational Policy, 28*(1), 96–125.

Moll, L. C. (2006, April). *The cultural mediation of thinking: Reconsidering a key Vygotskian concept* Paper presented at the Scribner Award Speech at the annual meeting of the American Educational Research Association, San Francisco, CA.

Morales, P. Z., & Aldana, U. S. (2010). Learning in two languages: Programs with political promise. In P. Gándara & M. Hopkins (Eds.), *Forbidden language: English learners and restrictive language policies* (pp. 159–174). New York: Teachers College Press.

National Center for Education Statistics. (2014). *The condition of education 2014* (NCES 2014-083). Retrieved from *http://nces.ed.gov/pubsearch/pubsinfo.asp?pubid=2014083*.

No Child Left Behind. (2002). No Child Left Behind (NCLB) Act of 2001, Pub. L. No. 107–110, § 115, Stat. 1425.

Orellana, M. F. (2009). *Translating childhoods: Immigrant youth, language, and culture.* New Brunswick, NJ: Rutgers University Press.

Orellana, M. F., & Gutiérrez, K. D. (2006). What's the problem?: Constructing different genres for the study of English learners. *Research in the Teaching of English, 41*(1), 118–123.

Orellana, M. F., Martínez, D. C., Lee, C. H., & Montaño, E. (2012). Language as a tool in diverse forms of learning. *Linguistics and Education, 23*(4), 373–387.

Orellana, M. F., & Reynolds, J. (2008). Cultural modeling: Leveraging bilingual skills for school paraphrasing tasks. *Reading Research Quarterly, 43*(1), 48–65.

Oropesa, R. S., & Landale, N. S. (2009). Why do immigrant youths who never enroll in U.S. schools matter?: School enrollment among Mexicans and non-Hispanic whites. *Sociology of Education, 82,* 240–266.

Paris, D. (2011). *Language across difference: Ethnicity, communication, and youth identities in changing urban schools.* Cambridge, UK: Cambridge University Press.

Pratt, M. L. (1991). Arts of the contact zone. *Profession, 9,* 33–40.

Reyes, I. (2012). Bilteracy among children and youths. *Reading Research Quarterly, 47*(3), 307–327.

Ruiz, R. (1995). Language planning considerations in indigenous communities. *Bilingual Research Journal, 19*(1), 71–81.

Rumbaut, R. G. (2014). English plus: Exploring the socioeconomic benefits of bilingualism in Southern California. In R. Callahan & P. C. Gándara (Eds.), *The bilingual advantage: Language, literacy and the US labor market* (pp. 182–210). Bristol, CT: Multilingual Matters.

Schleppegrell, M., & O'Hallaron, C. L. (2011). Teaching academic language in second language secondary settings. *Annual Review of Applied Linguistics, 31*(1), 3–18.

Schonewise, E. A., & Klingner, J. (2012). Linguistic and cultural issues in developing disciplinary literacy for adolescent English language learners. *Topics in Language Disorders, 32*(1), 51–68.

U.S. Congress. (1964). *Civil Rights Act.* Retrieved from *www.eeoc.gov/eeoc/history/35th/thelaw/civil_rights_act.html*.

U.S. Supreme Court. (1974). Lau v. Nichols (No. 72-6520). Retrieved from *http://caselaw.findlaw.com/us-supreme-court/414/563.html*.

CHAPTER 6

What Research Says (and Doesn't Say) about Literacy for Youth with Disabilities

KELLY CHANDLER-OLCOTT, MICHELLE DUFFY,
and JOANNA M. ROBERTSON

As a musician herself, Joanna (third author) was excited to attend a performance of The Piano Guys, a group she knew well from their recordings. As with any live music, she expected to see the performers playing or singing what she heard and was therefore surprised to hear whole lines of music produced by neither performer. At first she was confused, wondering where the other music originated. Was this "cheating"? The musicians later showed the audience how they performed a line, recorded it, set it on a loop using technology, then added further layers in person. Once she understood this process, Joanna stopped trying to see who was playing which part of the music, or how, and just enjoyed the concert. But the experience invited many questions for her: What counts as music? As live music? Who decides? Was this form of music making more inclusive than the traditional, both for musicians and for audience members?

Over the past 20 years, parallel questions have been raised by teachers, researchers, families, and youth themselves around literacy for students identified with disabilities, including those with the most significant support needs (Erickson & Koppenhaver, 1995; Kliewer & Biklen, 2001; Kluth & Chandler-Olcott, 2008; Mirenda, 2003). What counts as literacy? What literacy practices and pedagogy are appropriate for which learners? Who decides what counts and who gets access to which contexts? Just as in Joanna's musical performance example, these questions are linked to the increasing availability and importance of digital technologies in contemporary life and to shifts in individuals' ability to envision new possibilities in communities built on particular assumptions and expectations.

FRAMING THE CHAPTER

In light of these trends, we review in this chapter a wide range of literature to offer instructional recommendations for teaching literacy to youth identified with disabilities. Before we do, let us describe how we established our parameters, defined key terms, and decided on a theoretical lens to inform our review.

First, we want to explain how we conceptualize the population under consideration. We use the term *youth* to refer to students in grades 5 through 12, grades in which literacy typically facilitates learning new content but might not be the driving focus for instruction. On occasion, we reference a study with younger participants, particularly if the findings address an area that has not been well researched with older learners. We recognize that grade-level designations can be reductionist, particularly for learners with unusual learning profiles, and that some placements, such as self-contained special education classrooms, may not be organized around grades at all. These complexities notwithstanding, most researchers still note grade level for study participants, so we do here as well.

We acknowledge that our phrase "identified with disabilities" is broad. Although we use examples that invoke a range of disability labels, we make no attempt to be comprehensive, partly because of space limitations, and partly because some disabilities implicate literacy more directly than others. We also acknowledge that individuals experience disability labels differently, both across and within categories. For example, a student identified with a learning disability in reading may, though not always, have different literacy needs than a student with Down syndrome who has an intellectual disability. Similarly, two students with the same autism label can have different strengths and needs: One might control oral language reliably but require support to decode even one-syllable words, while another might readily comprehend complex text but require an augmentative communication device to share those understandings. Complicating such labels further are the descriptors "mild," "moderate," and "severe" that often modify them. We find such phrases problematic, because they do not acknowledge that individuals may be construed as more or less disabled depending on the absence or presence of social and learning supports (Collins, 2003). They can also contribute to lowered expectations, because students identified with "severe" disabilities are far more likely to be excluded from literacy instruction than those categorized as "mild" or "moderate" (Koppenhaver & Erickson, 2003).

Given these concerns, we treat disability labels with skepticism in this chapter and in our teaching. A label might prompt us to ask questions about a learner's needs, but only interaction with that learner can provide the answers. Still, we retain the phrase "students identified with disabilities" rather than talking about "all students" or "students with diverse learning needs," because we want to ensure that teachers do not overlook literacy learners with disability labels or offload meeting their needs as someone else's responsibility. We see this as particularly important in secondary schools given their historical use of exclusionary practices such as tracking students by perceived ability (Jorgensen, 1998).

We chose the phrase "a wide range of literature" to make a similarly inclusive statement about the resources on which we draw for our recommendations. While we rely primarily on empirical research, we also cite, where relevant, narratives authored by people with disabilities. We cast this wide net for two reasons. First, the research literature is patchy, focusing more on some aspects of literacy, such as sight-word acquisition, and some populations, such as students identified with learning disabilities, than on others. Second, we want to position people with disabilities as the experts on their own lives, despite their perspectives having long been silenced or ignored in many school contexts (Kliewer, Biklen, & Kasa-Hendrickson, 2006). Our own teaching and research have been enriched by insights offered by autobiographies and memoirs, and we believe the same will be true for other educators.

We read and construct insights from this literature with a common commitment to presuming competence, an idea from disability studies in education (Biklen & Burke, 2006; Collins, 2003; Jorgensen, McSheehan, & Sonnenmeier, 2007). Such a lens applied to literacy insists that teachers regard all students, including—some might say especially—those with disability labels, as holding automatic and irrevocable citizenship in the literate community. Learners do not need to "earn" access to literacy instruction by demonstrating particular kinds of readiness associated with grade-level norms (Kliewer, 1998). Instead, teachers assume that all learners have a right to rich literacy instruction, will benefit from such instruction, and can contribute to others' literacy learning in social contexts—even if those benefits and contributions are not yet apparent in conventional ways. According to Biklen (2005),

> Failing to adopt this posture, the teacher would forever doubt whether to educate at all, and would likely be quick to give up the effort. Aside from the optimism it implies, another benefit of the presuming competence framework over a deficit orientation . . . is that when a student does not reveal the competence that a teacher expects, the teacher is required to turn inward and ask, "What other approach can I try?" (p. 73)

Collins (2003) highlights the sociocultural dimensions of this perspective, arguing that ability and disability, as well as literacy success and failure, are "not constant or perceived as solely located within individuals" but rather are produced via "the intersection of environment and individual" (p. 3). In this view, educators must create classroom and school environments that presume all students possess potential as literacy learners and offer necessary supports such that individuals can achieve that potential.

REVIEWING THE LITERATURE

In the pages that follow, we review the literature on teaching literacy to students identified with disabilities, including those with complex support needs, around three themes: teaching conventional literacy skills, providing access to the general education curriculum, and transforming the literacy classroom for all literacy learners. We see each of these areas as complementary and building on each other, rather than as separate or competing agendas.

Teaching Conventional Literacy Skills

In this section, we review literature on teaching conventional reading and writing skills in both typical classrooms and intervention settings to youth identified with disabilities.

Such skills include decoding and word recognition, fluency, comprehension, vocabulary, and writing, all critical building blocks in students' preparation for college and career readiness, citizenship, and membership in varied communities.

While word recognition and comprehension may seem "basic" at a time when educators are emphasizing 21st-century skills such as creativity and collaboration, it is important to note that many students, particularly those with lower-incidence disabilities, have had inadequate opportunities to develop either set of skills. Literacy has typically been taught to them through a functional approach intended to support social participation and employment (Katims, 2000). Students learned to recognize sight words for safety or for preparing meals, and they were required to demonstrate mastery of discrete skills, such as letter naming, before being permitted to access literacies associated with connected text. Educators made such instructional choices because they believed that learning higher-level literacy skills was too cognitively demanding for some students. Due to these beliefs, school was, to quote one of Kliewer and Biklen's (2001) participants, "not really a place for reading" for many youth.

Only recently have teachers and researchers explored broader possibilities for teaching students with disabilities to read and write. The literature on this topic is still limited in scope and often includes small participant samples. It suggests, nonetheless, that students with a range of labels can benefit from evidence-based approaches to teaching literacy, such as those recommended by the National Reading Panel (National Institute of Child Health and Human Development, 2000).

Providing Explicit and Systematic Instruction

Studies suggest that explicit and systematic instruction benefits literacy learners with disabilities. In being explicit, educators show students precisely what is to be learned. New skills are modeled, sometimes over many learning sessions, with many opportunities for guided practice (Allor, Gifford, Otaiba, Miller, & Cheatham, 2013). Teachers are explicit about how such skills transfer to authentic reading and writing. Although practicing skills in isolation can increase automaticity, these skills need to be practiced in real texts for real purposes as well. In being systematic, educators plan to present new skills in a logical order so that students can connect them. For example, students with and without disabilities begin phonics instruction by learning words with short vowels and single consonants before learning those with more complex vowel and consonant patterns (Copeland & Keefe, 2007). Systematic presentation of material ensures that no skills are skipped.

Explicit and systematic instruction can be used to teach students with disabilities how to take part in similar literacy practices as nonlabeled peers. Lundberg and Reichenberg (2013), for example, taught adolescents with intellectual disabilities to comprehend using text talks similar to reciprocal teaching (Palincsar & Brown, 1984), an approach widely used for students without such labels. The strategic components of reciprocal teaching—predicting, generating questions, clarifying, and summarizing—were taught separately over several weeks, and students were provided with precise words to begin statements, such as *first, then,* and *last* when summarizing. Instructors scaffolded students' use of these strategies during group discussions and gradually reduced support as appropriate. As a result, students increased their comprehension scores and took part in meaningful conversations about texts.

Explicit instruction in word analysis has been beneficial for the literacy development of students with disabilities. For instance, Harris, Schumaker, and Deshler (2011) improved the vocabulary knowledge of students with learning disabilities by teaching them to identify morphemes and use a word-mapping strategy when analyzing the morphemes. Similarly, Bhattacharya and Ehri (2004) increased struggling readers' ability to decode and spell multisyllabic words by teaching them to analyze syllables within words. Both interventions provided students with effective strategies for analyzing unknown words.

The benefits of explicit and systematic instruction were also demonstrated by De La Paz and Graham (1997). In their study, students with intellectual disabilities were taught mnemonics to help them in their composition of opinion essays. One mnemonic was DARE: "Develop your topic sentence, Add supporting ideas, Reject possible arguments for the other side, and End with a conclusion" (p. 173). The steps were taught explicitly to students through modeling and guided practice. Students were also given plenty of opportunity to practice the skills independently. This instruction led to the increase in length and overall quality of the students' writing pieces.

Our support of teaching conventional skills systematically and explicitly should not be confused with support of the so-called "reading readiness model," which limits students' access to instruction when their growth does not conform to the linear order of subskills considered essential for promotion to higher-order skills (Mirenda, 2003). Students should have opportunities to build literacy skills in all areas; perceived difficulty in one skill should not prevent students from working on another. This gatekeeping often takes place when teachers misunderstand communication difficulties. The literature on autism, for instance, includes examples of individuals whose difficulties producing oral language were misinterpreted as a need for intensive phonics training (e.g., Blackman, 1999). We recognize that all learners may not develop sophisticated conventional reading and writing skills, but case studies of unexpected success (Kliewer, 1998; Mukhopadhyay, 2000; Ryndak, Morrison, & Sommerstein, 1999) suggest that teachers and researchers struggle to predict with certainty who will and who will not succeed. We see it as far better, given these patterns, to work from what Donnellan (1984) called the least dangerous assumption, a criterion requiring educators faced with inconclusive evidence of a learner's capability to offer the curriculum and instruction they would wish they had provided if presented later with evidence of the person's competence. Such an assumption obligates us to provide varied literacy instruction for all students.

Finding and Filling the Gaps

When working with older students, keep in mind that while many youth have developed some literacy skills over the years, significant gaps in their knowledge may affect their ability to interact with texts. For example, one student may have developed a large sight-word vocabulary, without developing strong decoding skills to figure out unknown words. Another student may have learned to look back through a text for explicitly stated information to answer comprehension questions but not how to use textual clues to make logical inferences. Studies suggest that areas such as decoding, comprehension, fluency, and written expression can be taught to students with disabilities through carefully planned instruction, but one must first assess each student's particular strengths and needs to determine the areas for further instruction.

Without sensitive assessment, it is not only impossible to plan effective ways to meet students' needs, but it is also possible to overlook skills that were present all along. Take, for example, what transpired when Mims, Hudson, and Browder (2012) worked with students with autism and intellectual disabilities to improve their comprehension of biographies. Their four participants were considered by their schools to be nonreaders; as the study progressed, however, the researchers discovered that one student could, in fact, read. Because of a tendency for professionals not to presume competence in students with disabilities and the lack of appropriate assessments for students with more complex communication needs, "hidden" skills often go unrecognized. As Mims and colleagues warn, "students' ability to 'show what they know' can be limited by the opportunities provided" (p. 77).

We recommend responsive teaching driven by assessments of students' strengths and needs, not their disability labels. At times, though, a disability may be associated with a certain instructional focus. For example, many students with autism struggle more with reading comprehension than with decoding. Awareness of this pattern combined with individual assessment data can help identify effective instructional strategies. O'Connor and Klein (2004) found that helping 20 adolescents with autism to recognize the connection between pronouns and their antecedents increased students' comprehension scores. Their approach was grounded in knowledge of the literacy learning differences often associated with autism. It's important to note, however, that some students with autism would not need such an approach, and that students with other disabilities might also find it beneficial, depending on their learning profiles.

Educators must therefore avoid overgeneralizing with label-driven inferences. For instance, teachers sometimes exclude individuals with limited speech from decoding instruction because the students cannot physically produce the phonemes to "sound out" the words. Alternative approaches such as the nonverbal reading approach (Heller, Fredrick, & Diggs, 1999) can address this need, however. Students learn to use internal speech to segment and blend phonemes, then to point to the words they read in a set of choices. When students make errors, teachers look at the distractors chosen to assess misunderstandings and provide corrective feedback. More recent research suggests that the approach can be implemented via computer-assisted instruction, making it even more flexible (Coleman-Martin, Heller, Cihak, & Irvine, 2005).

When youth with disabilities have yet to develop the skills to read complex texts independently, this does not mean that they cannot learn higher-level skills associated with them. Educators can use interactive approaches such as read-alouds and shared reading to scaffold students' access to texts written beyond their levels of word recognition (Copeland & Keefe, 2007). Through such experiences, students interact with texts' language, structure, and messages, which, in turn, can benefit their development of comprehension skills, vocabulary, and content learning beyond what might be possible with texts at their independent reading level. Shurr and Taber-Doughty (2012), for instance, demonstrated how comprehension of age-appropriate texts could be improved for middle school students with intellectual disabilities through read-alouds in which additional picture supports and discussion of the material were incorporated. Hudson and Browder (2014) increased student comprehension by teaching nonlabeled peer tutors to read adapted text aloud to labeled students. Tutors were trained to ask comprehension questions and to use a prompting system to help partners identify areas of the text that would provide answers to the questions. Finally, numerous researchers have documented individuals with disabilities navigating print materials considered too difficult for them because of interest in the topic and/or background knowledge from other sources and experiences (Kliewer & Biklen, 2001; Ryndak et al., 1999; Sonnenmeier, Jorgensen, & McSheehan, 2005).

Summary

The literature reviewed in this section suggests the value of assuming that all students with disabilities, including those with significant support needs, can benefit from the well-designed literacy instruction that research supports for students without such labels. Instruction is likely to be most beneficial when it is systematic and explicit, yet organized to be responsive to individual needs. Some students may require specific formats for increasing skills, including drill-type components. At the same time, the literature provides evidence that a narrow focus on skills—particularly overemphasis on teaching decoding as a prerequisite to students' access to meaning-focused approaches—can hinder students' development.

Providing Access to the General Education Curriculum

In the previous section, we reviewed research on approaches to building conventional reading and writing skills for youth identified with disabilities. Some of those studies were conducted in classrooms, but most took place in intervention settings organized by researchers. In this section, we review literature on providing access to literacy as a necessary part of the general education curriculum enacted in school classrooms. This curriculum includes not just the literacies valued in English language arts, such as the study of genres, themes, and literary periods, but also what is known as *disciplinary literacy*—the ways of reading, writing, and communicating associated with success—in other subjects (Shanahan & Shanahan, 2008). Some educators question whether access to disciplinary literacy is appropriate for individuals with the most complex support needs, but a growing body of examples suggests both the importance and feasibility of facilitating such learning for all learners. As one mother explained while pushing for greater curricular access for her child:

> Curt needs to learn about more than grocery shopping. To really "function," he needs to read everything—literature, humor, science, you name it. It's a big world. (Kluth & Chandler-Olcott, 2008, p. 42)

Adaptations

Educators use several terms concerned with providing access to that "big world" through the general education curriculum. Historically, the term *modifications* has referred to changes in what individuals will learn, often documented in students' IEPs (individualized education programs). *Accommodations* are physical or environmental adjustments that do not change curricular expectations but rather reduce barriers to students' achieving such expectations. Such adjustments are often, though not always, provided to students with a 504 Plan rather than an IEP. The term *adaptations* is used more loosely, sometimes in place of *accommodations,* and at other times to describe adjustments for students with and without disabilities.

In this chapter, we use *adaptations* most of the time. We define it as changes in instructional delivery and/or the content and difficulty of material that are intended to support individuals' access to literacy instruction within the general education curriculum. We favor this usage because it frames making adjustments as an expected part of responsive pedagogy, rather than compliance with the law or concessions to a "needy" individual. As we see it, businesses and organisms thrive when they adapt to changing demands and contexts; so do teachers when they adapt their practices to address evolving understandings of their students' needs.

Some research in this area has focused on what happens when teachers adapt the general education curriculum for students placed in self-contained special education classrooms (Kesler, Tinio, & Nolan, 2014; Michalski, Hodges, & Banister, 2005; Rao, Dowrick, Yuen, & Boisvert, 2009). In these cases, teachers sought to increase intellectual rigor for their students, often eschewing published programs focusing solely on the most discrete conventional skills, while acknowledging that their students needed scaffolding to learn and use other literacies. For example, Michalski et al. (2005) documented how Michalski, a middle-level special educator, implemented adaptive instructional strategies to provide her cognitively delayed language arts students access to a unit on digital storytelling. The researchers speculated that students like Michalski's were rarely offered experiences with multimedia technologies because of teachers' perceptions that the required adaptations would be too extensive. Michalski did not find this to be the case, however. With colleagues, she brainstormed adaptations allowing each of her students, including some who had not previously written in complete sentences, to construct digital stories about their life experiences. All students used a web graphic organizer to develop their stories with detail and worked in cooperative groups for peer support. She also permitted varying story lengths, depending on students' topics and organizational skills, and encouraged some to read their scripts verbatim, while others used their pictures as a guide for less formal presentations. The adaptations allowed each student to meet the same high standard for communicating ideas through a combination of words, images, and audio.

Other research suggests that access to the general education literacy curriculum may be further enhanced when students learn in inclusive classrooms enrolling heterogeneous peer communities. Compelling support for this argument comes from Kurth and Mastergeorge (2012), who studied the impact of instructional context on 15 adolescents with autism labels, eight from self-contained special education classrooms and seven from inclusive general education classrooms. Teachers in both settings rated their students' autism severity similarly using an established scale, but the study revealed other significant differences. For example, students with autism participated in noninstructional activities such as breaks less than 10% of the time in general education, compared to 32% in self-contained settings. In inclusive classrooms, students accessed the core general education curriculum with grade-level or adapted materials 87.2% of the time but only 0.1% of the time in self-contained classrooms. The study hints that access to the general education curriculum in inclusive classrooms may boost literacy by raising curricular expectations and offering greater time on task.

Other researchers have illuminated how adaptations facilitated literacy learning for individuals moving to general education classrooms from self-contained settings (Biklen & Burke, 2006; Ryndak et al., 1999; Sonnenmeier et al., 2005). Ryndak and colleagues (1999) published a 7-year case study of Melinda, a young woman identified with multiple disability labels, who spent her elementary grades in special education classes in which her literacy instruction focused on phonics workbooks. Efforts by Melinda's parents led to her placement in general education as a seventh grader, supplemented by one-to-one support from a special educator and reading intervention in a lab with nondisabled peers. Over time, with help from Melinda and her family, Melinda's teachers and service providers learned to make adaptations that supported and extended her capabilities—for instance, when her science teacher provided copies of her lecture outline with key parts highlighted to aid Melinda's note taking. The resulting growth in skills and confidence allowed Melinda to pursue personally and socially meaningful literacies such as reading about her interest in Elizabethan England and sharing testimony about inclusion with state representatives. These successes allowed her to overcome initial resistance to adaptations that set her apart from her peers, leading to acceptance of the idea that "receiving assistance to learn new skills led to greater independence for her later" (Ryndak et al., 1999, p. 17).

Jorgensen (1998) provided many additional examples of curricular adaptations from Souhegan High School, where building-wide restructuring resulted in access to untracked core classes for all students. Teacher collaboration, including interdisciplinary teaming and coteaching by general and special educators, yielded responsive adaptations like those designed for Andrew, a 10th grader with an unspecified disability, who participated in an integrated unit on English and biology. To build background knowledge about cell division and reproduction that many students gleaned solely through text reading, Andrew and several peers watched a film that used computer simulations and magnification to illustrate the processes. Andrew reinforced vocabulary learning with word–picture cards, and he sequenced those cards into sentences as preparation for an oral presentation on the life processes of single-cell organisms using metaphors and analogies. Another student helped him to type the text he read. More accessible information sources, scaffolds to help him sequence his writing, and peer support allowed Andrew to engage in rich disciplinary learning that would otherwise have been impossible.

Assistive Technology

Other research has documented how the general education curriculum can be accessed via students' use of assistive technology (AT), that is, equipment or systems intended to improve the functional capabilities of individuals with disabilities (Copeland & Keefe, 2007; Sonnenmeier et al., 2005). AT can be situated on a continuum from no-tech (sign language) to low-tech (a pictured daily schedule) and high-tech (voice-recognition software). Some AT examples, such as a classroom ramp, have little direct relationship to literacy, while others, such as text-to-speech software, have more obvious reading and writing connections. Tools and approaches intended to address complex communication needs, such as unreliable speech, are among the most important ATs for literacy purposes; these are typically known as augmentative and alternative communication (AAC).

Students whose teachers address their communication difficulties with appropriate AAC often demonstrate unexpected, and even rapid, literacy growth. See, for instance, Ryndak's description of a districtwide restructuring effort around inclusion (cited in Copeland & Keefe, 2007). Ken and Victor, middle school boys identified with multiple disabilities, had received services in self-contained classes with communication systems that allowed them to make choices between two options only, using yes–no vocalizations or selecting one of two switches. When they were placed in general education classes with support from special education personnel and a formal credit-bearing peer program, it became clear that their "communication systems were inadequate" and did not reflect the literacy abilities that both boys had developed, in Ryndak's words, "*in spite of* the limited nature" (p. xii) of the literacy instruction they had been receiving for years. Within just a few months, Ken and Victor required an AAC system of 40 choices and counting to communicate across contexts with multiple partners. According to Ryndak, cases like these are contributing to a "growing recognition" among educators that a student's "expression of knowledge through the use of literacy" is "in no way diminished" (p. xiii) by the incorporation of AT.

Ryndak's assertion hints at long-standing debates within schools about adaptations for students with disabilities, including, but not limited to, those associated with AT. Adaptations that help students gain access to materials or the physical environment appear to create less controversy than those that compensate for cognitive skills deficits (Boone & Higgins, 2007). Few teachers would dispute, for instance, that a student with a visual impairment needs access to a screen reader, although some might point to that need—inappropriately, in our view—as justification for excluding the student from general education. Questions more typically arise for teachers related to adaptations intended to provide what Naraian and Surabian (2014) call "intellectual and social access" (p. 333), those enabling greater participation in the classroom's learning and literacy practices. Naraian and Surabian argue that teachers should be guided in such cases by one question: "How will the tools I select grant the student greater control in determining the ways in which she or he can participate in mainstream classroom experiences and achieve desired educational outcomes?" (p. 338). Such a stance positions learners with disabilities as competent to peers and, just as important, to themselves.

Teachers may find, however, that their answers to Naraian and Surabian's (2014) question change given different learning outcomes. For example, it makes good sense to offer an ebook with a text-to-speech option to a student who has not yet learned to decode words if the goal is to further comprehension skills applied to grade-level text. This adaptation allows the student to read the book at a pace similar to that of his or her peers and to participate in text-based discussion. But such an adaptation should not preclude that same student from receiving targeted and explicit decoding instruction at another time and in another context.

Summary

The literature reviewed in this section suggests the value of providing rich access to the general education curriculum for all youth to build content knowledge and disciplinary literacies. Adaptations, including those utilizing AT, enable meaningful participation in heterogeneous learning communities by literacy learners with varying needs. Such adaptations are best designed via collaboration among teachers, families, and youth themselves, as each constituency offers different vantage points on what supports will be most beneficial in fostering greater independence over time.

Transforming Literacy Pedagogy for All Learners

In previous sections, we have reviewed research on teaching conventional reading and writing skills and providing access to the general education curriculum. We argue that both are necessary and not mutually exclusive for students with disabilities. But we recognize that most secondary schools are not prepared to facilitate such work, because of their organizational structures and the conceptualizations of literacy and ability that undergird those structures. A small but growing body of literature grounded in inclusive schooling suggests how we might transform literacy classrooms to meet all learners' needs. We turn to that literature here.

The need for these new conceptualizations can be seen clearly in McCloskey's (2011) case study of Samson, a young man identified as learning disabled. As a second grader, Samson was placed in a self-contained classroom because of his struggles with reading. McCloskey met him prior to his sixth-grade year, when his parents sought help to address his continued status as a "nonreader." Samson shared that he had previously received accommodations such as having his tests read to him, but McCloskey found little evidence of "any discussion with Samson or his family about *how* to teach Samson to read" (p. 734). Over 3 years, McCloskey tutored Samson weekly, and he responded well to the kinds of explicit instruction we recommended earlier. In her view, the difference maker was not the skills and strategy instruction alone but rather its combination with critical deconstruction of Samson's identity as disabled, particularly his belief that he alone was responsible for his literacy struggles. She concluded that successful literacy instruction for learners like Samson must explicitly address the impact of their segregation and help them negotiate "the stigma attached to the designation of 'being' disabled" (p. 732). We see McCloskey's study not only as a guide to organizing possible intervention for older students who need to learn literacy skills after many years of failure but also as a clarion call to construct learning environments that will not produce failure or stigma in the first place.

Reconceptualizing Who Belongs

One way to construct such environments is to conceptualize classrooms in ways that enfranchise all students. Collins (2003) demonstrates poignantly that the presence of students with disabilities in a heterogeneous learning community does not automatically confer belonging; such inclusion without disruption of deficit-oriented perspectives on disability can marginalize labeled literacy learners in harmful ways. Other researchers document more positive outcomes in inclusive settings, particularly when teachers focus acceptance and appreciation for difference (Jorgensen, 1998; Kliewer & Biklen, 2001; Ryndak et al., 1999; Sonnermeier et al., 2005). Teachers can often take cues in how to create such welcoming environments from students, as was the case in Kliewer and Biklen (2001). These researchers describe a classroom of fifth graders who welcomed Rebecca, a preliterate and primarily nonverbal student with autism, into their midst. Undaunted that their new peer did not speak, a group of girls initiated note passing to engage with her. This idea at first appeared naive to the teacher, but, to her surprise, the students quickly learned how to adapt their notes to facilitate Rebecca's responses. The process incorporated Rebecca into the community and suggested approaches the school's speech therapist used to provide Rebecca greater access to the curriculum. Both Rebecca and her nonlabeled peers redefined the classroom's rules of social engagement and learned more about communicating effectively.

This study and others (Biklen & Burke, 2006; Harris, 1994; Ryndak et al., 1999) suggest that when students with disabilities are welcomed into inclusive classrooms, their presence and their contributions can model literacy used to promote fairness and equity. One example comes from Harris's (1994) case study of Christine, a ninth grader with

Down syndrome, who, at her own and her parents' insistence, began attending general education classes after years of segregated schooling. Christine's participation in a journalism class improved her conventional literacy skills; it also led to her eventual assumption of a weekly column in the school newspaper that allowed her to share her perspectives on school and community issues. On one occasion, she used her column to speak out against the exclusion of a student with cerebral palsy from general education, raising important questions about diversity, fairness, and belonging.

Other studies suggest that the playing field can be leveled and identities can be reconstructed in heterogeneous classrooms when the meaning making approaches are new for everyone (Edmiston, 2007; Faux, 2005; Joy & Murphy, 2012). Faux (2005), for instance, documented how adolescents with disabilities created multimedia stories using TextEase 2000, a software program that gave them the opportunity to capitalize on their artistic and verbal strengths. Though these learners self-identified at the start of the study as having weak literacy skills, they had no preconceived ideas about their abilities with the new software and thus were able to abandon some supports, such as asking other to scribe, that they typically used with print-based writing. Faux concluded, "As they had not learned that multimedia literacy was an area of weakness for them, they did not try to avoid this style of 'writing'" (p. 177). Instead, they became actively engaged in valuable literacy instruction that might have stymied them in another context. As explained by Edmiston (2007), students' disability labels are reinforced throughout their schooling and "children have little power or authority to interpret or challenge their status as disabled" (p. 343). Even as young children, students accept these self-images as incompetent learners. These identities are constantly reinforced as they grow toward adolescence unless there is a powerful disruption of this thinking, such as what Faux (2005) described for the adolescents in her study.

Another example comes from French-as-a-second-language classes for Canadian sixth graders studied by Joy and Murphy (2012). According to these researchers, it is traditional in Canada, where French is one of two national languages, for French to be taught intensively over multiple months as students transition from elementary to middle school. Nearly all learners begin with similar background knowledge and a shared interest in the language. The assumptions undergirding instruction, for instance, that social interaction enhances intellectual development and that language must be used across contexts, were supportive of including learners with various profiles, including those with disabilities. The classes used varied approaches, including peer discussion, teacher modeling, dramatic presentations, and cross-curricular projects. Researchers reported that students with disabilities had more success with French reading and writing than with other curricular areas, partly because of the instructional variety and partly because the inclusive climate created in the classes allowed for new kinds of identity construction: "They are not afraid to make mistakes because they know everybody is making them and the fear of being laughed at or ridiculed is not there because they are all trying. They are more risk-takers because everybody's risk-taking" (p. 112).

Expanding Conceptions of Literacy

An important component of the instructional variety described by Joy and Murphy (2012) was students' ability to learn and demonstrate their learning through multiple modalities. A transformative pedagogy that helps youth with disabilities see themselves as competent literacy learners needs to value multiple literacy practices within the classroom curriculum. As we articulate what literacy pedagogy should look like for students with disabilities, we must assume a definition of what counts as literacy that is inclusive of multiple modes of representation and accepting of multiple literacy practices. Such a conception has much in common with Universal Design for Learning (Rose & Meyer, 2002). Adherents of this framework argue that building multiple means of (1) representation, (2) action and expression, and (3) engagement into instruction for all learners initially is preferable to (and will reduce the need for) retrofitting individual adaptations later.

A number of studies demonstrate the value of multiple representations for diverse literacy learners. MacLean (2008), for instance, observed that elementary students with diverse needs were more easily integrated into inclusive classroom communities, "whereas in secondary schools these students are often given the more marginalized status of 'visitor' to the mainstream classroom" (p. 75). She also noted that acceptance of multiple forms of representation, including gestures, sound, and images, was more prevalent in preschool and elementary classrooms. In light of these patterns, she studied adolescents with several disability labels, including some with multiple diagnoses, as they were led through a series of art activities. Participants learned the language of visual art to produce imaginary and actual artwork to tell their own stories.

Some of the most sustained work around expanding conceptions of literacy has been done by O'Brien (2012) in two different contexts, an afterschool literacy laboratory and a media-rich language arts class for seventh graders. His work in these settings shows how "students lacking in print-centric competencies according to formal tests" succeed with what O'Brien calls "multimediating," using and creating media (p. 74). In both projects, students pursued literacy practices, including print reading and writing, Web browsing, and even video gaming, to create sophisticated media projects showcasing their inquiry into self-selected topics. Like McCloskey (2011), O'Brien discovered that the identity reconstruction associated with this success motivated students to tackle and sustain conventional reading and writing tasks that they might otherwise have abandoned out of frustration or a desire for self-preservation. His case studies of individual learners highlight that "literate competence is not a static, universal phenomenon" (p. 77). Instead, it is socially situated and "relies on new tools like digital technologies that redefine texts and literacies" (p. 77). Access to, and increasing control over, multiple representations helped students to redefine themselves as they redefined what it meant to be literate.

Although O'Brien's (2012) framework is an inclusive one, his study participants were primarily nonlabeled students and students with high-incidence disabilities such as attention deficit disorder and learning disabilities. Other researchers, however, have demonstrated that students with lower-incidence disabilities—and often more complex support needs—also benefit from access to wider modes of representation, particularly when those modes are available to all students in inclusive classrooms and not merely as adaptations for labeled individuals (Jorgensen, 1998; Ryndak et al., 1999). Sonnenmeier et al. (2005), for instance, demonstrated the benefits for all learners of what they called an "immersion approach" to AAC, one in which all students in class with Jay, a young man with autism, had copies of the core vocabulary overlay for Jay's communication device on their desks. Such an approach benefited Jay's ability to communicate while reinforcing vocabulary acquisition in multiple modes for his peers.

The transformed pedagogy described in this section has highlighted contexts in which the instruction that benefited students with disabilities could be (and often was) offered to all the students in the inclusive classroom. Students took up the instruction in their own way, and the employment of adaptations, though necessary supports for youth with disabilities, did not necessarily mark individuals as different. In particular, the use of multimedia and multimodal technologies as part of typical classroom expectations helped to "normalize" the experience of students identified with disabilities. The same iPad might be used by a student with a disability as an AT and by a nonlabeled peer as a research tool. One student might use a laptop to dictate a story, while another might use it to type a final draft. The varied employment of such tools in inclusive settings helps challenge the idea that one use should be viewed as an adaptation marking a deficiency, and the other as mastering a new skill. As many technological devices increase in capability and decrease in cost, the line between assistive and information–communication technologies will likely blur further, perhaps ceasing to be a useful distinction. Teachers can further challenge this dichotomy by highlighting technology-mediated adaptations in daily life, such as doctors' use of dictation software to document medical histories or Kindle owners' use of reading enhancements built into their devices.

Summary

The literature reviewed in this section suggests the value of transforming literacy classrooms to welcome all students. Educators must push past simply allowing students with disabilities to be present in the literacy classroom, and instead find ways to position them as meaningful and contributing members of their classroom communities. As educators create environments that help students identified with disabilities resist cultural stereotypes of disability that have become rooted in their identity, students gain access to the classroom, which allows them to "exercise agency and alter their social positions within peer communities" (Naraian & Surabian, 2014, p. 339). By expanding notions of literacy, we can create more inclusive spaces. Promoting the use of multiple modalities and incorporating technology can further help to level the playing field. Studies suggest that this can be better achieved when all students are viewed as working toward goals and when students with and without disabilities use various tools and resources to meet their needs.

CONCLUSION

Scholars who espouse presuming competence call for educators to resist deficit perspectives and assume possibilities for the students with disabilities in their care. What we realized while writing this chapter, however, is that teachers must apply the same assumptions of agency and capability to themselves. They must presume their own competence when teaching literacy to all students, including those with complex support needs. They must be confident that deep knowledge of individuals, sensitive assessments, and collaborative relationships with other adults will help them devise responsive, inclusive pedagogies that are appropriate for every literacy learner, even those whose conventional skills are limited (so far).

We realize that it may be challenging to take such a stance, particularly given traditional expectations that teachers of labeled students will implement discrete, expert-designed programs with fidelity. What the literature reveals, however, is that such programs often fail to yield meaningful participation in literate communities. Instead, we call for teachers to design responsive, comprehensive literacy programs for learners they come to know well, programs that include but are not limited to interventions focused on conventional literacy skills. Research hints at promising directions for such work, but it is far from conclusive about the details. As the parenthetical material in our chapter title suggests, we acknowledge the gaps and limitations in that research, hoping that such candor will encourage readers to draw on it carefully, guided by their own expertise and lived experience.

Part of why we find Joanna's encounter with The Piano Guys so fascinating is that it pushes us to transcend narrow notions of who needs what support to succeed and, furthermore, who gets to determine that definition of success. A musician with a physical disability might integrate prerecorded and live music as an adaptation allowing her to perform in public, just as a literacy learner with unreliable speech might use text-to-speech software to share a written contribution with classroom peers. But The Piano Guys did not require such an adaptation; they chose it because it enabled them to make music in new and different ways. Similarly, while some adaptations we have discussed in this chapter are necessary to provide access to conventional skills and the general education curriculum for students with disabilities, other approaches to reading and writing might be chosen, by labeled and unlabeled students, if they were options within inclusive classrooms enacting broad conceptions of both literacy and ability. In such cases, we might find ourselves as teachers feeling the same surprise and pleasure that Joanna felt in the audience when we experience the new and unexpected forms of literacy students perform.

REFERENCES

Allor, J., Gifford, D., Otaiba, S., Miller, S., & Cheatham, J. (2013). Teaching students with intellectual disability to integrate reading skills: Effects of text and text-based lessons. *Remedial and Special Education, 34*(6), 346–356.

Bhattacharya, A., & Ehri, L. (2004). Graphosyllabic analysis helps adolescent struggling readers read and spell words. *Journal of Learning Disabilities, 37*(4), 331–348.

Biklen, D. (2005). *Autism and the myth of the person alone.* New York: New York University Press.

Biklen, D., & Burke, J. (2006). Presuming competence. *Equity and Excellence in Education, 39,* 1–10.

Blackman, L. (1999). *Lucy's story: Autism and other adventures.* Brisbane, Australia: Book in Hand.

Boone, R., & Higgins, K. (2007). The role of instructional design in assistive technology research and development. *Reading Research Quarterly, 42*(1), 135–140.

Coleman-Martin, M., Heller, K., Cihak, D., & Irvine, K. (2005). Using computer-assisted instruction and the nonverbal reading approach to teach word identification. *Focus on Autism and Other Developmental Disabilities, 20*(2), 80–90.

Collins, K. (2003). *Ability profiling and school failure: One child's struggle to be seen as competent.* Mahwah, NJ: Erlbaum.

Copeland, S., & Keefe, E. (2007). *Effective literacy instruction for students with moderate or severe disabilities.* Baltimore: Brookes.

De La Paz, S., & Graham, S. (1997). Strategy instruction in planning: Effects on the writing performance and behavior of students with learning disabilities. *Exceptional Children, 63,* 167–181.

Donnellan, A. (1984). The criterion of the least dangerous assumption. *Behavioral Disorders, 9,* 141–150.

Edmiston, B. (2007). Mission to Mars: Using drama to make a more inclusive classroom for literacy learning. *Language Arts, 84*(4), 337–346.

Erickson, K., & Koppenhaver, D. (1995). Developing a literacy program for children with severe disabilities. *The Reading Teacher, 48,* 676–687.

Faux, F. (2005). Multimodality: How students with special educational needs create multimedia stories. *Education, Communication and Information, 5*(2), 167–181.

Harris, M. L., Schumaker, J. B., & Deshler, D. D. (2011). The effects of strategic morphological analysis instruction on the vocabulary performance of secondary students with and without disabilities. *Learning Disability Quarterly, 34*(1), 17–33.

Harris, T. (1994). Christine's inclusion: An example of peers supporting one another. In J. S. Thousand, R. A. Villa, & A. I. Nevin (Eds.), *Creativity and collaborative learning: A practical guide to empowering students* (pp. 293–304). Baltimore: Brookes.

Heller, K. W., Fredrick, L. D., & Diggs, C. A. (1999). Teaching reading to students with severe speech and physical impairments using the nonverbal reading approach. *Physical Disabilities: Education and Related Services, 18*(1), 3–34.

Hudson, M. E., & Browder, D. M. (2014). Improving listening comprehension responses for students with moderate intellectual disability during literacy class. *Research and Practice for Persons with Severe Disabilities, 39*(1), 11–29.

Jorgensen, C. (1998). *Restructuring high schools for all students: Taking inclusion to the next level.* Baltimore: Brookes.

Jorgensen, C., McSheehan, M., & Sonnenmeier, R. (2007). Presumed competence reflected in students' educational programs before and after the Beyond Access professional development intervention. *Journal of Intellectual and Developmental Disabilities, 32,* 248–262.

Joy, R., & Murphy, E. (2012). The inclusion of children with special educational needs in an intensive French as a second-language program: From theory to practice. *Canadian Journal of Education, 35*(1), 102–119.

Katims, D. S. (2000). Literacy instruction for people with mental retardation: Historical highlights and contemporary analysis. *Education and Training in Mental Retardation and Developmental Disabilities, 35*(1), 3–15.

Kesler, T., Tinio, P., & Nolan, B. (2014). What's our position?: A critical media literacy study of popular culture websites with eighth grade special education students. *Reading and Writing Quarterly, 32*(1), 1–26.

Kliewer, C. (1998). *Schooling children with Down syndrome.* New York, NY: Teachers College.

Kliewer, C., & Biklen, D. (2001). School's not really a place for reading: A research synthesis of the literate lives of children with severe disabilities. *Journal of the Association for Persons with Severe Handicaps, 26,* 1–12.

Kliewer, C., Biklen, D., & Kasa-Hendrickson, C. (2006). Who may be literate?: Disability and resistance to the cultural denial of competence. *American Educational Research Journal, 43,* 163–192.

Kluth, P., & Chandler-Olcott, K. (2008). *A land we can share: Teaching literacy to students with autism.* Baltimore: Brookes.

Koppenhaver, D., & Erickson, K. (2003). Natural emergent literacy supports for preschoolers with autism and severe communication impairments. *Topics in Language Disorders, 23*(4), 283–292.

Kurth, J., & Mastergeorge, A. (2012). Impact of setting and instructional context for adolescents with autism. *Journal of Special Education, 46* (1), 36–48.

Lundberg, I., & Reichenberg, M. (2013). Developing reading comprehension among students with mild intellectual disabilities: An intervention study. *Scandinavian Journal of Educational Research, 57*(1), 89–100.

MacLean, J. (2008). The art of inclusion. *Canadian Review of Art Education: Research and Issues, 35,* 75–98.
McCloskey, E. (2011). The impact of labelling and segregation on adolescent literacy learning. *International Journal of Inclusive Education, 15*(7), 729–742.
Michalski, P., Hodges, D., & Banister, D. (2005). Digital storytelling in the middle childhood special education classroom: A teacher's story of adaptations. Retrieved from *www.bgsu.edu/content/dam/bgsu/education/teaching-and-learning/gear-up/documents/digital-storytelling-in-the-middle-childhood.pdf.*
Mims, P. J., Hudson, M., & Browder, D, M. (2012). Using read-alouds of grade-level biographies and systematic prompting to promote comprehension for students with moderate and severe developmental disabilities. *Focus on Autism and Other Developmental Disabilities, 27*(2), 67–80.
Mirenda, P. (2003). "He's not really a reader . . .": Perspectives on supporting literacy development in individuals with autism. *Topics in Language Disorders, 23*(4), 270–281.
Mukhopadhyay, T. (2000). *Beyond the silence.* London: National Autistic Society.
Naraian, S., & Surabian, M. (2014). New literacy studies: An alternative frame for preparing teachers to use assistive technology. *Teacher Education and Special Education, 37,* 330–346.
National Institute of Child Health and Human Development. (2000). *Report of the National Reading Panel: Teaching children to read: An evidence-based assessment of the scientific research literature on reading and its implications for reading instruction* (NIH Publication No. 00-4769). Washington, DC: U.S. Government Printing Office.
O'Brien, D. G. (2012). Struggling adolescents' engagement in multimediating: Countering the institutional construction of incompetence. In D. E. Alvermann & K. A. Hinchman (Eds.), *Reconceptualizing the literacies in adolescents' lives* (3rd ed., pp. 71–91). New York: Routledge.
O'Connor, I. M., & Klein, P. D. (2004). Exploration of strategies for facilitating the reading comprehension of high-functioning students with autism spectrum disorders. *Journal of Autism and Developmental Disorders, 34*(2), 115–127.
Palincsar, A. S., & Brown, A. L. (1984). Reciprocal teaching of comprehension-fostering and comprehension-monitoring activities. *Cognition and Instruction, 1*(2), 117–175.
Rao, K., Dowrick, P., Yuen, J., & Boisvert, P. (2009). Writing in a multimedia environment: Pilot outcomes for high school students in special education. *Journal of Special Education Technology, 24* (1), 27–38.
Rose, D., & Meyer, A. (2002). *Teaching every student in the digital age: Universal Design for Learning.* Alexandria, VA: Association for Supervision and Curriculum Development.
Ryndak, D., Morrison, A., & Sommerstein, L. (1999). Literacy before and after inclusion in general education settings: A case study. *Journal of the Association for Persons with Severe Handicaps, 24*(1), 5–22.
Shanahan, T., & Shanahan, C. (2008). Teaching disciplinary literacy to adolescents: Rethinking content-area literacy. *Harvard Educational Review, 78*(1), 40–59.
Shurr, J., & Taber-Doughty, T. (2012). Increasing comprehension for middle school students with moderate intellectual disability on age-appropriate texts. *Education and Training in Autism and Developmental Disabilities, 47*(3), 359–372.
Sonnenmeier, R., Jorgensen, C., & McSheehan, M. (2005). A case study of team supports for a student with autism's communication and engagement within the general education curriculum: Preliminary report of the Beyond Access model. *Journal of Augmentative and Alternative Communication, 21,* 101–115.

CHAPTER 7

The Development of Literate Identities and Practices across a Decade
Families, Friends, and Schools

CATHERINE COMPTON-LILLY

In September of 1996, 6-year-old Alicia walked into my first-grade classroom. Ten years later, I interviewed her and her mother, Ms. Rodriguez. When Alicia was in grade 1, her mother described her as "the type of child that loves school." To illustrate her point, she spoke about what happened when school was closed:

> "When [Alicia's] out of school she's like, 'I can't wait 'til we get at school.' I'm looking at her like, 'OK, Alicia you're off for Saturday, Friday, the long school vacation. You know, when they close school. [And] you [are] going [to] think about the day that we go back?' She's like, 'It's spring, I have so many friends.'"

Ms. Rodriguez recognized that some of Alicia's enthusiasm for school was related to her interest in "socializing with her friends." However, after a decade of loving school, Alicia's views changed during grade 11, when she was placed in a special classroom that was located in a distant corner of the high school and isolated from the other students. When asked if she still liked school, Alicia reported, "I do when I be in regular school with everybody."

In this chapter, I explore how scholars have addressed the various ecological systems that inform literacy identities and practices. Bronfenbrenner (1976, 1995a) conceptualized an ecological model of development as a system for "exploring as-yet-uncharted domains that offer promise for enhancing scientific understanding of the conditions and forces that shape human development through the life course" (p. 621). I begin by providing an overview of Bronfenbrenner's model, which situates development within layered systems that include microsystems, mesosystems, exosystems, macrosystems, and chronosystems. I then review how other scholars have addressed these systems to explore issues related to identity construction and literacy practices. Finally, I draw on Alicia's experiences to illustrate the interaction of these systems over time.

BRONFENBRENNER'S MODEL AS A FRAME FOR REVIEW

In this chapter, I explore how literacy scholars have addressed each layer of Bronfenbrenner's model—microsystem, mesosystem, exosystem, macrosystem, and chronosystem—alongside dimensions of Alicia's story. While these scholars have made significant contributions to the field of literacy, most do not directly connect their work to Bronfenbrenner's model. In addition, most of these scholars do not explore how people operate across multiple ecological systems and across time. By reviewing how scholars have portrayed particular ecological systems, then exploring Alicia's experiences across the full set of systems, we can explore how these layered ecological systems operate together and across time.

When considering development, Bronfenbrenner was interested in the increasingly complex reciprocal interactions that occur among objects and symbols within people's immediate environments. Particularly relevant to the current review, he wondered about the effects of proximal processes involving increasingly complex reciprocal interactions among people, object, and symbols over extended periods of time (Bronfenbrenner, 1979).

While time was addressed in Bronfenbrenner's early articulation of ecological theory (1994) via the "process–person–context–time (PPCT) model" (p. 38), the chronosystem was later recognized (see Bronfenbrenner & Morris, 2006) as a critical and distinct ecological system. The chronosystem highlights how temporality—historical time and experiences over time—operate and affect the ways people develop and make sense of their worlds. Chronosystems recognize both change and consistency in people and in the contexts they inhabit. Chronosystems involve the transitions that people make that affect developmental changes for themselves and their families (Bronfenbrenner, 1986). Bronfenbrenner (1977) pointed to the work of Elder (1974) and his analysis of the distinctive effects the Great Depression had on people's lives. Elder (2001) was particularly interested in how developmental mechanisms—advantages, disadvantages, transitional experiences, and turning points—affect people across time.

Bronfenbrenner (1977) emphasized that development does not take place outside of contexts and that multiple factors are constantly operating on individuals in interactive and nonlinear ways (Magnusson, 1995). Changes occur over time in terms of people's roles, activities, and the places they inhabit. Bronfenbrenner refers to these as ecological transitions that occur when a "person's position in the ecological environment is altered as the result of a change in role, setting, or both" (Bronfenbrenner, 1979, p. 26). These changes might involve "marriages, births, graduations, divorces, and deaths" (Bronfenbrenner, 1977, p. 525).

As Bronfenbrenner (1976/1995b) explained, lives and development are embedded in and affected by powerful historical forces, conditions, and events. Timing is a critical factor. *When* things happen can have significant effects on people's developmental trajectories. Events that coincide with culturally defined ages and role expectations have different effects than events that come too late or too early. Finally, the experiences of family members are intertwined with how individuals respond to transitions and life events.

While his model has been applied extensively to the experiences of young children, Bronfenbrenner (1976) noted the paucity of research that applied his model to middle childhood and adolescence. As he maintained, "Developmental transitions are not limited to the early years but recur, in various forms throughout the life of the learner" (p. 13). In particular, he noted the tendency for scholars to conduct cross-sectional rather than longitudinal studies. Bronfenbrenner worried that, as a result, "inquiry can shed little light on the learning process as a developmental experience" (p. 13).

Understandings about how multiple ecological systems interact are particularly relevant to the challenges faced by students from historically underserved communities. While much has been written about the achievement debt (i.e., Ladson-Billings, 2006), and the effects that living in marginalized, high-poverty communities have on children, much less is known about how effects operate and cumulate over time. Because little is understood about the ways mesosystems, exosystems, and macrosystems act upon individual children, it has been far too easy to blame parents and communities for problems that exist in underserved and underresourced communities. In addition, these accounts generally fail to recognize the strengths and remarkable forms of resilience that children in underserved communities develop (Coll et al., 1996; Coll & Szalacha, 2004).

I am in the unique position of having followed across a decade seven African American children from a high-poverty community. The children were my former students. They sat in my first-grade classroom. I have been honored to be able to talk with the children and their families across time and have crafted a set of counternarratives that challenge prevailing accounts that blame poor parenting and belligerent students. I believe Bronfenbrenner's model provides a unique framework for highlighting both the debilitating effects of growing up in a high-poverty community and the multiple ways in which families worked to sustain themselves and navigate their worlds (Coll et al., 1996; Coll & Szalacha, 2004).

IDENTITY CONSTRUCTION AND LITERACY PRACTICES IN SCHOLARLY LITERATURE AND FOR ALICIA

In the following sections, I review research that has explored identity construction and literacy practices for adolescent learners. Although these researchers do not directly cite Bronfenbrenner's model, my interest lies in the ecological systems that they reference and explore. Following a review of existing research related to each ecological system, I draw on Alicia's experiences to explore the multiple and intersecting ecological systems that have contributed to her development over time. As a student attending underfunded, inner-city schools in a high-poverty community, Alicia faced challenges as she has moved through school. The elementary school she attended, and where I taught, Rosa Parks Elementary School, was on the state list of schools under registration review and was threatened with closure if scores in reading did not improve during the initial year of the study. By the time Alicia was in fourth grade, the No Child Left Behind Act (NCLB; 2001) had been implemented, and statewide English language arts (ELA) tests were in place. In elementary school, we had a school sentry who monitored the hallways and removed students from classrooms if their negative behaviors escalated; as she entered middle school and high school, Alicia faced increased surveillance and regulation at school.

The Fight and the Microsystem of School

Microsystems involve face-to-face settings that entail physical, social, and symbolic features that invite, permit, or inhibit various types of engagement over time. Within microsystems, we can observe the enactment of proximal processes that Bronfenbrenner described as the "mechanisms of organism–environment behavioral interaction that drive development, and the profound ways in which these mechanisms are affected by characteristics of the developing person and the environmental context" (Bronfenbrenner, 1979, p. 626).

A vast number of scholars have explored various microsystems that engage adolescents with literacy and identity construction. These microsystems include adolescents' multimodal and digital practices at school (Mills, 2010), literacy practices outside of school (Moje, Overby, Tysvaer, & Morris, 2008), technology-mediated literacy practice outside of school (Chandler-Olcott & Mahar, 2003), instant messaging (IM) practices (Lewis & Fabos, 2005), and composition practices within a fanfiction community (Black, 2005).

For example, Chandler-Olcott and Mahar (2003) both explored and documented the adolescents' purposes for engaging in technologically mediated literacy practices. In addition, they explored the online communities of practice that inform and surround these practices. Specifically, they focused on two focal students, Rhiannon and Eileen; data—including interviews, fieldnotes, artifacts, and email exchanges—were collected for 18 months. Through this study, Chandler-Olcott and Mahar documented how students incorporated materials from media texts and borrowed various designs to create their own online compositions. In particular, they noted the mentor relationships that accompanied these literacy practices as adolescents provided each other with guidance and feedback. Similarly Black (2005) explored the literacy composition practices of English language learners (ELLs) in an online fanfiction community. She maintained that participation on the fanfiction site enabled "ELLs to forge connections with other fans and to establish a social base within this discourse community" (p. 120). In short, fanfiction sites were identified as supporting intertextual literacy practices, and linguistic and cultural hybridity, and therefore informing identity construction for youth. In both of these studies (Black, 2005; Chandler-Olcott & Mahar, 2003), we witness adolescents operating within microsystems that involve online communities.

For Alicia, my first-grade classroom was a microsystem. It was a large room with a book corner and a carpeted area, where children sat facing an easel. The children entered every morning, found books to read with their friends and were eventually called to the carpeted area collectively to read poems and stories. They were then sent to their tables to write, while I worked with small groups of students as they read. The physical layout of the classroom, including the book corner and the easel, provided opportunities for reading and writing, and allowed children to move around the room or work at tables, where social interactions were encouraged.

To further explore the microsystems that have accompanied Alicia's journey across time, I start at the end, with a critical event that occurred during Alicia's junior year of high school. Alicia had always been a good student. For the prior 9 years, she had consistently been described as a talkative student who never got into trouble at school. In December of grade 11, Alicia was involved in a fight in which the school sentry was injured. As a result, she was placed in a separate classroom of six to eight students and isolated from the other students for the remainder of the school year. Apparently one of the teachers at Alicia's school learned about Alicia and her friends through her own daughter's MySpace page. Alicia's mother blamed this teacher for creating the situation.

> "Two of the girls that was on the [web]page were having problems with her daughter. What she did was set up the whole thing, and [this teacher said] that they were in a gang. And passed it around the school [and] to the other teachers [and] to the students. Yeah. Right? What came of that, so far [is] four of those girls got jumped and one was Alicia. And what she's telling me is that because of that, and they consider them as a gang, [because] they always hang together. I'm like, how [do] you ask to get jumped by 10, 15 people? She was jumped by 10 or 15 girls.
>
> "What happened was Alicia was going up the stairs. The girl was, you know, how they get bumped in the hallways. Coming in the exit, the girl fell down the steps. When the girl fell on the steps, everybody looked and they started laughing. She wasn't hurt. So everybody laughed. She got mad. So she waited until she seen her friends come upstairs and then started her crap.
>
> "Alicia went to go up the steps. The girl ran up the steps, grabbed Alicia from behind and pulled her down. And when Alicia came down she almost fell. So she jumped. And when she jumped, she landed on her feet and that's when the girls [started] swinging and then Alicia starts swinging back and all her friends jumped in. Now in the process they're saying that one of the sentries got hurt and the whole nine [yards] but you're are blaming her for something she didn't do. . . . But [Alicia] never been in no fight. She has got her grades up, she started getting A's and B's. She was doing so good this year. Because she's like, 'Oh Mom, I'm like I'm almost out. I getting ready for college. Yeah. I'm smart, smart, smart. My grades are going to be killing.' She brought home her report card and I'm like, 'You didn't fail no classes?' 'No,' she said, 'I passed all my classes.'"

According to Ms. Rodriguez's account and my longitudinal observations, Alicia was a good student who got caught up in a bad situation. Despite her strong academic record, Alicia spent the rest of the school year in a sequestered classroom with six to eight of her peers and was required to arrive at school after all of the other children were in class, and she was not allowed to leave the isolated wing of the building where her classes were held. The school's actions were part of their anti-gang polices.

Thus, what occurred during face-to-face interactions between two groups of girls and a school sentry reflect the microcosm of this underfunded, inner-city high school. Bronfenbrenner (1979) described these as the "mechanisms of organism–environment behavioral interaction" (p. 626) that operated within a local context. In particular, these interactions occurred in an overcrowded stairwell when large numbers of students were changing classes. It is a highly surveilled space marked both via the presence of the school sentry and the actions of a teacher who was monitoring her daughter's MySpace page.

Friends, Gangs, and the Mesosystems of School, Home, and Peers

Mesosystems entail linkages across more than one microsystem. Bronfenbrenner (1994) refers to a mesosystem as "a system of microsystems" (p. 40). In short, microsystems interface, resulting in synergy, conflict, and/or convergence. In addition to interactions within the mesosystem, interactions also occur across ecological systems, creating domino effects. For example, Bronfenbrenner (1976) argued that changes in ecosystems could affect practices within microsystems, which in turn affect mesosystems via changes in the relationships among microsystems. Thus, mesosystems are continuously responsive to interactions and relations across systems.

Mesoystems, involving interactions across microsystems, have been explored by literacy and identity scholars (Leander & McKim, 2003; Moje, 2002; Moje et al., 2008; Mills, 2010; O'Brien, 2001; Vasudevan, 2006). For example, Moje and her colleagues (2008) examined the relationship between literacy practices that occur outside of school and classroom instruction. Drawing on a 9-year longitudinal study that focused on the experiences of 79 youth and included surveys, interviews, observations, achievement scores, and other school data, they identified tensions between in-school and out-of-school literacy practices, noting that students often read and wrote extensively outside of school. However, these practices were generally invisible to teachers and unconnected to school literacy practices. They argued that "what and why young people read and write outside of school may affect their continuing literate development" (p. 147) and that educators should draw upon these practices to improve educational experiences for adolescents. Leander and McKim (2003) challenge the bifurcation of online and offline spaces. They document the "traveling of practices" (p. 211) of adolescents across online and offline spaces highlighting "flows of objects, texts, and bodies" (p. 211) as online and offline activities "interpenetrate" (p. 218). Both of these analyses highlight mesosystems as they entail interactions across the microsystems of in-school–out-of-school and online–offline spaces.

The data brought to the current analysis of Alicia's school trajectory involve interactions across three microsystems: family, school/classroom, and peers constituting the mesosystems of interest. In some cases, the labels placed on people, the assumed causes of problems, and the interpretations of these events were drastically different across the microsystems. Mesosystems are evident in Ms. Rodriguez's account of the fight, in which we witness tensions involving conflicting interpretations as Alicia and her friends are constructed as gang members.

When we spoke, Alicia told me about her friends "I in a club, you know, because I had to help my goons out. You know goons [are the] people that you fight with. And [they my] friends, I fight with my friends." While Alicia noted that the group had a name and colors, she insisted that they were not a gang.

> "No, not, not my home girls. They don't [be] like 'Oh, we're going to go shoot somebody. We're gonna go stab [someone].' We don't do that. Like girls fight us sometimes. You know, you just gotta do what we [do]. We beat them up, because you know they start with us."

Thus, Alicia distinguished between her "home girls" and a "gang" by insisting that they only fought when they had to protect themselves. Perhaps even more interesting was how she and her mother described the group as comprised of childhood friends.

> ALICIA: My friends, we been friends since nursery school. And we just been friends from there.

MS. RODRIGUEZ: These are her friends like she was like, since second grade. It was second grade. They grew up together. Of course they're going to be friends. So now, I got to fight with them [the school administrators] because they probably think she's in a gang. Then they probably think that she asked for this. You know. No, she didn't ask for this.

Based on these accounts, it is clear that the school and the home had very different conceptions of Alicia and her friends. What Alicia and Ms. Rodriguez viewed as longstanding friendships and alliances that kept Alicia safe within the hallways of an urban high school, teachers and school staff viewed as a gang that needed to be controlled and dismantled. This mesosystem references problematic relationships across microsystems—in this case, relationships among home, school, and peers that are laden with tension and characterized by mistrust and surveillance.

Significantly, conflicts between the microsystems of home and school operated across the 10-year study. When Alicia's younger sister Quanzaa was in kindergarten, Ms. Rodriguez told the following story:

"Quanzaa has lost [her] gloves and I had just bought her pair of gloves and find out [she] lost them. And I said, 'When I get paid I'll buy you another pair,' right? Her teacher assumed I was on welfare. [She] tell her to tell her mother, 'When she get her check to buy you another pair of gloves.' And I went to school and told her, 'Let me explain something to you, OK? I work, everyday. Don't tell my child to tell me that. OK, when I get some money I'll go buy her a pair of gloves. I don't need you or nobody else to tell me that. I know her hands are cold. That's why most of the time she wear my gloves but I take them from her when I got to go to work, thank you. I walk her [to school] then I take them from her, then I go on to work because most of the time when they leave from school my girlfriend husband is down there and he drive them home. I don't get no ride home. I walk.' So she looked at me like, excuse me, I'm sorry. 'That's OK, be careful.'"

Ms. Rodriguez was incensed that the teacher would assume that she did not know that her child needed gloves and had assumed that the family was receiving welfare:

"A lot of teachers in a lot of schools . . . say this is the ghetto, right? And they say a lot of people is in the ghetto so they assume everybody is on welfare. And they'll say 'When your mother get her check tell her to buy you so and so.' And that's embarrassing for the kid."

Four years later, Ms. Rodriguez again named the assumptions that accompany being a parent in a high-poverty community. Speaking about teachers, she noted, "They figured most young Black people are either out there selling drugs or doing drugs and they think because you live in the ghetto, you got to act like the ghetto. But that's not true."

Thus, while Alicia's fight in high school was a significant and consequential event, mesosystems involving home and school had been fraught with tension across the decade. These tensions often related directly to the ways families and children were positioned by teachers and school personnel and have resulted in sedimented layers of distrust.

Curricula, Testing, Surveillance, and the Exosystems of Urban Schooling

Exosystems reference contextual factors that impact individuals, yet they are not part of individuals' immediate contexts. They include policies, institutional expectations, and laws. While individuals encounter these dimensions of context, they do not participate directly in the creation or the implementation of these contextual dimensions. Exosystems can involve policies and situations related to the employment of family members, social welfare systems, and urban development initiatives. As Bronfenbrenner (1986) reported, exosystems also surround and define school and have significant effects on students. Thus, school policies related to discipline, curricula, assessment, and graduation have indirect yet real effects.

Vasudevan (2006) documents how assessments, such as the Test of Adult Basic English, defined one student as having low literacy skills and as being a struggling student. Through her case study, she documented how teacher–student collaborations about topics of interest to the student challenged deficit labels by revealing the abilities that students bring to classrooms. Similarly, O'Brien (2001) challenged characterizations of some adolescents as being "at risk." He described how multimodal literacy practices could be accessed to provide students with opportunities to present themselves as "competent, creative and artistic" (p. 4), in contrast to official assessments that relied on standardized achievement systems.

Rosa Parks Elementary School was a mammoth school that served over 1,200 children from the lowest socioeconomic-level community in the city. At the time, Alicia attended Rosa Parks Elementary School, we were under registration review and were slated to be closed by the State if our reading and math tests scores did not improve at the end of the year. As part of the registration review process, school administrators were replaced, a new reading program was adopted, auditors from the State Education Department visited our school, and an official report was written.

When Alicia was in fourth grade, NCLB (2001) and its accompanying regimen of mandated tests was implemented. By the time Alicia graduated, she was required to pass a graduation examination. Although Alicia was affected by these policies, neither she nor her family was directly involved in their creation or implementation. Other relevant policies referenced in the longitudinal dataset relate to welfare, transportation, and law enforcement policies. The lives of people living in high-poverty communities are often affected by regulations and policies that have humiliating and degrading effects. Many of these policies are related to social services and health, as well as the availability of community resources, including shops, libraries, parks, recreational facilities, and community organizations. As Alicia and her older brothers grew up, moved out, and had their own children, they were increasingly affected by policies related to social services, health care, and employment. Eventually, their relationships with schools shifted from being students to being the parents of children attending schools. Legal policies were also encountered through incidents of police profiling and when one of Alicia's older brothers was briefly incarcerated.

When Alicia was in first grade and our school was subjected to monitoring by the State Education Department, a system of surveillance that was imposed on the school and the teachers. During that year, we were inundated with efforts to standardize and monitor instruction, which included a new and required basal reading program, mandated lesson plan formats that were reviewed weekly, and an ever-shifting set of reading assessments. Over the course of the year, multiple reading assessments were proposed, implemented, and abandoned, causing teachers to scurry to prepare students for ever-changing expectations and creating stress and anxiety. The information presented below is drawn from field notes taken during the first year of the longitudinal study.

The school year opened with a very poorly delivered, 2-day orientation presented by consultants from the basal reading company. My field notes described the sessions:

> They put a couple overheads on the screen, but the little boxes on them were meaningless. A few boxes, a few arrows, and all of the trendy words—"parents," "intervention," "assessment"—were there but there was nothing interesting or intriguing about what was presented. [Our school administrator] was furious. I am certain central office will hear about this!

The consultants tried to sell the program and convince us that the new reading program was the answer to all our reading woes. As teachers, we found the presentation insulting. I quoted one consultant as saying, "At first it is OK to hang on to some of the practices you have used in the past. But soon you will wean yourself from that other stuff [and just use our program]." This discourse of adoption and fidelity became alarming when a teacher was criticized for using a poem that was not part of the basal program, despite the fact that our district had not purchased the poetry charts that accompanied the reading program.

This focus on fidelity led to surveillance of our daily lesson plans. Each Monday we were required to submit our lesson plans to administrators who evaluated them using a checklist. In particular, administrators wanted us to indicate when we taught isolated skills including grammar, vocabulary, phonics, and spelling. I resorted to listing page numbers in my lesson plans to make clear how I was using the basal reader in my daily instruction. However, even my inclusion of page numbers did not satisfy my administrator, who continued to criticize my plans for not adhering to the teachers' manual. As I noted in my field notes, I suspected that the actual intent was "for all of our lesson plans to share the same format so that we could demonstrate continuity to the State Education Department [when they visited and] so that administrators could easily talk about what [the] teachers were doing."

Perhaps most distressing was the multiple and ever-changing series of assessments that were imposed on children. In January, administrators mandated that we conduct "skills assessments" with all children. In March, the reading specialist showed up with a list of colors that she asked our students to read. By April, we were required to use the placement test that accompanied the basal reading series. In June, we were notified that the students would be evaluated based on a running record and retelling of a story. Throughout the year, the assessments shifted, keeping us unsure about what counted.

By the time Alicia was promoted to grade 5, NCLB (2001) was in its second year and my former students had taken the new state-mandated ELA test during the previous year. By eighth grade, state-mandated testing was part of school. While rhetoric of social justice circulated, claiming that testing would ensure that all children met high academic standards, Ms. Rodriguez disagreed. During one interview, she turned to her children, who were sitting nearby, and explained:

"They making it harder for you all to get out [of high school]. And the dropout rate is so, so bad. It was already bad. . . . 'Cause you got a lot of kids that need help and they [teachers] ain't helping them. . . . They're not getting the education that they should. You got to teach them how to take this test and what's going to be on this test. . . . It's becoming too hard for them kids and so they dropping out. Because if they [do] not learn, if the teacher's not teaching them, and [then] they sit there and feel like they's stupid and they're not stupid."

In this section, I have focused on exosystems related to educational policies and instructional expectations that defined Alicia's school experiences. While Alicia was not directly involved in creating or negotiating these policies, educational policies related to curricula and testing affected what she was taught and how she was assessed. As ours was an underperforming school, surveillance that was ostensibly enacted to ensure student learning ultimately had negative effects as teachers struggled to meet increasingly stringent policies related to lesson planning, curricular fidelity, and assessment. As noted earlier, surveillance of students was also evident in Ms. Rodriguez's description of Alicia's fight. Both the teacher who monitored her daughter's MySpace account and the presence of the school sentry attest to the high levels of surveillance that were enacted in high school.

It is important to note that school policies represent only a sampling of the exosystems that affected Alicia and her family. Over the 10 years that Ms. Rodriguez participated in the project, she spoke of policies related to employment when after years of working towards her credentials for working in as an early childhood educator, and eventually opening own child care center, she was forced to close her center after one of her employees struck a child. Ms. Rodriguez also described the humiliation involved in having to apply for social services and the unregulated housing codes that caused her to seek a new apartment. Finally, she often noted the increasing loss of community resources, including the closing of her neighborhood library. Thus, exosystems had continuous and significant effects on Alicia and her family that both included and extended beyond education.

Culture, Race, Resilience, and the Macrosystems of Family

Macrosystems are less concrete than exosystems and are located within local communities and families. Bronfenbrenner described macrosystems as entailing "the economic, social, educational, legal and political systems, of which micro-, meso-, and exosytems are the concrete manifestations" (Bronfenbrenner, 1977, p. 515). Bronfenbrenner later refers to the macrosystem as a "societal blueprint" (1994, p. 40) that involves how people see the world. Macrosystems invoke an understanding of culture, the invocation of customs, and ways of valuing, believing, and knowing that reference what others might call ideologies. Macrosystems also entail the recognition of available material resources and opportunity structures.

Various macrosystems have been examined by literacy and identity scholars (Chandler-Olcott & Mahar, 2003; Moje, Ciechanowski, Kramer, Ellis, Carrillo, & Collazo, 2004; Morrell, 2002). Morrell focused on popular culture, which he described as a "terrain of exchange" (p. 73) between subordinate and dominant groups that provides a "logical connection between lived experiences and the school culture for urban youth" (p. 73) educators can use to motivate and empower adolescent learners. Moje et al. (2004) focused on funds of knowledge and discourses that operate within communities via networks and relationships that "shape ways of knowing, reading, writing, and talking" (p. 38). In their study, which focused on 30 children between the ages of 12 and 15, they identified funds of knowledge and discourses related to parents' work, travel, health, the environment, peers, online practices, and popular culture. As Moje and her colleagues explained, "It is critical to examine not only knowledges and Discourses themselves but also the funds in which knowledge and Discourses are generated" (p. 41). While what adolescents know and can do is important, it is also critical that we attend to the cultural spaces within which ways of understanding the world are generated. Thus, macrosystems entail the invisible ways of being, thinking, and valuing that affect how people make sense of their worlds.

In Alicia's family, I identify several prominent macrosystems. Some overlap with community norms and values, others are uniquely fostered within Alicia's family. Relevant macrosystems in Alicia's family include the high value placed on reading, being able to "deal with" the system, and an explicit critique of the deficit discourses that were often voiced about poor African America families who live in communities that Alicia's mother referred to as the "ghetto."

Unlike exosystems, macrosystems do not entail written policies and rules. They reflect people's values and beliefs, including those related to literacy. Macrosystems can also be spaces where resilience to adversity and the ability to negotiate difficult ecological systems are fostered and developed (Coll et al., 1996; Coll & Szalacha, 2004). The development of resilience is evident in Alicia's family members both in terms of the shared value they placed on reading and in the ways they actively and collaboratively dealt with racism.

On my first visit to Alicia's home, an appliance-size box of books was brought out from the back room. Alicia and her siblings gathered around to show me the board books, Little Golden Books, Dr. Seuss Books, discarded library books, and old school textbooks that filled the box. This box of books was an early clue about the value placed on literacy in Alicia's home. Not only did these books regularly circulate among Alicia and her brothers, but other books circulated among family members across the longitudinal study. When Alicia was young, she and her siblings exchanged books from *The Goosebumps Series* (Stine, 1992–1997) that were brought home from school libraries and borrowed from friends. Ms. Rodriguez exchanged books with her friends and eventually shared many of these with her children.

When Alicia was in 11th grade, she read one of her mother's books, then brought it to school, and several of her friends read the book. Eventually Alicia's younger sister, Quanzaa, got the book and took it to school. When her mother asked Quanzaa where he book was, Quanzaa explained, "I only took one book. Jen got my book. Ashley had your book. [She] gave me my book. Then, I gave her a book."

In addition to this circulation of books, when the younger children were learning to read, older siblings were expected to help:

> Ms. Rodriguez: When she's [Alicia's] reading along, she comes to me. And if she don't come to me she goes to one of her brothers [for help]. (interview 1/4/97)

MS. RODRIGUEZ: I believe if they didn't have their support of their brothers and their family, I don't think they would do as well [with reading]. (interview 9/6/00)

MS. RODRIGUEZ: (*addressing Alicia and Quanzaa*) You have people [to help you with reading]. (interview 2/1/01)

The importance of reading books was a shared value in the macrosystem inhabited by members of this family. Reading was not only viewed as an important skill that would serve them throughout life, but it was also recognized as a source of pleasure.

Macrosystems in Alicia's family also entailed beliefs and practices related to race. In particular, as the mother of four young men, Ms. Rodriguez was particularly concerned about how her sons presented themselves. As Ms. Rodriguez reported, "They figure most of the time the Black kids, a lot of them, they have a parent that don't care. So you have to actually show them that 'Uh-uh, no, this is a parent that do care.'"

Concerns about race, language, and the assumptions that might be made about Ms. Rodriguez and her children were voiced across the study. In general, family members shared a suspicion and distrust of officials, including police and in some cases teachers and school administrators. When Alicia was in grade 1, Ms. Rodriguez described how she made sure that her sons knew how to talk "proper." She explained:

"You got to test them out every now and then. Now this one [points to one of her sons sitting nearby] when he goes to a job interview he can do it because he always proper. But them [motions to her other sons in the next room] I gave [them a test] to see whether they can do it. And I was like 'Now go talk to so-and-so and so-and-so.' And he [her son] was like 'What—?' I says 'Now you got to walk the talk like you got some sense.' He goes up to him [and says], 'Excuse me' . . . and I'm sitting there looking at him like [thinking] now this is the same kid that works his mouth all over town. . . . So I know that they can make that conflict and I'm glad about it because it's easier for them. It's not, it won't be hard as they grow up changing. When they get to work, then when they get home 'OK chill,' all right fine [you can speak informally]. I'm glad they can do it though."

Issues related to race extended to police profiling. Ms. Rodriguez asked one of Alicia's older brothers to tell me about a recent incident that occurred when he and his brother were walking to the corner store. Police officers stopped them, searched their book bags, and pushed them up against the police car. Alicia's brother told the police, "You can put me in the cop car if you want to. I'm gonna treat you like you're treating me. You're treating me like a little kid. So I'm going to treat ya'll like one. It doesn't matter to me." Ms. Rodriguez was upset about the assumptions that the officers had made about her sons. "Just because you're walking and you look like something that don't mean you are. And they stereotype people and that's what I just can't get behind. . . . I'm like 'Nope.'" Family members described racism and profiling as pervasive in this community. As Ms. Rodriguez explained, "Yeah, they do it *all* the time to *all* of us."

The significance of race extended to the family's book selection practices. When Alicia was in grade 5, Ms. Rodriguez identified the African American writer Donald Goines (1973) as her favorite author: "He is a Black author. . . . He write about his life." Ms.

Rodriguez passed on the relevance of reading and race to her children. Leon read *Mama* (McMillan, 1987) after his mother finished; *Mama* is the story of an African American woman struggling to raise five children in a poverty-stricken urban community. Alicia read it a few years later. The book described earlier, which both Alicia and Quanzaa read, also featured African American characters in an urban context.

Interestingly, Alicia seemed to develop her interest in books that featured African American characters over time. In fifth grade, Alicia enjoyed reading books from the Babysitters' Club and explained that it did not matter that the books did not have Black protagonists. By middle school, she was exclusively choosing books with African American characters. While she rarely remembered the books she read in high school, she spoke extensively about *Kindred* (Butler, 2003), a book about an African American woman who is transported back to the time of slavery. Alicia explained:

> "It's interesting and crazy at the same time. . . . Because the lady go back in time and she comes back, she sees people older and older and older. And they think she's a slave when she go back in time but she not. And she can't be with her husband like she wants to because he White and she Black. That book's crazy."

Beliefs about reading and race are deeply ingrained in this family. Not only is reading valued and the ability to negotiate racism important in the daily lives of family members, but the confluence of reading and race is significant in terms of the types of stories read and the ways these stories contribute to developing resilience and the ability to navigate situations in which racism, assumptions about people of color, and inequitable economic and social opportunities exist. In particular, these narratives provide examples of African American people negotiating difficult situations and finding ways to survive and in some cases thrive. Thus, the macrosystem not only captures the ways beliefs and values intersect with everyday experiences, but it also provides resources that support children as they move forward within their lives.

Chronosystems

Chronosystems reference how temporality—including larger social histories and lived experiences—operate and affect how people develop and make sense of their worlds. Chronosystems invite consideration of how people experience change and consistency across time.

Research related to the chronosystem is best illustrated by the work of McLeod (2000, 2003). McLeod (2000) engaged in longitudinal research with adolescents from ages 12 to 18 to examine how gender and social class affect identity formation. Her work cuts across various ecological systems as she explores macrosystems related to cultural expectations and positionings related to class and gender alongside exosystems—specifically, school expectations and policies that affected students. Temporality is addressed as she explores how students describe themselves as maturing individuals, and in the ways they consider their futures, as well as documenting change and the formation of habitus over time. In my own work (Compton-Lilly, 2011, 2013, 2014), I have also explored literacy practices and identity construction over time.

For Alicia, the chronosystem references a vast array of temporal dimensions. We witness continuities related to the assumptions that have consistently been made about

Alicia, her family, and her peers, school policies that focus on surveillance and test scores, and family values related to negotiating race and reading. We also witness ongoing discontinuities among home, school, and peer interpretations of events and practices. Alicia's story includes points of transition as she moved from my first-grade classroom through elementary school and into high school. Over time, busy days in a single classroom with opportunities to read and write with other children morphed into multiple teachers, changing classrooms, and crowded hallways. Finally, we encounter the changing expectations of society. In school, Alicia endured the NCLB era with its standardized tests and skills-based instruction. Her family persevered through the welfare reforms of the 1990s and the more recent curtailment of social services, school funding, and public resources (i.e., libraries), especially in poor communities.

CONCLUSIONS

The studies presented in this review, including Alicia's case study, explore the various ways that ecological systems operate during adolescence as identities are constructed and literacy practices are refined. As noted earlier, many scholars have referenced the various systems that are relevant to the experiences of adolescents. Alicia's story has provided an illustration that highlights the complexity that accompanies events occurring within the microsystem of school. We witness a fight occurring in a school hallway as more than Alicia's bad behavior. This event, occurring within the microsystem of a school hallway, is related to a mesosystem that has historically featured tensions between home and school is reflected in assumptions made about Alicia, her family, and her community. Exosystems increasingly highlight surveillance through both unrelenting attention to test scores and ever-increasing monitoring—via book bag checks, school sentries, hallway sweeps, and even MySpace pages. While in first grade, teachers were the focus of surveillance; by high school students were also targeted.

As Sontag (1996) noted, Bronfenbrenner recognized that his theory had more readily been applied to explorations of children's experiences within and across multiple contexts than to the explorations of development. In particular, Ramey, Krauss, and Simeonsson (1989) maintained that many scholars have drawn on Bronfenbrenner's model to make "sweeping statements about systems" (p. v) rather than to explore meticulously how systems interact and affect development. Much of Bronfenbrenner's theorizing about interactions and negotiations across systems has been neglected, as have his discussions about the contributions that individuals, families, and communities make to ecological systems. In short, few scholars have provided either a "comprehensive treatment of the ecological paradigm" (Sontag, 1996, p. 322) or an analysis of the child and his or her experiences across ecological contexts. It is my hope that Alicia's story invites us to think about how adolescents are situated in layered systems of influence and within time.

REFERENCES

Black, R. W. (2005). Access and affiliation: The literacy and composition practices of English-language learners in an online fanfiction community. *Journal of Adolescent and Adult Literacy, 49*(2), 118–128.

Bronfenbrenner, U. (1976). The experimental ecology of education. *Educational Researcher, 5*(9), 5–15.
Bronfenbrenner, U. (1977). Toward an experimental ecology of human development. *American Psychologist, 32*(7), 513–531.
Bronfenbrenner, U. (1979). *The ecology of human development: Experiments by nature and design.* Cambridge, MA: Harvard University Press.
Bronfenbrenner, U. (1986). Ecology of the family as a context for human development: Research perspectives. *Developmental Psychology, 22*(6), 723–742.
Bronfenbrenner, U. (1994). Ecological models of human development. In M. Gauvain & M. Cole (Eds.), *Readings on the development of children* (2nd ed., pp. 37–43). New York: Freeman.
Bronfenbrenner, U. (1995a). The bioecological model from a life course perspective: Reflections of a participant observer. In P. Moen, G. H. Elder, & K. Lüscher (Eds.), *Examining lives in context* (pp. 599–618). Washington, DC: American Psychological Association.
Bronfenbrenner, U. (1995b). Developmental ecology through time and space: A future perspective. In P. Moen, G. H. Elder, & K. Lüscher (Eds.), *Examining lives in context* (pp. 619–647). Washington, DC: American Psychological Association.
Bronfenbrenner, U., & Morris, P. (2007). The bioecological model of human development. In R. M. Lerner (Ed.), *Handbook of child psychology* (pp. 793–828). Hoboken, NJ: Wiley.
Butler, O. E. (2003). *Kindred.* New York: Beacon Press.
Chandler-Olcott, K., & Mahar, D. (2003). "Tech-savviness" meets multiliteracies: Exploring adolescent girls' technology-mediated literacy practices. *Reading Research Quarterly, 38*(3), 356–385.
Coll, G. C., Lamberty, G., Jenkins, R., McAdoo, H. P., Crnic, K., Wasik, B. H., et al. (1996). An integrative model for the study of developmental competencies in minority children. *Child Development, 67*(5), 1891–1914.
Coll, G. C., & Szalacha, L. A. (2004). The multiple contexts of middle childhood. *The Future of Children, 14*(2), 81–97.
Compton-Lilly, C. (2011). Time and reading: Negotiations and affiliations of a reader, grades one through eight. *Research in the Teaching of English, 45*(3), 224–252.
Compton-Lilly, C. (2013). Literacy and identity construction across time and space: The case of Jermaine. *Journal of Adolescent and Adult Literacy, 56*(5), 400–408.
Compton-Lilly, C. (2014). The development of writing habitus: A ten-year case study of a young writer. *Written Communication, 31,* 371–403.
Elder, G. H. (1974). *Children of the great depression.* Chicago: University of Chicago Press.
Elder, G. H. (2001). Families, social change, and individual lives. *Marriage and Family Review, 31*(1 & 2), 177–192.
Goines, D. (1973). *White man's justice, Black man's grief.* New York: Holloway House.
Ladson-Billings, G. (2006). From the achievement gap to the education debt: Understanding achievement in US schools. *Educational Researcher, 35*(7), 3–12.
Leander, K., & McKim, K. (2003). Tracing the everyday "sitings" of adolescents on the Internet: A strategic adaptation of ethnography across online and offline spaces. *Education, Communication, and Information, 3*(2), 211–240.
Lewis, C., & Fabos, B. (2005). Instant messaging, literacies and social identities. *Reading Research Quarterly, 40*(4), 470–501.
Magnusson, D. (1995). Individual development: A holistic, integrated model. In P. Moen, G. H. Elder, & K. Lüscher (Eds.), *Examining lives in context* (pp. 19–60). Washington, DC: American Psychological Association.
McLeod, J. (2000). Subjectivity and schooling in a longitudinal study of secondary students. *British Journal of Sociology, 21*(4), 501–521.
McLeod, J. (2003). Why we interview now—reflexivity and perspective in a longitudinal study. *International Journal of Social Research Methodology, 6*(3), 201–211.

McMillan, T. (1987). *Mama*. New York: Houghton Mifflin.
Mills, K. A. (2010). Shrek meets Vygotsky: Rethinking adolescents' multimodal literacy practices in schools. *Journal of Adolescent and Adult Literacy, 54*(1), 35–45.
Moje, E. B. (2002). Re-framing adolescent literacy research for new times: Studying youth as a resource. *Reading Research and Instruction, 41*(3), 211–228.
Moje, E. B., Ciechanowski, K. M., Kramer, K., Ellis, L., Carrillo, R., & Collazo, T. (2004). Working toward third space in content area literacy: An examination of everyday finds of knowledge and discourse. *Reading Research Quarterly, 39*(1), 38–70.
Moje, E. B., Overby, M., Tysvaer, N., & Morris, K. (2008). The complex world of adolescent literacy: Myths, motivations, and mysteries. *Harvard Educational Review, 78*(1), 107–154.
Morrell, E. (2002). Toward a critical pedagogy of popular culture: Literacy development among urban youth. *Journal of Adolescent and Adult Literacy, 46*(1), 72–77.
No Child Left Behind Act (NCLB). (2001). Retrieved from *www.ed.gov/nclb/landing.jhtml*.
O'Brien, D. (2001). "At-risk" adolescents: Redefining competence through the multiliteracies of intermediality, visual arts, and representation. *Reading Online, 4*(11).
Ramey, L. C., Krauss, M. W., & Simeonsson, R. J. (1989). Research on families: Current assessment and future opportunities. *American Journal on Mental Retardation, 94*(3), ii–vi.
Sontag, J. C. (1996). Toward a comprehensive theoretical framework for disability research: Bronfenbrenner revisited. *Journal of Special Education, 30*(3), 319–344.
Stine, R. L. (1992–1997). *The goosebumps series*. New York: Scholastic Press.
Vasudevan, L. M. (2006). Looking for angels: Knowing adolescents by engaging with their multimodal literacy practices. *Journal of Adolescent and Adult Literacy, 50*(4), 252–256.

PART II
LOCATING ADOLESCENT LITERACIES

CHAPTER 8

Constructing Literacies in Secondary English Language Arts Curriculum
Discourses, Histories, Ethics

MARY JUZWIK, JENNIFER LYNN VANDERHEIDE, KATI MACALUSO, AMANDA SMITH, NATASHA PEREZ, SAMANTHA CAUGHLAN, MIKE MACALUSO, and CORI MCKENZIE

Winter break was winding down, and I (Cori) had exactly 1 week to fill in the contours of the unit on reading curriculum and instruction that my colleagues and I would teach in our secondary English methods course. I had a good sense of where the unit needed to go, but when it came to figuring out how to introduce the unit, I was at a loss. I had assumed that on that first day I would be able to rely on the way Jim Burke (2012) discussed reading in the course textbook, *The English Teacher's Companion, Fourth Edition*; as I reread the chapter, however, I realized that it was not going to work for my class.

The problem—if you can call it a problem—was that after spending a semester with my students, I realized that they were deeply enmeshed in discourses and assumptions about literacy espoused by the New Literacy studies. These preservice teachers were passionate about valuing the literacy practices students use outside of the classroom and about supporting students as they use these practices to make sense of themselves and the world around them. They planned to use hip-hop and film, Twitter and young adult (YA) literature in their curriculum, and they wanted all of their students to know that all languages and literate practices are important, meaningful, and beautiful. In short, my preservice teachers had learned to recognize and value the teeming multiplicity of literacies in students' lives.

Because I had gotten a sense of my students' commitment to valuing the pluralism in their classrooms, I could almost hear their critique of the Burke chapter on reading, as I reviewed it. I could see them reading the section titled "Reading: Past, Present, and Future" and getting worked up over Burke's concern with the way radio, TV, and the Internet have shaped reading. I could imagine them, for example, being infuriated by the fact that Burke frames Internet literacy practices as destroying our "old linear thought process" and contributing to a "slow erosion of our humanness and our humanity" (Carr, cited in Burke, 2012, p. 139). I could see them challenging the Burke text: "Who are you to determine what kinds of literate practices are best for humanity?" And when Burke details the work of scholars who have bemoaned the fact that schools "kill" students' desire to read books, including the "classics" that "offer wisdom . . . and 'imaginative rehearsals for the real world,' " (Gallagher, cited in Burke, 2012, p. 140), I could hear my students arguing that songs, advertisements, film, and oral histories could all offer wisdom and "imaginative rehearsals" for the world. As I read on and on in this chapter, I realized that my students would read Burke as "old school"—as embracing a definition of literacy that felt foreign, strange, and problematic.

We don't think Cori's teaching dilemma is anomalous; we think it is illustrative. According to one ongoing study, the Burke (2012) text is one of the two most widely used English methods texts in secondary English teacher preparation today (Caughlan, 2015). And acclaimed English educator Deborah Appleman (2011) salutes the book as one of the field's most important and enduring texts. Yet, like many popular textbooks, it does not consistently present "cutting-edge" scholarly understandings of one of the most central constructs of the English language arts (ELA): literacy. Thus, the tension Cori experienced between her students' pluralistic conceptualizations of reading and the narrowed, traditional notions of reading being advanced in this portion of *The English Teacher's Companion* serves to encapsulate the dilemmas that we, as former English teachers and practicing English teacher-educators, experience regularly: How do we articulate robust and scholarly understandings of literacy (or literacies, as Cori's students want to recognize) in relation to the secondary school curricular entity known as "English language arts"? This chapter invites readers into our ongoing exploration of this question.

FROM "LITERACY" TO "LITERACIES"

We define *literacies*, in the plural, as socially situated events, practices, and traditions of knowing about, understanding, feeling about, identifying with, valuing, co-constructing and/or participating in the use of *discourse(s)*. We define *discourse*, in turn, as language-in-use.[1] If literacies are always embedded in, emerging from, and actively shaping cultural, economic, ethical, ethnic, emotional, historical, ideological, linguistic, political, racial, religious, and other large- and small-scale contextual forces (e.g., Cushman, 2011; Heath, 1983; Kirkland, 2013; Street, 1984), it follows that different literacies—and their sponsors—historically evolve in processes of struggle with one another (Brandt, 2001). This struggle manifests along a continuum from implicit tension to open conflict, depending on the level of explicit theorization of values attached to competing literate practices/traditions (Gee, 2012).

This definition, and the tradition of New Literacies scholarship from which it emerges, serves to highlight the pluralism, the myriad literate practices in individual and

---

[1] We define literacy broadly here, following the spirit of current work in New Literacies Studies, in a way that does not restrict literacy to *written* language-in-use. It is worth noting, however, that not all members of our author team find this definition helpful or useful for their work. This broad definition does, however, allow us to make a clearer argument about the tensions we have experienced as students and scholars of literacy who also work in secondary ELA teacher education.

collective life. This pluralistic stance on literacy responds to, and resists, a still-dominant psychological perspective often assumed for purposes of schooling: that literacy is a singular, linear, developmental process similarly experienced by all individuals, as well as by all cultures progressing toward modernity. Taking this stance allows us to foreground issues of how, and by whom, different literacies are valued or devalued. Such a broad, pluralistic definition of literacy also allows us to frame the secondary ELA curriculum as one (of many) sites where situated literate practices occur, develop, and enter into struggle. With "one (of many) sites," we refer not only to English as one of many school subjects but also to the many sites in young people's and teachers' lives where situated literate practices occur, develop, and enter into struggle. Other such sites have been the topic of a good deal of New Literacies studies scholarship: families; virtual affinity groups; athletic teams; musical, theatrical, and other artistic troupes; churches and other religious or spiritual networks; workplaces; libraries; and so on.

Among the school subjects, however, English occupies an interesting position in relation to literacy/ies, because it is where "literacy" has traditionally been assumed to be taught, notwithstanding the growing push-back against this assumption in recent years, often under the banner of "disciplinary literacies." Conceiving of the ELA curriculum as a primary site for the construction of literacies raises questions of how literacies have come to be defined in secondary English. It also opens up the possibility that literacies might be constructed very differently in ELA classrooms.

ELA CURRICULUM IN HISTORY: READING, WRITING, SPEAKING

The contemporary idea of the English language arts (i.e., a school subject defined around the domains of reading, writing, speaking, and listening) can be traced to a book written by B. A. Hinsdale, who became a professor of education at the University of Michigan after a long career as teacher, principal, school superintendent, and Protestant pastor. His *Teaching the Language Arts: Speech, Reading, Composition* (1897) put forth the idea of the *language arts* as a curricular domain inclusive of the arts of reading, writing, and speech. This manner of construing the ELA arts as a school subject has been remarkably durable for over a century in the United States. The Common Core State Standards (CCSS) similarly map the literacy terrain of U.S. secondary English (National Governors Association Center for Best Practices & Council of Chief State School Officers, NGA & CCSSO, 2010) into the categories of reading (literature and informational text), writing, speaking and listening, and language. Many have worked to reimagine the ELA curriculum during the last decades of the 20th century and early into the 21st century (e.g., Langer, 1995; Mahiri, 1998; Morrell, 2005). However, most such efforts, carried out by university researchers, have failed to seed a widespread change in the lived curriculum of secondary English.

CHAPTER OVERVIEW

This chapter maps how literacies have been—and might be—constructed historically, ethically, and discursively across the curricular domains of "ELA." To frame this mapping, we first illuminate a central struggle shaping the construction of literacies in ELA, between

- The pull of pluralization (including both students' lives and languages, and the proliferating diversity of textual practices and modalities in which they engage).
- The pull of standardization aiming to narrow, reduce, and "school" the diversity of literacies included and valorized in the ELA curriculum.

We then consider how literacies are and have been constructed within the domains of reading/literature, writing, and speaking in the ELA curriculum.[2] In light of this domain mapping, we imagine how literacies might be (re)constructed across ELA curriculum domains to respond to pluralist literacies in our society in generative, imagination-opening ways. In the spirit of reimagining ELA, we conclude with a discussion of emerging and possible future directions for conceptualizing literacies across the ELA curriculum.

CONTEXTUAL FORCES SHAPING LITERATE PRACTICES IN THE U.S. ELA CURRICULUM

If, as we assume, literacies are embedded in, emerging from, and actively shaping ideological, historical, linguistic, racial, ethical, economic, political, cultural, ethnic, and other large- and small-scale contextual forces, then it only makes sense to ground our discussion of how literacies are constructed in ELA in at least some of these fields of force. Two fields of force (among many) in this particular historical moment frame our argument. First are the diverse languages, literacies, and life worlds of students in contemporary U.S. classrooms and the diversity and complexity of texts that circulate in their lives. Second, standardization looms large in the rhetoric surrounding the current state of curriculum, assessment, and pedagogy in schooling generally, and in ELA specifically. These fields of force often collide in English teacher preparation programs and classrooms alike—a theme explored throughout the chapter.

Languages, Literacies, and Pluralism

Student Language Diversity and Literacies

Our discourse-focused definition of literacy builds on scholarship in sociolinguistics that positions language as fluid rather than fixed, responsive rather than determined, and creative rather than rote (e.g., Blommaert & Rampton, 2012). This stance illuminates how, historically, "English" in the language arts has been constructed to mirror society at large, where only one variety, the standard edited English variety (i.e., Dominant American English), is valued in schools, businesses, and workplaces. Critical and decolonizing orientations to language study, historically marginalized languages, and multilingual practices have reached a new level of prominence as scholars push back on the ways that

---

[2] Because our definition of literacies centers language-in-use (i.e., discourse) and because we center discourse in our conceptualization of the English *language* arts curriculum, we choose to weave a discussion of language throughout these domains, rather than pulling it out as a domain of ELA in its own right (e.g., as the Common Core does).

powerful majorities have used existing language hierarchies and strategies of linguistic imperialism to marginalize nondominant language speakers (e.g., Canagarajah, 1999). This work also foregrounds the relationship between people's languages and identities as fundamental to their senses of self, their self-efficacy, and their ethical orientation to the world, so much so that disparaging a student's language can have long-lasting and damaging effects on his or her learning and achievement in school (e.g., Paris, 2011).

Shifting perceptions of what *language* is and does, then, impact understandings about literacy. Like literacies, language is not something we *have*, but rather something that we *do*; people *language and translanguage* (e.g., Pennycook, 2010)—what might be called the "languaging" perspective. Instead of language conceptualized as only a discrete set of skills, attention turns instead to speakers, relationships, practices, purposes, and processes by and through which language happens. Secondary students never come to school without language, although they may use a nondominant language or another discursive variation that makes sense in their world. The shifting demographics in U.S. schools (e.g., two languages are increasingly becoming the new norm in U.S. households (U.S. Census Bureau, 2011),[3] moreover, require an assumption of difference, in which difference resides not just in the language but in the ideological, historical, linguistic, racial, ethical, economic, political, cultural, and/or ethnic forces(s) interacting with students' grammars, vocabularies, and discourses as they engage in secondary ELA. Students' diverse worlds evoke and prepare them for many different literacies—many different ways of knowing, feeling, understanding, being, valuing, and ultimately *languaging* in the classroom.

Textual Diversities and Literacies

If language and other dimensions of difference are assumed to shape constructions of literacies in ELA classrooms, then so too are the diverse modes and text types shaping language use in students' and teachers' lives. *Multimodality* is one term that has been used to describe this textual pluralism. While the term *mode* has a considerable, and at times checkered, past in the history of writing instruction, for our purposes in this chapter, we identify a representational or communication mode when "a person and a community treats something as able to express and represent meanings" (Rowsell, 2013, p. 3). This stance seems ethically vital, because it (re)distributes power to know, value, and demonstrate knowledge and emotion across the widest possible span of people and communities. It embraces epistemic and semiotic diversity, favoring multiplicity over singularity. Hence, the *multi* serves an important role in the term *multimodal*, beyond just suggesting that there are many ways to communicate. Rather, it affirms the fact that a multitude of ways of knowing and representing knowledge are not only legitimate but also preferable.

A rich history of research on multimodality threads through literacy studies, and has penetrated the ELA to some extent. The New London Group (1996), for example, pushed literacy scholars and educators to consider a broader range of modes as texts. Literacy scholars continue to theorize about multimodality and to consider implications for ELA (e.g., Leander & Boldt, 2013; Pahl & Rowsell, 2012). One outcome of the scholarly interest in multimodality is its appearance throughout the last decade in university syllabi for ELA courses geared toward pre- and inservice teachers. Many English teacher-educators

---

[3]For further information about shifting linguistic demographics of U.S. households, see *www.infoplease.com/ipa/a0762163.html#ixzz3zs6ubikk*.

would say it is critical to prepare future teachers to help students develop literacy skills across modes. However, many teachers feel that they remain underprepared to teach students multimodal literacy skills and confront challenges when doing so (Ajayi, 2011). For example, they grapple with how English classrooms and curricula remain deeply committed to modes entrenched in "traditional" literacy practices sanctioned over 100 years ago. Yet teachers like Cori and her students, who recognize ELA as a scene of struggle about whose literacy "counts," recognize that the sanctioned "modes-as-usual" in ELA functioned historically, and continue to function, to maintain status quo positions of power and privilege for those who are male, White, and wealthy, by excluding "the other"—people of color, women, the poor, immigrants.

And so, many schools seem not truly interested in multimodality, because taking it seriously would require a tectonic shift in philosophical and ethical commitments. It would require reconfiguring whose modes and engagements with texts are sanctioned and practiced in secondary English. Therefore, sanctioned modes of reading and writing print, alphabetic text, in English, have remained remarkably stable as the semiotic currency in U.S. English classrooms since the time of Hinsdale. Often, when the ELA curriculum invokes multimodality, it signifies something more akin to learning styles. For example, music or visuals or the movement of bodies become an entry point for material (e.g., a poetry unit begins with musical lyrics as a "bridge" to writing and reading traditional poetry). These so-called "modes" are leveraged in the service of moving students toward greater skill with traditional literacy practices. Such activities serve the project of developing traditional modes of engaging alphabetic print text rather than helping students expand their literate repertoires, their representations of what they know and feel, what they can do with language, and, indeed, how their use of language shapes and is shaped by their identity. Thus, while multimodality is, at the very core, about epistemic, ontological, emotional, and representational inclusivity, English as a school subject often remains tied to the singular and the exclusionary. This exclusionary narrowing continues as the standardization movement in school systems around the world rages on.

Standardization

We lack space to review the full history of standardization(s) in the United States or globally, so we focus our discussion on the movement that began in the United States in the late 20th century. The moral panic over student achievement prompted by the *A Nation at Risk* report resulted in an unlikely confederation of social conservatives, business leaders, and neoliberal reformers seeking to save education from educators (National Commission on Educational Excellence, 1983). The NGA encouraged states to define the domains of the core subjects, including ELA, and to test students across each state in particular grades to assess how schools were doing in meeting the standards. According to these reformers, once teachers and students could identify the target, they would work to hit it (e.g., Pearson & Hiebert, 2014).

Two engines drove the standardization movement: the impetus toward critical thinking and innovation to create a smarter citizenry and workforce that would continue to keep America the leader of the information economy (Reich, 1991), and the desire to hold schools and districts accountable for teaching all students foundational skills and common knowledge. National subject-matter organizations, such as the National Council of Teachers of English (NCTE), attempted to lead the movement in their own particular areas, but trying to forge consensus within such pluralistic organizations was a contentious process, and few were happy with the results (Mayher, 1999). Within the states, constructivists warred with formalists; multiculturalists, with those committed to preserving the canonical literary heritage; and self-expressionists warred with utilitarians. The result was a series of political compromises that produced definitions of the domain of English that would have looked very familiar to Hinsdale and his contemporaries. Under the pressure of competing visions, the vision of English familiar to the business leaders and politicians who fondly recalled their grammar lessons and struggles with Shakespeare won out (Caughlan & Beach, 2007). This pattern continues today: Pearson (2013b), found that when research did not offer a definitive path for sequencing learning goals in the CCSS, choices were largely made on the basis of what had gone before.

It was, however, not the standards as written that had the greatest impact on the English curriculum and on literacy practices in the classroom, but the standards as tested. If the standards presented a limited view of the ELA, the standardized tests that assessed achievement to standard narrowed the curriculum still further. Neither all standards nor all topics listed in standards would be tested. The speaking and listening standards were the first to fall. Some states attempted to standardize the assessment of public speaking skills, and still others tried to standardize the assessment of writing portfolios (Pearson, 2013a), but these efforts were largely abandoned as time-consuming, expensive, and lacking in scientific validity. The forms of assessment that have persisted throughout the standardization movement reflect a rather narrow concept of what it means to be literate. For example, the part of the test labeled "writing" in some tests consists of multiple-choice items in which students have to locate errors in punctuation or choose the correct conjunction for a sample sentence. This very pattern is replicated in the new writing portion of the Scholastic Aptitude Test (SAT). The literacy skills required to succeed in many state standardized ELA tests were limited to low-level reading comprehension of short passages, recognizing the standard form of the language, and writing five-paragraph essays in response to decontextualized prompts. Literate activity in too many ELA classrooms moved toward teacher-centered recitation around texts and drills of grammar and vocabulary (Srikantaiah, Zhang, & Swayhoover, 2008), practice writing of short essays to prepare for tests (Dawson, 2013), and close reading of multiple-choice questions in the attempt to make students more test-savvy, particularly in low socioeconomic status (SES) districts (Sunderman, Tracey, Kim, & Orfield, 2004).

Though little scholarship between 1985 and 2012 has centered on the preparation of English teacher candidates to address standards (Pasternak, Caughlan, Hallman, Renzi, & Rush, 2014), evidence suggests that standardization will continue to impact the construction of literacies as it infiltrates teacher education programs. The most commonly assigned texts in ELA methods classes make only perfunctory references to standards—with Burke's text being a notable exception—but this rhetoric seems to be changing with the implementation and assessment of the CCSS. During the period when standards were being developed and implemented, however, English educators did publish commentary mostly critical of standards, both the very idea of standards and specific standards. Both progressive and traditional educators leveled this criticism (e.g., Rush & Scherff, 2011; Stotsky, 2012). Despite the criticism, the forms of literacy foregrounded by the Common Core reproduce the historically enduring—and fairly narrow—ways of defining and constructing literacy in ELA, narrowing the field of literate possibilities for English classrooms in an ever-more-pluralistic world.

CONSTRUCTING LITERACIES WITHIN THE DOMAINS OF ELA

With an eye on the tension between ever-expanding discourses of students, families, and communities on the one hand, and the ever-narrowing forces of standardization in early 21st-century schooling on the other, we turn to a discussion of how literacies are constructed within three enduring domains of ELA curriculum—reading, writing, and speaking. We focus on these three domains not necessarily because we wholeheartedly endorse them as the best way to imagine or delineate secondary English, but because they remain dominant in the practice(s) of categorizing and doing on-the-ground secondary English. In light of our definition of literacies, in the plural, it's worth keeping in mind that these sites of literate practice struggle with one another for prominence, not only in the English classroom but also in society at large (e.g., Brandt, 2014).

Reading

Considering how literacies are constructed within the curricular domain of reading in secondary ELA seems to warrant a consideration of the *what* (texts, both within and beyond alphabetic print), the *how* (the particular pedagogical approaches that teachers of reading and literature enact), and the *why* (the ends or larger purposes that reading and literature serve). While the texts included in secondary English curriculum have been expanding to include informational and other sorts of reading, here we primarily focus on reading in relation to "literature," because of its long-standing place in the secondary curriculum, and because it highlights the place of "verbal art" within ELA. In the interest of space, we also choose to limit our discussion to the *what* and the *why* of the literature curriculum, while recognizing that curriculum theorists would argue that the aims and content of the curriculum always carry with them a set of pedagogical implications.

Despite the different permutations of what might be possible at the various intersections of the content, purposes, and pedagogies of literature instruction, scholars have referred to the secondary literature curriculum as a relative still life (Grossman, 2001). Indeed, research has shown that the presence of canonical texts in the curriculum has remained remarkably stable, despite calls to vary the titles and kinds of texts taught in schools. For the most part, students have been reading the same content in English classrooms for the past several decades (Applebee, 1993; Grossman, 2001; Stotsky, 2010). A recent survey of book-length works taught in secondary schools found an increase in the diversity of multicultural, YA, and contemporary literature, yet the top 10 most commonly taught works (e.g., *Romeo and Juliet, The Great Gatsby, The Odyssey,* and *To Kill a Mockingbird*) has remained relatively unchanged. These trends within secondary ELA classrooms certainly paint a picture of stability in favor of written alphabetic print and a Western, White, male author population, despite the range and variety of verbally artful texts (e.g., song lyrics, images, videos, young adult literature) that students are taking up outside of schools.

But, as much as literature and reading in the secondary ELA classroom have remained a relative still life, the many and oftentimes competing purposes of literature instruction suggest greater tension and mobility in the field of English education. Caughlan (2007), for example, has written about the use of literature to "mediate pastoral relationships"—a practice "related to using literature to mold the values and dispositions of students" (p. 185). These more ethical invocations of reading and literature instruction have roots in a 19th-century Sunday school pedagogy that employed literature to cultivate not only students' minds but also their hearts and souls by interpolating them into Protestant Christian moral traditions (Brass, 2011). Dixon (1967) and others advocated for a "growth model" of literature instruction, with literature functioning in that model as a vehicle for students to process personal experience and grow as human beings.

While the purposes of literary instruction outlined earlier conceive of literature as capable of shaping the self, the literature curriculum has also been used to shape communities, nations, and other collectives. Anagnostopoulos, Everett, and Carey (2013) identify the ELA curriculum as a site for building and maintaining cultural memory, looking in particular at the use of Lee's *To Kill a Mockingbird* as a source for constructing cultural memory of race and racism in the United States. As other examples, Spiegelman's *Maus* and Wiesel's memoir *Night* have become increasingly popular in middle and secondary classrooms as means of remembering the atrocities of the Holocaust. As these examples suggest, literary instruction often aims to disrupt, inform, or affirm students' beliefs and understandings about the past. Haddix and Price-Dennis (2013) reference the possibilities and potential for multicultural and urban fiction to challenge preconceived biases and to better come to know diverse peoples. Similarly, Appleman (2009) has argued, "Our responsibility as literature teachers is to help make the ideologies inherent in . . . texts visible to our students" (p. 3) through the use of specific literary lenses, so that readers may become more ideologically aware. For these spokespersons and others like them, literature serves as a catalyst for collective remembering and social change.

Many rationales for teaching literature seem to position literature instruction as a scene for inspiration, disruption, empathy, personal growth, and so forth. A more technocratic reason for teaching literature, elaborated upon and backed by the writers of the CCSS, seems to narrow the possible activities, actions, and events that emerge from reading literature. The purposes of informational and literary reading look almost identical in standards put forth by the Common Core, with the verbs *analyze* and *determine* constituting the only two actions involved in reading. This treatment of reading—both literary and informational—as a vehicle for analysis aligns the domain of reading and literature with the primary aspiration of the Common Core: college and career readiness.

Perhaps, then, a central question that might guide investigation and consideration of the domain of literature and reading in ELA, and its role in constructing literacies, is "For *whom* is literature being taught?" The U.S. Conference on English Education envisions the persons engaged in the literary curriculum of ELA as "creative," as "contributors to the cultural, social, and economic health of their communities," and as "fully participating and critically aware citizens of our democracy in a complex, diverse, and increasingly globalized world" (*What is English Education?*, 2005, paragraph 2). This last point, in particular, which reminds us of the role that reading literature might play in students' participation in a *complex, diverse,* and *increasingly globalized* world, suggests to us that the domain of reading and literature cannot afford to be the "still life" that scholars have described. In an age of increasing linguistic, religious, and cultural pluralism, teachers and teacher-educators would do well to advocate for texts that reflect an increasingly globalized and cosmopolitan world, and to structure their pedagogy around rationales that allow students to enact the skills, dispositions, inquiry, and so forth, that are part and parcel of living in a pluralistic society.

Writing

Like reading, the writing that students do in school, what is assigned and taught, and what counts as writing are influenced by a constellation of forces, including those discussed earlier—language diversities, multimodality, and standards/standardization. These various forces have led to tensions in secondary ELA classrooms as schools, teachers, and students act within conflicting systems. Digital tools in particular have afforded sweeping changes in how people compose, who reads what they write, and the impact an individual's writing can have in the world.

Although the forms and uses of writing have changed greatly out of school, like reading, writing in school tends to look relatively similar to writing decades ago (e.g., Langer & Applebee, 1987), resulting in a gap between students' in-school and out-of-school compositional practices. Even when adolescents make use of digital tools, they often use technology to do the same types and forms of writing traditionally taught in secondary classrooms. In a study of argumentative writing instruction in 33 high school ELA classrooms, Newell, Bloome, and Hirvela (2015) found that most of the teachers neither assigned argumentative writing that was multimodal nor made use of digital tools beyond Internet research or word processing to do that writing. However, research and our own experience in classrooms has shown that some teachers are providing students with opportunities to compose digitally and multimodally, to compose in nontraditional genres such as fanfiction, and to reach out to audiences beyond the classroom (Hicks, 2013; Rish & Caton, 2011). As many English educators are integrating digital literacies into methods courses, we see great potential for writing in classrooms to more closely align with the types of writing adolescents do now and will compose out of school.

Another tension constructing writing in classrooms is that of writing as form versus writing as content. The CCSS (NGA & CCSO, 2010) imposed three genres onto school writing: narrative, exposition, and argumentative writing, with a particular emphasis on argumentative writing in the secondary grades. The language of these standards focuses more on the elements of these forms rather than on the content of the writing or the social goals students accomplish as they write. As Hillocks' (2005) research has shown, the demands of standards and standardized assessments directly influence writing instruction in secondary classrooms, suggesting that school writing may continue to be limited to narrow conceptualizations of these three types of writing. Hillocks (2005) lamented the typical focus on form in secondary classrooms, pointing to the influence of standardized tests and the nature of fill-in-the-blank forms as quick and somewhat effective test preparation. Our own time in classrooms supports Hillocks's findings that classroom writing is often reduced to formulaic texts rather than a means of building students' ideas or a method for participating in the classroom and beyond (Newell, VanDerHeide, & Wynhoff Olsen, 2014). These forms can include particular elements, such as the inclusion of various dimensions of Toulmin's (1958) argumentative model, and can even extend to strict organizational structures, such as the five-paragraph essay (Johnson, Thompson, Smagorinsky, & Fry, 2003). Although many of the forms students write in English classes do not reflect any type of writing in the "real world," these classroom-based forms persist, because they are well suited to standardized writing tests.

Additionally, defining how writing is constructed is also made difficult by the contextualized nature of literacies, so that what writing is and what counts as writing is constructed within highly particular classroom contexts (Heath & Street, 2008). Anyone who spends time in classrooms understands how each classroom community creates differing literacy practices, so the writing students do and how they do it will vary from classroom to classroom. However, rather than celebrating the diversity of writing across classrooms and the agency students bring as meaning makers in these spaces, national standards and standardized assessments push to make writing similar across all classrooms in our country and ensure that all students can write well in the same way and at the same time. This standardization is complicated even more by the fact that, as researchers, teacher-educators, and teachers, our field lacks a common understanding of what it means to learn to write (Applebee, 2000; Behizadeh & Engelhard, 2011), resulting in a variety of teaching and assessment practices. Across the previous century, writing studies has shifted from various understandings of what writing is and what it means to learn to write, from textual qualities such as grammar and syntax, to writing processes, such as the cognitive processes involved in drafting and revision, to flexible participation in social and rhetorical contexts. Teachers, in turn, have shifted their pedagogical focus from textual characteristics, such as using isolated grammar and mechanics worksheets, to approaches more centered on the writing process.

Speaking

The curricular domain of speaking may fare best among the three ELA domains when literacies are broadly construed to extend beyond the purview of written alphabetic print. Indeed, the pluralist push of students' diverse languages and literacies suggests an increasingly important role for speaking in the ELA curriculum. Yet student speaking seems more ephemeral, and therefore less measurable, than student writing. Perhaps for this reason, alongside the contention surrounding "students' right to their own languages" in US schools, speaking is often relegated to an instrumental use in secondary English: "talking to learn" (Britton, 1989) rather than "learning to talk" (Alexander, 2008). In the United States, speaking often becomes the medium through which learning happens in the secondary ELA curriculum (as well as other subject matters) rather than the stuff to be learned. To consider how literacies are constructed in relation to speaking in ELA curriculum, it is worth exploring both approaches to speaking—speaking as the ELA curricular content focus and speaking as an instructional instrument of other ELA curriculum domains.

The curricular content of speaking as a focus in secondary English has historical roots in the Western rhetorical tradition, which grounded Hinsdale's (1897) ideas about "speech" as a domain of ELA. Aristotle (1991) defined *rhetoric* as the ability to find the means of persuasion in any given situation and Quintilian (1958), deeply indebted to Isocrates before him, advanced an ethical purpose of rhetorical education by advocating that it produce "a good man [sic] speaking well" (12.1.1). Quintilian's methods of rhetorical education, still widely circulated in 19th- and early 20th-century U.S. schools and colleges, included carefully sequenced, cumulative practice with exercises designed to teach students a systematic method for speaking well (Murphy, 1987). For example, students imitate others' use of spoken language by memorizing, paraphrasing, or transliterating a speech from one language to another. They retell fables. They impersonate, or speak in the character of, a given person. They prepare and deliver deliberative speeches (arguing whether an action should be taken or not) and forensic speeches (arguing whether or not historical or fictional persons are guilty of some wrongdoing). The interplay among reading, writing, and speaking is constant, with "critical listening an important adjunct" skill (Murphy, 1987, p. xxiv). Such a curriculum generally focused on lengthy speeches and sustained discourse in the "public sphere" rather than on expressive talk, such as intimate narratives about everyday personal experience.

As rhetoric fell out of fashion across the 20th century, secondary ELA came to focus more on speaking as an instrument for learning across the ELA curriculum. Particularly after the Dartmouth Seminar in 1966, the idea of *talking to learn* got taken up enthusiastically in the United States (Dixon, 1967). In the early 1970s, college composition scholars and teachers advanced the idea that all students should have opportunities not only to talk to learn but also to engage in learning talk in their own languages and dialects (Students' Right to Their Own Language, 1974). While the historical document focused largely on African American language (AAL) speakers in the United States, the idea of students' Rights to Their Own Languages has taken on new meanings in our pluralistic, transnationally connected, multilingual society.

Continuing this focus on speaking as instrument in ELA curriculum, the 1990s saw the advent of a conversational turn in speaking. Drawing upon the work of Bakhtin (e.g., 1981), Nystrand, with Gamoran, Kachur, and Prendergast (1997) documented a correlation between dialogically organized instructional environments (identifiable by authentic teacher questions, teacher uptake of student responses, student questions, and open discussion) and student literacy achievement growth in reading comprehension. Marshall, Smagorinsky, and Smith (1995) conceptualized classroom discourse as a "speech genre" (Bakhtin, 1986), highlighting how teachers could productively model talk moves in small-group literary discussions. Juzwik, Nystrand, Kelly, and Sherry (2008) alternatively suggested the importance of conceptualizing classroom discourse as a meta-genre comprised of genres such as narrative, argument, exposition, and so on. It follows that different genres of speaking in ELA classrooms might support practice and development in reading and writing different genres (e.g., written argument in Nystrand & Graff, 2001).

Connecting the instrumental function of speaking to its (potential) function as curricular content to be learned, practiced, and performed, Smitherman (1977)—who coauthored "Students Right to Their Own Language" (1974)—further documented how AAL speakers' forms of talk enact complex verbal artfulness. By comparing the oral language practices of African American speakers to the literary practices of African American writers, Smitherman (1977) showed how AAL speaking was functionally akin to the verbal arts often being studied or produced in secondary English. Lee (1993) amplified this insight to show how spoken AAL (e.g., signifying) could support students' cognitive development of literary understanding. More broadly, conversational narrative talk can function as verbal art in its own right. Juzwik and Sherry (2007) showcased a middle school ELA classroom in which teacher and students performed narrative verbal art as a mode of responding to literature. Rather than merely "analyses" of literature (e.g., NGA & CCSSO, 2010), such speaking acts were performances of verbal art and functioned like the literary narratives under study.

Learning to speak "correct" English—circulating, powerful, and exceedingly narrow definitions of what it means to be a "good man [sic] speaking well"—has been a burden and legacy of ELA against which many English teachers and teacher-educators have struggled. Many want to embrace and celebrate literacies in the plural in ELA classrooms. We ourselves cringe when, in response to learning our identities as "English teacher," someone says, "Oh, I had better watch my grammar!" And so it has seemed simpler to focus on speaking as curricular instrument versus curricular goal. Yet we gladly find the Common Core calling for the "ability to listen attentively to others so that [high school graduates] are able to build on others' meritorious ideas while expressing their own clearly and persuasively" (NGA & CCSSO, 2010, p. 48). Implied in this statement, as we interpret it, is oral communication across all manner of difference. Learning to articulately, appropriately, and powerfully speak, and learning to listen attentively and critically seem especially vital skills and dispositions in an ever more pluralistic world in which acts of speaking, reading, and writing intertwine to help people accomplish actions in the world.

(RE)CONSTRUCTING LITERACIES TO (RE)ENVISION THE ELA CURRICULUM

Our vision for constructing literacies in ELA classrooms foregrounds the lived experiences of young people and the plurality of language and literacy practices in which they engage in and out of the classroom. Although tension between standards and the diverse lived literacies of adolescents will likely persist, we believe secondary ELA classrooms can be spaces in which students meet and exceed the standards while expanding their participation in local and global literacy practices. Here we move somewhat in reverse relative to our earlier discussion, beginning with language and moving to speaking, writing, then reading.

A Discourse-Centered Vision of Secondary ELA Curriculum

Our vision for the centrality of discourse and languaging in the ELA curriculum is certainly not new (e.g., Students' Right to Their Own Language, 1974; Heath, 1983; Morrell, 2005), but it has yet to be embraced on the ground in secondary ELA curriculum in the United States—including in ELA teaching textbooks like Burke's. It moves beyond rules and narrow standards of linguistic correctness toward considerations of the kinds of speaking, writing, and reading appropriate within various social worlds. It places at the center of the ELA curriculum the different ways diverse peoples use language; the values attached to these practices; the different accents, vocabularies, grammars, discourses, and varieties that exist; how various discourse practices come to be seen as verbally artful across cultural (and others sorts of) worlds; and what these differences and diversities mean and how they act in and on the world. Such a curricular shift may involve students and teachers noticing and even studying how languages and literacies are used in the communities from which students hail, acknowledging the many different ways of knowing, feeling, being, and languaging in everyday life; and incorporating these discoveries as units of study and discussion in the ELA classroom. The reframing of language difference as a resource can lead to asset-based pedagogies that welcome students' myriad languages into the classroom. We feel a sense of urgency in centering this more expansive view of discourse in ELA as a way of helping all students thrive, not only in ELA classrooms, but in their academic lives more generally.

Envisioning Speaking in Secondary ELA Curriculum

If the capacity to artfully construe and attentively listen to oral language is taken as a central aim of speaking in ELA, then what kinds of talk should students learn and practice in English? To be sure, the disciplinary discourse practice of ELA includes "language about language" and study of how discourse works. But more importantly, it involves the cultivation and performance of the kind of flexible verbal artfulness heralded and taught by Quintilian (1958) and others in the Western rhetorical tradition. Perhaps returning to some of the wisdom of that tradition (if not its narrowing and marginalizing legacies) might be helpful for cultivating some of these capacities. When English is understood as the humanities discipline concerned with the "how" of the verbal arts—inclusive of all manner of orally, digitally, and iconically mediated language—then teachers and curriculum and standards developers need to think about critical questions: What does it mean to hold students, who hail from linguistically and culturally pluralistic backgrounds, to some kind of English-discipline-specific spoken discourse features? Does, or should it, mean that everyone speaks "dominant American English" (i.e., everyone sounds the same)? We don't think so. We envision preparing students for communication and engagement with verbal arts of all kinds, across differences of all kinds (e.g., linguistic, ethnic, religious) in the ever-expanding universe of global discourse. As a discipline concerned with the verbal arts, it seems that English is especially well-poised (1) to appreciate, savor, and delight in the wide diversity of verbal artfulness that students bring to the classroom when invited and inclined to do so and (2) to expand students' capacities to speak artfully and appropriately in a variety of given situations, perhaps most especially encounters with diverse others.

Envisioning Writing in the Secondary ELA Curriculum

An alternative answer to the question, "What is writing in secondary ELA classrooms?" could be answered by a model of writing development proposed by Applebee (2000): *writing as participation in social action*. Applebee did not explicitly define or illustrate this model but suggested elements such as learning to write within a particular academic or social domain or classroom context, participating and acting in this domain or context with writing, and using writing to negotiate identity within cultural contexts. Rather than constructing writing as texts that students create in order to fulfill the demands of an assignment or a standard, ELA classrooms could construct writing as action that youth take as they participate in social worlds. These domains could be local, such as the school or local community, or larger, such as ongoing social conversations or the disciplines of literature or rhetoric. Writing as social action has the potential to afford students the opportunity to compose in real-world modes appropriate and effective for the given domain, allow students to write about meaningful content, and grow in their identity as writers. As an example, Jennifer VanDerHeide studied a teacher whose argumentative writing unit ended in the students collaboratively writing a letter to the principal requesting the privilege of leaving the school building at lunch. Together, the students gathered data for their argument, including published studies on learning and movement, as well as surveying teachers and students in their school. Through this collaborative writing, students learned how to participate in argument, how to conduct research and incorporate evidence into writing, and how to write to a particular audience; in the end, the principal did change the policy.

Envisioning (Literary) Reading in the Secondary ELA Curriculum

What is entailed in conceiving of literature as more than a vehicle for narrow analysis in an age of increasingly plural languages, identities, and texts? We imagine that entering a work of literature might be comparable to what Leander (as cited in Zancanella, 2007) described as figurative migration, where students might "trace the routes of moving people, moving culture, and moving texts" (p. 76). In the high school classrooms Michael Macaluso has visited, he observes teachers treating the literature curriculum as Applebee imagined it: as conversation across difference. One teacher, in describing her course plan, described her literature curriculum, consisting of texts such as Amy Tan's *Joy Luck Club*, Zora Neal Hurston's *Their Eyes Were Watching God*, and Steinbeck's *Of Mice and Men*, as allowing students to enter into different times, places, and experiences that afforded alternative points of view. If that sort of vision for literature instruction—a vision that conceives of reading as entering into relationships across time, space, and experience—is one that English educators wish to uphold, then a whole host of new questions begins to surface. Is reading—as suggested by the inclusion of standards increasingly devoted to informational texts—aimed toward knowing and understanding? In interviews with avid readers, Kati Macaluso has heard students, teachers, and librarians describe particular reading experiences as "haunting," "spine-tingling," "heartbreaking." And so we envision literature as a language *art*. Might individuals and communities participate in the language *arts*, then, by reading for the same reasons they find themselves visiting an art gallery or attending a live theatrical performance—to experience? to imagine? to inspire and feel? Our vision for reading instruction, like our discourse-centered, pluralized notion of literacies, invites teachers and students alike to live life in all its fullness and complexity.

CONCLUSION

Tensions between standardization and pluralization are those in which ELA teachers find themselves enmeshed every day in classrooms across the country. While policymakers attach ever-higher stakes to student proficiency on tests that "measure" achievement of narrow standards, the students who are to become proficient in these ways are ever-more engaged by forms of literacy not recognized by established ELA curricula and standards. This reality is not necessarily an unbridgeable gulf. Many students and parents value mastering discourses of power they see as gates to education, jobs, and so forth. Likewise, most teachers understand 21st-century literacies as moving targets. However, if we do not figure out how to bridge the divides between the pluralistic literacies beyond the classroom and the artificially constructed and constrictive literate practices of the traditional ELA classroom and practices, the school subject English may go the way of Latin and Greek at the end of the 19th century: widely acknowledged as culturally valuable and cognitively challenging but, in the end, obsolete.

REFERENCES

Ajayi, L. (2011). Preservice teachers' knowledge, attitudes, and perception of their preparation to teach multiliteracies/multimodality. *The Teacher Educator, 46*(1), 6–31.

Alexander, R. (2008). *Toward dialogic teaching: Rethinking classroom talk.* Cambridge, UK: Dialogos.

Anagnostopoulos, D., Everett, S., & Carey, C. (2013). "Of course we're supposed to move on, but then you still got people who are not over those historical wounds": Cultural memory and US youth's race talk. *Discourse and Society, 24*(2), 163–185.

Applebee, A. N. (1993). *Literature in the secondary school: Studies of curriculum and instruction in the United States* (NCTE Research Report No. 25). Urbana, IL: National Council of Teachers of English.

Applebee, A. N. (2000). Alternative models of writing development. In R. Indrisano & J. R. Squire (Eds.), *Perspectives on writing: Research, theory, and practice* (pp. 90–111). Newark, DE: International Reading Association.

Appleman, D. (2009). *Critical encounters in high school English: Teaching literary theory to adolescents* (2nd ed.). New York: Teachers College Press.

Appleman, D. (2011). The living library of NCTE. *English Journal, 101*(1), 48–52.

Aristotle. (1991). *On rhetoric: A theory of civic discourse* (G. A. Kennedy, Trans.) New York: Oxford University Press.

Bakhtin, M. M. (1981). *The dialogic imagination* (M. Holquist, Ed.; C. Emerson & M. Holquist, Trans.). Austin: University of Texas Press. (Original work published 1953)

Bakhtin, M. M. (1986). *Speech genres and other late essays* (V. W. McGee, Trans.; C. Emerson & M. Holquist, Eds.). Austin: University of Texas Press. (Original work published 1953)

Behizadeh, N., & Engelhard, G. (2011). Historical view of the influences of measurement and writing theories on the practice of writing assessment in the United States. *Assessing Writing, 16,* 189–211.

Blommaert, J., & Rampton, B. (2012). Language and superdiversity. Retrieved from *www.mmg.mpg.de/fileadmin/user_upload/documents/wp/wp_12-09_concept-paper_sld.pdf.*

Brandt, D. (2001). *Literacy in American lives.* New York: Cambridge University Press.

Brandt, D. (2014). *The rise of writing: Redefining mass literacy.* New York: Cambridge University Press.

Brass, J. (2011). Historicising English pedagogy: The extension and transformation of "the cure of souls." *Pedagogy, Culture and Society, 19*(1), 153–172.

Britton, J. (1989). *Language, the learner, and the school.* Portsmouth, NH: Heinemann. (Original work published 1969)

Burke, J. (2012). *The English teacher's companion, fourth edition: A completely new guide to classroom, curriculum, and the profession.* Portsmouth, NH: Heinemann.

Canagarajah, A. S. (1999). *Resisting linguistic imperialism in English teaching.* Oxford, UK: Oxford University Press.

Caughlan, S. (2007). Competing cultural models of literature in state content standards. In D. W. Rowe, R. T. Jimenez, D. L. Compton, D. K. Dickinson, Y. Kim, K. M. Leander, et al. (Eds.), *56th yearbook of the National Reading Conference* (pp. 178–190). Oak Creek, WI: National Reading Conference.

Caughlan, S. (2015). [Required texts in United States ELA methods course syllabi]. Lansing, MI: Unpublished raw data.

Caughlan, S., & Beach, R. (2007). Fissures in standards formulation: The role of neoconservative and neoliberal discourses in justifying standards development in Wisconsin and Minnesota. Retrieved from *http://epaa.asu.edu/epaa/v15n18.*

Cushman, E. (2011). *The Cherokee syllabary.* Norman: University of Oklahoma Press.

Dawson, C. (2013). Writing in the English language arts. In A. N. Applebee & J. A. Langer (Eds.), *Writing instruction that works: Proven methods for middle and high school classrooms* (pp. 28–49). New York: Teachers College Press.

Dixon, J. (1967). *Growth through English: A report based on the Dartmouth Seminar, 1966*. Reading, UK: National Association for the Teaching of English.

Gee, J. (2012). *Social linguistics and literacies: Ideology in discourses* (4th ed.). New York: Taylor & Francis.

Grossman, P. L. (2001). Research on the teaching of literature: Finding a place. In V. Richardson (Ed.), *Handbook of research on teaching* (4th ed., pp. 416–432). Washington, DC: American Educational Research Association.

Haddix, M., & Price-Dennis, D. (2013). Urban fiction and multicultural literature as transformative tools for preparing English teachers for diverse classrooms. *English Education, 45*(3), 247–283.

Heath, S. B. (1983). *Ways with words: Language, life and work in communities and classroom*. New York: Cambridge University Press.

Heath, S. B., & Street, B. V. (2008). *On ethnography: Approaches to language and literacy research*. New York: Teachers College Press.

Hicks, T. (2013). *Crafting digital writing: Composing texts across media and genres*. Portsmouth, NH: Heinemann.

Hillocks, G. (2005). At last: The focus on form vs. content in teaching writing. *Research in the Teaching of English, 40,* 238–248.

Hinsdale, B. A. (1897). Teaching the language-arts: Speech, reading, composition. Retrieved from *http://babel.hathitrust.org/cgi/pt?id=aeu.ark:/13960/t10p1gw4q;view=1up;seq=8)*.

Johnson, T. S., Thompson, L., Smagorinsky, P., & Fry, P. G. (2003). Learning to teach the five-paragraph theme. *Research in the Teaching of English, 38,* 136–176.

Juzwik, M. M., Nystrand, M., Kelly, S., & Sherry, M. B. (2008). Oral narrative genres as dialogic resources for classroom literature study: A contextualized case study of conversational narrative discussion. *American Educational Research Journal, 45*(4), 1111–1154.

Juzwik, M. M., & Sherry, M. B. (2007). Expressive language and the art of English teaching: Theorizing the relationship between literature and oral narrative. *English Education, 39*(3), 226–259.

Kirkland, D. (2013). *A search past silence: Literacy in the lives of young black men*. New York: Teachers College Press.

Langer, J. A. (1995). *Envisioning literature: Literary understanding and literature instruction*. New York: Teachers College Press.

Langer, J. A., & Applebee, A. N. (1987). *How writing shapes thinking: A study of teaching and learning* (NCTE Research Report No. 22). Urbana, IL: National Council of Teachers of English.

Leander, K., & Boldt, G. (2013). Rereading "A pedagogy of multiliteracies": Bodies, texts, and emergence. *Journal of Literacy Research, 45*(1), 22–46.

Lee, C. D. (1993). *Signifying as a scaffold for literary interpretation: The pedagogical implications of an African American discourse genre*. Urbana, IL: National Council of Teachers of English.

Mahiri, J. (1998). *Shooting for excellence: African American and youth culture in new century schools*. Urbana, IL: National Council of Teachers of English.

Marshall, J., Smagorinsky, P., & Smith, M. (1995). *The language of literary interpretation: Patterns of discourse in discussions of literature*. Urbana, IL: National Council of Teachers of English.

Mayher, J. (1999). Reflections on standards and standard setting: An insider/outsider perspective on the NCTE/IRA standards. *English Education, 31*(2), 106–121.

Morrell, E. (2005). Toward a critical English education: Reflections on and projections for the discipline. *English Education, 37*(4), 312–322.

Murphy, J. J. (1987). Editor's Introduction. *Quintilian on the teaching of speaking and writing: Translations from books one, two, and ten of the Institutio oratoria.* Carbondale: Southern Illinois University Press.

National Commission on Educational Excellence (NCEE). (1983). *A nation at risk: A report to the nation and the Secretary of Education.* Washington, DC: Author. Retrieved from *www2.ed.gov/pubs/NatAtRisk/risk.html.*

National Governors Association Center for Best Practices & Council of Chief State School Officers (NGA & CCSSO). (2010). *Common Core State Standards for English language arts and literacy, history/social studies, science, and technical subjects.* Washington, DC: Authors. Retrieved from *www.corestandards.org/wp-content/uploads/ela_standards.pdf.*

New London Group. (1996). A pedagogy of multiliteracies: Designing social futures. *Harvard Educational Review, 66*(1), 60–92.

Newell, G., Bloome, D., & Hirvela, A. (2015). *Teaching argumentative reading and writing in high school English language arts classrooms.* New York: Routledge.

Newell, G. E., VanDerHeide, J., & Wynhoff Olsen, A. (2014). High school English language arts teachers' argumentative epistemologies for teaching writing. *Research in the Teaching of English, 49*(2), 95–119.

Nystrand, M., with Gamoran, A., Kachur, R., & Prendergast, C. (1997). *Opening dialogue: Understanding the dynamics of language and learning in the English classroom.* New York: Teachers College Press.

Nystrand, M., & Graff, N. (2001). Report in argument's clothing: An ecological perspective. *Elementary School Journal, 101,* 470–493.

Pahl, K., & Rowsell, J. (2012). *Literacy and education: Understanding the new literacy studies in the classroom* (2nd ed.). London: Sage.

Paris, D. (2011). *Language across difference: Ethnicity, communication, and youth identities in changing urban schools.* New York: Cambridge University Press.

Pasternak, D. L., Caughlan, S., Hallman, H., Renzi, L., & Rush, L. (2014). Connecting past, present, and future: What is the state of the teaching of English in the 21st century? *Review of Education, 2*(2), 146–185.

Pearson, P. D. (2013a, April). *Assessment and the Common Core: Will our tests support or subvert our vision of deeper learning of English/language arts?* Paper presented at annual meeting of the International Reading Association, San Antonio, Texas. Retrieved from *http://textproject.org/assets/library/powerpoints/pearson-ira-2013-assessment-and-the-common-core.pdf.*

Pearson, P. D. (2013b). *Research and the Common Core: Can the romance survive?* Webinar presented for TextProject, January 25, 2013. Retrieved from *http://textproject.org/archive/webinars/common-core-state-standards-webinar-series-2/research-and-the-common-core-can-the-romance-survive.*

Pearson, P. D., & Hiebert, E. H. (2014). *Understanding the Common Core State Standards.* Santa Cruz, CA: Text Project. Retrieved from *http://textproject.org/assets/library/papers/pearson-hiebert-2013-understanding-the-ccss.pdf.*

Pennycock, A. (2010). *Language as a local practice.* New York: Routledge.

Quintilian. (1958). *The institutio oratoria* (Vols. I and II). Loeb Classic Library (H. E. Butler, Trans.). Cambridge, MA: Harvard University Press.

Reich, R. (1991). *The work of nations: Preparing ourselves for 21st-century capitalism.* New York: Knopf.

Rish, R., & Caton, J. (2011). Building fantasy worlds together with collaborative writing: Creative, social, and pedagogic challenges. *English Journal, 100,* 21–28.

Rowsell, J. (2013). *Working with multimodality: Rethinking literacy in a digital age*. New York: Routledge.

Rush, L. S., & Scherff, L. (2011). Opening the conversation: Thoughts on English teacher preparation and renewal with Patricia Lambert Stock, Ruth Vinz, and David Schaafsma. *English Education, 44*(1), 3–12.

Smitherman, G. (1977). *Talkin and testifyin: The language of Black America*. Detroit, MI: Wayne State University Press.

Srikantaiah, D., Zhang, Y., & Swayhoover, L. (2008). *Lessons from the classroom level: Federal and state accountability in Rhode Island*. Washington, DC: Center on Education Policy.

Stallworth, J., & Gibbons, L. (2012). What's on the list . . . now? A survey of book-length works taught in secondary schools. *English Leadership Quarterly, 34*(3), 2–3.

Street, B. V. (1984). *Literacy in theory and practice*. Cambridge, UK: Cambridge University Press.

Stotsky, S. (2010). *Literary study in grades 9, 10, 11: A national survey*. Association of Literary Scholars, Critics, and Writers. Retrieved from *www.alscw.org/publications/forum/forum_4.pdf*.

Stotsky, S. (2012, December 11). *Issue brief 3800: Common Core Standards' devastating impact on literary analysis and critical thinking*. Retrieved from *http://thf_media.s3.amazonaws.com/2012/pdf/ib3800.pdf*.

Students' Right to Their Own Language. (1974). Retrieved from *www.ncte.org/library/nctefiles/groups/cccc/newsrtol.pdf*.

Sunderman, G. L., Tracey, C. K., Kim, J., & Orfield, G. (2004). *Listening to teachers: Classroom realities and No Child Left Behind*. Cambridge, MA: Civil Rights Project, Harvard University.

Toulmin, S. E. (1958). *The uses of argument*. New York: Cambridge University Press.

U.S. Census Bureau. (2011) . *Detailed language spoken at home and ability to speak English for the population 5 years and older by states: 2006–2008*. Retrieved from *www.census.gov/hhes/socdemo/language/data/acs*.

What is English education? (2005). Retrieved March 16, 2006, from *www.ncte.org/groups/cee/positions/122898.htm*.

Zancanella, D. (2007). Dripping with literacy, a jazz-fueled road trip, a place to breathe. *English Journal, 97*(2), 71–78.

CHAPTER 9

Diverse Youth, New Teachers, and "Picturing" Literacy
Using Photovoice to "Partner" Our Way to Adolescents' Perspectives on Literacy

KRISTIEN ZENKOV, LAUREL TAYLOR, and JIM HARMON

The Exact Moment

"[Jerome] was practicing a dance routine and preparing for the Youth Explosion that was coming up. This picture shows his determination and practice while he was running then jumping off the stage. I wanted to get his picture, but couldn't capture him in midair. He kept getting mad but ended up doing it over and over again, until we finally got this action shot. This proves that even frustration should not get in the way of doing what you want, love, and enjoy."—Tamara

Tamara was a high school student, one of many young people in our Ohio and Virginia English high school and middle school classrooms and in the dozens of sites where we have conducted our photovoice project—"Through Students' Eyes" (TSE)—over the past decade. Photovoice (Wang & Burris, 1997)—also known as participatory photography—is a method that provides youths with a means to influence the policies and programs that affect them. Participants are asked to represent their points of view or to address issues in their communities by taking photographs, discussing them together, developing narratives to go with their photos, and conducting outreach or other action.

Tamara's story was a complicated one. She was a talented writer and a "waterfall" talker: Once she started sharing, she had a staccato delivery that made it difficult to understand what she was saying. Across the year that we worked with her in Jim's 10th-grade English class, she spent as much time in Jim's room as she could. She seemed to hunger for adult attention that, we speculated, filled the void of maturity she felt when surrounded by her peers.

When we met Tamara, Jim was her English teacher in an inner-ring Cleveland suburban high school, and Kristien was a local university literacy and teacher education faculty member committed to engaging with youths and preservice and inservice teachers as coteachers and coresearchers. We knew little about her until she agreed to participate in our photo elicitation project, and we began to meet with her in the one-to-one writing conferences that are now a cornerstone of our literacy efforts—one youth, one listening teacher–researcher, and a dedicated private interaction. When we posed our elicitation queries about photographs she had taken, Tamara was eager to respond and would take our rambling notes and turn them into fluid, wisdom-filled sentences.

Ultimately, we turned our interest in working with Tamara into practice and research inquiries about the nature of literacy and literacy instruction. These practice-based research lessons now inform many of our collaboratively conducted writing instruction and scholarly efforts with youth (Note: In this chapter we use the terms *youth, adolescents, young people,* and *students* interchangeably; in virtually all instances we are referring to students between ages 13 and 19). But these experiences and insights also now guide and are driven by our literacy education and research efforts with new teachers, offering notions of what counts as literacy curricula and literacy pedagogies that are mediated by these novice literacy educators.

OUR STUDENTS AND THEIR LITERACY RELATIONSHIPS

Our photo elicitation literacy project with youth began over a decade ago in a United Nations of schools in urban northeast Ohio, with students hailing from more than 40 countries in the classes Kristien was coteaching with veteran city educator and chapter coauthor, Jim, and the youth participating in our then-new TSE project. The majority of these young people had been born into families and communities in which formal education too often seemed as foreign an institution as English was a language. Most were children of multiple generations of high school dropouts—or "pushouts"—and the result appeared to be that their appreciation for our English instruction and for school in general was limited at best.

For much of the decade since that first TSE project, Kristien has worked with youths and other veteran teachers in mid-Atlantic exurban communities and schools with very distinctive and diverse demographic profiles that will be the norm throughout the United States in the not-too-distant future. These closely packed small cities outside the United States capital have experienced considerable demographic shifts, at their most extreme moving from 5% to almost 35% English language learning (ELL) students, while simultaneously seeing a substantial increase in immigrant youth. The families whose children have populated the classrooms where Kristien has served as a coteacher and research partner with both young people and their classroom teachers were arriving from as close as our major city's inner-ring suburbs—where housing costs are increasingly unaffordable—and from as far away as Guatemala, El Salvador, Korea, and Russia.

Similar to Jim's Midwestern urban students, school and its foundational language simply do not *mean* to these youth and their families what they do to so many of their teachers. Perhaps the most obvious evidence of this large-scale shift in our communities' relationships to school is the fact that the high school dropout rate for ELLs in the United States now consistently hovers above 30% for Hispanic 16- through 24-year-olds born outside of the United States. This percentage is approximately four times the proportion of 8% of 16- through 24-year-olds as a whole who formally and most often permanently disengage from our educational systems (Chapman, Laird, Ifill, & KewalRamani, 2011; National Center for Education Statistics [NCES], 2009).

The community in which Kristien and Laurel now collaborate on these literacy intervention and research projects is home to students from an even wider variety of backgrounds than the youth with whom Kristien worked in previous contexts. These young people might appear—physically—to be very similar to the adolescents in both urban Ohio and exurban northern Virginia, because they are a majority minority, with racial, ethnic, and linguistic profiles that are strikingly similar to the students in those Cleveland classrooms. Yet a closer examination of their academic demographics reveals that they are arriving in our high school having found considerable success in their previous schooling and English instruction experiences. Unlike too many of our urban Midwestern students, there is little chance that these young people will drop out of high school, and college is virtually a given in their futures.

While we have worked as coteachers and coresearchers in three very different communities over the past decade, all of our student populations have faced a strikingly similar—and increasingly common—reality. Jim's students struggled with school and the traditional examples of literacy practices we shared with them because of their previous *negative* encounters with school. Our exurban northern Virginia students were still learning about what school and its literacy endeavors might mean while they were confronting what must have seemed like an endless series of new cultural norms—most often while attempting to assist with their family members' similar cultural and economic challenges. And Laurel's mid-Atlantic inner-ring suburban students were similarly disengaged from school and our writing practices, because their current approaches to education had rewarded them with academic accolades and "good" grades but had done little to promote authentic connections to writing or learning. These youths' relationships to our schools' literacy practices seem to be equally complex and fragile.

LAYERS OF CULTURAL AND LITERACY GAPS

As we considered and coordinated this project over the past 10 years and in these three settings, we were impressed again and again by the fact that our students' experiences with school and traditional literacy instruction were almost everything ours were not. Perhaps because our own experiences with school and literacy instruction and particularly writing have, it has seemed, always been so positive and so clearly rooted in our personal rather than only our student or professional identities, even after decades of teaching in such contexts we are still learning that our students' and their family members' relationships to school and literacy are often different from and more complicated than our own. These are realities that we now work to acknowledge and honor on a daily basis, both as a foundational principle and as a regular feature of our teaching and research practices. These are also realities that we work to bridge through our collaboratively facilitated photovoice inquiries into youths' perspectives.

This commitment to responding to our increasingly diverse youths' limited relationships to writing and school with our practice-based teaching and research practices was born of a number of factors and histories, including the realities of our students' lives that we briefly described earlier. Initially, we were more desperate than intentional with this project, humble enough to acknowledge that we did not know why students were so often disengaged from our literacy tasks. We were simultaneously excited to find each other—veteran literacy teachers and teacher-educators willing to partner around our explorations of youths' perspectives on school and literacy from very different perspectives, while playing different but intersecting professional roles.

In this chapter we first briefly explore the theoretical and research origins of our collaborative research work as boundary-spanning literacy teachers and teacher-educators. We then detail the intervention-oriented, literacy-focused photovoice examinations of youths' perspectives on school and literacy with which we have been involved, followed by some recent findings of these practice-based studies. We next turn to the more recent, embedded notion of practice-based literacy research with which we have engaged—which focuses on not only the concepts of literacy that have resulted from our work with youth but also the examples of literacy education pedagogies born of practice-based studies that have been facilitated by us and mediated by preservice literacy educators.

Perhaps the most significant outcomes of our examinations are neither the traditional findings that have resulted from our collaborative, curriculum-based studies nor those findings determined as a result of the explorations conducted as parallel youth intervention and literacy teacher education efforts, with preservice teachers (PSTs) serving as instructional and research partners. As we examine in the discussion section of this chapter, the most compelling results of our research may be the models of merged, praxis-focused literacy education and research that we have devised and the concepts of literacy, literacy practice, and literacy scholarship that have evolved.

As we noted earlier, we have long been conscious of the cultural mismatch between us and our high school students. We do not reflect the diversity or racial, ethnic, or language traits of our students. And we are culturally and demographically more similar to the almost universally White, native English-speaking future teachers with whom we work and for whose literacy instruction practices we are responsible (Sleeter, 2008).

Through our practice-based research with each other, PSTs, and diverse youth, we recognize that the dilemmas and gaps we—skilled, veteran teachers and teacher-educators—are encountering are ones the future teachers who often accompany Kristien into these schools and communities will soon face in their own classrooms. We are more conscious than ever before that we have a responsibility not just to bridge the gap between diverse youths' and our own veteran teachers and teacher-educators' notions of literacy and effective literacy instruction. We might—or *must*—also, simultaneously, do so *for* and *with* the next generation of classroom-based literacy educators.

THE FOUNDATIONS OF OUR WORK

Our research efforts are rooted in a range of beliefs and theoretical elements. We arrived at these through our own extensive teaching experiences and our explorations of other scholars' and practitioners' theories of literacy and writing instruction. We highlight these foundational elements here and later in this chapter detail others that ground our extension of this work into practice-based literacy scholarship mediated by PSTs.

Echoing the perspectives of other, current literacy theorists, we believe that *all* writing is personal and that every writing act is inseparable from each individual's writing identity, whether or not we are consciously considering such personas or connections while we are engaged in any element of a writing process (Gonzales, Moll, & Amanti, 2005; Zumbrunn & Krause, 2012). We also believe that if we are to guide youth toward the deepest, healthiest, and most empowering of lifelong relationships to writing, we must provide them with opportunities to develop their own languages and voices every day, in and out of our classes (Noguera, 2008). Finally, we also believe that writing—or, more accurately, *composing*—is the most foundational of skills that we must facilitate our students in acquiring (Haddix & Sealey-Ruiz, 2012). This latter conviction is not merely a case of subject matter fandom, but an intentional, learned, and political conviction rooted in the reality that writing is simultaneously a *consumptive* and a *creative* act.

Of course, these principles and views are embedded in and echoed by the work of innumerable education and literacy theorists. Proponents of culturally responsive teaching have long called on educators to address the cultural mismatches between components of students' lives and schools in an effort to facilitate students' academic success while building teachers' cultural competence (Esposito & Swain, 2009; Gay, 2010; Journell & Castro, 2011). Such notions of curriculum and pedagogy acknowledge that many students need assistance developing—inventing and enacting—critical counternarratives about their cultures, their literacy and general academic abilities, and the relationships between these and their school experiences (May & Sleeter, 2010; Paris, 2012).

The idea that students' experiences should be core elements in any curriculum also relies on the principles of critical pedagogy, which suggest that our teaching acts should support institutional conditions and societal structures that facilitate student empowerment (Kincheloe, 2004). Critical pedagogy identifies a central purpose of schools—and, by extension, of literacy education—as the preparation of an educated and politically engaged citizenry, even as the democratic citizenship objective remains a key component in intense debates over curriculum (Ayers, 2004; Kincheloe & McLaren, 1998). We enact a critical pedagogical stance through our use of critical literacy approaches, through which we call on youth to interrogate texts and their purposes (Cammarota & Fine, 2008; Morrell, 2007).

The rapid demographic changes in the communities where we have conducted our project are representative of the shifts in constituents, their relationships to school, and their language and literacy capacities that virtually every U.S. teacher will face in the future (Cruz & Thornton, 2013; Lucas & Grinberg, 2008). For these youth, "literacy" means something different than it did for us as PreK–12 students and for the educational institutions by which we are now employed. Numerous scholars have documented the expanding nature of "literacy," where "texts" come in forms as diverse as music, Web-based media, texting, and social networking tools (Christenbury, Bomer, & Smagorinsky, 2009; Kress, Charalampos, & Jewitt, 2006; Moje, Overby, Tysvaer, & Morris,

2008). Literacy theorists commonly recognize that our instructional methods must rely on the expanded notions of "text" with which our students are familiar and with which they must be fluent in order to be successful in professional, community, and citizenship contexts in the future (Mills, 2010; Vasudevan, DeJaynes, & Schimier, 2010).

Finally, research has consistently revealed how students' literacy development plays a primary role in their decisions to remain in or reject school (Lan & Lanthier, 2003; Somers, Owens, & Piliawsky, 2009; U.S. Department of Education, 2007). Recent studies have documented how schools' curricular responses to diverse populations' low traditional literacy rates contribute to overall school disengagement (Ivey & Broaddus, 2007; Zenkov, 2009; Zenkov, Bell, Ewaida, & Lynch, 2012). Ultimately, we are attempting to serve youth who have very different *literacies* in the English language and the media through which it is communicated (Martínez-Roldán & Fránquíz, 2009).

In an effort to understand diverse youths' perspectives on school and engage them in meaningful school activities, researchers are considering students' points of view on our foundational educational institutions (Cook-Sather, 2009; Cushman, 2010; Easton & Condon, 2009; Yonezawa & Jones, 2009). These scholars' inquiries rely on a "youths as experts" orientation, acknowledging that young people can be participants in their own learning and discern ways that can help them navigate their academic experience (Biddulph, 2011; Schultz, 2011; Torre, Fine, Stoudt, & Fox, 2012). Many student voice inquiries are also grounded in the methods of youth participatory action research (YPAR), a form of experimental research conducted within a participatory community, with the goal of addressing an area of concern and identifying actions that can improve the quality, quantity, and equity of outcomes (Fine, Torre, Burns, & Payne, 2007; Mediratta, Shah, & McAlister, 2009). YPAR focuses on "critical youth engagement," helping young people—especially those from economically disadvantaged and immigrant communities—to understand and address conditions of structural injustice (Bautista, 2012; Kellett, 2009; Zeller-Berkman, 2007).

When we began our project, we appreciated the potential application of a multimodal notion of literacy with youth who we thought may not be comfortable sharing their perspectives through traditional, language-focused inquiries (Connolly & Kress, 2011; Gold, 2004). After a decade of implementing our practice-based photovoice research project, we have contributed to growing scholarship that has documented how critical perspectives on youths' and family and community members' relationships to school and our literacy practices might be discovered through the use of alternative, visually oriented research methods (Bell, Zenkov, Ewaida, & Lynch, 2011; Piper & Frankham, 2007; Zenkov, Ewaida, Lynch, Bell, & Harmon, 2013).

Our search for non-language-based methods ultimately led us to a consideration of photographs as text and a photovoice method, which has proven effective for engaging diverse youth and providing them with authentic means to share their perspectives (Ajayi, 2009; Bell, 2008; Hicks, 2013; Wang, 2006; Zenkov & Harmon, 2009). Image-based tools motivate students to develop an awareness of and share personal insights related to their school experiences (Doda & Knowles, 2008; Smyth, 2007; Zenkov, Bell, Lynch, et al., 2012). These explorations have helped us and the audiences of our scholarship to understand factors related to the success and failure of students in our ELA classes, while resulting in habits of thinking, reading, writing, and speaking for youth that go beyond surface meanings and dominant myths to understanding sociological phenomena (Fobes & Kaufman, 2008; Harper, 2005; Hibbing & Rankin-Erickson, 2003; Zenkov, 2009).

METHODS

These foundations in critical literacy, youths' perspectives, YPAR, and multimodal notions of literacy evoked the tools of our project, through which we have hoped to help middle and high school-level students consider their relationships to school and literacy, become better writers, and inform us about effective writing instruction (Kress, 2006; Streng et al., 2004). We have implemented this project with more than 1,000 diverse young people—averaging 30 participants per school- or community-based implementation. Our project always calls on youth to take and to consider digital photographs and related reflections to illustrate and describe what they perceive as the purposes of school and writing and reading, the supports for their school and literacy achievement and engagement, and the obstacles to their literacy and school success.

With each project we either provide participants with digital "point-and-shoot" cameras or use smartphones or computer tablets to take pictures, after offering them rudimentary instruction in camera operation and photo composition. We then lead youth on "photo walks" around their schools and neighborhoods, modeling the photo elicitation process. For our 1-day projects, each participant takes an average of 30 images, and for the multisession versions youth typically take approximately 100 images—all in response to the three project questions:

1. What is the purpose of school/reading/writing?
2. What helps you to be successful in school or with reading/writing?
3. What gets in the way of your school/reading/writing success?

We usually preface these visual explorations by having youth complete questionnaires addressing these questions, and we often conduct interviews with participants to help them further articulate their thinking. Following at least one or, ideally, multiple photo walks, we work with students to examine, select, discuss, and write about their photos. We review photographs with participants in one-on-one and small-group gatherings, discussing images as a part of the elicitation process—asking questions such as "What do you like about this photograph?" and "What does this photo mean to you?" We transcribe youths' oral reactions to images and help them edit their reflections on the photos that they feel best answer the project questions. Collectively, project participants have shot more than 15,000 images and after multiple draft reflections, these adolescents have written about approximately 4,000 of these in paragraph-length reflections.

At the conclusion of these projects, we—the authors of this chapter and the teacher partners with whom we work in each project or classroom site—collaboratively analyze the content of the images and writings youth have identified as their most compelling responses, coding prevalent visual and descriptive themes in adolescents' visual and written data (Kemmis & McTaggart, 2000; Patton, 2002; Rose, 2006). Most often we then collectively complete a framed content analysis of the entire set of each project's images and the accompanying reflections (Pole, 2004; Van Leeuwen & Jewitt, 2001), paying attention to students' answers to our research questions. Given our literacy focus, we most frequently reconsider our general content analysis notes, these visual and written data, and our interactions with young people through the lens of what these suggest about our writing curricula and pedagogies.

For this chapter, we have returned to images and reflections and to our planning and observation notes from projects we have conducted in the past decade, considering themes upon which we are only beginning to report. The data we have analyzed included approximately 1,200 photograph and reflection combinations. While we have documented numerous findings, themes related to notions of literacy, and effective literacy instruction in these data, here we highlight three literacy-related premises that have most recently and consistently emerged—that simultaneously offer insights into notions of literacy and literacy instruction.

Our findings' themes are sometimes evoked by youths' pictures and reflections, and at other times are explicitly illustrated by youths' photos and compositions. Given the space limitations of this chapter, we have abbreviated our descriptions of these themes below and introduced each with youths' images and writings, then have supplied a brief narrative summary of the pedagogical practice we identified through our analyses. Presenting our findings in this way not only venerates our practice-based approach and commitment to a respectful consideration of youths' perspectives but it also illustrates the "trustworthiness" threshold of findings that is commonly an element of such examinations (Fine et al., 2007). Such explorations aim for descriptive or illustrative results rather than generalizable discoveries, with the goal of informing educators' practices and paying attention to data drawn directly from youths' experiences (Mediratta et al., 2009).

LITERACIES AND PEDAGOGIES

No Quick and Dirty Writing Assessments

Family Signs

"This is a picture of my cousin, D'Angelo. . . . He is throwing up the 'King-Kennedy' sign because he represents King-Kennedy. People join gangs because they want to get back at other people who jumped their friends. His mother was born at King-Kennedy. . . . [I] don't want to join a gang because when gangs start fighting and then you have to represent your 'hood, then people start shooting . . . and then you'll get shot, and you'll think, 'I shouldn't have joined that gang.'"—Allen

Allen might have been barely 8 years old when he found his way into the community art gallery where we conducted our first version of TSE with Jim's students. We had intended to implement the project in Jim's school, but he had been one of more than 1,000 teachers the district laid off at the end of the previous school year due to a steadily shrinking enrollment. Allen noticed the constant stream of adolescents heading into the gallery space every other Saturday and simply wanted something else—something more—to do. He was a precocious young man, with an awareness of the world that belied his tender years.

We know now that the concepts of literacy, the examples of literacy content, and our assessments of students' writing should be anything but the decontextualized, "quick and dirty" assignments that are typical in many schools. If we want literacy to matter to youth—in school and beyond—and to be recognized as that most foundational tool of achievement and empowerment, then our writing instruction and assessment need to be rooted in notions of relationship rather than in tourist-like interactions. Perhaps the most obvious examples of such relationship-oriented literacy instruction and assessment practices are the series of one-to-one photo elicitation conferences we now conduct with youth in our project. While such structures may not seem to fit into most literacy teachers' school days or class periods, we may only be able to forge authentic connections between youth and their writing—and between adolescents and us, their teachers—if we rely on instructional procedures that are just *that* personal.

Local and Global Writing Assessments

Piggy Bank

"High school for me is similar to a fashion show. We put on our best clothes every day to walk the halls, and like any great fashion show it takes money. For some students, getting money is only a matter of asking their mom and dad, and others work part time jobs or get gigs cutting grass and shoveling driveways in the winter. But this gets in the way of what we truly come to school for, to learn. I think having to worry about what you're wearing and getting money gets in the way of getting an education."—Amber

Amber was the kind of student about whom most teachers dream. She seemed well-suited to school—she took impeccable notes in class, scored well on tests, and was always willing to contribute to discussions and activities. We first encountered her in her sophomore English Honors class, and we almost immediately thought that she seemed destined for bigger and better things. But almost as quickly as she gained our attention and admiration, she unwittingly pulled something of a disappearing act—one with which we have become too familiar with our diverse students and our writing instruction efforts. It was through her involvement in our project and study that she reappeared.

We must be clear: Amber never disappointed with her performance in class or our project—with the everyday assignments or what we have come to consider the "local" in her writing and learning and in our teaching. In fact, even when she became involved in our photovoice project, Amber willingly explored her relationship to school and reading and writing. And it was actually through her previously cited reflection that she articulated—and *taught* us—that a focus on the immediate in her school life, represented by fashion, was one of the most troubling elements of her writing performance and relationship and our writing instruction. If you considered Amber's behavior and execution on any 1 day, you might have judged her to be a young woman who needed no further academic support, who, in the moment and likely in the long-term, had it all figured out. She appeared to be someone teachers did not need to spend their time attempting to challenge, not someone who might vanish from our teacher radar.

Through this "local" focus, Amber's relationship to literacy and our teaching practices had become rote—in that automatic, established sort of way—and her literacy products meant *less* as a result. What our photovoice project—with its metacognitive focus on school and literacy and our assumption that youth can (or even should) offer insights into our notions of literacy and literacy instruction—provided was a chance and structures for us and youth to go "global." To take a broader perspective on literacy, our own and our students' notions of literacy, on their relationships to literacy and writing instruction, and on the ultimate ends of our writing instruction efforts.

Many would view Amber's reflection on fashion as grounds for an immediate change in school policy, for requiring students to wear uniforms. But what she and we most appreciated was that these inquiries and methods enabled us to *pause* in our notions of literacy and our writing instruction practices, and provided a chance for Amber to think more about school and what it *should* look like. Fashion and those traditional, everyday writing tasks and performances were the "local" element—who these youth and we *appeared* to be. The "global" was the *real* you, the one developed as a result of being open to making mistakes, the long-term you.

Amber reminded us of the extent to which youths' writing identities have been established by the time they reach high school, and how final their relationships to writing seem to be. We know now that one of the only ways to begin to work to change these identities and relationships and to move youth toward more positive orientations toward writing is through small steps and more authentic "local" writing assignments and assessments. In both whole-group writing instruction and in the writing conferences we conduct, we focus on a youth and a single piece of his or her writing, and a single element of each composition. Youths' writing efficacy is best improved through our laser-like concentration on the local.

These writing assessments are local, too, in the sense that they are conducted with just one student and one teacher or caring adult. While some subjects can be taught in large-group settings, this is often not the case with writing, particularly for youth who are disengaged from these tasks. Or, perhaps more accurately, some of the most foundational elements of writing instruction and writing engagement are best taught through local rather than large-group instruction. Such local—one-on-one—writing instruction calls on us as teachers and teacher-educators to advocate for school and classroom structures that *allow* for such methods.

After we have worked with youth over some length of time, we also use these one-to-one writing conference structures to conduct global writing assessments. We consider that single writing element or one of a student's writing goals across at least two examples of his or her writing and discuss the evidence of growth. Just as with the writing elicitation conferences we described earlier under the quick and dirty writing assessments theme, we recognize that such global evaluations are difficult to implement—mostly due to the time and classroom structures they require—but our students have taught us that they are foundational to effective literacy education efforts.

Due, Not Done

Mobile Home

"This picture that I've taken is called 'Mobile Home' and it represents the purpose of school for me. The reason why this picture is my purpose of being in school is, I don't want to grow up to be a homeless person. I want to set a strong and stable foundation for my family and live in a nice wonderful home that's safe for me and my family, and the way I'm going to start building that foundation is to finish school and go to college."—Eon

It did not take long after we met Eon in his sophomore English class to realize that behind his dramatic comic/tragic facade there was a brilliant young man with a short fuse. We learned that Eon was often on a mission to prove that he was far more than what you might assume about him, and he would challenge his peers' often innocently shared constructive feedback about his writing with what we can only explain as rage. Indeed, it seemed Eon felt persecuted by so many around him and perceived that very few people in his life *really* knew who he was.

As we grew genuinely to appreciate Eon's sarcastic and tongue-in-cheek humor, we often feared that his lack of impulse control would eventually get him into serious trouble—he had no qualms with being angrily aggressive with his peers and teachers alike, often for slights of which only he was aware. It was only when we read the reflection on the previously cited image that we began to understand the source of his fury: His deep-seated insecurity was rooted in the transience of his home life. Our solution to serving Eon better as his English and writing teachers, to getting to know him differently and better, and to helping him create richer and more proactive sense of his anger and pain was to invite him to participate in our project. We hoped to give him a means through which he was actually *asked* to voice his concerns about school as a part of school, instead of while *interrupting* school. And we hoped, too, that we might be able to get past the dismissive anger he felt and the defensive stance so many of our students very reasonably presented in response to our writing tasks, instruction, and feedback.

In these exchanges with Eon, and with so many of our students, we have learned that we must emphasize and reteach the notion that challenges to and constructive criticism on their writing does not represent the entirety of who students are or who they will become as writers or in life. We know now that they are dealing with so many experiences in their English classes that could contribute to the negative writing relationships they have developed and the rehearsed, indifferent, and even contemptuous attitudes they share. Somehow, we as writing teachers must find a way through these experiences and relationships—with the youth by our sides—and trust that they will find a more positive connection to writing on the other side.

One of the biggest mistakes we make as writing teachers is failing to communicate to students that our writing projects are never done: They are just due. These youth do not need additional pressure to perform, on demand, with our writing tasks. Rather, they require a developmental orientation to their writing growth, and they need teachers to forgive their writing struggles and look past their limited writing success and limited writing relationships. It is infinitely more important that our students are aware of and can articulate the nature of their writing relationships, growth, and achievement than it is that we—their teachers—can describe these realities. Such awareness offers youth not only opportunities for writing success in our classes or our practice-based photovoice interventions and research projects but also chances for achievement and the ongoing development of positive writing identities. When students leave our classrooms, *we* will not be with them to inform their writing efforts; their awareness and senses of efficacy will guide their writing relationships and endeavors.

FOUNDATIONS AND METHODS OF PARTNERING WITH PRESERVICE TEACHERS

We recognize that our collaborations as university- and school-based teachers, teacher-educators, and scholars are not the norm in our field. We feel fortunate that both our personal and professional instincts and our professional experiences as educators have been rooted in that boundary-spanning notion and in teaching, teacher education, and research practices that require us to cooperate. We came of age professionally in the era when "professional development schools" (PDSs) and school–university partnerships were increasingly common structures. We have continued this partnership focus across the past decade—an orientation that has gained favor and been formalized as a professional expectation in the most recent standards of the Council for the Accreditation of Educator Preparation (CAEP), the primary accreditation body in the teacher education field.

To a greater extent than ever before in the history of teacher education in the United States, we are being called on to design and implement programs that are rooted in "clinically rich" experiences. Federal and state educational policies increasingly highlight the need for strengthened connections between teacher education course work and clinical practices (Imig & Imig, 2008; Levine, 2006). As well, CAEP Standard 2 calls on colleges and universities to develop partnerships with area schools, which are the primary sites of preservice teachers' clinical training (CAEP, 2013). School- and university-based teacher-educators, scholars, and policymakers are united in their recognition that prospective teachers should have opportunities to explore the realities of PreK–12 education while being exposed to reflective practices that might revolutionize the classroom space (Grossman, 2010; Ronfeldt, 2012).

This shift toward a greater focus on preservice teachers' clinical preparation and a sense of shared responsibility among school- and university-based educators for the effective training of future teachers paralleled our decision to involve future teachers intimately in Kristien's classes in our explorations of youths' perspectives on school and literacy. We recognized that teacher education programs must provide PSTs with the tools and experiences necessary to be successful in our increasingly diverse, dynamic educational climates (Levine, 2006; Zeichner & Conklin, 2008). We surmised that "success" in these contexts might be defined by these new teachers' entrenched beliefs that schools should be places where all constituents—including the youth and PSTs themselves—are given the opportunity to become researchers into their own schooling experiences and to develop clear senses of their identities as learners. McIntyre (2009) recently asserted that "if we want student teachers to learn to engage, as part of their normal professional practice, in an informed intellectual analysis of their teaching and of how it can be improved, they need to learn this during their professional education as something that they do in schools" (p. 606).

We recognized the role of our practice-based projects for merging with our heightened teacher education concerns and for facilitating PSTs' experiences in classroom settings in which the voices of adolescents are integral—rather than tangential—factors in determining the nature of effective instruction. And we began to understand that teacher candidates might engage shoulder-to-shoulder as researchers with school- and university-based mentors. Of course, this "shoulder-to-shoulder" notion parallels the teacher–PreK–12 student coresearcher practices that are the core of our photovoice explorations.

Our goal remains an intervention-based research project that assumes that our literacy instruction will matter more to youth and the world if we intimately involve adolescents in the scholarship of teaching. And while the research literature on youths' perspectives on school has grown considerably, few of these inquiries have been implemented with—or, more importantly, by—the future teachers who will soon serve these diverse youth. We hypothesized that these methods might support our future teachers' effective clinical preparation and offer us new insights into notions of literacy and writing instruction practices. Our project has always been rooted in boundary-spanning teaching practices, with university faculty engaged in the coteaching of middle and high school classes, and classroom teachers involved as active researchers of their own practices rather than the subjects of such scholarship. But more recently, we have extended these inquiries and considerations of youth as experts on our literacy instruction and school into a literacy teacher education activity.

Guided by these commitments, policy shifts, and revised teacher education standards, for the past 4 years we have involved approximately 130 preservice teachers in our project implementations and practice-based examinations. These future teachers were enrolled in a field-based elective teacher education class, through which we visited three schools each year, with each novice educator partnering with one youth in each site—a total of approximately 400 young people. We intentionally selected the most diverse elementary, middle, and high schools as the sites for these projects, but we focused primarily on our existing PDS schools and collaborating teachers as our project homes and partner teachers. The students in these schools included youth from working-class middle and high schools in exurban and urban communities, adolescents who had recently arrived from mostly Central American home countries and were gradually being integrated into English-only classrooms, and a large percentage of African American youth.

These future teachers matched the profile of most new teachers across the United States: The majority were traditional White, middle-class college students, an average of 20 years old, from our immediate region, and hoping to teach in the very schools they had attended. These PSTs cofacilitated this study, working with us—the veteran teachers and teacher-educators—helping youth to complete photographic explorations and reflective writings based on the images they took and selected. While the primary data of these versions of the project were these adolescents' images and writings, we also called on future teachers—our co-researchers—to complete inclass reflections, pre- and postproject questionnaires, and "synthesis projects," in which they considered the intersections and tensions between their own and youths' perspectives on the purposes of, supports for, and impediments to school and literacy engagement and achievement. We content-analyzed these data for themes related to these future teachers' points of view on teaching writing and their learning about youths' literacy practices, and we use images from these preservice teachers' projects to illustrate the brief results below.

LITERACIES AND PEDAGOGIES MEDIATED BY PRESERVICE TEACHERS

"Use Words That Feel Good in My Ears"

Preservice teacher Caroline included the cover of Dr. Seuss's *One Fish, Two Fish, Red Fish, Blue Fish* to accompany a paragraph she entitled "Use Words That Feel Good in My Ears." She explained that a 10th-grade ELL with whom she had worked in our project had shared with her how the comments teachers used when offering feedback on his writing did not, in his words, "feel good." When Caroline asked more about what this student meant—eliciting his ideas, asking those evocative questions—it became clear that he understood "feel" in multiple ways, both in terms of the brief, harsh, and unconditional feedback from teachers he was accustomed to receiving on his writing, and in terms of the fact that he did not always understand what too many teachers would assume were basic directions, in English, which was still a new language to him.

This theme was one of the most prominent of the insights our preservice teacher students and research partners shared in their final projects. They repeatedly expressed surprise at—and a new awareness of—the fact that language was not just something we use in school, but that it can be a cultural barrier to our students' senses of academic efficacy. So many of our teacher candidate collaborators had little experience with students who attend urban schools and may experience challenges unlike those they faced in other school settings. And that when youth say they want teachers to clarify their expectations "well," they mean they want teachers to explain with a kind and patient tone, and to appreciate that learning about assignments while learning about school, about new social structures, about a new community, and about a new culture is really about learning seven languages at once.

"Youth Need to Fill Their 'Social Quotas'"

School as Prison

"The clock on the wall ticks down the sentence of the class. It's a constant reminder that schools can act as prisons when teachers don't teach, when students are forbidden to collaborate on what they are 'taught.' . . . To be completely restricted from speaking during a class defeats the purpose of school. In school you should be taught and able to collaborate on the things you are told by the teacher. Getting an education means that you get some time to learn what your peers comprehend and to compare notes."—Jon

Future teacher Sara chose the previous photograph to illustrate one of the key lessons she learned about effective teaching through our project—which was also a primary theme about notions of literacy and literacy instruction that we have discovered in these preservice teachers' synthesis projects from the past 4 years. In her interactions with sixth graders at a Title I school, Sara heard not just the student with whom she worked one-on-one; it seemed that the majority of these youth explicitly express a need to have what she called their "social quota" met during school. The young people were articulate about the fact that they felt that they had very reasonable needs to interact with their peers in school, often because the circumstances of their home lives meant that there were not sufficient chances outside of school to do so.

In our conversations with Sara and her preservice peers, we discussed what they were beginning to recognize as a social "void," which was not a deficit view of these youth or their families or communities, but a hunger for the interaction of which these young people were conscious. These youth appreciated, too, that they were demanding attention from teachers who were often busy or even overwhelmed by the needs—academic and social—of entire classes of students. But, echoing the earlier reflection that Jon composed several years ago, these future teachers offered critiques of the restrictions teachers place on youths' social interactions in class and school, when they might, instead, appreciate the many literacy learning opportunities that might result from these social interactions.

These preservice teacher-mediated insights reminded us that school is an unavoidably social venture—and one in which we *require* youth to participate and in which school is the foundation for youths' engagement in life *beyond* school, which is social in almost every way. Such realities highlight that "literacy" in school is a foundational content and process—not one that is reserved for our English classes. It now seems obvious that our notions of literacy instruction—particularly for diverse youth for whom school and our traditional literacy instruction mean such different things than novice teachers would expect—are in need of some dramatic and ongoing rethinking.

"Keeping Me Away from the Classroom Door" or "Learn—Don't Believe—Things about Students"

Hannah—another future teacher with whom we have recently partnered—selected a photo of one of the young men with whom she worked to illustrate the two quotes that she had transcribed during her conversations with him. The picture is of this young man—"Derek"—and a school security guard; we have chosen not to share this image out of respect for Derek's concern about possible negative repercussions. Derek described the troubling dynamics among teachers, the nonteacher adults in his school, and the youth whom he and we have encountered repeatedly, but who shocked these future teachers and were found by them to be almost criminal. These reflections revealed important insights about the notions of literacy and literacy pedagogies with which we should be operating.

For these youth, teachers simply knowing their names was not enough to make them feel welcome and remain in and engaged with school. These diverse, too often disenfranchised adolescents were not looking for miracles or lottery tickets or lightning strikes to instantly enhance their relationships to school and our literacy practices: They were seeking momentary connections, consistent but brief attention, and some semblance of a relationship with their teachers. In the words of Hannah, they wanted teachers to *learn*— not *believe*—things about them. For youth for whom school is still a new institution—or one in which they have not found much safety or success—cautious engagement is the norm, particularly in those classes where language and writing are the primary capital. And in these settings, where our literacy content and pedagogies are the focus, even a momentary negative exchange with a teacher can be damning.

Even more troubling to our preservice teacher project participants was the negative, impeding roles other adults in our schools could play with these youths' school attendance and literacy engagement and achievement. These future teachers highlighted, and we have heard echoed, too many times how office personnel and security guards may—in the name of "just doing their jobs"—make already reluctant school attendees take that next small step toward dropping out. In the words of this young man, such exchanges often were what was "keeping me away from the classroom door." Adults whom most of us would consider peripheral to students' school and literacy lives sometimes have a greater impact on these relationships than do their teachers. This insight reminds us that literacy and literacy instruction must be considered in that community school manner, with an eye toward the continuum of literacies with which youth are proficient and an awareness that our students' literacy relationships are impacted as much by environmental factors as by our daily lessons.

DISCUSSIONS AND CONCLUSIONS

After more than a decade of implementing these practice-based inquiries into youths' relationships to literacy with each other—our school and university teacher colleagues—and with future PreK–12 teachers, we believe that we are our most effective literacy educators and that our diverse middle and high school students are most engaged and empowered as writers when we approach them with the stances of humility and invitation that are the hallmarks of our YPAR photovoice projects and scholarship. We speculate that these stances are effective because our students are so accustomed to being approached by teachers and other adults in much less reverent ways. We are increasingly conscious of our dual roles as English teachers and literacy teacher-educators and of the possibilities and obligations we have to embed our work with youth in our teacher education efforts.

Our pedagogical strategies and studies appeal to a unique combination of theoretical frames, scholarly traditions, and teaching methods. We look to these traditions out of urgent necessity, as we are simultaneously attempting to address the literacy concerns of the adolescents who fill our classrooms and the literacy education concerns of the preservice teachers who will one day serve these youth. Such emphases require a willingness to look beyond subject, research, professional, and pedagogical customs and silos. Crafting our own literacy research and pedagogical modes is akin to the multimodal authoring by which our students are motivated. This is one of the conclusions we draw from these practice-based endeavors: Literacy educators and diverse youth are united by a need to play these creative roles and engage in these compositional acts. And the most effective notions of literacy and literacy education curricula and research might require teachers and scholars to engage in an ongoing consideration of seemingly disparate fields for sources of their methods.

We initially involved preservice literacy educators in our practice-based efforts because we were convinced—after years of implementation of these projects—that these were methods that future teachers needed to understand, both for the insights into youths' points of view they could gain and for the pedagogical processes we were modeling. We invited these future teachers to assist us, too, because we recognized that there is strength in numbers—that these preservice teachers could facilitate those one-on-one photo elicitations and writing conferences with young people much more efficiently than we could alone. But we are conscious now that involving preservice teachers—who are much closer in age and culture to the youth we are all trying to serve—may in part be our acknowledgment that we may not be the best bridges between the literacies these young people have and the literacies toward which we must guide them.

The richest and most frequently appearing concepts of literacy and literacy education of which we are now aware are rooted in notions, processes, and the results of inquiry. Inquiries that begin with and result in acknowledgments that no one set of constituents—university faculty, veteran teachers, preservice teachers, or even youth—has absolute expertise about the literacies or literacy pedagogies with which we should be functioning. Such literacy research efforts and pedagogies do not assume that adult perceptions are the lenses of authenticity; rather, these curricula and pedagogies are intimately related to listening to and learning from students' ideas about school, their places in it, and the subject matter they study.

Our use of photovoice methods affords us opportunities to interrupt many of the assumptions that all of these constituents make about what literacy is and how it should be taught. Ultimately, such multimodal inquiries into literacy require that educators, community members, and policymakers view the literacy curriculum and curriculum development as reflexive processes utilizing media with which children and young people are already proficient. The core of our project and orientation is the almost counterintuitive practice of asking students—rather than telling them—about the nature of school, curricula, and teaching practices. By assuming that youth should consider these natures, educators make the very different and positive conjecture that they can do so. This approach is rooted in the principle that educators must never assume that a student's failure to engage with curriculum or to complete a school task is evidence that he or she is not interested or is incapable of learning the material or completing work. The collective findings of these blended practice-based projects—drawn from distinct studies conducted by two very different populations of educators and researchers—reveal that effective writing instruction for diverse learners begins not with traditional, narrow notions of writing but with students' lives, and even with the lessons these youth might teach us.

These interventions and examinations are also grounded in notions of partnership that have long histories in the PDS movement and community schooling, and that are increasingly highlighted by practitioners and policymakers as foundational to our schools', communities', and colleges' most effective operation. The school and literacy engagement and achievement stakes are so very high for our increasingly diverse middle and high school students, and for the future teachers whom they will one day meet in our schools. The nature of youths' questions about our literacy practices and curricula and about our schooling institutions are rooted in cultural learning curves that have perhaps never before been appreciated—at least not systematically, by our school districts, teacher training methods, classroom practices, or societal traditions. The critical notions of literacy curricula and pedagogies that will best serve these students—and their teachers—may, then, only be developed through continued explorations of adolescents' ideas about school and their places in it—which might ultimately and absolutely be tied to notions of a "partnership literacy."

Ultimately, we speculate that the notions of literacy and literacy education with which we should be operating are *not* those that are drawn from the findings of these partnership- and practice-based studies and projects. These outcomes—the results of our fairly standard research analyses—are the *answers* to questions we have posed to diverse adolescents about how literacy might matter to them. These are extrapolated through our adult literacy teacher and teacher-educator scrutiny, through mechanisms that we control and with which we are proficient and experts. The concepts and curricula of literacy by which we must be guided are, instead, found within or comprise the inquiries themselves. The answer *is* the asking, and our students must be the leaders of our picturing and partnership endeavors.

REFERENCES

Ajayi, L. (2009). English as a second language learners' exploration of multimodal texts in a junior high school. *Journal of Adolescent and Adult Literacy, 52*(7), 585–595.

Ayers, W. (2004). Embers of hope: In search of a meaningful critical pedagogy. *Teacher Education Quarterly, 31*(1), 123–130.

Bell, A., Zenkov, K., Ewaida, M., & Lynch, M. (2011). *Seeing* students' perspectives on "quality" teaching: Middle school English language learners' pictures and "at risk" high school youths' voices. *Voices from the Middle, 19*(1), 32–40.

Bell, S. E. (2008). Photovoice as a strategy for community organizing in the central Appalachian coalfields. *Journal of Appalachian Studies, 14*(1–2), 34–48.

Bautista, M. (2012). *Pedagogy of agency: Examining youth participatory action research as a tool for youth empowerment and advocacy*. Doctoral dissertation, UCLA, Los Angeles, California.

Biddulph, M. (2011). Articulating student voice and facilitating curriculum agency. *Curriculum Journal, 22*(3), 381–399.

Cammarota, J., & Fine, M. (2008). Youth participatory action research: A pedagogy for transformational resistance. In J. Cammarota & M. Fine (Eds.), *Revolutionizing education: Youth participatory action research in motion* (pp. 1–12). New York: Routledge.

Chapman, C., Laird, J., Ifill, N., & KewalRamani, A. (2011). *Trends in high school dropout and completion rates in the United States: 1972–2009* (NCES Report No. 2012-006). Washington, DC: U.S. Department of Education, National Center for Education Statistics.

Christenbury, L., Bomer, R., & Smagorinsky, P. (Eds.). (2009). *Handbook of adolescent literacy research*. New York: Guilford Press.

Connolly, E. M., & Kress, G. (2011). *The incorporation of multimedia and multimodal learning tools into the teaching of research: A case study of digital storytelling in a high school English class*. New York: Edwin-Mellen.

Cook-Sather, A. (2009). *Learning from the student's perspective: A methods sourcebook for effective teaching*. Boulder, CO: Paradigm.

Council for Accreditation of Educator Preparation (CAEP). (2013). *CAEP accreditation standards*. Washington, DC: Author.

Cruz, B. C., & Thornton, S. J. (2013). *Teaching social studies to English language learners* (2nd ed.). New York: Routledge.

Cushman, K. (2010). *Fires in the mind: What kids can tell us about motivation and mastery*. San Francisco: Jossey-Bass.

Doda, N., & Knowles, T. (2008). Listening to the voices of young adolescents. *Middle School Journal, 39*(3), 26–33.

Easton, L., & Condon, D. (2009). A school-wide model for student voice in curriculum development and teacher preparation. In A. Cook-Sather (Ed.), *Learning from the student's perspective: A secondary methods sourcebook for effective teaching* (pp. 176–193). Boulder, CO: Paradigm.

Esposito, J., & Swain, A. N. (2009). Pathways to social justice: Urban teachers' use of culturally relevant pedagogy as a conduit for teaching social justice. *Perspectives on Urban Education*, 6(1), 38–48.

Fine, M., Torre, M. E., Burns, A., & Payne, Y. (2007). Youth research/participatory methods for reform. In D. Thiessen & A. Cook-Sather (Eds.), *International handbook of student experience in elementary and secondary school* (pp. 805–828). Dordrecht, The Netherlands: Springer.

Fobes, C., & Kaufman, P. (2008). Critical pedagogy in the sociology classroom: Challenges and concerns. *Teaching Sociology, 36*, 26–33.

Gay, G. (2010). *Culturally responsive teaching: Theory, research, and practice* (2nd ed.). New York: Teachers College Press.

Gold, S. J. (2004). Using photography in studies of immigrant communities. *American Behavioral Scientist, 47*(12), 1551–1572.

Gonzales, N. E., Moll, L., & Amanti, C. (Eds.). (2005). *Funds of knowledge*. Mahwah, NJ: Erlbaum.

Grossman, P. (2010). *Learning to practice: The design of clinical experience in teacher preparation*. Washington, DC: American Association of Colleges for Teacher Education.

Haddix, M., & Sealey-Ruiz, Y. (2012). Cultivating digital and popular literacies as empowering and emancipatory acts upon urban youth. *Journal of Adolescent and Adult Literacy, 56*(3), 192–198.

Harper, D. (2005). What's new visually? In N. K. Denzin & Y. S. Lincoln (Eds.), *The Sage handbook of qualitative research* (3rd ed., pp. 747–762). Thousand Oaks: Sage.

Hibbing, A. N., & Rankin-Erickson, J. L. (2003). A picture is worth a thousand words: Using visual images to improve comprehension for middle school struggling readers. *The Reading Teacher, 56*(8), 758–770.

Hicks, T. (2013). *Crafting digital writing: Composing texts across media and genres*. Portsmouth, NH: Heinemann.

Imig, D. G., & Imig, S. R. (2008). *From a traditional certification to competitive certification: A twenty- five year perspective*. In M. Cochran-Smith, S. Feiman-Nemser, & D. J. McIntyre, (Eds.), *Handbook of research on teacher education: Enduring questions in changing contexts* (3rd ed., pp. 1009–1016). New York: Routledge, with the Association of Teacher Education.

Ivey, G., & Broaddus, K. (2007). A formative experiment investigating literacy engagement among adolescent Latina/o students just beginning to read, write, and speak English. *Reading Research Quarterly, 42*(4), 512–545.

Journell, W., & Castro, E. L. (2011). Culturally relevant political education: Using immigration as a catalyst for civic understanding. *Multicultural Education, 18*(4), 10–17.

Kellett, M. (2009). Children as researchers: What we can learn from them about the impact of poverty on literacy opportunities? *International Journal of Inclusive Education, 13*(4), 395–408.

Kemmis, S., & McTaggart, R. (2000). Participatory action research. In N. K. Denzin & Y. S. Lincoln (Eds.), *Handbook of qualitative research* (2nd ed., pp. 567–605). Thousand Oaks, CA: Sage.

Kincheloe, J., & McLaren, P. (1998). Rethinking critical theory and qualitative research. In N. Denzin & Y. Lincoln (Eds.), *The landscape of qualitative research* (pp. 260–299). Thousand Oaks, CA: Sage.

Kincheloe, J. L. (2004). *Critical pedagogy primer*. New York: Peter Lang.

Kress, G. (2006). *Reading images: The grammar of visual design*. New York: Routledge.

Kress, G., Charalampos, G., & Jewitt, C. (2006). *Multimodality teaching and learning*. Royston, GA: BookEns.

Lan, W., & Lanthier, R. (2003). Changes in students' academic performance and perceptions of

school before dropping out of schools. *Journal of Education for Students Placed at Risk, 8*(3), 309–332.
Levine, A. (2006). *Educating school teachers.* Washington, DC: Education Schools Project.
Lucas, T., & Grinberg, J. (2008). Responding to the linguistic reality of mainstream classrooms: Preparing all teachers to teach English language learners. In M. Cochran-Smith, S. Feiman-Nemser, & D. J. McIntyre, (Eds.), *Handbook on teacher education: Enduring questions in changing contexts* (3rd ed., pp. 606–636). New York: Routledge.
Martínez-Roldán, C. M., & Fránquíz, M. E. (2009). Latina/o youth literacies: Hidden funds of knowledge. In L. Christenbury, R. Bomer, & P. Smagorinksy (Eds.), *Handbook of adolescent literacy research* (pp. 323–342). New York: Guilford Press.
May, S., & Sleeter, C. E. (2010). *Critical multiculturalism: Theory and praxis.* New York: Routledge.
McIntyre, D. (2009). The difficulties of inclusive pedagogy for initial teacher education and some thoughts on the way forward. *Teaching and Teacher Education, 25,* 602–608.
Mediratta, K., Shah, S., & McAlister, S. (2009). *Community organizing for stronger schools: Strategies and successes.* Cambridge, MA: Harvard Education Press.
Mills, K. A. (2010). A review of the "digital turn" in the new literacy studies. *Review of Educational Research, 80*(2), 246–271.
Moje, E. B., Overby, M., Tysvaer, N., & Morris, K. (2008). The complex world of adolescent literacy: Myths, motivations, and mysteries. *Harvard Educational Review, 78*(1), 107–154.
Morrell, E. (2007). *Critical literacy and urban youth: Pedagogies of access, dissent, and liberation.* New York: Routledge.
National Center for Education Statistics (NCES). (2009). *The condition of education: 2009.* Washington, DC: National Center for Education Statistics/Institute of Education Sciences.
Noguera, P. A. (2008). The schools we need. In *The trouble with Black boys: . . . And other reflections on race, equity, and the future of public education* (pp. 161–250). San Francisco: Jossey-Bass.
Paris, D. (2012). Culturally sustaining pedagogy: A needed change in stance, terminology, and practice. *Educational Researcher, 41*(3), 93–97.
Patton, M. Q. (2002). *Qualitative research and evaluation methods* (3rd ed.). Thousand Oaks, CA: Sage.
Piper, H., & Frankham, J. (2007). Seeing voices and hearing pictures: Image as discourse and the framing of image-based research [Special issue]. *Discourse: Studies in the Cultural Politics of Education, 28,* 373–387.
Pole, C. (Ed). (2004). *Seeing is believing?: Approaches to visual research* (Vol. 7). New York: Elsevier.
Ronfeldt, M. (2012). Where should student teachers learn to teach?: Effects of field placement school characteristics on teacher retention and effectiveness. *Educational Evaluation and Policy Analysis, 34*(1), 3–26.
Rose, G. (2006). *Visual methodologies: An introduction to the interpretation of visual materials.* Thousand Oaks, CA: Sage.
Schultz, B. D. (Ed.). (2011). *Listening to and learning from students.* Charlotte, NC: Information Age.
Sleeter, C. E. (2008). Preparing White teachers for diverse students. In M. Cochran-Smith, S. Feiman-Nemser, & D. J. McIntyre, (Eds.), *Handbook on teacher education: Enduring questions in changing contexts* (3rd ed., pp.559–582). New York: Routledge.
Smyth, J. (2007). Toward the pedagogically engaged school: Listening to student voice as a positive response to disengagement and "dropping out"? In D. Thiessen & A. Cook-Sather (Eds.), *International handbook of student experience in elementary and secondary school* (pp. 635–658). Dordrecht: Springer.
Somers, C., Owens, D., & Piliawsky, M. (2009). A study of high school dropout prevention and

at-risk ninth graders' role models and motivations for school completion. *Education, 130,* 348–356.

Streng, J. M., Rhodes, S. D., Ayala, G. X., Eng., E., Arceo, R., & Phipps, S. (2004). *Realidad Latina*: Latino adolescents, their school, and a university use photovoice to examine and address the influence of immigration. *Journal of Interprofessional Care, 18*(4), 403–415.

Torre, M. E., Fine, M., Stoudt, B., & Fox, M. (2012). Critical participatory action research as public science. In H. Cooper & P. Camic (Eds.), *APA handbook of research methods in psychology* (pp. 171–184). Washington, DC: American Psychological Association.

U.S. Department of Education. (2007). *The Nation's Report Card: Reading 2007* (NCES Report No. 2007-496). Washington, DC: U.S. Government Printing Office.

Van Leeuwen, T., & Jewitt, C. (Eds.). (2001). *Handbook of visual analysis.* Thousand Oaks, CA: Sage.

Vasudevan, L., DeJaynes, T., & Schimier, S. (2010). Multimodal pedagogies: Playing, teaching and learning with adolescents' digital literacies. In D. Alvermann (Ed.), *Adolescents' online literacies: Connecting classrooms, digital media, and popular culture* (pp. 5–25). New York: Peter Lang.

Wang, C., & Burris, M. A. (1997). Photovoice: Concept, methodology and use for participatory needs assessment. *Health Education and Behavior, 24*(3), 369–387.

Wang, C. C. (2006). Youth participation in photovoice as a strategy for community change. *Journal of Community Practice, 14,* 147–161.

Yonezawa, S., & Jones, M. (2009). Student voices: Generating reform from the inside out. *Theory Into Practice, 48*(3), 205–212.

Zeichner, K., & Conklin, H. G. (2008). Teacher education programs as sites for teacher preparation. In M. Cochran-Smith, S. Feiman-Nemser, & D. J. McIntyre (Eds.), *Handbook on teacher education: Enduring questions in changing contexts* (3rd ed., pp. 269–289). New York: Routledge.

Zeller-Berkman, S. (2007). Peering in: A look into reflective practices in youth participatory action research. *Children, Youth and Environments, 17*(2), 315–328.

Zenkov, K. (2009). The teachers and schools they deserve: *Seeing* the pedagogies, practices, and programs urban students want. *Theory Into Practice, 48*(3), 168–175.

Zenkov, K., Bell, A., Ewaida, M., & Lynch, M. (2012). Seeing how to "ask first": Photo elicitation and motivating English language learners to write. *Middle School Journal, 44*(2), 6–12.

Zenkov, K., Bell, A., Lynch, M., Ewaida, M., Harmon, J., & Pellegrino, A. (2012). Youth as sources of educational equity: Using photographs to help adolescents make sense of school, injustice, and their lives. *Education in a Democracy, 4,* 79–98.

Zenkov, K., Ewaida, M., Lynch, M., Bell, A., & Harmon, J. (2013). Picturing culturally relevant literacy practices: Using photography to see how literacy curricula and pedagogies matter to urban youth. *International Journal of Multicultural Education, 15*(2).

Zenkov, K., & Harmon, J. (2009). Picturing a writing process: Using photovoice to learn how to teach writing to urban youth. *Journal of Adolescent and Adult Literacy, 52*(7), 575–584.

Zumbrunn, S., & Krause, K. (2012). Conversations with leaders: Principles of effective writing instruction. *The Reading Teacher, 65*(5), 346–353.

CHAPTER 10

The Power of Fostering Pleasure in Reading

MICHAEL W. SMITH, JEFFREY D. WILHELM, and SHARON FRANSEN

We became English teachers because we love to read. Yet we worry that the goal of developing curricula and instruction designed to foster a love of reading in students is losing ground, at least in the United States. Consider that the first sentence in the section on aims on the first page of the *National Curriculum in England: English Programmes of Study* (United Kingdom Department for Education, 2014) reads as follows: "The overarching aim for English in the national curriculum is to promote high standards of language and literacy by equipping pupils with a strong command of the spoken and written language, and to develop their love of literature through widespread reading for enjoyment." In contrast, the first sentence of the *Common Core State Standards for English Language Arts and Literacy in History/Social Studies, Science, and Technical Subjects* (National Governors Association Center for Best Practices & Council of Chief State School Officers [NGA & CCSSO], 2010), the closest thing the United States has to a national curriculum, explains that the purpose of the standards is "to help ensure that all students are college and career ready in literacy no later than the end of high school" (p. 3). There is no mention of pleasure or enjoyment here or anywhere else in the document.

Murphy (2012) decries such a neglect of pleasure:

> If pleasure is recognized as not merely important to life, but central to it, then one would imagine that educational systems all around the world, in turn, would have taken this premise to heart in the design of educational spaces and in pedagogical engagements. Certainly, as histories of play and culture reveal, pleasure was central to the educational thinking of the celebrated thinkers of the past . . . Yet, across the past 140 years or so of organized education in Canada and the United States, pleasure and literacy education have been only occasional partners." (p. 318)

Our purpose in this chapter is to argue that neglecting the power of pleasure significantly undermines our efforts to educate our students. More specifically, we begin with a discussion of what pleasure in reading is, explain why it is important, theorize why it has been so neglected in the United States, then consider how it might be achieved.

WHAT PLEASURE IN READING IS

Reading for pleasure, according to Clark and Rumbold (2006), "refers to reading that we to do of our own free will anticipating the satisfaction that we will get from the act of reading. It also refers to reading that having begun at someone else's request we continue because we are interested in it" (p. 5). Nell's (1988) *Lost in a Book: The Psychology of Reading for Pleasure* is an examination of that satisfaction that avid readers derive from their reading. On the basis of a variety of studies, Nell builds a model of what he calls *ludic reading,* that is, the state of deep engagement avid readers experience while reading books for pleasure. He describes ludic reading this way:

> These are the paired wonders of reading: the world creating power of books, and the reader's effortless absorption that allows the book's fragile world, all air and thought, to maintain itself for a while, a bamboo and paper house among earthquakes; within it readers acquire peace, become more powerful, feel braver and wiser in ways of the world. (p. 1)

He then articulates that the antecedent conditions needed for that engagement include reading ability, a positive attitude to reading, and the appropriate book, in terms of both its match to the reader's ability and its match to the reader's interest. He argues that if those antecedents are in place, a reader will choose to begin reading. According to Nell, once a reader has begun reading, he or she pays a kind of effortless attention to the text (the continuing impulse to read), employing both automated reading skills and consciously controlled comprehension processes. The results, says Nell, are the physiological and cognitive changes that he describes in the previous quotation.

Both Clark and Rumbold (2006) and Nell (1988) seemingly assume that reading pleasure comes in only one variety. Others, however, delineate different kinds of pleasure, perhaps none more famously than Barthes (1975) in *The Pleasure of the Text.* Barthes makes a distinction between pleasure and bliss (*jouissance*). The text of pleasure, he says, "contents, fills, grants euphoria: the text that comes from a culture and does not break with it, is linked to a comfortable practice of reading" (p. 14). The text of bliss, in contrast, provides a dramatically different experience. It "imposes a state of loss . . . , unsettles the reader's historical, cultural, psychological assumptions, the consistency of his tastes, values, memories, brings to a crisis his relation with language" (p. 14).

As Sumara (1996) points out, by translating *jouissance* as bliss, the English translation of Barthes's work loses the explicit sexual connotations of the French, the implication of "playful eroticism" (p. 62) inherent in the word. Sumara explores the experience of *jouissance* he and his fellow reading group members experienced as they read *The English Patient,* illustrating how it requires "learning to be uncomfortable; learning to live with ambiguity, learning to tolerate the resistance of the literary fiction itself" (p. 70).

In our own work investigating the nature of reading pleasure (Wilhelm & Smith, 2014), we have taken a different approach. Barthes's distinction between the text of pleasure and the text of bliss sets up a hierarchy that we have come to question. According to

Barthes, conventional or familiar texts yield a kind of pleasure he doesn't much admire, a pleasure that's safe and comfortable. Experimental or unfamiliar texts, on the other hand, produce a more admirable kind of pleasure, a pleasure that is challenging and unsettling. However, our research analyzing the nature and variety of pleasure experienced by avid readers of texts marginalized by schools—romances, vampire stories, horror, dystopian fiction, and fantasy—suggests that these familiar texts can produce profound and surprising pleasure.

In our study, we conducted a series of interviews with 14 avid eighth-grade readers of those marginalized genres and then worked to get a more in-depth understanding of the pleasure provided by each particular genre by doing a case analysis of one or more older adolescents. Drawing on Dewey's (1913) delineation of different forms of educative interest, we found that our participants experienced four distinct kinds of pleasure: the pleasure of play, the pleasure of work, the pleasure of figuring things out, and the social pleasure of both affiliating with other readers and using one's reading to name oneself. We illustrate our findings by drawing on our interviews with three committed readers of vampire stories, a kind of text often dismissed by teachers and parents alike.

We called the immersive and absorbing experience of entering a story-world the pleasure of play, following Dewey (1913, p. 21) who writes that play "puts itself forth with no thought of anything beyond." Here's one of our informants describing that she derived that pleasure from her reading of vampire stories, focusing specifically on the Twilight series:

> "What draws people to Twilight is that it is relatable. Young characters. Teenagers. Relationships. Love. The dangers of love. You need it [love] so bad but it is dangerous and can slay you. That's the interest of teenage girls. Feelings—Bella's feelings can be related to. So intense. Most of what I read in school I cannot relate to. Like *1984*. There was NOTHING I could relate to. I wasn't interested in entering into the story. But I am so interested in entering into Twilight because it is about me right now. I can relate to it."

Because Twilight was "relatable" to her, she could experience the intense visceral pleasure of entering the story.

Whereas play puts itself forth with no thought of anything beyond itself, in work, according to Dewey, "The thought of the finished product and of the use to which it is to be put may come to [the child's] mind, but so as to enhance [the child's] immediate activity of construction" (p. 79). Perhaps our most striking finding is that our participants took pleasure from using their reading to help them construct the kind of people they wanted to become, a kind of pleasure we termed *inner work*, following Jungian scholars such as Robert Johnson who explain that inner work "is the effort by which we gain an awareness of the deeper layers of consciousness within us and move to an integration of the total self" (p. 13). Here's another informant manifesting her awareness of how she uses her reading of vampire stories to do such inner work:

> "Being a teenager is partly about struggling to be more adult and have more adult relationships. . . . I think a real struggle of more adult relationships is making sure they are life-giving in both directions. I mean, we all have these needs so you have to be careful about not being a vampire and sucking someone else dry, or hurting

and discarding them. But you have to be really careful not to let someone do it to you, too, like dominate you, just because you like being liked or feeling attractive or whatever. I think it's a real danger."

A third kind of pleasure is the intellectual pleasure of figuring things out. Dewey (1913, pp. 83–84) writes: "When any one becomes interested in a problem as a problem, and in inquiry and learning for the sake of solving the problem, interest is distinctively intellectual." A third informant explained how she derived that pleasure from reading vampire stories:

"Most of the main vampire characters become good at least to some degree. Lothaire [the protagonist of the vampire novel *Lothaire*] starts as evil and murderous and the plot goes for three-quarters and then he becomes . . . well, not good, but a grayish area—ending the book neutral. . . . So it's not like humans 'being good and vampires being bad.' There is always struggle between good and evil vampires and good and evil within a vampire. Authors give them different species names. Put them in different armies. Sometimes they right out say these are good, these are bad, sometimes they make you figure it out and in those books the goodness and evilness are more complicated and that is more interesting and fun."

The final kind of pleasure we identified was social pleasure. As Dewey (1913) points out, "social interest . . . is a strong special interest" (p. 84). We found that social pleasure has two dimensions: connecting with others and differentiating oneself from others. Our first informant explains both. She notes that while reading vampire stories,

"You just get sucked into it—you focus just on the experience. You come to like the characters and being with them. . . . It's not like I'd want to hang out with the characters in real life but I like being with them as a reader. And I like being with other readers being with them [the characters]."

She connects with the characters and with her fellow readers who are also experiencing that connection. But she also takes pleasure in using her reading to stake her identity and differentiate herself from others:

"So many male people say 'Twilight is just so dumb.' [They] can't believe you like 'that crap.' But we can resist them and say, 'Hey we love it.' We are not afraid to like it because of people who don't like it. Most of them have never read the books anyway; they just think they know what they are about. But we know and we like going back at them."

WHY PLEASURE IS IMPORTANT

Whatever conception of pleasure one adopts, we would argue that it is quite obvious that pleasure can play a powerfully motivating force in reading. Moreover, that motivation can have profound effects. We are especially compelled by *Social Inequalities in Cognitive Scores at Age 16: The Role of Reading* (Sullivan & Brown, 2013), a sophisticated analysis that draws on data collected in the 1970 British Cohort Study, which is following the lives of more than 17,000 people born in England, Scotland, and Wales in a single week of 1970. As a result of their analysis, Sullivan and Brown offer what we see as a startlingly important conclusion:

> Our findings . . . [suggest] that children's leisure reading is important for educational attainment and social mobility . . . and suggest that the mechanism for this is increased cognitive development. Once we controlled for the child's test scores at age five and ten, the influence of the child's own reading remained highly significant, suggesting that the positive link between leisure reading and cognitive outcomes is not purely due to more able children being more likely to read a lot, but that reading is actually linked to increased cognitive progress over time. From a policy perspective, this strongly supports the need to support and encourage children's reading in their leisure time. (p. 37)

The increased cognitive progress is what accounts for the surprising finding that leisure reading is also correlated with increased math performance.

Perhaps we should not have been so surprised by Sullivan and Brown's findings. In his blog (*http://skrashen.blogspot.com/2013/09/new-evidence-for-power-of-reading.html*), Stephen Krashen points out that Sullivan and Brown's work is consistent with his own work. For example Krashen, Lee, and McQuillen's (2012) study suggests that "providing more access to books can mitigate the effect of poverty on reading achievement" (p. 30). However, as they point out, access alone is not enough. Children have to take advantage of that access, something, we would argue, that depends on their deriving pleasure from so doing. In their analysis of Programme for International Student Assessment (PISA) results, Kirsch and his colleagues (2002) report a similar result:

> Levels of interest in and attitudes toward reading, the amount of time students spend on reading in their free time and the diversity of materials they read are closely associated with performance in reading literacy. Furthermore, while the degree of engagement in reading varies considerably from country to county, 15-year-olds whose parents have the lowest occupational status but who are highly engaged in reading obtain higher average reading scores in PISA than students whose parents have high or medium occupational status but who report to be poorly engaged in reading. This suggests that finding ways to engage students in reading may be one of the most effective ways to leverage social change. (p. 3)

Engaging students in reading appears to be one of the most formidable tools educators have to contribute to a more equitable society. It appears that fostering pleasure in order to encourage students' subsequent leisure reading is a crucially important educational goal.

WHY IS PLEASURE SO NEGLECTED?

If pleasure is so important, why is it so neglected? Cremin, Mottram, Collins, Powell, and Safford (2014) argue that "few countries appear to acknowledge the potential potency of enhancing children's independent reading, their pleasure in reading and engagement as readers" (p. 18) and they point their fingers at a foregrounding of the "narrow assessment" of reading skills. Gallagher (2009) makes a similar argument, contending that "schools value the development of test-takers more than they value the development of readers" (p. 5). Undoubtedly, current assessment practices have had an impact, but it seems quite clear that other arguments against pleasure have long existed.

Dewey (1913) begins his analysis of educative interest by analyzing the arguments that would be brought in what he called the "educational lawsuit" (p. 1) of interest versus effort. The plaintiff, he explained over a century ago, would offer an argument something like this:

> Life is not a merely pleasant affair, or a continual satisfaction of personal interests. There must be such continual exercise of effort in the performance of tasks as to form the habit of dealing with the real labors of life. Anything else eats out the fiber of character and leaves a wishy-washy, colorless being; a state of moral dependence, with continual demand for amusement and distraction. (p. 4)

The language may be a bit old-fashioned, but we have heard modern versions of this argument in the schools with which we work.

Radway (1986) explores another character-related argument against pleasure. She notes that mass-produced popular culture texts, the kinds of texts in which most readers take pleasure are seen as "capable of degrading, indeed, of corrupting those who enjoy it" (p. 7). As Nell (1988) points out, the cultural bias against popular cultural texts is so great that the participants in his studies on average rated over 40% of the reading they did as trash, with a doctoral student in English literature rating over 90% of his reading as such. The bias against what's popular is reflected in the books that are available to students in their schools. Worthy, Moorman, and Turner (1999), for example, concluded that "by an overwhelming margin, the students in our study preferred materials that have been traditionally scorned by literary critics and many educators" (p. 23). As a consequence, "there is an ever increasing gap between student preferences and materials that schools provide and recommend" (p. 23). This gap can only undermine the inclination to read and in so doing reduce the potential for students to experience the transformational benefits reading can bring.

A focus on reading pleasure as a major aim of instruction runs afoul of preparation for high-stakes tests and on the cultural bias against both interest as an appropriate motivator and the highly popular texts that many readers find pleasurable, biases that exist both within and outside schools. Yet the power and importance of pleasure is clear enough for schools and teachers to strive to resist those biases.

HOW TO CULTIVATE PLEASURE

Although, as Clark and Rumbold (2006) state, the investigation of "reading for pleasure has not been a research priority" (p. 9), a number of studies have addressed it in some fashion or another. We identified those studies by searching on both education-related databases and Google Scholar using the key words "pleasure" and "reading." We then also searched for "independent reading," "free choice reading," and "summer reading." Second, we read through reference lists of relevant studies in search of additional pertinent studies, especially those that were frequently referenced. Some of these searched led to studies that also focused on motivation or attitudes related to reading. The findings from these studies paint a consistent pattern. We discuss a handful of them that we have found evocative, then do a cross-study analysis to elucidate that pattern, focusing primarily on those published in journals and not on book-length works.

Cremin and her colleagues (2014) undertook perhaps the most extensive and certainly the most focused study of how to foster a reading for pleasure pedagogy. Their study included teachers of beginning readers to teachers of students as old as 11, so it explores the effects of pleasure reading on both emergent and developing readers. The study had two phases. The first was a survey of 1,100 teachers on their reading and teaching practices. The second was extensive work in 27 schools to support the development of a reading for pleasure pedagogy that ultimately centered on four core practices:

- reading aloud to the class for pleasure rather than for instrumental literacy teaching purposes;
- creating diverse, supportive and social reading environments;
- talking about books and making recommendations to individuals and the whole class;
- creating frequent opportunities for children to read independently for pleasure and giving them choices about what to read. (Cremin et al., 2014, p. 90)

The linchpin in their efforts was working with teachers to reflect on their own reading and to develop a richer knowledge both of materials that are available and of children's everyday reading practices. They conclude with this recommendation:

Reading for pleasure and reader engagement urgently require a higher profile to foster readers who not only can, but who choose to read and who grow as readers, as learners, and as young people as a result. This is not an optional extra but a basic requirement and one which deserves increased professional attention. (Cremin et al., 2014, p. 159)

Ivey and Johnston (2013) studied the impact of a program designed to take up Cremin and colleagues' (2014) challenge to foster pleasure and reader engagement. Their study was based on the premise that middle school students who are given the opportunity to select personally meaningful reading will become engaged readers. They conducted their study in five middle-grade classrooms with teachers who had committed to giving students control both of the materials they selected to read from the 150–200 titles available in each classroom library and of how they would respond to that reading. The teachers devoted class time to independent reading, teacher read-alouds, and student responses to their reading.

The primary data for the study were 71 end-of-year interviews. They found that students read for extended periods of time both in and out of school, and outside of sanctioned times, for example, after a teacher had moved on in activities or after parents had told a student to go to bed. According to Ivey and Johnston (2013), students' engagement extended beyond the time they spent reading, for students reported deep involvement in their reading, manifested in their talking about books in English class, in other classes, in the lunch rooms, at home with family members, and with friends from other schools. Those interactions led both to the deepening of existing friendships and the development of new ones, perhaps because students reported what Ivey and Johnston term an *expanded social imagination,* that is, "the ability to imagine what is going on in others' minds and to imagine the logic of social interaction" (p. 262). In addition, students began to relate to teachers on a reader-to-reader basis, rather than on a teacher–student basis. One teacher explained it this way:

> They are so excited about what they're reading, and they love what they're reading. They sit and tell you everything. They don't care whether you know the book or not. They don't love the affirmation. They just want the avenue to talk. (Ivey & Johnston, 2013, p. 261)

Students also reported a host of academic benefits, from increased reading and writing abilities to an increased knowledge of the world. Significant increases in performance on the state's standardized reading assessments suggest that the students were not overstating the case. In short, Ivey and Johnston (2013) documented significant shifts in how students saw themselves as readers and an increased understanding that through the exercise of their agency, they could shape their futures beyond their identity as a reader.

Strommen and Mates (2004) also take up the issue of reading identity. They administered a 10-page survey to a total of 151 sixth- and ninth-grade students to determine whether they could categorize them as readers or not-readers, that is, as students who can read but choose not to and then did follow-up interviews with an equal number of readers and not-readers. The readers talked about reading in terms of the pleasure they took from it. The not-readers also saw reading as important, but they talked about it in terms of purpose rather than pleasure. That is, they saw reading as a means to some functional end, for example, improving their vocabulary or filling out a job application.

Strommen and Mates's (2004) research questions focused on the factors that supported the development of readers. Not surprisingly, readers had regular interaction about books with members of their social circle who read for pleasure. Those interactions demonstrated the pleasure people can take from reading, helped the readers choose their future reading, and connected the readers to the culture of book lovers.

McKool (2007) also investigated the difference between avid readers and those who choose not to read outside school, through the use of a survey instrument and follow-up interviews. Like Strommen and Mates (2004), McKool found that "avid readers . . . were more likely to see adults or siblings reading novels and other materials more associated with pleasure" (p. 122). She also found that students reported few opportunities in school for informal discussions about what they were reading. However, avid readers did talk positively about uninterrupted reading time when they were given choice about what to read. Unfortunately, the reluctant readers reported that they were seldom given real choices, because their teachers prohibited them from reading from their favorite materials, for example, comic books or magazines.

Gabriel, Allington, and Billen (2012) take up the issue of students' preferred reading materials in a fascinating way. One hundred ninety-seven middle schoolers were given surveys about their leisure reading habits. Then about half were randomly selected to choose two free magazine subscriptions from a list of 31 magazines. During and after that time, additional surveys and interviews were conducted about how, when, and why they read the magazines they chose.

Gabriel and her colleagues (2012) found that that students tended to read their magazines on the very day that the magazines arrived. They argue that this behavior suggests that "the novelty factor is a consistent reason to initiate leisure reading" (p. 187). From this finding they make two suggestions about how teachers work with more conventional materials: Unveil new books in a classroom in installments, and simulate the thrill of receiving a mailing by periodically "delivering" a book to a particular student and making it clear that it was chosen just for him or her.

The students in the Gabriel et al. (2012) study read to deepen existing areas of expertise rather than to develop new ones, and they took pleasure in exporting what they read into their conversations, a finding consistent with one we (Smith & Wilhelm, 2002) made in our examination of the literate lives of young men both in and out of school. They argue that this finding suggests the importance of providing opportunity for informal talk about what students are reading, including their out-of-school reading.

Although magazines suffer from the same negative bias as do other popular cultural materials in the eyes of many teachers and parents, Gabriel and her colleagues (2012) found that students were applying just the kind of strategies teachers seek to develop in their work in school when they were reading outside school. They argue that this suggests that magazines can be a powerful instructional resource that contributes to the goal of cultivating capable and engaged readers.

Pitcher and her colleagues (2007) are more sanguine about the possibility of schools positively affecting students' attitudes toward reading. The 11 authors worked together to revise the Motivation to Read Profile, which is used with elementary school-age students to create the Adolescent Motivation to Read Profile, then administered it to students in eight sites in the United States and Trinidad. When they asked, "Have any of your teachers done something with reading that you really enjoyed?," students responded by citing reading aloud, literature circles, sustained silent reading time, and being given the opportunity to choose their own books. The interviews also made it clear that teachers' enthusiasm can have a tremendous positive impact on the way students feel about their reading. Teachers who shared their knowledge of and enthusiasm for reading positively affected students' attitudes. The authors make it clear that that knowledge ought to include an understanding of the multiple literacies in which students are involved outside class, so that they can include reading material of varied formats in the classroom.

Pruzinsky (2014) shares his efforts to cultivate a positive attitude toward reading in his International Baccalaureate (IB) classroom. Despite the rigors of the IB curriculum, he argues that it is essential to give at least 15 minutes a day of free reading time. During the class reading time, Pruzinsky suggests conferring with students to show them that their reading matters. He also advocates the importance of promoting the reader through book talks and through sharing his own reading life. He further notes that his efforts depend on having a strong classroom library. In concert, these efforts work to create what he calls a "reading sanctuary" (p. 29).

Lee (2011) also shares her efforts to develop a successful, sustained silent reading (SSR) program. She notes that encouraging students to read for pleasure involves more than just allowing them time in school to read, although providing that time is indeed important. She worked to create a conducive environment for reading and, as Ivey and Johnston (2013) suggest, allowed purposeful, quiet talking as long as it did not distract others. She also calls for developing a classroom library that includes a wide selection of texts from different genres and reading levels. She suggests not requiring students to bring materials to class because some may not have access to texts and others may not want to be seen with texts. She explains, "If our goal is truly to mentor students in their reading and to encourage them to read more, then we have to trust and honor the reader's interests," (p. 213) and tells the story of a student who brought in a catalogue from Cabella's as his text for SSR. She accepted his choice and in time he moved to hunting magazines and eventually to nonfiction survival stories. She also notes the importance of encouragement, especially in making reading recommendations. Rather than requiring some kind of accountability mechanism, she found that conferring and mentoring were more effective in promoting reading. Finally, she suggests allowing students who are enthusiastic about a book the option of sharing their enthusiasm through some kind of self-selected follow-up activity.

Lapp and Fisher (2009) take the impact of school a step further in their case analysis of their own 11th-grade class. They, too, discuss the power of choice, but the choice they provided their students was embedded in a more structured framework. More specifically, their inquiry-based curriculum was built around essential questions, such as "What's your life worth and to whom?" and "What are the consequences of your decisions?" (p. 557). The instruction they provided was designed to ensure student engagement and involvement through instructional tasks such as whole-class jigsaws, reciprocal teaching, book clubs, online chats, independent reading, poetry raps, and plays. They used a variety of different kinds of texts to engage students in the questions, from novels to newspapers, and had a weekly book club. They also provided time for independent reading of books chosen from a list constructed for each unit. Students compared what they were reading in the novels with the facts being presented in the nonfiction and the news articles being read by the whole class.

Lapp and Fisher (2009) report that their students took ownership of the topic and were actively engaged in the work of the class, even to the point of bringing in new texts to contribute to the inquiry. Lapp and Fisher conclude that the students' "enthusiastic participation cemented for us the fact that adolescents, just like adults, will read if the book is a good read, if the book is accessible, and if they can have some ownership in the selection" (p. 559).

Lapp and Fisher's (2009) findings about their 11th graders are consonant with those that emerged from the Guthrie, Hoa, Wigfield, Tonks, and Perencevich (2005) investigation of their concept-oriented reading instruction (CORI) with much younger children. They argue that *situational interest*, that is, the interest that one derives from a particular reading experience "may be re-experienced for another book in a series, or an alternative text on a slightly different topic. If the situational experience is accompanied by delight, and learning, the opportunity for developing long-term motivation may occur" (p. 93).

A centerpiece of the CORI model is that students were free to choose the reading they did that related to the concept under investigation from a wide array of texts of different genres. In addition, students were able to collaborate with classmates, to interact with challenging texts, and to engage in hands-on activities connected to literacy.

PUTTING IT ALL TOGETHER

Taken together, these studies paint a rather uniform picture of what teachers and schools can do to foster pleasure in reading. The first principle is to provide time for reading, both independent reading by students and read-alouds by teachers. As we tell the preservice and inservice teachers with whom we work, time is a zero-sum game. That is, every minute one spends doing something is a minute one cannot spend doing something else. The teachers in the studies we cite here demonstrated their commitment to a reading for pleasure pedagogy by devoting time to it. Frequent opportunities to read were a centerpiece of each classroom, and as Pitcher and her colleagues (2007) discovered, students appreciated that time.

Second, all of the studies indicate the importance of choice, although there were some differences among the choices provided. Cremin and colleagues (2014), Ivey and Johnston (2013), Pitcher and her colleagues (2007), and Pruzinsky (2014) all talk about allowing students a wide choice of books. Lapp and Fisher (2009) and Guthrie et al. (2005) talk about choice, but in their cases, the choice is somewhat more restricted, in that students' selections need to be relevant to the inquiry the class is pursuing. McKool (2007), Gabriel and her colleagues (2012), and Lee (2011) push the envelope a bit further by suggesting the importance of giving students real choices of the materials they most want to read, including magazines, comic books, and the like. Though the studies differed somewhat in the nature of the choice they suggest providing, they were united in proclaiming the critical importance of providing more choice of reading materials than students typically get in school.

A third component of a reading for pleasure pedagogy, according to these studies, is providing students opportunities for informed conversations about their reading. Reading is so often thought of as a solitary act. That's quite clearly not the case in the studies we have presented here. Cremin and her colleagues (2014) explain the importance of spontaneous talk about books. Ivey and Johnston (2013) document that the students in their study talked about books in English class, in other classes, in the lunchroom, at home with family members, and with friends from other schools. Interestingly, students shared instances of when they talked about their books with kids to whom they would otherwise not have spoken. The importance of talk is so great that in an article on the implications of her research, Ivey (2014) notes that teachers should "expect that students will want to talk, allow it to happen even during 'silent' reading, and arrange for it to happen regularly with the whole class, prioritizing what students bring to the conversation from their own reading" (p. 169).

Finally, all of the studies reviewed here document the importance of enthusiastic and knowledgeable teachers who, as readers themselves, model their reading and share their passion for it. These knowledgeable and enthusiastic teachers become conversational partners, book recommenders, and the recipients of students' recommendations. They open up their classes to a wide array of texts that their students enjoy. They create a culture of book loving in their classrooms.

Of course, it's important that schools help prepare students to be career and college ready. But we worry that this vision of the future results in too narrowly understanding what's important for students. This narrow understanding undermines important goals such as promoting lifelong reading, while at the same time undermining our capacity to meet goals such as those expressed in the Common Core State Standards. These goals are profound cognitive achievements that cannot be achieved without engagement and practice over time. This engagement and practice will not occur without the motivational power of pleasure.

Studies from around the globe teach us that students' inclination to engage in reading for pleasure outside school is a powerful predictor of their life chances. Other studies document the importance of reading for pleasure in the immediate situation. Understanding what reading pleasure is, resisting the forces that have turned schools away from it, and taking affirmative steps to cultivate it will help students reap the myriad benefits of reading, both now and throughout their lives.

The good news is that those steps are within teachers' control: providing time for free reading, respecting the reading choices students make, creating a context that allows for conversations about reading both among students and between students and teachers, and sharing themselves as a fellow reader. The stakes are too high not to take them. Murphy (2012) puts it this way:

> When pleasure and reading are companions, we know very well that children become engaged readers and are likely to continue to read throughout their lives. With this knowledge in hand, despite the waning influence of pleasure in relation to reading in schools across much of the twentieth century, we have an ethical obligation to 'do well' with what we know about the relationship between reading and pleasure. (p. 326)

In short, pleasure needs to be central to our practice.

REFERENCES

Barthes, R. (1975). *The pleasure of the text* (R. Miller, Trans.). New York: Hill & Wang.
Clark, C., & Rumbold, K. (2006). *Reading for pleasure: A research review*. London: National Literacy Trust.
Cremin, T., Mottram, M., Collins, F. M., Powell, S., & Safford, K. (2014). *Building communities of engaged readers: Reading for pleasure*. London: Routledge.
Dewey, J. (1913). *Interest and effort in education*. Boston: Houghton Mifflin.
Gabriel, R., Allington, R., & Billen, M. (2012). Middle schoolers and magazines: What teachers can learn from students' leisure reading habits. *The Clearing House: A Journal of Educational Strategies, Issues and Ideas, 85,* 186–191.
Gallagher, K. (2009). *Readicide: How schools are killing reading and what you can do about it*. Portland, ME: Stenhouse.
Guthrie, J., Hoa, L., Wigfield, A., Tonks, S., & Perencevich, K. (2005). From spark to fire: Can situational reading interest lead to long-term reading motivation? *Reading Research and Instruction, 45,* 91–117.
Ivey, G. (2014). The social side of engaged reading for young adolescents. *The Reading Teacher, 68,* 165–171.
Ivey, G., & Johnston, P. (2013). Engagement with young adult literature: Outcomes and processes. *Reading Research Quarterly, 48,* 255–275.
Johnson, R. (1986). *Inner work*. New York: Harper & Row.
Kirsch, I., de Jong, J., LaFontaine, D., McQueen, J., Mendelovits, J., & Monseur, C. (2002). *Reading for change: Performance and engagement across countries: Results from PISA 2000*. Paris: Organisation for Economic Co-operation and Development. Retrieved from www.oecd.org/edu/school/programmeforinternationalstudentassessmentpisa/33690904.pdf.
Krashen, S., Lee, S., & McQuillan, J. (2012). Is the library important?: Multivariate studies at the national and international level. *Journal of Language and Literacy Education* [Online], 8(1), 26–38.
Lapp, D., & Fisher, D. (2009). It's all about the book: Motivating teens to read. *Journal of Adolescent and Adult Literacy, 52,* 556–561.

Lee, V. (2011). Becoming the reading mentors our adolescents deserve: Developing a successful sustained silent reading program. *Journal of Adolescent and Adult Literacy, 55*(3), 209–218.

McKool, S. S. (2007). Factors that influence the decision to read: An investigation of fifth grade students' out-of-school reading habits. *Reading Improvement, 44,* 111–131.

Murphy, S. (2012). Reclaiming pleasure in the teaching of reading. *Language Arts, 89,* 318–328.

National Governors Association Center for Best Practices & Council of Chief State School Officers (NGA & CCSSO). (2010). *Common Core State Standards for English language arts and literacy in history/social studies, science, and technical subjects.* Washington, DC: Authors.

Nell, V. (1988). *Lost in a book: The psychology of reading for pleasure.* New Haven, CT: Yale University Press.

Pitcher, S. M., Albright, L. K., DeLaney, C. J., Walker, N. T., Seunarinesingh, K., Mogge, S., et al. (2007). Assessing adolescents' motivation to read. *Journal of Adolescent and Adult Literacy, 50,* 378–396.

Pruzinsky, T. (2014). Read books. Every day. Mostly for pleasure. *English Journal, 103*(4), 25–30.

Radway, J. (1986). Reading is not eating: Mass-produced literature and the theoretical, methodological, and political consequences of a metaphor. *Book Research Quarterly, 2,* 7–29.

Smith, M. W., & Wilhelm. J. (2002). *"Reading don't fix no Chevys": Literacy in the lives of young men.* Portsmouth, NH: Heinemann.

Strommen, L. T., & Mates, B. F. (2004) Learning to love reading: Interviews with older children and teens. *Journal of Adolescent and Adult Literacy, 48,* 188–200.

Sullivan, A., & Brown, M. (2013). *Social inequalities in cognitive scores at age 16: The role of reading.* London: Centre for Longitudinal Studies.

Sumara, D. (1996). *Private readings in public: Schooling the literary imagination.* New York: Peter Lang.

United Kingdom Department for Education. (2014). National curriculum in England: English programmes of study. Retrieved from *www.gov.uk/government/publications/national-curriculum-in-england-english-programmes-of-study/national-curriculum-in-england-english-programmes-of-study.*

Wilhelm, J. D., & Smith, M. W. (2014). *Reading unbound: Why kids need to read what they want and why we should let them.* New York: Scholastic.

Worthy, J., Moorman, M., & Turner, M. (1999). What Johnny likes to read is hard to find in school. *Reading Research Quarterly, 34,* 12–27.

CHAPTER 11

Disciplinary Literacy
A Multidisciplinary Synthesis

DAVID G. O'BRIEN and LISA ORTMANN

Academic literacy has recently limited its scope to the particular literacy practices and discourses of the academic disciplines of science, social studies, mathematics, and English studies. However, as the academic literacy focus has narrowed, the perspectives from within these disciplines have widened to consider new pedagogical representations of the disciplinary knowledge taught in secondary schools and higher education. Thus, the theoretical frameworks and definitions of literacy within disciplines are vast yet not clearly understood.

In this chapter, we discuss different perspectives on academic literacy for adolescents, drawing from within and outside of the field of literacy education. We consider how perspectives have shifted in response to the focus on disciplinary literacy and explore how the inclusion of digital and multimodal texts has contributed to some emerging perspectives. We include our research and that of our colleagues throughout the chapter to clarify how each framework has been represented and applied to studies of literacy within academic disciplinary areas. In much of our own work, we have collaborated closely with our school-based colleagues, observing, interacting with students, and synthesizing and reflecting during professional learning community (PLC) time and summer study sessions, leading to curricular modifications that feed back into this collaborative cycle. Also, in response to the recent criticism of the content literacy era of "infusing" sets of generic strategies or other instructional routines into instruction, we have purposely, especially in our most recent work, worked to develop changes in curricula, instruction, engagement, and assessments based on day-to-day work from within classrooms.

ACADEMIC LITERACY TRADITIONS AND TRAJECTORY

We use *academic literacy* as the broad category under which we include clearly defined approaches to literacy instruction such as content-area reading, writing across the curriculum, content literacy strategy instruction, academic language, and most recently, disciplinary literacy and its various enactments within the core subject areas. Although there are other instructional approaches we could discuss, the aforementioned have had traction in secondary schools and K–12 education policy, and maintain status in the current conversations regarding literacy instruction in secondary schools.

We also include digital literacies as part of academic literacy, particularly the affordances of digital texts and multimodality (Wilson, 2008). For each approach, we discuss the developing frameworks, with a focus on how these influence instructional approaches and how they have been studied. Through this review, we hope to shed some light on the relationships between the applied/emerging frameworks in recent scholarship and the realities for adolescents in schools. By highlighting exemplars of practice-based research in disciplinary teaching and learning environments we hope to open up the conversation about academic literacy to include a wider variety of frameworks and approaches.

How Has Academic Literacy Been Conceptualized?

The formal inquiry into academic literacy, which spans about 50 years (further back if one includes study skills) is neither new nor clearly defined (Moore, Readence, & Rickelman, 1983). With adolescent learners, the term *literacy,* as it is framed and discussed in major research syntheses and policy reports over the last decade (e.g., Biancarosa & Snow, 2006; Kamil, 2003), usually does not refer to literacy or literacy studies broadly speaking, but rather to reading and reading pedagogy, although there is also a large body of work on academic writing (e.g., Hyland, 2000; Geisler, 1994). Within the body of work labeled as *adolescent literacy,* academic literacy is a considerable component.

Academic literacy, whether informed from literacy and reading studies (e.g., Alvermann & Moore, 1991; Moje, 2008; Shanahan & Shanahan, 2008, 2012), writing studies (Hyland, 2000; De La Paz & Wissinger, 2015), functional language perspectives (Fang & Schleppegrell, 2010), discourse studies (Gee, 2000), academic language (Anstrom et al., 2010; Townsend, 2015), or the psychology of teaching and learning (Alexander & Jetton, 2000; Van den Broek, 2010), involves inquiry into how literacy and learning intersect. For example, pedagogically oriented work in academic language (e.g., Townsend, 2015), content literacy (e.g., Alvermann, Gillis, & Phelps, 2012), and writing across the curriculum (Ochsner & Fowler, 2004) all focus on facets of how literacy and language are implicated in learning and share some instructional assumptions and approaches. The field of literacy studies with a focus on reading is quite diverse, ranging from cognitive perspectives rooted in educational psychology to sociocultural perspectives ranging from anthropology and sociology to linguistics and discourse processing (O'Brien & Rogers, 2015).

Academic literacy is also situated within composition studies in educational contexts. Writing scholars have moved from an exclusive focus on cognitive processing models (e.g., Flower & Hayes, 1981) to consider frameworks of writing in the content areas (e.g., Bangert-Drowns, Hurley, & Wilkinson, 2004) and discourses as situated within broader discourse communities for whom people write (e.g., Lave & Wenger, 1991; Stockton, 1995). These scholars address questions of who "owns" writing instruction (Buzzi, Grimes, & Rolls, 2012; Monroe, 2003); the nature of argumentation, reasoning, and rhetoric within the various disciplines (De La Paz & Wissinger, 2015; Wolfe, 2011); and the successful use of discipline-specific language structures in students' academic writing performances (Lester et al., 2003).

The field of composition studies is undergoing a shift of focus from generic writing instruction, commonly referred to as *writing across the curriculum* (WAC), to *writing in the disciplines* (WID), which is a more discipline-specific approach. Although the two terms are sometimes used interchangeably, these approaches have different implications for the role of writing and writing instruction in higher education. While WAC emphasizes the commonality and portability of writing practices, WID emphasizes the differences among disciplines (Monroe, 2003). Scholars of writing instruction in higher education have argued that writing in the disciplines must align with the particular practices and curriculum goals of the specific programs of study. This shift in focus has moved writing instruction from within English and communications studies departments to disciplinary programs and departments across the college (McLeod & Soven, 2006). WID efforts have opened the doors between disciplines to include interdisciplinary cluster teaching, in which writing and disciplinary faculty collaborate on instructional goals and assessments for a cohort of students co-enrolled in their courses. Studies have found this model more effective than stand-alone writing courses in helping students reach high levels of discipline-specific writing (Watts & Burnett, 2012).

Critical literacy and literature scholars also study academic literacy, but through the use of critical frameworks that address how students engage with the inherent power dynamics in producing and consuming texts according to their discursive properties and uses within social discourse communities (Appleman, 2014). These scholars apply critical discourse theories and analysis methods to the study of texts, social practices, and the broader political/institutional discourses that exist in literacy teaching and learning contexts (Gee, 1999, 2012; Hodge & Kress, 1988; Kress & Van Leeuwen, 2001). Critical discourse analysis and critical literacy studies have offered the field of adolescent literacy ways of examining historical contexts, as well as multiple discourses within single interactions, and ways to connect the social world with the linguistic expressions of teaching and learning. Although most studies grounded in critical literacy frameworks are concerned with visions of literacy that connect the examination of societal power structures within texts to personal and social transformation and justice (e.g., Garcia, Mirra, Morrell, Martinez, & Scorza, 2015), some literary scholars have applied critical literacy frameworks in studies of how to support the access to academic literacy of traditionally marginalized adolescents. Park (2013) concluded that academic literacies must be defined as both the *knowledge* of how texts are written and interpreted and the *capacity* to manage school-based reading and writing tasks.

The shifting of content literacy to disciplinary literacy was marked largely by the spring 2008 issue of the *Harvard Educational Review*, which focused on adolescent and disciplinary literacy. In the issue, Draper (2008) critiqued the traditional notion of strategies instruction and content literacy courses and advocated for reconstructing disciplinary literacy as a collaborative practice between content and literacy educators; Shanahan and Shanahan (2008) drew distinctions between the specialized reading that experts within disciplines do, as well as how reading is characterized by content reading professionals; Moje, Overby, Tysvaer, and Morris (2008) noted the importance of metadiscourse in showing adolescents how to navigate various disciplinary discourses, while emphasizing the importance of multiliteracies, motivation, and engagement across disciplines; and Conley (2008) argued that strategies included in popular content literacy textbooks are untested in terms of equipping students with cognitive strategies they need to read independently and strategically for their own purposes.

This more recent perspective on academic literacy is predicated on the assumption that literacy professionals' outside-in approaches, particularly those of importing "generic" strategies into disciplines, have been ineffective (Fang & Schleppegrell, 2010; Shanahan & Shanahan, 2012). Instead, disciplinary literacy instruction should go beyond the "infusion" of generic cognitive strategies to a view of texts and literacy practices as part of overarching, metadiscursive frameworks for articulating how and why the purposes, uses, and forms of texts vary among content areas (Wilson, 2011). Because each discipline has distinct ways of engaging in inquiry, presenting evidence, and expressing arguments, secondary content literacy instruction should focus on sense-making and understanding, as well as engage students in authentic disciplinary activities (Draper & Broomhead, 2010).

Cross-disciplinary collaboration among literacy professionals and content-area teachers is assumed to result in stronger disciplinary literacy instruction. An improved understanding of how insiders within the discipline define and enact literacy practices is the expected outcome of interdisciplinary collaboration. However, there is no definitive evidence supporting this insider collaborative position. For example, studies that have examined cross-disciplinary collaborative efforts in secondary and higher education teaching contexts have found power issues relating to the positional authority of team members, conflicting pedagogical beliefs, and presumed hierarchies of the disciplines' barriers to successful literacy integration (Emerson, MacKay, MacKay & Funnell, 2006; Jacobs, 2010). Additionally, teachers of academic disciplines do not always view themselves as disciplinary insiders, and instead situate their identities within their world of work as educators (Jacobs, 2010; Wilson, 2011). Although cross-disciplinary collaboration can change teachers' attitudes toward the literacies of their disciplines (Emerson et al., 2006), the goals of literacy teachers and disciplinary teachers often do not align (Bazerman, 2005; Buzzi et al., 2012). Additionally, scarce physical resources, time, and the organization of high schools and colleges into often-divisive departments make the reality of these cross-disciplinary partnerships an almost insurmountable challenge.

The Role of Texts: From Textbooks and Print to Digital and Multimodal Affordances

As textbooks emerged as a text genre at the end of the 19th century, they became synonymous with compulsory rather than popular reading (Shapiro, 2012). Textbook commercial publishing, now mostly controlled by four large companies, does not have to worry about engaging students as an audience; rather, they must market textbooks to school districts via state adoption boards, local school boards, curriculum directors, and teachers and administrators (Shapiro, 2012; Sewall, 2005). In short, textbooks were never designed to be appealing to students, even though they do contain some sophisticated learning designs such as advance organizers, including multiple graphic overviews and guiding questions, selected vocabulary for preteaching concepts, and marginal glosses. Yet textbooks and related materials persist as dominant artifacts of the theoretical and instructional frameworks of disciplinary domains and discourses.

Beyond the "print-centric era" are disciplinary discourse communities that represent more shared understanding through the creation of collaborative, portable, disciplinary texts. One discourse community member reads a text and annotates it; the next member writes an updated text that infuses the annotated text but reshapes it to a new argument. Yet another member reads the newest text and argument and goes back to rework a text written weeks or even years before that was posted online. This collaborative fluidity of portable texts affords intertextuality, particularly of intersection of reading and writing (Bloome & Egan-Robertson, 1993) but from an intermedial perspective, which draws on the ability to read and write media and depends on facility in the use of a range of symbol systems and knowledge of the affordances of various modes of expression (e.g., Semali, 2005).

This intermediality is but one example of how digital spaces drastically change what is meant by disciplines, texts, and intertextual connections within and across disciplines (Beach & O'Brien, 2015). *Disciplinary literacy* involves teaching young people "how to access, interpret, challenge, and reconstruct the texts of the disciplines" (Moje, 2008, p. 100) rather than looking at texts as repositories of domain knowledge. With digital technologies and online spaces, students are afforded access to more texts than ever before, as well as tools to author traditional and multimodal texts themselves. From this perspective, digital work moves "beyond the linguistic" (Jewitt, 2005, p. 315) to a theory that acknowledges many elements of meaning (Cope & Kalantzis, 2000; Kress & Van Leeuwen, 2001). In some of our work with adolescents, we have used the affordances of digital, multimedia production to engage and redefine the agency and sense of creative expression of what they were learning; they made intertextual connections by designing projects with traditional print and other media (O'Brien, 2012).

Disciplinary Literacy and Policy

Relative to early literacy, adolescent literacy, including academic literacy, has received little attention nationally based on the popular discourse and press about the urgency of early literacy instruction (Alvermann, 2002; Biancarosa & Snow, 2006). This early literacy/early intervention focus, with its assessment and accountability narrative, has dominated policy concerns (Luke & Woods, 2009). Part of the public discourse about early literacy arises from the false binary that has been sustained: Children learn-to-read by the end of primary grades, then they proceed to apply what they know in reading-to-learn, which carries them through school and into college and the workplace. Nevertheless, the No Child Left Behind Act of 2001, although targeting early literacy, because of its magnitude in bringing a national literacy reading crisis to the fore, did have an impact on adolescent literacy (Conley & Hinchman, 2004).

The "crisis of adolescent literacy," which is part of a newer narrative in the last decade (Kamil, 2003), and many reports following it, has brought a renewed call to action but, again, has had relatively little impact on overall policies that support academic literacy. Nevertheless, there are federally funded programs and calls for fundable models focusing on academic literacy specifically tied to college and career readiness (e.g., U.S. Department of Education Office of Special Education Programs) and similarly targeted foundation grants (e.g., Great Lakes College Readiness Grants).

The attention to the importance of literacy in subject-area learning articulated in the grades 6–12 section of the English language arts Common Core State Standards (CCSS) is the latest push for more attention to academic literacy in social studies/history, science, and technical subjects. Web pages focusing on academic literacy for both children and adolescents are multiplying, mostly due to state and district responses to the CCSS. But the response to the CCSS has taken many forms, from revisiting content literacy approaches and infusing strategies into disciplines to cut-and-dried text and instructional practices defining disciplines, to calls simply just to add more reading and writing to content classes. Unclear in all of this activity related to the CCSS is who is responsible for setting up collaborative approaches drawing on both disciplinary insider knowledge and that of literacy professionals. A significant policy problem is the questionable assumption that English language arts teachers are particularly equipped to understand academic literacy. On a positive note, because of the inclusion of a disciplinary literacy focus in the CCSS, there is also increased interest in the role that academic literacy can play in elementary schools (e.g., Shanahan & Shanahan, 2014). Even literature study, which is typically associated with narrative texts, is being reconfigured to include more of a focus on nonfiction and informational texts, and is catalyzed by the CCSS (Appleman, 2014).

In science and mathematics education, national attention has shifted to an integration of disciplines as a new approach to teaching the science and mathematics academic standards, and specifically attending to the desire to build "STEM literate" students (Wojnowski & Pea, 2014). The case for science, technology, engineering, and mathematics (STEM) reform has been made most recently by President Obama in his 2013 State of the Union Address, in which he called for 10,000 of America's "Master teachers" of the STEM disciplines to work together to improve the state of STEM education. The national educational policy discourse since then has turned to enabling and inspiring today's students to select future degrees and careers in STEM fields, thus building a stronger STEM workforce. The Next Generation Science Standards (NGSS) proposes an interdisciplinary approach to teaching the STEM disciplines, and outlined within these standards are literacy-specific practices, processes, and reasoning strategies of the disciplines of science, engineering, and mathematics. As national K–12 education policy continues to shape what is essential to students' learning within academic disciplines, it is important that education scholarship consider and present the views of academic literacy that have been well-established within and outside the fields of literacy, K–12 education, and higher education more broadly.

DISCIPLINARY LITERACY FRAMEWORKS

Sociocultural Learning Theories

The role of literacy in learning in the disciplines is implicated in how we think of learning as situated, from cognitive to sociocognitive, to linguistic, to sociocultural frameworks. The earliest inquiry into sociohistorical schooling by Vygotsky and his students (Cole, 1990) is based on the postulate that humans, as learners, are different from other animals because their psychological processes are culturally mediated, historically situated, and arise from practical activity (Wertsch, del Rio, & Alvarez, 1995). Additionally, the mediational power of various tools, from words, signs, and language to objects, to digital apps, can profoundly change understanding and engagement. Human beings do not learn anything in isolation; rather, they live in socially and culturally defined communities in which understanding is mediated by artifacts. Cultural artifacts, which are tools, include language and literacy, along with more traditional notions such as objects.

But literacy in school, rather than being considered as a mediational tool, has been appropriated mostly as a way to communicate and access relatively narrow content with constrained forms of reading and writing (Gee & Hayes, 2011). The social practice of reading an academic text can frustrate students, because the uses of academic language can restrict students from constructing knowledge freely. Although this chapter is mostly about frameworks and approaches that support adolescents' access to academic language, both oral and written, we must acknowledge that academic language is also socially constructed for the purpose of excluding learners from playing "in the game" (Gee & Hayes, 2011), with rules constructed by each subject area. More importantly, these socially constructed subject-area "games" are not a realistic representation of how teachers, who are only superficially aligned within disciplines based on subject-area teaching assignments, transcend discipline-specific language in multidisciplinary inquiry. In actuality, outside of subject areas as social constructions of disciplines, people who engage in multidisciplinary collaboration are concerned less with producing and consuming discipline-specific knowledge than in thinking in new ways and solving problems in innovative ways.

One way to break free from the traditional socially constructed versions of disciplines in school as exclusionary games is to use reading and writing as part of activities to mediate new understanding. Socioculturally oriented notions of mind and understanding can be defined by participation in activity, and activity can be placed at the core of engagement and learning in school, especially activity that is connected to the lives, including social and cultural roots, of students (Roth & Lee, 2007). For example, in a study of the use of "new literacies" pedagogy for engaging struggling adolescent learners in junior high (O'Brien, Beach, & Scharber, 2007), we used cultural historical activity theory (Engeström, 2006; Roth & Lee, 2007) to ground a project focusing on studies of place. Students created multimodal productions depicting important places, ranging from hometowns to neighborhoods, to places in school. They picked visual, audio, or print to comment on the places in VoiceThread. As part of the project they studied the importance of place, the multimodal representation of it, and how various modes of expression afforded different meanings and ways of their engaging peers and us. The activity was grounded by a sociohistorical importance of the activity to the students. That and other projects within the study promoted both student engagement and learning beyond the traditional print-based curriculum.

Social and Functional Linguistics

Scholars who take a social and functional linguistic view of disciplinary literacy (e.g., Fang & Schleppegrell, 2010; Nagy & Townsend, 2012) prefer a discursive and textual approach; that is, they look at linguistic features of texts that are unique within disciplines and how those texts embody discursive features and academic language of disciplines. The interest in the functional linguistic structure is predicated on some of the ideas we express elsewhere in terms of discourse, but with a focus on written expression. Scholars who work within this framework take the position that disciplinary specialists use language in specific ways to present information to develop arguments, to infuse certain perspectives, and to create specialized texts with the linguistic characteristics compatible with these approaches (e.g., Fang, Sun, Chiu, & Trutschel, 2014). Two approaches to practice are evidenced in work within this framework: (1) work to sensitize teachers to the disciplinary language of texts through functional language analysis (FLA) (Fang & Schleppegrell, 2008; Nagy & Townsend, 2012) and (2) work in which students scaffold understanding of academic language in texts, often with an approach to academic vocabulary (e.g., Nagy & Townsend, 2012). This work indicates that targeting specific academic language in texts, by augmenting what teachers know about it, accompanied by explicit instruction with students, produces gains in disciplinary knowledge. Into the digital realm, affordances such as multimodality can make academic language accessible through the production and use of media (Gee & Hayes, 2011), for example, creating multimodal texts that represent academic vocabulary and concepts more richly.

Disciplinary Discourse Communities

Other interpretations of disciplinary literacy are drawn from a theory of discourses as situated within social communities of practices (Lave & Wenger, 1991) and discourse communities that participate within broader disciplinary discourses (Hyland, 2012). This approach rests on an assumption of learning within disciplines as an apprenticeship model; to understand a discipline, one must be indoctrinated as a member of its academic discourse community (Hyland, 2000, 2012). Implicit in disciplinary membership is participation in the observable practices in published, written discourse, as well as acceptance into the broader academic and social practices of the discipline. Hence, disciplinary literacy is cast as a "collective social practice" that is both socially shaping and being shaped by the discipline (Hyland, 2000). Similarly, scholars of rhetoric and the technology of texts, like Geisler (1994), have argued that many academic texts afford and sustain both expert and naive interpretations, with expert interpretation reserved for those inside the discourses and social practices of the profession.

These insider "implied readers" are not who literacy scholars think they are, nor do they read like we think they might. Geisler (1994) contends that in order to understand disciplinary literacy, we need to understand the cultural practices from within the discipline. The challenge of using discourse frameworks for studying the cultural practices of disciplinary insiders is that where disciplines (synonymous with Gee's [1990] "big D Discourses") are defined historically and rather abstractly, (little d) discourses are defined locally. Furthermore, what constitutes a discourse is constantly fluid and evolving (Gee, 1999). Although there may be common practices within a discourse community, the boundaries around a discourse are flexible, widening and narrowing, depending on the ways individuals introduce other discourses into the discourse community, thus changing discursive practices. Therefore, how the larger disciplines are taken up and recontextualized within these smaller, situated discourses in schools is of particular significance to theories of disciplinary literacy.

If we take an example from education in which disciplinary literacy would hypothetically be observed, we can trace how this challenge may play out. Imagine a high school biology classroom. We might say the biology teacher is charged with teaching the disciplinary practices of the discipline of biology, within the larger academic domain of "natural science"; however, she may not see herself as a disciplinary insider because she herself is not a biologist. Instead, she situates her identity within her world of work as a teacher. Furthermore, the biology teacher, being a particularly effective teacher, draws on multiple discourses in her attempts to teach the important concepts of her discipline. She uses multiple sources of information, various print-based and digital texts, and experiential learning situations; she requires students to represent learning by using multiple modalities, and engages students in inquiry-based projects to apply their knowledge. We could make the argument that each of these approaches accesses and requires students to participate in a variety of discourses, and that the totality of these constitutes the "discipline" of biology for her students. We wonder, where did "disciplinary" literacy begin and "generic" literacy end in this example? Furthermore, which discursive practices should be privileged on the unit exam in this teacher's classroom?

In acquiring disciplinary knowledge and skills, students encounter a "new and dominant literacy," often finding that their own writing practices are criticized by their teachers as they attempt to imitate a discourse (Hyland, 2000, p. 146). This is neither an effective nor a motivating learning stance. Students need to find ways to see their own discourse practices as opportunities, not limitations on their disciplinary learning. Hyland contends that the goal of imparting the literacy of the disciplines "involves developing a generative capacity rather than an adherence to rules, an exploitation of forms rather than compliance to them" (p. 148). Thus, a static and superimposed conception of what it means to "do a discipline" is counter to the classroom environments we want to promote.

In a 6-year project based on work in the Jefferson High Literacy Lab, David and his colleagues explored the discourse of possibility (O'Brien, 2012; O'Brien, Springs, & Stith, 2000) by engaging students in multimodal productions that confronted traditional notions of incompetence assigned to adolescents because they were labeled as "at-risk" learners and were unsuccessful with print-centric, schooled notions of literacy. At the same time they engaged in various disciplinary discourses while they explored project topics, critiqued dominant discourses associated with traditional notions of success in reading, and constructed new discourses of competence to support their work. The participatory culture of an effective classroom community like this one is exactly the kind of learning community we are finding in online environments today. In these environments, individuals draw from a variety of discourses in order to interact with individuals who draw from their own discourses. Together, in these online learning spaces, individuals read, negotiate, challenge, and re(present) disciplinary knowledge and disciplinary practices in ways that have never before been afforded through the traditional print-centric ways of disciplinary text production and consumption.

For example, in Lisa's research of disciplinary literacy in STEM-integrated learning in high school science classrooms, the discipline of engineering was positioned as a vehicle for students to apply their learning of particular physical science standards (Ortmann, 2015). In these classrooms, the science teachers modeled and scaffolded the discourse of physics; for example, they focused on the language of Newton's laws of motion as a means to evaluate the success of an engineering design. For many students, appropriating the dominant scientific discourse was a part of "doing school" and, with practice and repetition, students became somewhat successful at it. For the nontraditional students in the study, the use of this particular academic discourse was not just difficult—it was viewed as unnecessary.

In a classroom of ninth-grade immigrant students and English learners, a young man explained his experience working with a group of men to design and build a rainwater collection mechanism that could be used to collect and filter drinking water at a refugee camp. In his lived experience, engineering was about solving problems in the physical world through ingenuity and collaboration. Conversely, in the science classroom, engineering was about designing and constructing abstract "prototypes" out of Styrofoam and Bubble Wrap that represented the kinds of real-world solutions to social or physical problems actual engineers might design. This student's conceptual understanding of Newton's laws of motion and physics far exceeded that of his more traditional student peers; however, he did not take up the disciplinary discourse modeled in the classroom when communicating his ideas or evaluating the success of his design. Instead, he relied on a functional language and discourse, both in English and in his native language, to best convey his ideas to his peers and his teacher, and made use of multiple modes of representing knowledge. This case offers a counternarrative to the "disciplinary insider" point of view that legitimizes only one way of understanding and representing the content of a discipline. Although the student was unable to access a dominant, disciplinary discourse, he was able to develop a strong conceptual understanding of both Newton's laws of motion and the engineering design process.

Literacy from within the Disciplines

Emerging alongside the literature of disciplinary literacy constructed by the literacy education community are approaches to instruction emanating from the education community but from within disciplines, including scientific literacy, technological literacy, historical literacy, STEM literacy, and others. As education scholars across the disciplines have studied the role of academic texts and writing tasks of students in content-area courses, the notion of specific, disciplinary literacy texts and activities has taken hold, and each discipline is beginning to articulate what constitutes these practices and what defines their texts differently from texts in other disciplines. For example, historical literacy, with roots in Wineburg's (1991) work on the kinds of reasoning processes, texts, and practices in which historians engage when they read and write for historical purposes, was generated separately from the general academic literacy with roots in literacy education. This work gained significant attention in the field; consequently, other academics have started to replicate the study of the literacy practices of scholars within their disciplines (e.g., Kaiser & Willander, 2005).

Educational policy has played a significant role in defining the literacy from within disciplines. Roger Bybee's (1997) influential work on scientific literacy, situated within the current science education reform movement, advocates for a strengthening of science and mathematics instruction throughout the K–12 grades. Bybee's (2013) recent work in STEM integration also calls for a more substantial, useful curriculum in science that includes the impact of science and technology on society and the many social problems that have arisen due to limited resources and increasing global interdependence. Current policy in science education has evolved to draw attention to the "literacy" of science and technology (NGSS Lead States, 2013; National Research Council, 2012). Although the notion of scientific literacy has been around for decades, the goal of science education currently is scientific literacy for all students (Bybee, 2013).

The approaches to literacy within disciplines are reflective of a national social–efficiency value of preparing students for the literacy demands of college and careers in the STEM fields. In this discussion, what constitutes academic literacies is not always clearly defined, and when it is, the conversation relies on a traditional, print-based definition of functional literacy. In a study on integrating literacy into a physics course for prospective teachers, the science education researchers used this definition: "By integrating physics and literacy learning, we mean learning to speak clearly, listen closely, write coherently, read with comprehension, and make and critique media resources competently in physics contexts" (Van Zee, Jansen, Winograd, Crowl, & Devitt, 2013, p. 29). Similarly, Wilson, Smith and Householder (2014) argue that "engineering literacy derives from fundamental literacies, or the ability to locate, comprehend, evaluate, and produce discipline-specific texts" (p. 676). In their comparative case study on the use of engineering literacy in high school science classes, they examined how the traditional literacy practices of rereading and annotating, using cognitive strategies, recording ideas in writing, and providing and responding to feedback aided adolescents in their engineering design process. They found that the more of these literacy practices that students used in the initial stages of the engineering design activity, the more systematically they were able to address the constraints, criteria, and needs of the client in their final engineering solution, thus finding greater success on the engineering learning tasks.

In a recent review, Hillman (2014) outlined two prevalent approaches to mathematics literacy. These included Sfard's (2007) four-text features of mathematical words, narratives, visual mediators, and routines, and Kaiser and Willander's (2005) system of five levels of reasoning, which includes the five developmental levels of illiteracy, nominal literacy, functional literacy, procedural literacy, and multidimensional literacy, with the last representing mastery of mathematics as a discourse. In each of these examples, the examination of literacy in practice remains defined within traditional, print-centric views of literacy that do not take into account the social, digital, and multimodal frameworks from which literacy scholars are drawing in their own work.

Some literacy scholars take a social-efficiency approach to disciplinary literacy studies, that is, considering literacy as an important facet of the economic capital position on learning that connects success in school to economic growth, and educational achievement to success in global markets. Kiili, Mäkinen, and Coiro (2013) propose a framework for academic literacy in which the building of new knowledge and active citizenship rests at the core between the five literacy domains: disciplinary, innovative, digital, argumentative, and collaborative. The authors suggest that "these overlapping domains of literacy practices empower students to take a more active role in their local and global academic communities, while collaboratively building new knowledge for the betterment of society" (p. 226). In the framework they argue that although the literacy learning needs of adolescents should include disciplinary literacy, on its own, it does not provide a sufficiently balanced literacy approach. This is an important criticism of disciplinary literacy. Literacy is being inaccurately positioned in science, social studies, English, and mathematics education as a curriculum that can be packaged and clearly labeled for teachers. Most definitions of STEM literacy cover the social and economic needs of literacy taken up by the CCSS but overlook the social and personal purposes of literacy for adolescents (Zollman, 2012). There is a difference between preparing students to become *literate* and the processes of *literacy*. Conceptions of "STEM literacy" or other discipline-specific literacies, should not be viewed as content areas, but need to be deictic, composed of skills, abilities, factual knowledge, procedures, concepts, and metacognitive capacities (Zollman, 2012).

In the field of composition and rhetoric, the WID movement to house literacy instruction within the disciplines of study has been offered as a response to the fundamental purpose of obtaining a degree and graduating. Students focus on "the real curriculum," which is explained as the academic courses that make up the degree program, and represent course requirements that exist outside of that program of study (Buzzi et al., 2012). Though practical, a criticism of the WID approach is that teaching writing in a discipline-specific manner will fragment the humanistic mission of teaching speaking and writing in higher education, and lead students away from their personal concerns and voices. Fleury (2005) argues "in a [WID] approach—with its emphasis on singular, specialized disciplinary competence—students may miss the landscape, the multiple paths, perhaps even the multiple vehicles available to them as they move on in their academic work and beyond" (p. 74). In response to this criticism, Bazerman (2005) contests that the very act of studying discipline-specific forms of communication offers access to students otherwise excluded from academic communities, and provides them with ways to find their own voices, identities, and meanings within the disciplines. For him, "identities can grow, gain strength, and provide greater opportunities for social engagement as they assimilate the powers of the professions" (p. 89). This very same argument has been made by literacy scholars who take a sociocultural view of disciplinary literacy (e.g., Moje, 2008), functional linguistic perspectives (e.g., Fang & Schlepergrell, 2010), and the arguments from within the disciplines (e.g., Bybee, 1997). Improving students' access to the disciplines through a focus on academic literacy seems to be a unifying purpose for the shifts in K–12 policy and practice; however, what that looks like has yet to be determined.

CONCLUSIONS AND IMPLICATIONS

In this chapter, our aim has been to show the advantages of considering academic literacy as framed and studied from a multidisciplinary perspective. First, the complexity of a multidisciplinary view points to the futility of producing canned sets of definitions and practices fit to disciplines and the pitfalls of constructing binaries and artificial either–or distinctions such as generic or discipline-specific instructional approaches. On the practical end, seeking and using both theoretical and pedagogical practices from the range of disciplines that study and design academic literacy instruction, explore different notions of text, and foreground varying aspects of instructional language and discourse will provide a broader menu from which to choose to support adolescent learners.

Second, we emphasized the fluidity of academic literacy practices and content in relation to both purposes and activities, requiring the ongoing inquiry into day-to-day practices related to learning. The importance of a particular linguistic structure of the text, or the general tenets of how literacy should be defined and enacted within a discipline, is often subverted to the demands of particular tasks that define very constrained ways of reading and writing both within and across disciplines as they are articulated in school subjects. Not all practices can be defined as discipline-specific, or in terms of the ways a particular discipline situates texts, but rather in terms of completing assignments and responding to assessment rubrics.

For example, in a current professional development project with high school history teachers, we are working with our school-based colleagues to improve both the literacy engagement and academic literacy practices of students, with the goal of improving their postsecondary school success. The history classes, based on the International Baccalaureate curriculum, use a list of "command terms" in defining multiple ways of engaging with texts, thinking historically, assessing students' efficacy in arguing perspectives, and so on. At the top of one command list is the term *analyze*, which has this definition: "break down in order to bring out the essential elements or structure." With reference to academic literacy, "analysis" might tap generic approaches, possibly related to various types of comprehension, from recall to drawing inferences, to writing summaries; or it might tap discipline-specific practices tied to a functional language analysis unique to argumentation in history or how sourcing comparisons of primary texts might lead to understanding. So far, just a brief perusal and attempts to map command term processes to literacy practices related to learning are both intriguing and impossible. There are clearly ways of thinking, problem solving, and arguing within disciplines that do not fit congruently with our preconceptions generated from within literacy education. We continually talk with school-based colleagues about our preconceptions and definitions and about what we are learning that does fit; at the same time we are developing collaborative ways to work through these disciplinary definitions and constructs in terms of literacy to benefit the adolescents with whom we all work.

Additionally, in our professional development work with teachers, we have learned that academic literacy is as much about *accessibility* as *proficiency*. Students who do not understand when they encounter very complex history texts sometimes choose not to engage for many reasons, but mostly these two: (1) The text-based task is perceived as being so difficult that it might dissuade some students from reading; they might try to tackle the text minus the structured task (e.g., if they just read the text armed with important purposes) and both generic and discipline-specific strategies; and (2) because the task is considered too challenging as some students working with peers they perceive as more competent simply disengage from reading and defer to their peers to complete the reading and related task. The task itself defines and sometimes stifles possibilities offered by the text. Opening up the possibility of approaching texts at each student's unique, individual levels, defining purposes, and using stances and strategies that each feels confident in using, would open a new world of access to texts and participation in disciplinary discourse communities.

In our experiences, the most valuable window into academic literacy comes from working with our school-based colleagues as they conceptualize, plan, and construct lessons. Time spent in the field with teachers, observing and working with adolescents as they tackle assignments designed by teachers as specific articulations of academic literacy, and participating in regular discussions in PLCs, makes apparent how academic literacy is defined and enacted in day-to-day activities. In this ongoing work, we have explored how academic literacy, as created within disciplines, is often defined with sets of constructs, terms, and definitions that are incongruent with our previously constructed literacy categories. Some approaches to reading and writing might map directly onto generic reading, writing, and thinking approaches; some might be defined as "discipline-specific," and others defy any category. We hope that as we draw from multidisciplinary frameworks of academic literacy, ongoing collaboration with school-based colleagues will both clarify concepts and improve teaching and learning approaches.

REFERENCES

Alexander, P. A., & Jetton, T. L. (2000). Learning from text: A multidimensional and developmental perspective. In M. L. Kamil, P. B. Mosenthal, P. D. Pearson, & R. Barr (Eds.), *Handbook of reading research, Volume III* (pp. 285–310). Mahwah, NJ: Erlbaum.

Alvermann, D. E. (2002). Effective literacy instruction for adolescents. *Journal of Literacy Research, 34*(2), 189–208.

Alvermann, D. E., Gillis, V. R., & Phelps, S. F. (2012). *Content area reading and literacy: Succeeding in today's diverse classrooms.* New York: Pearson Higher Education.

Alvermann, D. E., & Moore, D. W. (1991). Secondary school reading. In R. Barr, M. L. Kamil, P. Mosenthal, & P. D. Pearson (Eds.), *Handbook of reading research: Volume II* (pp. 951–983). New York: Longman.

Anstrom, K., DiCerbo, P., Butler, F., Katz, A., Millet, J., & Rivera, C. (2010). *A review of the literature on Academic English: Implications for K–12 English language learners.* Arlington, VA: George Washington University Center for Equity and Excellence in Education.

Appleman, D. (2014). *Critical encounters in high school English: Teaching literary theory to adolescents* (3rd ed.). New York: Teachers College Press.

Bangert-Drowns, R. L., Hurley, M. M., & Wilkinson, B. (2004). The effects of school-based writing-to-learn interventions on academic achievement: A meta-analysis. *Review of Educational Research, 74*(1), 29–58.

Bazerman, C. (2005). A response to Anthony Fleury's "Liberal education and communication against the disciplines": A view from the world of writing. *Communication Education, 54*(1), 86–91.

Beach, R., & O'Brien, D. (2015). *Using apps for learning across the curriculum: A literacy-based framework and guide.* New York: Routledge.

Biancarosa, G., & Snow, C. E. (2006). *Reading next: A vision for action and research in middle and high school literacy, Second edition.* Washington, DC: Alliance for Excellent Education.

Bloome, D., & Egan-Robertson, A. (1993). The social construction of intertextuality in classroom reading and writing lessons. *Reading Research Quarterly, 28,* 305–333.

Buzzi, O., Grimes, S., & Rolls, A. (2012). Writing for the discipline in the discipline? *Teaching in Higher Education, 17*(4), 479–484.

Bybee, R. W. (1997). *Achieving scientific literacy: From purposes to practices.* Westport, CT: Heinemann.

Bybee, R. W. (2013). *The case for STEM education: Challenges and opportunities.* Arlington, VA: National Science Teachers Association.

Cole, M. (1990). Cognitive development and formal schooling: The evidence from cross-cultural research. In L. C. Moll (Eds.), *Vygotsky and education* (pp. 89–110). New York: Cambridge University Press.

Conley, D. T. (2008). Rethinking college readiness. *New Directions for Higher Education, 144,* 3–13.

Conley, M. W., & Hinchman, K. A. (2004). No Child Left Behind: What it means for U.S. adolescents and what we can do about it. *Journal of Adolescent and Adult Literacy, 48,* 42–50.

Cope, B., & Kalantzis, M. (Eds.). (2000). *Multiliteracies: Literacy learning and the design of social futures.* London: Routledge.

De La Paz, S., & Wissinger, D. R. (2015). Effects of genre and content knowledge on historical thinking with academically diverse high school students. *Journal of Experimental Education, 83*(1), 110–129.

Draper, R. J. (2008). Redefining content-area literacy teacher education: Finding my voice through collaboration. *Harvard Educational Review, 78*(1), 60–83.

Draper, R. J., & Broomhead, G. P. (Eds.). (2010). *(Re)imagining content-area literacy instruction.* New York: Teachers College Press.

Emerson, L., MacKay, B. R., MacKay, M. B., & Funnell, K. A. (2006). A team of equals: Teaching writing in the sciences. *Educational Action Research, 14*(1), 65–81.

Engeström, Y. (2006). Activity theory and expansive design. In S. Bagnara & G. Crampton Smith (Eds.), *Theories and practice of interaction design* (pp. 3–23). Mahwah, NJ: Erlbaum.

Fang, Z., & Schleppegrell, M. J. (2010). Disciplinary literacies across content areas: Supporting secondary reading through functional language analysis. *Journal of Adolescent and Adult Literacy, 53*(7), 587–597.

Fang, Z., Sun, Y., Chiu, C. C., & Trutschel, B. K. (2014). Inservice teachers' perception of a language-based approach to content area reading. *Australian Journal of Language and Literacy, 37*(1), 55–66.

Fleury, A. (2005). Liberal education and communication against the disciplines. *Communication Education, 54*, 72–79.

Flower, L., & Hayes, J. R. (1981). A cognitive process theory of writing. *College Composition and Communication, 32*(4), 365–387.

Garcia, A., Mirra, N., Morrell, E., Martinez, A., & Scorza, D. (2015). The council of youth research: Critical literacy and civic agency in the digital age. *Reading and Writing Quarterly, 31*(2), 151–167.

Gee, J. P. (1990). *Social linguistics and literacies: Ideology in discourses.* London: Falmer.

Gee, J. P. (1999). *An introduction to discourse analysis: Theory and method.* New York: Routledge.

Gee, J. P. (2000). Identity as an analytic lens for research in education. *Review of Research in Education, 25*(1), 99–125.

Gee, J. P. (2012). *Social linguistics and literacies: Ideology in discourses* (4th ed.). New York: Routledge.

Gee, J. P., & Hayes, E. R. (2011). *Language and learning in the digital age.* New York: Routledge.

Geisler, C. (1994). *Academic literacy and the nature of expertise: Reading, writing, and knowing in academic philosophy.* Hillsdale, NJ: Erlbaum.

Hillman, A. M. (2014). A literature review on disciplinary literacy. *Journal of Adolescent and Adult Literacy, 57*(5), 397–406.

Hodge, R., & Kress, G. R. (1988). *Social semiotics.* Oxford, UK: Polity Press.

Hyland, K. (2000). *Disciplinary discourses: Social interactions in academic writing.* Essex, UK: Pearson Education Limited.

Hyland, K. (2012). *Disciplinary identities: Individuality and community in academic discourse.* Cambridge, MA: Cambridge University Press.

Jacobs, C. (2010). Collaboration as pedagogy: Consequences and implications for partnerships between communication and disciplinary specialists. *Southern African Linguistics and Applied Language Studies, 28*(3), 227–237.

Jewitt, C. (2005). Multimodality, "reading," and "writing" for the 21st century. *Discourse: Studies in the Cultural Politics of Education, 26*(3), 315–331.

Kaiser, G., & Willander, T. (2005). Development of mathematical literacy: Results of an empirical study. *Teaching Mathematics and Its Applications, 24*(2–3), 48–60.

Kamil, M. L. (2003, November). *Adolescents and literacy: Reading for the 21st century.* Washington, DC: Alliance for Excellent Education.

Kiili, C., Mäkinen, M., & Coiro, J. (2013). Rethinking academic literacies. *Journal of Adolescent and Adult Literacy, 57*(3), 223–232.

Kress, G., & Van Leeuwen, T. (2001). *Multimodal discourse: The modes and media of contemporary communication.* London: Arnold.

Lave, J., & Wenger, E. (1991). *Situated learning: Legitimate peripheral participation.* New York: Cambridge University Press.

Lester, N., Bertram, C., Erickson, G., Lee, E., Tchako, A., Wiggins, K. D., et al. (2003). Writing across the curriculum: A college snapshot. *Urban Education, 38*(1), 5–34.

Luke, A., & Woods, A. (2009). Policy and adolescent literacy. In L. Christenbury, R. Boehmer, & P. Smagorinsky (Eds.), *Handbook of adolescent literacy research* (pp. 197–219). New York: Guildford Press.

McLeod, S. H., & Soven, M. I. (Eds.). (2006). *Composing a community: A history of writing across the curriculum.* Anderson, SC: Parlor Press.

Moje, E. B. (2008). Foregrounding the disciplines in secondary literacy teaching and learning: A call for change. *Journal of Adolescent and Adult Literacy, 52*(2), 96–107.

Moje, E. B., Overby, M., Tysvaer, N., & Morris, K. (2008). The complex world of adolescent literacy: Myths, motivations, and mysteries. *Harvard Educational Review, 78*(1), 107–154.

Moje, E. B., Stockdill, D., Kim, K., & Kim, H. J. (2011). The role of text in disciplinary learning. In M. L. Kamil, M. D. Pearson, E. B. Moje, & P. Afflerbach (Eds.), *The handbook of reading research, Volume IV* (pp. 453–486). New York: Routledge.

Monroe, J. (2003, Fall). Writing and the disciplines. *Association of American Colleges and Universities*, pp. 1–5.

Moore, D. W., Readence, J. E., & Rickelman, R. J. (1983). An historical exploration of content area reading instruction. *Reading Research Quarterly, 18*, 419–438.

Nagy, W., & Townsend, D. (2012). Words as tools: Learning academic vocabulary as language acquisition. *Reading Research Quarterly, 47*(1), 91–108.

NGSS Lead States. (2013). *Next generation science standards: For states, by states.* Washington, DC: National Academies Press.

National Research Council. (2012). *A framework for K–12 science education: Practices, crosscutting concepts, and core ideas.* Washington, DC: National Academies Press.

O'Brien, D. (2012). "Struggling" adolescents' engagement in multimediating. In D. E. Alvermann & K. A. Hinchman (Eds.), *Reconceptualizing the literacies in adolescents' lives: Bridging the everyday academic divide* (3rd ed., pp. 71–91). New York,: Routledge.

O'Brien, D., Beach, R., & Scharber, C. (2007). "Struggling" middle schoolers: Engagement and literate competence in a reading writing intervention class. *Reading Psychology, 28*(1), 51–73.

O'Brien, D., & Rogers, T. (2015). Sociocultural perspectives on literacy and learning. *Handbook of educational psychology* (3rd ed., pp. 311–322). New York: Routledge.

O'Brien, D. G., Springs, R., & Stith, D. (2000). Engaging at-risk students: Literacy learning in a high school literacy lab. In E. B. Moje & D. G. O'Brien (Eds.), *Constructions of literacy: Studies of teaching and learning in and out of secondary schools* (pp.105–123). Mahwah, NJ: Erlbaum.

Ochsner, R., & Fowler, J. (2004). Playing devil's advocate: Evaluating the literature of the WAC/WID movement. *Review of Educational Research, 74*(2), 117–140.

Ortmann, L. L. (2015). *Disciplinary literacies in STEM integration: An interpretive study of discourses within classroom communities of practice.* Doctoral dissertation, University of Minnesota, Twin Cities.

Park, J. Y. (2013). Becoming academically literate. *Journal of Adolescent and Adult Literacy, 57*(4), 298–306.

Roth, W. M., & Lee, Y. J. (2007). "Vygotsky's neglected legacy": Cultural–historical activity theory. *Review of Educational Research, 77*(2), 186–232.

Semali, L. (2005). Why media literacy matters in American schools. *Yearbook of the National Society for the Study of Education, 104*(1), 35–54.

Sewall, G. (2005). Textbook publishing. *Phi Delta Kappan, 86*(7), 498–502.

Sfard, A. (2007). When the rules of discourse change, but nobody tells you: Making sense of mathematics learning from a commognitive standpoint. *Journal of the Learning Sciences, 16*(4), 565–613.

Shanahan, C., & Shanahan, T. (2014). Does disciplinary literacy have a place in elementary school? *The Reading Teacher, 67*(8), 636–639.

Shanahan, T., & Shanahan, C. (2008). Teaching disciplinary literacy to adolescents: Rethinking content-area literacy. *Harvard Educational Review, 78*(1), 40–59.

Shanahan, T., & Shanahan, C. (2012). What is disciplinary literacy and why does it matter? *Topics in Language Disorders, 32*(1), 7–18.

Shapiro, A. (2012). Between training and popularization: Regulating science textbooks in secondary education. *Isis, 103*(1), 99–110.

Stockton, S. (1995). Writing in history narrating the subject of time. *Written Communication, 12*(1), 47–73.

Townsend, D. (2015). Who's using the language?: Supporting middle school students with content area academic language. *Journal of Adolescent and Adult Literacy, 58*(5), 376–387.

Van den Broek, P. (2010). Using texts in science education: Cognitive processes and knowledge representation. *Science, 328*(5977), 453–456.

Van Zee, B. E. H., Jansen, H., Winograd, K., Crowl, M., & Devitt, A. (2013). Fostering scientific thinking by prospective teachers in a course that integrates physics and literacy learning. *Journal of Science Teaching, 42*(5), 29–36.

Wade, S. E., & Moje, E. B. (2000). The role of text in classroom learning. In M. L. Kamil, P. B. Mosenthal, P. D. Pearson, & R. Barr (Eds.), *Handbook of reading research: Volume III* (pp. 609–627). Mahwah, NJ: Erlbaum.

Watts, J., & Burnett, R. E. (2012). Pairing courses across the disciplines: Effects on writing performance. *Written Communication, 29*(2), 208–235.

Wertsch, J. V., del Río, P., & Alvarez, A. (Eds.). (1995). *Sociocultural studies of mind.* Cambridge, UK: Cambridge University Press.

Wilson, A. A. (2008). Moving beyond the page in content area literacy: Comprehension instruction for multimodal texts in science. *The Reading Teacher, 62*(2), 153–156.

Wilson, A. A. (2011). A social semiotics framework for conceptualizing content area literacies. *Journal of Adolescent and Adult Literacy, 54*(6), 435–444.

Wilson, A. A., Smith, E., & Householder, D. L. (2014). Using disciplinary literacies to enhance adolescents' engineering design activity. *Journal of Adolescent and Adult Literacy, 57*(8), 676–686.

Wineburg, S. S. (1991). Historical problem solving: A study of the cognitive processes used in the evaluation of documentary and pictorial evidence. *Journal of Educational Psychology, 83*(1), 73–87.

Wojnowski, B., & Pea, C. (Eds.). (2014). *Models and approaches to STEM professional development.* Arlington, VA: NSTA Press.

Wolfe, C. R. (2011). Argumentation across the curriculum. *Written Communication, 28*(2), 193–219.

Zollman, A. (2012). Learning for STEM literacy: STEM literacy for learning. *School Science and Mathematics, 112*(1), 12–19.

CHAPTER 12

Misfits in School Literacy
Whom Are U.S. Schools Designed to Serve?

PETER SMAGORINSKY

For much of the history of U.S. education, schools were designed to meet the needs of members of society's upper class, preparing them for the rigors of college and the demands of corporate, social, and governmental leadership roles (Davis & Bauman, 2013). With this mission, the curriculum was canonical and narrow, with learning funneled through the assumption of American "exceptionalism" and the superiority of Western culture. This focus implicitly conveyed the message that anyone who didn't belong, or didn't fit, should drop out and get a job. (See Table 12.1 for the way in which one state, Georgia, has shown a gradual increase in the number of people earning high school diplomas.) The students' responsibility was to adjust to how schools operated given that formal education provided their primary conduit to the credentials and knowledge that would serve their careers well. Expecting the school to adjust to the students—especially those whose home lives required great adaptations to the expectations and practices of extant

TABLE 12.1. Georgia High School Graduation Rates

Year	Georgia adults with high school diplomas
1940	17%
1950	20%
1960	32%
1970	41%
1980	56%
1990	71%
2000	79%
2010	79%

educational traditions—would undermine its mission to prepare a college-ready student population that could ultimately rise to leadership roles in society. Given the difficulties of adaptation and questionable payoff for persistence, students from outside this elite subgroup often accepted the message, dropped out of school, and went to work.

Over time, a separate and ultimately competing vision of education arose in the United States: to reduce dropout rates and provide a comprehensive education for the broadest range of students possible, at least through the age of 16. Youth who did not fit the college-bound profile remained in school well beyond what had been required of their grandparents, even attending college when some systems went to open admissions in the 1970s, making college available to any high school graduate from a public university's designated feeder districts. Curriculum and instruction remained largely the same, however, with some adaptations to the more diverse student body now within schools' purview to educate. Such accommodations, however, have often been ridiculed by those for whom education remains a fairly elite enterprise (see, e.g., Morici, 2015). For every advocate of expanding and broadening the curriculum to include possibilities such as young adult literature that addresses issues of contemporary youth culture and society (e.g., Wolk, 2009), or diverse texts that speak to the experiences of students from outside the White Western canon (e.g., Fisher, 2007), a belligerent response has followed, claiming that rigor is being undermined and learning diluted by moves away from the most classic of educations (e.g., Stotsky, 1999).

My purpose in this chapter is to consider the fit between schools, particularly those adhering to "traditional" educational practices centered on formalism and factual knowledge, and the kinds of students they are now expected to educate and graduate. The education of diverse populations has raised questions about the degree to which various population subgroups have been served by the historical and current conduct of schooling. I next review research that documents the poor fit that many people have experienced with those educational structures that have endured well beyond their initial purpose of educating the elite for their inevitable societal leadership roles. With the recognition that all social categories are problematic, I organize this review around familiar classifications of race, gender, and social class. Based on this overview, I discuss the issues and suggest one implication that would help make school a more humane and enlightening place for students, teachers, and administrators.

RACE

Many researchers have begun to inquire into the reasons for differential school performance of racial groups in school. I am aware that "Big Five" racial theories (White, Black, Latin@, Asian, Native American) are entirely social constructions rather than true biological classifications (Delgado & Stefancic, 2013). I rely on them for this review because demographics are often categorized racially, even as I recognize the dubious benefits of adhering to what are now widely understood as questionable means of sorting people into groups given how much of the earth's population must be force-fit into the Big Five races, how much cultural and ethnic variety exists within each group, and how often mixed-race people are typically assigned to the lowest status race of their heritage, at times against their own sense of identity. Dissatisfied with the conclusions of White researchers such as Hernnstein and Murray (1994), who used intelligence test data to argue that Blacks are genetically inferior to Whites, these scholars have looked beyond traditional academic measures of literacy to reveal the ways in which youth compose and read texts outside the purview of the assessment machinery.

This effort to study literacy through investigations into authentic literacy practices in community settings rather than through achievement test data produced through forced school examinations got traction in the 1970s. In a decade-long linguistic ethnography, Heath (1983) studied Southeastern U.S. Piedmont residents, documenting the degree to which school expectations were matched with the home and community literacy practices of rural families. The Black neighborhood that she studied was oriented to play and performance, with silent, sequestered reading discouraged as antisocial and inappropriate to community life. Heath found that the expectations for silent compliance during reading lessons in school felt alien to children who were encouraged at home to get outside and interact with other people in the neighborhood, to engage in the performative practices of their community rather than the relatively asocial experience of silent reading.

Since then, scores of scholars, many of them from an African American heritage, have expanded on Heath's (1983) findings, investigating African American literacy development in a variety of regions and settings. These scholars (e.g., Kirkland, 2013) have found that although Black students are continually measured to have low and declining literacy rates in school, they live rich lives with print, spoken, and multimodal texts in their teeming literacy lives once outside the range of tolling school bells.

Kirkland (2014) makes a key distinction in considering how such opposing research-based conclusions could be found on the same population. School achievement tends to be measured in single-sitting examinations that are based on problems posed by test-makers, with scores computed for statistical manipulation. Ethnographies tend to be conducted outside school over time, with detailed documentation of social and cognitive processes through which self-chosen literacy goals are pursued, often with feedback, affirmation, critique, and other forms of response helping to shape literacy products, including readings. Such studies of Black students'—primarily urban in most research—literacy activities focus on what the youth consider to be authentic, meaningful processes and products, and typically find that literacy achievement is high, sustained, and of great social value. These literacy practices are characterized by their profoundly social qualities as youth perform for one another and use texts to position themselves in the midst of youth culture and others in their environments—a stark contrast to the solitary, detached manner in which their literacy is measured in response to culturally remote texts and tasks in school assessments.

Kirkland (2014) finds a set of related problems associated with relying on conventional school assessment to stand as definitive measures of literacy attainment. First, the literacy problems on which they are tested are not posed by the students. Rather, they are designed by adults paid to generate test problems that meet some psychometric standard for reliability across the whole testing population, often one dominated by middle-class students whose practices are more congenial to such testing. This approach of norming answers according to one dominant demographic produces feelings of alienation from the examinations, and consequently from school, on the part of those from other cultural groups given that school becomes associated with punitive testing that is indifferent to what the kids find important in their literacy lives.

Second, the exams assume that their test items are isomorphic across test-takers; that is, they are premised on the idea that the learning tasks they present to students are understood in the same manner by all within the test-taking population. In particular, the test designers tend to assume that the task *as they envision and intend it* is in turn taken up by all students in the same fashion in which they offer it. Newman, Griffin, and Cole (1989; cf. Smagorinsky, 2011) refer to this phenomenon as the problem of assuming a *task* or *problem isomorph* in which a learning problem is presented to people of different backgrounds in different settings, under the assumptions that this standardized procedure will be interpreted identically by all who encounter it, because that is how the designers believe it should work. The likelihood that the tests are constructed in relation to *autonomous texts*—texts with an inherent meaning that is not subject to reconstruction and instantiation of additional meanings by readers—is highly unlikely given the dubious nature of the assumption in light of virtually any social or constructivist perspective on textual composition and interpretation (for a general critique, see Nystrand, 1986; for an elaboration of a cultural theory of reading, see Smagorinsky, 2001).

Such attention to contexts is not only not available in the standardized world of assessment but it also obliterates such matters as "exogenous" or outside factors, particularly poverty, from the calculations, reifying the assumption that the tasks are isomorphic (Berliner, 2014). The ethnographic work assembled by Kirkland (2014), however, demonstrates that literacy practices and tasks are situated and constructed, and not amenable to standardized treatment.

Finally, school-based definitions of literacy are securely grounded in print, ignoring the vast compositional means available to youth elsewhere. Kirkland (2014) concludes that "as they age, Black males learn literacy less in school and more outside it. This literacy learning is defined less by print . . . and more by a variety of social and cultural assets/flows necessary for achieving meaning and message making important to their lives." As many have noted (e.g., Kajder, 2010), the Black population is one of many social groups in which print literacy serves as but one compositional tool among many in the digital world of the 21st century. What is starkly evident from Kirkland's (2014) comparison is the fact that young African Americans who are consistently measured as having low literacy in school assessments are reading and composing texts of great social value in nonschool contexts.

At about the same time that Heath (1983) conducted her study of Piedmont populations, Philips (1983) conducted her ethnographic study of the experiences of Warm Springs Indians on an Oregon reservation. These young people were often stereotyped as "silent" in school, yet they were found to be quite vocal on the playground, suggesting to Philips that the problem was not that Native Americans are silent, but that the structures and practices of schools provided such an alienating environment for them that they shut down. Since then, others (e.g., Four Arrows, 2013) have contended that Western approaches to schooling embody values of consumerism and disengagement from nature that continue to make school a hostile place for Native American students. As Deloria (1974) and many others have documented, the primary goal of the "Indian Schools" to which Native youth were sent a century ago, away from their families and heritage, was to eviscerate their Indian soul and replace it with sensibilities fully assimilated to White society, with their native languages forbidden and English required. For this cultural, ethnic, and racial group, the schooling experience has been one of colonization and oppression, with such seemingly routine practices as writing distrusted because of the manner in which written treaties were historically used to confiscate tribal lands through legal obfuscation and treachery (Belgarde, LoRé, & Meyer, 2009).

Other racial groups have been found to fit poorly with school as well. Moll (2000), for instance, found that Mexican American families in Arizona were oriented to cultural practices that made participation in school activities difficult. In home and community, families relied on *funds of knowledge,* or collective ways of knowing and acting in society, that were at odds with their schools' value on independent, competitive performance. At home, people might pool their resources to flourish as a social group, such as when they would pitch in to buy a vehicle so that many could travel to work together. They might trade services, such as exchanging mechanical work for food, as a way to gain collectively rather than compete individually. They might further share knowledge about newly posted jobs or other valuable information through which the community as a whole, rather than the individuals within it, benefits from opportunities. In school, however, such collaboration and group work were discouraged and indeed punished when collaboration was treated as cheating. This poor fit between community and school has been documented by many others since (e.g., Portes & Smagorinsky, 2010), particularly within the New Latin@ Diaspora, in which areas of the U. S. that have historically not hosted immigrant populations from Mexico and Mesoamerica become the destinations of refugees seeking work opportunities.

Immigrants in general have had a difficult time adjusting to U.S. schools. Fu and Graff (2009) look more deeply than the superficial gaze taken by policymakers to understand the immigrant experience, one that has no single pathway but is variable by ethnic and racial group, area of settlement, and much else. They argue that newcomers encounter circumstances much different from those cultivating the development of native-born youth. They often are placed in the role of translating for their elders, often in their capacity as workers in their family businesses. They often "become role models and surrogate parents for other young children in the community and their families. They care for their young siblings or cousins, take them to see doctors, and attend parent conferences" (p. 402). Taking on adult responsibilities both shows remarkable social, cultural, and linguistic competence in life outside school, and undermines school-sanctioned success, in that their familial duties may result in school absence, poor grades, and an increased likelihood of dropping out of school altogether (Perreira, Harris, & Lee, 2006).

Similar to Kirkland's (2014) account of African American youth, immigrant youth are not restricted to print literacy in their home and community lives. Fu and Graff (2009) find that the Digital Age, through which immigrant youth are immersed in a world of multiple literacies, helps to shape their identities as new Americans (cf. Vargas, 2006). Fu and Graff (2009) argue that "more research on popular culture and literacy identities for newcomers would illuminate their resilience and adroitness, thereby dispelling current and questionable conceptions of them as illiterate individuals in need of saving" (p. 402).

Policymakers rarely are privy to these rich literacy lives, because they rely on superficial data such as standardized test scores administered under alien and intimidating circumstances to make an absolute judgment about literacy development and achievement, and in turn, about teaching effectiveness. Yet those who study youth engagement with literacy in authentic (i.e., self-chosen) contexts consistently find that literacy comprises a critical aspect of their development and socialization. Even within school settings, careful observers have learned that taking kids' abilities at face value can lead to false and debilitating conclusions and assumptions. Primary school teacher Cynthia Ballenger (1999), for instance, when puzzled by the behavior of her Haitian immigrant children in her classroom, instead of forcing them to fit in the structures of conventional U.S. schooling, inquired into how they engaged with the world and adapted her teaching to accommodate their interactional styles and learning needs. But that solution—for teachers and schools to adapt to diverse learners, rather than for students to adapt to educational practices long engrained in schools—appears to be the exception rather than the rule, if the research base has accurately characterized how schools tend to be organized to the disadvantage of newcomers and others from outside the cultural mainstream.

The Asian racial group is often touted as a "model minority" culture, so successful that its members out-achieve Whites in academics and are therefore an ideal fit with U.S. schools. Asians are, for instance, the largest racial minority group at The University of Georgia, a surprising development given their relatively low numbers in the general state population (Shearer, 2015). Shearer clarifies that "the Asian category actually includes many ethnic and racial groups, comprising students of both Indian and Chinese descent," demonstrating the difficulty of using Big Five racial classifications for demographic purposes. Le (2012 online article), however, asserts that the "model minority" reputation is both mythic and overly homogeneous:

> It's true that 42% of all Asian American adults have at least a college degree, the highest of all the major racial/ethnic groups. It's also common for Asian American students to have the highest test scores and/or GPAs within any given high school or college cohort. But what usually gets left out is the fact that not all Asian Americans are the same. For every Chinese American or South Asian who has a college degree, the same number of Southeast Asians are still struggling to adapt to their lives in the U.S. . . . [Southeast Asians] have the highest high school dropout rates in the country. *Again, not all Asian Americans are the same.* (emphasis added)

Like other immigrant groups, Asian Americans are both highly diverse and include ethnic and national groups that have often waged war on one another, making them difficult to homogenize into one big, uniform race of people. As Le (2012) asserts, some Asian nationalities fit U.S. schooling patterns much better than others, have stronger familial models for school success, immigrate with differential cultural capital with which to undertake life on a new continent and in a new society, and in many ways disrupt the notion that they represent a stable and invariant racial group ready-made for school success. This assertion is supported by demographic data compiled by *Asian-Nation.org*, which provides the breakdown reported in Table 12.2. As this table makes clear, aggregating Asian American data for demographic purposes is quite unreliable given the variation in poverty levels, English language proficiency, and other factors that predict school success.

Furthermore, argues Yoo (2010), "People often assume that students with excellent academic performances have excellent psychological well-being. The model minority myth may motivate Asian American students to achieve higher test scores; but with often unfair and unrecognized burden, pressure, and discrimination, they may struggle emotionally feeling overwhelmed and socially disconnected" ("Doing Well vs. Feeling Well" section of online article, paragraph 1). This affective dimension of schooling, which runs throughout the literature on school engagement, remains unacknowledged by policymakers who believe that schools serve solely academic purposes, and that students' feelings about their relationships with school and its people are irrelevant to educational processes. Such a view is roundly contradicted by the sources I have consulted for this review.

TABLE 12.2. Socioeconomic Characteristics by Racial/Ethnic and Asian Ethnic Groups

Numbers are in percentages, except for income.

	Not proficient in English	Less than high school	College degree	Advanced degree	High skill occupation	Married, spouse present	Home-owner	Median personal income	Median family income	Living in poverty	Public assistance
Whites	0.7	15.3	25.3	3.0	21.4	64.5	78.2	$23,640	$48,500	9.4	1.3
Blacks	0.8	29.1	13.6	1.2	12.3	38.0	54.4	$16,300	$33,300	24.9	4.5
Latinos/Hispanics	30.3	48.5	9.9	1.6	9.6	56.3	52.4	$14,400	$36,000	21.4	3.5
Native American Indians	2.6	27.4	10.8	0.9	11.9	50.2	64.2	$14,500	$32,240	25.1	6.1
Indians	8.4	12.6	64.4	12.5	51.6	74.9	56.8	$26,000	$69,470	8.2	0.9
Cambodian, Hmong, or Laotian	44.3	52.7	9.2	0.4	9.8	66.6	53.3	$16,000	$43,850	22.5	9.9
Chinese	31.3	23.6	46.3	8.5	41.9	67.1	65.7	$20,000	$58,300	13.1	1.8
Filipinos	7	13.1	42.8	4.3	29.7	62.7	67.6	$23,000	$65,400	6.9	1.6
Japanese	10	9.5	40.8	4.6	32.0	60.7	70.8	$26,000	$61,630	8.6	0.9
Koreans	32.9	13.8	43.6	5.6	27.0	69.0	51.9	$16,300	$48,500	15.5	1.6
Pacific Islanders	7.1	21.7	13.6	1.6	13.8	61.4	48.1	$19,100	$50,000	16.7	4.4
Vietnamese	40.4	37.8	13.8	2.5	22.6	61.2	60.0	$16,000	$51,500	13.8	4.8

Note. Numbers are in percentages, except for income. From *www.asian-nation.org/demographics.shtml*. Reprinted by permission.

SOCIAL CLASS

Readers might infer that schools are designed to suit the White population well, given that non-White students tend to fit poorly with schools' social and academic emphases. Yet the White demographic is so large and varied that it is difficult to make any generalizations about the White population and its members' fitness for school. For many years, Whites were the only people likely to attend school at all, so presumably schools are suited to their orientation to literacy and school practices. Yet the White population attending school was not characteristic of the population at large, being more affluent and advantaged than most. I next review the challenges that face subpopulations within schools to illustrate how a great many White students feel just as distanced from mainstream school practices as do members of minoritized racial groups.

Heath's (1983) study of literacy practices in the Southeastern Piedmont region included two additional groups beyond the Black neighborhood featured previously. The other population of principal interest was the White fundamentalist Christian community, whose orientation to reading came through their engagement at home and church with the *Holy Bible*. In these settings, fundamentalist families learned that The Word is literally true and not to be disputed, a stance that enabled them to appropriate Biblical narratives and morals that stand above the questioning of human minds. This conception of the written text as essentially true and beyond question served these students poorly in school, where reading tasks required questioning and inference-making that violated the whole value system on which the children were being raised. Like the Black students studied by Heath, these students had developed home literacies that were at odds with those practiced in school, leading to poor academic performance in relation to the "mainstreamers," those more middle-class, less literally oriented families (often the children of teachers) whose home literacy events mimicked the sorts of reading practices emphasized in schools. These mainstreamers comprised Heath's third population, one whose youth fit school as conventionally carried out and were less likely to struggle through prior orientations that made silent, isolated reading with a critical stance difficult to undertake.

Other ethnographies have found similar struggles with other White population subsets. Eckert (1989), for instance, studied an upper Midwestern community school that enrolled a range of White students, from "jocks" to "burnouts." Jocks were those students who felt a strong affiliation with the school institution and bought into its values and activities. They might be athletes, as suggested by the term, but might include any youth who participated in the school's sponsored activities and events: clubs, student government, afterschool and extracurricular activities, and others. This demographic tended toward affluence, given that people who can spend time in extracurriculars rarely hold down jobs after school.

At the other end of the spectrum, Eckert (1989) found burnouts, those students who lacked a strong feeling of affiliation for school. Often from blue-collar families, they were oriented to the adult world of work and all of its trappings, such a smoking cigarettes. These students considered school an adolescent holding pen in which their path toward maturation was stunted by the control exerted by adults and student leaders. Their goal instead was to become financially independent by working in adult settings after school rather than staying in school and being treated like kids. The scripts of compliance embraced by the jocks were rejected by the burnouts, who cut class, hung out in parts of the building avoided by their affluent classmates, rejected academic rewards as worth pursuing, and left school for jobs once the final bell rang.

Eckert's (1989) study, though dated in some ways, retains currency in its general characterization of the manner in which students' levels of affiliation with the school institution, often following familial patterns, affect their willingness to accept school structures and practices as normative and fitting their rate of maturation. Students who reject the idea that school grades will have an impact on their future prospects tend to engage less with schoolwork than do those who accept the educational maxim that school performance sets the stage for the next step in life, often college. With little respect for the value of schoolwork, such students engage minimally with its demands, adding to the population of misfits who must remain in school until old enough to check out legally.

Eckert therefore argues that social class orientation is typically reproduced from generation to generation, with "the perpetuation of class inequalities through the funneling of children into their parents' place in society, and the enculturation of children into hierarchical social forms through explicit and implicit educational practices" (p. 7). This reproduction of the social division of labor channels youth toward particular types of experiences and outcomes through both explicit and implicit means, based on their social class of origin (see Williams, 1977).

People living in poverty—perhaps the social class most in need of educational support—find it difficult to escape the generational cycle implied by the notion of the reproduction of the social division of labor. Gorski (2013), who himself broke out of a low socioeconomic status (SES) background to become an educator, sees the problems as systemic: "We deny people in poverty access to equal educational opportunity, access to healthcare, and even access to air unspoiled by environmental hazards. We do this for generations and then, when some low-income youth don't do well on standardized tests or drop out of school or seem disengaged in class, we forget about these inequities and blame it on their 'culture'" (p. 54). Gorski has his sights set on the ways in which people of low (or no) income are pathologized in society at large, and in educational discourse in particular. This notion that the poor are agents of their own poverty has a long history in Western culture, in which income and character are often seen as mutually causal (Smagorinsky & Taxel, 2004, 2005). When poverty coexists with race, multiple factors collude to make it difficult to develop the resources required to elevate one's financial status such that it endures through succeeding generations.

The "culture of poverty" perspective on low/no-income people is well-evidenced in the work of Ruby Payne, a White, middle-class Midwesterner whose self-published books (e.g., 2013; the fifth edition of the book that made her a star on the inservice circuit) on educating poor children are both wildly popular among teachers and roundly excoriated by university theorists (see, e.g., Bomer, Dworin, May, & Semingson, 2008; Dudley-Marling & Lucas, 2009; Kunjufu, 2007; and many others).

This perspective on people in poverty is not new, and is not exclusively American. Honore-Antoine Fregier, speaking in Paris in 1840 (quoted in Smagorinsky & Taxel, 2005, p. 82), asserted that

> the poor and the vicious classes have been and will always be the most productive breeding ground of evildoers of all sorts; it is they whom we shall designate as the dangerous classes. For even when vice is not accompanied by perversity, by the very fact that it allies itself with poverty in the same person, he is an object of fear to society, he is dangerous.

In France, "les classes dangereuses" horrified the bourgeoisie, who believed them fated for lives of crime, not because of their circumstances but because of their moral deficiencies. Such a belief in the inherent moral decrepitude of people who lack money remains in society at large and in many policy positions. For example, many states receiving character education grants targeted people of low SES for character interventions designed to fix their personal deficiencies, which presumably will level the playing field so that their opportunities in life are the same as those of people of affluence (Smagorinsky & Taxel, 2004, 2005) in the sort of "no excuses" solutions offered, for example, by Jensen (2005), whose "brain-based" teaching ideas efface poverty as a factor in teaching and learning.

Much work in understanding poverty, while considering race, does not associate race with SES, even though the two are inextricably related (American Psychological Association, n.d.), a phenomenon known in sociological studies as "intersectionality." Undoubtedly, being a member of a racial minority group invites additional negative perceptions and assumptions to those that accompany low SES, leading to such overgeneralizations as the existence of a "thug class" permeating urban settings (as argued by Murray, 2001, among many others). One need not foreground race, however, to consider that low SES, whether urban, rural, or otherwise in location, produces systemic challenges for those who live under its oppressive conditions.

In school, students of low SES tend to be tracked into low-level classes in which pathologizing assumptions obtain (Entwisle, Alexander, & Olson, 2010). As Gorski (2013) notes, these students are most likely to be given a "basic" education administered through worksheets and other means of instruction designed to keep them quietly at work so as to presumably mute their thuggish tendencies. Yet such instruction makes school even more alienating than it is already, given that the students find schoolwork to be tedious, mind-numbing, and useless. Pedagogies of this sort are surely imposed on other students as well; their ubiquity in low tracks, however, virtually ensures that children and youth from low/no income families will find school to be a place in which they fit quite poorly.

SEX AND GENDER

Racial, ethnic, and cultural groups are not the only ones found to be at odds with how schools work. The American Association of University Women (AAUW; 1991) argued that schools shortchange girls by acceding to and reinforcing patterns suited to males, such as the tendency to argue against each other rather than to work relationally toward consensus and collaborative solutions. Schools, according to the report, reify extant social dynamics that privilege males over females in society at large, contributing to problems with self-esteem that lower girls' expectations over time and produce generational effects that perpetuate social hierarchies. This perspective, rooted in the first wave of feminist psychology launched by Gilligan (1982) and others, found that when men are entrusted with the task of defining matters such as morality, and do so by norming responses such that they correspond to those produced by male research samples, the research inevitably finds women to be lacking. In contrast, these feminist scholars posited that men and women are fundamentally different in their orientation to the world, such that male samples produce deficit conclusions about women, who are more likely to collaborate than compete.

The AAUW (1991) report, while getting great traction among university researchers and theorists, found less acceptance elsewhere. Sommers (2000)—a self-styled "equity feminist," in contrast to what she considers the "victim feminists" who authored the AAUW report—rebutted their claims, arguing that instead of seeking equity, feminist scholars were seeking to depress the growth of boys. Girls, she argued, in fact, outperform boys in just about every scholastic arena, raising questions about the degree to which boys are advantaged over girls. The discrepancy between girls' academic success in school and men's domination of the job market continues to vex those who see a causal relation between school achievement and work success, with patriarchal views and entrenched power elevating males in the workplace in spite of academic underperformance and its presumably predictive potential.

Given that the AAUW report is now nearly a quarter-century old, it's difficult to say whether the problems they identify existed at the time (per Sommers's [2000] critique), or if they persist today. There is at least anecdotal evidence that assumptions about girls' ability to work in STEM fields remain in place. In a book produced to accompany a new Barbie Doll, for instance, author Marenco (2013) provides the following question and answer:

Q: How many young women does it take to design and program a computer game?

A: None. Only boys know how to do that.

Techno-dolt Barbie tries to create a computer game, but crashes her laptop and calls upon friends Steven and Brian to fix it for her. The good news is that reviewers have uniformly excoriated the book on Amazon reviews. The bad news is that Eisenhower-era beliefs about girls' helplessness and boys' savvy have persisted well into the next century. If these assumptions are at work to any degree, then girls still face an uphill climb finding validation in the mixed company of school.

But Sommers (2000) and her feisty battle with other sorts of feminists is not isolated in thinking that schools are alienating places for boys. Smith and Wilhelm (2002), drawing on extensive interviews with teenage boys, found that they find the dry, dull reading assigned in schools to be repellant, and the isolating practices of schools to work against their desire to work on projects with friends. In contrast, the boys undertook reading for personal knowledge and interest outside school with vigor, particularly when it helped them with hobbies and pursuits such as playing video games. Indeed, the young men in their study reported that they preferred difficult texts and games that advanced their skills to those beneath their ability levels, a stance that contradicts assumptions about their rejection of school reading as too difficult. But the researchers conclude that school reading is repugnant to them not because of its difficulty, but because of its tedium and disassociation from their lives. If school provides a poor fit for girls, then it appears equally incommodious for boys.

Researchers into the school experiences of lesbian, gay, bisexual, transgender, and queer (LGBTQ) youth further find that school is an alienating place for those outside the male–female binary. Perhaps the most flagrant abuse concerns bullying by heterosexual students and teachers who cannot open their hearts to those of LGBTQ orientations (Miller, Burns, & Johnson, 2013). To Martino (2009), just including books with LGBTQ characters to promote acceptance is bound to fail. Rather, he asserts that a pedagogy that overtly interrogates heteronormativity is required to get students to understand the social construction of sexuality.

The heteronormative assumptions made by many in school institutions render those outside its spectrum into "others," who are viewed in deficit terms. Society has surely changed dramatically early in the 21st century in terms of legal shifts toward LGBTQ marriage, workplace rights, and other extensions of rights; the American Psychiatric Association's *Diagnostic and Statistical Manual of Mental Disorders* declassified homosexuality as a mental illness in 1973, nearly three decades after Kinsey, Pomeroy, and Martin (1948) found gay and lesbian orientations to be within the normal range of human sexuality. Yet obstacles remain in schools to feelings of affiliation by the typical LGBTQ student. Occasional national news of transgendered homecoming queens (see Nichols, 2013) and gay football players (see Pettigrew, 2015) give hope that, eventually, schools will become hospitable places for students across the sexual and gender spectra. Just as racism has persisted well beyond the Civil Rights laws of the 1960s, however, deficit views of LGBTQ youth, often fueled by the beliefs of religious extremists, continue to undermine the degree to which they find school to be a place that supports their growth. As with other youth who feel alienated by the school institution and its general population, the lack of feelings of belonging undermine engagement with curriculum and instruction, promote dysphoric feelings and thus reduce affiliation, contribute to feelings of depression and self-harm, and in general make school a difficult place to fit in and profit academically.

DISCUSSION

This chapter's titular question, "Misfits in School Literacy: Whom Are U.S. Schools Designed to Serve?," has no easy answer. My tentative conclusion is that schools serve the same people they were originally designed to accommodate: students of relative affluence who affiliate with the institution's promise that school achievement will pay off in life success. A century ago, these were just about the only people who persisted through to public school graduation. My own grandparents' generation was typical of that era. My mother's father left home at age 13—part of a great sweep of the first batch of children when his father remarried and his new wife wanted a new brood of her own to raise—to become a plumber's apprentice. My father's parents were refugees from Eastern European pogroms, and their two Belarussian-born sons were put to work as sign painters without attending school upon immigration to New York. My father and his U.S.-born brother attended school, with my father being the family's sole graduate from a secondary school. I focus here on males, because I am aware of no records of school attendance for my female ancestors of that era, although my mother, born in 1915, graduated from high school at age 15, earned an undergraduate degree, and was working on a master's degree when her studies were interrupted by marriage and her dedication to raising five children. She, however, was the exception in her own family and others like it.

Today, all would be required to stay in school through age 16 or 17 (see Wikipedia [n.d.] for a list of global compulsory education ages). Many might even stay through graduation. The website *governing.com* (2015) reports that most states now claim graduation rates of 55–75% for students who are economically disadvantaged, speak limited English, and are diagnosed as having disabilities. Whether this persistence is due to schools' greater accommodation to youth of difference, to the manipulation and falsification of statistics, or to schools' more aggressive policing of attendance is not answerable through the simple report of these rates.

If the work I have reviewed in this chapter suggests anything, however, it is that schools expect students to adapt to their institution more than schools accommodate a diverse range of students. This problem has been greatly exacerbated by the 21st-century accountability movement that has shifted attention from the imperative a few decades ago to celebrate diversity to a quite different charge: to standardize teaching, learning, and assessment according to the values of schools' most durable stakeholders. These remain the most affluent, typically White students. I was not able to locate any demographic data on the population of people involved in standardized test design, but my sense is that they are Whites from privileged backgrounds. When I did some consulting for the Educational Testing Service in the 1990s, that's about the only demographic I met in many visits to their New Jersey campus. Given continual concerns with cultural bias in standardized assessment—a seeming inevitability when uniformity is the goal—I can only assume that this problem remains intractable (see Padilla, 2001). Introducing the possibility of variation into a standardized system seems destined to produce confusion of the sort rarely accommodated in the policy world, at least in the ideal world in which policymakers seem perpetually to be ensconced, one that can fabricate assumptions—such as the canard that poverty is irrelevant to teaching and learning performance—so that the ideals of the system remain blissfully intact, if quite removed from reality.

The reality is that schools have always accommodated some students better than they accommodate others, perhaps most. The current effort at standardization is entrenching this problem further, making schools a place where too many kids struggle to fit within structures that suit them poorly. The problem of adaptation falls largely on students, and the greatest challenge for adaptation is required of those students who are least prepared to undertake it. In spite of the proliferation of posters featuring kittens of different colors accompanied by exhortations to celebrate diversity, then, schools remain primarily in the business of making students as similar as possible. Such an approach makes school more accessible to those already well-matched to its policies and practices, and less accessible to those whose home and community backgrounds, and possibly genetic disposition, in the case of the gender question, are least amenable to adaptation.

IMPLICATIONS

Traditionally, it is the role of the author to give research recommendations on what the scholarly community should investigate in order to better inform policy and pedagogy. The fact is, however, that for roughly 35 years, researchers have convincingly demonstrated that schools that adapt to students produce more enriching educations, and schools that remain rigid and dedicated to formalist, authoritarian instruction are exclusionary and alienating for the majority of students (for references, see the work cited throughout this chapter). I am not persuaded that more research demonstrating the same results will effect changes when policymakers rely on anecdotes, ideals, and ideology, and ignore libraries full of empirical studies. I'll relate a story told by Roy O'Donnell in the 1980s, concerning a young boy from O'Donnell's rural South. The boy, speaking to his elders, referred to a classmate as "iggernant." No, interrupted the adult; the term is *ignorant,* not *iggernant.* Nope, replied the boy. Ignorant, that's when you don't know nothin'. Iggernant—that's when you don't know nothin', *and you don't want to know nothin'.*

And that's who is developing and implementing educational policy and therefore shaping teaching practice: the "iggernant" among us. Journals produce volumes of work that are overridden by politicians' wishful thinking, all the way up to the U.S. Secretary of Education and his fanciful basis for his agenda (Ravitch, 2014). If this chapter has any implication that matters, it's not for more research. It's for policymakers to have some understanding of what they are doing by getting acquainted with what's already out there, so that they do not impose programs that work splendidly on paper but are disastrous to schools, students, teachers, and communities in terms of helping youth find school meaningful and educational.

REFERENCES

American Association of University Women. (1991). Shortchanging girls, shortchanging America. Retrieved February 18, 2015, from *www.aauw.org/files/2013/02/shortchanging-girls-shortchanging-america-executive-summary.pdf.*

American Psychological Association. (n.d.). *Ethnic and racial minorities & socioeconomic status.* Retrieved June 16, 2015, from *www.apa.org/pi/ses/resources/publications/factsheet-erm.aspx.*

Ballenger, C. (1999). *Teaching other people's children: Literacy and learning in a bilingual classroom.* New York: Teachers College Press.

Belgarde, M. J., LoRé, R. K., & Meyer, R. (2009). American Indian adolescent literacy. In L. Christenbury, R. Bomer, & P. Smagorinsky (Eds.), *Handbook of adolescent literacy research* (pp. 415–430). New York: Guilford Press.

Berliner, D. (2014). Exogenous variables and value-added assessments: A fatal flaw. *Teachers College Record, 116*(1), 1–31.

Bomer, R., Dworin, J. E., May, L., & Semingson, P. (2008). Miseducating teachers about the poor: A critical analysis of Ruby Payne's claims about poverty. *Teachers College Record, 110*(11), 2497–2531.

Davis, J., & Bauman, K. (2013). School enrollment in the United States: 2011. Retrieved February 19, 2015, from *www.census.gov/prod/2013pubs/p20-571.pdf.*

Delgado, R., & Stefancic, J. (Eds.). (2013). *Critical race theory: The cutting edge* (3rd ed.). Philadelphia: Temple University Press.

Deloria, V. (1974). *Behind the trail of broken treaties: An Indian declaration of independence.* Austin: University of Texas Press.

Dudley-Marling, C., & Lucas, K. (2009). Pathologizing the language and culture of poor children. *Language Arts, 86*(5), 362–370.

Eckert, P. (1989). *Jocks and burnouts: Social categories and identity in the high school.* New York: Teachers College Press.

Entwisle, D. R., Alexander, K. L., & Olson, L. S. (2010). Socioeconomic status: Its broad sweep and long reach in education. In J. L. Meece & J. S. Eccles (Eds.), *Handbook of research on schools, schooling and human development* (pp. 237–255). New York: Routledge.

Fisher, M. T. (2007). *Writing in rhythm: Spoken word poetry in urban classrooms.* New York: Teachers College Press.

Four Arrows. (2013). *Teaching truly: A curriculum to indigenize mainstream education.* New York: Peter Lang.

Fu, D., & Graff, J. M. (2009). The literacies of new immigrant youth. In L. Christenbury, R.

Bomer, & P. Smagorinsky (Eds.), *Handbook of adolescent literacy research* (pp. 400–414). New York: Guilford Press.

Gilligan, C. (1982). *In a different voice.* Cambridge, MA: Harvard University Press.

Gorski, P. (2013). *Reaching and teaching students in poverty: Strategies for erasing the opportunity gap.* New York: Teachers College Press.

Governing.com. (2015). High school graduation rates by state. Retrieved February 18, 2015, from *www.governing.com/gov-data/high-school-graduation-rates-by-state.html.*

Heath, S. B. (1983). *Ways with words: Language life, and work in communities and classrooms.* New York: Cambridge University Press.

Hernnstein, R. J., & Murray, C. (1994). *The bell curve: Intelligence and class structure in American life.* New York: Free Press.

Jensen, E. (2005). *Teaching with the brain in mind* (2nd ed., rev.). Alexandria, VA: Association for Supervision and Curriculum Development.

Kajder, S. (2010). *Adolescents and digital literacies: Learning alongside our students.* Urbana, IL: National Council of Teachers of English.

Kinsey, A. C., Pomeroy, W. B., & Martin, C. E. (1948). *Sexual behavior in the human male.* Philadelphia: Saunders.

Kirkland, D. E. (2013). *A search past silence: The literacy of young black men.* New York: Teachers College Press.

Kirkland, D. E. (2014, November). *The lies "big data" tell: Rethinking the literate performances of black males through a modified meta-analysis of qualitative "little" data.* Paper presented at the annual convention of the National Council of Teachers of English, National Harbor, MD.

Kunjufu, J. (2007). *An African centered response to Ruby Payne's poverty theory.* Sauk Village, IL: African American Images.

Le, C. N. (2012). A closer look at Asian Americans and education. Retrieved December 2, 2014, from *http://education.jhu.edu/pd/newhorizons/strategies/topics/multicultural-education/a%20closer%20look%20at%20asian%20americans%20and%20education.*

Marenco, S. (2013). *I can be an actress/I can be a computer engineer.* New York: Random House.

Martino, W. (2009). Literacy issues and GLBTQ youth: Queer interventions in English Education. In L. Christenbury, R. Bomer, & P. Smagorinsky (Eds.), *Handbook of adolescent literacy research* (pp. 386–399). New York: Guilford Press.

Miller, s. j., Burns, L. D., & Johnson, T. S. (Eds.). (2013). *Generation BULLIED 2.0: Prevention and intervention strategies for our most vulnerable students.* New York: Peter Lang.

Moll, L. C. (2000). Inspired by Vygotsky: Ethnographic experiments in education. In C. Lee & P. Smagorinsky (Eds.), *Vygotskian perspectives on literacy research* (pp. 256–268). New York: Cambridge University Press.

Morici, P. (2015, January 14). Obama's free community college plan: A bogus giveaway? Retrieved February 18, 2015, from *http://getschooled.blog.ajc.com/2015/01/14/obamas-free-community-college-plan-a-bogus-giveaway.*

Murray, C. A. (2001, February 6). Prole models. Retrieved June 16, 2015 from *www.aei.org/publication/prole-models.*

Newman, D., Griffin, P., & Cole, M. (1989). *The construction zone: Working for cognitive change in school.* New York: Cambridge University Press.

Nichols, J. M. (2013). Cassidy Lynn Campbell, transgender homecoming queen, poses for "NOH8" campaign. Retrieved February 19, 2015, from *www.huffingtonpost.com/2013/09/27/cassidy-lynn-campbell-noh8_n_4004877.html.*

Nystrand, M. (1986). *The structure of written communication: Studies in reciprocity between writers and readers.* Orlando, FL: Academic Press.

Padilla, A. M. (2001). Issues in culturally appropriate assessment. In L. A. Suzuki, J. G. Ponterotto, & P. J. Meller (Eds.), *Handbook of multicultural assessment: Clinical, psychological, and educational applications* (2nd ed., pp. 5–28). San Francisco: Jossey-Bass.

Payne, R. K. (2013). *A framework for understanding poverty: A cognitive approach* (5th ed.). Highlands, TX: aha! Process.

Perreira, K. M., Harris, K. M., & Lee, D. (2006). Making it in America: High school completion by immigrant and Native youth. *Demography, 43*(3), 511–536.

Pettigrew, C. (2015, February 18). "It gets better" for gay high school football player. Retrieved February 19, 2015, from *www.hlntv.com/video/2015/02/18/dalton-ray-wisconsin-football-player-comes-out-high-school-team-0*.

Philips, S. U. (1983). *The invisible culture: Communication in classroom and community on the Warm Springs Indian Reservation.* New York: Longman.

Portes, P., & Smagorinsky, P. (2010). Static structures, changing demographics: Educating for shifting populations in stable schools. *English Education, 42,* 236–248.

Ravitch, D. (2014, April 5). My favorite line from Arne Duncan: What is yours? Diane Ravitch's blog: A site to discuss better education for all. Retrieved June 10, 2015, from *http://dianeravitch.net/2014/04/05/my-favorite-line-from-arne-duncan-what-is-yours*.

Shearer, L. (2015, February 16). Minority student populations on the rise at UGA. Retrieved February 18, 2015, from *http://onlineathens.com/uga/2015-02-14/minority-student-populations-rise-uga*.

Smagorinsky, P. (2001). If meaning is constructed, what is it made from?: Toward a cultural theory of reading. *Review of Educational Research, 71,* 133–169.

Smagorinsky, P. (2011). *Vygotsky and literacy research: A methodological framework.* Boston: Sense.

Smagorinsky, P., & Taxel, J. (2004). The discourse of character education: Ideology and politics in the proposal and award of federal grants. *Journal of Research in Character Education, 2*(2), 113–140.

Smagorinsky, P., & Taxel, J. (2005). *The discourse of character education: Culture wars in the classroom.* Mahwah, NJ: Erlbaum.

Smith, M. W., & Wilhelm, J. D. (2002). *Reading don't fix no Chevys: Literacy in the lives of young men.* Portsmouth, NH: Heinemann.

Sommers, C. H. (2000). *The war on boys: How misguided feminism is harming our young men.* New York: Simon & Schuster.

Stotsky, S. (1999). *Losing our language: How multicultural classroom instruction is undermining our children's ability to read, write, and reason.* New York: Free Press.

Vargas, L. (2006). Transnational media literacy: Analytic reflections on a program with Latina teens. *Hispanic Journal of Behavioral Sciences, 38,* 267–285.

Wikipedia. (n.d.). School leaving age. Retrieved December 2, 2014, from *http://en.wikipedia.org/wiki/school_leaving_age*.

Williams, R. (1977). *Marxism and literature.* New York: Oxford University Press.

Wolk, S. (2009). Reading for a better world: Teaching for social responsibility with young adult literature. *Journal of Adolescent and Adult Literacy, 52*(8), 664–673.

Yoo, B. (2010). Unraveling the model minority myth of Asian American students. Retrieved from *www.education.com/reference/article/unraveling-minority-myth-asian-students*.

CHAPTER 13

Avoiding the Cheapest Room in the House
Dialoguing through Fear of Dialogical Practice

BOB FECHO, JENNIFER J. WHITLEY, and STEVEN J. LANDRY

DIALOGICAL CLASSROOMS

Paige Cole is an accomplished social studies teacher in northeast Georgia. For the past 7 years, she has taught in two school districts—and has won or been nominated for Teacher of the Year Awards for 5 of those 7 years. Additionally, Paige is a teacher consultant for her local site of the National Writing Project (NWP), a long-time and much-lauded (Jaxon, 2009; Lieberman & Friedrich, 2007; Lieberman & Wood, 2003) professional learning initiative for teachers. Through her NWP connections, Paige has served on national committees devoted to technology in classrooms, presented at national literacy conferences, cofacilitated weeklong institutes focused on literacy practice and technology, and developed and cofacilitated a successful summer institute centered on Holocaust studies, supported by a grant from New York City's Memorial Library. By all measures, Paige Cole is a highly qualified teacher. Yet, despite these accomplishments and accolades, Paige has moments of doubt as she tries to marry engaged and dialogical ways of learning with the increasing standardization of U.S. classrooms. As she wrote to fellow teachers in a chapter for a book focused on dialogical teaching practices:

> I do believe that fear has crept into our classrooms but do we have to let it in? The poet Hafiz (1999) admonished us to seek better lodging than in the tawdry rooms that fear inhabits. Fear is not the room I would like to keep residing in, with worry being my only companion. How many of us are putting ourselves in our own prisons? How many times have I given up on a dialogue before even entering it? How much of this is fear-based and what am I afraid of? (Cole, 2016, pp. 24–25).

Given her experience as an undergraduate and graduate student in progressive teacher education programs, Paige has developed not only an appreciation of dialogical teaching methods but also has honed and refined her abilities to teach in dialogical ways. Still, she sometimes allows fear to enter her classroom.

This chapter, then, is for Paige and for all the thoughtful and creative teachers and researchers who daily struggle to minimize the standardization and increase the multiple perspectives; who respect the imposed assessment tools, yet allow for a range of understandings; and who ready students for yearly testing, while also readying them for life's larger tests—the swift-paced, technological, and globalized existence we are creating. We follow this introductory case with a discussion of what we mean when we write *dialogical practice*, a quick survey of research on classroom dialogue conducted prior to 2000, and a brief explanation of our methods for reviewing the literature. We then delineate what research has come to tell us about teaching in dialogical ways, and we conclude our contribution to this book with a specific call for continued and necessary research that might better inform teachers about the potential and complexity of such work.

DEFINING DIALOGICAL PRACTICE

Building from the ideas of Freire (1970), Bakhtin (1981), Rosenblatt (1995), Gee (2012), and others, we offer the following as a working definition of dialogical practice that drove our search of the literature: "A dialogical classroom is one in which literacy is used to immerse teacher and students in an ongoing reflective conversation with the texts of their lives" (Fecho, 2011a, p. 5). This definition attempts to capture the depth of learning, the emphasis on language, the inclusiveness of all in the classroom, the sense of stretching across time, the care attributed to thought, and the importance of engaging with the world that we believe characterizes engaged dialogical practice. It should in no way be seen as definitive but should instead be viewed as a launching pad for future dialogue about the definition of dialogical practice.

Those of us who might call ourselves dialogical educators roughly divide into two camps. Like us, most dialogical educators straddle these theoretical stances, while perhaps adhering more to one than the other. One of those camps is occupied by educators who primarily build their pedagogy from the work of Brazilian educator Paulo Freire, from whose ideas much of the critical pedagogy framework has been derived. In a Freirian stance, asymmetrical issues of power dominate the landscape, and, as Eugene Matusov (2009) indicated, dialogue can occur only under certain conditions. Such dialogue springs from love of, humility before, and faith in others, and leads to a form of education based on problem-posing (Freire, 1970). It is this idea of problem-posing or questioning that positions the dialogue in a Freirian educational cosmos in apposition to what he has famously called *banking education,* or depositing "knowledge" inside the heads of students. In particular, banking education suppresses dialogue, whereas problem-posing education "regards dialogue as indispensable to the act of cognition that unveils reality" (p. 71).

Other dialogical educators, most of whom at least are acquainted with Freire's ideas, align more with the literary theories of Mikhail Bakhtin. As he considered the nature of discourse in novels, Bakhtin also developed ideas about language and learning. According to Bakhtin (1981), all meaning is made through response and in context. As such, meaning is constantly open to change. Given that individuals can't help but respond and that all response is based on prior response and pitched toward future response, we exist in an ongoing dialogue with all that we encounter daily. These dialogues are subject to *centripetal,* or unifying forces, and *centrifugal,* or individualizing forces. As such, humans alone and in groups simultaneously seek both common and personal understanding, and we do it through language that "enters a dialogically agitated and tension-filled environment of alien words, value judgments and accents, weaves in and out of complex relationships, merges with some, recoils from others" (p. 276). Language and the understandings we come to through language exist in this agitated environment of flux and uncertainty.

Given these differences, there is much that still connects Freire's theory and Bakhtin's theory. Chief among these connections is the idea that learners exist in a process of becoming. Freire (1970) described humans as being incomplete, with unfinished realities. But given the historical nature of humans—we grasp a sense of both the past and the future—we are then aware of being incomplete. As he explained, "In this incompletion and this awareness lie the very roots of education" (p. 72). As such, "immobility represents a fatal threat" (p. 72), and learners need to reference their history to better understand the present and future they are constructing.

Bakhtin (1981), writing from the orientation of language study, described the *living word*—language that is as malleable and changeable as any living organism. All language lives and shifts meaning within a context that "is directly, blatantly, oriented toward a future answer-word" while "forming itself in an atmosphere of the already spoken word" (p. 280). Learners bring worldviews and personal perspectives to all contexts but need to be willing to alter those views and perspectives as they encounter the world. Writing about the festivals of carnival, similar to contemporary Mardi Gras celebrations, where irreverence reigns, Bakhtin (1984) called them "feasts of becoming" that were "hostile to all that was immortalized and completed" (p. 10). These carnival spaces saw the "suspension of all hierarchical precedence" (p. 10) so, if only for a time, new relationships and ideas across socioeconomic classes could be established. In the theories of both Bakhtin and Freire, meaning is constructed within context and that context is about time as well as place.

Freire and Bakhtin also agree that there is power in naming the world, which is another way of saying that there is power in making meaning. Such an idea is base to Freire's (1970) work: "To exist, humanely, is to name the world, to change it" (p. 76). This naming the world is key to dialogue, which Freire called an "existential necessity," and argues that all people need access to this naming dialogue. To participate in dialogue is to participate in a generative act that is implied in Bakhtin's (1986) late work, in which he described humans as being "the witness and the judge" (p. 137), meaning that we both see and assess. It is through our witnessing and judging that we change the world, that whatever we bring our attention to—the sun, a stone, a leaf—takes on new meaning, depending on who is doing the looking and when and where they look. A stone may just be this hard thing underfoot to one person, evidence of geological origins to another, and a wonder of striated color to a third—or all three to the same person within different contexts.

To both expand and deepen the working definition we used at the start of this section—a *dialogical classroom* is one in which literacy is used to immerse teacher and students in an ongoing reflective conversation with the texts of their lives—we argue that engaged dialogical practice is (1) generative, (2) transactional, (3) process oriented, (4) open to interpretation and uncertainty, (5) steeped in complexity, and (6) positioned to question sociocultural and sociopolitical contexts. To teach in dialogical ways is to see not only writing and speaking as generative acts but also reading and listening, and when learners construct meaning through any of those literate activities, they are both shaping and being shaped by the texts they are constructing. Learning is viewed as a process across time, and because the process engages complex concepts with sociocultural and sociopolitical consequences, interpretations are multiple and certainty is rare. Somewhat similar to climate change deniers, there are education policymakers who have a more simplistic sense of classrooms. In response, we argue that dialogical processes are occurring in every classroom; it's the dialogical teacher who, understanding this reality, takes advantage of its possibilities.

The argument we won't make in this chapter is that teaching in dialogical ways is easy or always welcomed. There's a reason that despite the early arguments of progressive educators such as John Dewey (1902) and Carter G. Woodson (1933/2013), engaged dialogical practice remains marginalized in too many K–12 public and private schools in the United States. Perhaps the key reason for this marginalization lies in the argument that "problem-posing education does not and cannot serve the interests of the oppressor. No oppressive order could permit the oppressed to begin to question: Why?" (Freire, 1970, p. 74).

The same concern, etched in Bakhtin's (1981) terms, is to see the current focus on standardization as a skewing too far toward and past unification and into reification, thus limiting individual interpretation, creative understandings, and multiple perspectives. Whatever the reason, our review of practice-based research sketches what we know about the possibilities of engaged dialogical practice, while suggesting its limitations and pointing toward the need for more and richer research, as well as more and richer implementation.

THE RECENT HISTORICAL CONTEXT OF CLASSROOM DIALOGUE

Although we limited our exploration of dialogical practice primarily to research that has been done in the 15-year period since the start of the 21st century, a brief review of studies prior to that start date will help to create a historical context for the more current studies. In particular, this section points out differences between dialogue and dialogical pedagogy. In a Bakhtinian (Bahktin, 1981) sense, learners are always immersed in dialogue, which doesn't necessarily mean they are immersed in dialogical pedagogy. If teachers are unaware of the dialogical possibilities of the dialogue in their classrooms, meaning is still being made, but not necessarily in any systematic or intentional way that leads to multiple perspectives and complex understandings. Unless teachers provide structures and opportunities for considering, reflecting on, rethinking, connecting, and generating meaning, the bulk of the dialogical aspect of their classroom dialogue will be lost.

Much of the focus of research in the last one-third of the 20th century had to do with classroom dialogue or, termed another way, classroom discourse. For example, Howe and Abedin (2013), in their four-decade review of this literature, indicated that studies on initiation–response–feedback, or IRF (Sinclair & Coulthard, 1975), initiation–response–evaluation, or IRE (Mehan, 1979), and variations thereof have dominated studies of classroom dialogue. Such classroom participation channels dialogue through the teacher who initiates (Who is the main character of *Beloved?*), becomes the main receiver of the student response (Sethe), then provides feedback and/or evaluation ("Well done!"). Howe and Abedin (2013) go on to point out that although IRF/IRE is not a monolithic participation pattern and studies indicate the possibility of entertaining diverse perspectives (e.g., Bleicher, Tobin, & McRobbie, 2003; Dombey, 2003; Eggleston, 1983; Skidmore & Murakami, 2010), what they term *dialogic interaction* rejects this classic pattern and seeks either the withholding of feedback or the sharing of nonevaluative feedback (e.g., Chin, 2006; Delafield, 1999; Olitsky, 2007).

This work raises substantive questions. In particular, the studies cited earlier ask about who participates, in what ways, and to what ends. If IRF/IRE dominates participation patterns even into this second decade of the 21st century, as Howe and Abedin (2013) suggest, what does that mean for teachers who want to tug away from that pattern toward a more dialogical sense of participation? Howe and Abedin conclude that "much more is known about how classroom dialogue is organized than about whether certain modes of organization are more beneficial than others" (p. 325). As we shift into our discussion of practice-based research on dialogical practice, our intent is to focus on what we seem to know about what works and where the struggles and gaps may lie.

METHODS

The question of dialogical pedagogy often leads to a question of power. One of the elements of dialogical practice is a decentering of power. By remaining in constant reflection and ongoing inquiry, students and teachers co-construct tentative understandings, multiple perspectives, and negotiated directions for learning. Along similar lines, Marilyn Cochran-Smith and Susan L. Lytle (2009) argued that research, too, contains inherent hierarchies that may be interrupted by asking ourselves: *What counts as research?* We agree that, despite what we call our work,

> the goal is not to produce findings.... Rather, the goal is to create access for all learners to equitable and stimulating learning opportunities; to identify levers for needed change in people, institutions, and systems; and to act in ways that respect and honor the participation of various constituencies whose lives are implicated in the educational practices and policies under consideration. (p. 142)

In short, our purpose in this chapter is to consider and unpack *dialogical practice* through the research of others under our cohesive lens, but working with a broad conception of what counts as research. Although our emphasis in culling these studies to support practice was to focus on traditional university-based research, we also included other works that contained classroom descriptions of practice.

We began this research with two questions in mind: (1) What is dialogical practice, and (2) What does dialogical practice look like? Using our university's multisearch feature, we sought peer-reviewed pieces written within the last 15 years that included the terms *dialog* pedagogy*, *Bakhtin*, and/or *inquiry-based pedagogy*. After each search, we read, annotated, and interacted with the pieces that attempted to provide possible answers to our questions. We met three times during our inquiry in order to touch base, asking ourselves: (1) What does this literature say about dialogical practice?; (2) What questions do these pieces raise?; and (3) What is missing here?

During our second meeting, we realized how relatively little classroom research has been done on dialogical practice and, keeping the words of Cochran-Smith and Lytle (2009) in mind, broadened our search to find more of such work. After combing through our university's online database and other outlets, such as Google Scholar, we found 41 pieces that fit the parameters of our search. Throughout the rest of this piece, we explore what we saw, understanding that our unpacking of the aforementioned questions comes from our own contexts—we do not seek to provide a "how-to" guide for dialogical practice, but instead work with and through what we saw in the dialogical work of others and ourselves.

DISCUSSING RESEARCH ON DIALOGICAL PRACTICE

Early in this chapter, we laid out these characteristics of engaged dialogical practice: (1) generative; (2) transactional; (3) process oriented; (4) open to interpretation and uncertainty; (5) steeped in complexity; and (6) positioned to question sociocultural and sociopolitical contexts. If the intent is to create a dialogical practice that is responsive to these characteristics, then what in the literature provides us insight into the possibility of doing so? Quite literally, what does it look like for classroom practice to be generative, transactional, and so on? Although we think certain studies illustrate one of these characteristics better than another, we also understand that the studies contained herein can't always be confined to a single category. Given the limitations of length, we have tried to show this multiplicity of connections as often as possible, but we suggest that readers bring their own interpretations to these many possibilities.

Generative Dimensions of Dialogical Practice

Although most, if not all, teachers would agree that writing and speaking are generative acts, we suspect a few too many don't see the generative aspects of reading and listening. But as Louise Rosenblatt (1995) explained, each of us who reads *Beloved* generates a text that is uniquely ours—one that is based on our cultural experiences, our various contexts, and the purposes for which we read. Even a text that we've read in the past becomes a new text due to our shift in context. It is this generative aspect of literate practices that helps keep classic literature relevant to less experienced and casual readers. The text they construct may not be the text the author had in mind, but it's a text that reflects their dialogue with the words, plot, characters, and images, as filtered through their experiences. When you multiply this activity by the total numbers in any classroom, the result is scads of perspectives, stances, takes, and beliefs about a single shared text.

Dialogical pedagogy lends itself to this generative learning process in that it encourages multiple encounters with text that then foster multiple interpretations. In a study by Anglin and Smagorinsky (2014), five high school seniors constructed interpretations of each of the five acts of Shakespeare's *Hamlet* through spoken word performances. In researching within her classroom, Anglin drew on Bakhtin's (1981) historical and contemporary sense of context that created a generative space for the students to experiment with both genre and interpretation. As the authors noted, "In order to produce their interpretive raps, the students engaged in dialogic processes in which they explored the play's meaning, considered rap conventions through which to express their interpretation, called on additional cultural knowledge to include in their texts, and jointly composed their poetic texts" (p. A51). In doing so, the students dialogued with the original text, with historical interpretations of that text, with each other and their class peers, and with Anglin herself. All this dialogue was done in service of engaging students in generating multiple interpretations of the work.

Dialogical spaces are generative in another sense: They create learning contexts—either face-to-face or online—that are fluid and dynamic (Groenke & Paulus, 2007; Hedberg & Brudvik, 2008; Juzwik, Nystrand, Kelly, & Sherry, 2008). Working quantitatively, Juzwik et al. sought to document teacher and student moves that seemed to spark and sustain more dialogical engagement. By video recording and observing a seventh-grade classroom—14 students total—working on a unit centered on the young adult novel *Make Lemonade,* the research team took note of the oral narratives shared by students and how they seemed to increase in number as the students responded to each other. According to the researchers, the oral narratives "became dialogic resources" (p. 1145) that led to more nuanced and informed understandings of text.

This generative sense of fluidity occurs online as well, although Groenke and Paulus (2007) remind us that the questions we ask have great import toward encouraging or discouraging dialogue. This study discussed a modified computer-mediated discourse analysis of the chat transcripts between 24 middle school students and the eight preservice teachers with whom they were paired and only met online. However, only three preservice teachers and their pairings were used in this analysis. As suggested by earlier studies, IRF/IRE patterns of discussion can facilitate dialogic inquiry if and when effective initiation and follow-up questions are posed and are responsive to evolving contexts.

In addition, Groenke and Paulus (2007) noted that questions that "promote dialogic inquiry in face-to-face discussions do not always transfer successfully to the CMC [computer-mediated communication]" (pp. 157–158). Perhaps most importantly, structure and the medium seem less necessary for dialogical inquiry than "overall patterns of discourse shaped by teachers' instructional goals" (p. 158). Unless teachers build into their lesson plans "dialogic patterns of knowledge-building, then discussion will most likely" be more monological than dialogical (p. 158). Simply put, we cannot expect generative dialogue to spring from barren soil.

Transactional Dimensions of Dialogical Practice

Rosenblatt's (1995) transactional theories discussed at the start of the previous section take in the concept of mutual shaping, which is to say that as readers shape texts through their experiences, the texts are shaping the readers' current worldviews and future experience. The more substantive the text and the more we engage with it intellectually and emotionally, the greater the mutual shaping. Although transactions are always occurring, engaged dialogical practice lifts these transactions to the surface and allows for a meta-awareness.

The transactional nature of dialogical classrooms is well illustrated by work done by Gallagher and Ntelioglou (2011), who pulled data from the first year of a larger, 4-year, international, multisite ethnographic project trying to understand student engagement. They analyzed ethnographic field notes, teacher interviews, and student dramatic writing and performance pedagogy in order to argue that high school students who were engaged in "extensive dialogue and interaction that helped them to think both aesthetically and critically" were more successful in the drama classroom, creating a more "dynamic," and "literacy-rich" classroom space (p. 324). Thus engaged in this mutual shaping, students were better able to interpret and bring meaning to their dramatic work.

Researchers Vadeboncoeur and Luke (2004) looked closely at one classroom transcript in which students and their preservice teacher were "struggling to come to grips with ideologies, values, and critical understandings of a world around them clearly undergoing geo-political and cultural change" (p. 203) immediately after September 11, 2001. Part of a larger ethnographic study of a university–school partnership that focused on the teaching and learning of youth labeled *at risk*—although the authors disparage the term—the one transcript presented is representative of six different class discussions. Although there were many times that the preservice teacher didn't take advantage of "teachable moments," the researchers noted that the students responded better when they were engaged with open-ended questions, especially in a context of intertextuality in which they could make connections. This idea of intertextuality—of essentially dialogue across texts—seems conducive to a transactional learning process.

Process-Oriented Dimensions of Dialogical Practice

The generative and transactional dimensions of a dialogical practice discussed to this point feed into the emphasis on process in such teaching practices. Falling back on our theoretical framework, we reiterate that Freire (1970) and Bakhtin (1981) see all of us in a process of becoming marked by incompleteness and a wish—perhaps even a need—to make meaning in ways that fill in some, if not all, of the gaps caused by our incompleteness. This idea is not orientation toward process at the expense of product; rather it's a reemphasis that *how* we create and *what* we create are, themselves, in constant dialogue.

The work of Boyd and Markarian (2015) vividly illustrates the *how* of dialogue in relation to the *what* of dialogue. Conducted as part of a larger study, the researchers monitored a third-grade classroom of 18 students. The process behind dialogue (e.g., patterns of talk such as turn-taking norms, who gets to set agendas, and to what degree are those agendas taken up by others) were brought under their magnifying glass. In the words of the researchers, "dialogic talk functions to model and support cognitive activity and inquiry and supportive classroom relations, to engage multiple voices and perspectives across time, and to animate student ideas and contributions" (p. 273). Again, briefly put, process informs product and back again.

The process of identity construction, particularly among adolescents, is prominent in the literature (e.g., Cuenca, 2010; Hallman, 2012; Stables, 2003). One such study was conducted in Australia by Ryan and Johnson (2009) in a state secondary school, chosen because its English work programs were informed by critical pedagogy in relation to visual and multimodal texts. The participants were three White, middle-class, male and female, 16- to 17-year-old students "for whom emancipation or issues of social justice were *not* immediately or personally relevant" (p. 249, emphasis in original). Three overarching discourses were identified in the data: *discourses of youth* that resist conformity, *intentional discourses of schooling* that support conformity, and *discourses of society* that are controlling. Ultimately, Ryan and Johnson concluded that "teachers need to encourage students to explore their processes of subjectification, whereby they examine and understand why they make the decisions they do" and "how historical intertextual chains have shaped, and continue to shape their behaviours, actions and language use" (p. 258). Immersed as they are in a living example of the play of centripetal and centrifugal forces, students need to acknowledge the process in order to navigate it toward becoming more self-aware.

Also working with identity construction, Beatrice Ligorio (2010) highlighted ways that cultural psychology, educational psychology, and identity psychology transact. Working from dialogical self theory (DST; Hermans & Hermans-Konopka, 2010) and a constructivist view of conceptualized learning as building knowledge, Ligorio argued that schools are sites for change, but students aren't often given a voice "because they are not yet equipped with the necessary tools and resources to do so," but if they could express their voices "in the Bakhtinian sense," then "more understanding of how learning experience affects identity" (p. 93) would enrich classroom practice. She asserted that identity construction should be considered as part of the overall dialogical learning process.

The process-oriented dimensions of dialogical practice as they apply to writing processes were validated by the research we uncovered (e.g., Morgan & Beaumont, 2003; Van der Scaaf, Baartman, Prins, Oosterbaan, & Schaap, 2013). Along those lines, Morgan and Beaumont (2003) made a case for a dialogical approach to argumentation using a chat room and middle school students as key to their research design. By using role play and the staged performance of collaborative discussion to support the online chat room discussions, teachers in the study were able to engage students in dialogical approaches that immersed them in literate practice and in an ongoing conversation with the texts of their lives. To this end, the authors saw the chat room as a mediating space between speech and writing.

Dimensions of Dialogical Practice that Open It to Interpretation and Uncertainty

With so much learning activity in progress, there is a tendency for dialogical classrooms to venture into the realm of uncertainty. At the start of this chapter, we introduced you to Paige Cole, an accomplished teacher who believes in and often enacts a dialogical practice, but who, like most teachers, is beset by the limitations of standardization. Reflecting on this struggle, Paige wrote of having attended a workshop facilitated by teacher-educator Sheridan Blau:

> Blau also told us "The more you understand, the more questions you have." This statement, though I believe it, is not exactly what many people want to hear. The more questions we have, the more uncertainty exists. The more uncertainty may lead to more anxiety and I think many of us want answers. Many of us want things to be quantifiable or measurable so we feel like we have some sense of control. We are left vulnerable when we do not have it all figured out, that is until we learn to live in a more dialogical space. (Cole, 2016, pp. 22–23)

It is our sense that Paige's words reflect what many other teachers feel and experience. On the one hand, there's the inclination to create opportunities for multiple interpretations of literature and life situations; on the other hand, that uncertainty can breed an openness that feels disconcerting at best in this age of accountability.

Fortunately, there is some solid research that not only undergirds the importance of understanding uncertainty but also embraces students' need as learners to enter into uncertainty and dialogue through it. To begin, research on DST (Hermans & Hermans-Konopka, 2010) emphasizes that individuals can react to uncertainty by seeing it as something to be dreaded or as something rife with opportunity. Significantly, their work illustrates that dialogue "copes with uncertainty by *going into this uncertainty* rather than avoiding it" (p. 46, emphasis in original). We recognize that, not unlike turning a car into the direction of the skid on an icy road, this advice feels counterintuitive. Nevertheless, dialoguing through uncertainty "opens a range of possibilities that . . . remain flexible and susceptible to change during the process itself" (p. 46). By recognizing the complexity of issues at hand and seeking multiple interpretations and perspectives, we open learning spaces to a wider and more considered range of possible pathways toward understanding.

Brian Edmiston's (2014) research resonates profoundly with DST by using dramatic approaches to dialoguing through uncertainty. Working with students, from kindergartners through high school seniors, Edmiston engages them in various role-playing, scenario-acting, and idea-building strategies, all designed to help students make meaning through dialogical activity. Taking a somewhat embodied literacies approach, his dialogical practice shows teachers how to situate learning in real-life, authentic spaces. As such, his efforts show how *place, space,* and *play* are all important aspects of the classroom dialogues happening there. For example, Edmiston's research indicates how *ensemble tasks*—a term borrowed from theater groups in which actors play many parts and work more cohesively—can bring individual and group tensions to the surface for examination and promote eventual rethinking of intent and purpose.

Working in a mathematics classroom in Trinidad, Steven Khan (2007) established a dialogical community that introduced interpretation and uncertainty to learning associated with that content area. Textbooks and instructional materials represented some voices in that classroom, but Khan placed them in dialogue with his students and himself as they shifted away from "'mirroring the textbook,' 'cloze questions,' and a reliance on rules . . . as substitution for mathematical reasoning" (p. 1). Instead, Khan's study created a mathematics classroom that extended beyond the individuals to a place where the participants "are engaged in a polyphonic discourse with their teachers, their peers, their cultural resources, their schools, their families and themselves" (p. 35).

Dimensions of Complexity within Dialogical Practice

Multiple interpretations and uncertainty, almost as a given, seem to exist within complex contexts. What Mary Louise Pratt (1991) and Gloria Anzaldua (1987/2007) have configured as *contact zones* and *la frontera,* or the borderlands, respectively, are spaces of rich yet often daunting complexity. Classrooms are such places. Teachers working within this complexity frequently seek, through dialogical practice, more nuanced understandings of what happens there. They do this searching despite obstructions placed before them by policymakers and administrators. As Trevor Stewart (2012) noted in his study of six literacy teachers, such obstruction to dialogical practice "made it difficult . . . to engage in dialogue with the policy mandates they received" (p. 376). However, despite such push back, thoughtful teachers continue to wade into these complex spaces.

A study by Olga Dysthe (2011) describes such a teacher, Jean, and the tensions she faced when trying to use dialogical pedagogy in a test-centered high school classroom. Presented as a case study, the aim of Dysthe's chapter was to demonstrate not the difficulties of dialogical pedagogy when centered in a standards-based space, but the benefits of it when one tries. The problem lies within the standards-based formula, though, as it situates a teacher as the "authoritative" presence in the room, which becomes an obstacle to overcome in order to encourage dialogue among students.

One of the three authors of this chapter—Bob Fecho—developed a collaborative study with four high school teachers—Paige Cole, whom you've met, as well as Ian Altman, Angela Dean, and Lisa Hall. All have written about their experiences of trying to work dialogically in standardized schools (Fecho, Falter, & Hong, 2016). Their classroom practices, like that of Jean earlier, indicated that such teaching is possible and necessary, if not always easy to pull off. Working within a range of tensions—globalization and localization; the personal and the academic; the conflicting agendas of stakeholders; the mainstream and the margins; the ethical and the legal; the expedient and the desired—Angela, Ian, Lisa, and Paige at various times throughout the year needed to pay attention to one, some, or all of these tensions.

Events that transpired in the classrooms of these four teachers had caused a certain amount of wobble (Fecho, 2011b) in the equilibrium between the opposing forces, and conditions were ripe for tensions skewing to one side or the other. As such, "wobble" is a calling to attention, a provocation of response. When something wobbles—a wheel on a car, a glass of wine on a waiter's tray, a child's top, the Earth on its axis—we notice and are often moved to act. Angela, Ian, Lisa, and Paige all experienced various degrees of wobble through the academic year and, across a continuum of success and consistency, were able to dialogically call attention to issues with their practices and with their students.

Eugene Matusov (2009) adds to our understanding of complexity when he argues that all teaching revolves around dialogical relations. For him, it is never a question of whether or not to teach dialogically, but more a question of how to be a better and more cognizant dialogical teacher. His work in classrooms and with preservice teachers illustrates the ways teachers daily must recognize and build from the dialogical dimensions already inherent within all classrooms. Quite simply, "good teaching requires dialogue" (p. 80). But the dialogue must be entered with self-awareness, because "if . . . the teacher does not expect to learn something new from his or her student" then the potentiality of dialogue is limited (p. 84).

Dimensions of Sociocultural/Sociopolitical Questioning within Dialogical Practice

It's no great surprise given that dialogical practice has its roots in the critical theories of Freire (1970) and the carnival theories of Bakhtin (1984) that many teachers want to use it to help students explore issues related to race, gender, class, and other sociocultural factors. It is also those kinds of discussions that, as noted earlier in the chapter, keep some teachers from wanting to work dialogically, because they fear such discussions will float beyond their control. In this final section devoted to practice-based research, we examine what the literature can tell us about teaching in ways that call societal norms into question.

Some research seems to point toward what we lose when we don't exploit the dialogical possibilities in our classrooms. In the case study of Isaac, a student from northeast Georgia, Bob Fecho (2013) focused on a bipolar student and the transactions he made with other texts and his world. He used the student's own precocity for writing as a way to understand Isaac through the lens of a literacy educator. Essentially, Isaac wrote as a way to understand himself existentially, but too frequently teachers did not see the meaning-making potential of such writing. Fecho suggested that teachers should not "limit experience and dialogue in the classroom, because this can hamper the construction of meaning" (p. 135). Allowing for divergent interpretations, writing opportunities, and dialogue provides for a "greater range of access for developing understanding" (p. 135). Isaac used "all means and modes at his disposal to make sense of conditions that seemed random and grossly unjust. . . [He used] dialogue for existential purposes" (p. 135). Sadly, much of this writing was done outside of school and beyond the knowledge of most of his teachers.

In another study, Maren Aukerman (2012) explored the implications of a dialogical classroom space in relation to critical literacy, pushing for what she deemed "critical literacy as dialogic engagement" (p. 46). After an analysis of trends in critical literacy practices, she offered her addition to the field, noting "that pedagogies oriented toward critical literacy as dialogic engagement can offer intentional space for the unfolding of social heteroglossia" (p. 46), that is, a multiplicity of languages. She offered three implications for her theoretical research: (1) educators need to consider how their experiences constrain the goal of critical literacy; (2) classroom spaces should de-center teacher authority, as well as textual authority; and (3) teachers must recognize that there will never be one acceptable response to texts, especially in a critical literacy-based classroom, as there are so many unique contexts that inform our students' reading of texts.

Like Aukerman (2012), Brian Ort and Carl Burgchardt (2013) suggested that critical pedagogy is problematic if not situated within a dialogical space. Otherwise, it sometimes succumbs to Freire's (1970) banking model. In other words, if we teachers limit texts to specific meanings, we also limit our students' responses. Another researcher, Amy Brown (2011), performed a qualitative study in an attempt to answer the question, "What might a critical, democratic, or humanizing education look like in the context of neoliberal education reforms?" (p. 3). Using participant observation, interviews, and classroom observation, in addition to holding seven cultural circle meetings, she analyzed urban fiction and high school students' dialogical responses to it in order to call into question the current educational model and increase student engagement.

Morrell's (2004) and Duncan-Andrade and Morrell's (2008) research and teaching consistently speak to the use of dialogue to question asymmetrical power relationships. Although Bakhtin's and Freire's work have relevance in contemporary classrooms, their ideas can seem idealistic to teachers facing top-down mandates to standardize their instruction and testing. Morrell's (2004) piece responded to such concerns and encouraged a pedagogy that asks students not only to inquire into the classroom but also to "question the actual tests themselves" (p. 91). Duncan-Andrade and Morrell (2008) created a range of activities both during and beyond school hours that continuously provided opportunities and expectations for students to question not only the sociopolitical contexts in which they lived but also their own collusion in the process. In all his work, Morrell emphatically urged "teachers, teacher educators, and researchers to become advocates and activists for diverse modes of instruction" (2004, p. 91), especially as U.S. educational reform becomes more and more standardized. We couldn't agree more.

MOVING FORWARD

That dialogical practice is possible and doable, even in today's overly surveilled classrooms, is not a debatable question. Clearly, as the research detailed earlier indicates, thoughtful and caring teachers are able to work in dialogical ways. We hesitated, however, to use the adjective *innovative* to modify *teachers*. To call these teachers *innovative* is to marginalize them, to intimate that they need to be something more than thoughtful and caring, to somehow push them out there on the fringes of acceptable classroom practice. We don't believe, and we argue against the idea, that to enact dialogical practice, someone has to be seen as a rebellious or as magically creative and inventive.

Instead, and we think the research bears this out, aware and engaged dialogical practice can and should take place in any classroom in which the teacher believes in its potential and wants to enact it. In our experience working with the many teachers who populate the diverse sites of the NWP, a kind of double standard exists (Fecho et al., 2016). On the one hand, teachers feel they must, for many rational and imagined reasons, adhere to what often becomes rigid ways to handle whatever set of standards have been imposed on their classrooms. Given the high stakes often weighing on such adherence, we understand the plight of these teachers and the choices they often make.

Yet in conversation with many of these teachers, we frequently hear a longing on their part to teach to a higher and self-imposed set of standards. They want to teach in ways that help students generate their own understandings of text and add them to the understandings generated by others in the class. These teachers want their students not only to question the beliefs of others but also to call their own beliefs into question, to engage in the idea of wobble (Fecho, 2011b), with the intent of creating better-informed learners. They hunger for complex discussions about sociocultural issues, and not as disembodied, abstract discussions, but in dialogues that connect the lives of students to these discussions. They want, simply put, to honor the standards but to enact dialogical practice in service of them.

So that's the conundrum: to live in fear that to teach in ways that many teachers feel is in the best interests of their students might place their own job security at risk. What researchers and teacher-educators can do to support teachers in dialoguing past these fears is to continue studying and publishing what we learn about dialogical practice. In our survey of the literature, we discovered it is far easier to uncover theoretical discussions and advocacy pieces than to uncover empirical research. Assuredly, there is such work out there, but substantially more is needed, especially if those of us who believe in dialogical practice want to counter the master narratives indicating that standards are best taught through direct instruction.

In particular, we need to know more about the ways K–12 students dialogue among themselves and across groups. Although there seems to be a fair amount in the research literature about intergroup dialogue at the postsecondary level, "less is known about the impact of intergroup dialogue with adolescents" (Aldana, Rowley, Checkoway, & Richards-Schuster, 2012, p. 120). Many more critical examinations of classroom practice need to occur as well. Teachers and teacher-educators need multiple layers of descriptions and analyses of dialogical practice, in a wide range of contexts and enacted with a wide range of students. Nor should such research only tell the good news. The research we have reveals that teaching in dialogical ways makes classrooms more complex. That increased complexity is not necessarily a bad thing, because it compels teachers and students to think about what they are learning and how they are learning it, but it helps if teachers, through the research literature, enter a more aware dialogical practice with their eyes open.

What we've just outlined is a way for teachers and teacher-educators to work in tandem and to be more dialogically proactive. The more systematic and intentional (Cochran-Smith & Lytle, 2009) teachers and teacher-educators can be at describing and analyzing the dialogical dimensions of their practices, the greater will be the groundswell in terms of solidly establishing such practice in more classrooms. Teacher study groups and even whole schools could engage in practitioner research that would be effective, not to mention, professional dialogical learning, because it would be grounded in the classrooms of teachers. Teacher-educators can do their part by conducting methods and other preservice classes through dialogical means, and publishing their own practitioner research. Although it's useful to have teachers-to-be read about and try to imagine dialogical practice, it's far more practical to have them do so within a classroom in which they experience that practice as they read about it.

As Paige indicated at the start of this chapter, fear comes even to the confident teacher and can prevent many from further developing the dialogical dimensions of their practices. She acknowledges that to teach in dialogical ways is to invite complexity into the classroom:

> Dialogical teaching is harder to practice than the banking model. The dialogical classroom can be messy and, if done poorly, can be disastrous. . . . And, to correct a misconception, dialogical teaching is not a free-for-all. There is planning, grading, and then struggling and questioning it all. I continually ask myself: Did I create a situation where students could learn? (Cole, 2016, p. 22).

We're actually encouraged to see Paige raise these questions. It's the kind of self-questioning that a dialogical teacher should routinely conduct. She went on to explain that as a result of the collaborative research project with which she was involved, she "became more aware of when I was creating a space for dialogue and when I was holding court. The room came alive when it was dialogical," but a key event that she narrated left her wondering if such work was "meaningful for everyone" (Cole, 2016, p. 22).

What we hope we have done in this chapter is provide insight into how teachers in dialogue with their students can make their classrooms come alive. Having supported many teachers who attempt to work in dialogical ways in standardized classrooms, and having also enacted dialogical practice in our classrooms, we understand how doubt, concern, and fear can creep into and undermine the process. We've been there, and we've felt those feelings. The idea, and the research bears this out, is to not deny those emotions brought on by uncertainty, but instead to press into that which feels uncertain, all the while leaving oneself open to the many learning opportunities that these moments of "wobble" present. In doing so, all of us who try to teach in dialogical ways should continue, like Paige, to wonder what doing so means for us and for every student, parent, administrator, and other stakeholder we invite into the dialogue.

REFERENCES

Aldana, A., Rowley, S. J., Checkoway, B., & Richards-Schuster, K. (2012). Raising ethnic–racial consciousness: The relationship between intergroup dialogues and adolescents' ethnic–racial identity and racism awareness. *Equity and Excellence in Education, 45*(1), 120–137.

Anglin, J. L., & Smagorinsky, P. (2014). Hip-hop Hamlet: Hybrid interpretive discourse in a suburban high school English class. *Dialogic Pedagogy: An International Online Journal, 2*, 41–59.

Anzaldua, G. (2007). *Borderlands/La frontera*. San Francisco: Aunt Lute Books. (Original work published 1987)

Aukerman, M. (2012). "Why do you say yes to Pedro, but no to me?": Toward a critical literacy of dialogic engagement. *Theory Into Practice, 51*(1), 42–48.

Bakhtin, M. (1981). Discourse in the novel. In M. Holquist (Ed.), *The dialogic imagination: Four essays* (C. Emerson & M. Holquist, Trans.; pp. 259–422). Austin: University of Texas Press.

Bakhtin, M. (1984). *Rabelais and his world* (H. Iswolsky, Trans.). Bloomington: Indiana University Press.

Bakhtin, M. (1986). *Speech genres and other late essays*. Austin: University of Texas Press.

Bleicher, R. E., Tobin, K. G., & McRobbie, C. J. (2003). Opportunities to talk science in a high school chemistry classroom. *Research in Science Education, 33*(3), 319–339.

Boyd, M. P., & Markarian, W. C. (2015). Dialogic teaching and dialogic stance: Moving beyond interactional form. *Research in the Teaching of English, 49*(3), 272–296.

Brown, A. (2011). Consciousness-raising or eyebrow-raising?: Reading urban fiction with high school students in Freirean cultural circles. *Penn GSE Perspectives on Urban Education, 9*(1). Retrieved from www.urbanedjournal.org/archive/volume-9-issue-1-fall-2011/consciousness-raising-or-eyebrow-raising-reading-urban-fiction-hi.

Chin, C. (2006). Classroom interaction in science: Teacher questioning and feedback to students' responses. *International Journal of Science Education, 28*(11), 1315–1346.

Cochran-Smith, M., & Lytle, S. (2009). *Inquiry as stance: Practitioner research for the next generation*. New York: Teachers College Press.

Cole, P. (2016). Paige's story. In B. Fecho, M. Falter, & X. Hong (Eds.), *Teaching outside the box but inside the standards: Making room for dialogue* (pp. 15–27). New York: Teachers College Press.

Cuenca, A. (2010). Democratic means for democratic ends: The possibilities of Bakhtin's dialogic pedagogy for social studies. *Social Studies, 102*(1), 42–48.

Delafield, B. (1999). Lessons: Philosophy for children. In I. Parker (Ed.), *Critical textwork: An introduction to varieties of discourse and analysis* (pp. 53–64). Buckingham, UK: Open University Press.

Dewey, J. (1902). *The child and the curriculum*. Chicago: University of Chicago Press.

Dombey, H. (2003). Interactions between teachers, children and texts in three primary classrooms in England. *Journal of Early Childhood Literacy, 3*, 37–58.

Dysthe, O. (2011). Opportunity spaces for dialogic pedagogy in test-oriented schools: A case study of teaching and learning in high school. In J. White & M. Peters (Eds.), *Bakhtinian pedagogy: Opportunities and challenges for research, policy, and practice in education across the globe* (pp. 69–88). New York: Peter Lang.

Duncan-Andrade, J. M., & Morrell, E. (2008). *The art of critical pedagogy*. New York: Peter Lang.

Edmiston, B. (2014). *Transforming teaching and learning through active dramatic approaches: Engaging students across the curriculum*. New York: Routledge.

Eggleston, J. (1983). Teacher–pupil interactions in science lessons: Explorations and theory. *British Educational Research Journal, 9*, 113–127.

Fecho, B. (2011a). *Writing in the dialogical classroom: Students and teachers responding to the texts of their lives.* Urbana, IL: National Council of Teachers of English.

Fecho, B. (2011b). *Teaching for the students: Habits of heart, mind, and practice in the engaged classroom.* New York: Teachers College Press.

Fecho, B. (2013). Literacy practice and the dialogical self: Isaac making meaning. *Journal of Constructivist Psychology, 26*(2), 127–136.

Fecho, B., Falter, M., & Hong, X. (Eds.). (2016). *Teaching outside the box but inside the standards: Making room for dialogue.* New York: Teachers College Press.

Freire, P. (1970). *Pedagogy of the oppressed.* New York: Continuum.

Gallagher, K., & Ntelioglou, B. Y. (2011). Which new literacies?: Dialogue and performance in youth writing. *Journal of Adolescent and Adult Literacy, 54*(5), 322–330.

Gee, J. P. (2012). *Social linguistics and literacy. Ideology in discourses.* New York: Routledge.

Groenke, S. L., & Paulus, T. (2007). The role of teacher questioning in promoting dialogic literary inquiry in computer-mediated communication. *Journal of Research on Technology in Education, 40*(2), 141–164.

Hafiz. (1999). Your mother and my mother. In *The Gift: Poems by the great Sufi master* (D. J. Ladinsky, Trans.). New York: Penguin.

Hallman, H. L. (2012). Rhetoric of the future: Writing and identity at a school for pregnant and parenting teens. *English in Education, 46*(1), 38–55.

Hedberg, J. G., & Brudvik, O. C. (2008). Supporting dialogic literacy through mashing and modding of places and spaces. *Theory Into Practice, 47,* 138–149.

Hermans, H., & Hermans-Konopka, A. (2010). *Dialogical self theory: Positioning and counter-positioning in a globalizing society.* New York: Cambridge University Press.

Howe, C., & Abedin, M. (2013). Classroom dialogue: A systematic review across four decades of research. *Cambridge Journal of Education, 43*(3), 325–356.

Jaxon, K. D. (2009). *Constructing a stance toward inquiry lessons from the National Writing Project.* Berkeley: University of California.

Juzwik, M. M., Nystrand, M., Kelly, S., & Sherry, M. B. (2008). Oral narrative genres as dialogic resources for classroom literature study: A contextualized case study of conversational narrative discussion. *American Educational Research Journal, 45*(4), 1111–1154.

Khan, S. K. (2007). *Dialogical relations in a mathematics classroom.* Unpublished Master's thesis, Queen's University, Kingston, ON, Canada.

Lieberman, A., & Friedrich, L. (2007). Teachers, writers, leaders. *Educational Leadership, 65*(1), 42.

Lieberman, A., & Wood, D. R. (2003). *Inside the National Writing Project: Connecting network learning and classroom teaching* (Vol. 35). New York: Teachers College Press.

Ligorio, M. B. (2010). Dialogical relationship between identity and learning. *Culture and Psychology, 16*(1), 93–107.

Lyle, S. (2008). Dialogic teaching: Discussing theoretical contexts and reviewing evidence from classroom practice. *Language and Education, 22*(3), 222–240.

Matusov, E. (2009). *Journey into dialogic pedagogy.* Hauppauge, NY: Nova Science.

Mehan, H. (1979). *Learning lessons: Social organization in the classroom.* Cambridge, MA: Harvard University Press.

Morgan, W., & Beaumont, G. (2003). A dialogic approach to argumentation: Using a chat room to develop early adolescent students' argumentative writing. *Journal of Adolescent and Adult Literacy, 47*(2), 146–157.

Morrell, E. (2004). Bakhtin's dialogic pedagogy: Implications for critical pedagogy, literacy education, and teacher research in the United States. *Journal of Russian and East European Psychology, 42*(6), 89–94.

Olitsky, S. (2007). Promoting student engagement in science: Interaction rituals and the pursuit of a community of practice. *Journal of Research in Science Teaching, 44*(1), 33–56.

Ort, B. L., & Burgchardt, C. R. (2013). On critical–rhetorical pedagogy: Dialoging with *Schindler's List*. *Western Journal of Communication, 77*(1), 14–33.
Pratt, M. L. (1991). Arts of the contact zone. *Profession, 91,* 22–40.
Rosenblatt, L. (1995). *Literature as exploration* (5th ed.). New York: Modern Language Association.
Ryan, M., & Johnson, G. (2009). Negotiating multiple identities between school and the outside world: A critical discourse analysis. *Critical Studies in Education, 50*(3), 247–260.
Sinclair, J., & Coulthard, M. (1975). *Towards an analysis of discourse: The language of teachers and pupils*. London: Oxford University Press.
Skidmore, D., & Murakami, K. (2010). How prosody marks shifts in footing in classroom discourse. *International Journal of Educational Research, 49,* 69–77.
Stables, A. (2003). Learning, identity and classroom dialogue. *Journal of Educational Enquiry, 4*(1), 1–18.
Stewart, T. T. (2012). English teachers, administrators, and dialogue: Transcending the asymmetry of power in the discourse of educational policy. *English Education, 44*(4), 375–393.
Vadeboncoeur, J. A., & Luke, A. (2004). Who's/whose at risk?: Answerability and the critical possibilities of classroom discourse. *Critical Discourse Studies, 1*(2), 201–223.
Van der Schaaf, M., Baartman, L., Prins, F., Oosterbaan, A., & Schaap, H. (2013). Feedback dialogues that stimulate students' reflective thinking. *Scandinavian Journal of Educational Research, 57*(3), 227–245.
Woodson, C. G. (2013). *The mis-education of the Negro*. New York: Tribeca Books. (Original work published 1933)

PART III
ADOLESCENT LITERACIES AND MULTIPLE TEXTS

CHAPTER 14

Missing in Action
Learning from Texts in Subject-Matter Classrooms

CYNTHIA GREENLEAF and SHEILA W. VALENCIA

For the last several decades, researchers, classroom educators, and policymakers have targeted strategies for improving adolescent literacy achievement. Nevertheless, across the nation, few students reach literacy levels that enable them to develop interpretations, think critically about texts, make evidence-based arguments, or assemble information from multiple texts into a coherent understanding of a topic. While this set of circumstances may not be news, it should continue to concern us all. Despite new awareness of the literacy learning needs of adolescents, new policies aimed at advancing literacy skills for middle and high school students, new understandings of the unique demands of discipline-specific texts and literacy practices, and new standards focused on literacy instruction across the grade levels and subject-matter classes, we've made little progress over the past several decades. We believe that one fundamental reason students are not making progress in gaining advanced levels of literacy is that they have very little opportunity and support to use texts for purposeful learning in the subject areas, and thereby to gain needed dispositions, strategies, and skills.

Our purpose in this chapter is to contribute to the existing literature about this state of affairs. We are not naive. We recognize that many factors contribute to the persistent problem of engaging middle and high school students in learning from and with text, including widely varied engagement and reading proficiencies, lack of appropriate instructional resources, limited know-how among subject-area teachers, and competing commitments that undermine a sustained focus on reading to support learning and increasing independence. Ultimately, we know that solving the problem of learning from text will require simultaneous attention to all of these. And we recognize that doing so will unsettle the normative ways of teaching in middle and high schools. But we argue that doing so is foundational to improving outcomes for all students.

In this chapter, we draw on our distinct experiences over two decades to fill some of the gaps in research about how texts are actually used in disciplinary teaching and learning (Moje, Stockdill, Kim, & Kim, 2011), giving what Pearson and Gallagher (1983) have called an "existential description" of reading in the secondary subject areas. We target the perennial problem of learning with and from text in subject-area classrooms, share successful strategies we've undertaken, and make several recommendations that we feel are sensible and workable in the context of today's schools.

DISCOVERING THE MIA TEXT

Over two decades ago, one of us (Greenleaf, 1995) worked with a high school faculty serving a high-poverty, culturally and linguistically diverse population of students to collaboratively develop and study interdisciplinary project-based curricula. A ninth-grade unit, for instance, positioned students as various members of a community struggling to decide the best method of producing energy. Inspired by research on deeper, engaged learning, the curricula included discussion-based pedagogies, small-group work, and frequent opportunities for speaking and writing on curricular topics.

We found that although students were eager to participate in the projects (they attended class!), took up ways of talking that embodied their roles, and parroted information from class lectures or oral presentations given by visiting experts, their knowledge about the actual content of the units remained embarrassingly thin. We realized that students weren't reading, or weren't comprehending, the texts we had so carefully collected and provided to them. Texts, and the information, concepts, and points of view they provided on the topics linked through the carefully designed interdisciplinary units, were conspicuously missing in the action (MIA) of students' learning.

Investigating this problem, we soon found that many subject-area teachers had abandoned texts, teaching around them in many inventive ways. Classroom observations, interviews, and individual reading assessments of ninth graders revealed that students did not have texts assigned in many of their classes. Instead, they received lecture notes, or copied them from the board. When texts were used, teachers often read aloud to the class, or worse, had students read aloud round-robin to make sure all students "had access." Even in literature classes, students often listened to audiotaped renditions of a work, and just as often, viewed the film version of a book or play to keep pace with assigned reading. In situations in which course readings were assigned, and when they were circumvented through in-class oral renditions, teachers summarized the content for students with great regularity, allowing students to "pass" as readers by latching onto the work teachers did for them and the contributions of other students in class "discussions."

These same students demonstrated considerable variability in their reading abilities and familiarity with different types of reading materials inside and outside the school context. On the one hand, they read familiar types of out-of-school materials containing complex ideas, sentence structures, and arcane information (about video games, cosmetics, style, music, etc.) with considerable ease. On the other hand, their reading and comprehension of academic texts was unexpectedly and dramatically varied. Julio, for example, read Nicaraguan poetry at home, and in his English as a second language (ESL) class had many teacher-supported opportunities to make sense of literature. Yet in history, he copied notes from the board to learn content. Faced with an informational text about trade, he stumbled over sentences and text structures, his former fluency and interpretive prowess giving way to struggle. We began to see patterns in the reading we explored with case study students.

Open-ended surveys about reading behaviors and attitudes of 155 ninth-grade students told us how they defined reading. Good readers, they said, read fluently aloud. They read quickly. Good readers knew all the words they would encounter in a text beforehand. "They have to know more vocabulary words first." "They have to know how to pronounce words well." Good readers just (magically) understood the text. Few students mentioned the kinds of strategic problem solving readers do to make sense of texts (Greenleaf, Schoenbach, Cziko, & Mueller, 2001). One day in class we saw a student drop her textbook noisily onto the desktop at the beginning of the period. Her assigned reading included a section on the Armenian genocide. "Is there anyone here from Armenia?" she demanded. Another student complained about a text the class was reading, "It seems like they write this way to keep people like me out." Frequent experiences like these told us that these high school students did not expect to be challenged to read and understand worlds outside of their own experiences (Schoenbach, Greenleaf, Cziko, & Hurwitz, 1999). Echoing the responses we had seen on the survey, students seemed to have learned that what counted in school was having the correct answers (knowing already), not learning, or knowing how to learn, something new.

In these studies, we found that the vast majority of high school students in the diverse, urban settings where we worked had problems with comprehension, not decoding, of the texts they might encounter in school. They brought life experiences to bear on the interpretation of texts that were familiar to them, some of which they might encounter in school. Unexpected funds of knowledge came into view, like Julio's reading of poetry, when we listened to students making sense of a variety of texts. Yet students were profoundly inexperienced with many academic materials and text types. They became passive in the face of these materials, showing us that they did not expect to comprehend these sorts of things. Most importantly, we began to see that their reading facility with any given text was a direct measure of their experience with similar sorts of material, rather than their ability, and that their experience with such texts was a clear gauge of their opportunities to read, and learn from reading, in school.

THE ENDURING PROBLEM OF THE MIA TEXT

As we move to the present, the photocopied lecture notes teachers used to hand out have given way to glossy PowerPoint slides. Subject-area textbooks embed integrated literacy strategies into learning activities rather than relying only on end-of-chapter questions. Some schools and districts have elected to "go paperless," and students may have Chromebooks and iPads to access the myriad resources on the Internet. Technology has made it easier than ever for students to access a great variety of text, as well as to bypass reading and thinking by simply cutting and pasting text from elsewhere. New reading interventions and design-based implementation research have targeted disciplinary literacy practices, critical thinking, and deep comprehension. Yet in our ongoing work with teachers and students, and in our observations of subject-area classrooms across the middle and high school grades, we find text to be missing, still, in the action of learning.

The MIA Text in Project-Based Learning

In 2010, Valencia joined a multidisciplinary team of educational researchers and high school content teachers on an iterative design-based implementation research (DBIR) project (Penuel, Fishman, Cheng, & Sabelli, 2011) to develop, implement, and study a rigorous approach to project-based learning (PBL) in the Advanced Placement (AP) U.S. Government and Politics course.[1] The main objective was deep, transferable conceptual learning, rather than the broad content coverage and fast pace of many advanced courses (Parker et al., 2013). Also we aimed for engagement and success for the wide range of students now being encouraged to take AP courses under the banner of "AP for all"—not simply equity of access but equity of outcomes as well. After 2 years of pilot work and impending implementation in high-poverty urban schools, literacy issues surfaced and loomed large. Teachers and researchers wondered how literacy issues were interacting with their goal of deep content learning.

We set out to study the literacy contexts in these classrooms with the aim of designing, with our teacher collaborators, strategies to help students learn from texts. From 2010 to 2012, we used a combination of classroom observations, videotaped lessons, and interviews to study teachers in six schools across two states. Shockingly, we found that the majority of students, more than 70%, rarely read the course textbook, although teachers frequently assigned it for homework. They didn't need to read it to get a good grade, because teachers delivered the same information in class. As one student told us, "The information we get from all the PowerPoint [lectures] that he gives us is pretty much what we would read in the book. . . . We sort of read the textbook through him." Similar to Greenleaf, we observed teachers using a variety of work-arounds, including lectures, videos, Internet sources, and short handouts, to avoid relying on students to read the textbook.

We rarely observed in-class activities that involved extended reading—either supported by the teachers or student directed. The exception was the rare instance in which teachers arranged for students to use computers in the school library, because most classrooms had only one or two available, and many students didn't have access to the Internet at home. Few, if any, supplemental resources were available to teachers or students other than the occasional teacher-constructed or downloaded handout.

Much of the course reading was cast as homework. Assignments were expected to be completed individually and were framed as tasks to be completed for accountability rather than resources to be understood and used. Concerned about content coverage, teachers typically assigned entire textbook chapters (often more than 30 pages each), telling students, for example, "Read Chapters 16 and 17 in the textbook to prepare for a quiz," or they assigned reading from handouts with directions such as "Read the court case and write a one-third page summary." Directions like these were procedural rather than substantive—students were told the tasks they needed to complete, but they weren't oriented to the important ideas they needed to learn or how the knowledge would be useful to them. We soon realized that teachers rarely did more than skim the readings before they assigned them. Consequently, they were largely unaware of the content, the structure, or the challenges these textbook chapters presented for their students, nor did they devote class time to discussing the readings or the challenges students may have encountered.

We also observed that because students often lacked academic content knowledge about government and politics, and because related topics were common in everyday discourse, many students used their life experiences and simple logic to engage in discussion and project tasks when they should have been using knowledge they learned in the course (e.g., federalism, politics, interest groups, Constitutional reasoning, case law). Teachers

---

[1] We added AP Environmental Science in the following year, and, later, AP Physics.

were encouraged when students participated in debates and discussions, regardless of the depth of their understanding.

Like Greenleaf and colleagues (2001), we found that most students enrolled in the "open" AP Government (APGOV) classes had strong decoding skills but had difficulty with comprehension and with general and subject-specific vocabulary. Yet very few students recognized or reported that reading was difficult. They didn't connect understanding with reading. Students were compliant note takers, copying verbatim from slides, but they were confused about what to note from lectures or videos. One student told us, "I just pretty much write down what I thought was important . . . which was kind of difficult . . . because what I think is important may not be what [the teacher] thinks is important." All-in-all, we found that text played a limited role in students' learning.

The MIA Text in Classroom Observations

At about the same time Valencia was studying the AP PBL classes (Valencia & Parker, 2015), Greenleaf and colleagues (Litman, Marple, Greenleaf, Charney-Sirott, Bolz, et al., in press) approached highly regarded middle and high school teachers of literature, history/social studies, and science, asking to see lessons in which reading played a central role. They observed and videotaped 71 lessons taught by 34 teachers from 22 urban and suburban schools in two states, analyzing the lessons with an eye toward how much instructional time was devoted to working with texts versus teacher lecture, close reading to build disciplinary knowledge versus fact acquisition, and high-level tasks such as cross-text synthesis and argumentation (Litman et al., in press).

Findings from this study paint a brighter picture of reading and text use than does Greenleaf's earlier work and more recent studies (e.g., Valencia & Parker, 2015; Vaughn et al., 2013). Teachers allocated three times as much class time to working with texts as to lecture. Belying secondary teachers' often held beliefs that literacy tasks impinge on subject-matter learning, literacy tasks in the observed lessons generally had a disciplinary, knowledge-building focus. Half of all close reading involved disciplinary knowledge building (50% of the time), and argumentation and cross-textual analysis frequently involved disciplinary knowledge building (67 and 86% of the time, respectively). However, fact acquisition dominated when content was delivered by teachers.

These findings were clearly a result of targeting lessons in which reading played a central role, taught by highly regarded subject-area teachers. Thus, they offer what could be a best-case scenario of literacy opportunity to learn in middle and high school subject areas. It is therefore all the more noteworthy that working with text was no guarantee of a literacy focus: The majority of time allocated to working with text focused on disciplinary knowledge-building activities that did not actively engage students in making sense of the texts. While half of all lessons included some close reading, only 28% of class time was allocated to students actively thinking about and working with texts. And while analysis of these lessons documented more frequent use of texts than previous studies of content-area instruction, the *centrality* of texts to the authentic intellectual work of learning was quite limited, and teachers continued, in subtle ways, to deliver the content and even do the thinking.

For example, as they monitored students' progress in both small-group work and whole-class discussions, teachers would draw students to the needed information and even to their own conclusions or interpretations of texts through leading questions and selective uptake of students' contributions to discussions. Teachers would knit together and reinterpret, translate, and elaborate on students' contributions, adding new information as they orchestrated these "discussions." Seeking to engage students in discussion, through their talk, teachers nevertheless did the work themselves of reading and interpreting and knowledge building *for* students. As one high school history teacher realized about the way she had orchestrated discussion of a primary source document,

> "When I was writing things down on the board, they were coming from my words. I was giving them guiding questions. I'm building the bridge and they are just putting in the stones. They are part of it, but I took away some of their independence. I've come a long way from not lecturing off of power points, but I'm uncomfortable to go to the place where they don't feel successful."

ADDRESSING THE CONDITIONS OF SECONDARY SUBJECT-AREA CLASSROOMS

In our interpretation of this landscape, two scenarios are emerging. One replicates what Greenleaf found decades ago and what Valencia found more recently—that many secondary, subject-area teachers and their students are circumventing texts altogether, even when curricula are carefully designed to be rich and thoughtful. The other is a more subtle version of this problem: Even when texts figure into the classroom, they are not often engaged by teachers and students as sources and resources for learning. By and large, subject-area teachers are doing the bulk of the intellectual work as they deliver information and content to students in a variety of traditional, multimedia-saturated, and technologically supported ways, as well as more indirect interactions around texts. Students themselves are not digging into texts to make sense of them, even when they talk around and about them, and work with them in assigned tasks. Subject-area teachers admit they have great difficulty expecting and supporting students to learn from and with texts. Dependency on lecture, skating on the surface of texts, and information delivery masquerading as classroom discussion, rather than independent learning and deep engagement with texts, is the default.

Although relatively few studies have examined how texts are actually used in subject-area classes (Moje et al., 2011), our current studies confirm and extend what others have found. In a study of instructional time use in high school classrooms, Fisher (2009) found that students spend the majority of class time in listening activities such as lecture and film. Similarly, studies confirm that lecture has been and remains the dominant mode of instruction in both college-preparatory and general-track classes (ACT, Inc., 2006; O'Brien, Stewart, & Moje, 1995; Vaughn et al., 2013), yet teachers assign significant amounts of textbook and trade book reading (ACT, Inc., 2013; Applebee, 1993; Bain, 2006; Reisman, 2012). When students do interact with text, studies paint a picture of perfunctory reading activities that only require students to look up isolated pieces of information to fill in worksheets (Alvermann & Moore, 1991; Bloome, 1994; Fisher, 2009; Hartman & Dyer, 1992) or gain just a broad-based, basic understanding (Kiuhara, Graham, & Hawken, 2009). And, contributing to this, several studies confirm our finding that secondary teachers provide scant support for reading comprehension (Ness, 2008, 2009; Snow, 2002).

In our view, teachers' work-arounds are understandable reactions to the current state of affairs. They do not believe students will, or can, read the complex materials in their subject-area classes, and there is content that students need to know before moving on in a lesson or unit. They do not know how to break the entrenched habits of high school learning and engage students with academic reading, nor do they have the knowledge or support they need to scaffold student learning or help students develop needed skills. And they have few text sources available. Small wonder that subject-area teachers reach for efficient alternatives to ensure that students are exposed to needed content. Students' work-arounds are equally sensible. They do not know how to make sense of the texts in front of them—small wonder, given their lack of opportunity to learn to use text for learning. And they actually don't need to work with text, since teachers "deliver" the information and the thinking to them. Most concerning is that students are not compelled or inspired to take on meaningful reasons to learn from text.

For many literacy educators, this enduring state of affairs is explained by the fact that the texts (often textbooks) of subject-area classes are dry, unnecessarily complex, and disengaging; that students lack the necessary skills and strategies to engage with academic materials; and that the content literacy strategies offered to subject-area teachers fail to reflect authentic disciplinary practices. We agree that these areas need attention. Yet more puzzling is that despite an abundance of research and professional development efforts focused on improving instructional materials and teaching literacy strategies at the secondary level (both disciplinary and general), there has been only limited take-up on a broad scale, leaving high school practice relatively unchanged for more than three decades. We suggest, then, that the more fundamental problem we have documented—the absence of learning from text in the subject-area classroom—should take precedence in efforts to improve students' abilities to build knowledge, think critically and deeply, develop evidence-based arguments, and assemble information from texts into coherent understandings.

Our evidence suggests three on-the-ground issues that must be addressed to make headway on this problem. First, and most pressing, is shifting the emphasis to *using texts* rather than avoiding them. Both teachers and their students must be committed to reading and learning from texts in their subject-matter classes. If students aren't reading, grappling with text in front of them, and expecting to learn from text, then all the disciplinary literacy strategies in the world—analysis, argumentation, contextualizing, and the like—will not facilitate learning.

Second, both teachers and students need support and practice using texts for learning. This includes helping teachers knowledgeably analyze and select texts (and segments of texts) and plan for their purposeful use, based on the learning opportunities they support. It also includes supporting teachers to implement instructional routines that bring together the content and conceptual learning required for specific courses and the literacy strategies to learn in that class and beyond. Similarly, students need to develop, with teacher support, strategies and dispositions to dig into texts as sources of meaningful learning.

The third issue is one that we believe may account for the slow progress in facilitating learning from text—feasibility at the scale needed to address the problem. Recent approaches of the literacy research community may target reform that is optimal without adequately considering what is feasible for real teachers working in real school contexts—a tension that was acknowledged and seriously deliberated when the National

Council on Education Standards and Testing (NCEST, 1992) was created to advise Congress on the "desirability and feasibility" of national standards and tests. Although we appreciate efforts to demonstrate the promise of innovative ideas, we are concerned that many are not feasible and, as a result, have limited take-up in the contexts of most classrooms. For example, whereas literacy researchers may expend enormous effort designing and implementing a single teaching unit, lasting only a few weeks to a month (e.g., Moje & Speyer, 2014; De La Paz et al., 2014), teachers need strategies that can be used throughout an entire course. Some projects attempt to improve literacy proficiencies such as comprehension strategies and general academic vocabulary through curricula that are not specific to any particular subject area or course (Snow, Lawrence, & White, 2009; Schumaker, Deschler, & McKnight, 2002; University of Kansas Center for Research on Learning, 2004), but subject-matter teachers must attend to the development of concepts and skills specific to their courses. Other projects, including our own, have developed a whole year's worth of curriculum to replace existing units or courses or yearlong literacy intervention curricula, efforts that are both painstaking and labor intensive (Greenleaf, Hale, Charney-Sirott, & Schoenbach, 2007; Guthrie, Wigfield, & Perencevich, 2004; Monte-Sano, De La Paz, & Felton, 2014; Parker et al., 2013; Vaughn et al., 2013) but not easily scalable. In some cases, these designed interventions depend on researcher-constructed text materials or adapted (i.e., shortened and simplified) primary documents, an approach that we suspect may engage students in the short run but not adequately prepare them for the complexity of materials ahead and around them (De La Paz & Felton, 2010; Moje et al., 2004; Wineburg, Martin, & Monte-Sano, 2011), and equally important, fail to help teachers use textbooks and the limited assortment of text-based resources available in their classrooms.

Some designed interventions justifiably rely on substantial professional development efforts (Greenleaf & Schoenbach, 2004; University of Kansas Center for Research on Learning, 2004). Without question, teachers orchestrate and mediate the learning opportunities of their students, and to demand shifts in instruction through means such as new standards, without a concomitant investment in teacher learning, strikes us as utter folly. Similarly, some of the recent curricular interventions are designed to be educative for teachers, supporting new understandings and instructional practices that can be generalized beyond a specific course (Greenleaf, Hale, Charney-Sirott, & Schoenbach, 2007; Schoenbach & Greenleaf, 2009; Valencia, Adams, & Nachtigal, 2016). Even so, our own efforts in designing professional learning and in design-based implementation research have enabled us to understand more fully what is at stake in shifting the normative practices endemic to high school teaching and learning, and in foregrounding the role of texts and literacy in deep learning. We are therefore sobered by the enormous outlay of resources such design work involves and the necessary spread of the work beyond the few settings where we, and others, have been able to work.

Recognizing these realities, what then can we do to make significant headway on the project of literacy development at the secondary grade levels? Even as curriculum and design work moves forward on various fronts, we believe we must muster the strategies, resources, and will to focus work on the problem of fostering learning from text in everyday subject-area classrooms. We therefore offer a "modest" proposal aimed at what we think are feasible, field-tested strategies for gaining traction on this enduring problem: actually getting text used to learn necessary content, concepts, and ways of thinking in specific high school classes. We recognize even as we write this hopeful sentence that *feasible* will not necessarily mean easily done. But we hope our proposal is indeed modest, in that it may be both simpler and more feasible than the many elaborate endeavors under way that may be temporary and impractical fixes in the schools we know, with their limited resources and funding. Below, we draw on our research and multiyear work with teachers to offer first, the conceptual and focus shift we are calling for and second, practical strategies to enhance text-based teaching, student engagement, and learning in middle and high school.

A MODEST PROPOSAL: FOSTERING ENGAGED ACADEMIC LITERACY

We believe that gaining traction on the MIA text will require a sustained focus on fostering students' dispositions and strategies for what we have called *engaged academic literacy* (Schoenbach & Greenleaf, 2009). Engaged academic literacy describes the ability to approach complex texts for purposeful inquiry, with a range of productive learner dispositions and problem-solving strategies at the ready. Engaged academic literacy is in view when students work actively with one another, with teachers, and independently to understand challenging texts and construct new knowledge in ways that have meaning for them and that build on their knowledge, experience, creativity, and questions. In our view, such literacy practice is not merely the exercise of "the basic reading and writing skills taught in a conventional literacy medium during elementary and middle school years" (Holbrook & Koenig, 2000, p. 265) applied to learning information from expository texts. Nor do we mean "generic literacy skills," as they are often described, for example, in Shanahan and Shanahan's (2008) formulation of "intermediate literacy" as the generic comprehension strategies, basic fluency, and vocabulary skills common to many tasks, in contradistinction to "Disciplinary Literacy," in which skills are specialized to specific academic subject areas. Rather, we consider engaged academic literacy to involve an epistemological stance toward using texts to drive one's own learning.

This notion of engaged academic literacy builds on Norris and Phillips's (2003) description of *fundamental* literacy and the work of Greenleaf and colleagues in designing the Reading Apprenticeship instructional framework (Schoenbach, Greenleaf, & Murphy, 2012). We believe the inquiry orientations and negotiation of meaning that Norris and Phillips describe, as well as the dispositions to grapple with complexity and marshal stamina in the face of challenge that Greenleaf and colleagues have integrated into the Reading Apprenticeship framework, will be vital to students' ability to drive their own learning from course texts and from the texts they encounter in school and beyond. Such literacy moves beyond formulations of basic, intermediate, or so-called "generic" literacy skills. Rather, such strategies and dispositions are *generalizable,* and in that way fundamental to many contexts students encounter. Any act of reading is situated by the nature of the texts, tasks, specific reader characteristics, and sociocultural context surrounding it; therefore, situating class texts in subject-area learning tasks and framing such activity as inquiry situates the reading in the subject matter and discipline. From this perspective, no reading can be seen as "generic"—that is, nonspecific to the text, task, reader, subject matter, and context. As soon as such reading is framed as inquiry, as soon as texts are specific to subject matter, as soon as texts are linked to meaningful learning tasks, engaged academic reading becomes specifically disciplinary in nature.[2] Engaged academic literacy is inquiry-driven, problem-solving reading, grounded in subject matter/disciplinary learning, with texts that are representative of a range of materials students encounter in their years of study.

Our focus on fostering engaged academic literacy calls for a profound epistemological shift—that teachers engage students with reading in order to inquire, to learn, to question, to think, and to grapple, rather than to carry out perfunctory displays of knowledge or information retrieval. Such epistemic commitments are all too often foreign to secondary schooling. We have seen that approaching texts for purposeful inquiry helps students to develop dispositions for learning engagement and problem solving that we believe can empower them to enter academic texts, the subject matter, and ultimately disciplines, as legitimate peripheral participants (Lave & Wenger, 1991) in academic endeavors. Such epistemological framing repositions texts of all types, including school texts (e.g., textbooks, Internet sources, reference books, teacher-developed resources), as well as texts more particular to the content and discipline (e.g., the Constitution, science reports, economic and social accounts of phenomenon, case studies, primary sources) as resources for inquiry and learning. We believe such an inquiry orientation toward reading, coupled with text-based problem-solving strategies and dispositions, allows students to bootstrap their way into learning new things, into deciphering and interpreting new and complex texts, and ultimately, perhaps, into practicing and acquiring the kind of reasoning processes central to their learning in content classrooms and in academic disciplines.

Having called for a focus on engaged academic literacy, entailing what we believe is a profound epistemological shift and purposeful inquiry orientation toward the use of text in subject-area learning, we turn now to strategies to launch and sustain such work. Here, we draw on approaches we have used in our design research and professional development efforts. We present practical ideas to implement engaged academic literacy, offering tools and approaches for (1) planning instruction that purposefully integrates the *use of texts* for subject-area learning, rather than avoiding them, and (2) implementing instructional routines that develop students' learning dispositions and facilitate subject matter and disciplinary learning. While recognizing the everyday contexts of schools, their teachers, and their students, we aim with these suggestions to shift instruction toward engaged academic literacy in the service of subject-area learning. Such an approach will, we believe, recognize and draw on the expertise of teachers who know the core topics and concepts central to the courses they teach, in order to generatively create ongoing opportunities for students to use text for subject-area learning.

PLANNING ROUTINES TO SUPPORT ENGAGED ACADEMIC LITERACY

The approach we have taken to encourage *use* of texts by teachers and students is to assist teachers in helping their students learn *from texts* the content they are trying to teach. This way, the burden of teaching isn't borne solely by teachers' lectures, films,

---

[2] We understand the recent focus on providing students more opportunities to engage in literacy practices that more authentically reflect the epistemologies and reasoning processes of specific disciplines. We ourselves have worked to design such opportunities for students. We are making a distinction here between the teaching of specific disciplinary literacy practices and epistemologies, and fostering an epistemic stance of inquiry toward texts and learning of specific subject matter, more globally. We suspect the latter is in fact essential, *fundamental* even, to the former.

and the like, and students are not passive receivers of information. Instead, teachers have resources available to them—texts of various kinds—that can help, and students are supported to actively grapple with ideas presented in those texts. Staying with our commitment to work within everyday constraints—to make the work feasible and scalable—we assume that teachers will depend mainly on the text resources they already have in their classrooms. Generally this includes the textbook, some online sources that can be downloaded and distributed, website sources students can use online when computers are available, and supplemental materials or handouts teachers have accumulated over time. We work to help teachers use these materials selectively, to link them to purposeful subject-area learning goals, and to augment them, as needed, to meet these goals. This entails an important shift in the way subject-area teachers plan for instruction, building the groundwork for engaging texts as resources for inquiry and learning.

Reading with the Learner and the Curriculum in Mind

As we found in our various studies, teachers in the subject area do not read the texts they assign to students, as a matter of course. They may scan the pages of a textbook chapter to see what information it holds in preparation for a lesson. Therefore, to orchestrate and support students in learning from text, teachers must get in the habit of closely reading class texts, whether a textbook chapter, a monograph, something downloaded from the Web, or a newspaper article they think may be relevant. We ask teachers to read with an eye toward potential points of confusion their students may encounter—assumptions about background, vocabulary, complex concepts, disciplinary discourse patterns, and so forth—so they can help students work with these during text-based discussions (see Schoenbach, Greenleaf, & Murphy, 2016). At the same time, teachers also read with an eye toward their curricular priorities, identifying how a text presents important concepts and ideas, as well as unpacking arcane language or complex sentences, and interpreting graphics and visuals essential for students' knowledge building. The inquiry questions we ask teachers to respond to as they read potential course materials include:

- "What did you do to make sense of this text?"
- "What challenges does the text present to learners?"
  - "Vocabulary, word knowledge, topic knowledge, disciplinary understandings?"
- "What opportunities to learn does the text present?"
  - "Content learning opportunities?"
  - "Literacy learning opportunities?"

Aligning Texts and Learning Tasks

In addition to developing habits of reading course texts with student learning in mind, teachers need to align specific lesson and unit goals with texts that are available, an approach we call *text–task alignment* (Valencia, Wixson, & Pearson, 2014). Planning for text–task alignment requires teachers to attend simultaneously to three factors. First, teachers identify specific core content and concepts they want students to learn. Although this sounds fairly straightforward, we have found it to be challenging, requiring deep knowledge of the subject matter and related disciplines (see Parker & Lo, 2016, for a discussion of content selection), as well as decisions about the content and processes that can be treated lightly and those that need more in-depth attention.

Second, teachers carefully read the available text-based resources (e.g., textbook, online sources, handouts, newspaper article) to determine how to use them purposefully and strategically in ways that both guide and challenge students, motivating them to learn from text rather than to work around it. Here, we ask teachers to review potential sources with an eye toward the specific learning goals they have identified. Frequently, teachers find that it's unnecessary for students to read entire textbook chapters or Internet sources—that *portions* ("chunks") such as segments of textbook chapters, particular graphics, text found at particular Internet sites, specific articles or amendments to the Constitution, and so forth, align with their teaching priorities.

Finally, the selected text(s) or sections of texts and the teachers' objectives are brought together in a meaningful task that requires students to *use* their text-based knowledge in an immediate and relevant way—not simply accumulate facts. The task should require students to *apply* (often in collaboration with peers) their text-based understandings. The point is that reading and writing assignments should be aligned with the information students will need and the tasks they will complete. This way, knowledge and process objectives, text, and task are a coherent whole—they work together to scaffold learning of important course content. If students are asked to read and deeply comprehend any text, they should be clear about what they are expected to learn and how that learning will be used. As one student reminded us, "There has to be a point to the reading."

Compare the specificity of this text–task alignment example to an assignment in which students are simply told, "Read Chapter 13":

Teacher Content Objective: Students will understand the issues that were discussed at the Constitutional Convention and the various positions held by the delegates.

Task: Students are assigned to take on the role of a specific delegate to the Constitutional Convention in order to learn about the Federalist and Anti-Federalist perspectives represented. Then they role-play a series of deliberations at the Convention.

Text Reading 1: Use the website (XXXX) to find out about your delegate (educational background, political leanings, constituency, family history, etc.) in order to determine his positions on issues that will be debated and discussed at the Constitutional Convention.

Text Reading 2: Read textbook pages 000–000 on issues deliberated at the Constitutional Convention. Then, using the information you learned about your delegate (See Text Reading 1), hypothesize your delegate's position on each of the issues. Be prepared to debate delegates who have a different position, using evidence from your readings.

Engaging and Augmenting the Textbook as a Resource for Learning

Our approach to instructional planning is not intended to suggest that general background information from textbooks and other sources is unimportant, or that available texts are optimal sources. We are well aware of (and share) the many criticisms of textbooks—their density, "inconsiderate" text and structure (Armbruster & Anderson, 1985), encyclopedic breath instead of conceptual depth. We recognize, however, that these resources may be all teachers have. We also understand from our investigations with teachers and adolescents in reading novels, magazines, webpages, electronic manuals, nutrition labels, and tax forms, that most texts in the real world present real challenges to comprehension. They address selective audiences, and they refer to and demand knowledge that readers may or may not hold. They create barriers to understanding by virtue of the mismatch between text and reader. Textbooks, while holding considerable power and authority in our schools, do not seem fundamentally different from many texts in this respect. Those of us who have made our way through college preparatory courses in high school and go on to college to receive degrees and credentials have done so because we learned to learn from such texts. We are reluctant to deny that capacity to others. We elect, therefore, to focus our work on how texts, including textbooks, can best be used by teachers selectively, to support purposeful learning. Based on our experiences, we know that when teachers plan for instruction by closely reading such texts and aligning texts and tasks, even textbooks can become resources for meaningful student learning.

That said, as our earlier example of text–task alignment for the Constitutional Convention lessons indicated, we think a number of considerations are important for teachers to keep in mind as they plan for instruction that makes intentional use of texts. By closely reading and analyzing their course texts and materials, teachers may be surprised to find that the content they are assuming students will learn from these resources is actually missing. To use text as a resource for learning the valued content, teachers will therefore sometimes need to locate ancillary materials.

Considerations for Building Text Sets
- Provide varied entry points to address diverse learners.
- Begin with visuals from text materials to build concepts and engage interest.
- Select texts to draw on students' languages and experiences.
- Use selections about the same topic written at various levels of complexity.
- Intentionally vary the range of text types to represent the variety students will encounter.

Teachers may, for example, choose to use visual aids, such as maps, or historical documents, because these will be important sources of information in the subject area for students. We have assisted teachers to develop topically and thematically related text sets to meet all of these learning goals and instructional needs (see Schoenbach et al., 2012, Chapter 5). When teachers are guided by their instructional purposes and by habits of reading with learners in mind, they become attuned to the learning opportunities and challenges texts offer and are able to select appropriate texts efficiently from readily available resources, such as Internet sources, reference books, or alternative textbooks. At the same time, using texts for learning in the subject area does not mean students will learn necessary content by making one pass through any selected text. Providing students with opportunities to read selections multiple times as they move through learning tasks will also support them in gaining deeper comprehension and facility with texts.

INSTRUCTIONAL ROUTINES TO SUPPORT ENGAGED ACADEMIC LITERACY

These planning routines can be brought to life by using a small set of instructional routines that position texts as resources for collaborative inquiry and learning, and offer students support for engaged academic literacy. Below we describe routines for assigning reading, engaging students in metacognitive conversations to puzzle through texts, and generating text-based discussions for collaborative meaning making and subject-area learning. These routines are designed to build students' strategies and dispositions to deal with complexity and puzzlement, so that students will be equipped, when they leave the school building, with the tools, the ability, and the will to make their way through the varied and likely inconsiderate texts they encounter throughout their lives. Importantly, these routines bring texts and reading into classroom lessons in which teachers can provide guidance and support as students engage in the intellectual work of learning from text. Because these routines focus on approaching subject-area texts from a stance of inquiry and make use of subject-area texts for meaningful learning tasks, the work students carry out is necessarily situated in disciplinary purposes and text types.

Assigning Reading for Purposeful Learning

Building on the text–task alignment model, we work with teachers to design routines for assigning and using text-based information. Our aim is to address three dilemmas we identified from our data: (1) to ensure that students do the reading—to hold them accountable; (2) to have students use the reading to solve a problem or engage in a meaningful task; and (3) to provide teachers with opportunities to clarify or extend the reading and thinking *without lecturing about the same content,* which, we found, only caused students to not do the reading. Although these problems are more likely to arise with homework assignments, the approach can be used with any assignment—in class or out.

We created a framework for assigning text-based work (reading, research, etc.) that teachers use to *explain* the assignment, not simply give it. Specifically, the framework includes the *purpose* of the reading, how students will *use* it, and how they should go about the doing the work *(procedure).* Behind each category is the type of teacher planning described under text–task analysis—clarity of content priorities, disciplinary thinking, and a focus on application and inquiry. Many teachers post information in the format below in class and on class websites for students to refer to as they are engaged with texts. Overall, this process results in teachers assigning fewer pages (they prioritize depth of understanding over breadth) and students being more likely to complete the assignment successfully and learn from the text.

If the reading is assigned for homework, teachers follow up the next day with an application activity that requires students to apply what they were asked to read for homework and to discuss points of confusion. For example, the box below shows a homework reading assignment about Madison's model for the U.S. constitutional government. The following class period began with a "Homework Application" in which students first shared questions and confusions they encountered while reading (see "Metacognitive Conversations" below). Then, they discussed what they learned about Madison's Model and the position they would take, in their delegate role, on the model.

Purpose: Read pp. 48–51 in your textbook to learn about Madison's suggestions for structuring the new government. Specifically:
- What were the ideas he came up with?
- Why did he choose this type of structure?

Use: Tomorrow in class, in your role of delegate to the Constitutional Convention, you will need to explain each part of the model to the people of your state and to argue *for* or *against* them.

Procedure: Read the text and study the graphics. You will need both to understand the model. Then practice explaining the graphic in your own words, being sure you can explain the advantages and disadvantages of each part of the model.

When readings culminate in worthwhile learning tasks and demonstrations, reading tasks can be readily framed for purposeful inquiry. Not all reading and learning can wind up with an extensive demonstration project. However, inquiry framing is nonetheless an important aspect of instructional planning. Teachers must ask themselves, while planning, what purpose the reading will serve for students. And rather than simply assigning reading to acquire specific information, they must press for a larger purpose. Reading the Constitution becomes a very different enterprise when students are asked to make a decision about the constitutionality of a particular court decision, for example, compared to when they are simply preparing to take a test on the Articles. Similarly, students' experiences in a science lab can lead to questions they can be invited to resolve through assigned sections of a science textbook.[3]

The specificity of assignments such as these and, especially, the explicit recommended procedures are intended to serve as a model and scaffold for both teachers and students. Over time, and with experience, teachers should become more attuned to providing students with purposeful assignments matched to texts. Similarly, over time, and with both experience and teacher support, the need for explicit direction about procedures should fade as students develop a repertoire of strategies for engaging their assignments and learning from texts. And although the norm in high schools is to relegate a good deal of reading to out-of-class homework and research, our experiences suggest that the job of comprehending and building knowledge should happen in the classroom. We have witnessed positive shifts in the use of texts as teachers "flip" their classrooms to make reading a central in-class event in which students collaborate to learn with and from texts, with teachers at the ready to scaffold. But even when reading takes place away from classroom, the job of making meaning must be valued and explored in the classroom.

Building Dispositions for Engaged Academic Literacy through Metacognitive Conversations

This approach to assigning reading helps students see how the reading is related to learning tasks. However, to gather and focus the effort required for academic reading, we have seen that most adolescents will need support to develop new dispositions for approaching and engaging in the challenging sense-making involved in reading unfamiliar academic materials.

As we have argued elsewhere, these dispositions include characteristics such as curiosity, tolerance for ambiguity, and the expectation that one should be constructing understanding rather than passively carrying out prescribed procedures (Schoenbach & Greenleaf, 2009). Key student dispositions also include maintaining confidence in their own abilities and in the value of persistence, even while struggling through challenging text—for example, learning to approach unfamiliar text with what we have called a *code-breaking* stance. "This text may not have been written with your particular background knowledge and experiences in mind," we suggest, "but what can you make of it?" We therefore start the response to reading assignments, as we suggested earlier, by inviting students' own questions and confusions to drive small-group and class discussion. We have found that this simple approach supports students in developing dispositions to engage in reading in order to learn something new by turning the tables on what counts

---

[3] See *www.readingapprenticeship.org* for brief classroom videos illustrating this inquiry focus.

in class. Rather than having the right answers to teachers' questions, we make students' confusions and their own questions the starting point for learning.

Metacognitive Conversations: Turning the Tables on What Counts

Conversation Prompts

- "What was confusing in the assigned reading?"
- "Who else had that same confusion?"
- "Did anyone solve that problem?"
- "How did you figure that out?"

For example, before being able to understand the Bill of Rights that was ultimately ratified as part of the Constitution structuring the new government, students may need to clear up fundamental confusions: Does the Bill of Rights grant rights to citizens or prohibit the new government from encroaching on what were seen as the inalienable rights of citizens? To do so, they must grapple with the complex and arcane language expressions of the text itself. Consider, for example, the Establishment Clause: "Congress shall make no law respecting an establishment of religion, or prohibiting the free exercise thereof." What might the word *respecting* mean in this context? Why does a document begin with the phrase "Congress shall make no law?" If students feel they cannot voice confusions and solve comprehension problems, they will quickly disengage from reading and wait for others to tell them what the passages say and mean. Teachers play a vital part in this metacognitive conversation, encouraging students to solve the problems they have identified and drawing out issues they know students will need to grapple with but have not yet acknowledged.

Metacognitive conversation routines make the invisible processes of puzzlement and sense-making visible to all learners in the classroom (download lesson resources at *www.readingapprenticeship.org*). Importantly, these routines are social, *conversations* within the class around texts, in which students share their questions, confusions, and problem solving in a community of other learners similarly engaged and sharing their reading, thinking, and inquiry processes. Such conversations invite the resources students bring in the form of language practices, experiences, knowledge, curiosities, disaffections, and difficulties to enlarge the conversation and inform the problem solving in the classroom. Students learn to engage in thinking alongside text, working collaboratively to figure things out. Engaging in inquiry around reading puzzlements and problem solving can therefore help students figure out how to read unfamiliar and complex texts. At the same time, engaging in this work in class can help teachers understand unexpected sources of challenge in subject-area texts for particular students, including struggles teachers need to know about, misconceptions that need to be cleared up, and inventive new solutions that they hadn't considered.

Over time, as the class gains experience sharing stumbling blocks to comprehension and problem solving through them, the teacher can focus on these prompts to deepen students' learning:

- "Who had trouble with the language in that piece? Me, too. What did you struggle with?"
- "What do you make of those two maps?"
- "Did anyone figure out how *citizen* was being defined here?"

Supporting Collaborative Meaning Making through Text-Based Discussion

Metacognitive conversations about questions, confusions, and problem solving spill naturally into meaning-making discussions focused on linking readings to learning goals and application tasks. There are a number of text discussion routines, adaptations of the Socratic Seminar, for instance, that can productive. Our focus has been to ensure that discussions are designed to *make use* of texts, as the "Aligning Texts and Tasks" and "Assigning Reading" routines suggest. Framing text-based discussion as inquiry in relation to subject-area learning goals is essential. In addition, in our experience, there are three common pitfalls that get in the way of the robust learning that can occur through such discussion.

First, students have very little experience engaging in academic discussion given the teacher-centered instruction that is most commonly offered in secondary-level subject areas. They need support to learn to talk to each other rather than orient toward the teacher. By the same token, teachers need new tools and habits to avoid taking on the lion's share of the intellectual work *for* students. Second, students need discussion tasks that require them to ground their discussion in the text itself. Students need to learn to cite the text, orienting discussion members to specific locations in the text, so that all are able to refer to the relevant passage as they consider a group member's commentary, reasoning, and thinking. Third, although it may seem unnecessary to mention, this means that the text must be present and in the hands of students when text-based discussions occur. Surprisingly often, we have seen students be asked to discuss a text, without requiring that the text be present as part of the discussion. When there is no text to consult, students understandably stay on the surface level in their discussions, offer vague generalities, and are unable to adjudicate different possible interpretations.

Sentence Frames to Support Student-to-Student Text-Based Discussion

ASKING QUESTIONS

- "When I read . . . on page 000, I wondered . . ."
- "After I read . . . on page 000, I got confused about . . . , because . . ."
- "On page 000, I could not understand . . ."
- "Do you think it makes sense on page 000 that . . ."
- "I wonder what . . . means on page 000?"

OFFERING EVIDENCE

- "I think one reason is on page 000, where it says . . ."
- "I don't think . . . could be true, because on page 000 it says . . ."
- "If . . . is true, then that is a good reason to believe that . . . may be true."
- "Even . . . may be true, on page 000, . . . provides evidence for the opposite."

BUILDING ON IDEAS

- "I agree with your idea that . . . and I would like to add . . ."
- "I like your idea that. . . . Do you think that means . . ."

- "I have a different idea. To me, the evidence of . . . on page 000 means . . ."
- "Do you agree that there is a connection between . . . and . . . ?"

Teacher Talk to Elicit and Support Student Thinking

INVITE THINKING

- Ask questions that do not presume everyone has the same ideas.
  - "What do you think?"
  - "What did you make of . . . ?"
  - "What was especially interesting for you?"

PROBE FOR ELABORATION

- Help students share or uncover why they may have offered a particular idea.
  - "Help us understand your thinking on that."
  - "Can you tell us a little more?"
  - "What in the text makes you say that?"
  - "Can you give us an example?"

EXTEND THE DISCUSSION

- Ask questions that explicitly focus students on responding to others' ideas.
  - "Does everyone agree?"
  - "Did anyone else have a similar problem?"
  - "What might be another way to look at that?"

LINK

- Help students connect to previous learning.
  - "How might this relate to . . . we read about earlier?"
  - "What connections to previous lessons/units come to mind?"
  - "How does this help us understand . . . ?"

Inviting students to share their questions about texts opens the way for authentic inquiry framing. By documenting the questions that students raise, teachers can link class discussions of text back to these questions: "What evidence did you find in this passage about whether the Bill of Rights is meant to grant rights to citizens or limit the power of the new government? Can you point us to that in the text?" and "What do others think? Does anyone have additional or contrasting evidence to add?" Over time, text-based discussion becomes internalized, with the teacher only asserting norms of student-to-student discussion if things go awry. What's more vital is for teachers to keep a watch on their own tendencies to answer questions and resolve problems for students, because these are well practiced and automatic. We find that teachers benefit from these discursive tools, learning how better to support and hold students accountable for course readings and to orchestrate true text-based discussions. They increasingly turn students back to the texts to answer their own questions, expect students to support their assertions with textual evidence, and support students' interpretations and thinking about the implications of the texts they read as they carry out learning tasks. Students, for their part, come to engage reading and discussion of readings as part of a learning process and gain experience grappling with the kinds of texts they will continue to encounter in and out of school.

CONCLUSIONS

In this chapter we make a case for a shift in focus for literacy educators toward, first and foremost, engaging teachers and students in *using text for learning* in the subject-area classroom. We offer strategies for aligning texts and learning tasks, purposefully assigning reading and tasks aligned to meaningful content learning, and fostering metacognitive conversations and text-based discussions that we believe will go a long way toward building students' dispositions and competence as readers of complex materials. We promote a view of engaged academic literacy as an epistemic stance that can support students in taking a code breaking stance to puzzle their way into new territories bounded by unfamiliar text types, literacy practices, disciplines, and discourses. We acknowledge, honor, and support teachers' commitments to their subject areas in these suggestions. We also acknowledge the real conditions of often underresourced schools in which teachers and students carry out the work of teaching and learning, recognizing the limitations these conditions place on what is both possible and likely. At the same time, we recognize the real need to break with tradition in school culture, disrupting the normative practices and lecture modalities that place students in passive roles, while teachers deliver a steady stream of information. Supporting real reading to learn will demand real intellectual activity on the part of students.

Our experiences designing and implementing curricula and interventions draw us to this set of ideas and strategies as practical, scalable, feasible, and responsive to teachers' needs. We admit that getting these modest shifts in practice to occur is not a small endeavor. If our work in schools has taught us anything, it is that the collaboration and partnership of subject-area teachers will be vital to this enterprise. Working together with subject-area teachers has allowed us to draw on their expertise, foregrounding their understandings of what is important in the subject area and about particular topics to inform the selection of texts and the design of learning tasks. Working together in partnership has also supported teachers' generative capacity to align texts and learning tasks, to select and augment texts, to identify challenges and opportunities that texts present, and to support student engagement in learning. Perhaps the most important strategy to launch and sustain an effort to put texts to work in the service of students' learning, then, is this: to develop long-term partnerships with subject-area teachers, in which the investigation of course texts and their relationship to students' subject-area learning can be taken up collaboratively.

Ultimately, we are convinced by students themselves to continue to press for engaged academic literacy in subject-area classrooms. We have seen that reading of course materials, including textbooks, becomes an altogether different experience for students when we are able to support teachers to read potential course texts with learning in mind, to align texts and learning goals, to select parts of texts that are most germane to learning tasks, and to supplement existing resources as needed to accomplish learning goals. Furthermore, when students are supported to puzzle through unfamiliar texts through metacognitive conversations and collaborative meaning-making discussions, they tell us that formerly obtuse texts come alive for them. LaKeisha explained to us, "When you read, there should be a little voice in your head like a storyteller is saying it. If it's not there, then you're just lookin' at the words." Even the history textbook, a chronological compendium of historical events, can become something new in such a changed classroom learning environment. As Jason told us, wide-eyed, "I understand the book more now. I read differently—I basically get into the story, into the heart of it.... The stuff you read in the history book? These things really happened to people!"

We are persuaded of the urgency of this work by the many students who have described their experiences learning to read complex subject-area texts as life-changing events. As Jeraldo wrote to his teacher, "When I first came to this class I was scared. I have discovered that I have the courage to read stuff that I couldn't read.... I feel like a smart young man who can do anything I set my mind to. Nothing anyone says can hurt me because I have the knowledge to school them." We think, as a field, we have the knowledge to solve the problem of the MIA text, bringing texts and reading into the heart of student learning.

ACKNOWLEDGMENTS

Funding for the PBL project reported here was by the George Lucas Educational Foundation, the Spencer Foundation, and the National Science Foundation. We are grateful to the funders, the PIs on the project (Walter Parker and Susan Nolen), as well as the Knowledge in Action team for their support. Funding for Greenleaf's early classroom observations was provided by The Stuart Foundations. The recent observations were supported by the Institute of Education Sciences, U.S. Department of Education, through Grant R305F100007 under the auspices of the Reading for Understanding Initiative. The opinions expressed are those of the authors and do not represent views of the Institute or the U.S. Department of Education.

REFERENCES

ACT, Inc. (2006). *Reading between the lines: What the ACT reveals about college readiness in reading.* Iowa City, IA: Author.

ACT, Inc. (2013). *ACT National Curriculum Survey 2012: English language arts.* Iowa City, IA: Author.

Alvermann, D. E., & Moore, D. W. (1991). Secondary school reading. In R. Barr, M. L. Kamil, P. B. Moie, & P. D. Pearson (Eds.), *Handbook of reading research* (Vol. 2, pp. 951–983). New York: Longman.

Applebee, A. N. (1993). *Literature in the secondary school: Studies of curriculum and instruction in the United States.* Urbana, IL: National Council of Teachers of English.

Armbruster, B. B., & Anderson, T. H. (1985), Producing "considerate" expository text: Or easy reading is damned hard writing. *Journal of Curriculum Studies, 17,* 247–263.

Bain, R. B. (2006). Rounding up unusual suspects: Facing the authority hidden in the history classroom. *Teachers College Record, 108*(10), 2080–2114.

Bloome, D. (1994). Reading as a social process in a middle school classroom. In D. Graddol, J. Maybin, & B. Stierer (Eds.), *Researching language and literacy in social context* (pp. 100–129). Bristol, PA: Multilingual Matters.

De La Paz, S., & Felton, M. K. (2010). Reading and writing from multiple source documents in history: Effects of strategy instruction with low to average high school writers. *Contemporary Educational Psychology, 35*(3), 174–192.

De La Paz, S., Felton, M., Monte-Sano, C., Croninger, R., Jackson, C., Deogracias, J. S., et al. (2014). Developing historical reading and writing with adolescent readers: Effects on student learning. *Theory and Research in Social Education, 42*(2), 228–274.

Fisher, D. (2009). The use of instructional time in the typical high school classroom. *Educational Forum, 73*(2), 168–176.

Greenleaf, C. (1995). *Humanities education, research, and language development* (HERALD): Project Report to the Stuart Foundations.

Greenleaf, C., Hale, G., Charney-Sirott, I. & Schoenbach, R. (2007). *Reading apprenticeship academic literacy curriculum*. San Francisco: WestEd.

Greenleaf, C. & Schoenbach, R. (2004). Building capacity for the responsive teaching of reading in the academic disciplines: Strategic inquiry designs for middle and high school teachers' professional development. In D. S. Strickland & M. L. Kamil, (Eds.), *Improving reading achievement through professional development* (pp. 97–127). Norwood, MA: Christopher-Gordon.

Greenleaf, C., Schoenbach, R., Cziko, C., & Mueller, F. (2001). Apprenticing adolescent readers to academic literacy. *Harvard Educational Review, 71*(1), 79–129.

Guthrie, J. T., Wigfield, A., & Perencevich, K. C. (Eds.). (2004). *Motivating reading comprehension: Concept-oriented reading instruction*. Mahwah, NJ: Erlbaum.

Hartman, D. K., & Dyer, P. A. (1992). *An existential description of reading methods and materials in the content areas*. Urbana, IL: Center for the Study of Reading.

Holbrook, M. C., & Koenig, A. J. (2000). Literacy skills. In M. C. Holbrook & A. J. Koenig (Eds.), *Foundations of education: Vol. 2. Instructional strategies for teaching children and youths with visual impairments* (2nd ed., pp. 264–312). New York: American Foundation for the Blind.

Kiuhara, S. A., Graham, S., & Hawken, L. S. (2009). Teaching writing to high school students: A national survey. *Journal of Educational Psychology, 101*(1), 136–160.

Lave, J., & Wenger, E. (1991). *Situated learning: Legitimate peripheral participation*. New York: Cambridge University Press.

Litman, C., Marple, S., Greenleaf, C., Charney-Sirott, I., Bolz, M., Richardson, L., et al. (in press). Text-based argumentation with multiple sources: A descriptive study of opportunity to learn in secondary English language arts, history, and science. *Journal of Learning Sciences*.

Moje, E. B., & Speyer, J. (2014). The reality of challenging texts in high school science and social studies. In K. Hinchman & H. K. Sheridan (Eds.), *Best practices in adolescent literacy instruction* (2nd ed., pp. 207–231). New York: Guilford Press.

Moje, E. B., Stockdill, D., Kim, K., & Kim, H. (2011). The role of text in disciplinary learning. In M. L. Kamil, D. Pearson, E. B. Moje, & P. P. Afflerbach (Eds.), *Handbook of reading research* (Vol. 4, pp. 453–486). New York: Routledge.

Moje, E. B., Sutherland, L. M., Krajcik, J., Blumenfeld, P., Peek-Brown, D., & Marx, R. W. (2004, November). *Reading and writing like scientists: Toward developing scientific literacy in project-based science*. Paper presented at the 82nd Annual Convention of the National Council of Teachers of English, Indianapolis, IN.

Monte-Sano, C., De La Paz, S., & Felton, M. (2014). *Reading, thinking, and writing about history: Teaching argument writing to diverse learners in the Common Core classroom, grades 6–12*. New York: Teachers College Press.

National Council on Education Standards and Testing (NCEST). (1992). *Raising standards for American education*. Washington, DC: U.S. Government Printing Office.

Ness, M. K. (2008). Supporting secondary readers: When teachers provide the "what," not the "how." *American Secondary Education, 37*(1), 80–95.

Ness, M. K. (2009). Reading comprehension strategies in secondary content area classrooms: Teacher use of and attitudes towards reading comprehension instruction. *Reading Horizons, 49*(2), 143–166.

Norris, S. P., & Phillips, L. M. (2003). How literacy in its fundamental sense is central to scientific literacy. *Science Education, 87*(2), 224–240.

O'Brien, D. G., Stewart, R. A., & Moje, E. B. (1995). Why content literacy is difficult to infuse into the secondary school: Complexities of curriculum, pedagogy, and school culture. *Reading Research Quarterly, 30*(3), 442–463.

Parker, W. C., & Lo, J. (2016). Content selection in advanced courses. *Curriculum Inquiry, 46*(2), 196–219.

Parker, W. C., Lo, J., Yeo, A. J., Valencia, S. W., Nguyen, D., Abbott, R. D., et al. (2013). Beyond breadth-speed-test: Toward deeper knowing and engagement in an Advanced Placement course. *American Educational Research Journal, 50*(6), 1424–1459.

Pearson, P. D., & Gallagher, M. C. (1983). The instruction of reading comprehension. *Contemporary Educational Psychology, 8*(3), 317–344.

Penuel, W. R., Fishman, B. J., Cheng, B. H., & Sabelli, N. (2011). Organizing research and development at the intersection of learning, implementation, and design. *Educational Researcher, 40*(7), 331–337.

Reisman, A. (2012). Reading like a historian: A document-based history curriculum intervention in urban high schools. *Cognition and Instruction, 30*(1), 86–112.

Schoenbach, R., & Greenleaf, C. (2009). Fostering adolescents' engaged academic literacy. In L. Christenburg, R. Bomer, & P. Smagorinsky (Eds.), *Handbook of adolescent literacy research* (pp. 98–112). New York: Guilford Press.

Schoenbach, R., Greenleaf, C., Cziko, C., & Hurwitz, L. (1999). *Reading for understanding*. San Francisco: Jossey-Bass.

Schoenbach, R., Greenleaf, C., & Murphy, L. (2012). *Reading for understanding: How reading apprenticeship improves disciplinary learning in secondary and college classrooms* (2nd ed.). San Francisco: Jossey-Bass.

Schoenbach, R., Greenleaf, C. & Murphy, L. (2016). *Leadership guide for Reading Apprenticeship*. San Francisco: Jossey Bass Wiley & Sons.

Schumaker, J. B., Deshler, D. D., & McKnight, P. (2002). Ensuring success in the secondary general education curriculum through the use of teaching routines. In M. A. Shinn, H. M. Walker, & G. Stoner (Eds.), *Interventions for academic and behavior problems II: Prevention and remedial approaches* (pp. 791–823). Bethesda, MD: NASP.

Shanahan, T., & Shanahan, C. (2008). Teaching disciplinary literacy to adolescents: Rethinking content-area literacy. *Harvard Educational Review, 78*(1), 40–60.

Snow, C. (2002). *Reading for understanding: Toward an R&D program in reading comprehension*. Santa Monica, CA: RAND Corporation.

Snow, C. E., Lawrence, J. F., & White, C. (2009). Generating knowledge of academic language among urban middle school students. *Journal of Research on Educational Effectiveness, 2*(4), 325–344.

University of Kansas Center for Research on Learning. (2004). *Strategic instruction model*. Retrieved from www.ku-crl.org/iei/sim/index.html.

Valencia, S. W., Adams, C., & Nachtigal, S. (2016, April). *Rigorous content learning: Making text-based learning real*. Paper presented at the annual meeting of the American Educational Research Association, Washington, DC.

Valencia, S. W., & Parker, W. C. (2015). Learning from text in an advanced government and politics course. *Citizenship Teaching and Learning, 11*(1), 87–103.

Valencia, S. W., Wixson, K. K., & Pearson, P. D. (2014). Putting text complexity in context: Refocusing on comprehension of complex text. *Elementary School Journal, 115*(2), 270–289.

Vaughn, S., Swanson, E. A., Roberts, G., Wanzek, J., Stillman-Spisak, S. J., Solis, M., et al. (2013). Improving reading comprehension and social studies knowledge in middle school. *Reading Research Quarterly, 48*(1), 77–93.

Wineburg, S., Martin, D., & Monte-Sano, C. (2011). *Reading like a historian*. New York: Teachers College Press.

CHAPTER 15

"No More Paperwork!"
Student Perspectives on Multimodal Composing in Response to Literature

KELLY WISSMAN

At the conclusion of a study exploring how eighth-grade students responded to the opportunity to create digital comics in their reading support class, I asked the students what advice they would give to English teachers to improve their teaching. Without a moment's hesitation, Abby (all names are pseudonyms), proclaimed, "No more paperwork!" Abby's exclamation reflected a consistent theme across the perspectives of the eighth-grade students. At a time when adolescents like Abby are expressing themselves in increasingly varied ways across multiple modes and across multiple platforms outside of school (Ito et al., 2010), print literacies continue to dominate their in-school learning experiences (Shanahan, 2013).

Young people orchestrate multiple modalities when composing and consuming a range of texts, from digital stories (Hull & Katz, 2006) to fanfiction (Black, 2009), from spoken word performance (Fisher, 2007) to online remixes, podcasts, and blogs (Ito et al., 2010). Even as numerous research studies and position statements argue that "the profession needs to work toward more sophisticated and challenging curriculum, instruction, and assessments that reflect a broader definition of reading proficiency" (O'Brien, Stewart, & Beach, 2009, p. 94), many adolescents attend schools in which traditional pedagogical models promote a "single, exclusive, and intensive focus on written language" (Kress, 2003, p. 156), and state and national testing profoundly shape their experience of English courses as print-focused and test-driven. As Miller (2010) argues, "In the context of the high-stakes testing frenzy, students often have fewer opportunities than ever to find purpose and make meaning in school and little space to use their multimodal literacy strategies for school learning" (p. 213).

Just as the semiotic richness and imaginative literacy practices with which students engage outside of school often find few outlets in school, students' own perspectives on their learning have been similarly missing from the broader conversations about the nature and purpose of literacy education. At the rollout of the Common Core State Standards by the National Governors Association, the authors of the standards lauded the broad participation of many groups who contributed to their development, noting, "Teachers, parents, school administrators and experts from across the country together with state leaders provided input into the development of the standards" (Common Core State Standards Initiative, 2015, p. 1). That students as a constituency were not included here reflects their long-standing marginalization in conversations about education and educational reform. This lack of input, as Cook-Sather (2002) notes, represents a significant loss of potential to inspire and instantiate educational and pedagogical change. As she argues, "As long as we exclude these perspectives from our conversations about schooling and how it needs to change, our efforts at reform will be based on an incomplete picture of life in classrooms and schools and how that life could be improved" (p. 3). Deliberate inquiry into students' perspectives and careful analysis of their experiences can provide important insights, especially within pedagogical endeavors informed by emerging understandings of literacy practices as multimodal and as embedded in students' lived experiences.

This chapter explores the literacy practices and multimodal compositions of adolescents. It is anchored in a study of adolescents' participation in a reading support class in which their teacher invited them to respond to the novel *The Outsiders* (Hinton, 1967), with the software program Comic Life. Informed by an understanding of literacy as an aesthetic, creative, and purposeful practice of meaning making and as situated within the social context, I analyze the range and variation of students' use of multiple sign systems to respond to literature and their perspectives on the role of multimodalities within their literacy learning. I explore how students responded to the opportunity to bring multiple sign systems into their literacy work in school, how this opportunity shapes and reflects their response to literature, and how they theorized this learning opportunity. Within interviews, I found students speaking very clearly to both the uniqueness and the importance of opportunities within school to draw on multiple sign systems and on their imaginations to express themselves and to deepen their literary engagement. In this chapter, therefore, I seek to underscore the importance of both listening carefully to students' perspectives and looking intently at their creative work.

Given the visual nature of the students' comics, as well as their perspectives on the creative experience of producing them, I ground the analysis within perspectives on arts, aesthetics, and literacies (Vasudevan, 2010) and within transactional theories of response to literature (Rosenblatt, 1982). I argue that (1) rich descriptions of students' digital composing processes, products, and perspectives can help us broaden conceptions of literacy teaching, learning, and assessment beyond a print focus, and that (2) perspectives from the arts and literary response can enhance our understandings of students' digital composing processes in response to literature.

CONCEPTUAL FRAMEWORK

The Arts and Literacy

Eisner's (2003) pioneering work theorizing about the value of the arts in education provides insights into how inviting multiple forms of representation into the classroom can enhance literacy education. In drawing connections between the arts and literacy, Eisner argues, "In much language teaching, pedagogy is directed in ways that are highly rule-abiding.... But we also need to promote the student's recognition that language has a melody, that cadences count, that tropes matter, that metaphors mean" (p. 342). Eisner notes that narrow focus on the linguistic aspects of literacy can constrict meaning making, writing, "Literacy itself can be thought of not as limited to what the tongue can articulate but what the mind can grasp. Thus, in this sense, dance, music, and the visual arts are languages through which both meaning and mind are promoted" (p. 342). Nicholson (1999) similarly argues for engaging the arts to build meaning and promote understanding, arguing that "the visual, performing, and practical arts, for example, offer more than an avenue for indulging in idiosyncratic and extraneous self-expression, but constitute a means of perceiving and conveying understanding" (p. 109). Both Eisner (2003) and Nicholson (1999) underscore meaning making as inherent to encounters with the arts and with literacy, goals that are often sidelined in "rule-abiding" and test-driven pedagogies focused on recall, summary, and comprehension. As Gadsden (2008) contends:

> Academic achievement is increasingly defined in relationship to students' gaining proficiency in specific "skills," for example, reading, writing, and arithmetic. In such cases, the unfolding of thinking processes often appears secondary to the act of producing "the right answer" and ultimately an outcome. (p. 32)

By calling attention to the cadence and melody of language (Eisner, 2003), by describing how the arts promote rich engagements with texts shaped by imagination, multiple points of view, and playfulness (Heath, 2004), and by exploring how the arts, poetry, and literature engage us in deep questions of the human experience (Greene, 1995), theorists point to possibilities for reenvisioning language and literacy education as oriented toward meaning making and expression. As Heath asserts, "The arts encircle learning with meaning and thereby make comprehension and engagement fundamental for participation" (p. 339). Dire concerns about adolescents' comprehension skills often animate broader policy discourses; however, Heath's statement adds an important nuance to this preoccupation. In the arts, comprehension is not an end in itself, but a fundamental aspect of participation in endeavors shaped by the pursuit of meaning. As I explore below, the students' visual representations of a scene from *The Outsiders* created opportunities for students both to express their understanding of the novel and to communicate that understanding through multiple sign systems.

Reading and Writing as Transaction

A consideration of the relationship between literacy and the arts provides a framework for analyzing how students in this study drew on multiple sign systems beyond the linguistic to render emotive, perceptive, and sometimes humorous responses to *The Outsiders*. At the same time, transactional theories of reading and writing also provide lenses for analyzing students' creative and meaning-making processes. Rosenblatt (1982) explored the relationship between the reader and the text, envisioning reading as "a transaction, a two-way process, involving a reader and a text at a particular time under particular circumstances" (p. 268). Rosenblatt argued that the meaning we take from reading is shaped by the purpose and stance we bring to the reading event. A reader's stance may fall along what Rosenblatt calls the aesthetic–efferent continuum, drawing from the Greek meaning of *aesthetic* ("to sense" or "to perceive") and the *efferent* ("to take away"). She contends that teachers tend to distract students from the "evocation" they create in their minds *while* they read, to answering questions *after* they read, noting that "the tendency in the teaching of literature has been to turn the student's attention away from the actual experience, and to focus on presenting a 'correct,' traditional interpretation, and on knowledge about technical devices or biographical or historical background" (Karolides, 1999, p. 165). Rosenblatt (1982) posits that while knowledge of literary terms can certainly help enrich the aesthetic transaction, they are "vacuous concepts without recognition of the importance of stance. . . . 'Form' is something felt on the pulses, first of all" (p. 276).

In the context of this study, I find Rosenblatt's theory of the aesthetic transaction to be especially illuminative. With this multisensory, experiential process of aesthetic reading, Rosenblatt (1982) contends that we are actually involved in a creative process ourselves, noting, "out of these ideas and feelings, a new experience, the story or poem, is shaped and lived through" (p. 269). A "lived-through experience" in reading, then, is not simply a "personal connection"; rather, it conjures up participation within the text itself *and* participation in the new poem we are creating while we read. As Faust (2000) contends, close analysis of Rosenblatt's writing on the experiential aspects of reading leads to an understanding that reading is "socially mediated composing process" (p. 22) and that reading is "constructive and creative in a manner analogous with authorship" (p. 22). Therefore, Rosenblatt not only highlights the experiential nature of reading but also positions the reader as a composer and author.

While Rosenblatt's theories of reading have long received widespread recognition in the field, her perspectives on writing have not been as fully considered. Even as she noted differences between reading and writing, she also offered some parallels between the two. In language similar to the language she used to describe reading, Rosenblatt (1989) contends, "Writing, we know, is always an event in time, occurring at a particular moment in the writer's biography, in particular circumstances, and under particular external and internal pressures. In short, the writer is always transacting with a personal, social, and cultural environment" (p. 163). Just as she describes the "live circuit" that exists between the reader and the text, she also emphasizes the "live ideas" that the writer draws on when he or she is composing, contending:

> Live ideas have roots drawing sustenance from writers' needs, interests, questions, and values; live ideas have tendrils reaching toward external areas of thought. A personally grounded purpose develops and impels movement forward. The quickened fund of images, ideas, emotions, attitudes, and tendencies offers the means for making new connections, for discovering new facets of the world of objects and events—in short for thinking and writing creatively. (p. 165)

Rosenblatt (1989) contends that writers draw upon and choose from their "linguistic-experiential reservoir" (p. 164) to compose and revise texts and that these writing processes are reflective of their "selective attention." Rosenblatt's understandings provide insightful analytical lenses for the students' processes of creating their comics as they selected images from a broad range of texts that had personal significance and cultural resonance.

In Rosenblatt's conceptualizations of both reading and writing, she attends to experience, feelings, creativity, and composing in ways that I see as having resonance with both the arts and with the students' perspectives on the Comic Life project. Given that Rosenblatt developed and refined her theoretical understandings at a time when digital and multimodal texts did not predominate in the ways they do now, my choice to include her prominently in this chapter may seem anachronistic. As I explore next, a growing body of empirical studies of students' engagements with multimodal literacies framed by theories of digital literacies, multiliteracies, and New Literacies offer very valuable insights into how students orchestrate multiple modes to make meaning and to expand conceptualizations of literacies. My analysis is informed by these understandings; however, the students in this study described their learning in language more closely aligned with the arts, self-expression, and literary response. As I explore below, students spoke enthusiastically and often about the opportunity to be creative, to use their imaginations, and to share their own perspectives on the novel. I therefore contend that Rosenblatt's theories provide a resonant and generative lens through which to consider the students' perspectives and their multimodal compositions.

Incorporating Multiple Sign Systems into English Language Arts

Many would argue that the educational field tends to promote reading practices closer to the efferent end of Rosenblatt's continuum, given the increase in standardized testing upon the passage of No Child Left Behind legislation and with the enhanced attention to nonfiction texts within the Common Core State Standards. Despite emphases on testing and print literacies, however, educators and researchers have documented classrooms in which students engage with the arts, literacy, and multiple sign systems (Albers & Harste, 2007). Using a multiliteracies framework, Broderick's (2014) study of the design and authoring processes within a high school literary arts magazine showcases not only how students traversed multiple sign systems and modes such as writing, music, and graphic arts to create the journal, but also engaged in "collaborative design" processes that profoundly shaped how the creative works were ultimately framed, represented, and presented. Smagorinsky (1997) documented the generative nature of the knowledge that emerged when adolescents interpreted literature through the arts, contending, "Drawing, dancing, and drama thus took on new roles as legitimate academic forms of representation aside from the linguistic symbols that had provided the basis for their language arts representation in the past" (p. 102). In these ways, the arts become not just "activities," or "add-ons" to fixed curricula, but essential tools for dynamic thinking and meaning making (Short, Kauffman, & Kahn, 2000).

Attention to multiple sign systems has shaped not only how students engage with and respond to print texts but also the inclusion of digital and multimodal texts, including graphic novels, fanfiction, and comics, within the curriculum (e.g., Carter, 2009; Dallacqua, 2012; Frey & Fisher, 2004). From a multiliteracies perspective, Danzak (2011) analyzed how English language learners explored identities through the production of their own comics as they read others' immigration stories and composed their own. O'Brien, Beach, and Scharber (2007) showed how "struggling" readers developed a richer sense of literate competence and engagement as a result of reading and writing a variety of digital and multimodal texts. Rish and Caton (2011) explored how adolescents studied the genre of fantasy fiction and engaged in collaborative and multimodal writing processes akin to the practices associated with fanfiction. Miller (2010) argued that digital video composing across multiple English classrooms is a "potent new literacy learning tool that leads to increased student engage and achievement" (p. 201), a finding also substantiated in Curwood and Cowell's (2011) research into students' creation of digital poetry, as well as Bruce's (2009) analysis of his own students' digital video composing processes. Jocson (2012) studied ninth-grade students' work with digital video projects, analyzing the students' innovative and considered approaches to "narrative assemblage" across modes. Further echoing the potential of incorporating multiple modalities into literacy education, Vasudevan, Schultz, and Bateman (2010) demonstrated how fifth graders claimed literate identities in deeply meaningful and transformative ways that altered not only their perceptions of themselves but also how others saw them. As they argue, for students who have been "disengaged from routine and disconnected curricula, the chance to break the norms and boundaries of school for the purposes of [multimodal] composing can have an impact on their relationship to school by allowing them to take on new identities as students and writers" (p. 457).

Even amid these promising and inspiring examples, however, the linguistic mode continues to be privileged within English language arts (ELA) curricula and assessments (Shanahan, 2013). The case studies presented in Miller and McVee's (2012) edited volume show the enormous potential of incorporating multimodalities into classrooms, while also documenting the tensions, dilemmas, and struggles that emerge for teachers as they bump up against state standards, high-stakes testing, and school cultures resistant to change. Reflecting the pervasiveness of print-based literacies in schools, Christianakis (2011) found that young people face many obstacles to reading and writing multimodal texts, documenting students' inventive, yet often thwarted, attempts at "smuggling in various semiotic sources, genres, and symbolic tools across semiotic borders to create multimodal texts that did not privilege alphabet writing or school-taught genres" (p. 49). Furthermore, while we have a small, yet growing, research base exploring multimodalities within creative writing classrooms (Callahan & King, 2011; Curwood & Cowell, 2011), we have fewer studies of multimodalities within the literature classroom. As a result, there is a need to know more about how young people use digital tools to respond to literature within schools when they are intentionally invited to do so, and how these tools can shape their own literary understandings.

RESEARCH CONTEXT, METHODS, AND DATA ANALYSIS

This chapter draws from a larger study exploring one teacher's efforts to incorporate multimodal literacies into her eighth-grade academic intervention support (AIS) reading classes within a semirural school over a 2-year period. AIS courses are designed to provide additional support for students in meeting state standards in ELA. In accordance with state education guidelines, students are placed in AIS classes if they score below the passing score on the ELA state exam. They take these reading support classes alongside their "regular" English classes until they achieve a passing score on the state exam. At the time of the study in this particular school, AIS teachers had a certain degree of freedom to design their classes in accordance with their instructional goals and student needs. Many AIS classes were characterized by a focus on literacy skills, including comprehension, vocabulary, and summary, often pursued through work with short literary passages or worksheets. Ms. Singh's AIS classroom was unique in its inclusion of both entire novels and multimodalities.

The data were collected during Ms. Singh's implementation of a unit on *The Outsiders* across her AIS classes. At the time of the study, Ms. Singh was in her third year of teaching in the United States after a lengthy teaching career overseas. Ms. Singh chose *The Outsiders* for this unit because she was familiar with the text, and because previous students had been very engaged by it. She was especially curious to see how students' engagement with the book would be shaped by incorporating Comic Life into the unit. With the assistance of the school's media specialist, Ms. Singh developed a project to incorporate multimodal literacies into her classes for a 3-month period, including approximately 1 month reading and discussing the novel and 2 months writing a script based on one scene from the novel and creating a multimodal representation of it with Comic Life software. Primary data collection took place when the students were invited to choose one scene from the novel, write a script with narration and key dialogue from the scene, search for images on the Internet to incorporate into their comic, and create a comic using Comic Life. With the exception of being prevented from choosing images from the 1983 Francis Ford Coppola movie based on the novel, few limitations were placed on the students' choice of images. Along with two research assistants, I collected data in Ms. Singh's reading support classes and from the 17 students within those classes who provided research consent. Data sources include fieldnotes from classroom observations approximately two times a week in three of the classes for 2 months during the Comic Life phase; interviews with the teacher; interviews with the students; scripts students wrote to represent a scene from *The Outsiders*; and the Comic Life comics they produced.

Initial analysis of the data was informed by the constant comparative method (Taylor & Bogdan, 1984) and multimodal data analysis (Jewitt, 2009). My research assistants and I began by open coding the comics, interview transcripts, and fieldnotes, naming and describing what we were noticing in the data. We then developed data analysis matrices to look across the 17 scripts and comics within categories such as scene selection, image choices, frame count, and color scheme. In conjunction with this coding, we also reread the interviews and field observations to ascertain how the students described their choices and intentions, as well as what we noticed in our fieldnotes regarding their composing processes. As we looked across the data in the process of axial coding, we identified emerging themes and patterns, including, the range and variation of the students' use of intertextualities; the range and variation of meaning making across multiple sign systems; and the students' perspectives on their learning as a result of engaging with multimodal literacies.

While this approach yielded important insights into the data, I felt something was missing in the analysis. As I began to look across the findings, I noted that theoretical lenses drawn from the arts, aesthetics, and literary response provided more nuanced understandings of the students' creative work and their perspectives on their learning. As I returned to the dataset with the perspectives and terminology found within this chapter's conceptual framework, I further refined the analysis. In my presentation of students' processes, products, and perspectives on digital composing in response to literature, I therefore employ analytical tools and perspectives drawn from two conceptualizations of aesthetics. First, I bring to bear perspectives on aesthetics from the arts field to consider the *aesthetic qualities* of students' comics. In this way, the analysis considers the "sensory, expressive, and technical characteristics" (Tavin, 2007, p. 41) of students' digital compositions as I pay attention to the presence and impact of image selection, color choice, overall design, and so forth, on students' meaning making in their comics and how they express it. Second, I bring to bear Rosenblatt's (1986) discussion of *aesthetic transactions* in both reading and writing as rooted in the senses, in perception, and within the students' social worlds. Drawing from what I see as these complementary perspectives on aesthetics in the fields of art and literary response, the following research questions therefore guide my inquiry in this chapter:

- How can analytical lenses attuned to the aesthetic qualities of the students' comics illuminate how students conveyed their understanding and expressed themselves in their comics?
- How can analytical lenses attuned to aesthetic transactions illuminate the nature of students' responses to the book in their comics?
- How can aesthetic lenses help further illuminate student perspectives on the role and affordances of multimodal literacies within this reading support class?

In conjunction with these research questions and the conceptual framework, I found case studies well suited to describing and interpreting how the students took up the opportunity to respond to literature through digital composing. A case study approach provides multidimensional looks at phenomena by drawing on multiple data sources (Dyson & Genishi, 2005). A case study approach was also particularly appropriate given my interest in student perspectives as case studies attempt to render "the complex world of lived experience from the point of view of those who live it" (Schwandt, 1994, p. 118).

STUDENT PORTRAITS

In the four portraits that follow, I analyze how students responded to the opportunity to bring multiple sign systems and digital tools into their literacy work in school, how this opportunity shaped and reflected their response to literature, and how they theorized this learning opportunity. By describing both the aesthetic qualities of their comics and the students' aesthetic transactions in the creation of them, I attempt to render cases attuned to the visual and experiential nature of the students' meaning-making processes and literary understandings.

Delia

Near the back of the row of computers, Delia stared intently at her computer screen, silently moving images around until she was satisfied. In interviews and at the end of class, she was talkative, demonstrative, and friendly, but while constructing her comic, Delia worked with a quiet focus and an air of seriousness. As the images, words, narration boxes, and dialogue bubbles accumulated on her page, Delia would at times let out a small sigh if their arrangement did not meet her expectations. Delia included the most frames in her comic of any student, and her comic draws most directly on comic book conventions, with impactful image choices, contrasting background colors, and bold fonts.

Delia recreated the deadly confrontation between the Socs and the Greasers in an empty park late at night. She explained that she constructed an image of the scene in her head and tried to imagine the sensory aspects of being there herself, noting, "I just like kind of pictured the whole scene in my head. I'd just close my eyes at that point and think about what it'd be like if I was just standing there." In visualizing the scene in this way, by putting herself directly within it, Delia's approach has resonance with how Rosenblatt (1982) describes the reader's transaction with words on a page: "We participate in the story, we identify with the characters, we share their conflicts and their feelings" (p. 270). Delia's comic is edged with menace and her choice of images, dialogue, and colors suggest the sense of danger Delia pictured in her head. She blends verbatim dialogue from the novel and invented narration, choosing to allow her characters to speak with the same voice they do in the novel, while using the narration boxes to add rhetorical power to the images she's chosen to represent the scene. She explains, "I took most of [my dialogue] from the book, but as I was looking at it, I thought it would be better to add more stuff to it so it wouldn't be exactly the same."

While Delia's comic deftly captures essential dialogue and the numerous plot points in her scene, her comic stands out for its visual acumen and Delia's awareness of how image selection creates tone, mood, and symbolic meaning. Delia chose an uncanny image of a grinning skull with a full head of hair to represent Bob, the menacing Socs gang member. The stylized representation of Bob as a pompadoured grinning skull is a powerful device that draws the eye and compels the viewer's attention throughout the pages of Delia's comic. A grinning skull has multiple intertextual meanings across time and genres, from its appearance in *Hamlet* to its more modern use in skateboarding logos. The grinning skull motif has long been symbolic of death; it is therefore particularly compelling for Bob, who is stabbed to death by Johnny as he attempts to drown Ponyboy in a park fountain. Delia's selection of a handsome boy with a swollen eye and a bloody lip to represent Johnny is suggestive of the violence he will endure at the hands of the Socs. Moreover, the image evokes sympathy and compassion, emotions that many readers of *The Outsiders* feel for Johnny, a good-natured character who is beset by tragedy. Thus, Delia conveys her understanding of the emotional appeal of Ponyboy and Johnny, while representing their entitled and violent antagonist with a sinister, and disturbing, image of death.

Throughout her comic, Delia's design, compositional, narrative, and color choices are suggestive of deeper themes within the novel and their symbolic impact. In describing how teachers might assist students in deepening and building on their aesthetic transactions with books, Rosenblatt (1986) argues, "The student should be helped to pay attention to the interfusion of sensuous, cognitive, and affective elements that can enter into the process of selective awareness and synthesis" (p. 127). While Delia's teacher did not give her direct instruction in attending to this "interfusion," it appears that the freedom to create a scene with the Comic Life software enabled Delia to attend to the deeply sensory aspects of the scene and to communicate emotional resonances and her cognitive understanding of it. In an interview, Delia commented, "I know that the book taught me that there a lot of things that aren't very fair in life and that bad things happen." Her comic communicates this understanding on even more visceral and powerful level as she communicates through imagery a deep understanding of the characters and broader themes of human conflict, tragedy, and death. As Eisner (2003) notes, she visually represents how "tropes matter, that metaphors mean" (p. 342).

Delia noted that the project revealed to her parts of herself she had not realized, saying, "It was really fun because I had no idea I could ever do that before. To be able . . . to find out that there's many different things you can do and then to be able to do something that was very creative, I thought that was pretty cool."

Tanya

During class in the computer lab, Tanya usually sat next to her close friend, Mara. The two often chatted quietly as they worked, and they would frequently take time to study one another's projects and make comments. For her comic, Tanya chose to represent the reflective conversation between Johnny and Ponyboy as they reminisce about the past and consider the difficult choices that lay ahead. While lacking the undertones of violence and conflict in Delia's work, Tanya's comic reflects a similar impulse to convey the emotional tenor of the scene through character selection. When asked the hardest part of the project, Tanya indicated that she in fact labored most over the choice of characters, exclaiming, "It took me forever! Like most of the class periods, I was just looking. I was like, 'No . . . no . . . no!" She went on to explain how she decided on anime characters:

> "I didn't want to choose people that everyone knew, like a lot of people chose Edward [from the *Twilight* movies] and things like that. I didn't want to do that. I like mine to be different from other people's, so like I wanted to do something unique and stuff. So, I thought that would be cool to do, and I thought that like these characters fit it perfectly, so I chose them."

Revealing she had little familiarity with anime prior to the project, Tanya said she thought the characters would work "perfectly" because of their large, soulful eyes and gentle features. She explained that she chose sketches of anime characters from fanfiction websites because they were "more original" than the "official" images.

To set the scene, Tanya places her two contemplative protagonists on a windswept beach. Another striking image of a sunrise painted in rich reds and golds captures the essence of the line, "Nothing gold can stay," from the Robert Frost poem that figures prominently in the boys' conversation. This image appears in most of Tanya's frames and seems almost to become a character itself. It fills the comic with melancholy beauty and sets a warm and reflective tone, very similar to how the sunrise in the novel elicits a philosophical conversation between the boys. The image of the beach, with its cold blues and deep purples, contrasts with the glowing sunrise and is suggestive of the uncertainty of the boys' coming adulthood. In the penultimate page of her comic, Tanya brings together in an uneasy tension on one page these compelling images: the warm sunrise, the cold beach, and the thoughtful characters. In addition to reflecting the emotional tenor prevalent in anime, there is also a sweeping cinematic quality to Tanya's comic, where color sets the mood of the scene and close-up facial shots predominate. Tavin (2007) notes that one definition of *aesthetics* refers to how encounters with the arts can promote a "heightened awareness, radiance of mind, or a moving disposition" (p. 41). Tanya's intentional choices in words, images, and color allowed her to create a comic in which she could express a heightened awareness of this turning point in the boys' lives.

Curiously, Tanya includes on the final page of her comic both the entire Frost poem and one frame composed as a flashback representing all the Greasers together as young boys. The flashback is presented in gray scale and has been modified by Tanya to feature horizontal lines running across it. Interestingly, there is not a flashback featured in the novel. By incorporating this flashback device, she not only takes her own creative license but also underscores the feeling of nostalgia and the passage of time imbued in the scene. As a creator of the comic, and also a writer of this new facet to the scene, Tanya transacts with the novel, with her own imagination, and with the images she has located in her Internet searches for the comic. Using Rosenblatt's (1989) transactional theory of writing, with all these resources at her disposal, Tanya has "the means for making new connections, for discovering new facets of the world of objects and events—in short for thinking and writing creatively" (p. 165).

Tanya herself spoke frequently of enjoying the opportunity to be creative in the project, noting:

> "I liked the freedom to rewrite the whole script.... I thought it was really fun to do because I like being creative and I liked how we got to like put the story into our own point of view, like how we would see it. So I thought that was cool. And mine was really different! ... Because I used like cartoon characters and anime and just like changed everything ... I learned that I'm a lot more creative than I thought I was."

Tanya underscored how important it was for her to be "creative" and "original," and that she valued the opportunity to see how others in the class expressed themselves, noting that she learned the most about other people in the class by the images they selected. Tanya also said she appreciated the collaborative and enjoyable nature of the learning in the project, contrasting it with the usual "deskwork" that characterized many of her other classes: "It didn't even feel like you were learning because you had so much fun, and the time just flew by."

George

George was a recent transfer from another district and a new student in Ms. Singh's class. His charismatic personality and dry sense of humor quickly earned him many friends among his classmates. George was so enthusiastic about the project that he encouraged many members of his extended family to read *The Outsiders* and additional novels by the same author. He also downloaded the Comic Life software to his home computer. He was the only student in the study who said his goal with his comic was to entertain his classmates. George chose to eschew the ready-made templates provided by the software and create his own, noting, "Mine's all custom." Due to technical glitches and power failures, George lost his comic on numerous occasions. A skilled multitasker, George went about the business of recreating the comic each time, often answering questions and offering suggestions to other students sitting next to him without even looking up from his computer.

For his project, George chose a scene in which three of the protagonists rush into a burning church to save children who have become trapped inside. Despite the gravity of this scene, George's project is infused with cleverness, humor, and irreverence. He chose, for example, to represent the character of Ponyboy with a youthful-looking centaur (a "pony boy"). George's comic is distinct not only in this tone but also in its narrative structure. He strings together of a series of intertextual popular cultural references that only loosely refer back to the scene he is representing. Some notable examples of these comedic nonsequiturs include his use of the cereal slogan "I'm coo-coo for Cocoa Puffs!," an image of the spokesman for the Subway chain of restaurants, and President George W. Bush's signature. In arguing for the inclusion and critique of popular texts and mass media images within art education, Tavin (2000) notes:

> Indeed, images from the postmodern landscape penetrate and pervade every aspect of all children's lives in the form of television programs, children's books, advertisements, movies, comics, toys, cereal boxes, video games, fashion merchandise, sport shoes, fast food paraphernalia, and architectural and public spaces. These pervasive, immediate, and sometimes ephemeral images construct student's consciousness and their sense of identity, politics and culture. (p. 193)

George's comic certainly suggests the pervasive nature of these images, while also reflecting *how* those images are used as storytelling devices in the "postmodern landscape." The comic's narrative style embodies the ethos of absurdist and satirical animated television programs such as *Family Guy* and *South Park*. In these shows, plotlines exist not so much to drive the story, but rather to showcase intertextual references. Stories often remain unresolved, with plotlines twisting so radically that it is often impossible to connect the beginning of an episode to its end. Containing no actual dialogue from the novel, George's comic is a pastiche of advertising slogans and icons transposed on a nominal plotline. While George refers back to the burning church throughout the narrative, the comic is punctuated by images and dialogue that do not link to the scene in immediately recognizable ways. George also seems to appropriate the laconic detachment of characters in these television shows in his characters, who coldly appraise and calmly comment on the burning church.

For George, his "linguistic–experiential reservoir" (Rosenblatt, 1989) is a highly intertextual, image-driven media landscape in which the very concept of "story" seems to be in question. Unlike Tanya's use of anime to represent her characters' deep emotion, George draws on a much more diverse and eclectic set of images for the purpose of entertainment. George's comic raises some interesting questions about what happens when the "aesthetic transaction" bumps up against postmodern detachment. Whereas Rosenblatt writes of deep, sensory, "lived through" experiences with texts, George's comic suggests more of a remove. His comic communicates a sense of the absurd and is propelled forward by a clever juxtaposition of images that continually disrupt attempts at linear and logical sense-making. In some ways, then, the aesthetic transaction may seem to be an antithetical conceptual lens through which to read George's composing processes; however, when he spoke of his image choices, it is clear that they had strong resonance for him. They also had a strong resonance for his classmates, the audience George had in mind when creating his comic.

George frequently expressed special appreciation for the social and creative aspects of the Comic Life unit, noting that for students, "it's fun and it gives them a break from deskwork [and to] . . . get . . . little hands-on with the computer and they get to, like, socialize while they work, too. And they just get to learn a new program, how it works and, and use their creative power." To George, the opportunities to draw on his "creative power" and to work collaboratively with other students were rare, yet highly valued, aspects of his in-school learning experiences.

Evan

Possessed with almost frenetic energy, Evan's interest was captured by many things but was not held for long by any one thing in particular. If Evan had a hallmark, it was his loud interruptions of both Ms. Singh and his fellow students. He reacted to class activities with bursts of engagement, at times working diligently and with seeming great interest in Comic Life, and at other times choosing instead to distract and tease other students. He was of two minds toward *The Outsiders,* declaring at one point that he "liked" the book, and at another deriding it as a "stupid" book. In class discussions of the book, it was clear Evan was not transported by the language or plot of the book, and he was disinterested in other students' interpretations. Evan refused to write the script for his scene without significant input and assistance from Ms. Singh. This lack of an aesthetic transaction with the book seemed to carry over into his work with the Comic Life software. After finding Elvis images and incorporating them into his comic, he did little experimentation with fonts, background color, or the inclusion of additional images to set the tone or add dimension to the scene. He expressed relief when the comic was finished and had little interest in making changes to it once he did.

Evan spoke often about the project as being "hard." While many students also used similar language, they focused on the limitations of the software program in terms of expressing the fullness of their creative visions. In her descriptions of the project, Delia, for example, used the words "hard" and "challenging" on numerous occasions, at one time even calling the project "excruciatingly difficult." Delia was frustrated when class time was limited and she was unable to correct what she saw as flaws in her comic, noting, "Hmm, well, one thing that I'd definitely change are the pictures because they look sort of foggy and you can't really see what it was, so I want to make it so they're more clear and you can see everything. . . . I think maybe if I'd have had a little more time then I'd feel better." By contrast, Evan described the difficulties as being rooted in what he "had to do," explaining:

> "We really had to analyze the book and find, like, facts about the people. We had to go back and find descriptions of the people, then we had to find pictures that fit the descriptions so we had to keep relooking, going back and forth. The most challenging was you had to keep going back and forth in the book, back to the scenes. When you messed up, you had to start all over again."

Evan uses "had to" six times in this response, a striking contrast to Delia's language when she reveals her own initiative and her concern for the aesthetics of her comic. Evan's statement is also illuminating in its focus on "going back and forth in the book" as a frustration, almost as a chore.

With his extended time in AIS classes, Evan was accustomed to the expectation that students follow directions and complete the work as requested, even if he rarely complied.

Despite the built-in freedom to take creative license and to work at his own pace and across modalities in this project, Evan took on what Rosenblatt might characterize as an efferent stance, searching the book for information to "take away" and import into his comic. Thus, Evan seemed to interpret the purpose of the assignment to align with the learning goals in more "rule-abiding" (Eisner, 2003) literacy classes: accuracy ("pictures that fit the descriptions"); literal understandings ("facts about the people"); and print-focused ("going back and forth in the book"). He did note the difference, however, between this project and his other experiences in AIS:

> EVAN: Well, we've never done big projects like this in AIS classes. It's always been like tests three times a week on the books we're reading. It's been a lot more fun this year with all this.
>
> RESEARCHER: And looking back, do you feel you've learned more with this kind of stuff or with tests?
>
> EVAN: Well, with this, because I actually get interested.
>
> RESEARCHER: How was it with the tests?
>
> EVAN: With the tests, I just kind of failed.

Evan speaks to how the nature of the learning in AIS shifted with the inclusion of multimodal literacies. Despite his aversion at times to the Comic Life project, here Evan seems to indicate that this kind of multimodal learning might hold his interest and perhaps interrupt his resignation to previous failures.

CONCLUSION

Students chose an eclectic mix of images and narrative styles that reflected diverse purposes and approaches to the Comic Life project. Most students in this study expressed an interest in, and knowledge of, making meaning in both linguistic and nonlinguistic modes. Analyzing the aesthetic qualities of the students' comics illuminates how they selected images, colors, and dialogue to set the tone, tenor, and mood of their scene, as well as to suggest deeper themes in and responses to the novel. As evidenced by their frequent talk of using their imaginations and being creative, many students were able to "discover what it is to make a shape, an image, to devise a metaphor, to tell a tale—for the sake of finding their own openings into the realms of the arts" (Greene, 1991, p. 39).

Drawing on transactional theories of reading and writing, parallels can be drawn between Rosenblatt's aesthetic–efferent continuum of reading and students' digital composing processes. In "aesthetic digital composing in response to literature," students draw on digital tools to create meaning, seeking out images, color, and design elements to express their interpretation of the book (Wissman & Costello, 2014). At times, these images and narrative structures are drawn purposefully from popular culture texts for which students have an affinity, as in George's comic that reflected the ethos of adult animated shows; at others times, images are chosen for their desired symbolic effect, as in Delia's choice of a grinning skull. The students describe their choices often in sensory, affective, and emotive terms, and their chosen images often serve to embody a feeling or mood. The narrative style or story structure also reflects an awareness of meaning making within genres, as in Tanya's choice of anime to suggest high emotion or George's display of intertextual postmodern juxtapositions to entertain his classmates. In aesthetic composing, the students' focus is on leveraging the cultural, digital, artistic, and personal resources at their disposal to express their response to the book.

In "efferent digital composing in response to literature" (Wissman & Costello, 2014), on the other hand, students are concerned with the literal and the accurate. The images chosen do not reverberate with meaning or significance to the composer. Students pay little attention to other semiotic affordances of the software program to express the affective dimensions of the scene or to render a heightened sensibility through font choice, background color, and so forth. Efferent digital composing is also a more solitary process in which the axis of the interaction is between the student and teacher. This composing stance can also reflect the reading stance, as it did in Evan's case, when he expressed a disinterest and lack of engagement with the novel. In efferent digital composing, there is a utilitarian quality to the process, an exercise to be completed with dispatch.

While I find Rosenblatt's theory helps to illuminate a range of insights into students' composing processes, I also see ways in which digital composing calls for an extension and enrichment of these understandings. In writing about the implications of her transactional theory of reading for teachers, Rosenblatt (1982) contends, "After our reading, our initial function is to deepen the experience. . . . We should help the young reader to return to, relive, savor, the experience" (p. 275). Rosenblatt offers a cautious appreciation for how the arts can "offer an aesthetic means of giving form to a sense of what has been lived through in the literary transaction" (p. 276), but she considers these prospects "only generally relevant to the reading purposes" (p. 275). In considering the students' reflections on the process of choosing their scene and creating their comics, there were times when students referenced the "evocation" that was created while they read: Students spoke of characters who captured their attention, of language choices that engrossed them, and of feelings that emerged for them as characters faced difficult decisions or loss. Many times, these evocations did drive their choice of the scene. Yet, in my view, the creation of the comic not only furthered their experience of the initial evocation but it also created new experiences and deeper responses. They transacted with not only their memory of the experience of reading the book but also with the new text they were creating on the screen to help further the transaction.

A second way in which digital composing may encourage an extension of transactional theories of reading and writing concerns the prominence of the visual. Rosenblatt (1981) often uses terminology connected to the aural, arguing that readers "pay attention to the sound, to the kinesthetic and emotive reverberations of the words, and thus to make a poem" (p. 17). In aesthetic digital composing, the visual is more predominant as students imagine the scene in their heads and search for images, sometimes finding ones that match the vision in their heads, but often finding unexpected images that add new dimensions to their understanding. Delia's choice of a grinning skull, for example, emerged from a search for a different kind of image, but its appearance in the search results connected to her sense of the scene and what she wanted to communicate about her character.

Third, another extension of Rosenblatt's theories can be found in how the notion of "live ideas"—those ideas drawn from past experiences with life and language—is shaped by the digital landscape in ways one may not have anticipated. The vast diversity, availability, and ubiquity of those images, evident in George's case, means that students are drawing from a churning set of influences to an unprecedented degree. Fourth, through digital composing processes that took place together in a shared space, with students often viewing and commenting on each other's comics as they were produced, the transaction with the book moved from the internal and private to the external computer screen and to the larger classroom community.

It may not seem notable that students coming of age with the proliferation of new technologies would be adept at digital composing; however, it is notable that the students grounded their descriptions of these efforts in the language of arts, self-expression, and creativity. Consistently speaking to how digital composing engendered new insights into themselves and their abilities to work hard and express themselves, the students focused less on the technical affordances of the software and more on what they were able to express about themselves with them. They also spoke continuously, and often with a degree of sadness, about how this kind of work was a rare experience throughout their educational careers.

The students' comics encourage us, as researchers and as teachers, to consider how young people take up opportunities to respond to literature across semiotic modes and to do so with digital tools in ways that deepen and extend the aesthetic transaction. I believe teachers, researchers, and policymakers alike have a responsibility to listen to students and to provide rich description of their creative processes, products, and perspectives. When students and student achievement are instead reduced to scores on standardized tests, understandings of teaching and learning, especially in regards to literature, are similarly impoverished. Within a media landscape that is ever-evolving, conventions are shifting regarding storytelling and narrative (Williams, 2009). As George's case suggests, we need to consider the implications of these changing narrative forms and story arcs within popular culture texts for school-based literacy teaching (Wissman, Costello, & Hamilton, 2012). These new kinds of narratives also underscore the need to reenvision assessments to capture the complexities of new literacies (O'Brien et al., 2009; Stornaiuolo, Hull, & Nelson, 2009) and the sophistication of the authors who compose with them.

As students in this study both reflected back on their evocations with the initial transaction with the book and recreated a scene through visual means, they participated in a "selecting, organizing, synthesizing activity" (Karolides, 1999, p. 164) that revealed and extended their responses to the book. I therefore contend that creativity, far from being ancillary to literary understanding, can in fact inspire and enrich it. Rosenblatt has long argued against teaching literature primarily from an efferent perspective, noting that it forecloses the aesthetic transaction and will therefore impoverish the analysis that could come after. As Rosenblatt (1981) writes, "If there has not been an aesthetic evocation, with the reader weaving the work out of the vital, organismic components of meaning, analysis will be like algebra, an intellectual exercise, and efferent analysis of components or devices in the text" (p. 20). Instead of drawing on Rosenblatt to engage in the now rote exercise of asking students to make a "text-to-self" connection or to produce a "personal connection" on demand, teachers could instead focus on creating reading contexts that support rich experiential transactions that can then serve as the basis for subsequent analytical work. Aesthetic digital composing of response to literature provides opportunities for students to tap into the experiential, sensory, and creative—the "felt on the pulses" (Rosenblatt, 1982, p. 276)—aspects of reading and writing, and to express and extend the fullness of their transactions with texts of all kinds.

ACKNOWLEDGMENTS

I would like to thank Sean Costello and Diane Hamilton for their hard work and insightful contributions in data collection and analysis. Portions of this chapter appeared in Wissman and Costello (2014). Copyright 2014 by the National Council of Teachers of English. Reprinted by permission.

REFERENCES

Albers, P. & Harste, J. (2007). The arts, new literacies, and multimodalities. *English Education, 40*(1), 6–20.

Black, R. W. (2009). Online fan fiction, global identities, and imagination. *Research in the Teaching of English, 43*(4), 397–425.

Broderick, D. (2014). Collaborative design: Participatory culture meets multiliteracies in a high school literary arts community. *Journal of Adolescent and Adult Literacy, 58*(3), 198–208.

Bruce, D. L. (2009). Writing with visual images: Examining the video composition processes of high school students. *Research in the Teaching of English, 43*(4), 426–450.

Callahan, M., & King, J. M. (2011). Classroom remix: Patterns of pedagogy in a techno-literacies poetry unit. *Journal of Adolescent and Adult Literacy, 55*(2), 134–144.

Carter, J. B. (2009). Going graphic. *Educational Leadership, 66*(6), 68–73.

Christianakis, M. (2011). Children's text development: Drawing, pictures, and writing. *Research in the Teaching of English, 46*(1), 22–54.

Common Core State Standards Initiative. (2015). Frequently asked questions. Retrieved from *www.corestandards.org/about-the-standards/frequently-asked-questions*.

Cook-Sather, A. (2002). Authorizing students' perspectives: Toward trust, dialogue, and change in education. *Educational Researcher, 31*(4), 3–14.

Cook-Sather, A. (2006). "Change based on what students say": Preparing teachers for a paradoxical model of leadership. *International Journal of Leadership in Education, 9*(4), 345–358.

Curwood, J. S., & Cowell, L. L. (2011). iPoetry: Creating space for new literacies in the English curriculum. *Journal of Adolescent and Adult Literacy, 55*(2), 107–117.

Dallacqua, A. K. (2012). Exploring literary devices in graphic novels. *Language Arts, 89*(6), 365–378.

Danzak, R. L. (2011). Defining identities through multiliteracies: EL teens narrate their immigration experiences as graphic stories. *Journal of Adolescent and Adult Literacy, 55*(3), 187–196.

Dyson, A. H., & Genishi, C. (2005). *On the case: Approaches to language and literacy research.* New York: Teachers College Press.

Eisner, E. W. (2003). The arts and the creation of mind. *Language Arts, 80*(5), 340–344.

Faust, M. (2000). Reconstructing familiar metaphors: John Dewey and Louise Rosenblatt on literary art as experience. *Research in the Teaching of English, 35*, 9–24.

Fisher, M. T. (2007). *Writing in rhythm: Spoken word poetry in urban classrooms.* New York: Teachers College Press.

Frey, N., & Fisher, D. (2004). Using graphic novels, anime, and the Internet in an urban high school. *English Journal, 93*(3), 19–25.

Gadsden, V. L. (2008). The arts and education: Knowledge generation, pedagogy, and the discourse of learning. *Review of Research in Education, 32*, 29–61.

Greene, M. (1991). Texts and margins. *Harvard Educational Review, 61*(1), 27–39.

Greene, M. (1995). *Releasing the imagination: Essays on education, the arts, and social change.* San Francisco: Jossey-Bass.

Heath, S. B. (2004). Learning language and strategic thinking through the arts. *Reading Research Quarterly, 39*(3), 338–342.

Hinton, S. E. (1967). *The outsiders.* New York: Viking.

Hull, G., & Katz, M. L. (2006). Crafting an agentive self: Case studies of digital storytelling. *Research in the Teaching of English, 41*(1), 43–81.

Ito, M., Baumer, S., Bittanti, M., Boyd, D., Cody, R., Herr, B., et al. (2010). *Hanging out, messing around, and geeking out: Kids living and learning with new media.* Cambridge, MA: MIT Press.

Jewitt, C. (Ed.). (2009). *The Routledge handbook of multimodal analysis.* New York: Routledge.

Jocson, K. M. (2012). Youth media as narrative assemblage: Examining new literacies at an urban high school. *Pedagogies: An International Journal, 7*(4), 298–316.

Karolides, N. J. (1999). Theory and practice: An interview with Louise M. Rosenblatt. *Language Arts, 77*(2), 158–170.

Kress, G. (2003). *Literacy in the new media age.* London: Routledge.

Miller, S. M. (2010). Reframing multimodal composing for student learning: Lessons on purpose from the Buffalo DV project. *Contemporary Issues in Technology and Teacher Education, 10*(2), 197–219.

Miller, S. M., & McVee, M. B. (Eds.). (2012). *Multimodal composing in classrooms: Learning and teaching for the digital world.* New York: Routledge.

Nicholson, D. W. (1999). The dominance of language in the curriculum: Issues of access, equity, and opportunity. *Equity and Excellence in Education, 32*(3), 105–110.

O'Brien, D., Beach, R., & Scharber, C. (2007). "Struggling" middle schoolers: Engagement and literate competence in a reading writing intervention class. *Reading Psychology, 28,* 51–73.

O'Brien, D., Stewart, R., & Beach, R. (2009). Proficient reading in school: Traditional paradigms and the new textual landscape. In L. Christenbery, R. Bomer, & P. Smagorinksy (Eds.), *Handbook of adolescent literacy research* (pp. 80–97). New York: Guilford Press.

Rish, R. M., & Caton, J. (2011). Building fantasy worlds together with collaborative writing: Creative, social, and pedagogic challenges. *English Journal, 100*(5), 21–28.

Rosenblatt, L. M. (1981). Act 1, Scene 1: Enter the reader. *Literature in Performance, 1*(2), 13–23.

Rosenblatt, L. M. (1982). The literary transaction: Evocation and response. *Theory Into Practice, 21*(4), 268–277.

Rosenblatt, L. M. (1986). The aesthetic transaction. *Journal of Aesthetic Education, 20*(4), 122–128.

Rosenblatt, L. M. (1989). Writing and reading: The transactional theory. In J. M. Mason (Ed.), *Reading and writing connections* (pp. 153–176). Needham Heights, MA: Allyn & Bacon.

Schwandt, T. A. (1994). Constructivist, interpretivist approaches to human inquiry. In N. K. Denzin & Y. S. Lincoln (Eds.), *Handbook of qualitative research* (pp. 118–137). Thousand Oaks, CA: Sage.

Shanahan, L. E. (2013). Composing "kid-friendly" multimodal text: When conversations, instruction, and signs come together. *Written Communication, 30*(2), 194–227.

Short, K. G., Kauffman, G., & Kahn, L. H. (2000). "I just *need* to draw: Responding to literature across multiple sign systems. *The Reading Teacher, 54*(2), 160–171.

Smagorinsky, P. (1997). Artistic composing as representational process. *Journal of Applied Developmental Psychology, 18,* 87–105.

Stornaiuolo, A., Hull, G., & Nelson, M. E. (2009). Mobile texts and migrant audiences: Rethinking literacy and assessment in a new media age. *Language Arts, 86*(5), 382–392.

Tavin, K. (2000). Just doing it: Towards a critical thinking of visual culture. *Perspectives in Critical Thinking, 110,* 187–210.

Tavin, K. (2007). Eyes wide shut: The use and uselessness of the discourse of aesthetics in art education. *Art Education, 60*(2), 40–45.

Taylor, S. J., & Bogdan, R. (1984). *Introduction to qualitative research methods: The search for meanings.* New York: Wiley.

Vasudevan, L. (2010). Literacies in a participatory, multimodal world: The arts and aesthetics of Web 2.0. *Language Arts, 88*(1), 43–50.

Vasudevan, L., Schultz, K., & Bateman, J. (2010). Rethinking composing in a digital age: Authoring literacy identities through multimodal storytelling. *Written Communication, 27,* 442–468.

Williams, B. T. (2009). *Shimmering literacies: Popular culture and reading and writing online.* New York: Peter Lang.

Wissman, K. K., & Costello, S. (2014). Creating digital comics in response to literature: Linking the arts, aesthetic transactions, and meaning-making. *Language Arts, 92*(2), 103–117.

Wissman, K. K., Costello, S., & Hamilton, D. (2012). "You're like yourself": Multimodal literacies in a reading support class. *Changing English: Studies in Culture and Education, 19*(3), 325–338.

CHAPTER 16

Let's Translate!
Teaching Literary Concepts with English Language Learners

KELLY PUZIO, CHRISTOPHER KEYES, and ROBERT T. JIMÉNEZ

In the middle school library, I (Kelly Puzio) sat around the table with five restless bilingual boys, identified by their teachers as struggling readers. One by one, they told me that they hated reading. They liked football, soccer, and comic books. Who was I to disagree? I hated reading most things when I was their age, too, and I would have played soccer all day. "That's good news," I said, "because this wasn't about reading; it was about using Spanish in school and translating." Miguel, who had his head down on the table the entire time, finally looked me in the eye.

On that first day, we read 10 pages of a young adult novel and translated two sentences from English into Spanish. Students translated the passages orally in no time, but the written translations took a lot longer. They liked using Spanish in school and wondered if it was really OK. They argued about words, laughed, and asked when it would be time to go. While most of their arguments were about specific words, we had a few good conversations about the main character of the novel—Martin. At the end of our hour, they agreed that this didn't feel much like reading. It was a lot more fun.

This vignette, drawn from our study of middle school students' translations to understand language arts concepts, is one way that teachers can value and use heritage languages in the classroom. In this vignette, one can see both the promise and challenge of using collaborative translation with students.

The changing demographics of school-age children provide an opportunity to create communities of support for students who speak multiple languages. Although the benefits of bilingual education are widely recognized (Adesope, Lavin, Thompson, & Ungerleider, 2010), many schools do not have the resources to implement bilingual programs. Whereas most efforts to support biliteracy require a bilingual teacher, we have developed an instructional strategy that builds on the cultural and literacy strengths that many bilingual students bring to school, one that even monolingual teachers can enact. Overall, we view collaborative translation as one way for teachers to help develop biliteracy and emergent bilingual students. With the goal of providing equitable access to grade-appropriate concepts situated in the local schools, we share in this chapter an instructional practice designed strategically to support the use of students' heritage language in school settings.

BACKGROUND

One of the most challenging yet rewarding dimensions of teaching is honoring the local knowledge embodied by students' social, cultural, and linguistic histories. Although the cultural and political values of bilingualism and multilingualism are accepted globally, schools in the United States rarely value or use students' heritage language in the classroom. Instead, educators often view a student's heritage language as a problem (Ruiz, 1984) and provide bilingual students with low-quality instruction. In direct contrast with these deficit views, we view heritage languages as valuable resources (Moll, Amanti, Neff, & Gonzalez, 1992) that can and should be used by general education classroom teachers. For this reason, we developed TRANSLATE (Teaching Reading And New Strategic Language Approaches To English learners). Later in this chapter, we explain how our instructional approach explicitly builds on all of the linguistic resources brought by students into schools.

In fact, the most current thinking in regard to bilingualism and the process of learning new languages is captured by the terms *translanguaging* (García & Wei, 2014) or *translingual practice* (Canagarajah, 2013). These scholars demonstrate that bilinguals have one linguistic repertoire that is artificially split apart by monolingual ideologies and institutionalized practices that "fail to authenticate a multilingual and heteroglossic reality" (García & Wei, 2014, p. 56). From this perspective, bilingualism can be thought of as a single language system rather than two or more separate language systems. These scholars claim that the blame for school failure of many language-minority groups is due to this sociopolitical inability to value this multilingual reality of students. Cummins (2000) has called for "specific forms of pedagogy" to support linguistically diverse students, so that they can learn the "basic skills assessed by most tests while at the same time they expand their personal, intellectual, and academic horizons" (p. 248). Canagarajah (2013) recognizes that theorization of translingual practices should be accompanied by pedagogical implementation (p. 12). TRANSLATE is one instructional approach to teaching reading comprehension to students who make use of more than one language in order to make meaning from text.

It is important to note that theorists of translingual practice/translanguaging argue that "all of us have translingual competence, with differences in degree and not kind" (Canagarajah, 2013, p. 8). A translanguaging view of language, therefore, erases the monolingual–bilingual dichotomy that categorizes human beings in limiting terms and recognizes that everyone who seeks to be understood by speakers of different languages is translanguaging. Such a perspective has radical implications for conceptualizing teaching and learning. Many of the examples presented in this chapter illustrate what translanguaging looks like when students who are learning English work to comprehend texts that often are created without considering students' unique linguistic strengths and needs. While informed broadly by translanguaging theory, our instructional approach is informed specifically by three area of research: (1) language as an important resource, (2) collaborative/cooperative learning, and (3) reading strategies.

First, our instructional design was influenced by the fact that translation is already a source of local knowledge in which many bilingual students engage daily, particularly for family members (Orellana & Reynolds, 2008). In our study, the students we worked with reported regularly translating orally for their parents and grandparents, in a variety of settings, such as the bank and the doctor's office. In addition, students also reported providing oral translations of written documents. When thinking about translation, we have found it helpful to distinguish between gloss and dynamic translations (Nida, 2004). A *gloss translation* focuses on formal equivalence or literal "word-for-word" correctness. In contrast, a *dynamic translation* uses language and cultural understanding that is most appropriate for the audience. For example, if translating the English phrase *to each his own*, a gloss translation in Spanish would be *a cada uno lo suyo*. Drawing on cultural and linguistic knowledge, a dynamic translation might be *cada loco con su tema* ("every crazy person (or nut job) has his or her obsession"). As a practical matter, most translations fall somewhere between these two extremes.

Although translating is a complex and authentic literacy practice, research on how translation can support classroom learning is scarce (see Jiménez et al., 2015, for a more in-depth discussion). We know that translation can facilitate transfer of heritage-language skills, allow students to make connections to what they already know, and enhance retention of new information (Williams & Snipper, 1990). However, schools seldom require bilingual and emergent bilingual students to engage in demanding tasks that are as complex as the translation they are doing in their daily lives. García and Wei (2014) recognize that "bilinguals have one linguistic repertoire from which they select features strategically to communicate effectively" (p. 22). This, they argue, is the essence of translanguaging. Although research on how translation can be used strategically in K–12 school settings is scarce, translation is a complex language and literacy practice in which many bilingual students participate outside of school. TRANSLATE seeks to recognize students' linguistic resources to create transformative social spaces.

Second, our instructional design is supported by the wide variety of research on students' reading, discussing, and negotiating in cooperative and collaborative groups (Puzio & Colby, 2013). While we have designed our particular intervention using a collaborative group structure—in which students participate jointly on a common task without prespecified roles—our instructional program was informed by an array of within-class grouping research. Historically, researchers have used a wide variety of terms to emphasize ways of organizing small-group activity (see Oxford, 1997, for an analysis of cooperative, collaborative, and interactive grouping). Because this body of research has informed our instructional program, we employ the term *peer-mediated learning* to denote a macrocategory that includes multiple forms of within-class grouping.

For bilingual students in particular, quantitative (August & Hakuta, 1998; August & Shanahan, 2006; Cheung & Slavin, 2005; Cole, 2014; Roessingh, 2004) and qualitative (Genesee, Lindholm-Leary, Saunders, & Christian, 2005; Gersten & Jiménez, 1998; Gersten & Baker, 2000; Lightbown, 2000) syntheses recommend using peer-mediated approaches to teaching and learning. While these reviews have focused on effective instruction for bilingual students and English language learners, each review argues that peer-mediated learning is a key component of effective instruction for bilingual students. Along with supporting academic development, in one review, Swain, Brooks, and Tocalli-Beller

(2002) argued that the richness of peer-mediated dialogue that occurs in collaborative grouping could support the development of second-language learning. Researchers have reported that peer-mediated learning supports academic growth, because collaborative dialogue promotes enhanced engagement and participation (Calderón, Hertz-Lazarowitz, Ivory, & Slavin, 1997; Klingner, Vaughn, & Schumm, 1988). Others have argued that it also facilitated language acquisition (i.e., reading, writing, listening, and speaking) and engaged bilingual students in authentic, comprehensible language purposes such as negotiating and seeking clarification (Swain et al., 2002; Gass, Mackey, & Ross-Feldman, 2005). In fact, Swain et al. (2002) conceive of discussion as a tool that mediates second-language acquisition. However, these researchers concur that explicit instruction in productive dialogue is required to support productive interaction patterns.

While both quantitative and qualitative research support the use of peer-mediated learning for bilingual students, it has also been described as a double-edged sword (Dunston, 2002). Even though students, on average, prefer (Elbaum, Schumm, & Vaughn, 1997) and benefit from peer-mediated learning, it can be difficult to implement well and, at times, can be marginalizing and hierarchical (Cohen, 1994; Poole, 2008). In any setting, the participation patterns in group interaction are not always equal (Goatley, Brock, & Raphael, 1995) and are influenced by multiple factors, including friendship (Alvermann et al., 1996; Evans, 2002), gender composition (Evans, Alvermann, & Anders, 1998), and the presence of bossy students (Evans, 2002). Although peer-mediated learning is accepted as a core component of effective instructional programs, descriptive research provides consistent evidence that peer-mediated learning is not an educational panacea.

Third, our work is also informed by the vast array of research on reading strategies. By carefully examining how students read, researchers have shown that proficient readers use a variety of strategies to interact with texts, such as asking questions, summarizing, and predicting. Likewise, this field has shown that teaching students to use these strategies supports comprehension. Research has shown that bilingual students use specific bilingual strategies when reading (Jiménez, 1997). While similar to sociocognitive reading strategies (e.g., summarizing, predicting, questioning), translation is rooted in students' social and cultural histories and may therefore be conceptualized as a sociocultural reading strategy. As a component of translingual practice, translating "can be creative, enabling, and offer possibilities for voice" (Canagarajah, 2013, p. 6) that may otherwise remain unrecognized and unvalued in the educational community.

DESIGNING COLLABORATIVE TRANSLATION

This instructional strategy originated with a design research project aimed to create and refine a bilingual reading strategy (Keyes, Puzio, & Jiménez, 2014). We began our investigation by grounding our understandings in the empirical and theoretical literature. Over the course of 2 years, we met biweekly to read and discuss literature on bilingualism, culturally relevant pedagogy, and different ways to incorporate students' heritage language in the classroom. This process was critical, because it helped us co-construct a common vision for the multitude of ways that educators have supported bilingualism and biliteracy; we also decided that we wanted to develop a strategy that could be used by monolingual teachers—the vast majority of today's teachers. We were particularly inspired by the work of Orellana, Reynolds, Dorner, and Mesa (2003) on paraphrasing, and we wondered whether translation might help students socialize and understand textual concepts.

To further refine and understand how collaborative translation can support student understanding of language arts concepts, we worked extensively with 23 students (over 100 hours) in two middle school settings. These students were identified by both schools as being bilingual and as below benchmark in reading. This instruction occurred in pull-out settings (e.g., library, extra classroom) and focused on language arts. In both schools, we requested bilingual students who—according to their teachers—were struggling readers. One of the students we worked with was also identified for special education services. While we read and discussed multiple texts with students, we focus our attention here on conversations about *Brothers in Arms* (Langan & Alirez, 2004). This fictional, young adult novel centers on Martin (Marty) Luna, a new student at Bluford High. After watching his little brother, Huero, get tragically killed during gang warfare, Martin seeks revenge and is caught up in a cycle of violence. When his mother and teacher try to reach out to him, Martin's anger and rage often take over.

We based our original instructional design on guided reading (Fountas & Pinnell, 1996), modifying it to include translation and discussion that encourage the use of the heritage language. In particular, we adopted the small-group setting, with the focus on comprehension and word work, prompting, and tailored instruction from guided reading. Building on this work, here is a brief description of collaborative translation:

- *Choosing appropriate texts*. Use grade-appropriate texts that focus on essential curricular topics from your standards. Consider the important themes and ideas from the text. What do you want students to learn from reading this text?

- *Connecting students to texts*. In small groups of students who share a common heritage language, teacher-guided discussion begins with students are asked about personal experiences that reflect a main theme in the story. For example, prior to reading about a character having an argument with his mother over a major life decision, the instructor might ask, "When was the last time you got mad at someone in your family?"

- *Independent reading*. Students are asked to read a section of text (usually two to three pages from a novel) silently and to identify its most important point. We have students read short sections of text independently to support students' comprehension of the wider text. In order to make sense, student translations should consider the wider text base (e.g., textual themes, character traits, character language).

- *Sharing the main idea*. Students share (orally or in writing) what they think is most important from the reading. This step is used to determine how well students comprehend the text before the translation activity.

- *Requesting translations*. The teacher identifies a short section of text for students to translate. As they become familiar with the goals of the activity, students may also be asked to select passages to translate. If students are asked to write out their translations, it's essential that students translate important and short texts (less than 20 words). While students can verbally translate quickly, it takes much longer to write translations down.

- *Sharing and critiquing translations.* Students are asked to discuss, explain, and justify their translation choices. In line with research on collaborative learning and peer scaffolding, we believe that peer interaction discussions and arguments supports enhanced learning.

To help educators understand and use collaborative translation with their students, we focus in this chapter on the translation components that are most novel. In addition, we share our thinking about the instructional planning and reasoning that precede collaborative translation—how to select and identify translation-worthy texts.

GETTING READY FOR COLLABORATIVE TRANSLATION

Supported by a deep understanding of their students, thoughtful language arts instructors begin with instructional goals. What do you want your students to learn? When selecting translation excerpts, this question is particularly important, because different text excerpts support different instructional purposes. For example, do you want students to reason about how characters develop and interact? Or are you supporting students' understanding and analysis of textual themes? These instructional goals, derived from the Common Core State Standards for English language arts (National Governors Association Center for Best Practices & Council of Chief State School Officers [NGA & CCSO, 2010), have implications for how you prepare to organize collaborative translation. Table 16.1 delineates thematic- and character-based approaches to understanding *Brothers in Arms*. In the table, we have included one textual excerpt per chapter. As a practical matter, we used two or three sentences from each chapter when discussing the text with students. In our work with bilingual students, we typically preidentified excerpts (teacher-chosen), and we suggest this as a starting point. As a possible form of differentiation, students might identify text excerpts themselves. Students who could, for example, choose passages such as the ones in Table 16.1 (and a translation of those passages) would demonstrate a deep understanding of how texts communicate themes and/or character development, and this might be a useful graphic organizer for students to construct before beginning a larger, extended composition.

Along with supporting textual concepts, the best translation excerpts were moderately challenging and linguistically rich. We observed that excerpts that communicated simple and straightforward information were translated quickly but rarely inspired discussion among students. Excerpts with rich, figurative, language, such as metaphors, idioms, and similes, supported sustained engagement and prolonged discussions about text. Along with being challenging, we think that these excerpts captured students' attentions because of their inherent disputability: There is often no "correct" way to translate idioms and metaphors across languages. In the novel, Martin is infatuated with a girl who gets angry. We asked students to translate his thoughts: "There was fire in her eyes, it actually made her look even prettier" (Langan & Alirez, 2004, p. 58). To translate "fire in her eyes," student debated among *fuego en sus ojos (fire in her eyes), el miraba como si tenia fuego (the look/he looked as if she had fire)*, and *en los ojos de ella parecía que eran con fuegos (in her eyes it seemed that they were fiery)*. These statements demonstrate students' initial attempts at rendering metaphorical English language text into Spanish. Often, initial attempts were ungrammatical, but the early versions provided a

TABLE 16.1. Translation Excerpts for Character and Thematic Units

	Thematic emphasis: Cycle of violence	Character emphasis: Heroic characters
Textual concept	Individuals and social groups often participate in cycles of violence, patterns of repeated and dangerous acts associated with violence, retribution, and revenge. The violent behavior is often learned as a child and then repeated as an adult or throughout generations, therefore creating a cycle.	A hero or heroine is a character who, in the face of danger and adversity, displays courage and the ability to sacrifice for some greater good. To face the danger, the heroic character often leaves home, acquires companions, and is confronted by his or her death. While the danger is not always defeated or vanquished, the character and his or her companions are changed in a lasting way.
Brothers in Arms	Martin lives in a violent community. After watching his brother get killed by gangbangers, he seeks revenge and gets caught up in many forms of violence.	Martin is a flawed hero. He leaves his home, acquires a new family (his gang) and pseudomentor, and faces death on multiple occasions. While he has many flaws, Martin acts heroically by leaving the gang and returning home.
Chapter 1	"Whoever shot him tore a hole through my heart too, a black hole that, instead of blood, gushed only a desire for revenge" (pp. 11–12).	"I didn't have time to think. I just grabbed him and turned so that my body covered his like a shield" (p. 9).
Chapter 2	"Even if I couldn't save him, I could take out the one who took him. That's just the way it goes on the street. I'd heard about it all my life, and now I was becoming it. A gangbanger" (p. 15).	"He looked nervous and had a slight waver in his voice. 'You better watch where you're walking or you could get hurt, homes'" (p. 24).
Chapter 3	"When people start treating you like a criminal, you start believing you are one" (p. 36).	"'Just chill for a while, homes. You started losing it the other night. I heard you laughing in your sleep. That's messed up,' Frankie said" (p. 32).

good basis for later discussion. The ungrammaticality of students' statements is an indication that students are actively "translanguaging," or making use of their full linguistic repertoire to more fully comprehend text (Canagarajah, 2013). While showing complex bilingual reasoning, these translations also demonstrate (to a bilingual teacher) that students interpreted "fire" literally rather than metaphorically. Most important, however, is the marked rise in engagement and in discussion of language that accompanied the student debate about the "fire in her eyes."

STUDENTS TRANSLATE ORALLY

When invited to translate passages from English into Spanish orally, students universally did so quickly and without instruction. During oral translations, students were deeply engaged and sometimes openly proud of their linguistic skills. Typically, after one student offered up a verbal translation, others would suggest different translations or refinements to specific words, syntax, or phrases. Importantly, especially for monolingual teachers, students did not require instruction about how to translate. As any teacher would imagine, student participation was dependent on multiple factors, especially patterns of friendship and perceived translation ability. Even so, applied linguists have identified some translation strategies, such as description wherein the translator might describe something for which that person lacks an exact equivalent in his or her other language. For example, the word *octopus* could be described as an animal that has eight legs (Atkinson, 1987).

When students translated sentences, they tended to create translations that went word by word (gloss translations). For example, in the novel, Martin joins a gang that initiates members by "jumping" or "beating" them in, with several gang members attacking the prospect simultaneously. As an important rite of passage, Martin knows that he must fight well and fearlessly. With the support of a bilingual teacher, the following example illustrates a conversation about Martin's experience after getting "jumped in":

INSTRUCTOR: Could you tell me how you would say this in Spanish, the sentence, "The pain I felt when Huero died was worse than anything this crew could dish out." How would you say that in Spanish?

VERONICA: *El dolor* [the pain].

SONIA: *El dolor que yo siento* [the pain that I feel].

INÉS: *Por dentro* [inside].

SONIA: *Por dentro, no es igual a cuando se murió Huero* [Inside, is not the same as when Huero died].

INSTRUCTOR: So you're saying, "*El dolor que yo siento . . .*" [The pain that I feel].

SONIA: *Por dentro, no es igual* [Inside is not the same].

INSTRUCTOR: *No es igual, ¿a qué?* [Not the same as what?].

SONIA: *Cuando se murió Huero* [When Huero died].

INSTRUCTOR: OK, OK. So, Marty's feeling pain inside from Huero dying, but where is the other pain coming from?

JULIA: The punches.

INSTRUCTOR: The punches, right? So which pain does he think is worse?

SONIA AND JULIA: Huero.

This kind of exchange was typical for our middle school students, whose verbal translations were highly collaborative endeavors. In this particular translation, in which students demonstrate the connection between Martin's physical and emotional pain, a bilingual teacher can also assess students' comprehension and prompt them to clarify their thinking. We view these gloss translations as a solid and perhaps necessary foundation toward more dynamic translations that incorporate the pragmatic linguistic background knowledge of bilingual students.

During this phase, the role of a monolingual teacher is somewhat different but nevertheless important. Although the monolingual teacher may not be able to understand what students are saying, he or she may be able to hear and detect different words and support student discussion of those differences before selecting a final translation. For example, a monolingual teacher might hear one student translate *friend* as *amigo* and another student translate *friend* as *compadre*. In addition, the monolingual teacher can also support participation by asking a variety of questions: "Do you have a different translation? Is there any other way that we might translate this?" While many monolingual teachers might fear that students are discussing nonacademic topics, we did not find this to be case. Students were excited to showcase their translation abilities, especially because it was something that the monolingual teacher could not do.

WRITING IT DOWN

After students translated the text orally, we invited them to write their translations on paper. Initially, we intended to have students write down *all* of their translations. However, from the very beginning, it became clear that the writing process for translating would take a long time. This is perhaps not surprising, because students have more experience translating orally in their families and communities. As such, teachers need to be strategic about when they ask students to write and when they ask students to translate orally.

Although we were concerned that students might not be able to write in their heritage language, someone has always been able to write, even in groups as small as three students. Interestingly, even students who underestimated their abilities in Spanish and claimed that they could not do it were actually able to write quite competently when the need arose (i.e., the person who normally wrote was absent). Also, with a bit of prompting, reflection, and support from instructor and peers, students often surprised themselves by discovering that writing in Spanish has many similarities with writing in English. In other words, they could transfer what they knew about writing in English to writing in Spanish, and vice versa. We see such a result as one of the beneficial side effects of the TRANSLATE instructional approach.

The following example illustrates several observations about the role of written translations. In this situation, four girls were placed in pairs, and each pair was given a different segment to translate. We chose text segments that portrayed Marty's transformation as he participated in the cycle of violence: "It was like I was dead inside, like my heart had turned gray and rotten once Huero passed away" (Langan & Alirez, 2004, p. 19). In the following conversation, the girls collaborate as they dissect this rich text into a meaningful translation:

>CAMELIA: How do you say *turn* in Spanish?
>
>FLOR: *Me voltié?* [I turned?] Turned, like turned.
>
>CAMELIA: Turned, like my heart had turned gray.
>
>FLOR: *Oh! Y mi corazón se volteó* [Oh! And my heart turned].
>
>CAMELIA: No, that doesn't make sense.
>
>FLOR: That doesn't make sense. *Cambió* [It changed].
>
>CAMELIA: *Volvió a gris* [It turned gray].
>
>INSTRUCTOR: *Cambió?* [It changed?]
>
>FLOR: *Y se volvió* [And it turned].
>
>INSTRUCTOR: *Se volvió?* [It turned?]

CAMELIA: *Como si estuviera cambiado* [As if it had changed].

SERENA: What is this word?

FLOR: *Levanté* [I got up].

INSTRUCTOR: *Levanté* [I got up].

SERENA: OK. What'd you say?

CAMELIA: *Mi corazón cambió color gris* [My heart changed to gray].

INSTRUCTOR: *Poniendo gris?* [Turning gray?]

CAMELIA: *Mi corazón* [My heart].

INSTRUCTOR: So when you picture his heart turning gray, what's really happening? Is his heart really turning gray?

FLOR: It makes sense if I write it like this.

CAMELIA: *Que su corazón se está volviendo* [That his heart is turning]. What's the right word?

INSTRUCTOR: What's the author trying to say? His heart's turning gray, he's becoming . . .

SERENA: Sad.

INSTRUCTOR: Sad. So instead of saying gray, maybe gloomy. His heart becomes gloomy, his heart's becoming sad. You can choose different words if that makes more sense.

CAMELIA: Like the gray . . .

YESENIA: Gray sky.

This conversation requires an intimate understanding of the text, as well as a good understanding of both languages. Here, the girls are experimenting with three Spanish words to represent the word *turned* as it relates to a metaphorical heart turning gray. They then try various grammatical and syntactical forms to best translate the meaning in the original segment, checking their work by asking if it makes sense. Although the girls have been paired, and each pair has a different segment to translate, they cannot resist involving everyone at the table in constructing their translation. This is important, because it suggests the importance of social interactions while translating in eliciting local knowledge for these students.

The functional role of the instructor is important. Whereas a monolingual instructor can invite students to compare and contrast words that are clearly different in their written form, a bilingual instructor can scaffold their entire translation. As the girls wrestle with choosing the best words, the instructor directs them to think about the text's metaphorical meaning. This is accomplished by asking students to explain their translation choices in terms of the larger text (i.e., "How do the words you choose reflect the personality of the character? How does that phrase relate to this theme from the book?"). The instructor supports students in creating dynamic translations that are not only grammatically correct but also reflect the character's tone and voice. This includes helping the girls recognize the metaphorical and connotative meanings of the original text. The final product required that the participants to negotiate and play with different words and sentence constructions. Following this conversation, students wrote the translation shown in Figure 16.1.

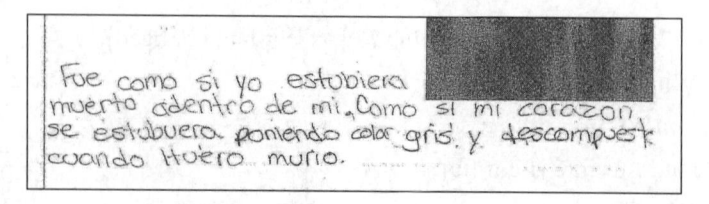

> Fue como si yo estubiera muerto adentro de mi. Como si mi corazon se estubuera poniendo color gris y descompuesto cuando Huero murio.

FIGURE 16.1. Student-produced translation.

EVALUATING TRANSLATIONS

One of the essential elements of collaborative translation is having students informally evaluate their translations. Writing translations down is not the end goal, from an interpretive perspective; it is really an opportunity for rich dialogue about textual concepts such as word meaning and choice, syntax, and comprehension. During this time, students reread their translations or the translations of others and answer a simple question: Does this make sense? Initially, making sense referred to choosing words that conform to conventional syntax and grammar. As shown below, the written artifact can and should become a touchstone for conversations about textual concepts and themes:

> INSTRUCTOR: So what are these two translations telling us about the story and telling us about what's going on with Marty?
>
> FLOR: He was cold. He didn't care about anybody. He just wanted to kill the person that killed his brother. He wanted to feel the pain.
>
> . . .
>
> CAMELIA: He's just sad. *Estoy apagada* [I am worn out].
>
> FLOR: The person feels.
>
> YESENIA: *Deprimido* [Depressed].
>
> . . .
>
> INSTRUCTOR: He says he's dead inside.
>
> YESENIA: *Está muerto* [He is dead].
>
> FLOR: Yeah.
>
> INSTRUCTOR: What's that called when we say he's dead inside?
>
> YESENIA: *Está muerto* [He is dead] . . . *Dentro de él* [Inside of him].
>
> CAMELIA: Hay una enfermedad de eso que [There is an illness that] . . . you can't move . . .
>
> YESENIA: Paralyzed. I mean, I know that word.
>
> . . .
>
> FLOR: *Como estaba en coma no se podia mover* [Like, he was in a coma, he couldn't move].
>
> YESENIA: Paralyzed. He's paralyzed.
>
> INSTRUCTOR: Paralyzed.

FLOR: Because he didn't want to move on, he wanted to stay there.

INSTRUCTOR: Is he really paralyzed?

FLOR: No.

INSTRUCTOR: What is paralyzed?

YESENIA: When you can't move at all.

CAMELIA: When you just . . .

INSTRUCTOR: But how is he paralyzed?

FLOR: Cause he doesn't want to move on from the person who killed his brother. He wants to. . . . He's stuck in there.

INSTRUCTOR: So is his body paralyzed or what is paralyzed?

STUDENTS: His mind!

INSTRUCTOR: His mind is paralyzed. OK.

FLOR: And his heart.

Here, the translation served as a springboard for a thoughtful discussion about Marty's emotional and psychological state. Students offer up the words *depression, coma,* and *paralysis* to describe Marty's interior life. From a pedagogical perspective, the wonderful thing about this conversation is that students were deeply involved in understanding Marty's character—a depressed teenager paralyzed by the death of his brother, someone dying inside because of all the violence. Their individual translations reached and stretched toward this larger understanding. Such intense reading and scrutiny of language is demanding work for the students, and in the discussion Camelia declares that she is *apagada* (worn out)! Despite its cognitive demand, students' engagement was very high when they discussed their writing.

During this phase, a monolingual teacher can support students to evaluate their translations by carefully examining written translations produced by different groups or pairs. As both a creative and an analytical task, students almost never construct the same written translation. By asking students to explain and justify the differences between these translations, a host of thought-provoking conversations will ensue. Typically, student conversations focus on the meaning of different words, but these discussions can support students' understanding of wider textual themes (as shown in the previous examples).

BECAUSE IT SOUNDS MORE LIKE A GANGBANGER

As students became more experienced at evaluating translations, *making sense* came to include creating translations that fit the broader text. Moving beyond syntactically and grammatically correct language, students evaluated the pragmatics of their translations. Working with the students, we developed an important translation criterion: Would this character say that? At one point, students were translating the following text: "Just chill for a while, homes. You started losing it the other night" (Langan & Alirez, p. 32). When translating the idiomatic expression "losing it," students debated three different options:

no estabas controlado anoche (you were not in control last night), *estabas perdiendo aquella noche* (you were losing that night), and *tú estabas volviendo loco* (you were turning crazy). After a lengthy discussion, the following conversation occurs:

> INSTRUCTOR: You think Frankie would say *estabas perdiendo aquella noche* [you were losing that night]. Can you tell me why?
>
> INÉS: Nope.
>
> INSTRUCTOR: No? There isn't a right or wrong answer here, it's really your guys' opinions. Thinking about what you know about Frankie, what do you think he would say?
>
> INÉS: *Tú estabas volviendo loco* [You were turning crazy], the third one.
>
> INSTRUCTOR: *Tú estabas volviendo loco.* Can you tell me why?
>
> INÉS: Cause he's like a gangbanger and like gangbangers don't say this.
>
> INSTRUCTOR: They don't say *estabas perdiendo aquella noche*?
>
> JULIA: I like the third one.
>
> INSTRUCTOR: You like the third one, too?
>
> SONIA: Yeah, me too.
>
> INSTRUCTOR: Because it sounds more like a gangbanger?
>
> SONIA: Yeah.
>
> INSTRUCTOR: OK, is there any change that we should make to this to make it sound even more like a gangbanger?
>
> SONIA: *Tú estabas volviendo loco,* I don't change.
>
> INÉS: *Te estabas, tú te estabas.*
>
> INSTRUCTOR: *Tú te estabas.* OK, that makes it more reflexive. Anything else? OK, so I think that this is really helpful to me and I think doing this may help us understand a little bit more about who Frankie is, and help us understand the story.

Although students are still focused on specific words, their framework for evaluating the translation is somewhat different. When Inés says, "He's like a gangbanger and gangbangers don't say this," she demonstrates that she has appropriated the character-based pragmatics criterion (Would this character say that?). Although the students do not use the precise literary terms or academic language, they are beginning to understand characterization, that novels portray characters in particular ways by using suitable language, diction, and dialogue.

DISCUSSION

In language arts classrooms, we sought to reimagine how teachers could support the engagement and learning of bilingual students in culturally responsive ways. While bilingualism and biliteracy are viewed as valuable goals, there is little practical guidance about how to use heritage languages in support of conceptual understanding, particularly in settings with monolingual teachers. Both monolingual and bilingual teachers can use collaborative translation to support student comprehension of the text, as well as to further students' linguistic development. We have used the collaborative translation activity. Along with promoting students' understanding of textual concepts, collaborative translation is one way that teachers might differentiate for bilingual students in linguistically diverse settings. While most forms of differentiation are based on complexity and interest, collaborative translation is based on students' heritage language.

With these goals and challenges in mind, we have tried to demonstrate that collaborative translation can help students to understand and reason about language arts concepts. We have discussed how to select text excerpts for translation, demonstrated that students can produce oral translations quickly, and have shown that discussions after translations (both written and verbal) are linguistically and conceptually rich. Like most language arts instructors, we believe deeply in inviting students to participate in tasks and activities that foster high engagement and high-quality dialogue. While students naturally focus on issues of grammar and syntax, teachers can support students to connect these discussions to textual themes and concepts.

While retaining a clear focus on language arts concepts, collaborative translation draws on the local knowledge that bilingual students bring to schools and can actively and positively develop greater bilingualism and biliteracy, which are valuable cultural and marketplace skills. Likewise, we believe that teenage bilingual and emergent bilingual students should know that many people make careers out of interpreting and translating between languages. They do this in schools, hospitals, and for international businesses. Along with supporting students to understand key textual concepts, collaborative translation may open students' eyes to an important life opportunity.

With a little preparation, translation can be integrated into many common language arts instructional strategies. While teachers regularly use text-based questions to support students' comprehension and interpretation of narrative texts, bilingual students might also translate important textual excerpts. Another common instructional practice is to organize small reading groups or literature circles. If there are three or four students with the same heritage language in a classroom, these students might construct a translated version of an important narrative scene. These dramatic reenactments might be written, performed, and/or video-recorded and then played back to the class. These creative productions would showcase bilingual students' linguistic strengths and celebrate multiple ways that language can be both functional and artful.

REFERENCES

Adesope, O. O., Lavin, T., Thompson, T., & Ungerleider, C. (2010). A systematic review and meta-analysis of the cognitive correlates of bilingualism. *Review of Educational Research*, 80(2), 207–245.

Alvermann, D., Young, J. P., Weaver, D., Hinchman, K., Moore, D., Phelps, S., et al. (1996). Middle and high school students' perceptions of how they experience text-based discussions: A multicase study. *Reading Research Quarterly*, 31(3), 244–267.

Atkinson, D. (1987). The mother tongue in the classroom: A neglected resource? *ELT Journal*, 41(4), 241–247.

August, D., & Hakuta, K. (1997). *Improving schooling for language-minority children*. Washington, DC: National Academy Press.

August, D., & Shanahan, T. (Eds.). (2006). *Developing literacy in second-language learners:*

Report of the National Literacy Panel on language-minority children and youth. Mahwah, NJ: Erlbaum.

Calderón, M., Hertz-Lazarowitz, R., Ivory, G., & Slavin, R. E. (1997). *Effects of bilingual cooperative integrated reading and composition on students transitioning from Spanish to English reading.* Baltimore: Center for Research on the Education of Students Placed at Risk (CRESPAR) at Johns Hopkins University.

Canagarajah, S. (2013). *Translingual practice.* New York: Routledge.

Cheung, A., & Slavin, R. (2005). Effective reading programs for English language learners and other language-minority students. *Bilingual Research Journal, 29*(2), 241–267.

Cohen, E. G. (1994). Restructuring the classroom: Conditions for productive small groups. *Review of Educational Research, 64*(1), 1–35.

Cole, M. W. (2014). Speaking to read: Meta-analysis of peer-mediated learning for English language learners. *Journal of Literacy Research, 46*(3), 358–382.

Cummins, J. (2000). *Language, power, and pedagogy.* Clevedon, UK: Multilingual Matters.

Dunston, P. J. (2002). Instructional components for promoting thoughtful literacy learning. In C. C. Block, L. B. Gambrell, & M. Pressley (Eds.), *Improving comprehension instruction: Rethinking research, theory, and classroom practice* (pp. 135–151). San Francisco: Jossey-Bass.

Elbaum, B. E., Schumm, J. S., & Vaughn, S. (1997). Urban middle-elementary students' perceptions of grouping formats for reading instruction. *Elementary School Journal, 97*(5), 475–500.

Evans, K. (2002). Fifth-grade students' perceptions of how they experience literature discussion groups. *Reading Research Quarterly, 37*(1), 46–69.

Evans, K. S., Alvermann, D., & Anders, P. L. (1998). Literature discussion groups: An examination of gender roles. *Reading Research and Instruction, 37*(2), 107–122.

Fountas, I. C., & Pinnell, G. S. (1996). *Guided reading: Good first teaching for all children.* Portsmouth, NH: Heinemann.

García, O., & Wei, L. (2014). *Translanguaging: Language, bilingualism and education.* New York: Palgrave Macmillan.

Gass, S., Mackey, A., & Ross-Feldman, L. (2005). Task-based interactions in classroom and laboratory settings. *Language Learning, 55*(4), 575–611.

Genesee, F., Lindholm-Leary, K., Saunders, W., & Christian, D. (2005). English language learners in U.S. schools: An overview of research findings. *Journal of Education for Students Placed at Risk, 10*(4), 363–386.

Gersten, R., & Baker, S. (2000). What we know about effective instructional practices for English language learners. *Exceptional Children, 66*(4), 454–470.

Gersten, R. M., & Jiménez, R. T. (1998). *Promoting learning for culturally and linguistically diverse students.* Belmont, CA: Wadsworth.

Goatley, V. J., Brock, C. H., & Raphael, T. E. (1995). Diverse learners participating in regular education "Book Clubs." *Reading Research Quarterly, 30*(3), 352–380.

Jiménez, R. T. (1997). The strategic reading abilities and potential of five low-literacy Latina/o readers in middle school. *Reading Research Quarterly, 32*(3), 224–243.

Jiménez, R. T., David, S., Fagan, K., Risko, V. Pacheco, M., Pray, L., et al. (2015). Using translation to drive conceptual development for students becoming literate in English as an additional language. *Research in the Teaching of English, 49*(3), 248–271.

Keyes, C. S., Puzio, K., & Jiménez, R. T. (2014). Collaborative translations: Designing bilingual instructional tools. *Journal of Education, 194*(2), 17–24.

Klinger, J. K., Vaughn, S., & Schumm, J. S. (1988). Collaborative strategic reading during social studies in heterogeneous fourth-grade classrooms. *Elementary School Journal, 99*(1), 3–22.

Langan, P., & Alirez, B. (2004). *Brothers in arms.* West Berlin, NJ: Townsend Press.

Lightbown, P. M. (2000). Classroom SLA research and second language teaching. *Applied Linguistics, 21*(4), 431–462.

Moll, L. C., Amanti, C., Neff, D., & Gonzalez, N. (1992). Funds of knowledge for teaching: Using a qualitative approach to connect homes and classrooms. *Theory Into Practice, 31*(2), 132–141.

National Governors Association Center for Best Practices & Council of Chief State School Officers (NGA & CCSSO). (2010). *Common Core State Standards for English language arts and literacy in history/social studies, science, and technical subjects.* Washington, DC: Authors.

Nida, E. (2004). Principles of correspondence. In L. Venuti (Ed.), *The translation studies reader* (2nd ed., pp. 126–140). New York: Routledge.

Orellana, M. F., & Reynolds, J. F. (2008). Cultural modeling: Leveraging bilingual skills for school paraphrasing tasks. *Reading Research Quarterly, 43*(1), 48–65.

Orellana, M. F., Reynolds, J., Dorner, L., & Mesa, M. (2003). In other words: Translating or "para-phrasing" as a family literacy practice in immigrant households. *Reading Research Quarterly, 38*, 12–34.

Oxford, R. L. (1997). Cooperative learning, collaborative learning, and interaction: Three communicative strands in the language classroom. *Modern Language Journal, 81*(4), 443–456.

Poole, D. (2008). Interactional differentiation in the mixed-ability group: A situated view of two struggling readers. *Reading Research Quarterly, 43*(3), 228–250.

Puzio, K., & Colby, G. T. (2013). Cooperative learning and literacy: A meta-analytic review. *Journal of Research on Educational Effectiveness, 6*(4), 339–360.

Roessingh, H. (2004). Effective high school ESL Programs: A synthesis and meta-analysis. *Canadian Modern Language Review, 60*(5), 611–636.

Ruiz, R. (1984). Orientations in language planning. *National Association for Bilingual Education, 8*(2), 15–34.

Swain, M., Brooks, L., & Tocalli-Beller, A. (2002). Peer-peer dialogue as a means of second language learning. *Annual Review of Applied Linguistics, 22*, 171–185.

Williams, J. D., & Snipper, G. C. (1990). *Literacy and bilingualism.* New York: Longman.

CHAPTER 17

Acquiring Processes for Responding to and Creating Multimodal Digital Productions

RICHARD BEACH, JILL CASTEK, and JOHN SCOTT

The use of digital media production tools for creating multimodal digital texts in the classroom has led to an increased interest in what adolescents learn through their participation in creating these texts (Bazalgette & Buckingham, 2013; Dezuanni, 2014). We define *multimodal digital texts* as those that combine different images, video, sound effects, music, and language to engage their audiences. While print texts, as evident in medieval manuscripts, have always been multimodal, the relative ease in using digital media production tools such as Glogster (a poster-making tool), Animoto (an animation tool), and iMovie (a video-making and editing tool) have enhanced the degree to which students can collaboratively create multimodal texts (Leander & Boldt, 2013).

In this chapter, we describe the sense-making processes associated with (1) responding to multimodal texts, (2) creating multimodal texts, and (3) assessing and fostering self-reflection of students' multimodal productions, and offer implications for instruction in each area.

RESPONDING TO MULTIMODAL DIGITAL TEXTS

Multimodal digital texts combine print with images, video, and audio/music to provide students with distinctive reading experiences. For example, the WordPlay Shakespeare iBooks, *Macbeth, Romeo and Juliet,* and *A Midsummer Night's Dream* include videos of performances juxtaposed next to the text. These videos can be stopped, rewound, or fast-forwarded as the reader desires. The text also incorporates modern translations and synopses of each scene and includes pop-up descriptions of characters. Readers can highlight, annotate, and share responses, and use search functions to locate specific language or ideas. These features combine with the text to convey multiple meanings and encourage the reader to reject a single interpretation (Coles & Hall, 2001). Multimodal content affects interpretive practices and creates new resources (and demands) on meaning making (Jewitt, 2002; Luke, 2003; Zammit, 2007). Thus, the inclusion of multimodal content within digital texts redefines reader, author, and text relations, and opens up new potentials for meaning making.

This research suggests that analysis of multimodal texts involves more than just analysis of texts themselves. Serafini (2015) conceptualizes multimodal texts as not only "visual objects" but also "multimodal events" and "sociocultural artifacts," involving recontextualizing of texts as

- *visual objects* by focusing on identifying use of certain visual elements such as use of images; creating inventories related to uses of borders, text boxes, color palette, horizontal or vertical design; and use of typography.
- *multimodal events* by focusing on elements of visual grammar related to perspectives, composition, use of frames, motifs, method of representation, associations, audience positioning, etc.
- *sociocultural artifacts* by applying analytical and ideological analyses to critically examine producers' intentions and audience response, analyze portrayals of gender, race, and power, and stereotypical representations. (p. 414)

Multimodal Tools Mediating Social Interactions

Multimodal elements offer students different points of entry into a text and alternative possible paths through it. Castek, Beach, Cotanch, and Scott (2014) studied sixth graders' use of Diigo (a collaborative digital annotation tool used with online texts). As students read, they added their own ideas and responses on expandable sticky notes. Particularly appealing to the sixth graders was that when they posted their yellow sticky note icons on the text, other students would then become intrigued with the idea of prying open the note to reveal their peers' annotations—an example of a sensory, multimodal appeal. The students' responses to and questions about the text served to make a single digital text both multiple and multimodal.

Students both raised questions and posted answers in their annotations. When they read each other's ideas, they built on each other's questions with their own annotations and connections. By reading each other's annotations, students were exposed to viewpoints that differed from their own, resulting in their appropriation of new ways to interpret ideas. Students used annotations for "integrating/connecting" and "inferring," and in the process applied their own personal experience and prior knowledge to the issue about which they were reading. As they engaged in the annotation and response practice using Diigo sticky notes, they became invested in the dialogue and better understood the content of the article.

As annotations were added, students collaboratively built on each other's ideas. The fact that students' sticky note annotations targeted specific sentences in the text indicated that students were able "determine important ideas," as well as "infer," "integrate," or "evaluate" specific information found in the text. Thus, the use of Diigo annotations produced a trail of thinking that students could readily share with others, including their teacher.

Digital devices offer new opportunities to navigate online texts. Simpson, Walsh, and Rowsell (2013) demonstrated that the affordances of touch allow for multimodal, multidirectional reading paths across and between texts. By tracking students' pathways through texts and interactions through touch, the researchers showed that it is possible to see navigation as evidence of the relationship between material and cognitive processes, which fosters meta-textual awareness. The effect of the reader making links to background experience and knowledge of other texts through intertexual referencing considers the logical connections students chose to make as they forged their digital reading paths. Multimodalities tap into the types of literacies that students use on a daily basis, often outside of the classroom, and are increasingly multisensory as devices that employ touch, such as smartphones, tablets, and other mobile devices, become the norm.

The Importance of Multimodal Literacies

Without the ability to employ multimodal literacies, students may have difficulty understanding and interpreting certain multimodal texts (Kress & Jewitt, 2003; Kress & van Leeuwen, 2001). An analysis of 16- to 9-year-old British students' responses to a 2006 political cartoon entitled "High Noon" portrayed George W. Bush as a cowboy walking down a western town street with a large vulture flying over his head labeled "Iraq." El Refaie and Horschelmann (2010) found that students had difficulty applying the multimodal literacies involved in linking the referents in the cartoon to the lived world. They lacked the interpretative skills and knowledge of the political context of the 2006 election, in which Democrats took over Congress due to critiques of the Iraq War. Thus, inferring a narrative about the relationship between Bush and the vulture, and making intertextual references to the meaning of the images, was absent. Teaching students the multimodal literacies of interpretation becomes vitally important in contexts such as these.

New technologies offer the possibility to build new relationships between readers and writers in a manner that challenges and breaks down some of the traditional distinctions that are drawn between consumers of information and producers of information. Online fanfiction forums, for example, enable readers to respond to texts in a variety of ways. Readers of these texts move between various identity categories, such as writer, reviewer, or editor of other fans' stories fluidly. As they read these texts, they critique and appreciate them. In the process, they become writing mentors involved in coaching others by posting comments, drawing pictures, adding content, and offering suggestions. Playing multiple roles as a reader, a guide, and/or a critic opens up new spaces reflecting on audience and process. This is important for the development of higher-order thinking.

Multimodal features open up new opportunities for response and appear to have several benefits. First, crafting responses can be a collaborative activity that draws on the strengths and resources that different students bring to the process. Although one individual may be stronger in critical thinking skills, another may excel in organizing ideas or adding detail, while still another may be more skilled in creative expression. By working together, students benefit from shared expertise as they engage in response activities (Castek & Cotanch, 2013).

Digital tools open up new possibilities for response. For example, using a screencasting app such as ShowMe or VoiceThread, students can view the same image or video clip to share ideas and react to one another (Beach & O'Brien, 2014). These apps include the ability to draw and audio-record on top of a digital image or video; viewers can then add their own audio, drawings, or written comments in response. These back-and-forth interactions spark additional reflections and deepen responses. Using video, graphics, audio broadcasts, drawings, images, and a host of other technological and multimodal resources may help students realize that meaning can be found and made in multiple places and through multiple modes.

CREATING MULTIMODAL DIGITAL TEXTS

As students learn to respond to multimodal digital texts, they are also creating multimodal digital texts. Students' know-how and experience, acquired from responding to multimodal texts, can then transfer to producing multimodal texts requiring students' knowledge of specific aesthetic and design aspects of a certain form or genre. In a unit on understanding and creating graphic novels, students first studied the features of the graphic novel, *Around the World* (Phelan, 2011), in terms of the use of panels, gutters, speech bubbles, and visual effects. The students then transferred their understanding of visual narrative development in the Phelan novel to their own productions (Napoli & Sychterz, 2015). For example, one student employed, as did Phelan, images of facial expressions to portray certain emotions, while another student employed box frames to convey the passage of time.

The ubiquitous use of mobile devices for creating images and videos combined with the shaping of content using apps such as Snapchat or Vine for multimodal self-expression makes this possible. As a result, students are using multimodal production as unfolding acts of becoming. Leander and Rowe (2006) suggest that in such production, "performance has no organizing center, frame, single meaning, or static pivot, but rather evolves and splinters in multiple directions, as do the identities of performers participating within it" (p. 435).

The portability of digital devices means that teachers or students have more opportunities to create content flexibly, in different contexts, within and outside of school. For example, teachers created "learning trails" for their students by taking photos tied to global positioning system (GPS) locations on virtual field trips (Li, Guo, Lee, & Negara, 2013). Sung and Mayer (2013) suggested that using an iPad to record data about solar cells in a school courtyard versus using a desktop computer in a science lab, led to higher levels of student engagement, perhaps because of the iPad's portability.

Uses of virtual reality tools such as Google Street View allows students to create alternative, multimodal, virtual representations of the material world (Burnett, Merchant, Pahl, & Rowsell, 2014), so that

> "Street View," therefore, can be seen as a figured world of practice which does not simply represent a material world, but captures it in a particular way. This perspective enables us to see texts as traces of social practice. They are objects that carry different identities sedimented (Rowsell & Pahl, 2007) within them: of their creators and revisers and of those who interact within and around them. Each brings their own personal meanings so that prior and contemporaneous material worlds live on in texts. (p. 96)

These multimodal virtual representations also bring to mind embodied experiences and evoke subjective associations (Burnett et al., 2014).

Digital devices' portability and ease of use have also enhanced students' ability to work collaboratively to produce multimodal texts and have led researchers to focus on identifying the learning processes involved in adolescents' collaborative processes such as

> scripting, casting, performance, set and costume design, musical composition, sound design, special effects, and the orchestration of all these and more into a single timeline [within] generic, institutional, technical, economic and historical dimensions of these choices. (Bazalgette & Buckingham, 2013, p. 98)

Responding to and Creating Multimodal Texts as Social and Rhetorical Events

Diana Masny (2009) posits that responding to multimodal texts involves making sense of a text as an event involving bodies, language, images, space, time, and experiences leading to the disruption of status quo perspectives, constituting new ways of becoming. In responding to and creating multimodal texts, students are engaged in new sense-making ways of *becoming other* through the experience of different, alternative perspectives for perceiving the world (Masny & Waterhouse, 2011). By engaging in multimodal literacies, adolescents experience becoming

> speakers, writers, artists, digital avatars: communities. Literacies are actualized according to a particular context in time and space in which they operate. Given the nomadic tendencies of literacies; they are not wed to *a* context, but are taken up in unpredictable ways across various contexts. Reading is both intensive (disruptive) and immanent. Literacies involve constant movement in the process of becoming Other. . . . In short, literacies are about reading, reading the world, and self as texts. (p. 292)

For adolescents, part of becoming "other" involves critiquing how they and other adolescents construct their identities through adopting popular culture media representations. This involves, for example, determining ways to resist how they are often portrayed in deficit, problematic ways as troubled or deviant. Adolescents may resist and disrupt these representations and explore alternative ways of becoming by selecting, reorganizing, and remixing images of these problematic representations through "modularity" to create new texts that critique the meanings associated with the original texts (Domingo, 2014). In the process, they are therefore recontextualizing these meanings (Van Leeuwen, 2008). One high school student noted how her creation of a documentary about her life experiences served to defy stereotypical assumptions about African American daughters of single mothers:

> I think if anything this documentary kind of showed me what I am, what I've become, because statistically, I'm not supposed to be the way I am, because you know people say that without a father figure in your life you are supposed to crave attention from boys. I mean that's what I hear and what I SEE on TV. . . . So I guess this doc has shown me who I am, because I am not like that. That's not something I was, I am, or am ever going to be. (Doerr-Stevens, 2015, p. 29)

In using her documentary to recontextualize and critique deficit media representation images of single-parent African American families, this student is portraying her identity as someone who was not adversely influenced by being the daughter of a single parent.

Engaging in multimodal production also entails creating a rhetorical event leading to consideration of potential audience uptake. This requires students to collaboratively select multimodal content that will appeal to their audiences. When seventh-grade students created public service announcements about issues of preservation facing the Chesapeake Bay (for posting on a class YouTube channel), they worked collaboratively in groups consisting of a director, producer, writers, and researcher to determine how to effectively employ certain rhetorical "hooks" to engage their audiences. They needed to determine how to communicate their point to their audience in a relatively short time given that their videos were 30 seconds or less (Griffith, 2015).

To recontextualize multimodal texts relative to achieving positive audience uptake, adolescents need a meta-language for determining how re-creating texts serves to achieve their rhetorical purposes (Unsworth, 2011). For example, the picture book *Flotsam* (Wiesner, 2006) is about a boy who finds a camera on the shore and portrays a history of underwater life (Unsworth, 2011). The book includes a series of zoom-shot images of the boy using a magnifying glass and microscope to determine the content of pictures from the camera. To create a book trailer promoting the book (see *http://tinyw.in/t72p*), students employed meta-language to reflect on how visual meanings through use of zoom shots in their video were similar and different. This approach reflected use of "transmedia navigation" across the use of different media (Jenkins, 2006). Similarly, eighth graders used Adobe Premiere editing software to create their own version of a scene in which Romeo is being chased across Verona to reach the dead Juliet, using clips from the *Romeo and Juliet* film by Luhrman (1996; Burn & Durran, 2006). In reflecting on their video production, students employed meta-language referring to the use of camera angles and types of shots to portray conflicts between characters (Unsworth, 2011).

Digital Storytelling, Identity, and Agency

The proliferation of digital technologies across everyday spaces affords not only new tools and capacities for meaning making but also new, dynamic contexts for sharing, consuming, and remixing digital artifacts as events. One key feature of multimodal artifacts has to do with the development of time (Bazalgette & Buckingham, 2013) that is evident, for example, in the use of editing to pare down video material given a focus on "duration as a dimension" (Dover, 2014). For instance, digital storytelling created through use of iMovie, Adobe Premiere, or VoiceThread has emerged as one such form of time-based media that often consists of a slideshow of images or short video clips, either originally created by the student or downloaded from Internet content hubs such as Google or photography repositories such as Flickr. This digital content is then arranged in a time line and visually meshed together through editing software transition effects such as "dissolve" or "wipe." The use of "old film" digital effects and animations and use of editing employing film scratches and static serves to create a nostalgic, historical visual effect. This visual layer is then edited to synch with an audio track, which might consist of a recording by the student of an original story, a popular song or original song composed in a music program such as Audacity or Garageband, or a voice recording layered on top of an instrumental track. The final product, represented as a video and closely resembling cinematic techniques such as montage, effectively blends together for the audience these visual and audio layers into a coherent viewing experience whose meaning is more than just the summation of its individual media components.

Because digital story production has often focused thematically on personal narrative and community representation, researchers have examined how students braid together modes and semiotic resources for expressing or performing cultural and social identities. This creative mobilization of diverse resources for telling one's story becomes a site for agentive action in the world, particularly for students and young artists from historically marginalized communities whose own voice and actions in the world are often silenced (Hull & Katz, 2006). By empowering students to author their own unique story using image, sound, voice, gesture, and editing techniques, digital video production motivates critical and reflexive identity work. Using a range of digital literacies allows adolescents to publicly demonstrate knowledge of popular culture and portray creative aspects of their identities, for example, by creating video remixes of songs or literary texts (Vasudevan, Schultz, & Bateman, 2010).

In collaboratively recontextualizing media representations, adolescents are also challenging familiar, hegemonic meanings associated with their everyday practices and spaces. For example, a group of students at Jefferson High School in Bloomington, Minnesota, created a video portraying how a member of a peer group is transported into a music video world within his school (Beach & Swiss, 2010). The video features his peers representing popular music video groups dancing in the school hallways. The student encounters a number of different groups, for example, the Beastie Boys, as he wanders in a confused daze through the school. Given his curiosity as to why he experienced this transformation of his school world, at the end of the video, he turns to a graphic novel to seek some explanation for his experience. He is then shown being again transported into the graphic novel world to become a black-and-white line drawing character.

These students were using video editing techniques to recontextualize their school world through combining video and music, as well as portraying how the main character is engaged in alternative experiences of becoming "other." They were effectively using digital video tools, for example, the graphic book editing feature, to portray the student's exploration of alternative identities.

Given the centrality of the body in adolescence, recontextualizing familiar practices and spaces often involves portrayals of affective experiences through embodied enactments with others (Ehret & Hollett, 2014; Leander & Boldt, 2013). The video opens with a group of five boys laughing at a brief video of a male student falling and injuring his body. This enactment of adolescent male bonding not only portrays the emotions of a shared peer-group experience but also is itself a commentary about adolescent male obsession with embodiment and physical deviations.

As the student encounters the music groups in the school hallways, the video emphasizes the main character's embodied reactions of running and stumbling through the schoolyard and hallways, portraying the character's sense of disruption of his familiar sense of his school world. When the student then enters into the graphic novel world, he experiences a further becoming within a media-cultural world that creates a momentary sense of solace.

Understanding the activity of creating this video therefore entails understanding the affective elements of use of digital tools to portray bodies acting in unpredictable, deviant ways as a commentary on the restrictions of school spaces. Others videos created in the same video production class portrayed the affective appeal of consumerist/popular culture on embodied ways of dressing, talking, gesturing, or walking associated with certain media celebrities, adopting, for example, "the look" of a Taylor Swift that constituted adolescent identities. Students also created parodies of advertisements portraying physical transformations from weak to strong or unattractive to attractive, and challenged the consumerist myth of the instant physical transformation through the use of a "miracle" product (Beach & Swiss, 2010).

While content hubs and image repositories online offer a seemingly limitless archive of potential resources from which students can curate visual representations for their stories, navigating these image banks requires the development of critical media literacies (Alvermann, Hutchins, & McDevitt, 2012), specifically in terms of how algorithms produce search results in which the particular cultural and social histories inscribed on these images are not always immediately visible amid their rapid and disperse circulation online. For example, students in South Africa, who created digital stories, employed mostly images and media curated from Google searches and YouTube (Hull & Scott, 2013). Students of color who wanted to use an image of a doctor or a lawyer to represent a future career path were confronted with search results that often yielded mostly White professionals, limiting their choices for self-representation (Hull & Scott, 2013).

In one particularly salient example from a collection of South African students' digital stories, a student used an image of former football Hall of Famer and once-accused murderer O. J. Simpson sitting in a courtroom, wearing a black leather glove to represent his desire to become a lawyer. Confused as to why the student would choose Simpson, whose celebrity and trial were unknown to the student, researchers discovered this curatorial choice likely occurred because the Simpson photo appears as a top search result on Google Images (Hull & Scott, 2013). Because Google's search algorithm organizes search results (at least in part) based on the popularity of an image associated with a specific key word, and because this photo appears prominently across the Web as a hallmark moment in one of the most televised court cases of that time, this student discovered the photo as one of only a few top results depicting a lawyer of color. While within the local viewing context of his peers, the Simpson image might be recognized only as representing an anonymous lawyer of color, once this student's story circulated across a global network, the image acquired new and unintended meanings, in turn shifting how viewers might interpret the piece as a whole.

Educators therefore need to recognize the constraints that both search algorithms and software place on how this agency manifests in the discovery, curation, and dissemination of digital artifacts. In the earlier South African example, while the Google search algorithm had a clear impact on how the student was able to tell his story and produce meaning, these constraints also open up crucial opportunities for dialogue, reflection, critical thinking, and the development of media literacy competencies.

In addition to producing digital stories, adolescents also consider how to disseminate and share their productions within certain communities of viewing as a means of "becoming other" identity performances (Halverson, 2010; Doerr-Stevens, 2015). As producers, adolescents need to be conscious of present and local, as well as future and global audiences, and, as audiences, they need to be conscious about cultural contexts and the producer's perspective. Such interventions include the use of public video sharing sites such as YouTube and Vimeo to expose these stories to a broader public, as well as the creation of digital storytelling that deploys custom social networking tools to connect storytellers and provide designated spaces where critical dialogue can occur about videos and video production.

Students develop critical media literacies through the process of learning to navigate social media channels in distributing their digital stories and selecting appropriate websites for intended audiences. By adding descriptions and tags to increase the visibility of their stories, and customization of viewing and commenting settings to avoid negative commentary from trolls or spammers (Brewster & Hereth, 2013), students learn to reach intended audiences and make conscious choices about feedback and distribution channels. Extending the work of digital video production to include distribution in this way also requires researchers and educators to expand on current methodological and assessment approaches, moving from analysis and evaluation of the content and form of a single artifact to how an artifact circulates and prompts interaction with others in online social contexts.

Video Responses as Multimodal Dialogue and Critical Remix

The circulation of digital videos across social media sites such as YouTube not only promotes diverse viewing experiences but also catalyzes response in the form of video remixes and video responses. Greek adolescents used their YouTube videos to share with large audiences their portrayals of the negative effects of the economic crisis in Greece on unemployment and psychological effects on Greek adolescents' lives, as well as their critique of the political power structures (Triliva, Varvantakis, & Dafermos, 2015). This "participatory culture" engages the active appropriation of videos and multimodal artifacts in generating new, related media, while also privileging new forms and styles of videos that feature "spreadability" as a crucial attribute (Jenkins & Ford, 2013). The use of the fragmentary nature of viral meme videos invites viewers to produce remixes which fill in these gaps or holes (Shifman, 2013).

Whether these gaps occur because of the shifting viewing contexts of online audiences, limitations in amateur video production techniques, or are purposefully constructed by video makers to provoke response, they help us recognize the connection between video forms and their potential reappropriation by others. This acknowledgment can inspire educators to imagine classroom video-making practices in new ways. For example, Adami (2014) describes how video responses on YouTube "[prioritize] transformations of forms over mutual understandings" and "undermine . . . the very notion of text as the means of exchange of meanings" (p. 241). Adami emphasizes how traditional ideas about communication breakdowns in vernacular video responses, where a desire on the part of interactants to "differentiate" themselves from others motivates creative performance over a demonstration of understanding. Through analysis of the different levels of relatedness among response videos on YouTube, Adami repositions agency as an act of individuation, in which the choices video creators make in connecting to or critiquing another video motivate the nature of their unique creative performance.

Although these responses take on various positions and motivations, they nonetheless invoke particular genres that frame meaning for the community of video responders based on shared knowledge of video genres. Given this shared knowledge, "subversive parodies utilize knowledge of how genres function through different semiotic channels and point our attention toward larger structures and rules that shape our rhetorical behavior" (Ray, 2013, p. 187). When considering how producers assemble multimodal semiotic resources in creating response videos, genre plays a critical role in shaping the meaning of a video not only as an individual artifact, but also, more importantly, as the relational meanings between videos connected across a viral video event.

Providing students the opportunity to engage with a viral video phenomenon in the classroom opens up new possibilities for critical inquiry. Rather than focusing on how viral videos gain visibility through portraying irresponsible or offensive behaviors, a more appropriate strategy might instead focus on how a response video contributes to advancing the intellectual and critical work of the community of learners. For example, in 2013 an electronic dance song by the artist Baueer, called "The Harlem Shake," spawned the Harlem Shake Meme, which began with a video of a man in a mask dancing to the song alone in a room, followed by a jump cut to everyone in the room dancing about wildly. Within 2 weeks of the discovery of this original video, over 12,000 video responses were created around the globe, most of which recreated or remixed this basic structure of the meme video.

However, as the meme rapidly spread across the Internet, with the most popular videos garnering views in the millions, the origin of the actual Harlem Shake dance was lost amid the profuse proliferation of the meme across the Internet. Unknown to many participants, Baueer's song had actually adopted its name from a popular dance born out of Harlem, New York, decades earlier. As the meme spread, people with knowledge of the deep cultural roots of the *real* Harlem Shake dance took issue with the Internet meme, citing it as just another example in a long tradition of mainstream, White communities appropriating and mocking African American cultural practices (Koehler, 2013). In this particular case, educators could seize this opportunity for students to participate in viral media by producing video responses that creatively reestablish this connection between the meme and the original dance, and to think more critically about other examples of problematic cultural appropriation and cultural marginalization. These skills can be put to use not just to understand and respond to pop cultural phenomena such as the Harlem Shake meme, but also to interact more effectively and generating online instructional tutorials, which can be brought into the classroom and shared among peers in creating self-directed communities of learners.

Using Audio in Multimodal Productions

Another multimodal method involves using tools such as iMovie or Audacity to combine or remix audio—music, sound effects, voice-overs, and so forth, with images/video to create multimodal productions. In using audio, it's important that sound effects and music not be perceived as simply an ancillary add-on to images or video, requiring an appreciation for how audio contributes to the meaning of images and video in multimodal production. This mixing of audio and images fosters what Lynn Shanahan (2012, p. 269), drawing from Chion's (1990, p. xii) notion of "conceptual resonance between image and sound," describes as learning how sound enhances the meaning of images:

> The sound makes us see the image differently, and then this new image makes us hear the sound differently, which in turn makes us see something else in the image, which makes us hear different things in the sound, and so on.

Students gain understanding of the meaning of audio or sounds by considering how sounds acquire certain meanings in their everyday lives. Walter Gershon (2011) posits that sounds function as "embodied knowledge" for helping students make sense of experience and spaces, as well as better understand certain group values. The sounds students experiences in urban settings—sirens, traffic noise, train signals, construction, and so forth, serve to define the meaning of urban spaces, just as the sounds of animals, birds, or other wildlife serve to define the meaning of natural spaces. To analyze how students can attend to sounds as "embodied knowledge," Gershon analyzed students engaged in a "sensory walk" in a park in which one student led another blindfolded by giving directions through the park to a tree in which listening to the crunching of leaves or the sound of a tree was recorded on a "sonic data strip" (p. 77).

Students draw on their knowledge of these cultural meanings of sound to produce audio-only texts through participation in projects such as the Youth Radio project in Oakland, California, which involved adolescents creating their own radio productions about topics associated with their own lives (Soep & Chávez, 2010, p. 47). These radio productions involve the use "converged literacy," that is,

> a space where various literacies pertaining to radio production and distribution—as well as distinct media forms, such as spoken-word poetry, digital photography, and personal interviews—coexist and merge into a single audio presentation where "the printed word is just the beginning (23, 47)." (Todorova, 2015, p. 49)

In one project, college students produced 13 short radio productions that were broadcast on a university campus and on an overseas radio station about their perceptions of multiculturalism; students also wrote essays describing their productions in terms of how they addressed issues related to multiculturalism in their productions (Todorova, 2015). These productions functioned as "soundscapes" that "involved the use of vocal and electronically generated sounds to express a feeling, make an impression, or tell a story" (p. 49). An analysis of six Filipino–British youths' creation of multimodal remix rap texts using Ulead, Photoshop, Cubase, and YouTube as "culture songs" identified how they combined traditional Filipino folk songs with hip-hop rhythm and rhyme along with logo animations featuring the colors red, blue, yellow, and white. This remix represented a meshing of the Philippine and the U.K. flags (Domingo, 2014) and portrayed the students' multicultural identity allegiances as acts of becoming.

Given that students may not be familiar with effective use of audio as a multimodal composing tool, they may need explicit instruction on how to effectively combine audio and images together to convey ideas. An analysis of one teacher's instruction associated with students using HyperStudio to create image productions found that because the students received no instruction in how to insert sound or music with the slides, the students did not employ narrative, voice-overs, or music to enhance their productions (Shanahan, 2012). Viewing sound as simply an add-on embellishment as opposed to an essential component of multimodal productions was a missed opportunity for deepening understanding of content. Instruction on use of sound as a multimodal composing tool would include analysis of the use of effective voice-overs or narration to convey certain meanings. One way to go about this is by masking the sound in multimodal texts and then having students compare differences between texts with versus without sound. In studying the relationship between music and story, Gaetan Pappalardo (2010) had her students view a video of John Williams conducting an orchestra in creating the soundtrack for the movie *Jaws* (Spielberg, 1975) to focus on how the music served to convey the story line.

Through such instruction, students learn to combine and remix audio with images and video. Students in a high school language arts class used GarageBand to create and record songs as members of an imagined band (O'Brien & Dubbels, 2010). They drew on poems, dialogue, and lyrics first to record their oral interpretation of lyrics on one GarageBand track, then added music and beats on another track to enhance the meaning of their lyrics.

ASSESSING STUDENTS' MULTIMODAL PRODUCTIONS

Given our focus on the processes students acquire through multimodal productions, assessing uses of those processes involves a focus on not only their final productions but also their reflections on the processes employed in creating their texts based on their goals and choices (Shipka, 2011). For such self-reflection, students can draw on criteria formulated by the National Writing Project (2011) Multimodal Assessment project: artifact (finished product), context, substance (content, quality, and significance of ideas presented), process management and skills, and habits of mind. For example, a student may reflect on how he or she employed certain processes, skills, and habits of mind, to create an artifact relative to the rhetorical context.

For assessing students' multimodal productions, as previously noted, drawing on the use of community-based shared knowledge of genre features suggests shifting assessment from what a student's individual text communicates on its own toward acknowledging the transformations and impact videos can have on a community of viewers and producers. Instead of evaluating only how effectively a student organizes multiple modes to convey meaning, educators should also value how effectively a student organizes these semiotic resources as social and rhetorical events to spark more response videos and engagement by other members of the community.

Fostering Students' Self-Reflection of Multimodal Production

A primary purpose of assessment is to foster students' self-reflection on how their multimodal texts are related to their rhetorical context. Gallagher (2014) posits that it is important that students perceive context not simply as a matter of conforming to the dictates of a task or space, but rather as something they perform through encounters between themselves and their audiences. To have students reflect on contextualizing as performance, he has students ask, "How (effectively) does the text perform contexts? How (well) does its interface stage encounters with users?" (p. 3). He cites the example of a first-year college student Brenda's reflections on the processes of creating her multimodal e-portfolio, "Putting Education under the Microscope," which included 20 images and links to 11 videos. Brenda was producing context through how she framed her e-portfolio as a digital book with a cover, introduction, preface, tabs to a table of context, and an afterword (all book-like components).

Drawing on course readings by Freire and Rodriques, Brenda invites the reader to grapple with questions about the purposes of education by asking, "What were/are your education complications?" (Gallagher, 2014, p. 7). She includes images portraying schooling, for example, a colorful drawing contrasted with an image of a drab, neglected school, as well as a word cloud with *critical thinking* as the predominate words. Brenda also includes what she describes as "a series of examples that cause the viewer to interact with images of historical and more outdated photographs of the education system as well as more modern ones" (p. 7). In reflecting on the process of creating her e-portfolio, she notes that, "I think having the ability to constantly go back edit, add, exchange and move around certain parts of my E-portfolio is extremely beneficial to my project" (p. 10). In essence, she invites her audience to identify with her performance as her understanding grows and evolves.

Using Digital Tools to Engage in and Model Self-Reflections

Students can also use screencasting apps such as ShowMe or Explain Everything to record think-aloud reflections about their work, for example, their reflections on their processes of responding to a text or playing a video (Abrams, 2014). The fact that these technologies are easy to use may serve as an incentive to engage in frequent metacognitive reflection. The use of these recordings over time can then be used to identify changes in students' thinking processes, for example, how students' responses to texts changed across the school year.

To model self-reflections, teachers can create videos demonstrating the self-assessment process, as instructors of a first-year online composition course did at Arizona State University (Rankins-Robertson, Bourelle, Bourelle, & Fisher, 2015). Based on the instructor's demonstration videos, students submitted self-reflections on their process of creating multimodal texts and discussed their sense of purpose, audience, genre, and use of materials as social and rhetorical events. One student created a profile of a citizen in a town and reflected on the evolution of the town for a local newsletter. The student reflected on her use of images to represent the citizen's responses to her interview questions. She also discussed her willingness to devote hours to editing her audio interviews given that she was going to share these with her family members, who were residents of the town. Her reflections contextualized her production and purpose, which involved making connections with her family. In another project, a student created a travel blog including commentary about changes in a Los Angeles theater from 1931 to 2009, using images of the lobby, the mezzanine, the stage, and other parts of the building. The student noted the importance of effective use of images to capture the historical shifts in the theater. Another student created an audio portrait of her parents' 25-year marriage using interview clips, with her parents' wedding song playing in the background. In her self-reflection, the student noted that she decided to switch back and forth between the two parents, so that her audience could compare her parents' perceptions of the same events. For giving feedback to these projects, the instructors used audio or screencasting tools, so that they could share their verbal comments, further demonstrating the use of multimodal production practices (Rankins-Robertson et al., 2015).

Given the layered complexity of multimodal digital productions, it is often difficult to provide written feedback to students' work, particularly with online courses. In giving feedback on students' videos, it can be more useful to employ video annotation tools such as YouTube Annotations or VideoAnt (*http://ant.umn.edu*) to target comments to specific images within a video, as well as screencasting tools such as Jing, Camtasia, or CamStudio for recording comments on students' work. Students in one study preferred video feedback, suggesting that it was more individualized, supportive, and detailed, and that it prompted more self-reflection than text-based feedback (Henderson & Phillips, 2015). Tools such as SoundCloud, Audacity, or Kaizena (for use with Google Drive files) can be used for providing audio feedback. Students in the McKittrick, Mitchum, and Spangler (2015) study perceived SoundCloud to be a useful tool for providing peer-feedback on students' multimodal writing, which suggests the process fostered self-reflection.

SUMMARY AND IMPLICATIONS FOR INSTRUCTION

In this chapter, we have explored the sense-making processes associated with (1) responding to multimodal texts, (2) creating multimodal texts, and (3) assessing and fostering self-reflection of students' multimodal productions. In addition, we have identified processes involved when adolescents respond to and create multimodal productions. We have focused on the processes of recontextualizing to critique status quo meanings of texts and the idea of performance through building connections with audiences.

While we have separated responding to and creating multimodal texts, it is essential that students be continually challenged to integrate the two processes (Beach, Anson, Kastman-Breuch, & Reynolds, 2015; for resources on integrating these processes, see *http://digitalwriting.pbworks.com*). As students take part in instruction that requires them to critique media representations, they acquire fundamental knowledge of audio and cinematic techniques that then transfer to creating multimodal productions. For example, high school students examined media representations of adolescents and found disparities between these media representations and their own experiences, resulting in the examination of the question as to how these representations actually influence their daily lives (Bruce, 2015). This analysis led to creating digital video portrayals of their uses of media, with many focusing on use of music and video games as shaping their identities. As suggested by Serafini's (2015) typology of specific elements of multimodal texts as "visual objects," "multimodal events," and "sociocultural artifacts," students benefit from acquiring meta-language through teacher and/or peer modeling of use of specific concepts related to use of camera shots, angles, and editing transitions, as well as audio, remix, and other features, for use in their video productions.

It is also important that students acquire different critical perspectives (Appleman, 2014) for analysis of problematic, stereotypical media representations in multimodal texts as "sociocultural artifacts" (Serafini, 2015), for example, asking students to reflect on how television ads portray only certain demographic groups, using certain products in ways that ignore disparities in race, class, and gender. After having such discussions, students are more likely to apply these critical perspectives when they experience emotions of anger or resentment in response of problematic representations (Lewis & Tierney, 2013).

Finally, students benefit from instruction that focuses on the aesthetic design aspects of multimodal texts, for example, studying the evolution of use of cinematic techniques in film history or changes in visual art across different artistic periods. Such instruction involves integration of art, literacy, and social studies, and serves as a powerful illustration of the use of multimodal texts to express ideas.

While the examples featured in this chapter provide suggestions for instructional implications, we intend that readers think creatively about the ways digital tools can be used for multiple instructional purposes. For example, we described how screencasting apps can be used flexibly for composition, self-reflection, and the delivery of teacher feedback. However, as the digital world continues to evolve, it is vital that our instructional practices demonstrate a commitment to our students' strengths and their needs, and not simply the use of the latest and greatest technologies. Keeping the focus squarely on our students will ensure that we prepare them for thoughtful and active participation in the literacy and learning communities that will define their futures through becoming an *other* in multimodal social and rhetorical events.

REFERENCES

Abrams, S. S. (2014). *Integrating virtual and traditional learning in 6–12 classrooms: A layered literacies approach to multimodal meaning making.* New York: Routledge.

Adami, E. (2014). "Why did dinosaurs evolve from water?": (In)coherent relatedness in YouTube video interaction. *Text and Talk, 34*(3), 239–259.

Alvermann, D. E., Hutchins, R. J., & McDevitt, R. (2012). Adolescents' engagement with Web 2.0 and social media: Research, theory, and practice. *Research in the Schools, 19*(1), 33–44.

Appleman, D. (2014). *Critical encounters in secondary English: Teaching literary theory to adolescents.* New York: Teachers College Press.

Bazalgette, C., & Buckingham, D. (2013). Literacy, media and multimodality: A critical response. *Literacy, 47*(2), 95–102.

Beach, R., Anson, C., Kastman-Breuch, L., & Reynolds, T. (2015). *Understanding and creating digital texts: An activity-based approach.* Lanham, MD: Rowman & Littlefield.

Beach, R., & O'Brien, D. (2014). *Using apps for learning across the curriculum: A literacy-based framework and guide.* New York: Routledge.

Beach, R., & Swiss, T. (2010). Digital literacies, aesthetics, and pedagogies involved in digital video production. In P. Albers & J. Sanders (Eds.), *Literacies, the arts, and multimodality* (pp. 300–320). Urbana, IL: National Council of Teachers of English.

Brewster, S., & Hereth, J. (2013). Chain reaction: A youth-driven, multimedia storytelling project. *Journal of Curriculum Theorizing, 29*(2), 26–34.

Bruce, D. L. (2015). Re-constructing and re-presenting teenagers: Using media literacy to examine cultural constructions of adolescents. *English Journal, 104*(3), 68–74.

Burn, A., & Durran, J. (2006). Digital anatomies: Analysis as production in media education. In D. Buckingham & R. Willett (Eds.), *Digital generations: Children, young people, and new media* (pp. 273–294). Mahwah, NJ: Erlbaum.

Burnett, C., Merchant, G., Pahl, K., & Rowsell, J. (2014). The (im)materiality of literacy: The significance of subjectivity to new literacies research. *Discourse: Studies in the Cultural Politics of Education, 35*(1), 90–103.

Castek, J., Beach, R., Cotanch, H., & Scott, J. (2014). Examining middle-school students' uses of Diigo annotations to engage in collaborative argumentative writing. In R. Anderson & C. Mims (Eds.), *Handbook of research on digital tools for writing instruction in K–12* (pp. 80–101). Hershey, PA: IGI Global.

Castek, J., & Cotanch, H. (2013). Examining 7th graders' tablet-created screencasts to promote safe driving: Reflections from a service learning project. In R. Ferdig & K. Pytash (Eds.), *Exploring multimodal composition and digital writing* (pp. 186–200). Hershey, PA: IGI Global.

Chion, M. (1990). *Audio-vision: Sound on screen.* New York: Columbia University Press.

Coles, M., & Hall, C. (2001). Boys, books and breaking boundaries: Developing literacy in and out of school. In W. Martino & B. Meyenn (Eds.), *What about the boys?: Issues of masculinity in schools* (pp. 211–221). Buckingham, UK: Open University Press.

Dezuanni, M. (2014). The building blocks of digital media literacy: Socio-material participation and the production of media knowledge. *Journal of Curriculum Studies, 47*(3), 416–439.

Doerr-Stevens, C. (2015). "That's not something I was, I am, or am ever going to be": Multimodal self-assertion in digital video production. *E-Learning and Digital Media, 12*(2), 164–182.

Domingo, M. (2014). Migrating literacies: Multimodal texts and digitally enabled text making. *Text and Talk, 34*(3), 261–282.

Dover, C. (2014, March 14). What is "time-based media"?: A Q&A with Guggenheim conservator Joanna Phillips [Web log post]. Retrieved from *http://tinyurl.com/o99gyor*.

Ehret, C., & Hollett, T. (2014). Embodied composition in real virtualities: Adolescents' literacy practices and felt experiences moving with digital, mobile devices in school. *Research in the Teaching of English, 48*(4), 428–452.

El Refaie, E., & Horschelmann, K. (2010). Young people's readings of a political cartoon and the concept of multimodal literacy. *Discourse: Studies in the Cultural Politics of Education, 31*(2), 195–207.

Gallagher, C. W. (2014). Staging encounters: Assessing the performance of context in students' multimodal writing. *Computers and Composition, 31,* 1–12.

Gershon, W. (2011). Embodied knowledge: Sounds as educational systems. *Journal of Curriculum Theorizing, 27*(2), 66–81.

Griffith, J. (2015). Writing public service announcements and genre-jabs. In V. Yenika-Agbaw & T. Sychterz (Eds.), *Adolescents rewrite their worlds: Using literature to illustrate writing forms* (pp. 29–49). Lanham, MD: Rowman & Littlefield.

Halverson, E. R. (2010). Film as identity exploration: A multimodal analysis of youth-produced films. *Teachers College Record, 112*(9), 2352–2378.

Henderson, M., & Phillips, M. (2015). Video-based feedback on student assessment: Scarily personal. *Australasian Journal of Educational Technology, 31*(1), 51–66.

Hull, G., & Katz, M. L. (2006). Crafting an agentive self: Case studies in digital storytelling. *Research in the Teaching of English, 41,* 43–81.

Hull, G., & Scott, J. (2013). Curating and creating online: Identity, authorship, and viewing in a digital age. In K. Drotner & K. C. Schrøder (Eds.), *Museum communication and social media: The connected museum* (pp. 130–151). New York: Taylor & Francis.

Jenkins, H. (2006). *Confronting the challenges of participatory culture: Media education for the 21st century.* Chicago: MacArthur Foundation.

Jenkins, H., & Ford, S. (2013). *Spreadable media: Creating value and meaning in a networked culture.* New York: New York University Press.

Jewitt, C. (2002). The move from page to screen: The multimodal reshaping of school English. *Journal of Visual Communication, 1*(2), 171–196.

Koehler, S. (2013, March 18). The problematics of the Fake Harlem Shake [Web log post]. Retrieved from *http://tinyurl.com/c7r7paf*.

Kress, G., & Jewitt, C. (2003). Introduction. In C. Jewitt & G. Kress (Eds.), *Multimodal literacy* (pp. 1–18). New York: Peter Lang.

Kress, G., & van Leeuwen, T. (2001). *Multimodal discourse: The modes and media of contemporary communication.* London: Edward Arnold.

Leander, K., & Boldt, G. (2013). Rereading "A pedagogy of multiliteracies": Bodies, texts, and emergence. *Journal of Literacy Research, 45*(1), 22–46.

Leander, K., & Rowe, D. (2006). Mapping literacy spaces in motion: A rhizomatic analysis of a classroom literacy performance. *Reading Research Quarterly, 41*(4), 428–460.

Lewis, C., & Tierney, J. D. (2013). Mobilizing emotion in an urban English classroom: Producing identities and transforming signs in a race-related classroom. *Linguistics and Education, 24,* 289–304.

Li, Y., Guo, A., Lee, J. A., & Negara, G. P. K. (2013). A platform on the cloud for self-creation of mobile interactive learning trails. *International Journal of Mobile Learning Organisation,* 7(1), 66–80.

Luhrman, B. (Director). (1996). *Romeo and Juliet* [Motion Picture]. United States: 20th Century Fox.

Luke, A. (2003). Literacy and the other: A sociological approach to literacy research and policy in multilingual societies. *Reading Research Quarterly, 38*(1), 132–141.

Masny, D. (2009). Literacies as becoming: A child's conceptualizations of writing systems. In D. Masny, & D. R. Cole (Eds.), *Multiple literacies theory: A Deleuzian perspective* (pp. 13–30). Rotterdam, The Netherlands: Sense.

Masny, D., & Waterhouse, M. (2011). Mapping territories and creating nomadic pathways with multiple literacies theory. *Journal of Curriculum Theorizing, 27*(3), 287–305.

McKittrick, M., Mitchum, C., & Spangler, S. (2015). The sound [sans] the fury": The efficacy of SoundCloud audio feedback in the writing classroom. *Journal of Teaching and Learning with Technology, 3*(2), 40–53.

Napoli, M., & Sychterz, T. (2015). Graphic novels come alive in a sixth-grade classroom. In V. Yenika-Agbaw & T. Sychterz (Eds.), *Adolescents rewrite their worlds: Using literature to illustrate writing forms* (pp. 148–162). Lanham, MD: Rowman & Littlefield.

National Writing Project. (2011). Planning to test the framework in practice [Web log post]. Retrieved from *http://digitalis.nwp.org/resource/2751.*

O'Brien, D., & Dubbels, B. (2010, May 13). Technology and literacy: Current and emerging practices with Student 2.0 and beyond [Web log post]. Retrieved from *http://tinyurl.com/7fxtoed.*

Pappalardo, G. (2010, November 15). Using music in the classroom to inspire creative expression [Web log post]. Retrieved from *http://tinyw.in/4udw.*

Phelan, M. (2011). *Around the world.* Somerville, MA: Candlewick.

Rankins-Robertson, S., Bourelle, T., Bourelle, A., Fisher, D. (2015). Multimodal instruction: Pedagogy and practice for enhancing multimodal composition online. *KAIROS, 19*(1). Retrieved from *http://tinyurl.com/lwauxuj.*

Ray, B. (2013). More than just remixing: Uptake and New Media composition. *Computers and Composition, 30,* 183–196.

Rowsell, J., & Pahl, K. (2007). Sedimented identities in texts: Instances of practice. *Reading Research Quarterly, 42*(3), 388–404.

Serafini, F. (2015). Multimodal literacy: From theories to practices. *Language Arts, 92*(6), 412–423.

Shanahan, L. (2012). Use of sound with digital text: Moving beyond sound as an add-on or decoration. *Contemporary Issues in Technology and Teacher Education, 12*(3), 264–285.

Shifman, L. (2013). *Memes in digital culture.* Cambridge, MA: MIT Press.

Shipka, J. (2011). *Toward a composition made whole.* Pittsburgh, PA: University of Pittsburgh Press.

Simpson, A., Walsh, M., & Rowsell, J. (2013). The digital reading path: Researching modes and multidirectionality with iPads. *Literacy, 47*(3), 123–130.

Soep, E., & Chávez, V. (2010). *Drop that knowledge: Youth Radio stories.* Berkeley: University of California Press.

Spielberg, S. (Director). (1975). *Jaws* [Motion Picture]. United States: Universal Pictures.

Sung, E., & Mayer, R. E. (2013). Online multimedia learning with mobile devices and desktop computers: An experimental test of Clark's methods-not-media hypothesis. *Computers in Human Behavior, 29*(3), 639–647.

Todorova, M. S. (2015). Dusty but mighty: Using radio in the critical media literacy classroom. *Journal of Media Literacy Education, 6*(3), 46–56.

Triliva, S., Varvantakis, C., & Dafermos, M. (2015). YouTube, young people, and the socioeconomic crises in Greece. *Information, Communication and Society, 18*(4), 407–423.

Unsworth, L. (2011). Comparing and composing digital re-presentations of literature: Multimedia authoring and meta-communicative knowledge. In L. Unsworth (Ed.), *New literacies and the English curriculum* (pp. 186–212). London: Continuum.

Van Leeuwen, T. (2008). *Discourse and practice: New tools for critical discourse analysis*. New York: Oxford University Press.

Vasudevan, L., Schultz, K., & Bateman, J. (2010). Rethinking composing in a digital age: Authoring literate identities through multimodal storytelling. *Written Communication, 27*(4), 442–468.

Wiesner, D. (2006). *Flotsam*. New York: Houghton Mifflin.

Zammit, K. (2007). Popular culture in the classroom: Interpreting and creating multimodal texts. In A. McCabe, M. O'Donnell, & R. Whittaker (Eds.), *Advances in language and education* (pp. 60–76). New York: Continuum.

CHAPTER 18

Adolescents Reading Graphic Novels and Comics
What We Know from Research

STERGIOS BOTZAKIS, RACHELLE SAVITZ, and DAVID E. LOW

In recent years, a growing number of literacy scholars has argued that comic books and graphic novels, which for the purposes of this chapter are called by the umbrella term *comics*, provide students of all ages with an ideal format for navigating wide ranges of literacies and modalities, and for taking an agential role in making meaning. The inherently multimodal medium of comics "raise[s] complex questions bearing on semiotics, linguistics, aesthetics, textuality, representation, epistemology, narrative, and spatiality" (Witek, 2009, p. 218) and disrupts the autonomous, monomodal definition of literacy overwhelmingly endorsed by the contemporary testing regimen (Jacobs, 2013; Low, 2012). The multiple literacies that students simultaneously enact via reading and writing/designing comics are indeed vastly significant in contemporary literacy contexts.

However, such a conception of comics has not always been prevalent in education research. The few education researchers who studied young people's comics reading found ill effects, including a cause of linear dyslexia (Mosse & Daniels, 1959) and distraction from more fortifying and instructive reading materials (Arlin & Roth, 1978). The images and limited amount of text have long painted comics as inferior or as simple texts that limit opportunities for students to read (Arlin & Roth, 1978). In particular, the images were said to distract readers from tracking text, and overall time spent reading comics detracted from time that could be spent reading materials that could enrich students' reading skills. Today, comics are being considered more as a unique medium in which the images and words both contribute to meaning making, and they fit into any discussion of what should "count" as literacy in- and out-of-school contexts (e.g., Carter, 2009). A visual and textual medium, comics of many varieties are immensely popular with children, youth, and adults throughout the world (e.g., Botzakis, 2009; Duncan & Smith, 2009; Pustz, 1999). Attending to readers' interactions with comics has been shown to be about more than just imparting visual literacy skills. According to Street's (1995) ideological model of literacy, such interactions may reveal much about students' diverse identities as literate beings. It may "provide opportunities for increasing engagement, developing meaningful connections, and fostering innovative approaches to teaching and learning" (Simon, 2012, p. 516).

Though it is unlikely that this work has had much of an impact on standardized English language arts curricula, especially with the types of literature and literacy instruction stressed the Common Core State Standards, there is currently a critical mass of scholarly literature discussing the benefits of employing comics in schools and in alternative learning spaces. Over the past two decades, researchers representing a variety of disciplines have argued that the medium of comics is not taken as seriously as it should be in schools, libraries, and museums; in college English, fine arts, and media classes; in academic scholarship; and by society at large (e.g., Carter, 2008; Connors, 2010; Esquivel, 2006; Griffith, 2010; Groensteen, 2009). In this chapter, we focus on the portion of this research corpus dealing with adolescent learners, both in and out of school.

IDENTIFYING PERTINENT STUDIES

Comics is a catch-all term that is contested by researchers and practitioners. The medium of comics is probably most accurately called *sequential art* (Eisner, 1985), defined as a series of artistic images and words intended to be read in a sequential order, but this terminology is not typically used in terms of education research. Comic books and comic strips are popular forms of the medium, though they are not typically held in high regard in terms of taste or worth (Wright, 2001). Eisner (1978) popularized the term *graphic novel* to refer to larger, self-contained works, such as his *A Contract with God and Other Tenement Stories*, and that term appears frequently in research by educators and librarians (e.g., Gavigan, 2011). However, some creators and authors eschew the graphic novel label, finding it a somewhat pretentious way of referring to "a long comic book that needs a bookmark and has to be re-read" (Spiegelman, cited in Spurgeon, 2011), and they prefer to call the medium either *comics* or *comix*. Still others (e.g., Thompson, 2008) use the term *graphica*, which is somewhat confusing, because the term has been used largely to pertain to charts, tables, and other visual displays of information.

Detailing all of these monikers is relevant to our process of identifying pertinent studies for this review. We conducted a total of nine searches using the Education Resources Information Center (ERIC) via EBSCO (Elton B. Stephens Co.). The first search produced a total of 62 articles and books, using the terms *graphic novels* and *adolescent*. The second search, using terms *graphic novels* and *middle school*, provided a total of 11 texts. The third search, using the terms graphic novels and high school, yielded 17 texts. The fourth search, using the terms *comic books* and *adolescents*, resulted in 28 texts. Using the terms *comic books* and *middle school*, the fifth search showed 11 texts. The sixth search six, using the terms *comic books* and *high school*, yielded 18 texts. The seventh search, using the terms *comic books* and *high school*, provided 33 texts. The eighth search, using the terms *comics* and *middle school*, yielded 14 texts. The ninth search, using the terms *comics* and *adolescents*, provided 21 texts. Some texts appeared in more than one search, and all articles and books were read for possible use of this research. The works chosen for this review all contained accounts of research studies pertaining to use of graphic novels, or comic books, in middle school or secondary literacy settings. We explore these studies in three major clusters: identity, diverse learners, and pedagogy.

COMICS, IDENTITY, AND POPULARITY

Increasingly, literacy research has examined the interaction of reading practices and identity, largely because expanded definitions of literacy require looking at more than the mechanical aspects of reading. As Moje (2008) suggested, "Rather than lamenting the alleged crisis of youth aliteracy (i.e., 'kids don't read anymore'), we should examine what young people do read and write," because "youths preferred texts are often multimodal" (p. 207) and not the pen-and-paper modes of communication typically associated with school. Contemporary views of adolescent literacy have cast light on how youth enact complex literacy practices, even if they are in nonschool contexts (Hull & Schultz, 2001).

An awareness of how comics reading may be bound into a student's identity was the focus of a study about Yusef, a teenage "connoisseur of comic books and reading" (Simon, 2012, p. 520). Yusef was described as being troublesome in high school and on a trajectory of failure when one of his teachers interviewed him and was able to make a relationship with this troubled student via comics. After learning about his interest in Marvel superhero comics, as well as manga, the teacher stopped seeing Yusef's drawings as transgressions against school and classwork. By being allowed to explore expression via drawing and creating his own comics for school assignments, Yusef succeeded beyond expectations and became much more involved in positive school behaviors, eventually being accepted into a prestigious academy of fine arts high school program. Being aware of how students enact their literate identities provided a tool for teachers to be more effective, where "as connoisseurs of particular forms of literacy, teachers [became] connoisseurs of their students" (p. 525).

Yusef's proclivities are not isolated, as many research studies, particularly those conducted in libraries (e.g., Bergin, 2005; Griffith, 2010) indicate that comics, graphic novels particularly, have been among the most circulated and checked out books among adolescents. What is more, making comics has been widespread in afterschool programs (Bitz, 2004; Khurana, 2005), where students engage in creating and distributing their works to each other and even beyond, to the communities where they live. Such activities show how making comics is just as integral to many adolescents' identities as reading them.

THE COMICS MEDIUM AND DIVERSE LEARNERS

Another hallmark of the research on comics in educational settings is growing attention to the unique properties of the "invisible art" (Heath & Bhagat, 1997) as they apply to the reading process. In particular, the format of comics with individual panels arranged in a sequence, divided by gutters, implies the passage of time and space, requiring the reader to make multiple inferences and cognitive jumps (McCloud, 1993). Such metacognitive activity is a hallmark of positive reading behaviors with traditional texts and an area in which students may struggle, but with comics this is done almost imperceptibly. Yang (2008) attributed the ease with which most readers make sense of comics to the concept of "visual permanence," in which "time progresses only as quickly as [one's] eyes move across the page" (p. 188). In effect, "the rate of information-transfer is firmly in the reader's control" (Yang, 2008, p. 188), and individualized reading occurs through the scaffolds built into in the text format.

The combination of words and images in comics provide an opportunity for scaffolding for some readers and also a new modality that interests and attracts more capable readers. It is important to note that comics have been shown to be a preferred medium of a variety of readers (Schwarz, 2006) of either gender (Moeller, 2011) across the lifespan (Botzakis, 2009; Dyson, 1994; Norton, 2003) and across languages (Cary, 2004), and for both struggling readers (Gavigan, 2011) and skilled ones (Botzakis, 2009, 2014). This last point in particular is worth noting, because the reputation of comics as childish or low-culture texts had made it easier for some to relegate them to second-class status or to be considered something that can be used as a palliative for struggling readers (e.g., Hallenbeck, 1976) and not as text choices potentially appropriate for all readers.

TEACHING WITH GRAPHIC NOVELS

Teachers have a variety of texts from which to choose when deciding what works best for their students and classroom curricula. Comics texts have been shown to be a motivational way to supplement and enrich the curriculum across all content areas (Tatalovic, 2009; Witek, 1989), to teach visual literacy (Connors, 2012), to provide students an opportunity to use technology in reading and creating their own graphic novels (Botzakis, 2014), and to furnish challenging texts that require higher-order thinking and address diverse and difficult themes (Boatright, 2010), all while teaching necessary literacy skills related to the Common Core State Standards and other standards required throughout the United States (Frey & Fisher, 2008).

Comics as Motivational Tools

One great appeal of comics is that they "resemble our nonvisual self-awareness, so we inherently identify with them, whereas we react to a more realistically drawn character as being separate from ourselves" (Sardone, 2012, p. 68); many students also consider them to be fun (Norton, 2003). The typical reader used the visual cues in a graphic novel or comic book to help him or her gain meaning, which in turn is motivation to keep reading for comprehension and not to give up when struggles arise. Additionally, providing students a choice of texts is a motivational factor to help students develop into lifelong readers (Allington, 2013; Alvermann et al., 2007); comics, especially graphic novels, have been shown to be texts that interest students of all ages.

Another positive feature of comics is their use of images, which many students seem to comprehend almost immediately (McCloud, 1993). Graphic novels and comic books are very common in current pop culture, through literature, movies, toys, and video games. Students have an additional advantage because they have genre awareness after being inundated with the characters, plots, and themes found in these different types of media and text (Morrison, Bryan, & Chilcoat, 2002; Schwartz & Rubinstein-Avila, 2006; Schwarz & Crenshaw, 2013). As the popularity of graphic novels has increased, these texts have been further "integrated with popular culture for children and adolescents via marketing and mass production" (Griffith, 2010, p. 182), and "educators have recognized both the artful complexities of these texts and their growing popularity among students, and have developed programs and practices to use them to foster learning and engagement" (Botzakis, 2009, p. 50).

One such educator conducted a study to determine what the typical middle school student wanted and liked to read (Edwards, 2009). Her findings indicated that middle school students were more inclined to read graphic novels, even when they were not interested in other types of books. These students also indicated that they enjoyed the format and were able to challenge themselves with higher expectations as they read.

Another educator, who offered graphic novels in book groups in a middle school elective class and found that students were adept at reading those texts, stated that "the jokes, the conclusions, and the characters made sense at once" (Seyfried, 2008, p. 46) to the students. He also found utility in using nonfiction articles about graphic novels and comic books in conjunction with those graphic novels; students were interested and engaged in learning about how the texts were created, why the author chose to include certain elements and leave out others, and why certain images were chosen. They also engaged in analyzing authors' word choices and text flow, as well as engaging more regularly in a type of close reading in order to understand the purpose and meaning of the graphic novels.

Comics and Visual Literacy

Multimodal texts abound in today's world, and students need to be able to analyze and interpret visual literacy as well as textual literacy (Frey & Fisher, 2008). Comics have been called "print precursors of hypertext—or perhaps are themselves an early form of hypertext" (Purves, 1998, p. 47), because they utilize both imagery and words to create meaning. Even though there now exist webcomics, that is, comics that are made and disseminated online (Moorefield-Long & Gavigan, 2012), common use of comics is not necessarily new in the "New Literacies" (Lankshear & Knobel, 2011). Still, they are multimodal texts that can provide avenues to connect traditional and electronic reading skills. Reading comics requires students to use the pictures and illustrations to infer the themes, ideas, characters, and underlying emotions found in the text. They must use the unwritten dialogue found in these illustrations to visualize and interpret the words that are presented. Put simply, reading comics requires reading images (Kress & van Leeuwen, 1996) and words simultaneously, and creating a conception of meaning that would not be possible from attending to either alone.

Education researchers have examined multiple aspects of how reading comics works in relation to visual literacy. Smetana, Odelson, Burns, and Grisham (2009) discussed in depth the benefits of how visuals complement the written word in terms of building comprehension. They stressed that readers must be able to "analyze how the use of color, light, shadow, and lines influence the tone and mood of the story" (p. 230) in the endeavor to understand comics texts. They continued by explaining that readers needed to derive information from the visuals, and not just the words, by looking at the facial and bodily expressions presented in the graphics to figure out the story and information to make inferences. The visuals help provide them the contextual support and clues to be able to comprehend the text.

Other research indicates that comprehending comics goes beyond being able to make inferences from pictures. Low (2012) examined how the visuals in comic books require the reader to "produce inferences in order to construct meaning, and position the reader in the role of co-author of the text" (p. 370), but he also added that students not only needed typical literacy skills used with traditional texts but also the ability to interpret and discuss the unique conventions of comic books, such as the relationship between panels and gutters. Understanding the grammar and components of comics was necessary for critically reading challenging, complex texts. In addition, these skills can also be extrapolated in a broader sense to compare different types of texts and the affordances offered by each. A number of researchers have espoused activities in which students "analyze how different media work and what the strengths and weaknesses of various media are for diverse purposes and audiences" (Schwarz & Crenshaw, 2013, p. 48). Graphic novels are relatively accessible texts that can be used as a means for students to begin to "read, comprehend, and analyze a variety of modes and forms of texts" (Rick, 2011, p. 35).

Creating Comics: Making Multimodel Texts

The ability to analyze the visuals that accompany the words often makes it easier to understand difficult concepts or texts (Boerman-Cornell, 2013), and being able to assume the information and conventions learned through analyzing visuals in comics can create a platform for expression in which students not only create their own comics but also gain insight into all manner of issues dealing with composition. For instance, Frey and Fisher (2004) used graphic novels to "create lessons in reading and writing that addressed the multiple literacies that students possessed and needed to develop" (p. 19) for their ninth-grade writing course that consisted of 32 struggling readers and writers from diverse backgrounds. They used novels written by Will Eisner (e.g., 1978), as these works' topics were relevant and familiar to the lives of students in the class and were predominantly short in length. While reading the texts, the focus was placed on comprehension, literary elements, and vocabulary. However, students were left to figure out the meaning of the ending on their own. Once the text was read, students were then required to write about it, in any way they chose. These authentic writings were then used for lessons in grammar and the writing process. The next step was for students to read the beginning of a text and create their own ending. The culminating activity was for the students to create their very own illustrated story, demonstrating all that they had learned about the writing process and literary elements.

When creating their own graphic works, students exercise their abilities in "creative writing, storyline development, various fine art skills, graphic design, document layout, and computer literacy" (Vega & Schnackenberg, 2006, p. 30). Some researchers (e.g., Hughes, King, Perkins, & Fuke, 2011)have identified the task of creating comics as a difficult enterprise where the "visual, textual, and spatial elements work together to create the sound effects and gestures that give deeper meaning to the narratives being told" (p. 602) through comics. Hughes et al. conducted two case studies with high school students in relation to reading and creating their own graphic novels, and found in both studies that by understanding the techniques used in graphic novels through the creation of their own, students were able to validate the idea and importance of understanding the combination of image and text. In addition, even though many of these students were proudly aliterate and found combining words and image to be a challenge, they were able to develop multimodal skills in ways that could be easily applied to both school and future workplaces.

In the interest of creating comics in a more traditional sense, Bitz (2004) started the Comic Book Project. It originally had 733 children work in teams to design original comic books in their afterschool programs, based on the premise that "a more thorough connection between arts and literacy is formed when children create their own comic books" (p. 575). Students were provided a Manuscript Starter that had been developed by Teachers College and Dark Horse Comics (Morris, 2004) as a template and were provided direct instruction on the creation of graphic novels by trained afterschool program staff. Once the manuscripts were complete, students were provided an additional template to create their actual comic book. The children were solely responsible for creating eight-page comic books, in color. An unexpected outcome of the program was the fact that students used the creation of the comic books as an outlet for troubles and experiences in their lives. Student and staff surveys given at the end of the program revealed that most students surveyed about the project felt it was educational and fun, as well as beneficial in improving literacy skills, especially writing.

Another set of educators (Morrison et al., 2002), identified the need both to provide a scaffold to support students' creations and to add a social component. They saw making comic books as an "opportunity for students to be creative in the presentation of their writing" (p. 759), in the hope that students would then "engage in greater literacy exploration than they otherwise would, due to the comics' popular and easily accessible format" (p. 759). They created an adaptable format meant for teachers to use in a variety of student groupings and age levels, and later had students share their works with each other in a sort of comics fair. This last social action was what they found most effective, providing an audience for whom students put extra care and craftsmanship into their work. They concluded that students learned "a great deal more from this approach than by traditional teaching methods" (p. 767).

Comics across the Curriculum

Comics have most often been used as vehicles for literary analyses in language arts classrooms, and as you will see below, although the extant research studies pertaining to adolescent students have been conducted in language arts classrooms, they also have applications in other content areas. Boerman-Cornell (2013) identified and discussed how graphic novels could be beneficial in the disciplines of math, social studies, science, art, health, and physical education, provided that teachers first make sure students understand that they will need to make inferences and predictions based on not only the words they read but also what they see in the illustrations presented. Increasingly, graphic novels are used in social studies classes, because they portray historical or biographic events, and they provide an alternative avenue to engage students in both arenas (Witek, 1989). Similarly, a growing number of science-focused graphic novels convey depictions of scientific processes or concepts, using image and words in ways similar to textbook diagrams, only with more depth (Tatalovic, 2009). It would be wise to heed Boerman-Cornell's (2013) advice in reading these words, and not to skip over the use of images in service of simple curricular coverage.

Seemingly mundane activities, such as reading comic books, have been shown to have educational applications in terms of learning and practicing language. Palumbo (1979) used Marvel comic books to teach basic literary concepts. He demonstrated how to use the illustrations in a comic book to "prompt the reader to explore the story more closely by inviting him [or her] to attend also to the narration and dialogue at the same time that they . . . visually reinforce the meaning of these story elements" (p. 2). The Marvel Comics examples he provided also showed how to teach "synopsis, dramatic fiction, exposition, flashback, foreshadowing, plot structure, climax, resolution, sub-plot, double, foil, characterization, irony, symbolism, allegory, metaphor, pathetic fallacy, personification, and allusion" (p. 3), while also addressing additional literary elements, vocabulary, and comprehension skills and strategies.

Many texts taught in literature classes are difficult for students to read and comprehend due to the difficult language and complex themes (Rick, 2011). Oftentimes, educators use graphic novel versions of these classics, which are complex and challenging in their own right (Hughes et al., 2011; Rice, 2012; Rick, 2011), to provide an alternative avenue for discussion and more abstract thinking activities (Smetana et al., 2009).

Perhaps the most widely available graphic novel adaptations are those of Shakespeare's plays, and it has been posited that they have been used mostly to avoid "getting lost in the complex language" (Sardone, 2012, p. 68). Educators Wolfe and Kleijwegt (2012) used Oscar Zarate's (2005) version of *Othello* to explore how the texts differed in terms of modalities, identifying how the graphic novel text was complex, only with the added component of visuals that brought "out the symbolism behind the words" (p. 31) and allowed readers to find literary meaning in the text. The authors addressed Zarate's visual craft as well, including his depiction of various symbolic images as clues throughout the text for the reader to depict Iago's psychological transformation when he becomes consumed by wanting the destruction of Othello. The added modality can serve as a scaffold for some students, or provide an added dimension of meaning and potential analysis for others.

Teachers have also used comics to help readers understand and comprehend classic literature via creating their own comic adaptations (Sardone, 2012). In particular, after reading *The Great Gatsby*, students were able to incorporate textual evidence from the novel to create a narrative from the viewpoint of a character other than the protagonist. By creating their own comic books, students were able to demonstrate their grasps of plot and characterization, as well find an opportunity to demonstrate a complex sense of reading comprehension in an innovative manner.

Comics in Thematic Units and Teaching Difficult Topics

Due to the fact that graphic novels and comic books may fall into diverse genres and can be used with many content areas, they are effective resources to contribute to interdisciplinary thematic units, which allow students to "see the links between various subjects, rather than just compartmentalizing knowledge for specific classes" (Vega & Schnackenberg, 2006, p. 36). Carter (2007) recommended the use of graphic novels in cross-curricular units among collaborating content-area teachers, supplemental to traditional texts already being used in the English language arts (ELA) classroom, and/or use of contact zone theory as a lens through which students and teachers "examine important issues from multiple social and personal points of view and to posit those views in a dialogic conversation with others who do the same" (p. 51). He also emphasized how graphic novels can be used to "expose injustice and examine complex social issues" (p. 51), much like young adult novels do.

The modes of communication and representation bound into the mechanics of sequential art allow a great range of expression, which can lead to more empathetic readings of texts and also facilitate mingling textual works and identity, as mentioned earlier.

Combining the two concerns about cross-disciplinary subjects and the potential for fostering readers' empathy, comics, and in particular graphic novels, are sturdy vehicles for addressing difficult themes and perspectives that appear in literature and history, such as social justice (Wolk, 2009), stereotypes (Rice, 2012), immigration (Danzak, 2011), differing cultures and diversity (Schwarz & Crenshaw, 2013), as well as ways to focus on important issues relevant to teens (Carter, 2007; Bitz, 2004). They provide a mediated, yet immediate experience (Warshow, 2001) that can make an impact on any reader.

For instance, a graphic novel such as Art Spiegelman's *Maus* (2003), a dual narrative about an artist trying to relate to his father and the father's account of surviving being interned in a concentration camp during World War II, opens up a space where readers can "better understand the horrors of the Holocaust through the complex humanity of the main characters" (Chun, 2009, p. 147). By reading a work like this, teachers and students both get to explore dimensions of literature, history, philosophy, and humanity in reference to harrowing, coded images that open up possibilities for understanding. However, not all works that promote such an immediate experience need be so harrowing. Schwarz and Crenshaw (2013) discussed how the graphic novel can be used as a *bildungsroman,* or coming of age novel. In these novels, "often the protagonist wanders in search of love, social justice, or the meaning of life, and on the journey to discovery he or she faces conflict with self, family, and society" (p. 47). Although not all graphic novels are so moving or relatable, many have such a potential to address the potentially difficult issues of social justice, diversity, adolescent development, and students' identity.

Learning Outcomes of College-Age Students

Although it has been demonstrably proven that comics are very popular with younger adolescent readers (Griffith, 2010), that they are interwoven with a number of readers' identities, and that they also stoke students' motivation to read (Norton, 2003), the research on the effectiveness of teaching using comics is virtually nonexistent in the field of adolescent literacy. However, there are some indications that older research populations may speak to that absence. One research study on first-year college students, who may be considered older adolescents, has offered evidence that comics "prove beneficial as a method of making connections, recalling information, enhancing memory, and stimulating interest" (Cirigliano, 2012, p. 29). In addition, findings from a questionnaire used in that study indicated that, as a whole, the college students found that using the graphic novel was entertaining, enjoyable, and informative, and that they would also like to use graphic novels in other classes. In another study with first-year college students, Short, Randolph-Seng, and McKenny (2013) found that students understood, recalled, and retained economic concepts more effectively when reading a graphic novel text in lieu of their traditional textbooks. Somehow, the combination of words and images made more of a lasting impression and promoted more long-term memory.

CONCLUSION: WHAT TEACHERS OUGHT TO KNOW ABOUT COMICS

The studies detailed earlier may shed light on the potential positive outcomes of teaching using graphic novels, but they do not address the issue that these texts require some attention in order to be used effectively as pedagogical resources. Connors (2012) addressed the fact that most teacher education programs do not actually train teachers to teach visual literacy, and that these teachers are often left "to their own devices to figure out how best to address a subject with which they may lack experience" (p. 72). He emphasized the need of a shared vocabulary in reference to the concepts of basic shapes, perspective, and left–right visual structure that are incorporated throughout graphic novels. Furthermore, it is suggested that teachers be familiar with comics conventions, including the arrangement, organization, and navigation of panels, the conventions and types of speech and thought bubbles, and how shading may convey tone (Boerman-Cornell, 2013).

As Carter (2008) wrote, "It is sound practice" to include comics in schools, and "integrating them is a step toward a realization of more democratic notions of text, literacy, and curriculum" (p. 47). Indeed, the medium of comics offers unique meaning-making affordances, and the fact that so many children, youth, and adults throughout the world genuinely *enjoy* interacting with comics should not be overlooked by educators (Botzakis, 2009; Tabachnick, 2009). Comics are low-tech, relatively cheap to procure, and easy to make, and they represent a format familiar to many students and their families across cultural and socioeconomic lines. Comics are "a medium treasured by countless youths across many cultures and which is inherently representative of multiple synchronous literacy practices, serving as a counter-narrative to the dominant discourse of single-definition school literacy curriculums" (Low, 2012, p. 371). In fact, the medium of comics, writes Monnin (2011), "asks us to rethink how we define reading and writing today" (p. xii). Attending to how and why adolescents are drawn to comics, and what they do with the medium, requires that educational researchers and practitioners take up the anthropological traditions of New Literacy studies, because comics literacies, like other literacies, are cultural and multimodal practices linked to the lived contexts within which people make and express meaning. Monnin (2011) warns, "A failure to adopt a pedagogy of multiliteracies," such as one including comics, "will only create a further gap between what kinds of literacies students interact with at home or at work and those they interact with at school" (p. xii). Taking up these texts offers opportunities for all types of adolescents, those who are skilled and those who struggle. What is more, because of the increasingly diverse set of creators, characters, and situations being represented in comics (Royal, 2012), many formerly underrepresented groups can now find familiar faces to follow and read about in the pages of comics.

REFERENCES

Allington, R. L. (2013). What really matters when working with struggling readers. *The Reading Teacher, 66*(7), 520–530.

Alvermann, D. E., Hagood, M. C., Heron-Hruby, A., Hughes, P., Williams, K. B., & Yoon, J. C. (2007). Telling themselves who they are: What one out-of-school time study revealed about underachieving readers. *Reading Psychology, 28*(1), 31–50.

Arlin, M., & Roth, G. (1978). Pupils' use of time while reading comics and books. *American Educational Research Journal, 15*(2), 201–216.

Bergin, M. (2005). Who is reading manga?: One high school's story. *Young Adult Library Services, 3*(4), 24–26.

Bitz, M. (2004). The Comic Book Project: Forging alternative pathways to literacy. *Journal of Adolescent and Adult Literacy, 47*(7), 574–586.

Boatright, M. D. (2010). Graphic journeys: Graphic novels' representations of immigrant experiences. *Journal of Adolescent and Adult Literacy, 53*(6), 468–476.

Boerman-Cornell, B. (2013). More than comic books. *Educational Leadership, 70*(6), 73–77.

Botzakis, S. (2009). Adult fans of comic books: What they get out of reading. *Journal of Adolescent and Adult Literacy, 53*(1), 50–59.

Botzakis, S. (2014). Graphic novels: Who likes them and why. Retrieved from *http://ohiorc.org/adlit/inperspective/issue/2014-02/article/vignette1.aspx*.

Carter, J. B. (2007). Transforming English with graphic novels: Moving toward our "Optimus Prime." *English Journal, 97*(2), 49–53.

Carter, J. B. (2008). Comics, the canon, and the classroom. In D. Fisher & N. Frey (Eds.), *Teaching visual literacy: Using comic books, graphic novels, anime, cartoons, and more to develop comprehension and thinking skills* (pp. 47–60). Thousand Oaks, CA: Corwin Press.

Carter, J. B. (2009). Going graphic. *Educational Leadership, 66*(6), 68–72.

Cary, S. (2004). *Going graphic: Comics at work in the multilingual classroom.* Portsmouth, NH: Heinemann.

Chun, C. W. (2009). Critical literacies and graphic novels for English-language learners: Teaching Maus. *Journal of Adolescent and Adult Literacy, 53*(2), 144–153.

Cirigliano, M. M. (2012). Exploring the attitudes of students using an edutainment graphic novel as a supplement to learning in the classroom. *Science Educator, 21*(1), 29–36.

Connors, S. P. (2010). The best of both worlds: Rethinking the literary merit of graphic novels. *ALAN Review, 37*(3), 65–69.

Connors, S. P. (2012). Toward a shared vocabulary for visual analysis: An analytic toolkit for deconstructing the visual design of graphic novels. *Journal of Visual Literacy, 31*(1), 71–92.

Danzak, R. L. (2011). Defining identities through multiliteracies: EL teens narrate their immigration experiences as graphic stories. *Journal of Adolescent and Adult Literacy, 55*(3), 187–196.

Duncan, R., & Smith, M. (2009). *The power of comics: History, form and culture.* New York: Continuum.

Dyson, A. H. (1994). The Ninjas, the X-Men, and the ladies: Playing with power and identity in an urban primary school. *Teachers College Record, 96*, 219–239.

Edwards, B. (2009). Motivating middle school readers: The graphic novel link. *School Library Media Activities Monthly, 25*(8), 56–58.

Eisner, W. (1978). *A contract with God and other tenement stories.* New York: Baronet Books.

Eisner, W. (1985). *Comics and sequential art.* Paramus, NJ: Poorhouse Press.

Esquivel, I. (2006). Graphic novels: A medium with momentum. *The Journal of Media Literacy, 53*(2), 33–39.

Frey, N., & Fisher, D. (2004). Using graphic novels, anime, and the Internet in an urban high school. *English Journal, 93*(3), 19–25.

Frey, N., & Fisher, D. (Eds.). (2008). *Teaching visual literacy: Using comic books, graphic novels, anime, cartoons, and more to develop comprehension and thinking skills.* Thousand Oaks, CA: Corwin Press.

Gavigan, K. (2011). More powerful than a locomotive: Using graphic novels to motivate struggling male adolescent readers. *Journal of Research on Libraries and Young Adults, 1*(3). Retrieved from *www.yalsa.ala.org/jrlya/2011/06/more-powerful-than-a-locomotive-using-graphic-novels-to-motivate-struggling-male-adolescent-readers*.

Griffith, P. E. (2010). Graphic novels in the secondary classroom and school libraries. *Journal of Adolescent and Adult Literacy, 54*(3), 181–189.

Groensteen, T. (2009). Why are comics still in search of cultural legitimization? In J. Heer & K. Worcester (Eds.), *A comics studies reader* (pp. 3–12). Jackson: University Press of Mississippi.

Hallenbeck, P. N. (1976). Remediating with comic strips. *Journal of Learning Disabilities, 9*(1), 11–15.

Heath, S. B., & Bhagat, V. (1997). Reading comics, the invisible art. In J. Flood, S. B. Heath, & D. Lapp (Eds.), *Handbook of research on teaching literacy through the communicative and visual arts* (pp. 586–591). New York: Macmillan Library Reference USA.

Hughes, J. M., King, A., Perkins, P., & Fuke, V. (2011). Adolescents and "autographics": Reading and writing coming-of-age graphic novels. *Journal of Adolescent and Adult Literacy, 54*(8), 601–612.

Hull, G., & Schultz, K. (2001). Literacy and learning out of school: A review of theory and research. *Review of Educational Research, 71*(4), 575–611.

Jacobs, D. (2013). *Graphic encounters: Comics and the sponsorship of multimodal literacy.* New York: Bloomsbury Publishing USA.

Khurana, S. (2005). So you want to be a superhero?: How the art of making comics in an after-school setting can develop young people's creativity, literacy and identity. *Afterschool Matters,* (4), 1–9.

Kress, G., & van Leeuwen, T. (1996). *Reading images: The grammar of visual design.* New York: Routledge.

Lankshear, C., & Knobel, M. (2011). *New literacies: Everyday practices and social learning* (3rd ed.). New York: Open University Press.

Low, D. E. (2012). "Spaces invested with content": Crossing the "gaps" in comics with readers in schools. *Children's Literature in Education, 43*(4), 368–385.

McCloud, S. (1993). *Understanding comics: The invisible art.* Northampton, MA: Tundra.

Moeller, R. A. (2011). "Aren't these boy books?": High school students' readings of gender in graphic novels. *Journal of Adolescent and Adult Literacy, 54*(7), 476–484.

Moje, E. B. (2008). Youth cultures, literacies, and identities in and out of school. In J. Flood, S. B. Heath, & D. Lapp (Eds.), *Handbook on teaching literacy through the communicative and visual arts* (Vol. 2, pp. 207–219). New York: Erlbaum.

Monnin, K. (2011). *Teaching early reader comics and graphic novels.* Gainesville, FL: Maupin House.

Moorefield-Lang, H., & Gavigan, K. (2012). These aren't your father's funny papers: The new world of digital graphic novels. *Knowledge Quest, 40*(3), 30–34.

Morris, C. (2004). Urban students create superheroes to battle real-life ills. Retrieved from *www.columbia.edu/cu/news/04/02/comic_book_project.html.*

Morrison, T. G., Bryan, G., & Chilcoat, G. W. (2002). Using student-generated comic books in the classroom. *Journal of Adolescent and Adult Literacy, 45*(8), 758–767.

Mosse, H. L., & Daniels, C. R. (1959). Linear dyslexia: A new form of reading disorder. *American Journal of Psychotherapy, 13,* 826–841.

Norton, B. (2003). The motivating power of comic books: Insights from Archie comic readers. *The Reading Teacher, 57*(2), 140–147.

Palumbo, D. (1979). *The use of comics as an approach to introducing the techniques and terms of narrative to novice readers.* Paper presented at the annual meeting of the Popular Culture Association in the South, Louisville, KY.

Purves, A. C. (1998). *The web of text and the web of God: An essay on the third information transformation.* New York: Guilford Press.

Pustz, M. (1999). *Comic book culture: Fanboys and true believers.* Jackson: University Press of Mississippi.

Rice, M. (2012). Using graphic texts in secondary classrooms: A tale of endurance. *English Journal, 101*(5), 37–43.

Rick, J. (2011). Educate the educators about graphic novels: Five tips for success. *Library Media Connection, 30*(2), 34–35, 38.

Royal, D. P. (2012). Drawing attention: Comics as a means of approaching US cultural diversity. In L. Dong (Ed.), *Teaching comics and graphic narratives: Essays on theory, strategy, and practice* (pp. 67–79). Jefferson, NC: McFarland.

Sardone, N. B. (2012). Teaching classic literature with comic books and virtual lit trips. *English Journal, 102*(1), 67–70.

Schwartz, A., & Rubinstein-Ávila, E. (2006). Understanding the manga hype: Uncovering the multimodality of comic-book literacies. *Journal of Adolescent and Adult Literacy, 50*(1), 40–49.

Schwarz, G. (2006). Expanding literacies through graphic novels. *English Journal, 95*(6), 58–64.

Schwarz, G., & Crenshaw, C. (2013). Old media, new media: The graphic novel as Bildungsroman. *Journal of Media Literacy Education, 3*(1), 47–53.

Seyfried, J. (2008). Reinventing the book club: Graphic novels as educational heavyweights. *Knowledge Quest, 36*(3), 44–48.

Short, J. C., Randolph-Seng, B., & McKenny, A. F. (2013). Graphic presentation: An empirical examination of the graphic novel approach to communicate business concepts. *Business Communication Quarterly, 76*(3), 304–321.

Simon, R. (2012). "Without comic books, there would be no me": Teachers as connoisseurs of adolescents' literate lives. *Journal of Adolescent and Adult Literacy, 55*(6), 516–526.

Smetana, L., Odelson, D., Burns, H., & Grisham, D. L. (2009). Using graphic novels in the high school classroom: Engaging deaf students with a new genre. *Journal of Adolescent and Adult Literacy, 53*(3), 228–240.

Spiegelman, A. (2003). *Maus: A survivor's tale.* New York: Penguin.

Spurgeon, T. (2011, December 19). CR holiday interview #1—Art Spiegelman. Retrieved from *www.comicsreporter.com/index.php/cr_holiday_interview_1_art_spiegelman.*

Street, B. V. (1995). *Literacy in theory and practice.* New York: Cambridge University Press.

Tabachnick, S. E. (2009). Introduction. In S. E. Tabachnick (Ed.), *Teaching the graphic novel* (pp. 1–15). New York: Modern Language Association of America.

Tatalovic, M. (2009). Science comics as tools for science education and communication: A brief, exploratory study. *Journal of Science Communication, 8*(4), 1–17.

Thompson, T. (2008). *Adventures in graphica: Using comics and graphic novels to teach comprehension, 2–6.* Portland, ME: Stenhouse.

Vega, E. S., & Schnakenberg, H. L. (2006). Integrating technology, art, and writing to create comic books. *Middle School Journal, 37*(4), 30–36.

Warshow, R. (2001). *The immediate experience: Movies, comics, theatre and other aspects of popular culture* (expanded ed.). Cambridge, MA: Harvard University Press.

Witek, J. (1989). *Comic books as history: The narrative art of Jack Jackson, Art Spiegelman, and Harvey Pekar.* Jackson: University Press of Mississippi.

Witek, J. (2009). Seven ways I don't teach comics. In S. E. Tabachnick (Ed.), *Teaching the graphic novel* (pp. 217–222). New York: Modern Language Association of America.

Wolfe, P., & Kleijwegt, D. (2012). Interpreting graphic versions of Shakespearean plays. *English Journal, 101*(5), 30–36.

Wolk, S. (2009). Reading for a better world: Teaching for social responsibility with young adult literature. *Journal of Adolescent and Adult Literacy, 52*(8), 664–673.

Wright, B. W. (2001). *Comic book nation: The transformation of youth culture in America.* Baltimore: Johns Hopkins University Press.

Yang, G. (2008). Graphic novels in the classroom. *Language Arts, 85*(3), 185–192.

Zarate, O. (2005). *William Shakespeare's Othello.* London: Can of Worms Press.

CHAPTER 19

Academic Language and Subject-Area Learning

ZHIHUI FANG

Learning in any modern discipline requires at least some interaction with written text, with some disciplines (e.g., history and English) more reliant on it for their social practices than others (e.g., art and music). This dependency becomes even more pronounced in subject-area learning, where content is presented in school to students primarily through textbooks and other written media (e.g., trade books, magazines, and online resources). These texts, as disciplinary and professional discourses recontextualized for educational purposes (Bernstein, 1975), are constructed in lexical, grammatical, and discursive patterns that students often find unfamiliar and difficult, if not alienating. These patterns, commonly referred to as *academic language* (or *academic registers*), are not barriers devised by experts for gatekeeping purposes (although they can effectively serve as gatekeepers that alienate those who have not mastered them), but they are functional for construing knowledge and value and for achieving particular rhetorical effects that are specific to particular genres and disciplines; at the same time, however, they are also a major source of reading and writing difficulties for many adolescents (Fang, 2012a; Fang, Schleppergrell, & Moore, 2013). This chapter reviews recent scholarship on the conception of academic language, the challenges academic language presents to adolescents in subject-area learning, and pedagogical approaches and strategies for addressing these new language demands.

CONCEPTUALIZING ACADEMIC LANGUAGE

The notion of academic language has received considerable attention in the literature on second-language learning and, more recently, in literacy education. Although a consensual definition of academic language has yet to emerge, most scholars associate it with the oral or written language required for doing academic work in school. At least three areas of scholarship contribute to the conception of academic language. The sociolinguistic work of the early 1980s (e.g., Heath, 1983; Michaels, 1981; Snow, 1983) shows that teachers have certain expectations about language use in school-based tasks (e.g., group sharing time, read-alouds, writing conferences) and that children who come from homes and communities where language use is different from school expectations are often disadvantaged and disempowered, leading to their lack of engagement in classroom literacy events and ultimately their literacy underachievement and school failure.

The idea that children's home, or everyday, language differs from school-based, or academic, language was brought to the forefront of educators' consciousness when Cummins (1981, 1984), working in bilingual settings with a focus on assessment issues, introduced a distinction between what he called "basic interpersonal communicative skills" (BICS) and "cognitive academic language proficiency" (CALP). BICS, or everyday language, refers to the language used on the playground, in the lunchroom, at birthday parties, or in other day-to-day social interactional contexts. CALP, or academic language, refers to the language used for effective participation in subject-area learning in school. According to Cummins, academic language is cognitively more demanding; hence, it takes much longer (5–7 years) to develop than everyday language (6 months to 2 years).

Cummins's binary distinction raises our awareness of the gap between everyday and academic language, and reminds us of the detrimental effects of conflating the two in assessing students' academic performance. At the same time, however, it has been criticized for privileging school-based language and for offering an impoverished view of everyday language (Haneda, 2014). Functional linguists (e.g., Gibbons, 2006; Schleppegrell, 2004) have worked to address this issue by foregrounding the role of context in language use. Drawing on Halliday's (1978, 1985) work on language in context (i.e., register), these scholars argued that academic language is best conceptualized along a continuum of mode, from contexts of informal spontaneous interaction to contexts of formal written communication. Emphasizing that language use varies according to context and purpose, they showed that the language that is functional for school (i.e., academic language) is different from the language that students use to socialize with family members and friends in their daily lives (i.e., everyday language). This difference, as summarized by Snow and Uccelli (2009), lies along the dimensions of interpersonal stance (detached and authoritative vs. involved and interactional), information load (concise and dense vs. redundant and sparse), organization of information (thing oriented vs. action oriented, embedded clauses vs. coordinate and subordinate clauses, within-text references vs. outside-text references), lexical choices (diverse, precise, and formal vocabulary vs. limited, imprecise, and colloquial vocabulary), and representational congruence (compact and incongruent grammar vs. simple and congruent grammar, abstract concepts as agentive subjects of sentences vs. animate entities as grammatical agents of sentences).

Academic language is not a monolithic or unitary construct, however. Its forms and functions vary by subject matter, task, purpose, and grade level, as different forms of knowledge and ways of meaning require different kinds of academic language. Although certain features of writing are commonly recognized as "academic," they manifest in different ways across different disciplines and social contexts. One reason for this variation is that academic communities are composed of individuals "with diverse experiences, expertise, commitments and influence" whose language and literacy practices are influenced by "the personal and interpersonal, as well as the institutional and sociocultural" (Hyland, 2004, p. 9). Academic language is also dynamic and evolving, reflecting the protean nature of knowledge and the multitude of forces that characterize the specific situation in which it is used. For example, deepening globalization has led to the growing presence of multilinguals (i.e., people using two or more language varieties), who bring their unique ideologies, identities, experiences, and rhetorical styles to their discursive practices. Such "codemeshing" or "translanguaging" (Canagarajah, 2013)—the simultaneous use of two or more language varieties in a single context—challenges the homogeneity of academic language, bringing about diversity and hybridity in the way language is used in academic and disciplinary settings. In light of this, Fang (2012b) suggested that academic language is best conceived of as the braiding of three strands of language—everyday language, abstract language, and metaphoric language (see Table 19.1 for examples and features of these language strands), with the shape of the braid determined by factors such as topic, context, and purpose. Figure 19.1 captures this braiding, linking language strands to the type of knowledge each strand typically construes and the literacy demands it presents. Any text is an instantiation of a particular braiding, with certain strands more heavily present in some texts than in others. Recognizing and responding to the different shapes and features of academic language are key to supporting students' academic work in school.

TABLE 19.1. Examples and Features of Three Language Strands

Strand of language	Example[a]	Feature
Everyday language	You can control the trains this way, and if you do that, you can be quite sure that they'll run more safely and more quickly, no matter how bad the weather gets.	• Sentence consisting of coordinate and subordinate clauses (*and, if, no matter how*) • Process oriented (*control, do, run, be, gets*) • Pronouns (*you, they*) as clause subjects • Colloquial vocabulary and phrases
Written language	If this method of control is used, trains will unquestionably be able to run more safely and faster, even when the weather conditions are most adverse.	• Sentence consisting of subordinate clauses (*if, when*) • Thing or concept oriented (*this method of control, trains, the weather conditions*) • Abstract (*this method of control, the weather conditions*) and concrete (*trains*) participants as clause subjects • Formal vocabulary and phrases
Metaphoric language	The use of this method of controlling unquestionably leads to safer and faster train running in the most adverse weather conditions.	• A single sentence with two long noun phrases (*the use of this method of controlling, safer and faster train running in the most adverse weather conditions*) linked by a causal verb phrase (*leads to*) • Abstract participants constructed in dense noun phrases (*the use of this method of controlling, safer and faster train running in the most adverse weather conditions*) • Formal vocabulary and phrases

[a]The three example sentences are taken from Halliday (1989, p. 79).

326 ADOLESCENT LITERACIES AND MULTIPLE TEXTS

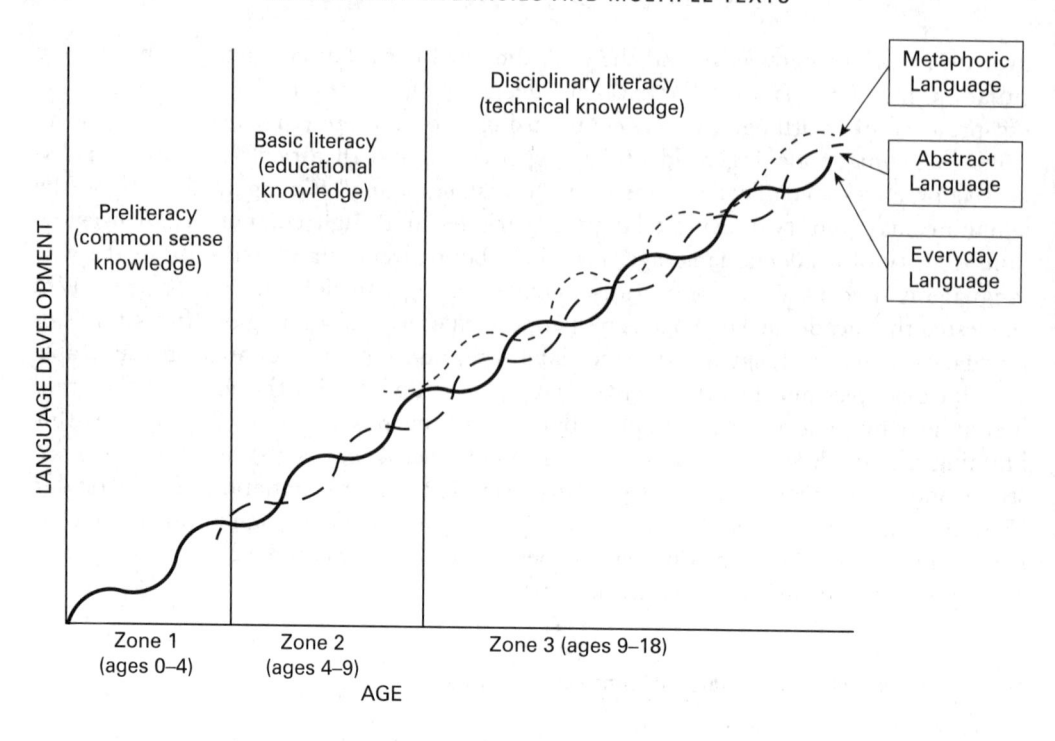

[Figure: A graph with LANGUAGE DEVELOPMENT on the y-axis and AGE on the x-axis, divided into three zones: Zone 1 (ages 0–4) labeled "Preliteracy (common sense knowledge)"; Zone 2 (ages 4–9) labeled "Basic literacy (educational knowledge)"; Zone 3 (ages 9–18) labeled "Disciplinary literacy (technical knowledge)". Three braided curves rise across the zones, labeled at the top right as "Metaphoric Language," "Abstract Language," and "Everyday Language."]

FIGURE 19.1. Academic language as the braiding of everyday language, abstract language, and metaphoric language. Adapted from Fang (2012b, p. 22). Adapted with permission from the author.

More recently, scholars have argued that the notion "academic language" needs to be expanded to "academic communication" to account for the multimodal and multisemiotic nature of today's school-based texts and students' expanding communicative repertoires inside and outside of school. Modern science texts, for example, contain "not just words in sentences and paragraphs, but tables, charts, diagrams, graphs, maps, drawings, photographs, and a host of specialized visual representations from acoustical sonograms to chromatography strips and gene maps" (Lemke, 2002, p. 24). As Haneda (2014) pointed out, communication in academic settings takes the form of not only natural language but also physical action, material artifacts, and other semiotic tools (e.g., graphs, diagrams, and images). In other words, academic language is only one of the communicative repertoires of academic communication. This means that attention to both linguistic and nonlinguistic means of communication is critical to ensuring students' success in school and beyond.

ACADEMIC LANGUAGE AND THE CHALLENGES OF SUBJECT-AREA LEARNING

Academic language is a kind of social language commonly associated with the social context of schooling (Gee, 2008). It is "the language through which school subjects are taught and assessed" (Schleppegrell & O'Hallaron, 2011, p. 3). As such, academic language presents a challenge to students who have limited experience with or little instruction in it. Recent statistics show that over two-thirds of adolescents struggle with reading and writing texts in subject areas, with English language learners and children from economically disadvantaged backgrounds disproportionately represented in this struggling population (National Center for Education Statistics, 2013). Although success in subject-area learning ultimately depends on content knowledge, language and literacy skills, and motivation, most literacy scholars agree that academic language presents a major obstacle to this success. In fact, the literacy and learning problems experienced by many adolescents have been attributed in large part to their struggle with academic language (Snow & Uccelli, 2009). What is it, then, about academic language that makes it daunting for students, particularly in subject-area learning at the secondary level? To illustrate the demands of subject-area reading and writing, I present several texts below that middle and high school students are expected to be able to read (see Table 19.2) or have written in response to academic tasks (see Table 19.3) in subject-area classrooms.

Table 19.2 features two texts. Text 1 is an excerpt from Chris Crowe's (2003) *Getting Away with Murder,* an award-winning trade book often used in middle school social studies classrooms, which details the kidnapping and murder of a Black teenager, the subsequent trial and acquittal of his two White killers, and the aftermath of these events for the civil rights movement. Text 2 is an excerpt from *A Window on Eternity,* a trade book suitable for high school environmental science. This book, written by two-time Pulitzer Prize winning biologist Edward Wilson (2014), describes the destruction and restoration of an important preserve in Mozambique, Africa.

TABLE 19.2. Sample Texts from Award-Winning Science and Social Studies Trade Books

Text 1 (social studies text)[a]	Text 2 (science text)[b]
The Emmett Till case was not the sole cause of the civil rights movement, but it was the final indignity that caused the flood of outrage to overflow the dam of racial injustice. Brinkley points out that Rosa Parks did not plan to initiate a bus boycott on December 1, 1955, but her own weariness from a lifetime of discrimination made her determined not to surrender her seat to a white person on a Montgomery city bus that evening. "A lifetime's education in injustice—" wrote Brinkley, "from her grandfather's nightly vigils to the murder of Emmett Till—had strengthened her resolve to act when time came." Parks's refusal to abide by the segregated busing laws in Montgomery led to the 381-day boycott of the city bus system, a boycott that brought Reverend Martin Luther King, Jr., to prominence, brought an end to segregated public transportation in Alabama, and marked the first nationally publicized action in the modern civil rights movement.	The near obliteration of the megafauna during the civil war and the massive poaching afterward had consequences for the remainder of the park's plants and animals that have only begun to be studied. With the zebra and antelope herds reduced to insignificance, too few grazers and browsers remained to trim the park's grasses and low-growing herbaceous vegetation. Only ground fires were left to fill that ecological role, and then mostly during the long, dry winter. Plants once kept short by constant feeding now grew higher. At the outset of the dry season, leaves and branches from bushes and trees that had fallen freely all the way to the ground were caught and held by the thickening layer of brush. The suspended detritus, kept away from ground moisture and dried by currents of air, became tinder for the lightning-struck fires. In the savannas and dry forests the flames that once hugged the ground now climbed to reach the canopies of the shrubs and trees, where, caught by the wind, they became wildfires that swept the land.

[a]From Crowe (2003, p. 114).
[b]From Wilson (2014, p. 39).

TABLE 19.3. Sample Texts Written by Middle and High School Students

Text 3 (biography)	Text 4 (report)
Do you want to hear about a woman scientists who lived for 101 years? Well, her name is Alice Hamilton. She was born in 1869 in Fort Wayne, Indiana, and died in 1970. She was an American pathologist. She worked to promote safer working conditions in industry. She conducted studies and did research for the state of Illinois, the U.S. government, and the League of Nations. Also, she became the first female faculty member at the Harvard Medical School (1919–1935). Wow, she did a lot. That was a big deal to be a faculty member of the Harvard Medical School, plus she was the first female there. I think that is pretty cool. Right now I am thinking that she was just born smart because she was educated at home most of her life, and then she went to a private school for girls for a few years. She received her medical degree from the University of Michigan, where she was one of the first women to get her medical degree. And then she continued her studies at the Johns Hopkins University in Baltimore, Maryland. Actually, she never stopped trying to learn new things. She was also a champion of workers' compensation laws. Cool, she started off so small, in her jobs I mean, and ended up so big. I wonder how she managed to do all that? I guess she just kept on trying until she succeeded.	How long have Alligators been on earth? No one really nows that question. But what we do now is that they love to eat a lot. Also they are anphibian but they like the water better compared to the pitchers I took, if they aren't in water they, are in swampy areas. Alligators can be very vicious so if you were to see one in the wild then don't panic, just walk away. Don't mess with them when it's mateing season because they are very carefull about their babies. If one was to start chasing you, run in a zigzag because they are very fast running straight, but there slow turning. A cool fact is that when you hold his mouth shut it want be able to open it's mouth but when it shuts his mouth it can chop of your arm. A baby can hold it shut but it is dangerous when his mouth is open. This amphibians are highly dangerous but very cool to study, there is a lot to know about this awesome creature and I will love to work with them some more.

Note. Students' original manuscripts are presented here without correction of misspellings or punctuation.

    Both texts in Table 19.2 deal with topics that are not "here and now," but are instead distant and specialized Text 1 interprets a historically significant event that happened some 60 years ago, and Text 2 provides an explanation for the devastation of biodiversity in a nature preserve in Africa. Accordingly, the language that constructs these sorts of knowledge is technical, dense, abstract, metaphorical, and hierarchically structured, patterning in ways that are not only different from everyday language but also specific to particular disciplines. Technicality in both texts is realized through a set of field-related terms that include, for example, *civil rights movement, racial injustice, discrimination, bus boycott, segregated busing laws, Rosa Parks,* and *Martin Luther King, Jr.* for Text 1 and *megafauna, herbaceous vegetation, ecological, plants, detritus, savannas,* and *currents of air* for Text 2. These terms convey meanings that are specific to the specialized fields of, respectively, civil rights movement and ecology.

    Density, on the other hand, is realized in long noun phrases with modifiers, prepositional phrases, embedded clauses, and nonfinite clauses. The long noun phrases in Text 1 include <u>the sole</u> cause <u>of the civil rights movement,</u> <u>Parks's</u> refusal <u>to abide by the segregated busing laws in Montgomery,</u> <u>the 381-day</u> boycott <u>of the city bus system,</u> <u>a boycott that brought Reverend Martin Luther King, Jr. to prominence,</u> and <u>the first nationally</u>

publicized action *in the modern civil rights movement*. Text 2 uses long noun phrases such as *the near obliteration of the megafauna during the civil war*, *the remainder of the park's plants and animals that have only begun to be studied*, *the park's low-growing herbaceous* vegetation, *the* outset *of the dry season*, leaves and branches *from bushes and trees that had fallen freely all the way to the ground*, *the thickening* layer *of brush*, *the lightning-struck* fires, *the* flames *that once hugged the ground*, *the* canopies *of the shrubs and trees*, and *wildfires that swept the land*. These noun phrases enable the author to pack a heavy load of information into the clause structure, substantially increasing the processing demand for the reader. Another grammatical pattern that also contributes to density is long sentences with multiple embedded, coordinate, and subordinate clauses, such as the last sentence of Text 1 (*Parks's refusal . . . the modern civil rights movement*) and the last sentence of Text 2 (*In the savannas . . . that swept the land*).

Abstraction is realized in nominalizations, that is, nouns or noun phrases that can be repackaged into more everyday expressions with verbs, adjectives, or clauses. Text 1 is populated with nominalizations such as *cause, indignity, the flood of outrage, the dam of racial injustice, boycott, weariness, a lifetime of discrimination, the murder of Emmett Till, resolve, refusal, prominence, end, transportation, action,* and *civil rights movement*. Text 2 also contains some, although much fewer, nominalizations, such as *obliteration, poaching, insignificance,* and *feeding*. These nominalizations allow the author to expand information (e.g., *Parks's refusal to abide by the segregated busing laws in Montgomery, the first nationally publicized* action), ascribe judgment (e.g., *the sole cause, the final indignity, the massive poaching, constant feeding*), package a series of events into an entity that is then reified as a specialized concept (e.g., *civil rights movement*), and facilitate discursive flow (e.g., *the near obliteration of megafauna and the massive poaching* in Text 2 re-presents as subject a series of ecologically devastating events that were described in the preceding chapter of the book so that discussion about the topic can continue in the current chapter).

A more subtle use of language in the two texts involves metaphorical realization of logical relations. In everyday language, logical–semantic links are typically realized in conjunctions (e.g., *because, but*). However, in Texts 1 and 2, these links are also indicated through clause embedding, as well as nominal, verbal, or prepositional expressions. For example, causation in Text 1 is realized in nouns (*the sole cause of the civil rights movement*), verbs (*that caused the flood of outrage, her own weariness . . . made her determined not to . . ., Parks's refusal . . . led to the 381-day boycott . . . , a boycott that brought . . . to prominence, brought an end to . . .*), and prepositions (e.g., *but her own weariness from a lifetime of discrimination*). Similarly, cause–effect relations in Text 2 are realized in nouns (e.g., *consequences*) and prepositions (e.g., *with the zebra and antelope herds reduced to insignificance*). These ways of construing causality and other logical–semantic relations make the logical links in the text much more difficult to discern, thus impeding comprehension for students who are typically more used to making logical links through conjunctions.

In terms of structure, Text 1 sandwiches concrete narration (what Brinkley said about Rosa Parks) between abstract interpretations (the first and the last sentences of the paragraph), whereas Text 2 presents a thesis (first sentence) that is subsequently explained and illustrated. These structures are reflective of the different purposes served by the two texts, with Text 1 focusing on interpreting historically significant events and Text 2 on explaining the reasons for the destruction of biodiversity in a nature preserve.

Taken together, the lexical, grammatical, and discursive patterns just described are motivated in that they enable disciplinary experts to construct knowledge and structure text in ways that conform to genre and disciplinary norms and achieve the author's purpose. They tend to co-occur to create a syndrome known as *academic language,* or more specifically, *historical language* or *scientific language.* While any of these features can be present in everyday language at any time, they rarely co-occur with regularity in the context of everyday quotidian conversation. As such, they tend to be unfamiliar to students, presenting a significant barrier to reading comprehension, above and beyond unfamiliar topics.

Not only do adolescents find academic language challenging to read and comprehend, many of them also struggle with using academic language to communicate in subject-area learning, as can be seen with the two texts presented in Table 19.3. Text 3 was written by a sixth-grade student in response to an assignment in her science class that required her to write a biography of a famous scientist who is her favorite and about whom she has read at least three books or articles. Text 4 was written by a ninth-grade student in response to his language arts teacher's request to write a report about one of his favorite state animals.

Both texts draw heavily on the lexicogrammatical and discursive resources of everyday language. In telling the life story of scientist Alice Hamilton or describing the attributes of alligators, the student writers use

- Interrogative sentences (e.g., *Do you want to hear about a woman scientists who lived for 101 years? How long have alligators been on earth?*).
- Imperative sentences (e.g., *Don't mess with them; then don't panic, just walk away*).
- First- and second-person pronouns (e.g., *I, you*).
- Colloquial expressions (e.g., <u>Well</u>, *her name is Alice Hamilton;* <u>Also</u>, *she became the first female faculty member; I think* <u>that's pretty cool</u>; <u>Wow</u>, *she did* <u>a lot</u>; *That was* <u>a big deal</u> *to be a faculty member . . . ,* <u>plus</u> *she was the first female there;* <u>Actually</u>, *she never stopped trying to learn new things;* <u>Cool</u>, *she* <u>started off so small</u>, <u>in her jobs I mean</u>, *and* <u>ended up</u> <u>so big</u>. *No one* <u>really</u> *nows that question; But what we do now is that they love to eat* <u>a lot</u>; <u>Also</u> *they are amphibian; A* <u>cool</u> *fact is . . . ; This amphibians are highly dangerous but* <u>very cool</u> *to study, there is* <u>a lot</u> *to know about this* <u>awesome</u> *creature and I will love to work with them* <u>some more</u>).
- Reference to writer's mental processes (e.g., *Right now I* <u>am thinking</u> *that . . . ;* <u>I think</u> *that's pretty cool;* <u>I wonder</u> *how she managed to do all that?* <u>I guess</u> *she just kept on trying*).
- Chaining syntax (e.g., *Right now I am thinking* <u>that</u> *she was just born smart* <u>because</u> *she was educated at home most of her life,* <u>and then</u> *she went to a private school for girls for a few years; Also they are amphibian* <u>but</u> *they like the water better compared to the pitchers I took,* <u>if</u> *they aren't in water they, are in swampy areas; A cool fact is* <u>that</u> <u>when</u> *you hold his mouth shut it want be able to open it's mouth* <u>but</u> <u>when</u> *it shuts his mouth it can chop of your arm*).
- Conjunctions to indicate temporal sequence (e.g., *right now, when, and then*) or other logical links (*also, because, so, but, if, until*).
- Pronouns with unclear or inconsistent references (e.g., *I wonder how she managed*

to do all *that*?; but what *we* do now is that they love to eat a lot; Don't mess with *them* when *it*'s mating season; If *one* was to start chasing you, run in a zigzag because *they* are very fast running straight. A cool fact is that when you hold *his* mouth shut *it* want be able to open *it*'s mouth but when *it* shuts *his* mouth *it* can chop of your arm).

In terms of organization, neither text has a logically well-developed structure. Instead, both texts are sustained mainly through the repetition of pronominal references (e.g., she, they, we, I). Much of information is presented haphazardly, especially in Text 4, with no clear indication of a particular ordering of a conceptual kind. No significance can be attached to the order of the sentences; they could occur in any order. The presence of these language features suggests that neither writer has firm control over academic language.

The difficulties that the students experience in using academic language can be summarized into three areas that Snow and Uccelli (2009) identified as (1) the challenge of representing the self and the audience, such as acknowledging the status of the audience, selecting an appropriate voice, signaling a specific relationship with audience, and indexing epistemological status of a claim; (2) the challenge of representing the message, such as selecting and participating in a genre, adjusting message to audience status, representing ideas, indexing source of information; and (3) the challenge of organizing discourse, such as using discourse markers to signal logical–semantic relations and making choices of reference. To these, a fourth area of challenge can be added, that of adhering to conventions of mechanics (e.g., spelling and punctuation) and basic grammar (e.g., subject–verb agreement, pronoun use), which is a particularly salient issue with Text 4. A further challenge is that facility in using academic language must be coordinated with additional cognitive accomplishments, such as genre mastery, command of reasoning strategies, and disciplinary knowledge, in order for any communication (e.g., writing) to be successful (Snow & Uccelli, 2009).

Understanding the language through which subject-area knowledge is constructed and the challenges this language presents to adolescents is key to success in subject-area teaching. It enables teachers to better scaffold students' literacy development and support their learning in subject areas. As Schleppegrell (2006) observed, "Recognizing the linguistic realizations of the challenges of disciplinary learning gives us power to raise students' consciousness about these features of language and thereby enable their participation in and contribution to the further development of knowledge" (p. 62). Teachers need strategies for promoting academic language development within the context of subject-area learning.

DEVELOPING ACADEMIC LANGUAGE IN SUBJECT-AREA LEARNING

Given the centrality of academic language to subject-area learning and socialization, it is essential that students develop facility in understanding and using it. All teachers have the responsibility to help students develop linguistic resources that enable them to learn and communicate what they have learned. This development work requires "experience, practice, motivation, and opportunity to interact and negotiate meaning" in authentic contexts for which academic language is functional (Schleppegrell, 2001, p. 455). It needs to take place in disciplinary contexts in which academic language is used for communicative purposes involving firsthand experiences of observing, manipulating, performing, and inquiring, as well as secondhand experiences of reading, writing, and talking; that is, academic language cannot be learned in a vacuum or in contexts in which it is rarely present. Embedding academic language work within authentic disciplinary experiences gives the work purpose, meaning, and usefulness, ensuring that language and content are not separate but are developed together.

One key to developing academic language proficiency is to provide ample opportunities for reading, writing, and talking about texts in subject areas. As students explore topics that are of interest to them and significance to the subject area, they read, discuss, reason with, question, evaluate, reflect on, and write about texts that are rich in content and comprise varied genres, registers, and modalities. Reading and responding to a wide variety of texts valued by disciplinary insiders (e.g., textbooks, trade books, journals, magazines, newspapers, websites, encyclopedias, wikis, and archived documents) maximizes students' exposure to academic language as it is used by experts to explore substantive issues in their fields, and is especially important for those who have limited experience with it in school or no access to it outside of school.

Immersion in academic language does not guarantee its mastery, however. Students need guidance in order to gain a deep understanding of its logic, structure, and functions. Such guidance can be provided through "explicit attention to language that is informed by knowledge about academic registers" (Schleppegrell, 2012, p. 413). According to Gee (2003), whereas children have an innate ability to acquire their mother tongue (everyday language), the process of learning a social language such as academic language is not itself biologically endowed. Similarly, Vygotsky (1934/1987) argued that "scientific concepts" (in the sense of being systematically organized), such as academic language, are learned primarily through instruction, requiring conscious awareness and intentional application. Taken together, these scholars suggest that teachers need to provide deliberate support to help students develop proficiency in academic language.

Such support has traditionally been given in the form of vocabulary instruction, as vocabulary knowledge is widely recognized as the key to unlocking the meaning of text. For example, Snow, Lawrence, and White (2009) described an approach to academic language development for students in grades 4–8 that focuses on academic vocabulary across the subject areas of social studies, science, mathematics, and language arts. The program, called Word Generation, teaches words that students are likely to encounter in school textbooks and on tests. It consists of weekly units, with each unit introducing five high-utility target words drawn from brief passages on controversial contemporary topics. Passages on controversial topics are chosen in order to stimulate conversation, debate, and inquiry, thus giving students an authentic opportunity to use academic language with target vocabulary. In each unit, target words are introduced at the beginning of the week, then revisited in a range of settings during the week to ensure that students have multiple exposures to these words in meaningful contexts. Students examine each target word as it is used in several subject areas in order to develop a multifaceted understanding of the word. They also learn to analyze words structurally, identifying prefixes, suffixes, roots, or cognates that may help them make connections with target words and make sense of the weekly passages. The program was found to improve students' text comprehension and content learning. Other evidence-based strategies for engaging adolescents in learning academic vocabulary have also been described, including word sorts, vocabulary journals, four squares, concept definition word maps, categories, word walls, vocabulary self-collection, picture puzzlers, music puzzlers, matching games, dice games, pictionades, Academic Taboo, and Action Jeopardy! (Fang, 2010; Gillis, 2014/2015; Larson, Dixon, & Townsend, 2013; Townsend, 2009).

But academic language is more than just vocabulary. Developing academic language proficiency involves learning not just skills for tackling complex words but also a repertoire of other skills that are similarly critical to subject-area reading and writing, such as unpacking complex or unusual sentences, uncovering agency, understanding connectives, identifying author stance and voice, tracking references, defining concepts, establishing a context, demonstrating credibility and membership, enacting interpersonal relationships, and calibrating discursive flow (Fang, 2016; Hyland, 2004). Fang (2008, 2010) described a handful of language-based tasks for developing some of these skills, including noun expansion and deconstruction, sentence completion, sentence combining and anatomy, analysis of thematic progression, and paraphrasing. These tasks, briefly described and exemplified in Table 19.4, can be used in read-aloud sessions, writing conferences, or other meaningful contexts, with language samples drawn from the texts students read or write in the units of study.

In addition to these general academic language skills, students also need to learn how and why academic language varies across genres and subject areas in order to develop disciplinary literacies. An approach that can help students develop these skills is "functional language analysis" (Fang & Schleppegrell, 2010). The approach, which has been shown to be effective in promoting both literacy development and content learning in subject-area classrooms (e.g., Achugar, Schleppegrell, & Oteiza, 2007), offers a set of linguistic tools that enable students to systematically explore meaning through detailed analysis and discussion of language patterns in the text. For example, students can identify the content (i.e., main ideas or what happened) of the text by analyzing the process (realized in a verb), participant (realized in a noun), and circumstance (realized in adverb and prepositional phrases) in each clause, with process analysis showing what events are presented (e.g., doing, describing, identifying, saying, or thinking), participant analysis revealing who/what is involved and has agency and who/what is not involved, and circumstance analysis indicating when, how, and why something happened. They can learn about how the text is organized by analyzing what begins each clause (e.g., time markers indicating chronology or abstract nouns indicating causes and effects), how clauses are combined (e.g., coordination, subordination, or embedding), and how cohesion is created and sustained (e.g., reference, conjunction). They can also infer author opinion, attitude, or voice by analyzing word choices, with, for example, analysis of intensifiers (e.g., *The general is a little/extremely disappointed*) and words with positive/negative meanings (e.g., *The oil price skyrocketed/plunged in recent weeks*) indicating how the message in the text is made more or less intense, analysis of adjectives and adverbs (e.g., *They are true friends. This effectively ends their friendship*) showing how meaning is made more or less precise, and analysis of nouns (e.g., *That rascal used to be my roommate*), verbs (e.g., *It is alleged that he stole the car*), adverbs (e.g., *The students were treated fairly at the camp*), adjectives (e.g., *That is disgusting*), and modals (e.g., *She may be sick. This can't be true*) revealing author judgment, appreciation, emotion, or engagement. These analyses, summarized in Table 19.5, promote close, critical reading of text, helping students more effectively access and critically evaluate the information they are expected to learn from the text; at the same time, they also illuminate the ways language is used as a

TABLE 19.4. Description of Language-Based Tasks

Name of task	Description	Purpose
Noun expansion and deconstruction	Students are given a noun (e.g., *solid*) and asked to compete in a language game called building "noun trains" by adding as many modifiers (before noun) and qualifiers (after noun) as possible (e.g., <u>a natural, nonliving</u> solid <u>with a definite chemical structure that is representable by a chemical formula</u>). Conversely, students deconstruct a long noun phrase such as "*the first nationally publicized action in the modern civil rights movement*" into its constituents of pointer (*the*), describer (*first, nationally publicized*), head (*action*), and qualifier (*in the modern civil rights movement*), recognizing the lexical and grammatical resources (e.g., article, adjective, adverb, prepositional phrase, embedded clause) that instantiate these functional constituents.	This task develops students' understanding of how information is packed to increase density in subject-area texts.
Sentence completion	Students are presented with a brief passage—such as "*During combustion, the carbon and hydrogen combine with oxygen in the air to form carbon dioxide and water. _____ releases energy in the forms of heat and light.*"—and asked to fill in the blank space with a noun or noun phrase (e.g., *this process*) that summarizes the previously presented information.	This task helps students gain insights into how information is synthesized or distilled in a way that also facilitates discursive flow in the text.
Sentence combining and anatomy	Students repackage a set of loosely connected sentences (e.g., *Bacteria use sulfur compounds to perform chemosynthesis. They live along portions of the mid-ocean ridges. In the mid-ocean ridges, superheated water either seeps or blasts from the crust. This is shown in Figure 14-7.*) into a more compact sentence (e.g., *Bacteria <u>that</u> perform chemosynthesis using sulfur compounds live along portions of the mid-ocean ridges, <u>where</u> superheated water either seeps or blasts from the crust, <u>as</u> shown in Figure 14-7.*), or vice versa.	This task helps students understand how information can be packaged and repackaged in ways that accommodate the needs of audience, style, author purpose, and discourse organization.
Analysis of thematic progression	Students examine what begins each clause (i.e., theme) and patterns of thematic progression (e.g., reiterating, zigzagging, or mixed) in a text. For example, this brief excerpt from a middle school environmental science textbook (*Recycling, along with reducing and reusing, also reduces the amount of trash that must be burned or hauled to landfills. The burning of trash, the trucks that haul trash to landfills, and even the landfills themselves all cause air pollution. To reduce air pollution, many people keep their cars well tuned. Well tuned cars use gas more efficiently and produce fewer pollutants.*) features a zig-zagging pattern of thematic progression. Specifically, the beginning of the second sentence (i.e., *The burning of trash, the trucks that haul trash to landfills, and even the landfills themselves*) summarizes what is presented toward the end of the first sentence (*the amount of trash that must be burned or hauled to landfills*); the beginning of the third sentence (i.e., *To reduce air pollution*) picks up what is presented toward the end of the second sentence (i.e., *... cause air pollution*); and the beginning of the fourth sentence (i.e., *Well-tuned cars ...*) continues the discussion of the topic presented at the end of the third sentence (i.e., *keep their cars well tuned*).	This task helps students learn how the choice of clause themes impacts the presentation of information and the creation of discursive flow.

(continued)

TABLE 19.4. *(continued)*

Name of task	Description	Purpose
Paraphrasing	Students work with a short but challenging chunk of text (e.g., *The location and operation of the camps were based on calculations of accessibility and cost-effectiveness—the hallmarks of modern business and administrative practice.*), using their own words to rewrite the text, with special attention to specialized vocabulary, nominalization, logical links, and long noun phrases (e.g., *The Nazis determined <u>where the camps were to be located</u> and <u>how they were to be operated</u> by <u>calculating</u> how <u>accessible</u> and <u>cost-effective</u> they are. This is <u>characteristic of how modern business and administration operate</u>.*).	This task encourages students to switch between everyday language and academic language, promoting the use of everyday language as a resource for making sense of academic language.

creative resource for making meanings in genre- and discipline-specific ways, thus giving students insights into and power for academic communication.

It is important to bear in mind that academic language is not the ultimate goal of learning; rather, it is a means to learning content, developing advanced literacies, and achieving other personal, intellectual, and social goals. This dictates that academic language instruction connect with not only subject-area content but also students' lives outside of school. That is, instructional practices involving academic language should engage students' interests, build on their everyday language and funds of knowledge, affirm their linguistic and cultural identities, promote collaborative problem solving, encourage strategic use of a range of material (e.g., artifacts) and semiotic (e.g., language, images) tools, and scaffold comprehension and production of language and text for diverse purposes and across different subject areas (Cummins, 2014; Haneda, 2014). For example,

TABLE 19.5. Functional Language Analysis Framework

Meaning focus	Questions to ask about text	Analysis strategies
Content: *Experiential meaning*	• What is the text about? • Who does what to whom, how, when and where? • What are the main ideas?	Analyze each clause, identifying the relationships constructed in nouns, verbs, adjectives, and other language features.
Organization: *Textual and logical meanings*	• How does the text weave meaning into a coherent message? • How is the text organized? • By what logic is the text structured?	Analyze what begins each clause, how clauses are combined, and how cohesion is created and sustained.
Style/Perspective: *Interpersonal meaning*	• How does the author infuse judgments and points of view? • What is the author's perspective? • How does the author interact with the reader? • What is the power or solidarity of the relationships among the participants (e.g., characters) in the text?	Analyze word choices for attitudes, evaluation, and authorial perspectives.

when teaching academic language to help students improve their writing, teachers should share and discuss the content and craft in well-written subject-area texts (e.g., literature or nonfiction prose), select only a few academic language features or skills to focus on at one time, scaffold the teaching with examples and explanations rather than formal definitions, make links between the linguistic features introduced and the effects they might have on meaning, provide multiple opportunities for students to discuss the linguistic features introduced, encourage imitation by offering model linguistic patterns for students to play with and eventually appropriate in their own writing, nurture students' ability to make informed choices in their writing and to see the process of writing as a process of designing meaning, promote playfulness innovation with language, celebrate the new things students have learned (or almost learned), and avoid taking over the ownership of student writing by imposing their own revisions and edits (Myhill, 2013; Weaver, 2010). These practices are more likely to succeed in improving students' engagement, language proficiency, literacy growth, and other learning outcomes.

IMPLICATIONS FOR TEACHING AND RESEARCH

Despite its importance, academic language has received surprisingly little attention in the reading/literacy research literature outside the realms of bilingual or second-language education. For example, not a single chapter was specifically devoted to academic language in the four volumes of *Handbook of Reading Research* (Pearson, Barr, Kamil, & Mosenthal, 1984; Barr, Kamil, Mosenthal, & Pearson, 1991; Kamil, Mosenthal, Pearson, & Barr, 2000; Kamil, Pearson, Moje, & Afflerbach, 2010) or the three editions of *Handbook of Research on Teaching the English Language Arts* (Flood, 1991; Flood, Lapp, Squire, & Jensen, 2003; Lapp & Fisher, 2010), both of which have been heralded as providing "comprehensive, authoritative" reviews of the field. This exclusion indicates a perennial lack of attention to academic language in the mainstream literacy research and in adolescent literacy scholarship. As Snow and Uccelli (2009) lamented, "Ironically, although academic language skills are widely cited as the obstacle to achievement for struggling readers in general, much of the empirical research on academic language has been done by those studying English Language Learners" (p. 113). Thus, it is worth reiterating that academic language is a barrier to school success not just for English language learners; it is indeed an issue that matters to all students and across all subject areas.

Foregrounding the role and challenge of academic language in subject-area learning augurs the need for teachers to develop new capacities. Specifically, in order to better scaffold students' academic language development in the service of their subject-area learning, teachers need to develop robust knowledge about how language works in their discipline, strong skills for planning engaging units of instruction that promote integration of language and content, and effective strategies for supporting exploration of language and meaning in daily instruction (Schleppegrell & O'Halloran, 2011). They also need to be familiar with the practices and worldviews of specific discourse communities, because acquiring academic language is, in essence, "a social process of enculturation into the values and practices of some specialist community" (Lemke, 2002, p. 21). These areas of expertise are not just for language or literacy teachers, they are also important for subject-area teachers, who are now expected to support language and literacy development at the same time they are promoting content learning (e.g., National Governors

Association Center for Best Practices & Council of Chief State School Officers [NGA & CCSSO], 2010). Teachers need to be able to engage students in discussion about text that raises their awareness about the way knowledge and value are construed through language (and other modalities) in the subject areas. Those who understand academic language, as well as its challenges in and relationship to subject-area learning, will be more effective in working with and supporting the diversity that is typical of students in today's classrooms.

As noted earlier, the teaching of academic language should be embedded within broader disciplinary experiences in which students engage in reading, writing, talking, observing, listening, viewing, inquiring, and performing related to the topics and ideas that are significant to the discipline. These experiences provide rich, authentic contexts in which academic language is used, both orally and in writing. When working with disciplinary texts, teachers can follow an instructional sequence that involves four stages: engaging with the text, zooming in on the text, playing with the text, and extending the text (Fang, 2016). In the first stage, teachers engage students in making sense of the text through reading, questioning, and discussion. Once students have gained a general understanding of the gist of the text, teachers can then zoom in on a particularly challenging but important segment (e.g., passage) within the text. In this stage, teachers engage students in reading the passage closely, sentence-by-sentence, identifying lexical and grammatical patterns within each sentence, elaborating on their meanings, and discussing their rhetorical functions in the text. In so doing, teachers explicitly draw students' attention to new and challenging academic language patterns, helping them expand their linguistic repertoires for making meaning with purpose across genres, registers, and disciplines. During the third stage, teachers design language-based tasks that highlight and reinforce key or new lexical, grammatical, or discursive patterns from the text. These tasks provide students with opportunities to "play with" academic and disciplinary language, helping them develop familiarity with and facility in using it. During the fourth stage, students write, first collaboratively and then independently, a new text appropriating or paraphrasing the key or new language resources from the text they have been reading closely. Teachers encourage imitation and "playful innovation" (Myhill, 2013) in language use as students work on communicating meaning in genre and discipline-specific ways.

As new methods and programs are being developed to promote academic language learning, there is a concurrent need to study rigorously the efficacy of these methods and programs. Such studies are especially pressing in an educational environment in which teachers are exhorted to adopt evidence-based practices. To date, there is robust evidence for a vocabulary-focused approach that emphasizes multiple exposure to words across multiple contexts, opportunities to practice and personalize word meanings, structural analysis, and visual support (e.g., Snow et al., 2009; Townsend, 2009). There is also emerging evidence that a functional focus on sentence and grammar in context is effective in promoting academic language and advanced literacy development, as well as content learning (e.g., Achugar et al., 2007; Jones, Myhill, & Bailey, 2013). However, given the persistent neglect of language and literacy in subject-area teacher education (Fang, 2014), much more work is needed to study effective ways of enacting a "language-based"/"linguistically informed" pedagogy (Fang & Schleppegrell, 2008; Fang, Schleppegrell, & Cox, 2006) or other pedagogical models (e.g., Cummins, 2014; Haneda, 2014) in a range of subject-area classrooms. This work is critical to preparing adolescents of varying abilities and from diverse backgrounds for college, career, and global citizenship.

REFERENCES

Achugar, M., Schleppegrell, M., & Oteiza, T. (2007). Engaging teachers in language analysis: A functional linguistics approach to reflective literacy. *English Teaching: Practice and Critique*, 6(2), 8–24.

Barr, R., Kamil, M. L., Mosenthal, P., & Pearson, P. D. (1991). *Handbook of reading research* (Vol. 2). Mahwah, NJ: Erlbaum.

Bernstein, B. (1975). *Class, codes and control: Theoretical studies towards a sociology of language.* New York: Shocken Books.

Canagarajah, S. (2013). *Translingual practice: Global Englishes and cosmopolitan relations.* London: Routledge.

Crowe, C. (2003). *Getting away with the murder: The true story of the Emmett Till case.* New York: Phyllis Fogelman Books.

Cummins, J. (1981). Four misconceptions about language proficiency in bilingual education. *NABE Journal*, 5(3), 31–45.

Cummins, J. (1984). *Bilingual education and special education: Issues in assessment and pedagogy.* San Diego, CA: College Hill.

Cummins, J. (2014). Beyond language: Academic communication and student success. *Linguistics and Education*, 26, 145–154.

Fang, Z. (2008). Going beyond the "Fab Five": Helping students cope with the unique linguistic challenges of expository reading in intermediate grades. *Journal of Adolescent and Adult Literacy*, 51(6), 476–487.

Fang, Z. (2010). *Language and literacy in inquiry-based science classrooms, grades 3–8.* Thousand Oaks, CA: Corwin Press, and Arlington, VA: NSTA Press.

Fang, Z. (2012a). The challenges of reading disciplinary texts. In T. Jetton & C. Shanahan (Eds.), *Adolescent literacy in the academic disciplines: General principles and practical strategies* (pp. 34–68). New York: Guilford Press.

Fang, Z. (2012b). Language correlates of disciplinary literacy. *Topics in Language Disorders*, 32(1), 19–34.

Fang, Z. (2014). Preparing content-area teachers for disciplinary literacy instruction: The role of literacy teacher educators. *Journal of Adolescent and Adult Literacy*, 57(6), 444–448.

Fang, Z. (2016). Text complexity in the U.S. Common Core State Standards: A linguistic critique. *Australian Journal of Language Literacy*, 39(3).

Fang, Z., & Schleppegrell, M. J. (2008). *Reading in secondary content areas: A language-based pedagogy.* Ann Arbor: University of Michigan Press.

Fang, Z., & Schleppegrell, M. J. (2010). Disciplinary literacies across content areas: Supporting secondary reading through functional language analysis. *Journal of Adolescent and Adult Literacy*, 53(7), 587–597.

Fang, Z., Schleppegrell, M. J., & Cox, B. E. (2006). Understanding the language demands of schooling: Nouns in academic registers. *Journal of Literacy Research*, 38(3), 247–273.

Fang, Z., Schleppegrell, M. J., & Moore, J. (2013). The linguistic challenges of learning across academic disciplines. In A. Stone, E. Silliman, B. Ehren, & G. Wallach (Eds.), *Handbook of language and literacy: Development and disorders* (2nd ed., pp. 302–322). New York: Guilford Press.

Flood, J. (1991). *Handbook of research on teaching the English language arts.* Mahwah, NJ: Erlbaum.

Flood, J., Lapp, D., Squire, J. R., & Jensen, J. M. (2003). *Handbook of research on teaching the English language arts* (2nd ed.). Mahwah, NJ: Erlbaum.

Gee, J. (2003). Opportunity to learn: A language-based perspective on assessment. *Assessment in Education: Principles, Policy and Practice*, 10(1), 27–46.

Gee, J. (2008). What is academic language? In A. S. Rosebery & B. Warren (Eds.), *Teaching science to English language learners: Building on students' strengths* (pp. 57–70). Arlington, VA: NSTA Press.

Gibbons, P. (2006). *Bridging discourse in the ESL classroom: Students, teachers, and researchers.* London: Continuum.

Gillis, V. (2014/2015). Talking the talk: Vocabulary instruction across the disciplines (or what to do instead). *Journal of Adolescent and Adult Literacy, 58*(4), 281–287.

Halliday, M. A. K. (1978). *Language as social semiotic.* London: Edward Arnold.

Halliday, M. A. K. (1985). *An introduction to functional grammar.* London: Edward Arnold.

Halliday, M. A. K. (1989). *Spoken and written language.* Oxford, UK: Oxford University Press.

Haneda, M. (2014). From academic language to academic communication: Building on English learners' resources. *Linguistics and Education, 26,* 126–135.

Heath, S. B. (1983). *Ways with words: Language, life and work in communities and classrooms.* Cambridge, UK: Cambridge University Press.

Hyland, K. (2004). *Disciplinary discourses: Social interactions in academic writing.* Ann Arbor, MI: University of Michigan Press.

Jones, S., Myhill, D., & Bailey, T. (2013). Grammar for writing?: An investigation of the effects of contextualized grammar teaching on students' writing. *Reading and Writing, 26*(8), 1241–1263.

Kamil, M. L., Mosenthal, P., Pearson, P. D., & Barr, R. (2000). *Handbook of reading research* (Vol. 3). Mahwah, NJ: Erlbaum.

Kamil, M. L., Pearson, P. D., Moje, E. B., & Afflerbach, P. (2010). *Handbook of reading research* (Vol. 4). New York: Routledge.

Lapp, D., & Fisher, D. (2010). *Handbook of research on teaching the English language arts* (3rd ed.). New York: Taylor & Francis.

Larson, L., Dixon, T., & Townsend, D. (2013). How can teachers increase classroom use of academic vocabulary. *Voices from the Middle, 20*(4), 16–21.

Lemke, J. (2002). Multimedia semiotics: Genres for science education and scientific literacy. In M. J. Schleppegrell & M. C. Colombi (Eds.), *Developing advanced literacy in first and second language: Meaning with power* (pp. 21–44). Mahwah, NJ: Erlbaum.

Michaels, S. (1981). "Sharing Time": Children's narrative styles and differential access to literacy. *Language in Society, 10*(3), 423–442.

Myhill, D. (2013). Playful explicitness with grammar: A pedagogy for writing. *Literacy, 47*(2), 103–111.

National Center for Education Statistics. (2013). *The condition of education 2013.* Washington, DC: U.S. Department of Education.

National Governors Association Center for Best Practices & Council of Chief State School Officers (NGA & CCSSO). (2010). *Common Core State Standards for English language arts and literacy for history/social studies, science, and technical subjects: Appendix A.* Washington, DC: Authors.

Pearson, P. D., Barr, R., Kamil, M. L., & Mosenthal, P. (1984). *Handbook of reading research* (Vol. 1). New York: Longman.

Schleppegrell, M. J. (2001). Linguistic features of the language of schooling. *Linguistics and Education, 12,* 431–459.

Schleppegrell, M. J. (2004). *The language of schooling: A functional linguistics perspective.* Mahwah, NJ: Erlbaum.

Schleppegrell, M. J. (2006). The challenges of academic language in school subjects. In I. Lindberg & K. Sandwall (Eds.), *Språket och kunskapen: att lära på sitt andraspråk i skola och högskola* [Language and knowledge: Learning a second language in school and college](pp. 47–69). Gothenburg, Sweden: Gothenburg University Institute for Swedish as a Second Language.

Schleppegrell, M. J. (2012). Academic language in teaching and learning. *Elementary School Journal, 112*(3), 409–418.

Schleppegrell, M. J., Greer, S., & Taylor, S. (2008). Literacy in history: Language and meaning. *Australian Journal of Language and Literacy, 31,* 174–187.

Schleppegrell, M. J., & O'Hallaron, C. (2011). Teaching academic language in L2 secondary settings. *Annual Review of Applied Linguistics, 31,* 3–18.

Snow, C., Lawrence, J., & White, C. (2009). Generating knowledge of academic language among urban middle school students. *Journal of Research on Educational Effectiveness, 2*(4), 325–344.

Snow, C., & Uccelli, P. (2009). The challenge of academic language. In D. R. Olson & N. Torrance (Eds.), *The Cambridge handbook of literacy* (pp. 112–133). New York: Cambridge University Press.

Snow, C. E. (1983). Literacy and language: Relationships during the preschool years. *Harvard Educational Review, 53,* 165–189.

Townsend, D. (2009). Building academic vocabulary in after-school settings: Games for growth with middle school English-language learners. *Journal of Adolescent and Adult Literacy, 53*(3), 242–251.

Vygotsky, L. S. (1987). Thinking and speech. In R. W. Rieber & A. S. Carton (Eds.), *The collected works of L. S. Vygotsky: Vol. 1. Problems of general psychology* (N. Minick, Trans.). New York: Plenum Press. (Original work published 1934)

Weaver, C. (2010). Scaffolding grammar instruction for writers and writing. In T. Locke (Ed.), *Beyond the grammar wars: A resource for teachers and students on developing language knowledge in the English/literacy classroom* (pp. 185–205). London: Routledge.

Wilson, E. O. (2014). *A window on eternity: A biologist's walk through Gorongosa National Park.* New York: Simon & Schuster.

CHAPTER 20

Young Adult Literature and Classroom-Based Research

GAY IVEY

Tyrell [by Coe Booth], it made me think, first, cause I was kind of raised in that kind of lifestyle. But as I looked at it, I looked at it like it was kind of hard, you know? But seeing how it was for somebody else, and seeing how it was for them to live it every day . . . to read about someone's life like that, it made me think. There's so many kids that brag about what they do and don't have. And then people like me, that didn't really having anything growing up at all. . . . Like I used to think that I was terrible. Now that I look at it, I felt that I was kind of important, because I was like, "this person got that, this person got this." I should look at it as even though I didn't have too many things when I was little, I should still be appreciative that I had my parents in my life.
—NYKEISHA, eighth grade

Adolescents read to make sense of the messiness and uncertainty of their past, present, and future lives, and the complicated relationships within those lives. In this chapter I focus on recent empirical studies set in classrooms in which young adult literature is the tool with which middle and high school readers and their teachers grapple with questions of identity and social significance. Engagement with young adult literature, although still rare as a literate practice in secondary classrooms, has substantial consequences in particular for students like Nykeisha, quoted above, who had not been well served by conventional literacy instruction, and whose mind was frequently occupied by the everyday complexities of her life outside of school.

Until quite recently, the *young adult* has, in essence, been left out of studies of young adult literature (Bickerstaff, 2008; Hayn, Kaplan, & Nolen, 2011). There is a substantial collection of research on the texts themselves (e.g., Curwood, 2013a; Petrone, Sarigianides, & Lewis, 2015; Wickens, 2011), some studies to explore teachers' uses of and dispositions toward multicultural literature (e.g., Ketter & Lewis, 2001) and examinations of how teachers' reading of young adult literature might help them understand

and respond to the realities of adolescents' personal, cultural, and social worlds (e.g., Faulkner & Latham, 2013; Glenn, 2012; Pytash, Morgan, & Batchelor, 2013). What has been missing is a close look at adolescents' relationships within young adult texts, particularly in classrooms, and therefore in relationships with others around their reading.

It is relatively easy to identify possible explanations for the shortage of classroom-based research on adolescents' uses of young adult literature. Most conspicuously, canonized literature still trumps all other texts in secondary English curricula. In spite of the fact that state and national standards do not require knowledge of particular authors and titles, assignment of the classics persists locally, a phenomenon Franzak (2008) referred to as the enforcement of "phantom policies," because they are neither official nor written, but instead are perpetuated by specific ideologies of what English as a school discipline is expected to accomplish. Lewis and Dockter (2011) suggest, though, that many English teachers may be caught between an urgency to focus on traditional practices, due to national standards and testing, and a desire to transform their classrooms into spaces that are responsive to contemporary cultural and social concerns of students.

In contrast to the sanctioned curriculum comprised of classic texts, Burroughs and Smagorinsky (2009) invoke Eisner's concept of the "null curriculum" (1994) to explain the use, or more accurately, the lack of use of young adult literature in English classrooms. The issues taken up by young adult literature, including questions of sexual identity, implications of drug and alcohol abuse, violence, and religion, among other topics considered controversial in school, are often explicitly omitted from the official curriculum, even though these are issues adolescents face regularly in their own lives. For researchers, then, it may be difficult to find secondary classrooms in which reading of young adult literature is pervasive.

Another possible reason that classroom-based research involving young adult literature is scarce is that nonprint forms of media comprise a sizable proportion of adolescents' reading (Bruce, 2009; Moje, Overby, Tysvaer, & Morris, 2008), and particularly for social reasons (Black & Steinkuehler, 2009). Recent case studies have included adolescents' social networks around young adult literature in virtual spaces (e.g., Curwood, 2013b), but not emanating from classroom practice. Thus, in recent years, students' out-of-school literacies, rather than school-sponsored reading, have been viewed as fertile contexts for empirical study.

YOUNG ADULT LITERATURE IN CLASSROOM-BASED STUDIES

The dearth of classroom-based research featuring young adult literature should not be interpreted as a lack of importance or value, however. In their call for a shift in the research from a primary focus on text analysis toward a serious examination of classroom use, Hayn et al. (2011) identified three overarching questions to be considered:

> What transactional occurrences happen between teachers and students?
> Between students and students?
> Between readers and texts? (p. 177)

In this chapter I explore recent research that begins to address these questions. I begin with a look at how a text might be considered "young adult" literature and a description of the types of texts researchers suggest that adolescents prefer. Then, I describe several relevant studies published in the past several years that document student experiences with young adult literature when it is prioritized within the curriculum. Although the quantity of studies is small, the findings are substantial enough to stir the conversation about adolescents' reading and how young adult literature could and should find a prominent place in secondary classrooms.

The Texts That Engage Adolescents

The paucity of young adult literature use in classrooms limits empirical knowledge of what adolescents want to read, and in fact, might even distort it. When Karen Broaddus and I (Ivey & Broaddus, 2001), surveyed over 1,700 sixth graders about their motivations to read, we asked students to name a particular title of a book they liked reading at school. We found that there was limited variation across responses, and particularly for students with the same teacher. We reasoned these were not actually the books they preferred, but instead, the titles they knew. Books made popular by movies also skew our perceptions of what engages young adults, specifically for youth across different cultural, ethnic, and linguistic groups. If we allowed the media to fully shape our impressions, we might believe, for instance, the most students prefer dystopian literature (e.g., *The Hunger Games*; Collins, 2008), and although certainly many adolescents enjoy these books, there is no evidence that they represent a majority. It is also likely that adolescent readers respond less positively to award-winning books (e.g., Newbery Medal) than do their teachers (George, 2008).

It is significant, then, that questions about the literature that engages students have been taken up in research. Of these, however, the questions about *why* students read particular kinds of books are the most useful. In general, what we know is that adolescents read to understand and construct their own identities and to explore perspectives on their social worlds, with particular emphasis on the intricacies of their relationships and who they wish to be in relation to others. In this way, what might be considered "young adult literature" depends on who is reading it and for what purposes. Although we typically think about this category as including books that are written for readers within the approximate ages of 12 and 18, we might count any book that, for an individual reader, helps to sort out matters of personal relevance. Kirkland (2011), for instance, argued that for young Black men, in particular, this means connecting with a particular character as an expression of self. One of the young men Kirkland studied, for instance, experienced total disengagement with *Beowulf*, but identified with *The Iliad*, proclaiming to classmates, "I am Achilles" (p. 205), providing evidence that some adolescents do find connection with characters in canonical literature. It is also the case that many adolescents want to read contemporary texts written for an adult audience but featuring young adults wrestling with personal issues or adults' reflections on experiences and decisions of their youth, such as former gang member Reymundo Sanchez's memoir, *My Bloody Life: The Making of a Latin King* (2000).

A more prevalent argument in empirical research, though, is that young adults are drawn to the texts with settings that resemble their own social realities and characters with familiar problems (Ivey & Broaddus, 2001; Moje et al., 2008). Adolescents use texts and characters, in some cases, as tools for thinking through present and future dilemmas, or as cautionary tales (Howard, 2011). For instance, a 14-year-old boy explained to me how reading *Homeboyz* (Sitomer, 2008), a story of gang-related violence, revenge, and redemption, made him think about life choices: "It really made me think of how your life can be really messed up like if you do the wrong thing, and you have to pay the consequences. So I've been thinking about that some. It kind of got to me." A female eighth-grade student I observed was brought to tears in class while reading that the male protagonist in *Perfect Chemistry* (Elkeles, 2008) callously referred to a sexual experience with a female character who cared deeply for him, as—in the students' words—"just a fuck." This caught her, and the female character with whom she identified, off guard. She immediately turned to her peers in class to talk about the implications of such a hurtful breach of trust, the specifics of which she was experiencing personally for the first time. Navigating emotions within problems that resonate with adolescence is an important reason for adolescent reading (Becnel & Moeller, 2015).

Adolescents also use texts to experience the perspectives of others and to consider the moral implications of this knowledge (Ivey & Johnston, 2013). In my research, students consistently describe shifts like this one from a ninth-grade student: "I never knew how alone some people feel, or what it's like to be in a mental hospital. Someone who attempts suicide, I don't know how they feel, so [reading] helps me understand how they feel, and it gives me new ways to view life." Although connecting to characters with familiar problems certainly pulls adolescent readers, they are also drawn to texts that expand their awareness of others.

The types of young adult literature addressing these purposes for reading—using characters as tools for life decisions and identity development, grappling with relationship problems, and expanding the social imagination in and out of narrative worlds—include a wide range and depends on individual readers. However, several general (and overlapping) categories are clear:

- Stories of characters or real people struggling with relationships and identities (e.g., *The Secret Story of Sonia Rodriguez*; Sitomer, 2008; *Gym Candy*; Deuker, 2007).
- Narratives set in complex and sometimes dangerous social worlds that young people must navigate (e.g., *Takedown*; van Diepen, 2013; *If I Grow Up*; Strasser, 2009).
- Stories told in first-person narration, allowing readers to see through the eyes of others and experience their personal and social dilemmas (e.g., *Every Day*; Levithan, 2012; *Glimpse*; Williams, 2010).
- Stories with shifting narrators, providing windows into multiple and often conflicting perspectives (e.g., *Leverage*; Cohen, 2011; *Jumping off Swings*; Knowles, 2009).

In the remainder of this section, I describe empirical studies in which these types of books were prioritized and made available in middle and secondary classrooms.

Young Adult Literature and Achievement: Grant Street Secondary School

Francois (2013a, 2013b) investigated the literacy-related experiences of students and teachers in an urban school that, on many accounts, was beating the odds. Over the period of several years, reading achievement and the literate culture at Grant Street Secondary School—a community where over 82% of students were considered to be economically disadvantaged—were dramatically transformed. Several years prior to Francois's study, reading achievement scores of students in grades 6–12 were low, and as Francois reports, most middle grades scores were the lowest in the state. However, after a schoolwide commitment to arranging for students' independent reading within a reading workshop framework, along with internally conceptualized and carefully concerted professional development, Grant Street exhibited a different profile: Students' reading growth was two to three times greater than the national norms, and students' dispositions toward reading remained stable, even as national trends have consistently demonstrated a downward turn throughout the middle and high school years.

Francois's yearlong investigation, including extensive observations in English and humanities classrooms, and teacher and student interviews, centered on understanding the nuances of practice that related to this growth and how participants (students, teachers, staff) perceived these practices. Although the specific use of young adult literature was not the focal point of this research, this case was a rare example of a setting that featured widespread use of texts that matter to adolescents in secondary classrooms.

At Grant Street, all students in grades 6–10 were provided with time to read books of their choosing every day, and students in grades 11 and 12 were given the opportunity to read self-selected texts for one class period each week. Students were granted access to a wide range of texts in expansive classroom libraries, and teachers became more knowledgeable about the books students preferred to read, which made it more possible for them to recommend books to particular students and to have rich conversations.

Although reading daily and achieving volume-related goals were expectations for all students, Francois determined that students were more likely persuaded by the relational richness associated with the reading culture at Grant Street, for instance, conversations about books with peers and teachers, recommendations passed between students and teachers, and impromptu book clubs that sprang up over shared interests. Francois attested to the fact that even though "independent reading" times in classroom were largely devoted to silent reading and conferences between teachers and students, social activity around books outside of class was quite common. In addition, the texts themselves offered a space for relationships, with students reporting that characters and the dilemmas they faced were tools for thinking through their own personal and social problems. An 11th grader in Francois's study (2013a), for instance, asserted that books gave him "a way out, showing a new way to tackle a problem in a similar situation. . . . [the character] applies a different way, a different method, a positive way to get out of it, and it makes you a better person overall" (p. 147).

In Francois's assessment, the changes in literacy at Grant Street, although initiated through commitment to a set of instructional practices and teacher learning around those practices, were due to the *humanizing* of reading instruction (Francois, 2013a, p. 30). Teachers attended to the interests and concerns of students by becoming knowledgeable about the books that mattered to them and making them accessible, building relationships, and supporting students' sense of agency.

Expanded Consequences of Reading Young Adult Literature

Peter Johnston and I (Ivey & Johnston, 2013) explored the perspectives of students whose English teachers made engaged reading—through student choices of young adult literature—the centerpiece of the curriculum. Two years prior to the study, all four eighth-grade English teachers in one middle school in a small mid-Atlantic U. S. town had decided to abandon all assigned reading in favor of self-selected, self-paced reading within a large collection of young adult literature. In addition to making choices about what to read, students were given the authority to decide how to respond (or not) to the books they read. In other words, there were no strings attached: no quizzes, book reports, projects, written responses, or minimum number of books to read.

A large number of books contained unadulterated details of contemporary social realities, texts that students would come to refer to as "disturbing" but highly engaging. Teachers began the year by gathering all students in the auditorium and presenting a series of book talks on some of the most preferred titles of the previous year's eighth-grade students; thereafter, teachers routinely introduced new books during regular class periods. Each class period began with substantial student reading time, followed by a teacher read-aloud of a young adult book, and ending with writing instruction.

We approached their examination of students' experiences in this context through the perspective that reading is a transactional experience involving the reader and the text (Rosenblatt, 1983), and that when students read self-selected young adult literature, they do so to make sense of their lives and their relationships with others and the world. Thus, we were especially attentive to transformations not only in students' reading but also in their personal, emotional, and social development.

Through end-of-year interviews with 71 students, supported by teacher interviews and classroom observations throughout the school year, we identified a range of outcomes students associated with engagement in young adult literature. Most prominently, students reported a substantial amount of engaged reading, not only in class but also across the school day and outside of school. For instance, one student reported, "I usually read, like, all the time at night. . . . If I hear [my parents] come upstairs, I'll, like, just put it under my covers, then they go away, and I'll start reading again" (Ivey & Johnston, 2013, p. 261). We surmised from our findings that if students were only reading during the time set aside in English class—which is 20 minutes a day in many contexts—they were not actually engaged but were likely just going through the motions of reading.

Students also described shifts in their identities, not only as readers but also as people, for instance, describing themselves as smarter and more intellectual. They reported reading widely, experiencing a sense of agency in their reading, stepping out of their comfort zones when it came to choosing books, and knowing more not just about books but about the world. They attributed greater emotional and academic self-regulation to their experiences around reading. Their comments suggested shifts in their sense of agency about their present lives, for instance, in committing to resist the self-destructive behavior they encountered in characters, and about their future lives, for instance, in believing they could go to college when they had not previously entertained that possibility.

One of the most salient findings, particularly compared to previous studies of reading that focused on reading for information and for individual reading achievement (e.g., Guthrie, Wigfield, & You, 2012), was the social thread that was prominent throughout students' experiences. Students reported widespread talk about books with peers, teachers, and family members, both in and out of school, and, in the process, making new friends as a result of joint interest in books. They described shifts in existing relationships, including decreased tension with parents, and the deepening of bonds with friends. Students perceived a heightened sense of trust with classmates. As one student put it:

> At the beginning of the year, you've known everybody, but you're not friends with everybody. And, like, once we started doing this, and everybody starts speaking out, and like, everybody's having conversations with each other about it, it seems like you're friends with everybody. (in Ivey & Johnston, 2013, p. 262)

Students' relational development was not limited to classroom communities and immediate family and friends, though. More broadly, students described shifts in their sense of others and of themselves in relation to others. These shifts were often rooted in students' experiences within the young adult literature they read, many of which offered perspectives that were unfamiliar to students, as described by this student:

> I thought [*Destroying Avalon*] was really good, really sad at the end. But it just makes you think about, to pay attention to how people react, to pay attention to how they're feeling about stuff. Like when you see people you don't really think . . . they have problems or whatever. But then some of the ones I've read, you can just understand people better. (Ivey & Johnston, 2013, p. 262)

Consistently, students reported these shifts in their social imaginations—their propensity to imagine the thoughts and feelings of others—beginning with characters in books and then with people in their social worlds outside of books. This is consistent with previous research on adults engaged in reading narrative (Bal, Butterman, & Bakker, 2011; Bal & Veltkamp, 2013; Johnson, 2011; Mar, Oatley, Hirsch, De La Paz, & Peterson, 2006). Relatedly, students suggested shifts in their sense of moral agency, that is, the belief that they could make a moral difference in the world, such as one student who shared that she had interrupted an instance of bullying on Facebook after reading the book *Hate List* (Brown, 2010).

Like the students in the study by Francois (2013a), the students in our study demonstrated growth in reading test scores; similarly, the change in scores was greater than the average change for other schools statewide taking the same test, and in particular, there was substantial growth for students considered economically disadvantaged. A major implication of our study, though, was that what students' reading of young adult literature does for test scores distracts us from the more meaningful consequences—the development of the whole person.

Engaged Reading of Young Adult Literature as a Collaborative, Transformative Process

Related to our study of the widespread consequences of engagement with young adult literature, we (Ivey & Johnston, 2015) conducted a second study tracing the evolution of practice in this same set of eighth-grade classrooms. Using a lens of third-generation cultural–historical activity theory (Engeström & Glaveanu, 2012; Sannino, Daniels, & Gutiérrez, 2009; Stetsenko, 2008), we examined the shifts in both individual and community practice and how they interacted across three activity systems: the community of teachers, classroom communities, and the moment-to-moment interactional processes.

In our earlier work (Ivey & Johnston, 2013), we explained that teachers ceded to students decisions about what to read—selecting from a vast collection of compelling young adult literature—and what to do with their reading, if anything. This follow-up study made clear the complexity of how classroom practices actually evolved. Although supporting students' sense of autonomy through providing good text choices and doing so with a no-strings-attached policy (e.g., no assignments connected to books) was a necessary condition for engagement, the shifts in practice—for both teachers and students—was due to more than simple changes in methods and materials. In short, the goals for teaching and learning changed; consequently, so did relationships and therefore the culture of this community.

We documented that literacy practices evolved from a focus on individual students becoming engaged in reading for the purposes of academic achievement to a focus on reading and conversation as a collaborative enterprise with the goal of socioemotional engagement inside and outside of books, in short, working on selves and relationships. These transformations happened as three evolving activity systems (teaching community, classroom community, moment-to-moment interactions) influenced each other across time. For instance, students learned more about each other through talking about books, leading to expansions of relationships and of available things about which to talk. Once teachers understood this, they arranged to make students more accessible to each other, for example, by changing the no-talking principle during student reading time, and allowing talk when necessary, and even encouraging it. Likewise, students' desks were moved out of rows facing the front of the classroom to clusters of desks facing each other. Rules and procedures were modified to suit the larger purposes of reading.

In addition, power relationships were flattened, as expertise about books was no longer the teachers' domain, but instead distributed across students. Teaching was also distributed as students recruited each other (and teachers) to read, made good recommendations, and helped each other sort through confusion as they read. Teachers' relationships with each other changed, too, as they began to see each other (and students) as resources for helping to perpetuate the literate practices across classrooms. For instance, teachers and students routinely visited other classrooms to find books and to seek out conversation partners around books. We concluded that although young adult texts were important tools, it was human agency and relationships that ultimately made classroom practices truly transformative.

IMPLICATIONS FOR INSTRUCTION

The existing research offers direction and promise for classroom practice. A primary interest of many people examining the links between research and practice is in "what works" to boost achievement. As the present studies indicate, if middle and secondary schools are concerned with improving reading test scores, then providing students with young adult literature that matters to them, giving them time and space to read, and pulling back on requirements related to reading constitute a strong beginning. In a related finding, in their survey of what adolescents say they read outside of school, Moje and her colleagues (2008) found that of all of the forms of text students reported reading—including a host of digital texts—only the reading of novels could be linked to higher reading achievement. In addition, Glaus's (2014) analysis of the contemporary young adult fiction she examined led her to conclude that these texts indeed meet, if not surpass, the criteria for complexity suggested by the Common Core State Standards (NGA &

CCSSO, 2010). In short, prioritizing young adult literature in classrooms makes sense if we want to influence achievement. To stop there, however, would be to create a cascade of missed opportunities.

A strong theme in empirical studies of school-based reading of young adult literature centers on why students read, that is, as a tool for identity development, social capital, and expanded relational understandings. Yet, all too often, young adult literature in the curriculum is valued only as a way to get students to read, primarily because of the link between time spent reading and reading achievement (e.g., Guthrie, Schafer, & Huang, 2001; Kirsch et al., 2002). Practical implications of such a view routinely focus on increasing time to read in school and challenging students to read a minimum number of books. But instructional programs that aim merely to increase students' volume of reading, with no attention to what students experience as they read, likely fail to facilitate the full range of social and personal implications of engagement with young adult literature as reported, for instance, in my own studies (Ivey & Johnston, 2013a, 2013b) reported in this chapter.

When students' reasons for reading are central to envisioning instruction, the cloth of experiences with text, both inside in relationships to characters, and outside in relationships with others, will more likely influence decisions about the place and function of young adult literature reading. Silent reading times would be replaced by social spaces wherein students not only read but also talk through, when necessary, issues introduced into the classroom community by personal and societal dilemmas students encounter in books. Coats (2011) described contemporary young adult literature as

> organized around the same sorts of tensions that preoccupy the physical bodies and emotional lives of its intended audience: tensions between growth and stasis, between and ideal world we can imagine and the one we really inhabit, between earnestness and irony, between ordinary bodies and monstrous ones, and perhaps most importantly, between an impulsive individualism and a generative ethics of interconnectedness. (p. 316)

It is no wonder that adolescent readers are compelled to talk about and through the narratives that speak to their lives and to which they speak back. Particular texts, then, become resources in conversations with others and in the ongoing conversations in the minds of adolescents. Consider this example from an eighth-grade classroom. Four girls I observed in conversation about *In Ecstasy* (McCaffery, 2009) expanded their discussion about differences between the two main characters and the relational problems they caused to a consideration of "other in their own school community. Ava confessed she struggled to approach classmates outside of her own social group, but also that this problem had been on her mind: "You look over to the one [cafeteria] table, and it only has those three girls that always sit alone, and you're like what do they talk about?" Neena added, "Like, I always wanted to be social with, you know, like the outcasts, like the outcasts of the outcasts." Shannon reiterated, though, how difficult that might be: "The only thing I don't like is, is like what Ava said. Even if you just like go to someone else's table and you just like try to have a conversation, it's almost like so awkward, like 'you're not in my clique,' and you don't know what to say." As the girls continued this line of thought, they made references to characters in other books they had read, movies, and other real-life instances as they further complicated the problem. Trudy suggested that the issue should be taken up in the larger community and that she saw it as a school's responsibility "to teach everyone to be supportive of everyone's differences." The girls are far from solving the issues, but these conversations and the perspectives of each other and the characters they encounter become a collection of voices in their ongoing thought and talk, and likely will influence their future actions.

Although no teacher appears in the previous conversation, it is clear that the teacher of these students has made particular instructional decisions that make possible their engagement with texts and with each other. First, the teacher did not demand that students read particular texts. It is difficult to locate research documenting widespread engagement with young adult literature in classrooms where the same text is assigned to all students. In the studies reviewed here, students made choices, although these choices were often influenced by peers and by teachers who had deep knowledge about individual students and about the books that matter to students. Second, in all of the studies, teachers pulled back on conventional forms of reading and literary instruction in favor of relational work with students and turning students toward each other as instructional resources. Third, classroom discourse around reading was not dominated by teacher-directed cognitive and metacognitive strategies talk, but was instead about the complex issues in the texts students were taking up in their lives. This is not to say that the processes of reading are unimportant in the curriculum, but it is situated differently in these classrooms. For instance, I recently described one such scenario in which a student spontaneously shared with classmates a strategy she created for getting through a particularly complex book:

> I go through the book and see what's in it, to see if it has parts or weird titles of chapters. And I looked through this book, and it has, like, six parts, and the titles of chapters are lyrics from songs. I do that with most of my books. I write the parts down on a piece of paper and use it as I read. (in Ivey, 2014, p. 168)

The teacher promptly invited and received examples of strategies from other students who had read a range of different texts, then made their thinking available to the whole class to be used as possible tools for future reading.

FUTURE RESEARCH ABOUT YOUNG ADULT LITERATURE

If the short but persuasive list of classroom-based studies on uses of young adult literature in middle and secondary schools tells us anything, it is that we need to pay attention to adolescents' reasons for reading. Although, in the studies reviewed here, students' reading achievement as determined by standardized test scores increased, it is clear that students read not to get better at reading but instead to make sense of their identities, their social worlds, and their futures. Furthermore, they did so while constructing social networks around their reading and through widespread conversation. It seems important that student-preferred young adult literature reading in school, as described in the studies presented here, shares qualities with both the print and nonprint reading and writing students report participating in within school and outside of school (e.g., Moje et al., 2008). If research is following adolescents to where literate activity is abundant, complex, and socially oriented, then virtual worlds are not the only environments rich for examination. Simply put, classrooms in which students are provided with a vast array of young adult literature, and where teachers cede to them choices about what to read and what to do with their reading, as well as time and space to talk, offer substantial possibilities for research.

There is much yet to be learned about adolescents' engagement with non-narrative forms of young adult literature and how these might be leveraged in learning across the school day. Although it is likely that students' general feelings about informational texts are less than positive (Guthrie, Wigfield, & Klauda, 2012), students are interested in reading about topics relevant to subjects such as social studies and science (Stockdill & Moje, 2013). If existing research that features students' use of narrative types of young adult literature is any indication, then the kinds of informational texts available to students, their purposes for reading, and the discursive environments in which they experience them, will weigh heavily into their levels of engagement and the consequences of their reading.

In addition, the social nature of adolescents' engagement with young adult literature and their propensities to talk, share, and recruit reading partners and groups around compelling texts offer a glimpse into how dialogic classrooms might be created in secondary schools and what this might mean for students' personal, relational, and intellectual development. In his pivotal study in eighth- and ninth-grade English classrooms, Nystrand (1997) found that most talk could be characterized as recitation, and student-generated talk was uncommon. We now know that when students experience a sense of agency in their reading—particularly when the curriculum allows them to grapple with the complex realities of their present and future lives—dialogic interactions are plentiful.

Finally, engagement with young adult literature in diverse classrooms, in particular, provides a space for deepening our understandings about the development of adolescents' individual and collective critical consciousness. Lewis (2000) argued for an expansion how we think about aesthetic reading, pushing students beyond simple instances of connection with characters or story events toward interrogating the social and political dimensions of text. Creating such a space would require populating classrooms with a range of perspectives, as was the case in classrooms such as those described in this chapter. These include texts that reflect the social and political tensions of contemporary life, as well characters that students come to care about, whose thoughts and emotions become available to readers, and the readers themselves, who, in the process of talk through and about books, reveal information about themselves that they might not otherwise reveal.

REFERENCES

Bach, J., Choate, L. H., & Parker, B. (2011). Young adult literature and professional development. *Theory Into Practice, 50,* 198–205.

Bal, P. M., Butterman, O. S., & Bakker, A. B. (2011). The influence of fictional narrative experience on work outcomes: A conceptual analysis and research model. *Review of General Psychology, 15*(4), 361–370.

Bal, P. M., & Veltkamp, M. (2013). How does fiction reading influence empathy?: An experimental investigation on the role of emotional transportation. *PLoS ONE, 8*(1), e55341.

Becnel, K., & Moeller, R. A. (2015). What, why, and how they read: Reading preferences and patterns of rural young adults. *Journal of Adolescent and Adult Literacy, 59*(3), 299–307.

Bickerstaff, S. (2008). Exploring the risks in Smack: Risky stories in young adult literature. In Y. Kim, V. J. Risko, D. L. Compton, D. K. Dickinson, M. K. Hundley, R. T. Jimenez, et al. (Eds.), *57th yearbook of the National Reading Conference* (pp. 107–118). Oak Creek, WI: National Reading Conference.

Black, R. W., & Steinkuehler, C. (2009). Literacy in virtual worlds. In L. Christenbury, R. Bomer, & P. Smagorinksy (Eds.), *Handbook of adolescent literacy research* (pp. 271–286). New York: Guilford Press.

Booth, C. (2007). *Tyrell*. New York: Scholastic.

Brown, J. (2010). *Hate list*. New York: Little, Brown.

Bruce, D. L. (2009). Reading and writing video. In L. Christenbury, R. Bomer, & P. Smagorinksy (Eds.), *Handbook of adolescent literacy research* (pp. 287–303). New York: Guilford Press.

Burroughs, R., & Smagorinksy, P. (2009). The secondary English curriculum and adolescent literacy. In L. Christenbury, R. Bomer, & P. Smagorinksy (Eds.), *Handbook of adolescent literacy research* (pp. 170–182). New York: Guilford Press.

Coats, K. (2011). Young adult literature: Growing up, in theory. In S. A. Wolf, K. Coats, P. Enciso, & C. A. Jenkins (Eds.), *Handbook of research on children's and young adult literature* (pp. 315–329). New York: Routledge.

Cohen, J. (2011). *Leverage*. New York: Dutton.

Collins, S. (2008). *The hunger games*. New York: Scholastic.

Curwood, J. S. (2013a). Redefining normal: A critical analysis of (dis)ability in young adult literature. *Children's Literature in Education, 44,* 15–28.

Curwood, J. S. (2013b). *The Hunger Games*: Literature, literacy and online affinity spaces. *Language Arts, 90*(6), 417–427.

Deuker, C. (2007). *Gym candy*. New York: Houghton Mifflin.

Eisner, E. (1994). *The educational imagination: On the design and evaluation of school programs* (3rd ed.). New York: Macmillan.

Elkeles, S. (2008). *Perfect chemistry*. New York: Walker.

Engeström, Y., & Glaveanu, V. (2012). On third generation Activity Theory: An interview with Yrjö Engeström. *Europe's Journal of Psychology, 8*(4), 515–518.

Faulkner, J., & Latham, G. (2013). Disturbing stories: Literature as pedagogical disruption. *English in Education, 47,* 102–117.

Francois, C. (2013a). Reading is about relating: Urban youths give voice to the possibility for school literacy. *Journal of Adolescent and Adult Literacy, 57,* 141–149.

Francois, C. (2013b). Reading in the crawl space: A study of an urban school's literacy-focused community of practice. *Teacher College Record, 115,* 1–35.

Franzak, J. K. (2008). On the margins in a high-performing high school: Policy and the struggling reader. *Research in the Teaching of English, 42*(4), 466–505.

George, M. (2008). Comparing middle grade teachers' and middle grades students' reactions to Newbery Award winners. *ALAN Review, 36,* 55–65.

Glaus, M. (2014). Text complexity and young adult literature: Establishing its place. *Journal of Adolescent and Adult Literacy, 57*(5), 407–416.

Glenn, W. J. (2012). Developing understandings of race: Preservice teachers' counter-narrative (re) constructions of people of color in young adult literature. *English Education, 44*(4), 326–353.

Guthrie, J. T., Schafer, W. D., & Huang, C. (2001). Benefits of opportunity to read and balanced reading instruction for reading achievement and engagement: A policy analysis of state NAEP in Maryland. *Journal of Educational Research, 94*(3), 145–162.

Guthrie, J. T., Wigfield, A., & Klauda, S. L. (2012). *Adolescents' engagement in academic literacy* (Report No. 7). Retrieved from www.corilearning.com/research-publications.

Guthrie, J. T., Wigfield, A., & You, W. (2012). Instructional contexts for engagement and achievement in reading. In S. L. Christenson, A. L. Reschly, & C. Wylie (Eds.), *Handbook of research on student engagement* (pp. 601–634). New York: Springer.

Hayn, J. A., Kaplan, J. S., & Nolen, A. (2011). Young adult literature research in the 21st century. *Theory Into Practice, 50,* 176–181.

Howard, V. (2011). The importance of pleasure reading in the lives of young teens: Self-identification, self-construction, and self-awareness. *Journal of Librarianship and Information Science, 43*(1), 46–55.

Ivey, G. (2014). The social side of engaged reading for young adolescents. *The Reading Teacher, 68*(3), 165–171.

Ivey, G., & Broaddus, K. (2001). "Just plain reading": A survey of what makes students want to read in middle school classrooms. *Reading Research Quarterly, 36,* 350–377.

Ivey, G., & Johnston, P. H. (2013). Engagement with young adult literature: Outcomes and processes. *Reading Research Quarterly, 48*(3), 255–275.

Ivey, G., & Johnston, P. H. (2015). Engaged reading as collaborative transformative practice. *Journal of Literacy Research, 47,* 297–327.

Johnson, D. (2011). Transportation into a story increases empathy, prosocial behavior, and perceptual bias toward fearful expressions. *Personality and Individual Differences, 52,* 150–155.

Ketter, J., & Lewis, C. (2001). Already reading texts and contexts: Multicultural literature in a predominantly white rural community. *Theory Into Practice, 40*(3), 175–183.

Kirkland, D. E. (2011). Book like clothes: Engaging young black men with reading. *Journal of Adolescent and Adult Literacy, 55*(3), 199–208.

Kirsch, I., de Jong, J., LaFontaine, D., McQueen, J., Mendelovits, J., & Monseur, C. (2002). *Reading for change: Performance and engagement across countries: Results from PISA 2000.* Paris: Organisation for Economic Co-operation and Development.

Knowles, J. (2009). *Jumping off swings.* Somerville, MA: Candlewick.

Levithan, D. (2012). *Every day.* New York: Knopf.

Lewis, C. (2000). Limits of identification: The personal, pleasurable, and critical in reader response. *Journal of Literacy Research, 32*(2), 253–266.

Lewis, C., & Dockter, J. (2011). Reading literature in secondary school: Disciplinary discourses in global times. In S. Wolf, K. Coats, P. Enciso, & C. Jenkins (Eds.), *Handbook of research on children's and young adult literature* (pp. 76–91). New York: Routledge.

Mar, R. A., Oatley, K., Hirsch, J., De La Paz, J., & Peterson, J. B. (2006). Bookworms versus nerds: Exposure to fiction versus nonfiction, divergent associations with social ability, and the simulation of fictional social worlds. *Journal of Research in Personality, 40,* 694–712.

McCaffrey, K. (2006). *Destroying Avalon.* Freemantle, Western Australia: Freemantle Press.

McCaffrey, K. (2009). *In ecstasy.* Toronto: Annick Press.

Moje, E. B., Overby, M., Tysvaer, N., & Morris, K. (2008). The complex world of adolescent literacy: Myths, motivations, and mysteries. *Harvard Educational Review, 78*(1), 107–154.

National Governors Association Center for Best Practices & Council of Chief State School Officers (NGA & CCSSO). (2010). *Common Core State Standards for English language arts and literacy in history/social studies, science, and technical subjects.* Washington, DC: Authors.

Nystrand, M. (1997). *Opening dialogue: Understanding the dynamics of language and learning in the English classroom.* New York: Teachers College Press.

Petrone, R., Sarigianides, S. T., & Lewis, M. A. (2015). The youth lens: Analyzing adolescence/ts in literary texts. *Journal of Literacy Research, 46*(4), 506–533.

Pytash, K., Morgan, D., & Batchelor, K. (2013). Recognize the signs: Reading young adult literature to address bullying. *Voices from the Middle, 20*(3), 15–20.

Rosenblatt, L. (1983). *Literature as exploration.* New York: Modern Language Association of America.

Sanchez, R. (2000). *My bloody life: The making of a Latin king.* Chicago: Chicago Review Press.

Sannino, A., Daniels, H., & Gutiérrez, K. D. (Eds.). (2009). *Learning and expanding with activity theory.* New York: Cambridge University Press.

Sitomer, A. L. (2008). *Homeboyz.* New York: Hyperion.

Sitomer, A. L. (2008). *The secret story of Sonia Rodgriguez*. New York: Hyperion.

Stetsenko, A. (2008). From relational ontology to transformative activist stance on development and learning: Expanding Vygotsky's (CHAT) project. *Cultural Studies of Science Education, 3*, 471–491.

Stockdill, D. B., & Moje, E. B. (2013). Examining the relationship between youth's everyday and social studies literacies and learning. *Berkeley Review of Education, 4*(1), 35–68.

Strasser, T. (2009). *If I grow up*. New York: Simon & Schuster.

van Diepen, A. (2013). *Takedown*. New York: Simon Pulse.

Wickens, C. M. (2011). Codes, silences, and homophobia: Challenging normative assumptions about gender and sexuality in contemporary LGBTQ young adult literature. *Children's Literature in Education, 42*, 148–164.

Williams, C. L. (2010). *Glimpse*. New York: Simon & Schuster.

PART IV
PEDAGOGIES OF ADOLESCENT LITERACIES

CHAPTER 21

How Practice-Based Research Informs Adolescent English Language Learners' Composing and Compositions

JILL FITZGERALD

Approximately 9% of the school-age population in the United States consists of English-language learners[1] (National Clearinghouse for English Language Arts, n.d.). Modern-day subject-matter classroom diversity has become the "new mainstream" (Enright & Gilliland, 2011). Writing, as one facet of language, promises many affordances for adolescent English learners beyond the academic advantages often cited (Williams, 2012). Composing can proceed at a slower pace than oral discourse, and printed language permits both "changeability" and endurance, scaffolding English language learning in ways that oral English lacks. Such features can encourage development of cognitive processes and procedures in relation to audience and purpose—processes and procedures that promote language acquisition. As well, final compositions generally require some degree of precision in various attributes of language use (e.g., voice, register, word choice), characteristics that may support and develop English learners' knowledge use and expansion as they plan, execute, monitor, and revise their compositions. Moreover, writing can involve construction, reconstruction, organization, reorganization, and consolidation of knowledge, and as such, is an excellent venue for learning (including learning in content areas) (e.g., Manchón, 2011).

However, although the U.S. English learner population is large and growing, little attention has been devoted to adolescent English learners' composing and compositions (e.g., Leki, Cumming, & Silva, 2008; Ortmeier-Hooper & Enright, 2011; Harklau & Pinnow, 2009). Instead, most second-language writing research has been done with

---

[1] The term *multicompetent* is a notable, and preferable, new term in the literature that embraces the affordances and benefits of multilingualism. However, since only one study was located in which native-language writing competence was examined, the predominant term in the literature, *English language learner,* is used in this chapter.

college-age students (Ortega & Carson, 2010). The importance of adept writing ability has not gone unnoticed by adolescent English language learners who report that as they transition from high school to college their greatest linguistic challenge is writing (Kanno & Grosik, 2012). Unfortunately, the extent to which current-day writing instruction actually occurs for adolescent U.S. English learners is not clear, although some evidence suggests that in the mid- to late-1990s it was highly variable, and English learners immersed in mainstream classrooms may not receive high-quality writing instruction (Harklau & Pinnow, 2009). Furthermore, writing instruction is one of the least addressed areas in teacher preparation (Enright, 2013; Harklau & Pinnow, 2009).

The primary aim of this research review is to address educational practices that nurture and enhance adolescent middle and high school English language learners' composing and compositions, especially for students living in the United States. Readers may additionally profit from recent research reviews of second-language writing that extend beyond practice-based research, adolescent English learners, and/or include studies accomplished outside of the United States, such as foreign-language learning about composing and compositions by Cumming (2016), Fitzgerald (2006), Harklau and Pinnow (2009), and Leki et al. (2008). Prominent themes permeate the current literature on adolescent English learner practice-based research and are represented in this chapter: A framework of important factors and issues for English learners' composing is needed when considering practices for composing and composition development; composing is a medium for language, and language is interwoven with culture and identity; and composing practice is situation-specific but can be influenced by macro-level factors such as school, state, and federal policy. A final theme in this chapter is that although the research is in its infancy, the findings suggest certain fundamental guidelines for practices related to adolescent English learners' composing and compositions.

ARTICULATING KEY FACTORS FOR SECOND-LANGUAGE COMPOSING AND COMPOSITION PRACTICE

Educators are more likely to support English learners' progress if they understand fundamental characteristics of composing and compositions when adolescents are writing in a second language, as well as when writing in their native language (cf. Leki et al., 2008; Zhu, 2010). Whether explicit or implicit, educators' practices are in some sense based on their theories of what approaches are most likely to enhance English language learners' composing and compositions (e.g., Leki et al., 2008). However, currently, no coherent theory exists for understanding the composing processes used by second-language learners and their compositions in general, or for adolescents specifically (Cumming, in press; Kroll, 2003; Leki et al., 2008; Zhu, 2010).

Short of offering a theory, to situate the review, critique, and implications of the practice-based research that follows, Figure 21.1 at least depicts a transactional framework of major factors involved in adolescent second-language composing and composition. The framework is called "transactional" to emphasize both the reciprocal and iterative ways that authors work with their presumed readers and the interplay among various factors involved in composing. The framework provides a way to consider goals for practice and research—what components and issues matter and should be addressed during practice and in research. The portrayal is briefly explained in the following

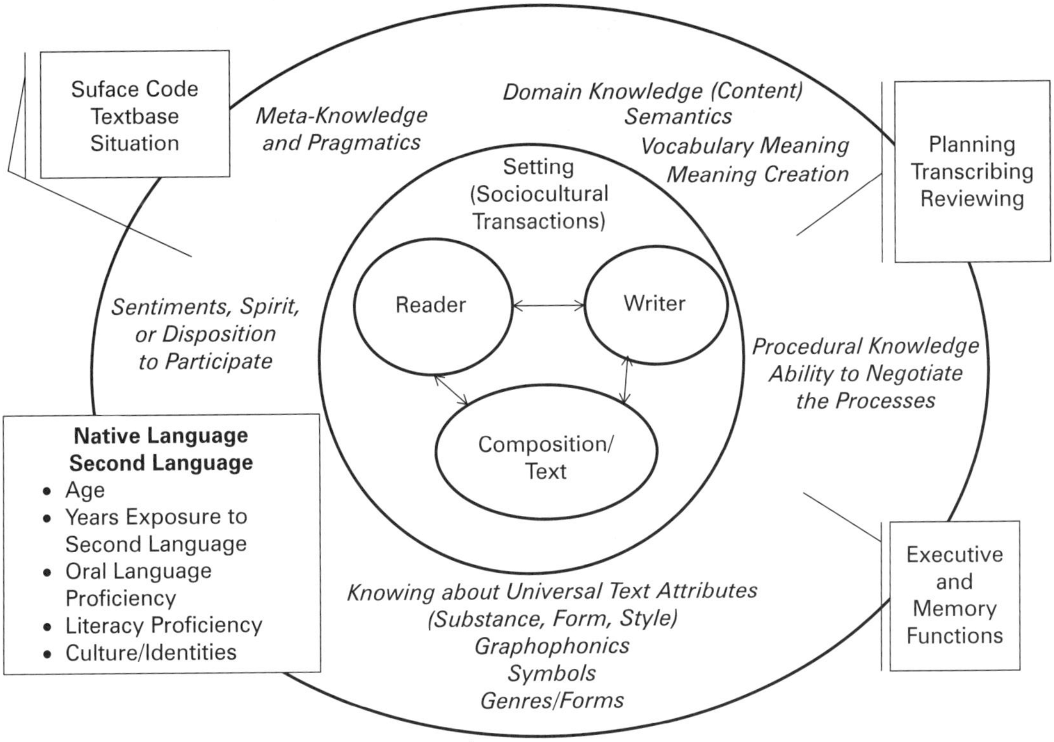

FIGURE 21.1. A framework for considering English language composing and composition. From Fitzgerald (2013). Copyright 2013 by Springer Science + Business Media. Adapted by permission.

sections (cf. Zhu, 2010, on the criticality of representing the writer, reader, text, context, and their interactions; Ivanič, 2004, on the importance of understanding composing and composition in increasingly broader contexts; Villalva, 2006, on the significance of an ecological framework). Most importantly, adolescent second-language learners' authoring is interwoven with significant issues associated with their immersion in a culture (or cultures) that is (are) generally different from the culture of their native language (Ortmeier-Hooper & Enright, 2011).

Sociocultural Factors

The term *sociocultural transaction* and the two-way arrows in Figure 21.1 represent the reciprocal influences that occur between an author and his or her imagined reader(s) whether composing in a native or a new language (e.g., Pugh et al., 2006), as well as the sociolinguistic contexts involved in the particular composing situation. Authorship involves negotiation of meaning with readers in particular circumstances for particular purposes (Nystrand, 1989). Students are social actors who write to engage in dialogues with their readers in some form or fashion. As writers compose, they consider what their readers might be thinking as they read parts of the composition, what their readers might need to know or find difficult in the text, how they might surprise or affect their readers in some way, and/or whether and how their readers might critique the text.

Schools, teachers, and peers become part of the social fabric of a composing culture, because they influence students and are in turn influenced *by* student authors through a wide range of micro- and macro-contexts, from school stated or implied policy for what counts as "good" writing and "good" curriculum and instruction, to teachers' understanding of second-language composing, to teachers' and peers' values for writing, and to ways teachers and students position and view themselves and each other in relation to their power to transform themselves, to engage, or to disengage (Englert, Mariage, & Dunsmore, 2006; Ivanič, 2004; Ortega & Carson, 2010). Students' and teachers' own identities as writers and readers of compositions are socially constructed through their own and "others'" images (Gee, 2000).

Cognitive Factors

The five types of knowledge in the outer circle in Figure 21.1 emphasize key mental processes involved in native- and second-language composing. They represent in-the-mind knowing about, knowing what, and knowing how of selected facets of writing (Fitzgerald & Shanahan, 2000):

1. Metaknowledge and pragmatics (e.g., Shell, Colvin, & Bruning, 1995) are about the functions and purposes of composing, for example, knowing that authors transact with readers, and monitoring meaning-production strategies.
2. Domain knowledge (world knowledge or prior knowledge) is the content or substance of what one knows.
3. Procedural knowledge is about knowing how to access, use, and create knowledge, as well as integrate various processes (Kellogg, 1994).
4. Knowledge about desirable characteristics of the written text in English (which themselves can vary from one culture to another) includes letter and word generation, requiring phonological and grapheme awareness and morphological understanding; sentence syntax—rules for constructing sentences (Kellogg, 1994); and syntax of larger chunks of text—organization, genre (Shanahan, 1984).
5. Last, sentiments, spirit, or disposition to read or write references individuals' creation and sharing of meanings with others—or not.

Cutting through any composing act, three levels of cognitive representation and activation occur: Authors use symbols (surface code, letters and syntax) to stand for their meanings; authors have meaningful propositions in mind that are free of surface code (called a *mental textbase representation*); and they consider content or "microworld" substance of the text (an internal model of the situation) (Kintsch, 1998). In addition, the trilevel activity occurs throughout planning, text generation, and reviewing (Hayes, 2006). Other mental activities are involved as well, such as working memory, short- and long-term memory, self-regulation, and executive control of multiple processes, and there are accompanying neurological bases (e.g., Hayes, 2006).

Composing Challenges and Affordances Specific to English Language Learners

While few studies have documented how language status factors function during second-language composing, the probable importance of several language status factors has been realized by researchers and practitioners, including the following: the age at which the student began learning the new language (e.g., Abrahamsson, 2012); the length of time the student has been learning the new language (cf. studies on the impact on oracy of time devoted to learning a new language [e.g., Abrahamsson, 2012; Muñoz, 2008]; the nature of the relationship between the new language and the native language (e.g., the degree to which each language is opaque vs. transparent; Koda, 2008); the degree of oral and literate proficiency in the native language (Harklau & Pinnow, 2009); and cultural compatibilities and incompatibilities connected to the two languages. Variations in these factors can have a significant impact on what sorts of practices are most likely to enhance an adolescent English language learner's composing and composition progress.

For adolescents, writing in English as a second language can be particularly challenging for additional reasons (Kormos, 2012). While research is sparse on both the challenges and the affordances for composing in the new language (e.g., Harklau & Pinnow, 2009), there are both sociological and cognitive indicators of the complexities that adolescent second-language learners bring to their authoring and compositions. Such sociological and cognitive factors are discussed in the following sections.

Language Status and Social Factors, Identities

A major, and very complex, issue for the adolescent English language learner as author is the pivotal role of identity formation. Identity formation is a central feature in adolescent development in general. Adolescence is a critical transitional period during which personal identities are formed. For English language learners, identities can be even more complicated, especially for new immigrants who are faced with pressures to assimilate while simultaneously preserving cultural origins (Fu & Graff, 2009). Composing itself requires authorship, and what is authorship of a composition if not an identity-defining moment (cf. Schoonen & Appel, 2005)? One's identity is tied up in language, and learning to write isn't simply about acquiring particular linguistic abilities (Matsuda, Canagarajah, Harklau, Hyland, & Warschauer, 2003; Ortmeier-Hooper & Enright, 2011). Authors shed light on how they see themselves and open themselves up to how readers see that identity, including possible criticism, as well as to perceptions of themselves as members of a linguistic minority immersed in an English-majority culture. For adolescent English language learners, composing can be one of many symbolic acts of negotiating social allegiance and identity (Ortmeier-Hooper & Enright, 2011). Transfer of writing ability that can occur across languages is entangled with an adolescent's former and new cultural values and attitudes about composing. One sign of that entanglement is *code switching* (using words from both languages within and across utterances) that can reflect the onset of one's identity hybridization as it is mediated by language (Zentella, 2002). The sounds, words, and syntax of a language represent meanings that are attached to one's cultural understandings. Code switching can serve as a threshold state in which an adolescent can represent an affiliation with two cultures through language.

Additionally, selected research evidence suggests there can be a disconnect between school and outside-of-school literacies for adolescent English language learners (García, 1999). U.S. high-school English learners have been documented doing a fair amount of writing outside of school, including journals and poetry to share with peers, while their school-based writing instruction does not involve such practices, favoring academic writing and standard use of mechanics (Fu, 1995; García, 1999).

Language Status and Cognitive Factors

From research predominantly conducted outside of the United States, several points may be relevant to the U.S. situation. It seems clear that second-language learners use their native language when writing in the new language as a means of easing the task (Ortega & Carson, 2010); there is some minimal evidence that native-language and second-language writing ability are correlated (Harklau & Pinnow, 2009); and individuals tend to compose in a second language using basically similar cognitions and procedures as those in their native language (Cumming, 2001; Fitzgerald, 1995). So although there is no specific evidence to support the claim for U.S. adolescent English learners, it also seems likely that they would experience some cross-language cognitions while composing. Intuitively, but yet to be researched, the cross-language cognitions could be facilitative types of transfer (e.g., "I know the word I want to use in Spanish, and I bet there's an English cognate for it. I'll try that"). By using native-language knowledge, English language learners may diminish the cognitive demands and manage the writing task to negotiate successful meaning creation (Harklau & Pinnow, 2009).

At the same time, native-language cognitive transfer may inhibit adolescents' fluency when writing in English. The presence of two languages, combined with the acquisition of new knowledge about semantics and syntax in the new language, can create considerable cognitive load, which in turn may result in a laborious composing task, generally requiring more processing time (Fitzgerald, 1995; Harklau & Pinnow, 2009). Adolescent English learners often must give more attention to creating surface code (spelling, syntax, vocabulary choice, and more) as opposed to elaborating the meanings they want to create (Harkau & Pinnow, 2009; e.g., "I want to create some suspense in this mystery I'm writing, but it's too much hard work. I need to spell everything in English correctly and make sure I get the verbs right first").

STUDY SELECTION CRITERIA AND STUDIES REVIEWED

Empirical research was included if it was published between 2000 and 2015 (dissertations, theses, and works such as Education Research Information Center [ERIC] documents were not included), and student participants were noted as middle-grade or high school second-language learners of English regardless of the term used to describe the participants (e.g., *language minority, English as a second language, bilingual, English language learner, dual language learner*). Additionally, studies were considered "practice-based" if students were taught something about composing by someone else (e.g., a teacher or peers) or students' composing practices were examined by researchers. Any practice-based setting could be included. For instance, a setting could be bilingual education, dual language education, English immersion with pullout English as a second language, or out-of-school situations, (e.g., writing in community centers).

Studies were included only if student participants were in the United States. Research conducted in varied international contexts is needed and certainly can inform the U.S. situation (e.g., Grabe & Kaplan, 1996). However, there is also some value in describing research findings as they may pertain to more specific situations, including specific nations and specific second languages. As portrayed in the preceding sections, the writing experience is always socially situated and impacted greatly by the contexts within which the learner lives and writes. Variation in individual backgrounds and contexts of composing is vast (Cumming, 2016). Among those various factors are the new language to be learned and culturally ingrained and/or respected pedagogical approaches. For instance, learning a new language in a foreign-language setting through course work restricts lived experiences with the new language, and students' motivations and views of "best" instructional methods can vary considerably across the globe. Even the localized U.S. focus itself results in a considerable amount of variation across situations. Consequently, while threads of commonality and differences can result from examining adolescent second-language writing research globally, there remains the possibility that results from one context could lead to inaccurate overgeneralization to another context.

Additionally, once studies were gathered using the preceding criteria, the rigor of the practice-based research method was considered to further filter studies for inclusion (cf. Alvermann, Simpson, & Fitzgerald, 2006). For qualitative research, reports generally had to include detail about study particulars; researcher reflectivity; primary data (e.g., quotes, stories); conclusions about what was learned; and discussion of how conclusions point to a wider discourse. For experiments or quasi-experiments, the design had to include a control or comparison group or normative data. For quasi-experiments, there also had to be some pretesting of outcomes of interest.

WHAT DID THE STUDIES REVEAL?

The body of U.S. adolescent English language writers' practice-based research is increasing, but there are still many unanswered questions. Thirty-six studies were collected for the present review, and the research questions may be loosely organized into five clusters based on the primary issue addressed: (1) describing English language learners' composing and composition, and its development (10 studies); (2) students' identity development as it interfaces with their composing and compositions (4 studies); (3) the influence of classroom and school practices, including an intersection with policy (16 studies); (4) outside-of-school practices (3 studies); and (5) professional development for teachers (3 studies).

The research was weighted heavily toward qualitative and case study examination of a wide variety of sociocultural issues (32 studies). Virtually all of the qualitative/case studies were grounded or framed in some way in a sociocultural perspective, and many were longitudinal. In general, they focused on the complexities of the social relationships among authors, readers, the multiple contexts in which they were embedded, and the sociocultural interactive nature of English learners' composing. Through case studies, the situated nature of composing, coupled with the wide variety of research issues addressed, advanced the beginnings of a rich set of understandings for particulars. The emphasis on the intersection of personal histories with socially situated contexts may represent an essential shift in the field toward new perspectives on adolescent second-language learners themselves, as well as what constitutes effective instruction (Cummins, 2009). One general statement that can be made is that the case studies tended to reveal some of the myriad complexities involved in English learners' composing, while exploring their challenges, but emphasizing their affordances and promise.

Only a very small number of experimental or quasi-experimental studies (4) was uncovered. In each case, teachers were taught a package of methods generally aimed at enhancing students' cognitive understandings of composing and compositions and involving explicit instruction, and evidence indicated that teachers faithfully implemented the methods.

How Does Composing in a New Language Happen and Develop?

The 10 studies that primarily addressed how adolescent English learner composing happens and develops focused on wide-ranging research issues within the topic. One conclusion as a result of comparing and contrasting across the seven studies, and from one study in particular (Valdés & Sanders, 2006), was that there was considerable variance in students' English composing status growth. For instance, during a 2-year study, three Spanish-speaking immigrant middle school students' English writing development varied according to the tasks performed and varied according factors such as their compositions' organization and mechanics (Valdés & Sanders, 2006). An explanation for the variant growth was that the students' composing and composition was dependent on their instructional settings, exposure to English outside of school, and/or other factors (e.g., personal histories).

Another conclusion was that adolescent English learners can implement important composing competencies that can go un-noticed by others. Villalva (2006) found that English learners actually engaged in English composing practices that reflected strengths, but they hid those practices from their teachers, because the practices differed from those expected in their mainstream classes.

Other researchers focused on composition challenges. For high school English learners, the greatest self-identified challenge for English writing was translating between two languages, followed by content generation (Beck, Llosa, & Fredrick, 2013). However, one researcher found that adolescent English learners in English-as-a-second-language classes (as compared to language-minority and native-English-speaking peers in regular language arts classes) may know and use certain linguistic features, such as English grammatical constructions, but fail to apply certain constructions when required for specific purposes (Reynolds, 2005). The implication was that the larger challenge was recognition of rhetorical appropriateness, an understanding that might grow with greater exposure to various rhetorical forms. Similarly, in another analysis of the same students' compositions, students in regular language arts classes (some of whom were formerly labeled English language learners) used more causal markers for one topic than another, whereas the students in the English as a second language classes used similar amounts of causal markers across the two topics (Reynolds, 2002). That is, the latter group did not cognitively differentiate the two topics, again suggesting a need for clearer understanding of different rhetorical structures during some phase of writing development. In a separate study (Danzak, 2011a), students generally appeared to apply a knowledge-telling strategy rather than strategically planning, composing, and revising their compositions in relation to task purposes and requirements.

Results of one study implied transfer of knowledge across English and Spanish composing and compositions for middle grade English learners (Danzak, 2011a). Linguistic analyses at the lexical, syntactic, and discourse levels across eight expository and narrative autobiographical compositions revealed similar uses of linguistic features for the two languages.

Finally, adolescent English learners' composing and composition growth over time may not be linear (Fu, 2009), and there is limited evidence of hybridization of processes, language, and/or genre, signaling a possible advancing phase in development. For instance, when examining think-alouds during composing, along with retrospective interviews and compositions themselves, a comparison between 10 high school English learners and 17 native-English-speaking peers revealed the English learners were far less likely than the peers to produce the target genre (Bunch & Willett, 2013; Beck et al., 2013). Their genres were "narrguments," that is, hybrids of narratives and argumentative exposition. The hybrid genre represented a phase in development during which students used known knowledge combined with new understandings—a positive progression toward mature exposition rather than evidence of incapability or "error." Similarly, code switching, that is moving between languages, represented another facet in a phase of development. It was found to be an important and useful coping strategy through which fourth- through 12th-grade English learners could scaffold transitional composing in the classroom (Fu, 2009) or on the Internet (Lam, 2004). As well, comparison of "errors" made by high school English learners and their native-English-speaking peers revealed that while both groups made more errors in social studies than in English language arts, the English learners displayed significantly higher error rates than their peers (Wilcox, Yagelski, & Yu, 2014). However, the researchers also noted the paradoxes involved in determining whether a verbal issue was an "error," that is, a mistake, or whether it represented a conceptualization that simply was different from the reader's expectation. That is, a question was raised as to whether some of the "errors" actually reflected a kind of developmental phase during which the English learner was transitioning to some new learning.

Identity Development Interfaces with Composing and Compositions

Four sets of researchers focused intently on student cases to examine how English language writers' identity was forged (or not) and intertwined with present and past experiences and self-identification. A consistent theme across the studies on identity was that adolescent English language learners engaged in multiple identities (e.g., with peers outside of school or in an English class), identities that were socially constructed by "other" individuals (e.g., peers, relatives, educators), then rejected or accepted by the student (Ortmeier-Hooper, 2013). In one case, composing on the Internet with a transnational peer group supported a student's developing identity as an English writer (Lam, 2000). Some students, such as Hoon, a native-Korean high school student, experienced their identity as English learners as stigmatization and were able to develop coping strategies that facilitated writing development (Yi, 2013). But in other cases, an English writer's identity may be rejected. Wisdom, a 14-year-old Nigerian refugee, experienced cultural dissonance with his writing teacher when his refugee identity was misperceived and "tested" through questioning. To discuss his sociopolitical past, Wisdom would have had to make himself vulnerable to criticism from someone outside his culture. The resultant tension impeded his development as a writer, because he did not want to take on the refugee identity in his classroom.

A clear message for practitioners that arises from the studies of identity development was that how students experience their past and their contemporary presence in society, school, and classroom matters relate not only to their composing and composition progress but also their personal dispositions toward writing and schooling. Case studies in this cluster revealed students who were aware of ethnic differences, encountered language discrimination, and, depending on their English writing expertise, displayed language preferences (Danzak, 2011b).

Influence of Classroom and School Practices

Again, although the 11 case or descriptive analyses, one formative experiment, and four experiments/quasi-experiments of classroom and school practices were wide-ranging in intent, some potential lessons emerged. First, how teachers interact with adolescent English learners and the language they use, as well as their involvement in students' language, may impact students' composing progress in several ways. Even in predominantly English immersion settings, interactions with bilingual and monolingual texts in an environment that is sensitive to the use of native language while developing English can sustain students as they move from high school into new settings (Kibler, 2014). Even students who start high school knowing no English may flourish academically and as writers when supported in certain classroom ways (Kibler, 2013).

Opportunities for students' writing development were created locally through experiences of both activity and perceptions of self and others (Kibler, 2013). For instance, results of a study of four immigrant adolescents suggested that writing practice accomplished in a native country may travel with them only if the social structures in the new situation encourage and permit access to original practices (Leonard, 2013). Students' literacy practices were destabilized and redefined by the social contexts they met along the way, suggesting that writing has high- or low-mobility forms, depending on the social (including classroom) structures encountered.

In a related vein, formal and informal conferences with students hold strong potential for advancing English learners' composing processes and composition. But how teachers perceive English learners and how they interact during conferences can be critical to students' success. For example, Kibler (2011) found considerable challenges inherent in the writing conferences across content areas she observed with English learners. On the whole, the conferences tended to be conducted on the teachers' grounds and were "difficult in-the-moment interpretive work" for both teachers and students, in which not much teacher–student negotiation occurred. The teacher used strategies to force the English learners to bring their knowledge into view—a strategy that generally can be positive—but for some English learners, doing so requires the risk of vulnerability. While the conferences in the study led to completion of composition products, they also introduced unresolved ambiguities into the conference interactions and students' understanding of them.

Second, selection of a wide variety of materials and topics relevant to adolescent English learners may be one key to their composing advancement (Kibler, 2013). For instance, during a formative experiment involving 14 adolescent English learners, researchers concluded that selecting materials and topics that met students' own purposes for both reading and writing was important, but the individualized nature of the fit (vs. a stereotypical formulation of cultural identity) was key (Ivey & Broaddus, 2007). The social practices of individual students' present and future lives led to engagement, so flexibility and variety in material selection was essential. Similarly, a packaged instructional approach called Complex Instruction, which revolved around composing as meaning making and involved small heterogeneous groups requiring use of a variety of textual resources, appeared to be related to adolescent English learners positive writing development (Bunch & Willett, 2013). Analysis of 40 English learners' compositions written in seventh-grade social studies classrooms revealed that the students' composing and compositions reflected strong intertextuality. The students exhibited potential affordances for meaning making by utilizing the many resources available to them, including other classroom and personal historical texts, and considering factors inherent in the targeted composition, such as register and genre.

Third, in a related vein, exposure to rich content-area topic depth and breadth may advance English learners' knowledge and compositions. At the same time, when structured in certain ways, content-knowledge advancement opportunities can be lost. When teachers exposed learners to a rich conceptual curriculum across content areas, students' experiences of academic writing socialized them into disciplinary norms for understanding content, academic language, and disciplinary compositions (Enright, 2013). However, another set of researchers emphasized the importance of carefully attending to the discourses expressed during the content-area experiences. Moje, Collazo, Carrillo, and Marx (2011) revealed three competing discourses in one project-based seventh-grade science classroom with 31 Latin@ students—the discourse of the science discipline itself, the instructional classroom discourse, and the students and teacher's social/everyday discourse. Moje and colleagues suggested that a more congruent third space could be created to bring together the three different discourses, and that, if created, that third space would enhance the students science learning and scientific writing. Fránquiz and Salina (2011) provided an example that may illustrate such a third space. During three history lessons on provocative topics of special interest to immigrant adolescents, digitized documents, document-based questions, and writing assignments (e.g., letters or similar forms) appeared to make the subject relevant and meaningful to the students. In turn, students were cognitively engaged and exhibited identity investment in their compositions.

Fourth, helping students to focus on language itself and to consider similarities and differences across texts and languages, using intertextuality as a tool for learning and writing, can empower English learners to be "agentive text makers" (Harmon, 2013). Systematic Functional Linguistics, a formalized approach whereby teachers helps students to analyze language itself, may enhance adolescent English learners' understanding of composing and composition beyond "doing the activity" (Spycher, 2007).

Fifth, when teachers learned about and implemented explicit instruction in cognitive strategies for writing, such as how to plan and set goals, how to tap prior knowledge, how to construct gist, how to revise for various purposes, and more, adolescent English learners tended to write compositions judged to be higher in quality and displaying desirable composition characteristics, such as more depth of interpretation, greater clarity of thesis, and better idea organization (Matuchniak, Olson, & Scarcella, 2014; Olson et al., 2012; Olson & Land, 2007).

Sixth, some evidence suggests that the sheltered instruction observation protocol (SIOP) model effectively enhanced adolescent English learners' writing proficiency, especially after 2 years of teacher participation in professional development that lasted 7 days in Year 1 and 3 days in Year 2 (Short, Echevarria, & Richards-Tutor, 2011). The SIOP is a general model for teaching subject-area curriculum. Teachers use a participatory approach with modeling, hands-on activities, cooperative mini-projects, and more, while teaching disciplinary content to English learners. While not specifically aimed solely at writing instruction, writing instruction is incorporated.

A final study highlighted the influence of macro-level contextual factors of policy, standards, and an accountability climate on classroom writing practices and norms, which in turn socialized adolescent English learners into narrow restrictive norms for academic writing (Enright & Gilliland, 2011).

Out-of-School Practices

Limited evidence suggests that some adolescent English learners may write outside of school at least to some extent. Latin@ children of working-class families in the United States often engage in collaborative writing activities in public spaces, such as the kitchen or the living room, involving parents, siblings, cousins, and extended family members (Gonzalez, Moll, & Amanti, 2005). Two teenage native Japanese sojourners in the United States spent considerable time on academic reading and writing outside of school, in large part to complete school assignments (Haneda & Monobe, 2009). They also sought private tutoring on Saturdays; they wrote mainly in Japanese, but also some in English. One high-school Korean immigrant drew on her voluntary, out-of-school writing for her creative writing class (Yi, 2010).

Other Studies Related to Adolescent English Learner Composing and Composition

Three additional studies addressed teacher professional development. If teachers are to advance English learners' composing and compositions, some understanding of the social and meaning-making functions, purposes, and inner workings of languages, especially the English language, may be important—not to teach English per se, but rather to enact lessons and to hear and respond to students in caring ways that can enhance both students' writing proficiency and their desire to take on an English (and native-language) writerly stance (e.g., Bunch, 2013). One approach to helping all teachers, but especially mainstream teachers, better understand their English learners' composing and composition needs is to invite teachers to analyze the language features that are central to their own discipline, an approach called *systematic functional linguistics* (SFL; Schleppergrell, Achugar, & Oteíza, 2004). The focus is on understanding how the discourse features both realize and are realized by the social and historical contexts in which the texts are written. Teacher-preparation SFL initiatives have been shown to be successful in advancing middle grade and high school teachers' knowledge of language (Aguirre-Muñoz, Park, Amabisca, & Boscardin, 2009; Schleppegrell et al., 2004). A second approach has been to ask teacher candidates who major in teaching English as a second language to blog with adolescent English language learners, with the specific purpose of better understanding the demands that high school academic writing places on the students (Baecher, Schieble, Rosalia, & Rorimer, 2013). The teachers-in-preparation became more aware of their own deficit connotations about the students' composing abilities, of the challenges the students faced, as well as the need for a high degree of interaction with students and their compositions.

Finally, it is worth noting that no adolescent English learner U.S. studies of feedback were located. As one means of assisting student writing development, provision of teacher (and to some extent, of peer) feedback on students' written compositions proliferates in U.S. secondary schools. However, the sparse research on such feedback with English learners has been accomplished predominantly with college-age students. Furthermore, studies of the effectiveness and roles of teacher feedback, taken collectively, have been inconclusive (Hyland & Hyland, 2006). The prior research confirms that some language-learning potential can be gained from corrective feedback, but the range of conditions under which it is effective and the extent of its potential are not clear—even for older students (Bitchener, 2012). As a result, uncertainties remain about the most effective forms of feedback for adolescent English language learners.

SUMMARY OF CONCLUSIONS FROM RESEARCH TO DATE

Practice-based research involving U.S. adolescent English learners' composing and compositions across the last 15 years is beginning to expand, but it remains thin. Few definitive conclusions can be drawn. However, tentative statements about practice may be offered—with a caveat to consider them cautiously due to very few studies having addressed a wide-ranging set of issues.

Researchers who studied *how adolescent English learner composing occurs and develops* found the following:

1. There was tremendous variability in students' English composing status and growth—likely due to contextual issues such as instructional setting (e.g., bilingual class vs. English immersion) and personal histories (e.g., length of time studying in the United States).
2. Adolescent English learners can display composing competencies that go unnoticed or are ignored by their teachers.
3. The greatest challenges may be translating between two languages, content generation, and recognition of rhetorical appropriateness.
4. Composing processes, procedures, and content knowledge may transfer across English and Spanish.
5. Development over time may not be linear, and hybridization of processes, language, and/or genre may signal advancing knowledge rather than misunderstanding, miscue, or error.

Regarding studies of *identity development*, a strong theme emerged: Adolescent English learners engage multiple identities, and some identities are socially constructed by others, then rejected or accepted by the student. For example, adolescent English learners may accept others' perceptions of them as "good" English writers, or they may reject peers' or teachers' perceptions that they are "struggling" or "transitional" English writers, even to the point of refusing teachers' requests or assignments.

Conclusions about *classroom and school practices* were as follows:

1. Teachers who evidenced respect for English learners' native language, their native cultural(s), and linguistic challenges in the U.S. setting provided sustenance and

encouragement to English learners' progress as authors. The central importance of that respectful climate permeated several studies and was reflected in classrooms in various ways, including provision of materials and topics that interfaced with students' own lives and purposes for composing, exposure to a wide variety of textual resources to support intertextuality, and encouragement to compose using students' own personal histories.

2. Selection of a wide variety of materials and topics relevant to adolescent English learners may be one key to their composing advancement.
3. Exposure to content-area breadth and depth may advance English learners' compositions under certain attendant conditions, such as provision of provocative topics relevant to student interests, digitized documents, and assignment of particular composition forms.
4. Helping students to focus on language itself, comparing similarities across texts and languages may lead to enhanced understanding of composing and compositions.
5. Explicit instruction in cognitive strategies for composing led to improved compositions.
6. The sheltered English classroom approach in the SIOP was effective for advancing adolescent English learners' writing proficiency.
7. Macro-level factors of policy, standards, and an accountability climate affected classroom writing practice and norms, which in turn impacted students' perceptions of composing and compositions.

Also, it appears that adolescent English learners may write *outside of school* to some extent—in native language and English, though such writing may be related to school assignments.

Finally, both *professional development* sessions in systematic functional linguistics and blogging with adolescent English learners enlightened educators' understandings of the English learners' composing challenges and affordances. Uncertainties remain about the most effective forms of *feedback* for English learners.

THEORY AND FUTURE RESEARCH

Some research findings support the transactional framework in the opening of this chapter for English learners' composing and compositions, including the need to account for sociocultural intersections, cognitive capacities, and language status interplay. At the same time, the framework is just that—it is not a coherent theorization of how various elements in the framework function alone or as they interact with other elements. One clearly missing element is accounting for the impact of broader policies on facets in the framework (e.g., Enright & Gilliland, 2011).

Much more research is needed on every factor and issue in the framework presented in the opening of this chapter. Of special note, there have been surprisingly few studies of content-area writing with adolescent English learners, of curriculum and instructional praxis (Leki et al., 2008), and of within-student, cross-language research (Ortega & Carson, 2010). All of these issues require much greater depth of examination. Also notably missing are studies of composition elements such as vocabulary choice and diversity, especially since English vocabulary repertoire is often considered to be a pivotal language ability (e.g., Snow & Uccelli, 2009). Finally, research on implementation of technological advances for English learner composing is needed (Cumming, 2016).

Three-fourths of the practice-based studies examined in this review addressed questions best examined through qualitative analyses. Notably understudied were cognitive issues and explicit instruction of cognitive abilities. As others have noted, each methodological paradigm has strengths, but the former often lack the power to examine cognitive issues carefully, while the latter often have an impoverished outlook on the role and impact of social issues (cf. Harklau & Williams, 2010). To make a meaningful impact on practice, both types of studies are needed, and in the present case, more emphasis on studies of explicit instruction in cognitive processes appears warranted.

Several research design issues also should be considered in the future. There is a strong need for researchers to attend closely to reliability of measures and coding methods, and to incorporate more than one writing sample in data collection, even for qualitative studies, because without multiple compositions, the extent of generalization to similar or different forms of compositions isn't knowable. A larger body of longitudinal studies would also inform the development of adolescent English learners' composing ability, as well as the contexts under which greater versus lesser development occurs. As well, conferring with practitioners and including them as coresearchers, especially for instructional studies, could ground research in practical issues and might particularly augment instructional methodologies.

Foundational Guiding Principles for Practice Arising from the Research Base

A return at this point, and periodically throughout the following sections, to the transactional framework of English learners' composing and composition factors is useful. A first point is that few of the specific factors and related issues raised in the opening framework have been studied. Consequently, we are left with more questions than answers. However, the current research findings do suggest some tentative foundational guiding principles for middle- and secondary-grade practices. The principles are in keeping with Cummins's (2014) literacy engagement framework, in which meaning creation is scaffolded, connections to English learners' lives are activated, identities are affirmed, and language is extended.

For many disciplinary teachers, the principles in the following sections likely require some rethinking about their instructional settings. Although disciplinary teachers nationwide may be slightly positive, on the whole, about inclusion of English learners in their classes, they also tend to hold English-as-a-second-language teachers responsible for English learners' language development, and some deny responsibility to modify their teaching for diverse learners (Polat & Mahalingappa, 2013). Disciplinary teachers are focused intently on content learning—a content that can be laden with complex concepts, and the texts of their classrooms are frequently written at or above grade level, and are often not "reader-friendly," even for native-English students. In many cases, the majority of the students in the classes are native-English speakers, or even when a large number of English learners are present, multiple native languages may be spoken. Although the principles suggested below could usefully pertain to all students, they do require some attention to, and modifications for, English learners, including considerable adaptation of materials and instructional approach.

- *Be mindful of how complex English language learner composing can be.* One of the most important implications of the work to date for practitioners, and one explicated in the opening transactional framework for adolescent English learner composing, is that while developing composing abilities for all adolescents can be complex, it is even more complex for adolescent English language learners. Consequently, a first guiding principle is that practitioners should keep the added layers of complexity in mind at all times.

- *Recognize that certain linguistic challenges, as well as affordances, can accompany English composing for new language learners.* Students at various stages of English development often are compelled to find what they intend to say in native language and figure out how to translate it to English, which can take additional processing time. Recognizing that delay or pause in composing can imply that cognitive work is ongoing may not only suggest the need to allow extended time to think but it may also encourage it. An implication is that providing sufficient planning, transcribing, and revision time is important, as is the opportunity for students to write in their native language while composing, before or during writing English, even when the teacher does not understand the native language (Cummins, 2009; Ortega & Carson, 2010). Given that composing processes, procedures, and content knowledge may transfer across languages, careful attention to processing time and to encouragement of native language use as much as possible is an asset to English learners, because it can enable students to use higher-order and critical thinking sooner than if they only trying to think in English (Cummins et al., 2005). As well, in instances where cognates exist across languages, encouragement to notice and use cognates may be helpful (Cummins, 2009).

- *Pay close attention to individual English language learners' personal characteristics; set expectations accordingly; and tailor composing activities, requests, and assignments.* As implied in the opening framework for English learners' composing, personal factors such as length of time studying in the United States, degree of native-language composing proficiency, and more, mean that there is tremendous variability in adolescent English learners' composing status and growth. Tailoring composing activities, requests, and assignments can assist student attitudes toward composing, as well as their composing and composition development.

- *Watch for hybridization examples in compositions that can signal English learners' composing development.* Realize that adolescent English learners' composing progress may occur in spurts and plateaus, and that it may not parallel typical development of native-English speakers. When working on the threshold between two languages, what might traditionally be taken to be "errors" may actually be hybridization that signals developmental progress. The "narrguments" noted in one study provide nice examples of a way in which English learners demonstrate developmental progress. Code switching is another example of hybridization. Variously called translanguaging," "languaging," "metrolanguaging," or "multilingual languaging," students use whatever linguistic capabilities are present to achieve communicative goals (Sebba, 2012). Mental processes of switching languages happen spontaneously while composing (see Cumming, 2013, for neurolinguistic evidence). Encouraging such hybridization and code switching as transitional status may enhance students' development.

- *Recognize that language and culture are identity laden, and vice versa.* Because language is inherently tied to culture, students transitioning into a new language and a new culture live in a threshold space, a space filled with tension. To adapt, they sometimes believe they need to give up something of themselves in their present and past to become something different. At a critical transition period for all adolescents, the English learner is especially vulnerable to exclusion, to being "different," to feelings of not belonging, and to criticism. Composing, as a key linguistic representation of cultural norms, when handled well, can be a source of comfort, an avenue for self-expression, and a self-perceived growth experience. Or it can be yet another source of tension. As suggested in the social transactional nature of the opening framework, when interacting with adolescent English learners, understanding their threshold space as language makers during composing can better situate teachers' and others' responses, questions, and conversations about composing and compositions, moving us to a place of caring support and genuine appreciation, which can in turn be perceived by students as concern for their well-being and growth.

- *Demonstrate respect for English learners' native language and culture through thoughtful provision of activities and materials.* Enable and encourage a wide variety of textual resources, including native-language resources before and during composing (Cumming, 2001). Consider topics that could be especially relevant to students' lives, including past and present cultures. This principle may be one of the most difficult to enact for disciplinary teachers (Grabe & Zhang, 2013). In many, if not most, instances, they will need to locate lower-level texts or texts written in native language so that their English learners can access the topics when their reading levels are below grade level. Other solutions could involve paired student learning and use of audiotapes and videos. A set of educational practices called "identity texts" also provides ways in which students with diverse language backgrounds share stories and information about their own cultural experiences and knowledge while composing, translating, and critiquing (Cummins & Early, 2011; cf. Gonzalez et al., 2005, regarding valorization of multilingual students' home and community culture and knowledge).

  Still, teacher energy and creativity are necessary in locating materials and restructuring lessons at least in minor ways if English learners are to progress as English authors.

- *Introduce adolescent English learners to disciplinary breadth and depth.* Content-area classrooms hold great promise for adolescent English learners' academic and composing advancement because they can contain interesting and evocative topics that draw students into learning. Disciplinary spaces can also be arenas for helping English learners to use composing to learn and organize content, as well as to learn disciplinary language and genres. In fact, in one study English learners' high school tracking into or out of more or less intense content-area high school courses was a better predictor of achievement than the students' English proficiency, suggesting that exposure to rich disciplinary knowledge was more critical for their academic progress than English proficiency (Callahan, 2005). At the same time, English learners in early and intermediate phases of learning English need some individualized or small-group scaffolding and instructional supports, such as selecting a subset of class goals for compositions so that new English learners can accomplish at least some, if not all, of the goals intended for native-English learners.

- *Learn about linguistic characteristics that differ across forms and genres, and help English language learners to do the same.* Develop metacognitive understandings of the English language, especially for features that are particularly salient within particular disciplinary areas (Cummins, 2014). Then help students to understand the features though lessons or mini-lessons during which texts written in the same and different forms are compared for similarities and differences. Where possible, compare to forms in native language. A result may be that students also develop metacogitive linguistic awareness, a framework factor known to be important to advancement of composing and compositions.

- *Implement explicit instruction in cognitive strategies for composing.* Various cognitive abilities in the opening transactional framework for composing were well supported in the work of Olson and colleagues (2012). Many examples of instructional goals and activities can be found there and in the SIOP.

REFERENCES

Abrahamsson, N. (2012). Age of onset and nativelike L2 ultimate attainment of morphosyntactic and phonetic intuition. *Studies in Second Language Acquisition, 34,* 187–214.

Aguirre-Muñoz, Z., Park, J.-A., Amabisca, A., & Boscardin, C. K. (2009). Developing teacher capacity for serving ELLs' writing instructional needs: A case for systemic functional linguistics. *Bilingual Research Journal, 31,* 295–322.

Alvermann, D., Simpson, M., & Fitzgerald, J. (2006). Research in teaching and learning in reading. In P. Alexander & P. Winne (Eds.), *Handbook of educational psychology* (pp. 427–451). New York: Guilford Press.

Baecher, L., Schieble, M., Rosalia, C., & Rorimer, S. (2013). Blogging for academic purposes with English language learners: An online fieldwork initiative. *Contemporary Issues in Technology and Teacher Education, 13,* 1–21.

Beck, S., Llosa, L., & Fredrick, T. (2013). The challenges of writing exposition: Lessons from a study of ELL and non-ELL high school students. *Reading & Writing Quarterly, 29,* 358–380.

Bitchener, J. (2012). A reflection on "the language learning potential" of written CF. *Journal of Second Language Writing, 21,* 348–363.

Bunch, G. C. (2013). Pedagogical language knowledge: Preparing mainstream teachers for English learners in the new standards era. *Review of Research in Education, 37,* 298–341.

Bunch, G. C., & Willett, K. (2013). Writing to mean in middle school: Understanding how second language writers negotiate textually-rich content-area instruction. *Journal of Second Language Writing, 22,* 141–160.

Callahan, R. (2005). Tracking and high school English learners: Limiting opportunity to learn. *American Educational Research Journal, 42,* 305–328.

Cumming, A. (2001). Learning to write in a second language: Two decades of research. *International Journal of English Studies, 1,* 1–23.

Cumming, A. (2013). Multiple dimensions of academic language and literacy development. *Language Learning: A Journal of Research in Language Studies, 63*(Suppl. 1), 130–152.

Cumming, A. (2016). Writing development and instruction for English language learners. In C. A. MacArthur, S. Graham, S., & J. Fitzgerald (Eds.), *Handbook of writing research* (2nd ed., pp. 364–376). New York: Guilford Press.

Cumming, A. (in press). Theoretical orientations to L2 writing. In P. Matsuda & R. Manchón (Eds.), *Handbook of second and foreign language writing.* Berlin: Mouton de Gruyter.

Cummins, J. (2009). Foreword. In D. Fu (Ed.), *Writing between languages: How English language*

learners make the transition to fluency, grades 4–12 (pp. ix–xii). Portsmouth, NH: Heinemann.
Cummins, J. (2014). Beyond language: Academic communication and student success. *Linguistics and Education, 26,* 145–154.
Cummins, J., Bismilla, V., Chow, P., Cohen, S., Giampapa, F., Leoni, L., et al. (2005). Affirming identity in multilingual classrooms. *Educational Leadership, 63,* 38–43.
Cummins, J., & Early, M. (2011). *Identity texts: The collaborative creation of power in multilingual schools.* London: Trentham Books.
Danzak, R. L. (2011a). The integration of lexical, syntactic, and discourse features in bilingual adolescents' writing: An exploratory approach. *Language, Speech, and Hearing Services in Schools, 42,* 491–505.
Danzak, R. L. (2011b). The interface of language proficiency and identity: A profile analysis of bilingual adolescents and their writing. *Language, Speech, and Hearing Services in Schools, 42,* 506–519.
Englert, C. S., Mariage, T. V., & Dunsmore, K. (2006). Tenets of sociocultural theory in writing instruction research. In C. A. MacArthur, S. Graham, & J. Fitzgerald (Eds.), *Handbook of writing research* (pp. 208–221). New York: Guilford Press.
Enright, K. A. (2013). Adolescent writers and academic trajectories: Situating L2 writing in the content areas. In L. C. de Oliveria & T. Silva (Eds.), *L2 writing in secondary classrooms: Student experiences, academic issues, and teacher education* (pp. 27–43). New York: Routledge.
Enright, K. A., & Gilliland, B. (2011). Multilingual writing in an age of accountability: From policy to practice in U.S. high school classrooms. *Journal of Second Language Writing, 20,* 182–195.
Fitzgerald, J. (1995). English-as-a-second-language learners' cognitive reading processes: A review of research in the United States. *Review of Educational Research, 65,* 145–190.
Fitzgerald, J. (2006). Bilingual writing in preschool through 12th grade: The last 15 years. In C. A. McArthur, S. Graham, & J. Fitzgerald (Eds.), *Handbook of writing research* (pp. 337–354). New York: Guilford Press.
Fitzgerald, J. (2013). Constructing instruction for struggling writers: what and how. *Annals of Dyslexia, 63,* 80–95.
Fitzgerald, J., & Shanahan, T. (2000). Reading and writing relations and their development. *Educational Psychologist, 35,* 39–50.
Fránquiz, M. E., & Salina, C. S. (2011). Newcomers developing English literacy through historical thinking and digitized primary sources. *Journal of Second Language Writing, 20,* 196–210.
Fu, D. (1995). *My trouble is my English: Asian students and the American dream.* Portsmouth, NH: Heinemann.
Fu, D. (2009). *Writing between languages: How English language learners make the transitions to fluency: Grades 4 to 12.* Portsmouth, NH: Heinemann.
Fu, D., & Graff, J. M. (2009). The literacies of new immigrant youth. In L. Christenbury, R. Bomer, & P. Smagorinsky (Eds.), *Handbook of adolescent literacy research* (pp. 400–414). New York: Guilford Press.
García, O. (1999). Educating Latino high school students with little formal schooling. In C. Faltis & P. Wolfe (Eds.), *So much to say: Adolescents, bilingualism, and ESL in the secondary school* (pp. 61–82). New York: Teachers College Press.
Gee, J. (2000). Identity as an analytic lens for research in education. *Review of Research in Education, 25,* 99–125.
Gonzalez, N., Moll, L., & Amanti, C. (2005). *Funds of knowledge: Theorizing practices in household, communities, and classrooms.* Mahwah, NJ: Erlbaum.
Grabe, W., & Kaplan, R. (1996). *Theory and practice of writing: An applied linguistic perspective.* Harlow, UK: Longman.

Grabe, W., & Zhang, Z. (2013). A critical component of English for academic purposes teaching and learning. *TESOL Journal, 4,* 1–24.

Haneda, M., & Monobe, G. (2009). Bilingual and biliteracy practices: Japanese adolescents living in the United States. *Journal of Pacific Communication, 19,* 7–29.

Harklau, L., & Pinnow, R. (2009). Adolescent second-language writing. In L. Christenbury, R. Bomer, & P. Smagorinsky (Eds.), *Handbook of adolescent literacy research* (pp. 126–139). New York: Guilford Press.

Harklau, L., & Williams, G. (2010). Practicing theory in qualitative research on second language writing. In T. Silva & P. K. Matsuda (Eds.), *Practicing theory in second language writing* (pp. 93–111). West Lafayette, IN: Parlor Press.

Harmon, R. (2013). Literary intertextuality in genre-based pedagogies: Building lexical cohesion in fifth-grade L2 writing. *Journal of Second Language Writing, 22,* 125–140.

Hayes, J. R. (2006). New directions in writing theory. In C. A. MacArthur, S. Graham, & J. Fitzgerald (Eds.), *Handbook of writing research* (pp. 28–40). New York: Guilford Press.

Hyland, K., & Hyland, F. (2006). Feedback on second language students' writing. *Language Teaching, 39,* 83–101.

Ivanič, R. (2004). Discourses of writing and learning to write. *Language and Education, 18,* 220–245.

Ivey, G., & Broaddus, K. (2007). A formative experiment investigating literacy engagement among adolescent Latina/o students just beginning to read, write, and speak English. *Reading Research Quarterly, 42,* 512–545.

Kanno, Y., & Grosik, S. A. (2012). Immigrant English learners' transitions to university: Student challenges and institutional policies. In Y. Kanno & L. Harklau (Eds.), *Linguistic minority students go to college: Preparation, access, and persistence* (pp. 130–147). New York: Routledge.

Kellogg, R. (1994). *The psychology of writing.* New York: Oxford University Press.

Kibler, A. (2011). "I write in a way that people can read it": How teachers and adolescent L2 writers describe content area writing. *Journal of Second Language Writing, 20,* 211–226.

Kibler, A. (2013). "Doing like almost everything wrong": An adolescent multilingual writer's transition from high school to college. In L. C. de Oliveria & T. Silva (Eds.), *L2 writing in secondary classrooms: Student experiences, academic issues, and teacher education* (pp. 44–63). New York: Routledge.

Kibler, A. K. (2014). From high school to the Noviciado: An adolescent linguistic minority student's multilingual journey in writing. *Modern Language Journal, 98,* 629–651.

Kintsch, W. (1998). *Comprehension: A paradigm for cognition.* New York: Cambridge University Press.

Koda, K. (2008). Impacts of prior literacy experience on second language learning to read. In K. Koda & A. M. Zehler (Eds.), *Learning to read across languages: Cross-linguistic relationships in first- and second-language literacy development* (pp. 68–96). New York: Routledge.

Kormos, J. (2012). The role of individual differences in L2 writing. *Journal of Second Language Writing, 21,* 390–403.

Kroll, B. (Ed.). (2003). *Exploring the dynamics of second language writing.* Cambridge, UK: Cambridge University Press.

Lam, W. S. E. (2000). L2 literacy and the design of the self: A case study of a teenager writing on the internet. *TESOL Quarterly, 34,* 457–482.

Lam, W. S. E. (2004). Second language soecialization in a bilingual chat room: Global and local considerations. *Language Learning and Technology, 8,* 44–65.

Leki, I., Cumming, A., & Silva, T. (2008). *A synthesis of research on second language writing in English.* New York: Routledge.

Leonard, R. L. (2013). Traveling literacies: Multilingual writing on the move. *Research in the Teaching of English, 48,* 13–39.

Manchón, R. M. (2011). Writing to learn the language: Issues in theory and research. In R. M. Manchón (Ed.), *Learning-to-write and writing-to-learn in an additional language* (pp. 61–82). Amsterdam: Benjamins.

Matsuda, P. K., Canagarajah, A. S., Harklau, L., Hyland, K., & Warschauer, M. (2003). Changing currents in second language writing research: A colloquium. *Journal of Second Language Writing, 12,* 151–179.

Matuchniak, T., Olson, C. B., & Scarcella, R. (2014). Examining the text-based, on-demand, analytical writing of mainstreamed Latino English learners in a randomized field trial of the Pathway Project intervention. *Reading and Writing, 27,* 973–994.

Moje, E. B., Collazo, T., Carrillo, R., & Marx, R. W. (2001). "Maestro, what is 'quality'?": Language, literacy, and discourse in a project-based science. *Journal of Research in Science Teaching, 38,* 469–498.

Muñoz, C. (2008). Age-related differences in foreign language learning. Revisiting the empirical evidence. *International Review of Applied Linguistics in Language Teaching, 46,* 197–220.

National Clearinghouse for English Language Arts. (n.d.). OELA (Office of English Language Arts): Fast Facts: Profiles of English Learners (ELs). Retrieved from *www.ncela.us/files/fast_facts/oela_fastfacts_profilesofels.pdf.*

Nystrand, M. (1989). A social-interactive model of writing. *Written Communication, 6,* 66–85.

Olson, C. B., Kim, J. S., Scarcella, R., Kramer, J., Pearson, M., van Dyk, D. A., et al. (2012). Enhancing the interpretive reading and analytical writing of mainstreamed English learners in secondary school: Results from a randomized field trial using a cognitive strategies approach. *American Educational Research Journal, 49,* 323–355.

Olson, C. B., & Land, R. (2007). A cognitive strategies approach to reading and writing instruction for English language learners in secondary school. *Research in the Teaching of English, 41,* 269–303.

Ortega, L., & Carson, J. (2010). Multicompetence, social context, and L2 writing research praxis. In T. Silva & P. K. Matsuda (Eds.), *Practicing theory in second language writing* (pp. 48–71). West Lafayette, IN: Parlor Press.

Ortmeier-Hooper, C. (2013). "She doesn't know who I am": The case of a refugee L2 writer in a high school English language arts classroom. In L. C. de Oliveria & T. Silva (Eds.), *L2 writing in secondary classrooms: Student experiences, academic issues, and teacher education* (pp. 9–26). New York: Routledge.

Ortmeier-Hooper, C., & Enright, K. A. (2011). Mapping new territory: Toward n understanding of adolescent L2 writers and writing in US contexts. *Journal of Second Language Writing, 20,* 167–181.

Polat, N., & Mahalingappa, L. (2013). Pre- and in-service teachers' beliefs about ELLs in content area classes: a case for inclusion, responsibility, and instructional support. *Teaching Education, 24,* 58–83.

Pugh, K. R., Frost, S. J., Sandak, R., Gillis, M., Moore, D., Jenner, A. R., et al. (2006). What does reading have to tell us about writing?: Preliminary questions and methodological challenges in examining the neurobiological foundations of writing and writing disabilities. In C. MacArthur, S. Graham, & J. Fitzgerald (Eds.), *Handbook of writing research* (pp. 433–448). New York: Guilford Press.

Reynolds, D. W. (2002). Learning to make things happen in different ways: Causality in the writing of middle-grad English language learners. *Journal of Second Language Writing, 11,* 311–328.

Reynolds, D. W. (2005). Linguistic correlates of second language literacy development: Evidence from middle-grade learner essays. *Journal of Second Language Writing, 14,* 19–45.

Schleppegrell, M. J., Achugar, M., & Oteíza, T. (2004). The grammar of history: Enhancing content-based instruction through a functional focus on language. *TESOL Quarterly, 38,* 67–93.

Schoonen, R., & Appel, R. (2005). Street language: A multilingual youth register in the Netherlands. *Journal of Multilingual and Multicultural Development, 26,* 85–117.

Sebba, M. (2012). Multilingualism in written discourse: an approach to the analysis of multilingual texts. *International Journal of Bilingualism, 17,* 97–118.

Shanahan, T. (1984). Nature of the reading–writing relation: An exploratory multivariate analysis. *Journal of Educational Psychology, 76,* 466–477.

Shell, D. F., Colvin, C., & Bruning, R. H. (1995). Self-efficacy, attribution, and outcome expectancy mechanisms in reading and writing achievement: Grade-level and achievement-level differences. *Journal of Educational Psychology, 87,* 368–398.

Short, D., Echevarrìa, J., & Richards-Tutor, C. (2011). Research on academic literacy development in sheltered instruction classrooms. *Language Teaching Research, 15,* 363–380.

Snow, C., & Uccelli, P. (2009). The challenge of academic language. In D. Olson & N. Torrance (Eds.), *The Cambridge handbook of literacy* (pp. 112–133). Cambridge, UK: Cambridge University Press.

Spycher, P. (2007). Academic writing of adolescent English learners: Learning to use "although." *Journal of Second Language Writing, 16,* 238–254.

Valdés, G., & Sanders, P. A. (2006). Latino ESL students and the development of writing abilities. In C. R. Cooper & L. Odell (Eds.), *Evaluating writing: The role of teachers' knowledge about text, learning and culture* (pp. 249–278). Urbana, IL: National Council of Teachers of English.

Villalva, K. E. (2006). Hidden literacies and inquiry approaches of bilingual high school writers. *Written Communication, 23,* 91–129.

Wilcox, K. C., Yagelski, R., & Yu, F. (2014). The nature of error in adolescent student writing. *Reading and Writing, 27,* 1073–1094.

Williams, J. (2012). The potential role(s) of writing in second language development. *Journal of Second Language Writing, 21,* 321–331.

Yi, Y. (2010). Adolescent multilingual writers' transitions across in- and out-of-school writing contexts. *Journal of Second Language Writing, 19,* 17–32.

Yi, Y. (2013). Adolescent multilingual writer's negotiation of multiple identities and access to academic writing: A case study of a Jogi Yuhak student in a US high school. *Canadian Modern Language Review, 69,* 207–231.

Zentella, A. C. (2002). Latino/a languages and identities. In M. Páez & M. Suárez-Orozco (Eds.), *Latino/as: Remaking America* (pp. 321–338). Berkeley: University of California Press.

Zhu, W. (2010). Theory and practice in second language writing: How and where do they meet? In T. Silva & P. K. Matsuda (Eds.), *Practicing theory in second language writing* (pp. 209–228). West Lafayette, IN: Parlor Press.

CHAPTER 22

Teaching and Learning Literary Argumentation in High School English Language Arts Classrooms

GEORGE E. NEWELL, DAVID BLOOME,
and the ARGUMENTATIVE WRITING PROJECT[1]

In recent decades scholars and teachers alike have critiqued the hegemony of text-based, literary argumentative essays by challenging the assumption that the text is primary and possesses a relatively determinate meaning. For instance, the certainty of literary arguments based in New Critical analyses has given way to calls for "a multidimensional diversity of response—to elicit and encourage differences rather than consensus" (Marshall, 1990, p. 177). However, classroom instruction and research-based accounts of teaching writing and literature often ignore the complexities of cultures, classrooms, assignments, and other media that might facilitate or thwart opportunities to learn how to think deeply and critically about "literary experience" (Faust, 2000; Langer, 2011; Rosenblatt, 1938, 1978). Accordingly, over the last 30 years many scholars and teachers alike have called for "a more complex examination of the assumptions and expectations about readers, [writers], authors, and text as they are situated within specific personal and cultural contexts" (Applebee, 1993, p. 116).

In this chapter we proffer a conceptual framework for the teaching and learning of "literary argumentation" for both instructional and research purposes that takes seriously the challenge of rethinking the bases of the construct of literary argumentation. For purposes of this review, literary argumentation is grounded in the questions "How might this text be read here, now, among us (the people present)?" and "How might it be read in the future, in other spaces, among other people?" Put another way, how students might read and understand a text is shaped by the teacher's willingness to explore the

---

[1] The members of the Argumentative Writing Project are George Newell, David Bloome, Alan Hirvela, Tzu-Jung Lin, Min-Young Kim, Brenton Goff, SangHee Ryu, Larkin Weyand, Eileen Buescher, and Seung Yon Ha.

warrants and backing for the interpretations presented during instructional conversations to allow for an open and public consideration. This notion of literary argumentation as an ever-shifting social construction of meaning and significance within a context has implications for teaching and learning of literature, as well as argumentation. Our central argument is that because a range of discursive practices exists within the generic notion of literary argumentation, a conceptual review and description of research and classroom practices can provide a fuller and deeper conceptualization. Before considering a range of alternative frameworks for teaching and learning literary argumentation and argumentative writing, we briefly describe our 5 years of collaborative research with high school English language arts (ELA) teachers that have led us to reframe how literary argumentation might be conceptualized.

A 5-YEAR JOURNEY WITH ELA TEACHERS

The Argumentative Writing Project's (AWP) initial study of teaching and learning in ELA classrooms funded by the Institute of Education Sciences (IES) began in 2010 with collaborative work with 31 teachers in a range of school districts in central Ohio. Using field research employing ethnographic methods, we studied each teacher during a single instructional unit on argumentative writing. Fundamentally, we regarded the teachers as collaborators as we tried to understand what was happening in their classrooms, what they found challenging and compelling about argumentation, and what kinds of instructional conversations and activities supported student learning. In many cases, the collaborating teachers enabled us to understand the current instructional contexts and the significant challenges with which teachers identified and to which they responded. In other cases, experienced and well-informed teachers introduced us to new considerations of the role of argumentation not as one more instructional unit but as a way to organize and integrate the ELA curriculum.

One of the more significant intellectual shifts in our thinking about argumentation and argumentative writing was a move from concerns focused largely on structural issues (How can students' argumentative writing be improved with changes in instruction?) to a social practices perspective (How in this classroom is argument defined, understood, and experienced as a set of social constructions and ways of acting, using language, thinking, valuing, and feeling?) (Newell, Bloome, & Hirvela, 2015). As we began to realize the "situatedness" of what counts as argumentative writing, we reframed our work with a social practices perspective to understand what we had previously conceived as cognitive activity within a social setting. We realized that the uniqueness of the social processes of classrooms, like other social contexts, reveals the shared social beliefs, norms, expectations, and ways of acting and interacting, within which particular social practices are adopted and adapted. We began to understand that what we were studying as social practices was what is considered argumentative writing, and how teachers and students do argumentative writing within and across the varied social contexts of classrooms.

As part of this initial project we also began to understand some of the challenges teachers and students encounter with literature-related argumentative writing. In spite of the fact that the teachers, selected as excellent writing teachers in their respective schools, had a deep commitment to their students' academic learning, they often faced challenges that our current IES project has begun to explore:

- Although the teachers had an understanding of argumentation and some of its components, in general, their conceptual understanding was singular and their knowledge of formal structures was focused on claims and evidence. For example, although the teachers understood the nature of argumentation in general, they lacked knowledge of literary argumentation and the possible ways that arguing might be a way of knowing literature. That is, they often viewed argumentation as similar to a persuasive argument or as a way to present a fully formulated interpretation rather than as a potential strategy for learning, building consensus, or creating new knowledge.

- The dominance of teacher presentations about argument inhibited the epistemology of argumentation as an extended, in-depth, reasoned exchange. As a result, teachers' explanations of argumentation and ways of developing an argument lacked deep and compelling ways of talking with students about their efforts to compose and revise their argumentative writing. This was particularly challenging in the case of literary argumentation, in that teachers tended to treat literary texts as sources of information rather than as explorations of experience and new understandings (Rosenblatt, 1938, 1978).

- Some of the teachers we studied taught argumentation in separate, distinct, and relatively brief instructional units that left argumentation and argumentative writing isolated from other components of their ELA instruction, such as literature instruction, language study, and reading. The more effective ELA teachers had either constructed or were constructing their classroom curricula with argumentation as the centerpiece for much longer periods of time—in some cases for the entire school year—and at least periodically linking it to literary study.

As we began the second phase of our work with another IES grant in Spring 2014, we made three significant decisions regarding our research agenda. First, we focused on literary argumentation in particular, as opposed to argument about the broad social, political, or personal topics we had observed in our earlier study. Second, with a deeper and more complex notion of argumentation, we decided to study each teacher in a single classroom across an entire school year to understand the possible trajectories of teacher change and student learning over time. Third, to work even more collaboratively with teachers, we studied literary argumentation with them during a 2-week summer workshop and across the school year in monthly teacher meetings to learn a range of approaches to argumentation and to plan an argument-based inquiry approach to ELA.

In our collaborations with classroom teachers, we defined *literature-related argumentative writing* as critical and analytic thinking about literary texts, rhetorical production, and social practice involving the identification of a thesis (also called a *claim*), supportive evidence (empirical or experiential), and assessment of the warrants. Although school writing includes a range of genres and functions, teaching and learning argumentative writing in high school ELA classrooms is of particular significance. There is an emphasis in the Common Core State Standards (CCSS; National Governors Association Center for Best Practices & Council of Chief State School Officers, 2010) on argumentative writing in secondary schools, based on the premise that argumentation and argumentative writing facilitate success in higher education and career opportunities, as well as foster intellectual development and critical thinking. (See DeStigter, 2015, for a critique of the emphasis on argumentative writing in the CCSS).

In our study of 40 ELA teachers over 5 years, we found that teachers enacted instruction with a range of approaches. Beliefs about what literary argumentation is, and in turn, what students should learn about argumentative writing and how they should learn it, tended to privilege differing orientations in the field of ELA in general and literature instruction in particular. In conceptualizing what we learned from our collaborations with these 40 ELA teachers, we build on McCormick's (1994) analysis of approaches to reading theory and teaching of literary texts. McCormick employed Eagleton's (1996) notion of the "ideological signification" of any act of reading. This includes a set of assumptions regarding what is significant and valued within a social formation. Thus, in this chapter, we hope to unravel the ideological significations of a range of ways of researching and teaching literary argumentation in high school ELA classrooms by asking what is the ideological and epistemological glue that holds these approaches together. We discuss four heuristic frames for teaching and learning literary argumentation in the next section.

FOUR FRAMES FOR TEACHING AND LEARNING ARGUMENTATIVE WRITING

Although there are commonalities, making an argument varies across academic disciplines and professional communities (Bazerman & Paradis, 1991; Voss, Perkins, & Segal, 1991). How one makes and composes an argument in mathematics, for example, differs from how one does so in history, physics, biology, and literature. However, our focus is on high school ELA classrooms and particularly on the study of literature, where reading and writing are closely intertwined. By high school, 80% of the writing that students do is writing about literature (Applebee, 1993). The study of literature itself is varied, with some approaches emphasizing the aesthetic and structural qualities of literature (Frye, 1957) or disciplinary ways of knowing literature (Fahenstock & Secor, 1991). Other approaches consider the quality and depth of individual response to literature (Rosenblatt, 1978), while still others emphasize literary argumentation as a practice and way to reflect upon the world (McCormick, 1994). Thus, within the field of literary studies, what constitutes an effective argument varies (Fahenstock & Secor, 1991), and students must learn diverse approaches to written argumentation (Wilder, 2002). Within the realities of classroom life, school, and district policy (Grossman, Thompson, & Valencia, 2002), teachers' and students' argumentative epistemologies (Newell, VanDerHeide, & Wynhoff Olsen, 2014) and teachers' literacy practices (Bloome, Carter, Christian, Otto, & Shuart-Faris, 2005) contribute other factors in teachers' efforts to negotiate goals for argumentative writing about literature with their students (Beck, 2006; Wilder, 2002).

Based on conceptions of literary argumentation within the field of English studies and ELA as they are presented in theoretical (Eagleton, 1996) and pedagogical (Appleman, 2009; Beach, 1993; McCormick, 1994) literatures, as well as how they are enacted in high school ELA classrooms (Applebee, 1993), we describe four different orientations or "frames" (Tannen, 1993) for teaching and learning literary argumentation: formalist, disciplinary, reader response, and social practice (see Table 22.1). Each frame presents its own fundamental differences for adequacy of response and interpretation, the role of teacher and student (as reader), and what is of significance in discoursing about literature. *Framing* (Tannen, 1993) refers to the structure of expectation within an interaction,

TABLE 22.1. Identifying Features and Theorists for Four Frames of Literary Argumentation

Framing	Unit of meaning for warrants	Focus of argumentation	Literary theorists	Educational theorists/researchers
Formalist	Text itself—how the text works	Interpretations based on close textual reading	Brooks & Warren (1938); Empson (1930)	Johannessen, Kahn, & Walter (2009); Lewis & Ferretti (2009)
Disciplinary	Application of disciplinary tools for interpretation	Interpretations through invocations of a set of special *topoi* (e.g., ubiquity) and literary reasoning	Fahenstock & Secor (1988); Rabinowitz (1997)	Foster (2003); Lee (2007); Wilder (2002)
Reader response	Reader in transaction with text	Interpretations as beginning in an evocation which becomes the bases for response	Rosenblatt (1938, 1978)	Beach & Marshall (1990); Langer (2011); Probst (2004)
Social practice	Social interaction within particular contexts	Interpretations shared and negotiated within a social process	Bakhtin (1981); Fish (1980)	Faust (2000); Lewis (2001)

that is, what activity is being engaged in and how teachers and students mean what they say and write. For our purposes, framing is a heuristic to consider ways of taking from texts (Heath, 1983) as conceptualized theoretically, pedagogically, and practically during teaching and learning of literary argumentation. Additionally, each frame has its own underlying assumption regarding the location and the process of literary meaning—in the text, within disciplinary ground rules, in reader–text transactions, or in the social interactions among readers. Put another way, each frame assumes its own unique way of warranting a literary argument.

The Formalist Frame

We have named this frame "formalist" to capture how a text might be read (as a form or structure), as well as how an interpretation within this frame can be argued (as a focus on the form or structure of the literary text). However, we realize that there are differences between Russian formalism and the American New Criticism emerging in the late 1930s and into the 1950s. Given the dominance of the New Criticism in American high schools (Applebee, 1993), it is this theory of literary understanding that fits with our use of formalism. Eagleton (1996, p. 42) points out that "the poem [text] meant what it meant, regardless of the poet's intentions or the subjective feelings the reader derived from it." The key to the formalist frame is an underlying assumption about the centrality of the text as an object for analysis and as a preset structure into which students might fit their literary arguments—often referred to as the five-paragraph-theme (Johnson, Smagorinsky, Thompson, & Fry, 2003).

Within the classroom, the practice of a formalist approach is much more difficult to identify in a pure form. Even as formalists might insist on concerns with form or text structure, they realize that the reader must rely on literary conventions, leaving the reader as a key part of sense-making. For example, Lewis and Ferretti (2009) included children with learning disabilities who they "trained" to apply text-analytic strategies as they composed highly structured literary arguments. Their study points to a key question within the formalist framework: What are students learning about literature and about argumentation when asked to use preset structures that include genre-specific elements of literary discourse in their essays? Lewis and Ferretti developed a writing format using the acronym "THE READER," which includes

> a **THE**sis, they [students] must back up that thesis with **REA**sons, they should include **D**etails as illustrations of those reasons (direct quotes or direct reference to the literary passage), they should **E**xplain how those quotes and references are related to their reasons or thesis, and they should **R**eview their main points in a conclusion. (p. 263)

Johannessen, Kahn, and Walter (2009) offer an example of how students might be helped to develop an interpretive argument by providing a clear scaffold within which students may first develop their skills, then apply them in new situations. They occupy a somewhat unique position in the high school (and college) pedagogical literature in that they make the transition between thinking and writing, but their highly structured approach is text-based and seems to focus on understanding what an author "means" in a work ("Write a statement of the author's [poet's] generalization") rather than on how an individual reader can come to a well-reasoned interpretation through a transaction with the text. Thus, despite their stated intention, Johannessen et al. do not really offer a way for students to move from personal response to literary argument.

Although such formalist instruction might prepare students well for an assessment requiring brief written responses, the fact that students are forming an argument using preset formats may short-circuit a deeper understanding of text about which they are writing. Perhaps most important, this is the kind of instruction in literary argumentation that Applebee (1981, 1984, 1993; Applebee & Langer, 2013) has been concerned about for decades. Hillocks (2005) has complained about ELA teachers' "obsession with form," which, he argues, has prevented them from taking the content of students' writing seriously.

In our classroom observations and in interviews with teachers and students, a formalist frame is typically a key component of literary argumentation. For example, the collaborating teachers often point out that it is essential to begin with preset forms for students "to get started." Although, as researchers, we agree that the teachers must start somewhere, and formal argumentative structures are one logical beginning, we have also noticed that once text structures such as the five-paragraph theme become part of the instructional conversation and then are reinforced by assessments (requiring students to demonstrate that they know where to locate the thesis statement), teachers and students find a shift toward other approaches to literary argumentation quite challenging.

The Disciplinary Frame

Within the area of disciplinary literacy is a range of perspectives highlighting the different disciplinary traditions, theoretical stances, and research foci that undergird current work on disciplinary literacy pedagogy (Moje, 2007). In her extended review of this work, Moje presents both theory and research related to four types of disciplinary literacy pedagogy that provide students with access to (1) expert subject-matter knowledge; (2) disciplinary knowledge they care about, generated in response to their own everyday concerns and interests; (3) disciplinary knowledge and ways of knowing that are usable in everyday life; and (4) disciplinary ways of producing knowledge via oral and written texts. Her central argument is that

> scholars operating from any one of the disciplinary literacy perspectives work from the stance that to learn deeply in a subject matter, young people need to have access to the way that conventions of disciplinary knowledge production and communication can be routinely or more explicitly challenged and reshaped by other forms or practices of knowing; such knowledge gives young people the power to read critically across various texts and various disciplines. (p. 37)

We think that this captures a long-standing assumption about the value of "disciplinary literacy," and Moje develops a rather sophisticated argument for a lengthy "apprenticeship in text practices" and raises a key issue for us: The explicitness of disciplinary ways of knowing how to make a literary argument, for example, has to be more than simply displaying disciplinary knowledge as repositories of reproduced facts and strategies; it also must include tools for producing and constructing new understandings.

Although Lee (2007) does not refer to her approach to teaching literary reasoning as an apprenticeship, she has actively pursued such pedagogical and curricular developments in her research program focused on the literary education of low-income African American youth. Lee's construct of cultural modeling situates subject areas as cultures and seeks to tease out the demands of discourse in subject areas such as English. She then looks for spaces to link students' everyday discourses and practices specifically for the purpose of enhancing academic discourse and literary development. Studying in her own classroom, Lee has demonstrated how a teacher with deep knowledge of students' backgrounds and ways with words could link those experiences and ways to the practices valued in the discipline.

Wilder's (2002) observational study of college writing teachers and students supports Lee's (2007) thesis that more successful students, at least implicitly, know and recognize the underlying assumptions for literary arguments of which less successful students seem largely unaware. Wilder found that teaching assistants and instructors regularly employed *topoi*, or common warrants, that is, the unstated premises used to tap into what a reader of literary criticism might value in lectures and discussions about literature but often left implicit. Additionally, students who were most successful in the class were able to distinguish the literary criticism passages that contained the special *topoi* from the linguistic texts that did not. Students who were less successful in this class, those getting C's or lower, were not able to make this distinction. Although the study did not allow Wilder to draw clear conclusions about the effects of *topoi* invocations in student essays on students' overall success in the class, she did find that students who identified the purpose of writing arguments about literature as fundamentally persuasive in nature were more likely to be successful in the class.

The work of the three scholars just described raises important issues for both "academic literacies" in general and literary argumentation in particular. As we understand their arguments for teaching students disciplinary literacy, knowledge and practices from academic disciplines such as ELA and English studies, they seem to assume what Lea and Street (2006) describe as "academic socialization." This refers to students' acculturation into disciplinary and subject-based discourses and genres. "Students acquire the ways of talking, writing, thinking, and using literacy that typified members of a disciplinary or subject area community" (p. 369). However, this model assumes that since academic practices are stable and reproducible, students learn to write, read, and take action in an academic discipline unproblematically.

The observational studies and interviews we conducted as part of the AWP offer a different notion of academic learning, one that includes issues of power and epistemology (similar to Lea & Street, 2006). For example, in an interview about writing a literary argument about a short story, Randy (all references to teachers, students, and skills are pseudonyms) described his experience developing an interpretive claim about the story:

> RANDY: OK. What I am going to tell you is the way I do it, and not like my teacher wants me to. I see myself as a more creative type and I like to be reflective about my reading. So when I read Hemingway's story I am thinking maybe he is too. So this is why I wanted to write about his way of writing about characters. You know, creative and stuff. I didn't want to get into what was his intentions are about so and so or what he should or should not write about. I just wanted to write about how he thought about his own life, like through his characters . . . how he used his writing to reflect.
>
> FIELD RESEARCHER: Tell me how your way is different from what your teacher is expecting.
>
> RANDY: Oh, it's not just her [the teacher]. At this school you need to read and write as if you are in college, and, you know, writing for professors who are experts and you have to impress them. This means, OK, like what does he [the writer] mean when he uses a metaphor or some other term, like that. But with me it's more about thinking about what's going on with me when I am not in school too. That's what I mean about being creative . . . just expressing yourself and being reflective.

Randy's comments reveal boundaries that he sees between academic literacies and out-of-school literacy practices; he likes "to be reflective about my reading." Yet he intends to blend his academic life with life outside of school. Rather than understanding how Randy is constructing a literary argument as part of his socialization into the discipline of literary studies, we think it is more compelling to see his "writerly" moves (Harris, 2006) as interweaving literacy practices he learned in school with practices from other domains of his life. Moreover, Randy provides an example of how literacy practices with which he identifies in his life outside of school are ones that resonate in one way or another with some of the academic literacies that mediate learning in his ELA class. Also, students' identities as students, as writers, and as thinkers are at play. "Fundamental to networking literacy practices across boundaries in this way is the extent to which the subject positions held out to students by academic literacies resonate with their sense of who they are and who they want to be in other domains of their lives" Ivanič & Satchwell, 2007, p. 121), as they did for Randy.

The Reader-Response Frame

With the advent of the process-oriented approaches to writing instruction in the 1970s and early 1980s, scholars and teachers alike began to consider new ways of extending such approaches to other areas of the ELA curriculum. As part of the process-oriented movement in writing, a constructivist framework seemed to offer an alternative to teaching that emphasizes the reproduction of others' ideas and the transmission of an objective and culturally sanctioned body of knowledge. Within this new framework instruction becomes more a matter of helping students learn to construct, interpret, and argue for themselves (Britton, 1970; Griffin & Cole, 1984; Langer & Applebee, 1986).

In Applebee's (1993) survey of literature instruction in U.S. schools, he included a chapter called "Writing and Literature," in which he was not so optimistic regarding such a constructivist shift. When teachers were asked in a survey to list their most typical writing assignment in their classrooms, they reported text-based essays by a wide margin over essays focused on a reader's personal response or interpretation. In addition, the most frequently used instructional techniques for writing about literature remained very traditional: written comments, assignment of a grade, and correction of errors in mechanics. Applebee concluded, "Thus, although it is clear that process-oriented instruction is broadly recognized as an appropriate approach to teaching writing, it does not seem to have led to drastic reformulation of what teachers do, at least in the context of writing about literature" (p. 171).

Based on 5 years of study in 40 ELA classrooms, we know that there are specific instructional principles and practices grounded in process-oriented instruction that contribute to student learning of argumentation (Newell et al., 2015). However, to realize more fully the potential of these activities, the field of ELA needs a sophisticated conceptualization of these principles and practices for argumentative writing and how to incorporate those into an ELA program. Put another way, rather than sample lessons or lists of process-oriented activities, ELA teachers will benefit more from a fundamental reconceptualization of teaching argumentation and argumentative writing. We think reader-response theories hold a great deal of promise, but this optimism is tempered by two issues. First, there is little agreement among scholars and teachers alike regarding what knowledge of literary text is (personal, textual, cultural, etc.) and what argumentation might become. Second, an empirical basis for developing a reader-response framework for literary argumentation is thwarted by dualistic thinking about readers, texts, and their relationships. We examine these issues below.

During one of the monthly teacher meetings the AWP held last school year, we (teachers and field researchers) read and discussed an article titled "From Story to Essay: Reading and Writing" (Petrosky, 1982) published in *College Composition and Communication*. Petrosky argues for the need to connect reading and writing with a focus on literature; that is, a focus on the relationships among reading, response to literature, and composition. He further argues "that our comprehension of texts, whether they are literary or not, is more an act of composition—for understanding is composing—than of information retrieval, and that the best possible representation of our understandings of texts begins with certain kinds of compositions, not multiple-choice tests or written free responses" (p. 19). After we tried out Bleich's (1975) "response heuristic" (recommended by Petrosky) during our meeting by writing about and then discussing our understandings of a poem, one of the teachers took a deep breath and began to criticize Petrosky's focus on subjective response (using Bleich's response heuristic) to a text. He argued that in his school, and in his teaching experiences, a rather more text-based, objective interpretation was a key part of literature-related argumentative writing.

To better understand this teacher's response, it is necessary to consider the part of the article that triggered the teacher's concern. In a section near the end, Petrosky describes "Dan" as one of his more successful case study students, in that Dan effectively and imaginatively used the heuristic. Here is the excerpt to which the teacher responded: "But the [Dan's essay] responses were not only moving, they had explanatory power because they used examples and illustrations derived from associations as a way of revealing the readers' mental maps that were guiding their responses" (p. 33). The teacher complained that this is precisely what he was trying to ensure that his students' avoid, that is, the uses of subjective experience with the text as a way to make a literary argument. To clarify the issue, the teacher was concerned that "writing about literature then becomes about the student's own life, with the text ignored." In the discussion that ensued, it became evident that some of the teachers had not considered "subjective experience" while reading a text as a legitimate way to argue for a literary interpretation, while others had not had the opportunity to consider how personal experience *might be* a legitimate warrant for literary interpretations.

A Reconceptualization of Reader Response as a Social Construction

Faust (2000) describes the tension the teachers articulated this way: "Literary experience is defined implicitly as a dualistic interaction whereby reading subjects interpret textual objects" (p. 20). He further argues that some of the most highly regarded theorists and researchers in ELA have engaged in the same dualistic thinking. Faust then makes a move that provides a compelling clarification to this long-standing tension. He first eschews two commonly held interrelated assumptions: first, that teachers should avoid subjectivism in students' arguments, and second that pedagogical efforts should insist on interpretive consensus, since literary works contain timeless and universally valid truth claims. Following Dewey and Rosenblatt, Faust then argues for a new vision of the classroom as a "marketplace of ideas" in which teachers would assist students in negotiating their differences by foregrounding the sociocultural context in which reading events take place. They would teach students how to use writing and speaking to textualize their responses as readers of literature. In addition teachers would require students to reflect on and question those responses in light of their own and others' emerging concerns. "Overall students would be encouraged to view the experience of reading with others as an opportunity to achieve thoughtful responses testifying to their enhanced awareness of multiple possibilities for making meaning with literature" (Faust, 2000, pp. 28–29). In the next session, we take up what we refer to as a "social practice" frame, as a way to think of literary argument as "the experience of reading with others."

The Social-Practice Frame

Many, although not all, scholars have treated written literary argumentation as if there is a relatively consistent set of cognitive and linguistic skills and processes that define an effective argument, regardless of variation in contexts. Although there has been recognition that there may be different ways of engaging in argument (Berrill, 1996; van

Eemeren, Grootendorst, & Henkemans, 2002), different ways of teaching argumentative writing (Ramage, Bean, & Johnson, 2007; Toulmin, Rieke, & Janik, 1984), and different kinds of argument text schemes (Walton, Reed, & Macagno, 2008), to date there has been little attention to viewing argumentative writing as a set of social practices that vary across and within social institutions, social settings, and social situations.

In our view, the teaching of literary argumentation and argumentative writing involves not only a concern for effectively teaching and learning a written genre, acquiring argument schemata, and specific tactics and strategies, but also learning how to engage in the social practices associated the academic ELA domain, including literary education. These social practices—particular ways of using spoken and written language, and other semiotic systems within particular social situations—involve ways of reasoning, sharing ideas, expressing opinions, exploring perspectives, inquiring into the human condition, constructing texts, generating insights, establishing social relationships, expressing social identities, and using spoken and written language. These practices are essentially social in at least two ways. The teaching and learning of argumentative writing are social because argumentative writing is essentially, and by definition, communication and engagement with others; and it is social because teaching and learning are essentially social as teachers and students interact with each other, constructing new knowledge and new understandings. In our view, social practices are constantly evolving, and the enactment of a social practice within any specific social event always involves an adaptation of the social practice (to borrow from Bakhtin [1981], the enactment of a social practice always involves a reflection and refraction of that social practice).

To illustrate key concepts in conceptualizing the teaching and learning of literary argumentation as a social practice, we draw on a longitudinal study of an 11th-grade International Baccalaureate (IB) ELA classroom that is part of our current study of teaching and learning literary argumentation. Using ethnographic-oriented methods, including interviews with teachers and students, video recordings of classroom observations, fieldnotes and the analysis of classroom work, we studied the ways Ms. Hill orchestrated the teaching and learning of literary argumentation. Ms. Hill (a mixed-race female with 12 years of teaching experience) had taught IB English for 3 years at the start of the study. The school's distinction was due to a reputation for academic excellence and various options for participation in both advanced placement (AP) and IB programs across a range of content areas. Ms. Hill's 11th-grade IB English class (26 students; 16 White and 10 other ethnicities) was embedded in a "humanities" program, an advanced or "high level" IB option that students could self-select for the study of literary analysis. The majority of Ms. Hill's students enrolled in other AP and IB courses offered at the high school. According to a school practice, Ms. Hill and her students have a 2-year span (11th and 12th grades) to work together and develop a mutual understanding of one another, as well as literary analysis. In conversations, Ms. Hill often used "literary analysis" to describe the focus on her 11th-grade ELA course.

In a series of lessons in late September 2014, Ms. Hill engaged her IB 11th-grade students in a "Slip or Trip?" activity (Hillocks, 2011) to introduce argumentation into her curricular conversation, "to make sure that they learned the terms for argument and how claim, evidence and warrant can be used in their writing." After these initial sessions, she began folding the terms into her teaching of what she referred to as "analytic essay writing about literature." Ms. Hill reported that initially, she "felt skeptical" about argumentation: "The Toulmin model just seemed like one more way to structure essays, and

I assumed my 11th graders already knew a form." Gradually, however, as she read her students' writing, considered ways of teaching literary analysis, and met with one of the field researchers weekly to discuss the role of argumentation in her classroom, she began to realize that just renaming the ingredients of a preset form was "not really analysis. In fact, I am beginning to feel like argument is analysis but in a more tangible form that I can actually teach."

It is important to understand that Ms. Hill appropriated the Toulmin-based criteria after responding to her students' revised summer writing projects. In an interview, she commented, "This is when I realized that I had to be more clear and specific about what I meant by analysis. Argument is analysis, and now I have a way to communicate what I mean by analysis rather than assuming they know or that it was some mysterious idea." After 2 months of instruction focused on the elements of argument, Ms. Hill pivoted from "learning to argue" to "arguing to learn." That is, as her students began to appropriate the concept of argumentation, she shifted from structural issues (how to compose and organize an argumentative essay) to ideational issues (how to use argumentation as a heuristic for literary analysis and understanding). Below, we describe Ms. Hill's initial efforts to integrate elements of the Toulmin (1958/2003) model with literary analysis. What we highlight is not simply the use of structural elements such as claim, warrant, and evidence as an analytic frame but an underlying argumentative epistemology and ontology grounded in pursuit of communicative rationality (Habermas, 1990). More simply stated, Ms. Hill orchestrates the instructional conversation in a way that facilitates the use of argumentation for deep understanding of a literary work and for appreciating and incorporating multiple perspectives.

Near the end of October, Ms. Hill and her students engaged in an instructional conversation about the short story "Indian Camp" (Hemingway, 1925). Ms. Hill had two interrelated purposes: to prepare the students to write a literary argument and to engage them in exploratory talk about the theme of dominance. Briefly, in this story, the first of the Nick Adams series, a country doctor has been summoned to an "Indian" camp to deliver a baby. At the camp, the father is forced to perform an emergency caesarean section using a jackknife, with Nick, his son, as his assistant. Afterward, the woman's husband is discovered dead, having slit his throat during the operation. Many critics describe "Indian Camp" as a story of initiation: Nick's father exposes his young son to childbirth and, unintentionally, to violent death. Yet, as we see in the instructional conversation, rather than a story of initiation, Ms. Hill frames an analysis of the story using the theme of dominance. We view her stance and the task that she gave the students as an iteration of the question "How might this text be read?"

After about 20 minutes of announcements and a summary of the previous session, Ms. Hill asked the students to "take out your homework on 'Indian Camp,'" which required students to list examples of dominance in "Indian Camp" and to identify evidence, warrants, and backing for each example. She then asked the students to work briefly in groups of four to "come up with the top two examples . . . that you guys can agree on and then we will share-out."

The small peer group discussions focused mostly on students telling each other what they did and what examples they found. There was little depth to the discussion and little engagement of the students with each other's ideas. For example, in one of the peer groups, the students discussed whether they had used page numbers and quotes or just listed the example; they read through their lists of examples, noting whether they had

had the same ones on their lists, but never discussed why they did or did not have any particular example on a list.[2]

About 25 minutes into the lesson, Ms. Hill stopped the small peer groups and began a whole-class discussion, which was organized with Ms. Hill asking questions or making comments and students responding to her. On occasion, she provided an evaluation—"I agree"—although mostly she repeated, revoiced, or summarized a student response, and on occasion juxtaposed it with the comment of another student who had a different view. She wrote on the whiteboard the terms *evidence, warrant,* and *backing,* and throughout the discussion wrote bits from students' comments that fit into each.

In order to understand what happened during this event, it is important to recognize that the theme of dominance is not necessarily inherent in the story text, which is merely to say that the story can be read otherwise and, indeed, many literary critics have read it otherwise, and there is no evidence that Hemingway intended to foreground the theme of dominance. What Ms. Hill has done is to ask that the students to read the story in a particular way, to read it as a story of dominance, and to read it framed as readers making an argument about the meaning of the text. It is in this sense that argumentation is a framework for literary analysis in responding to the question "How might this text be read?"

The discussion of the story continued as Ms. Hill probed the students' reading of the text as a story of social dominance. Much of the instructional conversation involved students sharing their ideas; the students built on each other's ideas and there was little disagreement. Many of the students argued that there is a theme of male dominance and contributed additional evidence and warrants in support of that claim. Some of the warrants involved premises about individual behavior (e.g., calling women a derogatory name), background experiences of the students (their experiences with doctors), other stories they have read that are (or could be) related (other stories by Hemingway), and some involve institutional structures (e.g., the lack of women doctors and what constitutes professional behavior). About 36 minutes into the hour-long lesson, Greg questioned whether the particular example of the doctor saying that he ignores the woman's screams is evidence of male dominance.

> GREG: I was just gonna say, we were arguing whether or not the first example [the doctor saying he ignores the woman's screams] is really about male dominance over female dominance.
>
> TEACHER: OK. Tell me why.
>
> GREG: Some of us [in the small group] were saying that he [the doctor] had to push aside screams for the operation rather than "I hate females and I am going to ignore the screams." But that [inaudible] . . .

In the exchange that followed, it became evident that not all the students were in agreement with the assumption that "Indian Camp" can be interpreted and critiqued using compliance as a cultural code—or, we might say, as a warrant for interpreting the doctor's behavior as he tended to the birth. Greg (and at least one other group member) assumed that under the circumstances (attending to a birth), the doctor's action were both appropriate and necessary. But what is happening here is more complex than students disagreeing with each other and offering counterarguments.

Starting with Greg's comment and continuing to the end of the lesson, the students and Ms. Hill responded to each other's comments by alternatively arguing about the place of male dominance and racial dominance in the events of the story and the strength of the warrants that can be made for these claims. We use the term *alternatively arguing* to characterize what is happening in this instructional conversation rather than counterargument because the effort does not appear to be an attempt to convince others that one perspective is correct and another is wrong (or less justified); rather, that the students and teacher are exploring the text—how it might be read—adding layers of meaning and insight.

It is not easy to engage in the teaching and learning of literary argumentation (or in any subject-matter area) as a set of social processes and practices of discovering and exploring complex ideas that value and respect multiple perspectives. It requires shifting social relationships from being competitive to being a coherency of heteroglossia; it requires redefining knowledge as situated, multiple, and continuously evolving; and it requires redefining oneself as continuously a learner with and among others. It requires prizing an open mind (but not an empty one). It requires understanding argumentation as process and social practice rather than a product. And all of these moves require redefining pedagogy and curriculum.

The Significance of Warranted Assertability

In an interview with Ms. Hill about the instructional conversation on "Indian Camp," she pointed out, "This is the first time I really saw the value of warranting an argument. Now I see that this is getting at the hidden areas of the story—what I want them to talk about but they never do." This comment brings us to what we understand as the key element of literary argumentation: How students might read and understand a text is shaped by the teacher's willingness to explore the warrants and support the interpretations proffered during instructional conversations to allow for an open and public consideration. For instance, when another group of students raised an alternative explanation for the doctor's seemingly callous behavior toward the mother in terms of how doctors need to act during a dangerous medical procedures, rather than rejecting this claim as irrelevant to the assumption of his domineering behavior, she asked the students to unpack their warrants: "If you have an argument that you are going to argue against, then you need to back it up with something. And you're saying that . . . [gestures toward the group] it is just a scream, and he's a doctor, and as doctor you have to block it out." We understand the move captured in the phrase "And you're saying" as a revoicing that signals the value of offering new ideas that open a space for what Barnes (1976) calls "exploratory talk."

There is, however, another dimension to how Ms. Hill and her students consider the warranting behind different and multiple interpretations that might address concerns of relativism, a criticism often heard in objections to reader-response theory (Faust, 2000). We would argue that Ms. Hill's efforts to have students unpack and present their ideas for their peers to consider (and perhaps critique) contributes Dewey's (1941) notion of "warranted assertability" that may challenge relativistic claims. Rosenblatt (1994) offers warranted assertability to argue against claims of extreme relativism. In doing so, she maintains the notion of literary argument as a social construction within specific contexts: that warranted assertability depends on "shared criteria concerning methods of investigation and kinds of evidence" (p. 1078). For instance, Ms. Hill allowed her students to negotiate their differences by foregrounding the sociocultural context in which reading events take place: She requests that the student who offers an alternative interpretation of the doctor's behavior explain to his peers what he assumes about the doctor's actions as "professional." Put another way, Ms. Hill asks that he textualize his reaction as a reader of literature by sharing the criteria for his warrants, to consider and question those reactions in light of his own and others' emerging concerns. In general terms, students are encouraged to view the experience of reading with others as an opportunity to achieve thoughtful responses testifying to their enhanced awareness of multiple possibilities for making meaning with literature.

TOWARD A THEORY OF TEACHING AND LEARNING LITERARY ARGUMENTATION

In this chapter we have considered the role of literary argumentation in high school ELA classrooms within four different frames: formalist, disciplinary, reader response, and social practice. Each framework has a particular notion of academic learning and interpretation of literature—from issues of how texts work to how readers consider how they might respond to a text; how disciplinary literacy might take student beyond their current understandings; and finally, how the interweaving of social practices such as reading, writing, and talking might foster explorations of culturally significant issues such as power relations and social dominance. Clearly, ELA is not in need of another theory of reading or interpreting literature—as this chapter demonstrates, we have these in abundance. Rather, what the field needs is a theory of practice in the teaching of literature, a vision that would account for some of the tensions among ways of arguing and interpreting literature and at the same time help teachers consider what they will do Monday morning. Graff (1992) has defined theory as "what erupts when what was once silently agreed to in a community becomes disputed, forcing its members to formulate and defend assumptions that they previously did not even have to be aware of" (p. 53). Although ELA class members do not always talk openly about it, the field is currently at a point of consensus breakdown, especially in these times of CCSS, statewide assessments, teacher evaluations, and significant divisions in both the field of composition studies and literary studies as an academic discipline. What ELA needs is a "kind of reflective discourse about practices" that may prove productive.

To move toward a theoretical framework for teaching literary argumentation, the AWP has begun to develop two interrelated principles in our collaborative work with high school ELA teachers. First, within the realities of school structures and conventions, a theory of teaching would have to have a coherent theory of learning that recognizes the interrelatedness of the social practices of reading, writing, and discussing that are often part of classroom life. For example, if process-oriented approaches to writing assume that students must find their own way into a topic, then literature instruction must include argumentation as a way for students to make their ways toward evocations that become the basis of their responses that are, in turn, tried out during instructional conversations within an interpretive community (Faust, 2000). We have argued that the teaching and learning of argumentation involves a complex set of social, communicative, philosophical, and intellectual (reasoning) practices that are constituted through the use of spoken language, written language, and related semiotic systems (e.g., visual displays). Rather than conceptualizing teaching and learning as one set of processes and practices and argumentation as another set, we see them as inseparable and mutually defining. That this social practice view of argumentation stands in contrast to a view of literature teaching and learning as a way to monitor students' interpretations as correct, monolithic, and teacher-centered is self-evident. Instead, ELA needs a productive way to proceed toward a theory of teaching that values the social dimensions of literacy and centrality of social practice in learning.

Second, and perhaps more importantly, a theory of teaching grounded in literary argumentation as a social practice would need to account for the differences among teachers. As Britton (1988) has pointed out,

> what matters most is that teachers should intuitively behave in ways that facilitate learning. But their intuitive responses to what happens in the classroom are strengthened when by reflection they cumulatively build their own rationale for what they are doing. That is to say, they need to theorize from their experience ... finding reasons, ways to explain both their failures and successes. And once they have begun theorizing in this way, they can selectively make use of other people's thinking, other people's theories, and the evidence of research. (p. 16)

A major effort of the AWP is to provide teachers with time and opportunity to make that move into theory through a summer workshop, collaborative data analysis, postobservation debriefings, interviews, and monthly teacher meetings. One aspect of this work is to offer and to encourage teachers to imagine a new range of alternative frames for teaching and learning literary argumentation.

ACKNOWLEDGMENTS

This chapter is based on support provided by the Institute of Education Sciences, U.S. Department of Education, through Grant No. 305A100786 to The Ohio State University (Dr. George E. Newell, Principal Investigator). The opinions expressed in this chapter are those of the authors and do not represent views of the Institute or the U.S. Department of Education. We also gratefully acknowledge support from the Center for Video Ethnography and Discourse Analysis and the Department of Teaching and Learning at The Ohio State University.

REFERENCES

Applebee, A. N. (1981). *Writing in the secondary school*. Urbana, IL: National Council of Teachers of English.
Applebee, A. N. (1984). *Contexts for learning to write: Studies of secondary school instruction*. Norwood, NJ: Ablex.
Applebee, A. N. (1993). *Literature in the secondary school: Studies of curriculum and instruction in the United States*. Urbana, IL: National Council of Teachers of English.
Applebee, A. N., & Langer, J. (2013). *Writing instruction that works: Proven methods for middle school and high school classrooms*. New York: Teachers College Press.
Appleman, D. (2009). *Critical encounters in high school English: Teaching literary theory to adolescents*. Urbana, IL: National Council of Teachers of English.
Bakhtin, M. M. (1981). *The dialogic imagination: Four essays* (M. Holquist, Ed., C. Emerson & M. Holquist, Trans.). Austin: University of Texas Press.

Barnes, D. (1976). *From communication to curriculum*. Harmondsworth, UK: Penguin Education.
Barnes, D. (2008). Exploratory talk for learning. In N. Mercer & S. Hodgkinson (Eds.), *Exploring talk in school* (pp. 1–15). Los Angeles: Sage.
Bazerman, C., & Paradis, J. (Eds.). (1991). *Textual dynamics of the professions: Historical and contemporary studies of writing in professional communities*. Madison: University of Wisconsin Press.
Beach, R. (1993). *A teacher's introduction to reader-response theories*. Urbana, IL: National Council of Teachers of English.
Beach, R., & Marshall, J. (1991). *Teaching literature in the secondary school*. Orlando, FL: Harcourt Brace Jovanovich.
Beck, S. W. (2006). Subjectivity and intersubjectivity in the teaching and learning of writing. *Research in the Teaching of English, 40*(4), 413–460.
Berrill, D. B. (Ed.). (1996). *Perspectives on written argument*. Creskill, NJ: Hampton.
Bleich, D. (1975). *Readings and feelings: An introduction to subjective criticism*. Urbana, IL: National Council of Teachers of English.
Bloome, D. (2015). The role of talk in group-based activity in classrooms. In N. Markee (Ed.), *The handbook of classroom discourse and interaction* (pp. 128–141). Hoboken, NJ: Wiley.
Bloome, D., Carter, S., Christian, M., Otto, S., & Shuart-Faris, N. (2005). *Discourse analysis and the study of classroom language and literacy events: A microethnographic perspective*. Mahwah, NJ: Erlbaum.
Britton, J. (1970). *Language and learning*. London: Allen Lane.
Britton, J. (1988). Writing, learning, and teacher education. In J. S. Davis & J. D. Marshall (Eds.), *Ways of knowing: Research and practice in the teaching of writing* (pp. 15–44). Urbana, IL: National Council of Teachers of English.
Brooks, C., & Warren, R. P. (1938). *Understanding poetry*. New York: Harcourt Brace Jovanovich College.
DeStigter, T. (2015). On the ascendance of argument: A critique of the assumptions of academe's dominant form. *Research in the Teaching of English, 50* (1), 11–34.
Dewey, J. (1941). Propositions, warranted assertability, and truth. *Journal of Philosophy, 38*(7), 169–186.
Eagleton, T. (1996). *Literary theory: An introduction*. Minneapolis: University of Minnesota Press.
Empson, W. (1930). *Seven types of ambiguity*. London: Chatto & Windus.
Fahenstock, J., & Secor, M. (1991). The rhetoric of literary criticism. In C. Bazerman & J. Paradis (Eds.), *Textual dynamics of the professions: Historical and contemporary studies of writing in professional communities* (pp. 77–96). Madison: University of Wisconsin Press.
Faust, M. (2000). Reconstructing familiar metaphors: John Dewey and Louise Rosenblatt on literary art as experience. *Research in the Teaching of English, 35*(1), 9–34.
Fish, S. E. (1980). *Is there a text in this class?: The authority of interpretive communities*. Cambridge, MA: Harvard University Press.
Foster, T. C. (2003). *How to read literature like a professor*. Fort Mill, SC: Quill.
Frye, N. (1957). *Anatomy of criticism: Four essays*. New York: Atheneum.
Graff, G. (1992). *Beyond the culture wars: How teaching the conflicts can revitalize American education*. New York: Norton.
Griffin, P., & Cole, M. (1984). Current activity for the future: The zo-ped. In B. Rogoff & J. Wertsch (Eds.), *Children learning in the zone of proximal development* (pp. 45–64). San Francisco: Jossey-Bass.
Grossman, P., Thompson, T., & Valencia, S. (2002). The impact of district policy on beginning teachers. *ERS Spectrum, 20*, 12–22.
Habermas, J. (1990). *Moral consciousness and communicative action* [Moralbewusstein und

kommunikatives Handeln]. (C. Lenhardt, S. W. Nicholsen, & T. McCarthy, Trans.). Cambridge, MA: MIT Press.

Harris, J. D. (2006). *Rewriting: How to do things with texts.* Logan: Utah State University Press.

Heath, S. B. (1983).*Ways with words: Language, life, and work in communities and classrooms.* Boston: Cambridge University Press.

Hemingway, E. (1925). Indian Camp. In E. Hemingway, *In our time* (pp. 15–19). New York: Scribner's.

Hillocks, G., Jr. (2005). At last: The focus on form vs. content in teaching writing. *Research in the Teaching of English, 40*(2), 238–248.

Hillocks, G., Jr. (2011). *Teaching argument writing, grades 6–12: Supporting claims with relevant evidence and clear reasoning.* New York: Heinemann.

Ivanič, R., & Satchwell, C. (2008). Boundary crossing: Networking and transforming literacies in research processes and college courses. *Journal of Applied Linguistics, 4*(1), 101–124.

Johannessen, L. R., Kahn, E. A., & Walter, C. C. (2009). *Writing about literature (theory and research into practice).* Urbana, IL: National Council of Teachers.

Johnson, T. S., Smagorinsky, P., Thompson, L., & Fry, P. G. (2003). Learning to teach the five-paragraph theme. *Research in the Teaching of English, 38*(2), 136–176.

Langer, J. A. (2011). *Envisioning knowledge: Building literacy in the academic disciplines.* New York: Teachers College Press.

Langer, J. A., & Applebee, A. N. (1986). Reading and writing instruction: Toward a theory of teaching and learning. *Review of Research in Education, 13*, 171–194.

Lea, M., & Street, B. (2006). The "Academic Literacies" model: Theory and applications. *Theory Into Practice, 45*(4), 368–377.

Lee, C. (2007). *Culture, literacy, and learning: Blooming in the midst of the whirlwind.* New York: Teachers College Press.

Lewis, C. (2001). *Literary practices as social acts: Power, status, and cultural norms in the classroom.* New York: Routledge.

Lewis, W. E., & Ferretti, R. P. (2009). Defending interpretations of literary texts: The effects of topoi instruction on the literary arguments of high school students. *Reading and Writing Quarterly, 25*(4), 250–270.

Marshall, J. (1990). Writing and reasoning about literature. In R. Beach & S. Hynds (Eds.), *Developing discourse practices in adolescence and adulthood* (pp. 161–180). Norwood, NJ: Ablex.

McCormick, K. (1994). *The culture of reading and the teaching of English.* Manchester, UK: Manchester University Press.

Moje, E. B. (2007). Developing socially just subject-matter instruction: A review of the literature on disciplinary literacy teaching. *Review of Research in Education, 31*(1), 1–44.

National Governors Association for Best Practices & Council of Chief State School Officers (NGA & CCSSO). (2010). *Common Core State Standards for English language arts and literacy, history/social studies, science, and technical subjects.* Washington, DC: Authors.

Newell, G. E., Bloome, D., & Hirvela, A. (2015). *Teaching and learning argumentative writing in high school English language arts classrooms.* New York: Routledge.

Newell, G. E., VanDerHeide, J., & Wynhoff Olsen, A. (2014). High school English language arts teachers' argumentative epistemologies for teaching writing. *Research in the Teaching of English, 49*, 95–119.

Petrosky, A. R. (1982). From story to essay: Reading and writing. *College Composition and Communication, 33*(1), 19–36.

Probst, R. E. (2004). *Response and analysis: Teaching literature in secondary school.* Portsmouth, NH: Heinemann Educational Books.

Rabinowitz, P. J. (1997). *Before reading: Narrative conventions and the politics of interpretation: The theory and interpretation of narrative series.* Columbus: Ohio State University Press.

Ramage, J. D., Bean, J. C., & Johnson, J. (2007). *Writing arguments: A rhetoric with readings* (5th ed.). New York: Longman.
Rosenblatt, L. M. (1938). *Literature as exploration.* New York: Appleton-Century-Crofts.
Rosenblatt, L. M. (1978). *The reader, the text, the poem: The transactional theory of the literary work.* Carbondale: Southern Illinois University Press.
Rosenblatt, L. M. (1994). The transactional theory of reading and writing. In R. B. Ruddell, M. Ruddell, & H. Singer (Eds.), *Theoretical models and processes of reading* (pp. 1057–1092). Newark. DE: International Reading Association.
Tannen, D. (1993). *Framing in discourse.* New York: Oxford University Press.
Toulmin, S., Rieke, R. & Janik, A. (1979). *An introduction to reasoning.* New York: Macmillan.
Toulmin, S. E. (2003). *The uses of argument.* Cambridge, UK: Cambridge University Press. (Original work published 1958)
Van Eemeren, F. H., Grootendorst, R., & Henkemans, A. F. S. (2002). *Argumentation: Analysis, evaluation, presentation.* London: Routledge.
Voss, J. F., Perkins, D. N., & Segal, J. W. (Eds.). (1991). *Informal reasoning and education.* Hillsdale, NJ: Erlbaum.
Walton, D., Reed, C., & Macagno, F. (2008). *Argumentation schemes.* New York: Cambridge University Press.
Wilder, L. (2002). "Get comfortable with uncertainty": A study of the conventional values of literary analysis in an undergraduate literature course, *Written Communication, 19*(9), 175–221.

CHAPTER 23

Adolescent Literacy and Collaborative Inquiry

ROBERT SIMON and AMIR KALAN

In a teacher education classroom in Toronto, groups of middle school students, teacher candidates, and university researchers, members of our research collaborative, the Teaching to Learn Project (Simon et al., 2014; Simon & the Teaching to Learn Project, 2014), discuss projects developed from curricula they coauthored for Art Spiegelman's graphic novel *Maus: A Survivor's Tale* (1986). *Maus* documents Spiegelman's father's recollections of the Holocaust and the author's own struggles to come to terms with what it means to be the child of a Holocaust survivor. Youth and teachers involved in the Teaching to Learn Project collectively worked through what historian Dominick LaCapra (1998) has referred to as the "delicate relationship between empathy and critical distance" (pp. 4–5) in the process of responding to Spiegelman's text, a book that reflects profound human suffering. Through collaborative inquiries, the group attempted to challenge the traditional notion that curriculum is developed *for* students (or for teachers), and instead aimed to work *with* students to meaningfully engage with issues that mattered from individuals' perspectives.

We also coresearched this process. Building on a cross-site partnership between a middle school in the Toronto District School Board and our university, we involved youth and teachers in the process of inquiry. This included data collection, as well as inviting participants to document their understandings through writing, film, video, and conceptual art. This multifaceted collaboration allowed us to explore how adolescents individually and collectively imagine alternative ways of engaging with a text such as *Maus*, while at the same time providing a space for teacher candidates to develop pedagogical practices from listening to and collaborating with students who participated with them on our research team.

In preparation for writing curriculum, students and teachers responded to *Maus* in different forms, ranging from essays to artwork. For example, one group shared a diorama they created to express empathy with victims and survivors of the Holocaust and outrage at the continued prevalence of anti-Semitism provoked by Holocaust deniers (see Figure 23.1). A large white box papered in "White Pride" propaganda, the diorama included cutouts through which recreated scenes from the book could be seen. In their presentation about their project to the larger group, one of the youth described these holes as representing "the holes in [Holocaust deniers'] stories. They are kind of making up facts, and it's not really true at all." Another student described the inside of the box as their attempt to portray "what actually happened in the Holocaust. It's supposed to be a scene in just like a regular town in Poland, and how the Holocaust affected it." These scenes portrayed suffering experienced by Polish Jews, constructed with paper, velum, paint, collage, and cardboard: figures of Jews depicted as mice hanging in a public square or huddled in an attic crawl space, hiding from Nazi soldiers.

Critical collaborative inquiries can generate the empathy, solidarity, and activist responses intended by writers such as Spiegelman (1986), who share their difficult histories in literary works. One student noted, "I had learned about the Holocaust before, but what I got out of this project was how emotionally connected people were." Another student emphasized the impact of intergenerational collaboration: "I liked working with the teacher candidates because it's good to hear input not only from people your age but also from people who are older." One of the teachers noted, "I appreciated the risk the students took in the projects that they did. It was great to see what learners are capable of doing when given the chance."

FIGURE 23.1. Youth and teacher candidates author curriculum for *Maus* and coresearch the process: Plan and final diorama exploring empathy and Holocaust denial, 2015.

This research partnership suggests questions related to the function of collaboration in literacy research:

What role might collaborative inquiry play in helping individuals make sense of texts?

How can teachers and students in a research context work together across differences to gain more nuanced understandings of our shared social world?

How might participatory research be a means of mobilizing multiple perspectives in learning from adolescents' diverse literacy practices, in and out of school?

What are the potentials of collective research of this nature for actualizing curricular, pedagogical, and social change?

In this chapter we explore how university researchers work with youth, families, community members, and teachers across a professional lifespan to investigate adolescent literacy pedagogy. Situating our understandings of adolescent literacy as a complex of practices taken hold of locally for diverse social and political purposes (Street, 1995), we call for attention to critical, collaborative, participatory, inquiry-based investigations in literacy, which we believe have renewed significance in a policy context dominated by more positivistic paradigms of research and professional practice. First, we define collaborative practitioner inquiry, highlighting key dimensions of participatory forms of research. We then review literacy research in which inquiry-based collaborations are taken up for diverse purposes, using varied methods, and taking place in a range of social and institutional contexts. Finally, we return to the example of the *Maus* project in our conclusion to illustrate the potential of collaborative research as a means of deepening our understandings of adolescent literacy and our approaches to teaching adolescents in increasingly transnational and multimodal contexts of teaching and learning.

THEORETICAL FRAMEWORKS

Our understanding of collaborative research in adolescent literacy is informed by the conceptualization of practitioner inquiry as an epistemological and methodological *stance* on practice. This notion of *inquiry as a stance* (Cochran-Smith & Lytle, 2009) suggests the relational and ideological dimensions of collaborative research, highlighting how and who researchers are relative to others, as well as emphasizing the larger political purposes of their work. Practitioner inquiry hinges on the epistemological notion that in educational research the *insider* position of teachers should receive particular attention. Most educational research has traditionally been conducted by outsiders and might therefore lack perspectives that can only be provided by insiders—including educators and youth whose experiences and perspectives are embedded in sites of practice. Through an analysis of alternative ways teachers record and present their research—from more traditional venues, such as journals or essays, to less traditional approaches, such as oral inquiry processes used to analyze student works (Martin & Schwartz, 2014; Simon, 2013; Strieb, Carini, Kanevsky, & Wice, 2011) or arts-based curriculum inquiries such as those we highlight in the example that opens our chapter—Lytle and Cochran-Smith (1992) emphasize that "school-based teacher researchers are themselves knowers and a primary source of generating knowledge about teaching and learning for themselves and others" (p. 447). Though this claim may seem obvious—who, after all, is better positioned to experience literacy teaching and learning than educators and students themselves?—the argument that teachers are well positioned to research practice remains radical in educational contexts marked by heightened accountability, surveillance of teachers, promotion of unified standards, the rise of so-called "value-added" evaluation models (Clayton, 2013; Darling-Hammond, Amrein-Beardsley, Haertel, & Rothstein, 2011), and reentrenched scientism in research on teaching that promotes epistemic hierarchies.

We note here a key characteristic of many forms of practitioner inquiry: a tendency to initiate different forms of collaboration in order to challenge dominant institutional structures and their hierarchical organization:

> Practitioner inquiry shares a sense of the practitioner as knower and agent of educational and social change. It also fosters new kinds of social relationships that assuage the isolation of teaching and other sites of practice. This is especially true in inquiry communities structured to foster deep intellectual discourses about critical issues. (Cochran-Smith & Lytle, 2009, p. 37)

Accordingly, we explore the collaborative possibilities for investigating critical aspects of adolescent literacy experienced by different teacher inquiry communities, teacher–researcher collaborations, and youth participatory action research initiatives. We have organized our overview of collaborative research in adolescent literacy by how the teachers and researchers involved in these projects name their work, how they situate their projects conceptually or ideologically, what research paradigms they draw upon, and how they understand the audiences for their research. In our analysis we were guided by a framework suggested by Lytle (2000), who highlights the ways in which practitioner researchers situate themselves in connection to the *legacies* that inform their work; their *location* or *positionality* as researchers; the local *communities* and broader *neighborhood* of the research, teaching, or social action within which they are situated; and, ultimately, the manner of change or work in the world toward which their inquiries are *oriented*.

The term *legacy* highlights the backgrounds of practitioner researchers in two specific ways: first, an educator's personal background and how it is connected to his or her practice and research; and second, the research paradigms and the traditions of inquiry practitioners come from and bring with them into the field. Thinking about educators' legacies within their sites of practice naturally invites reflections on their positionality in relation to participants and objects of inquiry or what Lytle (2000) refers to as their *location* in their research, which she describes as " 'positions relative to other systems or organizations, and thus the particularities of school context and collegial relationships, stance on practice, relationships with students, questions and etiologies of questions as well as their perceptions of the complex relationships of teaching and research" (p. 705).

Unlike other methodologies, practitioner inquiry commonly takes place in *community*; practitioner researchers often work in collaboration or relationship with others situated within sites of practice that host or benefit from their inquiries. Although each community has its unique nature, different communities are either directly or in subtle ways connected to each other. Communities learn from each other, cooperate, compete, and are often shaped by conflicts or micropolitics that can produce "constructive controversy" (Achinstein, 2002, p. 448). Mobilizing these processes in communities of inquiry, educators partner with others to address feelings of "disequilibrium and conflict" (Anderson & Saavedra, 1995) in their practices and communicate their visions of educational change with neighboring communities.

Acknowledging the deeply local nature of literacy (Street, 1995) and teaching, Lytle (2000) argues for a reconceptualized and reinvigorated notion of the local in literacy research in relation to the concept of *neighborhood* (drawing on Moshenberg, 1996), which she describes as "a conceptual space or vicinity in which the salient concern is not an essentialized identity but rather one's *location relative to others*" (p. 709; emphasis added). Finally, she suggests a need to consider *orientation* in practitioner inquiry, which "takes into account the intricacies of genre, topic, purpose, and audience" (p. 699). In our gloss, a consideration of *neighborhood* and *orientation* foregrounds what and who collaborative research in adolescent literacy is ultimately for, as well as its locus of change, whether at individual, institutional (classroom, university, district, or school-based), or broader social levels.

COLLABORATIVE INQUIRY AS A MEANS OF INVESTIGATING LITERACY FOR AND WITH ADOLESCENTS

For adolescents, literacy encompasses a range of practices in and out of school, shaped by culture, ideology, and identity, mobilized for an array of critical purposes (e.g., Alvermann, 2007; Dickar, 2004; Elkins & Luke, 1999; Mahiri, 2004; Moje, 2002; Moje, Young, Readence, & Moore, 2000; Vasudevan & Campano, 2009; Winn, 2015). In this section we provide a brief overview of how collaborative inquiry has been taken up by educators to explore adolescent literacy practices and literacy pedagogy for adolescents. This includes school- and classroom-based inquiries by literacy teachers, conducted with colleagues and students (e.g., Broderick, 2014; Cone, 2002; Waff, 1995); the work of teacher inquiry communities (e.g., Jones, 2014; Riley, 2015; Simon, 2015a); participatory action research with adolescents (e.g., Wright & Mahiri, 2012; Morrell, 2006); and cross-site collaborations, like the *Maus* project we described previously, that entail partnerships across institutional and community-based contexts (e.g., Campano, Ghiso, & Sánchez, 2013).

School- and Classroom-Based Collaborative Inquiry

As teacher researcher Cynthia Ballenger (2009) has explained, literacy educators often face what she terms *puzzling moments* in their practices, for instance, when they feel doubtful about their approaches to teaching diverse adolescents, when tensions emerge in the classroom, or when students raise unpredictable questions or appear reluctant to communicate their reactions to shared texts. In response to these uncertainties, teachers engage with different forms of intentional inquiry, often in collaboration with students, through which they (1) identify moments of dissonance, (2) adopt a systematic approach to collect data that can shed light on their questions, and (3) take an inquiry stance and consciously reflect on dissonant moments in ways that inform others and feed back into their own practices (Pincus, 2001). Moreover, many dissonant moments occurring in middle or secondary literacy classrooms are somehow rooted in sensitive issues such as cultural and linguistic difference, race, ethnicity, class, gender, equity, access, and accountability. Teachers themselves also have different *legacies*. They and their students frequently come from different ethnic, cultural, and intellectual backgrounds, which require complicated forms of identity negotiation when they have to deal with moments of doubt, disharmony, or uncertainty.

Activist literacy teachers often use feelings of dissonance as catalysts for inquiry with colleagues. Joan Cone (2002), for example, became concerned with what she and colleagues came to regard as the "caste-like" academic tracking of students into ability groups in her California school's English program (p. 1), in particular African American males, who were the majority in her "low"-ability ninth-grade classes even though they did not represent a majority of the school's population. Her inquiries with colleagues in her department led them to wonder about their own complicity in the "co-construction" of low achievement in English classes (Cone, 2005). They attempted to address these inequities by creating heterogeneous classes and opening advanced placement classes to any student with the desire to enroll. Cone's scholarship records how faculty members needed to call into question their own perceptions of adolescents' literacy abilities to accompany structural changes, coming to recognize how adolescents' perceived "failure" and "achievement" in literacy are social constructs that impact teachers' interpretation of adolescents' literate abilities and students' placement and performance in school. Cone and her colleagues' inquiries resulted in a dramatic increase in the number of Latin@ and African American adolescents who qualified for the University of California and California State entrance requirements. In spite of this progress, Cone notes that her school district reinstated tracking under the auspices of meeting "adequate yearly progress" under No Child Left Behind (Cone, 2005).

Many teacher researchers have explored collaborative inquiries with students into the intersections of language, identity, and social justice. Following in the tradition of June Jordan (1988), Fecho (2000) explored language and power with his African American and Caribbean American students. Inspired by students' concerns about the marginalization of Black English in the curriculum, Fecho (2000) documents how their yearlong collaborative inquiry moved beyond "an assignment to be completed solely because I had requested it" to become a "personal need to be filled through academic means" (p. 369) that helped him to recognize how adolescent literacy and language is closely connected to issues of identity and culture. Diane Waff (1994, 1995) and her students engaged in female-only conversations they called "girl talk" sessions, as well as conversations about gender in mixed-gender classrooms. Their collective inquiries brought to the surface how gendered talk influences girls' social and academic identities and self-perceptions. In her classroom-based inquiries, Linda Christensen (2000, 2009) documents how adolescents mobilize language, including poetry, as a means of exploring their family legacies and cultural histories within a broader social justice curriculum. Christensen and Dyan Watson (2015) note that inviting students to use poetry as a vehicle for exploring issues that matter to them allows "students' lives—the 'landscape and bread' of their homes, their ancestors, their struggles and joys—[to be] invited into classrooms as subjects worthy of study" (p. 3).

Collective inquiries with adolescents often inform teachers' curricular and pedagogical choices as well as their own stances as educators. Like Cone, Smokey Wilson (2007) investigated the persistent overrepresentation of African American students in remedial courses in a community college context. Wilson inquired into her students' experiences of schooling and what she terms the "literacies of college" they need to be successful.

For example, Wilson documents her inquiries with a student who described being publicly shamed in school for being a struggling reader. This experience prompted Wilson to explore material questions related to her students' experiences of school failure and her own responsibility as an educator. "I needed to know why the remedial classes were almost always filled with African American students. Why were they almost never in the classes reading Thoreau's *Walden* . . . ? Why did some learners succeed while others continued old patterns?" (p. 3). Lalitha Vasudevan (2006/2007) describes her inquiries of a student with whom she worked in a program designed to support adolescents who had prior encounters with the juvenile justice system. Vasudevan explains how they became co-learners who "read the world" (Freire, 1970/2005) together, developing a relationship through shared research into the students' interest in Kawasaki motorcycles. Each of these cases demonstrates how educators' inquiries with students inform their understandings of adolescent literacy, as well as their approaches to teaching literacy to adolescents.

In addition to feeding into pedagogy and deepening relationships with students who are repositioned as co-inquirers, teachers' collaborative research sometimes involve theorizing about literacy to speak back to conceptualizations proliferated by university researchers (Simon, Campano, Broderick, & Pantoja, 2012). To take one example, Debora Broderick's (2014) research documents how she and her students adopted a multiliteracies approach in their creation of a high school literary arts journal, *Concrete Voices*. Broderick's project not only facilitated multimodal literacy practices but it also invited her colleagues and other educators to "re-think the at-risk label" (p. 198). Broderick takes up the notion of participatory culture from Jenkins, Purushotma, Weigel, Clinton, and Robinson (2009, p. 59), a vision of classrooms as spaces in which "everyone knows something, nobody knows everything, and what any one person knows can be tapped by the group as a whole." Ultimately, Broderick retheorizes multiliteracies in terms of her students' collaborative inquiries. She argues that what she terms *collaborative design* is "a theoretical hybrid approach that captures the complexities of both the creation of multimodal texts and the rich communities from which they flourish" (Broderick, 2014, p. 198). The work of Broderick and other classroom-based researchers who have co-inquired with colleagues and youth indicates how critical, participatory inquiries in classrooms shift attention from individualized, deficit orientations to reposition students and teachers as knowledgeable and integral to the research process (Vasudevan & Campano, 2009; Morell, 2006).

Literacy Teacher Inquiry Communities

The examples of Cone (2002, 2005), Broderick (2014), and others suggest that, for literacy teachers, working within and against the constraints of everyday teaching can be daunting. As Snow-Gerono (2004) notes, "It is not always, not even usually, acceptable in schools to ask questions about mandates handed down from district or state administrators" (p. 242). As a result, teachers might creep into isolation to "fend off the disruptions and distractions that so often come from being too caught up in an overwhelming system" (Hobson, 2001, p. 175). Inquiry communities can be a means for literacy teachers to combat isolation and develop critical solidarity with colleagues, inspired by Freirean (1970/2005) problem-posing and problem solving-processes that reveal power dynamics and help them to address equity issues in schools (Ritchie, 2012; Simon, 2015a; Simon & Campano, 2013).

Slavit and Nelson (2005) describe *"supported teacher collaborative inquiry* as a model of professional development that includes long-term support for teacher-led inquiry in a group setting" (p. 2) in which "teachers have the opportunity to share beliefs, instructional perspectives, and co-construct new meaning around notions of pedagogy" (p. 3). Drawing on her experiences as a literacy teacher researcher over many years, Waff (2009, p. 70) documents how communities help teachers move "out from the isolation of the classroom to the shelter of inquiry communities that provided safe spaces for real dialogue, the sharing of stories, [and] relationships with colleagues." Rather than merely mollifying teachers' concerns, inquiry communities create spaces for colleagues to "generate new knowledge that helps teachers make a difference in improving student learning" (p. 70), supporting critical self-reflexivity into issues of race, power, and social contexts of schooling and informing critical literacy pedagogy for adolescents.

As we noted previously, literacy teachers' collaborative inquiries are often sparked by moments of uncertainty or dissonance (Ballenger, 2009; Pincus, 2001); teacher inquiry communities can "provide a shift to uncertainty and appreciation for dialogue in collaboration" (Snow-Gerono, 2005, p. 249). Inquiry communities also encourage individuals to develop critical and culturally relevant curriculum for adolescents. For example, the Bread Loaf Teacher Network, a technology-facilitated learning community for urban and rural literacy teachers in the United States, has supported educators to create "innovative online projects designed to promote culturally sensitive and transformative literacy" (Bread Loaf Teacher Network, n.d.; see also Goswami & Stillman, 1987). Teacher inquiry communities differ from most professional development programs in that they are organized by teacher researchers themselves to tackle tangible problems they contend with, predicated on horizontal rather than hierarchical conceptions of knowledge generation (Campano, Honeyford, Sánchez, & Vander Zanden, 2010; Freire, 1970/2005), and may therefore be regarded as grassroots sources of educational innovation (Ghiso, Campano, & Simon, 2014).

Adolescent literacy teachers have initiated and participated in inquiry communities for an array of purposes. For example, teachers have created communities that meet regularly to improve their approaches to teaching diverse adolescents (Butler & Schnellert, 2012; Castle & Dickey, 2014; Snow-Gerono, 2005), especially by developing "new ways of looking at, listening to, and learning from their students" (Michaels, 2004, p. vii) in order to reflect on vital aspects of adolescent learning, literacy, or their own practices (Hobson, 2009). Some communities have been formed to discuss employing critical pedagogies in the classroom (Jones, 2014; Kramer & Jones, 2009; Rogers, Mosley, Kramer, & the Literacy for Social Justice Teacher Research Group, 2009) particularly to reengage disenfranchised students in classroom-based literacies (Jones, 2014; Riley, 2015; Waff, 2009). Literacy teachers gather together to experiment with research dissemination in a variety of forms, including fieldnotes, reflections, poetry, digital portfolios, artwork, and blogging, as well as more traditional forms of research presentation (Jones, 2014; Autrey et al., 2005). Many teachers organize inquiry communities around the shared goal of challenging normative structures and practices in schools. For example, Blackburn, Clark, Kenney, and Smith (2010) document the work of the Pink TIGers, an inquiry community of educators from urban, suburban, and rural schools, who came together to challenge homophobia, support teachers to create alliances with lesbian, gay, bisexual, transgender, and queer (LGBTQ) adolescents, and develop anti-homophobic practices in their classrooms.

Inquiry communities can encourage teachers to recognize how adolescents are already literate in ways that are often unrecognized in school (Simon, 2012). Riley (2015) documents a study group that she formed with five literacy teachers from different urban schools. She describes how participating teachers used this community as a space to define and enact critical literacy pedagogy. This included deepening their understandings of adolescent literacy and challenging dominant conceptions of what counts as literacy in school. For example, one teacher described her working definition of *adolescent literacy*, developed through shared inquiries with colleagues, which Riley, following Richardson (1997), rendered in the form of a data poem:

> When I think of it,
> when I think "literacy,"
> I just think about how students identify themselves
> and how they understand the world around them and how they view their place within the world around them.
>
> (Riley, 2015, p. 420).

This example suggests how inquiry communities can help teachers to work against the grain of dominant conceptions and practices, and to acknowledge and embody sociocultural perspectives on literacy that better account for adolescents' unique cultural histories, representational choices, and concerns.

Simon (2015b) documents the work of an inquiry community formed by teacher candidates who met regularly during their teacher education program and into their first 2 years in the classroom. These teachers used inquiries into adolescents' literacy practices to work against the grain of dominant narratives of urban adolescents' resistance or disengagement with literacy (Gadsden, Davis, & Artiles, 2009). One teacher explored how a student, who had appeared disengaged in class, cultivated a critical disposition rooted in his experiences of systemic injustices. She wrote about how this incident informed her own critique of schooling:

> There is a disjuncture between what students learn in schools, specifically literacy skills, and how it applies in their real lives. This difference of beliefs is striking, and I wonder if any of it has root in Will's questioning of his own education. . . . It is impossible to have faith in an institution if you believe it is not teaching what you think is important (Simon, 2015a, p. 243)

Local teacher inquiry communities are often supported by networks such as the National Writing Project (NWP), which connects universities and communities of educators, with the broader aim of using inquiry as a means of improving writing pedagogy. The NWP has promoted peer-to-peer professional development and research for inservice teachers in urban and rural sites across the United States since 1974 (Lieberman & Pointer Mace, 2010). Their principles position literacy teachers as knowledge generators and agents of change, considering the role of universities in supporting teachers who would like to improve conditions through reflection, inquiry, and theory-informed action. This emphasis on the impact of teachers as agents of change—particularly achieved through collective inquiry—is not accidental. The program consciously follows a teacher-centered agenda best manifested in its Teacher Inquiry Communities (TIC) Network.

In a study supported by the NWP, Jones (2014) collected stories from participating teachers in a TIC about how relationships with disenfranchised students have helped them to "cultivate a critical way of being" (p. 5). One of the teachers in this community described learning from the literacies and creative writing abilities of a student who, in spite of his prior struggles with academic writing, learned to navigate school barriers successfully with his teacher's help. Supporting teacher inquiries in local communities like this one, the NWP attempts to create channels of communication between teacher researchers in different sites of practice nationwide, with the following goals:

- To develop a more national and encompassing vision of teacher research for the NWP and the teaching profession as a whole
- To create a structure for the pooling of geographically and culturally informed knowledge that has national implications
- To increase the capacity of NWP sites to address issues of equity, access, and accountability, and serve as a mechanism to gather data that address those issues. (National Writing Project, 2015, n.p.)

Among numerous reports provided by the teachers and researchers involved in TIC, Castle and Dickey (2014) have written about "the power of collaborative teacher research" (p. 1). In their project, a group of female literacy teachers studied the literacy practices of their male students to understand why the boys did not engage with reading as much as the teachers expected. The teachers decided to share their frustration with their colleagues and to discuss the challenges they faced when inviting the boys to read. They formed a community of inquiry to reflect on their experiences more systemically.

The teachers took the following steps. They reviewed teacher research literature as a source of inspiration to learn about other teachers' experiences with the same problem, and to learn about the views, contexts, and methods of other teacher inquiry communities. They met as a community on a "No guilt!" basis, which let the teachers skip meetings and not feel guilty about it, although members hardly missed the gatherings. They created protocols to structure their approach to data collection and analysis. They brought fieldnotes to receive feedback from other members and collaboratively analyzed their data. Their collaborative inquiry revealed that "they had judged much of the content of boys' interests as not appropriate to express in school, or even 'gross' (such as boys' fascination with bodily functions and noises).... The findings forced the teachers to rethink gender and their own gender biases in teaching as well as in their personal lives" (p. 4).

Castle and Dickey (2014) describe the results of creating their teacher inquiry community as follows:

> It is never easy to admit the need to change. They were very surprised to find that boys' interests were so different from what they had been teaching. It is to their credit that their [the teachers'] high level of professionalism allowed them to recognize their own gender biases and decide change was necessary in their teaching in order to address the needs of boys and of all their students. (p. 5)

Castle and Dickey's (2014) study is an example of how inquiry communities can encourage teachers to recognize adolescents' literacy needs and interests, and equip them with the intellectual inspiration needed to challenge institutional restrictions and strengthen their positions as agents of change. Once teachers start collaborating through inquiry, everyday challenges, moments of confusion, or dissatisfaction with students' behavior can become catalysts for pedagogical and even structural reform. Castle and Dickey describe how inquiry allowed teachers to shift their focus from what they had previously regarded as male students' "gross" or "inappropriate" behavior toward an inquiry into their own biases as educators. In this respect, inquiry communities can help teachers to regard redefining their pedagogical principles not as a sign of weakness but rather as a natural part of their own identity negotiation and professional development.

Youth Participatory Action Research in Literacy

Youth participatory action research (YPAR) in adolescent literacy involves collaborations among educators, students, and community members, oriented toward investigating and addressing issues identified by youth themselves. Participatory action researchers value how the epistemologies, literacies, and social practices of adolescents and their communities impact the research process (Cammarota & Fine, 2008). YPAR actively relies on the knowledge adolescents bring with them into sites of learning (Cahill, 2007) and draws on indigenous understandings of collaboration and knowledge building (Tuck, 2009). As Guerrero, Gaztambibe-Fernández, Rosas, and Guerrero (2013) note, youth participatory action researchers do not study adolescents but work alongside them:

> YPAR entails action-oriented and critical work enacted in the best interests of youth by and with youth; YPAR values youth knowledge about their lived experiences and opens up community space for them to critically examine these experiences; YPAR considers youth capable of becoming critical researchers, public intellectuals, and proactive advocates of change. (p. 109)

As a result, Guerrero et al.'s (2013) research documents how adolescents in their project developed research literacy skills. Through YPAR, adolescents become inquirers: They read research literature, produce reports, correspond with adults, present their findings, and so forth. Morrell (2006) similarly describes YPAR as scholarship intending to "inspire multiple transformative outcomes including individual development and social action" (p. 7). Although knowledge generation through research is crucial in YPAR, "an equally important focus is the development of students' literacies through innovating and empowering classroom curricula and pedagogies. . . . Youth participatory action research seeks to develop young people as empowered agents of change through a process that also addresses larger issues of social inequality" (p. 7).

YPAR is a way to *humanize* (Paris & Winn, 2014) adolescent literacy research by placing researchers, teachers, and students on equal ground. In other words, YPAR involves regarding active participation in research not merely as the domain of an elite class of scholars but also as a fundamental human right (Appadurai, 2006), encouraging youth to use research as a means of making sense of their own literacy learning. YPAR is not only a way to study students' literacy practices, but is often a vehicle to generate engagement (Morell, 2006), a method of community building and creating opportunities for learning. YPAR in adolescent literacy often involves students of color (Bertrand, 2014; Guerrero et al., 2013; Livingstone, Celemencki, & Calixte, 2014), underprivileged, or marginalized students (Brown & Rodriguez, 2009; Fox, 2011) in order to help them take action to transform inequitable conditions they identify in their schools and communities.

YPAR connects with literacy in two ways. First, it involves students in the process of research, so that they can engage with literacy as researchers. Second, it helps students make sense of their literacy practices and become conscious of their learning processes and the sociocultural circumstances that foster or hinder them. An example of the former is the Positive Youth Development (PYD) program initiated by Wright and Mahiri (2012) to bring youth and adults together to try alternative curricular and pedagogical approaches that can create literacy development. PYD approaches attempt to engage students that have been marginalized by dominant pedagogical practices. Wright and Mahiri initiated a youth-led YPAR project in an urban community-based organization. In this project, they invited 10 community members including eight youth (ages 13–18) and two adult facilitators to study collaboratively the impact of project-based learning on the members' literacy practices. The project was to assess the needs of the community and to think of plans for development. Wright and Mahiri document how the project helped Pepe, previously resistant to traditional reading activities, eagerly engage with reading. "Pepe and two team members mapped neighborhood assets, read materials on the neighborhood's immigration and factory labor history, took notes during a walking tour of the neighborhood, and created a skit that illustrated the neighborhood's sociohistorical conditions and needs" (p. 126).

Next to creating opportunities for youth to engage with literacy, YPAR also invites participants to consciously take an inquiry stance on their lives and literacy practices. These projects can create opportunities for students, alongside teachers and researchers, to think about the factors that enhance or hinder their engagement with literacy in school. For instance, Livingstone et al. (2014) conducted a project in Montreal that brought together 16 Black adolescents and four adults (two researchers and two community workers) to study the educational challenges of Black students. The students attended research training sessions to become familiar with qualitative research methods and were invited to lead the project asking why some Black students did not feel successful at school. In the process of the research, they found out that the progress of Black youth was impeded by factors beyond classroom activities or individual interest in subjects. These factors included, school culture, and the socioeconomic conditions of students' neighborhoods.

Similarly, Brown and Rodriguez (2009) involved marginalized youth in the United States in investigations into everyday struggles that negatively impact their learning. Drawing on the work of Gutiérrez (2008) and others, Bertrand (2014) created a *third space* in which educational policymakers and a group of Black youth investigated how racism manifested itself in the educational system and hindered the educational lives of students of color. As these examples suggest, participatory research often involves the constructive disruption of institutional structures and practices (Cochran-Smith & Lytle, 2009), and therefore presents challenges to the status quo, as well as to individuals involved in YPAR, particularly researchers who situate their participatory projects within schools. Guerrero et al. (2013) described Proyecto Latin@, a YPAR project conducted in collaboration with a group of Latin@ students in the Toronto District School Board, in order to identify the challenges experienced by participating youth in navigating social and institutional barriers they faced. The research team experienced its own set of challenges in the process, including confronting "public expectations, community and media perceptions, negotiations of our roles as project co-facilitators, and the tensions that arise when attempting to embody the youth-centred principles of YPAR while delivering a senior social science credit course" (p. 105).

Irizarry and Brown (2014) document their school-based YPAR, including ARISE—Action Research into School Exclusion—a 2-year project involving Black and Latin@ adolescents who had experienced significant academic or disciplinary troubles. Though all youth in the project had been institutionally labeled as academically "disabled," "the research team chose to examine how particular experiences, beliefs, and actions, which are logical responses to economic, sociopolitical, and educational marginalization, get interpreted as 'disordered' " (p. 69). Findings from this research informed workshops for preservice teachers, as well as academic presentations, demonstrating how YPAR supports the learning of educators, as well as youth.

Cross-Site Collaborations in Literacy Education

Burridge, Carpenter, Cherednichenko, and Kruger (2010) employed Giddens's (1984) *structuration theory* to explain why their teacher education program at Victoria University in Australia was mainly structured around inquiry-based partnerships. A brief glance at *structuration theory* can help us better understand the necessity of initiating collaborations in educational research and explain how cross-site partnerships can maximize the impact of critical adolescent literacy research. If one regards the function, creation, and reproduction of social systems as caused by both *structure* and *agents*, the potential of human agency to reform systems becomes a valuable resource. Attention to the power of the agency of individuals working within and against a system can help teachers and researchers view education as a phenomenon not entirely shaped by structure. In other words, an emphasis on human agency re-renders education as a social practice with phenomenological and hermeneutic dimensions. A productive structure in this regard is a structure closely connected to individuals' beliefs, practices, textual backgrounds, and meaning-making processes, as opposed to a "well-made" structure engineered by experts to be imposed on teachers and students.

Using this theoretical framework, we might better appreciate the importance of cross-site collaborations in inquiry-based literacy education. As we have discovered in the process of working with students, teachers, and university researchers in the Teaching to Learn Project, initiating partnerships among individuals from different sites of practice and research has the potential to multiply the myriad experiences that people bring with them into learning and research communities, strengthening the human agency that can constructively challenge outmoded structures, practices, and curriculum. For example, the arts-based inquiries that resulted in students' intricate representation of trauma, empathy, and Holocaust denial we described at the outset of this chapter were informed by how individuals mobilized their diverse perspectives and experiences in the service of deepening their awareness in the process of designing innovative social justice curricula. This approach to inquiry is particularly meaningful in adolescent literacy research, since individuals' experiences are tightly bound with their literacy practices. In other words, if literacy is understood as practices grounded in sociocultural and sociopolitical contexts, simplified microscopic investigations may not be the best way to understand how people engage with literacy. Adolescents' literacy practices are multidimensional; happen within and across multiple sites (in and out of schools); are fostered or hindered by interactions at home, in their communities, at school, and among their peers; and include complicated textual exchanges. Accordingly, research on socially situated literacy practices benefits from cross-site, inquiry-based collaborations.

Similarly, in critical approaches to teaching and learning literacy, cross-site collaborations are powerful vehicles for encouraging students to broaden their views of literacy and to experience new forms of social action. If adolescents are regarded as potential "organic intellectuals" (Gramsci, 2010), they need to see their sites of learning as greater than the classroom. In documenting their research collaborations across school–university boundaries with youth, teachers, administrators, in an urban school district in the Midwestern United States, Campano et al. (2013) describe how cross-site, cross-cultural experiences help students regard education as a means of "[mobilizing] their cultural identities for critical ends" (p. 98).

Whereas traditional methodologies often favor a top-down model in which researchers carry out investigations in isolation and provide teachers and students with solutions, cross-site collaborations enable educators to restructure sites of learning for an organically formed "literacy vision" (Jetton, Cancienne, & Greever, 2008). Though such partnerships are not unproblematic (Pappas, 2005), cross-site research can allow communities, students, teachers, and researchers to democratically develop critical, community-oriented, and student-centered approaches to literacy learning. In other words, cross-site research is a form of *praxis inquiry* (Burridge et al., 2010), in which inquiry equals action, an attempt to reach out to communities and institutions to involve all the stakeholders in the process of education.

Most reports on cross-site, inquiry-based collaborations in adolescent literacy education focus on university–school partnerships (Campano et al., 2010, 2013; Comber, Kamler, Hood, Moreau, & Painter, 2004; Jetton et al., 2008; Zellermayer & Tabak, 2006). University–school collaborations are formed by researchers, teachers, and sometimes students coming together to reflect on pedagogical and literacy practices, and consequently to transform them. These collaborations sometimes take the form of participatory action research, or resemble inquiry communities supported by academics and researchers (Simon et al., 2014).

Park, Simpson, Bicknell, and Michaels (2015) describe a university–school partnership that studied the effectiveness of Poetry Inside Out (PIO), a literacy project designed to help English language learners in English-dominant schools improve their academic literacy by means of poetry and translation. The two English teachers (Simpson and Bicknell) and the two academics (Park and Michaels) believed that engaging with poetry and translation would help English learners see themselves as "linguistic and cultural beings who use language to participate in, and speak to, their worlds" (p. 51). PIO was designed "to create a playful and safe space where students can take risks and delve into facets of language such as word meaning, grammar/syntactic structures, metaphoric language, and nuances of rhythm or rhyme" (p. 51). Park et al. describe how teachers and researchers partnered in the research process:

> Together we developed two goals for our research: (1) document and reflect on the implementation of PIO with English learners, noting issues or questions that emerge for

the teachers, and (2) document and reflect on the kinds of student learning fostered by PIO. . . . The data collection and analysis were carried out by teachers and university-based researchers. (p. 52)

This suggests how university–school research collaborations can involve all partners in the research process, from design, data collection, and analysis, to research dissemination and even coauthorship.

One important form of university–school partnership involves collaborations with preservice teachers (Burridge et al., 2010; Fritz, Cooner, & Stevenson, 2009). Such partnerships allow teacher candidates to enter schools to engage with adolescents and reflect on their practices as teacher researchers while learning in the university. For example, collaborative inquiries in the Teaching to Learn Project coincide with a literacy methods course one of us teaches at University of Toronto, providing opportunities for new teachers to explore critical issues in teaching and learning alongside adolescents (Simon et al., 2014).

Cross-site collaborations, however, are not limited to university–school partnerships. These collaborations can include other institutions and individuals, such as governmental offices, museums, art galleries, factories, and professionals with different expertise, including visual artists (Simon & the Teaching to Learn Project, 2014; Goodman, 2015) and poets (Fisher, 2007; Jocson, 2005). Cross-site inquiries sometimes involve educators working together across their different institutions. Lewis (2009), a high school teacher in a border community in Arizona, describes a unique cross-continent inquiry into language, culture, and social justice involving herself, an English headmaster (Michael Armstrong), a college professor in South Africa (Lusanda Mayikana), and a primary school teacher in Lawrence, Massachusetts (Mary Guerrero). Influenced by the work of the Breadloaf Teacher Network (Goswami & Stillman, 1987), their inquiry involved students as coresearchers who, along with their teachers, shared "language memoirs" that provided Lewis (2009) with a "revolutionary forum" to learn from her students about their experiences of bilingualism, which in turn fed into her own practice as a bilingual educator (pp. 52–53).

Researchers and teachers involved in cross-site inquiries often adopt critical paradigms that value students' home languages and out-of-school literacy practices (Moll, Amanti, Neff, & Gonzalez, 1991), and utilize research as a catalyst for school or social change. Rogers et al. (2009) document the efforts of a teacher-coordinated collective comprised of teachers "across the lifespan," who collaborated with university-based educators and activists to explore how adolescents can mobilize critical literacy to "make changes in people's lives" (p. 22). In her investigation of adolescents' lives and literacies and innovative pedagogies in Harlem schools, Kinloch (2010) developed partnerships with youth, educators, and community activists who were involved in data analysis and authored response pieces to Kinloch's own research. Rogers, Morrell, and Enyedy (2007) describe how partnerships among university researchers and adolescents encouraged youth to develop identities as critical researchers. Kamler and Comber (2005) describe how early year and experienced teachers worked together in an inquiry community they formed to explore the roots of school inequities. This community provided a "discursive space where teachers could talk about poverty, violence, racism and classism" (p. 228), among other issues, with the goal of addressing the problem of unequal literacy outcomes. These examples demonstrate the role cross-site inquiries can play in critical literacy education, encouraging teachers to link adolescent literacy with social justice education (Miller, Beliveau, Destigter, Kirkland, & Peggy, 2008).

CONCLUSION

With these insights in mind we return to the vignette that opens this chapter. Middle school students, teachers, teacher candidates, and university researchers came together in the Teaching to Learn Project with the goal of designing critical literacy curriculum. We developed collaborations with adolescents to facilitate the emergence of activities that may engage students in meaningful ways with literature relating traumatic experiences, with the goal of challenging dominant top-down curriculum development processes. The project, at the same time, involved cross-site inquiry. We met in the students' classroom at their school; they attended teacher education classes at our university, and we visited an art gallery together. Our shared research was a part of the official curriculum for middle school students and assignments in teacher candidates' literacy methods course.

As illustrated by the examples we have reviewed throughout the chapter, collaborative inquiries in this community involve more than any single individuals' perspectives. To make the most of our collective experiences, youth and teachers shared family history narratives in small groups, describing their family's participation in or location during the Holocaust. They situated their own cultural legacies in relation to our shared inquiry, and communicated across differences of race, age, ethnicity, social location, and power. Youth and teachers worked side-by-side to develop ideas for teaching Spiegelman's (1986) *Maus,* and coresearched that process. This involved multimodal and multimedia approaches to documenting their learning, such as the diorama we described previously. Along the way, teachers were able to engage directly with adolescents' literate abilities as authors, literary critics, activists, and researchers. For many participating teachers, collaborative inquiry expanded their conceptions of literacy, pedagogy, and adolescents' abilities to contribute to the research process. In the words of one participating teacher candidate, adolescents' contributions to this collaboration "exceeded my wildest expectations."

Our experience, however, was far from a storm-free process of meeting students' needs, or of seamlessly co-articulating our perspectives on teaching *Maus*. Youth and teachers expressed a range of emotional responses to the text and the practice of coresearching and coauthoring the curriculum. Sarah Evis, a teacher who partnered with Rob Simon to initiate this research between her middle school students and his teacher education students, shared how one student, Anne, had an "epiphany" about the Holocaust in the process of creating a painting with other adolescents in her group, based on their research with teachers. Drawing on visual motifs from Spiegelman's text, Anne and her collaborators depicted Jews as mice being led to the gas chamber (see Figure 23.2). In an analytic memo, Sarah wrote:

> "Anne looked exhausted and close to tears. She said that she'd had a breakdown the night before. That was the word she used. (Interestingly, it works as a break in a barrier as well as an emotional event, but that's my observation). She said that it just hit her—her words I think—that it was all real. [Through the process of painting] . . . what had previously been abject, to protect herself emotionally, became real. . . .

FIGURE 23.2. Anne's painting.

I think that in a moment, at home the night before we talked, the safety of time and distance collapsed."

This collapsing of "the safety of time and distance" signals what LaCapra (1998) has described as the complex process of *working through* responses to the Holocaust by means of inquiry. Scholars in trauma studies, as well as scholars in literacy, such as Elizabeth Dutro (2013), have noted the insufficiency of language to capture the meaning of traumatic experiences (p. 302). For Anne, as for many others in our community, teachers and students alike, painting her response to *Maus* broke down commonly oppositional stances—assuming critical distance on the one hand or developing deeply empathic connections with their object of inquiry on the other (LaCapra, 1998). The choices that Anne and her collaborators made in their artwork helped them to mark key ideational aspects of the text. When she presented her painting to the larger group, another student asked Anne why she chose to paint the bodies white, "as if they are taking off their skin." Anne responded that she painted them white like the cats "to represent how [the Nazis] tried to reflect their image on other people." She noted that "the dead bodies are supposed to be faceless and nameless, 'cause a lot of people don't know what happened to their family," which Anne regarded as one of the most terrifying and tragic results of the Holocaust.

For researchers, working through collaborative inquiry involves complex emotional, as well as intellectual, labor. Anne's painting—along with collaborative textual responses made by other students, including research reports, oral presentations, artworks, websites, and videos—provides one example of what collaborative inquiries in adolescent literacy can offer. As we have highlighted throughout this chapter, these inquiries pay close attention to the cultural backgrounds of teachers and students, and the hermeneutic experiences they bring with them into the classroom (Simon & Campano, 2015). Individuals involved in collaborative projects come to regard adolescent literacy in broad terms and regard it as connected to students and teachers' lives and histories; they consequently remain sensitive to the positionality of researchers, teachers, students, administrators, and others involved in these projects. In other words, they reflect on teachers' legacies, students' communities, and the sociopolitical neighborhoods to which they belong, would like to communicate with, or wish to challenge (Lytle, 2000).

For teachers, inquiry-based collaborations can invite more democratic relationships in classrooms. Collaborative research in adolescent literacy is commonly action oriented, as well as inquiry driven. As a result, adopting collaborative inquiry as a pedagogical practice can be a starting point for transforming educational conditions, particularly for students who are most alienated or marginalized in mainstream schooling. Such inquiries also provide a means for teachers and students' to explore their own belief systems and interactions with language and literature. This work often raises more questions than it answers. In this sense, as well as others, collaborative inquiry may run against the grain of educational policies oriented toward certainties, and may be more concerned with managing teaching and measuring individual students' performances by narrow benchmarks than with working from and cultivating more capacious views of learning or literacy. By contrast, inquiry-based collaborations in adolescent literacy classrooms can create hermeneutic spaces in which teachers can reread and rebuild their own textual legacies and make better sense of their students' literate lives.

REFERENCES

Achinstein, B. (2002). Conflict amid community: The micropolitics of teacher collaboration. *Teachers College Record, 104*(3), 421–455.

Alvermann, D. (2007). Multiliterate youth in the time of scientific reading instruction. In K. Beers, R. Probst, & L. Rief (Eds.), *Adolescent literacy: Turning promise into practice* (pp. 19–26). Portsmouth, NH: Heinemann.

Anderson, G. L., & Saavedra, E. (1995). Insider narratives of transformative learning: Implications for educational reform. *Anthropology and Education Quarterly, 26*(2), 228–235.

Appadurai, A. (2006). The right to research. *Globalization, Societies, and Education, 4*(2), 167–177.

Autrey, T. M., O'Berry Edington, C., Hicks, T., Kabodian, A., Lerg, N., Luft-Gardner, R., et al. (2005). More than just a web site: Representing teacher research through digital portfolios. *English Journal, 95*(2), 65–70.

Ballenger, C. (2009). *Puzzling moments, teachable moments: Practicing teacher research in urban classrooms.* New York: Teachers College Press.

Bertrand, M. (2014). Reciprocal dialogue between educational decision makers and students of color: Opportunities and obstacles. *Educational Administration Quarterly, 50*(5), 812–843.

Blackburn, M. V., Clark, C. T., Kenney, L. M., & Smith, J. M. (2010). *Acting out!: Combating homophobia through teacher activism.* New York: Teachers College Press.

Bread Loaf Teacher Network. (n.d.). Bread Loaf Teacher Network. Retrieved from *www.middlebury.edu/blse/bltn.*

Broderick, D. (2014). Collaborative design: Participatory culture meets multiliteracies in a high school literary arts community. *Journal of Adolescent and Adult Literacy, 58*(3), 198–208.

Brown, T. M., & Rodriguez, L. F. (2009). *Youth in participatory action research.* San Francisco: Jossey-Bass/Wiley.

Burridge, P., Carpenter, C., Cherednichenko, B., & Kruger, T. (2010). Investigating praxis inquiry within teacher education using Giddens' structuration theory. *Journal of Experiential Education, 33*(1), 19–37.

Butler, D. L., & Schnellert, L. (2012). Collaborative inquiry in teacher professional development. *Teaching and Teacher Education, 28*(8), 1206–1220.

Cahill, C. (2007). The personal is political: Developing new subjectivities through participatory action research. *Gender, Place and Culture, 14*(3), 267–292.

Cammarota, J., & Fine, M. (2008). *Revolutionizing education: Youth participatory action research in motion.* New York: Routledge.

Campano, G., Ghiso, M. P., & Sánchez, L. (2013). "Nobody one knows the . . . amount of a person": Elementary students critiquing dehumanization through organic critical literacies. *Research in the Teaching of English, 48*(1), 97–124.

Campano, G., Honeyford, M., Sánchez, L., & Vander Zanden, S. (2010). Ends in themselves: Theorizing the practice of university-school partnering through horizontalism. *Language Arts, 87*(4), 277–286.

Castle, K., & Dickey, K. (2014). Boys' literacy study: The power of collaborative teacher research. *Voices of Practitioners, 9*(1), 1–7.

Christensen, L. (2000). *Reading, writing, and rising up: Teaching about social justice and the power of the written word.* Milwaukee, WI: Rethinking Schools.

Christensen, L. (2009). *Teaching for joy and justice.* Milwaukee, WI: Rethinking Schools.

Christensen, L., & Watkins, D. (2015). *Rhythm and resistance: Teaching Poetry for social justice.* Milwaukee, WI: Rethinking Schools.

Clayton, C. (2013). *Understanding current reforms to evaluate teachers: A literature review on teacher evaluation across the career span* (Prepared for the New York Association of Colleges for Teacher Education). Retrieved from *www.nyacte.org/documents/clayton_2013_teacher_evaluation.pdf*.

Cochran-Smith, M., & Lytle, S. L. (2009). *Inquiry as stance: Practitioner research in the next generation.* New York: Teachers College Press.

Comber, B., Kamler, B., Hood, D., Moreau, S., & Painter, J. (2004). Thirty years into teaching: Professional development, exhaustion and rejuvenation. *English Teaching: Practice and Critique, 3*(2), 74–87.

Cone, J. (2002, May 6). The gap is in our expectations. *Newsday.* Retrieved from *www.goingpublicwithteaching.org/jcone/gap_expectations.pdf*.

Cone, J. (2005). Co-constructing low achievement: A study of a senior English class at an urban high school (Monograph). Retrieved May 13, 2015, from *http://gallery.carnegiefoundation.org/collections/castl_k12/jcone/jc_monograph_edit.pd*.

Darling-Hammond, L., Amrein-Beardsley, A., Haertel, E. H., & Rothstein, J. (2011). *Getting teacher evaluation right: A background paper for policy makers.* Washington, DC: American Educational Research Association and National Academy of Education.

Dickar, M. (2004). Words is changin' every day: Langauge and literacy in the urban contact zone. In B. R. C. Barrell, R. F. Hammett, J. S. Mayher, & G. M. Pradl (Eds.), *Teaching English today: Advocating change in the secondary curriculum* (pp. 68–80). New York: Teachers College Press.

Dutro, E. (2013). Towards a pedagogy of the incomprehensible: Trauma and the imperative of critical witness in literacy classrooms. *Pedagogies: An International Journal, 8*(4), 301–315.

Elkins, J., & Luke, A. (1999). Redefining adolescent literacies. *Journal of Adolescent and Adult Literacy, 43*(3), 212–215.

Fecho, B. (2000). Critical inquiries into language in an urban classroom. *Research in the Teaching of English, 34*(3), 368–395.

Fisher, M. (2007). *Writing in rhythm: Spoken word poetry in urban classrooms.* New York: Teachers College Press.

Fox, M. (2011). Literate bodies: Multigenerational participatory action research and embodied methodologies as critical literacy. *Journal of Adolescent and Adult Literacy, 55*(4), 343–345.

Freire, P. (2005). *Pedagogy of the oppressed.* New York: Continuum. (Original work published 1970)

Fritz, A. E., Cooner, D., & Stevenson, C. (2009). Training new content area secondary teachers to teach literacy: The university/public school partnership. *Reading Improvement, 46*(1), 19–28.

Gadsden, V., Davis, J. E., & Artiles, A. J. (Eds.). (2009). Risk, schooling, and equity. *Review of Research in Education, 33*, 1–362.

Ghiso, M. P., Campano, G., & Simon, R. (2013). Grassroots inquiry: Reconsidering the location of innovation. *Language Arts, 91*(2), 105–112.

Giddens, A. (1984). *The constitution of society: Outline of the theory of structuration.* Berkeley: University of California Press.

Goodman, S. (2015). Facilitating student documentary projects toward 21-century literacy and civic engagement. Retrieved from *www.bankstreet.edu/occasional-paper-series/25/facilitating-student-documentary-projects.*

Goswami, D., & Stillman, P. (1987). *Reclaiming the classroom: Teacher research as an agency for change.* Upper Montclair, NJ: Boynton/Cook.

Gramsci, A. (2010). *Prison notebooks.* New York: Columbia University Press.

Guerrero, C., Gaztambibe-Fernández, R., Rosas, M., & Guerrero, E. (2013). Proyecto Latin@: The possibilities and limitations of a high-profile institutionally sponsored youth participatory action research project. *International Journal of Critical Pedagogy, 4*(2), 105–126.

Gutiérrez, K. D. (2008). Developing a sociocritical literacy in the third space. *Reading Research Quarterly, 43*(2), 148–164.

Hobson, D. (2001). Learning with each other: Collaboration in teacher research. In G. Burnaford, J. Fischer, & D. Hobson (Eds.), *Teachers doing research: The power of action through inquiry* (pp. 173–191). Mahwah, NJ: Erlbaum.

Hobson, S. (2009). Learning to listen: Creating socially just curricula for middle and high school classrooms. In R. Rogers, M. Mosley, & R. A. Kramer (Eds.), *Designing socially just learning communities: Critical literacy education across the lifespan* (pp. 65–75). New York: Routledge.

Irizarry, J. G., & Brown, T. (2014). Humanizing research in dehumanizing spaces: The challenges and opportunities of conducting participatory action research with youth in schools. In D. Paris & M. T. Winn (Eds.), *Humanizing research: Decolonizing qualitative inquiry with youth and communities* (pp. 63–80). Thousand Oaks, CA: Sage.

Jenkins, H., Purushotma, R., Weigel, M., Clinton, K., & Robinson, A. J. (2009). *Confronting the challenges of participatory culture: Media education for the 21st century.* Cambridge, MA: MIT Press.

Jetton, T. L., Cancienne, M. B., & Greever, B. (2008). The evolving roles of faculty learning communities: A university/high school literacy partnership. *Theory Into Practice, 47*(4), 327–335.

Jocson, K. M. (2005). "Taking it to the mic": Pedagogy of June Jordan's poetry for the people and partnership with an urban high school. *English Education, 37*(2), 132–148.

Jones, S. (2014). *Writing and teaching to change the world: Connecting with our most vulnerable students.* New York: Teachers College Press.

Jordan, J. (1988). Nobody mean more to me than you and the future life of Willie Jordan. *Harvard Educational Review, 58*, 363–374.

Kamler, B., & Comber, C. (2005). Turn-around pedagogies: Improving the education of at-risk students. *Improving Schools, 8*(2), 121–131.

Kinloch, V. (2010). *Harlem on our minds: Place, race, and the literacies of urban youth.* New York: Teachers College Press.

Kramer, M. A., & Jones, R. (2009). Establishing a critical literacy lab in an adult education center. In R. Rogers, M. Mosley, & R. A. Kramer (Eds.), *Designing socially just learning communities: Critical literacy education across the lifespan* (pp. 113–124). New York: Routledge.

LaCapra, D. (1998). "Acting-out" and "working-through" trauma: Excerpt from an interview with Professor Dominick LaCapra. Jerusalem: Yad Vashem Shoah Resource Center. Retrieved from *www.yadvashem.org/odot_pdf/microsoft%20word%20-%203646.pdf.*

Lewis, C. (2009). Using narrative as teacher research: Learning about language and life through personal stories. In D. Goswami, C. Lewis, M. Rutherford, & D. Waff (Eds.), *Teacher*

inquiry: Approaches to language and literacy research (pp. 43–68). New York: Teachers College Press.
Lieberman, A., & Pointer Mace, D. H. (2008). Teacher learning: The key to educational reform. *Journal of Teacher Education, 59*(3), 226–234.
Livingstone, A., Celemencki, J., & Calixte, M. (2014). Youth participatory action research and school improvement: The missing voices of black youth in Montreal. *Canadian Journal of Education, 37*(1), 283–307.
Lytle, S. L. (2000). Teacher research in the contact zone. In M. Kamil, P. Mosenthal, D. Pearson, & R. Barr (Eds.), *Handbook of reading research* (pp. 691–719). Mahwah, NJ: Erlbaum.
Lytle, S. L., & Cochran-Smith, M. (1992). Teacher research as a way of knowing. *Harvard Educational Review, 62*(4), 447–474.
Mahiri, J. (2004). *What they don't learn in school: Literacy in the lives of urban youth.* New York: Peter Lang.
Martin, A. C., & Schwartz, E. (2014). *Making space for active learning: The art and practice of teaching: Using Prospect Center's descriptive review of practice.* New York: Teachers College Press.
Michaels, S. (2004). Foreword. In Brookline Teacher Research Seminar, *Regarding children's words: Teacher research on language and literacy* (pp. vii–xii). New York: Teachers College Press.
Miller, s. j., Beliveau, L. B., Destigter, T., Kirkland, D., & Peggy, R. (2008). *Narratives of social justice teaching: How English teachers negotiate theory and practice between preservice and inservice spaces.* New York: Peter Lang.
Moje, E. B. (2002). Re-framing adolescent literacy research for new times: Studying youth as a resource. *Literacy Research and Instruction, 41*(3), 211–228.
Moje, E. B., Young, J. P., Readence, J. E., & Moore, D. W. (2000). Reinventing adolescent literacy for new times: Perennial and millennial issues. *Journal of Adolescent and Adult Literacy, 43*, 400–410.
Moll, L., Amanti, C., Neff, D., & Gonzalez, N. (1991). Funds of knowledge for teaching: Using a qualitative approach to connect homes and classrooms. *Theory Into Practice, 31*(2), 132–141.
Morrell, E. (2006). Critical participatory action research and the literacy achievement of ethnic minority groups. *National Reading Conference Yearbook, 55*, 1–18.
Moshenberg, D. (1996). Standing in the neighborhood. In J. Slevin & A. Young (Eds.), *Critical theory and the teaching of literature* (pp. 75–92). Urbana, IL: National Council of Teachers of English.
National Writing Project. (2015). About teacher inquiry communities network. Retrieved May 25, 2015, from *www.nwp.org/cs/public/print/programs/tic?x-t=about.view*.
Pappas, C. C. (2005). Making "collaboration" problematic in collaborative school-university research: Studying with urban teacher–researchers to transform literacy curriculum genres. In J. Flood, D. Lapp, & S. Brice-Heath (Eds.), *Handbook on teaching literacy through the communicative and visual arts* (2nd ed., pp. 215–231). New York: Simon & Schuster/Macmillan.
Paris, D., & Winn, M. T. (2014). *Humanizing research: Decolonizing qualitative inquiry with youth and communities.* Thousand Oaks, CA: Sage.
Park, J. Y., Simpson, L., Bicknell, J., & Michaels, S. (2015). "When it rains a puddle is made": Fostering academic literacy in English learners through poetry and translation. *English Journal, 104*(4), 50–58.
Pincus, M. (2001)."The circle of inquiry": From playing with the possible: Teaching, learning and drama on the second stage. Retrieved August 1, 2015, from *http://insideteaching.org/quest/collections/sites/pincus_marsha/c_of_i.htm*.
Richardson, L. (1997). *Fields of play: Constructing an academic life.* New Brunswick, NJ: Rutgers University Press.

Riley, K. (2015). Enacting critical literacy in English classrooms: How a teacher learning community supported critical inquiry. *Journal of Adolescent and Adult Literacy, 58*(5), 417–425.

Ritchie, S. (2012). Incubating and sustaining: How teacher networks enable and support social justice education. *Journal of Teacher Education, 63*(2), 120–131.

Rogers, J., Morrell, E., & Enyedy, N. (2007). Studying the struggle: Contexts for learning and identity development for urban youth. *American Behavioral Scientist, 51*(3), 419–433.

Rogers, R., Mosley, M., Kramer, M. A., & the Literacy for Social Justice Teacher Research Group. (2009). *Designing socially just learning communities: Critical literacy education across the lifespan.* New York: Routledge.

Simon, R. (2012). "Without comic books there would be no me": Teachers as connoisseurs of adolescents' literate lives. *Journal of Adolescent and Adult Literacy, 55*(6), 516–526.

Simon, R. (2013). "Starting with what is": Exploring response and responsibility to student writing through collaborative inquiry. *English Education, 45*(2), 115–146.

Simon, R. (2015a). "I'm fighting my fight, and I'm not alone anymore": The impact of communities of inquiry. *English Education, 48,* 41–71.

Simon, R. (2015b). "Just don't get up there and '*Dangerous Minds*' us": Taking an inquiry stance on adolescents' literacy practices in urban teacher education. In J. Lampert & B. Burnett (Eds.), *Teacher education for high poverty schools* (pp. 235–251). New York: Springer.

Simon, R., Brennan, J., Bresba, S., DeAngelis, S., Edwards, W., Jung, H., & Pisecny, A. (2014). Investigating literacy through intergenerational inquiry. In H. Pleasants & D. Salter (Eds.), *Community-based multiliteracies and digital media projects: Questioning assumptions and exploring realities* (pp. 159–180). New York: Peter Lang.

Simon, R., & Campano, G. (2013). Activist literacies: Teacher research as resistance to the "normal curve." *Journal of Language and Literacy Education, 9*(1), 21–39.

Simon, R., & Campano, G. (2015). Hermeneutics of literacy pedagogy. In K. Pahl & J. Rowsell (Eds.), *Routledge handbook of literacy studies* (pp. 476–482). New York: Routledge.

Simon, R., Campano, G., Broderick, D., & Pantoja, A. (2012). Practitioner research and literacy studies: Toward more dialogic methodologies. *English Teaching: Practice and Critique, 11*(2), 5–24.

Simon, R., & the Teaching to Learn Project: Bailey, A., Brennan, J., Calarco, A., Clarke, K., Edwards, W., Fujiwara, C., et al. (2014). "In the swell of wandering words": The arts as a vehicle for adolescents' and educators' inquiries into the Holocaust memoir *Night*. *Perspectives on Urban Education, 11*(2), 90–106.

Slavit, D., & Nelson, T. H. (2005). Dialogic teacher change: Two cases of supported collaborative inquiry. *Papeles de Trabajo sobre Cultura, Educación y Desarrollo Humano, 2*(2), 1–22.

Snow-Gerono, J. L. (2005). Professional development in a culture of inquiry: PDS teachers identify the benefits of professional learning communities. *Teaching and Teacher Education, 21*(3), 241–256.

Spiegelman, A. (1986). *Maus: A survivor's tale.* New York: Knopf.

Street, B. (1995). *Social literacies: Critical approaches to literacy in development, ethnography and education.* New York: Longman.

Strieb, L., with Carini, P., Kanevsky, R., & Wice, B. (2011). *Prospect's descriptive processes: The child, the art of teaching, and the classroom and school* (rev. ed.). North Bennington, VT: Prospect Archives and Center for Education and Research.

Tuck, E. (2009). Re-visioning action: Participatory action research and indigenous theories of change. *Urban Review, 41*(1), 47–65.

Vasudevan, L. (2006/2007). Looking for angels: Knowing adolescents by engaging with their multimodal literacy practices. *Journal of Adolescent and Adult Literacy, 50*(4), 252–256.

Vasudevan, L., & Campano, G. (2009). The social production of adolescent risk and the promise of adolescent literacies. *Review of Research in Education, 33,* 310–353.

Waff, D. (1994). Girl talk: Creating community through social exchange. In M. Fine (Ed.), *Chartering urban school reform* (pp. 192–203). New York: Teachers College Press.

Waff, D. (1995). Romance in the classroom: Inviting discourse on gender and power. *National Writing Project Quarterly, 17*(2), 15–18.

Waff, D. (2009). Coresearching and coreflecting: The power of teacher inquiry communities. In D. Goswami, C. Lewis, M. Rutherford, & D. Waff (Eds.), *On teacher inquiry: Approaches to language and literacy research* (pp. 69–89). New York: Teachers College Press.

Wilson, S. (2007). *"What about Rose?": Using teacher research to reverse school failure*. New York: Teachers College Press.

Winn, M. (2015). Exploring the literate trajectories of youth across time and space. *Mind, Culture, and Activity, 22*(1), 58–67.

Wright, D. E., & Mahiri, J. (2012). Literacy learning within community action projects for social change. *Journal of Adolescent and Adult Literacy, 56*(2), 123–131.

Zellermayer, M., & Tabak, E. (2006). Knowledge construction in a teachers' community of inquiry: A possible road map. *Teachers and Teaching, 12*(1), 33–49.

CHAPTER 24

Scaffolding Adolescents' Reading of Challenging Text

In Search of Balance

MICHAEL F. GRAVES

"Damn You, Neil Postman."
—ROBERT HOGAN

In 1970, Neil Postman, a Professor of Media Ecology at New York University, published an article titled "The Politics of Reading" in the *Harvard Educational Review*. In the article, Postman argued that too much emphasis is put on learning to read, that arguments for the importance of reading are flawed, that the printed word is out of date and being replaced by electronic media, and that privileging reading is in fact reactionary. Not surprisingly, the article garnered a good deal of attention, and several years later the International Reading Association republished the article, along with responses from authorities in the fields of reading and English education (Winkeljohann, 1973). Robert Hogan, then Executive Secretary of the National Council of Teachers of English, titled his response "Damn You, Neil Postman." I have used Hogan's title as an opening quotation not because this chapter deals with Postman but to suggest that, as you read this chapter, you may identify some contemporary luminaries to whom Hogan's sentiments might apply.

    I write this chapter because I am seriously concerned about a number of aspects of the Common Core State Standards (CCSS), aspects that in my judgment do not result in the Standards supporting a balanced approach to developing proficient and engaged readers, and are likely to present a particular challenge to adolescents who struggle with reading. As Smith, Appleman, and Wilhelm (2014) have noted, criticizing the Standards has become *de rigueur*. It has also become *de rigueur* to take the stance that the Standards have the potential to, in the words of Smith et al., "provide a real opportunity for progressive change in American education" (p. 2), a stance echoed by literacy leaders such as Arthur Applebee and David Pearson in their endorsements for Smith et al.'s book. The Standards certainly have enormous potential to influence education in the United States. In fact, since the Standards are currently adopted by over 40 states, since students in 28 states will take one of the tests designed to measure mastery of the standards this year (Hefling & Smyth, 2015), and since students in all adoption states will take the tests in the coming years, it is clear that this potential is already being realized and will be more fully realized in the future. However, I believe that this potential includes the possibility of significant negative effects.

Before continuing, let me state explicitly that I am in favor of having national standards. Both individual students and the United States as a whole should profit from having students throughout the country share educational experience. Also, I strongly support a number of the central tenets of the Standards. I believe, for example, that more time spent on informational text and serious attention to the text itself are worthy goals. At the same time, I believe that the current Standards are seriously flawed in a number of ways and that some of the instructional ideas associated with the Standards are, to again quote Smith et al., "just plain wrong headed and misinformed" (p. 2). In the remainder of this chapter, I first discuss three general criticisms I have of the Standards and the way in which they were introduced. I make these criticisms because I believe that they serve as a basis for seriously questioning specific aspects of the Standards. Following these general criticisms, I describe a conjunction of four emphases of the Standards that, taken together, create an imbalance that is likely to have dire consequences for many students, particularly for adolescents who struggle with reading. Finally, I describe an instructional framework for scaffolding students' reading of individual texts that I believe can be a helpful tool for teachers to use in counteracting the imbalance in the Standards.

THREE GENERAL CRITICISMS

My first general criticism is that the authorship, processes for developing the Standards, and funding sources were not made nearly as transparent as they should have been. Neither the basic Standards document (National Governors Association Center for Best Practices & Council of Chief State School Officers [NGA & CCSSO], 2010) nor the Standards website (*www.corestandards.com*) lists the authors of the report, adequately describes the process through which the Standards were developed, or acknowledges the funding source. To be sure, some of this information is discoverable. The *Revised Publishers' Criteria for the Common Core State Standards English Language Arts and Literacy, Grades 3–12* (Coleman & Pimentel, 2012) identifies Coleman and Pimentel as "two of the lead authors" of the standards; Pearson (2013) identifies Coleman and Pimentel as the designers of the standards; and the moderator for a presentation Coleman gave to a group of New York State educators (see Coleman, 2011) introduced Coleman as the "architect" of the standards. But surely the authors of a document should be clearly identified in the document itself.

Regarding the description of the processes for developing the Standards, the basic Standards document (NGA & CCSSO, 2010, p. 3) reveals only that the effort was led by the CCSSO and the NGA, received input from a variety of sources, and was refined through successive drafts and feedback. The Standards website (*www.corestandards.org/*

about-the-standards/development-process) provides a time line, notes that over 10,000 public comments were received, and in a series of links provides lists of feedback groups, work groups, and a validation committee. Although a number of leading educators served on these groups, the only concrete information I found about just what they did is that 24 of the 28 members of the Validation Committee signed off on the document.

Finally, as far as I can tell, neither the basic Standards document not the Standards website provides any information on the funding sources for the effort. As is the case with authorship, information on the funding source is available elsewhere. It was, as is now widely known, the Gates Foundation (see, e.g., "How Bill Gates Pulled Off the Swift Common Core Revolution" [Layton, 2014] and "Who Paid for the Common Core Standards?" [Ravitch, 2013]). Whether or not one agrees with Ravitch that it is dangerous to have a foundation such as the Gates Foundation funding the process, the argument that the funding source should be clearly revealed in the CCSS materials seems unassailable.

My second general concern is that the Standards specifically claim to be research-based, when in fact much of what they advocate is not. The introduction to the basic Standards document states that "the Standards are (1) research and evidence based" (NGA & CCSSO, 2010, p. 3), but beyond making that claim, the basic document makes no mention of research and in fact includes no references.

Appendix A (NGA & CCSSO, 2010, Appendix A, no date), which claims on the cover to include "Research Supporting Key Elements of the Standards," actually supports only a few tenets and thrusts of the Standards, and presents a good deal of information that is not based on research. For example, the first section of Appendix A, which deals with text complexity, presents strong research evidence that many high school graduates are not prepared to meet the demands of college texts, moderate evidence that K–12 texts are decreasing in complexity, and no evidence that increasing the complexity of the texts student read in elementary and secondary school will increase students' ability to read college-level texts (Pearson, 2013). This last matter, increasing the complexity of the texts student read in elementary and secondary schools, is of course, one of the central thrusts of the Standards. It is also one of the four specific emphases of the Standards that I question below. As another example, the section of Appendix A on vocabulary begins with a one-page section providing strong research support for matters such as the importance of vocabulary and the extent to which students learn vocabulary in context, but then the section includes three pages on Beck, McKeown, and Kucan's (2002, 2013) notion of three tiers of words, which is widely accepted and very popular with teachers but is in no way research based.

Another CCSS document, *The Common Core State Standards: Insight into Their Development and Purpose* (Conley, 2014), claims to include "a summary of the research base supporting the standards" but does not in fact include such research, instead providing what is listed as a link to the research, a link that simply leads back to Appendix A, which, as I just noted, supports only some parts of the Standards and includes a good deal of information that is not research based. In an analysis of the extent to which the Standards are research based, Pearson (2013) acknowledges that his analysis is "not a meta-analysis or even a classic review of the literature" (p. 237) and observes that "surely, something like a meta-analysis or an exhaustive research review ought to be done" (p. 237). My belief is that a substantial review of the research should have been conducted and reported as part of the development of the Standards, and before the vast majority of the over 100,000 schools, more than 3 million teachers, and more than 50 million student in the United States were asked to follow the dictates of the Standards.

My third general concern is that the Standards give far too little attention to student motivation and engagement. As research and theory (Guthrie, 2015; Guthrie & McPeake, 2013; Moje & Speyer, 2014; National Research Council, 1999, Stripek, 2002; Wentzel & Wigfield, 2009), classroom observations, and common sense make clear, motivation and engagement are absolutely crucial to success in reading and in learning generally. As teachers of adolescents recognize, and as Guthrie, Wigfield, and Klauda (2012) indicated in a recent survey, many adolescents have an aversion to reading difficult informational texts and very frequently refer to them as "boring." In the basic Standards document, the topic of motivating students comes up only twice, in a graphic on factors influencing text complexity that appears on pages 31 and 57. In Appendix A, the topic of motivating students again comes up in the same graphic on text complexity (p. 4), in a statement indicating that motivation is something readers bring to the act of reading (p. 7), in a paragraph acknowledging that motivation is a factor to consider in selecting texts (p. 9), and in three repetitions of a box indicating that motivation is one reader-task consideration (pp. 12, 14, 16). In the *Publishers' Criteria,* the topic of motivating students comes up three times. In the first instance, the authors refer to including "texts with complexity levels that will challenge and motivate students" (p. 4). In the second, they refer to constructing "questions and tasks that motivate students to read inquisitively and carefully" (p. 7). And in the third, they refer to including questions that "will motivate students to dig in and explore further" (p. 8). Clearly, the Standards are not mute on the subject of motivating students. Equally clearly, they give very little attention to this all-important factor.

A PERFECT STORM OF FOUR RELATED RECOMMENDATIONS

My more specific concern is with the combined effect of four recommendations or biases that are present in the Standards themselves, Appendix A, the *Publishers' Criteria,* and the pronouncements of prominent and influential spokespersons for the Standards, including David Coleman (see, e.g., Coleman, 2011, 2013) and David and Meredith Liben (see, e.g., Liben, Liben, & Etienne, 2012). Taken together, I firmly believe that these recommendations could create a "perfect storm," a truly catastrophic situation for struggling readers—particularly for the many adolescent struggling readers who are disaffected with school and with reading—and a serious, if not catastrophic, situation for more able and more engaged readers.

The four recommendations/biases with which I am concerned are the emphasis on challenging text, the insistence that *all* students read these challenging texts, the emphasis on close reading, and the deemphasis on supporting students as they read.

Certainly, students need to read challenging texts. However, students also need to read texts that are less challenging, and even texts that are easy. Reading less challenging and easy texts is vital for building automaticity, fluency, vocabulary, world knowledge, and positive dispositions toward reading.

Certainly, *all* students need to learn to read challenging text. However, while *all* students need to learn to read challenging text, students who struggle with reading are not going to become adept at reading challenging text simply by being required to do so. Students who struggle with reading need a lot of support in dealing with challenging text, are therefore going to take more time than other students in dealing with challenging text and, as a consequence, are not going to be able to deal with as many challenging texts as others.

Certainly, there is a place for close reading, but there is also a place for not-so-close reading, for reading material that is easily comprehended and enjoyable, and that provides the volume of reading that students need to build both their reading skills and the habit of reading as a lifelong pursuit. We also need to recognize that the enormous amount of time required for close reading of short texts dramatically reduces the time available for doing the volume of reading needed to build vocabulary and world knowledge. Coleman (2011), for example, suggests that a close reading of Martin Luther King's 6,000-word "Letter from a Birmingham Jail" would require at least 6 days.

Finally, it is certainly the case, as the Standards repeatedly stress, that students need to become independent, and that some texts should therefore be read without teacher support. However, some students require a good deal of support with many texts, and some texts require a good deal of support for many, if not most, students. The sink-or-swim approach that the Standards privilege simply does not square with what research reveals about how students learn (see, e.g., Bransford, Brown, & Cocking, 2000).

I need to make clear, it is not that the Standards and their proponents fail to recognize any of these concerns. It is a matter of balance, or rather imbalance: These concerns receive far too little attention. For example, the first three pages of Appendix A present a detailed argument for the emphasis on challenging text, noting that the demands of college, careers, and citizenship require that students read complex texts, that K–12 texts have declined in complexity over the past half-century, and that current instructional practices have not done enough to foster independent reading of complex text. At the bottom of one of those pages is a three-sentence footnote acknowledging that scaffolding is often appropriate. Even in that footnote, however, the authors note that the movement should always be toward decreasing scaffolding and increasing independence.

As another example, in describing a close reading of a 275-word segment of Linda Monk's *Words We Live By: Your Annotated Guide to the Constitution* (2003), Liben et al. (2012) begin the reading without any attempt to motivate students or provide directions for the reading. They simply have students read the passage silently and follow this with a teacher or a skillful reader reading it aloud. They do, however, note that depending on the difficulty of the text or skill of the students, teachers might do the oral reading first. Similarly, in discussing what to do with vocabulary, Liben and his colleagues suggest that most word meanings can be discovered by carefully considering the context. However, they note that if students are not likely to be able to discover the word's meaning from context, it may be necessary for teachers to explain and discuss some of them. Repeatedly, the emphasis is on providing as little assistance as possible.

As another example, in the *Publishers' Criteria*, Coleman and Pimentel specifically note that "all students, including those who are behind, have extensive opportunities to encounter grade-level complex text" (p. 3). They also note, however, that "students whose reading ability is developing at a slower rate also will need supplementary material that they comprehend without extensive support" (p. 3). Both statements are perfectly reasonable. But, again, it is a matter of balance. The importance of including complex and challenging text is addressed repeatedly throughout the document, frequently in bold type, while including less complex text is addressed only occasionally, and never in bold print.

Again, my concern is with balance and with what I see as an imbalance given the perfect storm of stress on challenging text, close reading, all students reading repeatedly and engaging in close reading of that challenging text, and all of this supported by as little scaffolding as possible. It seems likely that the first three of these thrusts are likely to influence educational practice in the United States for the foreseeable future, and that little can be done about that at the present time. In the remainder of this chapter, I deal with the fourth matter: supporting students' reading. Fortunately, although not emphasized in the Standards, many resources are presently available for supporting students reading. These include *Adolescent Literacy and the Teaching of Reading* (Appleman, 2010), *Developing Readers in Academic Disciplines* (Buehl, 2011), and *Best Practices in Adolescent Literacy Instruction* (Hinchman & Sheridan-Thomas, 2014). In the following pages, I describe a particular approach to supporting students' reading. It overlaps with many of the approaches described in the previously cited sources and elsewhere, but I believe it has some particular advantages in that it is supported by theory and research and is systematic, presenting a rather comprehensive set of activities teachers might use (including opportunities for before, during, and after students read a text), and offering options from which the teacher chooses based on the text students are reading, the students themselves, and the purposes for reading the text.

THE SCAFFOLDED READING EXPERIENCE

The approach described in this chapter is termed the *scaffolded reading experience*, or SRE, and book-length descriptions of it include those of Graves and Graves (2003), Fitzgerald and Graves (2004), and Appleman and Graves (2011). As shown in Figure 24.1, an SRE has two phases—a planning phase and an implementation phase. During the first phase—planning—the teacher considers the students, the selection they are reading, and the purposes for reading. During the second phase—implementation—the teacher selects those pre-, during-, and postreading activities that will lead students to a successful reading experience. The SRE framework is appropriate for virtually any combination of students, texts, and purposes; but the specific pre-, during-, and postreading activities, as well as the number of such activities that are employed in any particular situation, differ greatly. In general, with less proficient students, more difficult selections, and more challenging purposes, more scaffolding is needed. Conversely, with more proficient students, less difficult selections, and less challenging purposes, less scaffolding is needed.

The scaffolded reading framework is flexible and adaptable in that it presents a variety of options—possible pre-, during-, and postreading options—from which teachers choose those best suited to lead a particular group of students to success with a particular text and a particular goal or set of goals. These options are shown in Figure 24.2.

Prereading activities prepare students to read the upcoming selection. They serve a number of functions in helping students engage with and comprehend text. These include piquing students' interest in the selection, reminding them of things they already know relevant to the selection, and preteaching aspects of the selection that they may find difficult, such as complex concepts and troublesome words. Of course, students can read many texts without prereading assistance, but when texts are challenging or when the teacher want students to understand them deeply, prereading activities can set the stage for a truly productive and rewarding reading experience. Most of the prereading activities

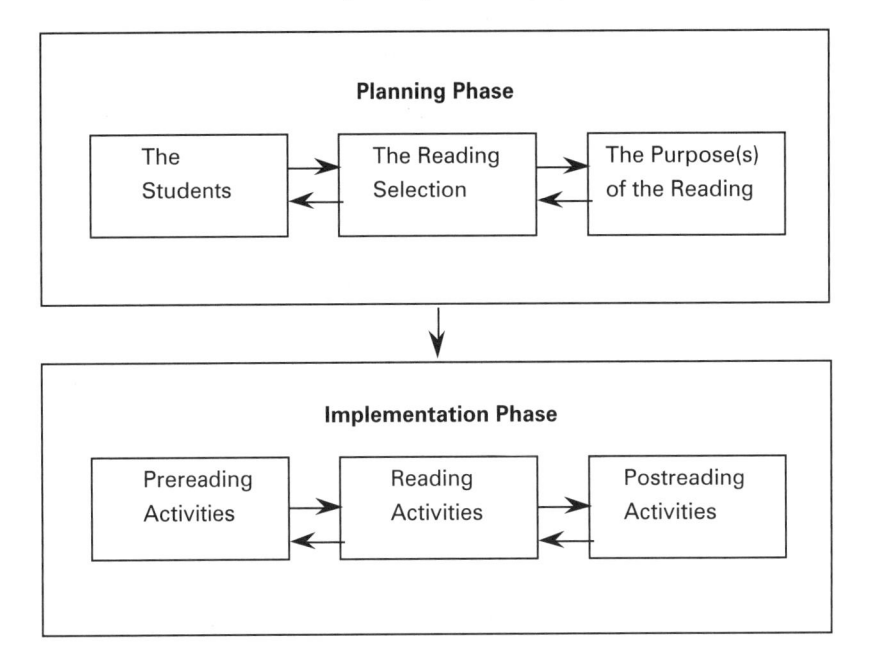

FIGURE 24.1. The SRE framework.

Prereading Activities	During-Reading Activities
• Relating the Reading to Students' Lives • Motivating • Activating Background Knowledge • Building Text-Specific Knowledge • Preteaching Vocabulary • Preteaching Concepts • Prequestioning, Predicting, and Direction Setting • Considering Literary Elements • Suggesting Literacy Lenses • Using Students' Native Language • Involving English Language Learners' Communities, Parents, and Siblings • Suggesting Strategies	• Silent Reading • Reading to Students • Supported Reading • Traditional Study Activities • Student Oral Reading • Modifying the Text
	Postreading Activities • Questioning • Discussion • Writing • Drama • Artistic and Nonverbal Activities • Application and Outreach Activities • Reteaching

FIGURE 24.2. Optional activities in an SRE.

shown in Figure 24.2 are self-explanatory, but a few may deserve clarification. The activities include both "Activating Background Knowledge" and "Building Text-Specific Knowledge," because in some cases students already have the requisite knowledge to deal with a passage, while in other cases that knowledge needs to be taught. "Preteaching Vocabulary" and "Preteaching Concepts" are distinguished, because teaching words for which students already have concepts is a radically different and easier task that teaching words representing new and potentially difficult concepts. The "lenses" referred to in "Considering Literary Lenses" are perspectives though which students can examine a text, such as reader response, archetypal, social power, gender, and deconstruction perspectives (see Appleman, 2014, for descriptions of these and other lenses). To avoid repetition, the two activities specifically designed for English language learners ("Using Students' Native Language" and "Involving English Language Learners' Communities, Parents, and Siblings") are listed only among the prereading activities. However, they are equally useful as during-reading and postreading activities. Finally, the key word in "Suggesting Strategies" is *suggesting*. While teaching comprehension strategies is an important part of fostering adolescent literacy, SREs are designed to foster learning from text.

During-reading activities include both things students themselves do as they are reading and things teachers do to assist students as they are reading—students' reading silently, teachers reading to them, students' taking notes as they read, and the like. A few during-reading activities deserve further explanation. "Silent Reading" is deliberately listed first, because this is the most frequent mode of reading that students use outside of school and it should therefore be the most frequent mode of reading in school. "Supported Reading" refers to activities that focus students' attention on particular parts of a text as they read it. For example, students might complete a semantic map of key concepts as they read an expository passage. "Modifying the Text" refers to activities such as presenting material on audio- or videotapes, simplifying the text, or having students read only part of it.

Postreading activities provide opportunities for students to synthesize and organize information gleaned from the text so that they can understand and recall important points. They also provide opportunities for students to evaluate an author's message, his or her stance in presenting the message, and the quality of the text itself. And they provide opportunities for students to respond to a text in a variety of ways—to reflect on the meaning of the text, to compare differing texts and ideas, to engage in a variety of activities that will refine and extend their understanding of what they learn from the text, and to apply what they have learned to the world beyond the classroom. As before, a few of these postreading activities may profit from further explanation. "Drama" includes any performance, including short plays, skits, pantomimes, and Readers' Theatre. "Application and Outreach Activities" include things such as cooking something after reading a recipe and organizing a drive to collect winter coats after reading an article on people in need of winter clothing.

Having said all this and having listed 25 possible activities in Figure 24.2, I want to stress that I am not suggesting that more supportive activities is better than fewer of them, or that adolescents should routinely be supported with SREs. Students should frequently read material without teacher support, particularly without prereading support, or "fronting" as it is sometimes called. I am in full agreement with authorities like Pearson (2013) and Shanahan (2012), who note that teachers sometimes provide too much support, particularly too much prereading support, but that is not an argument that they should provide too little support. When students cannot competently complete a reading task on their own, they need the support that will lead them to a successful reading experience rather than to failure and frustration.

THE THINKING BEHIND SREs

The impetus for developing the SRE was an insight explained by Jenkins (1979) in what he termed a *tetrahedral model of learning*. Jenkins observed that a number of psychological experiments that appeared to be investigating the same phenomena produced quite different results. As explained by the tetrahedral model, the outcome of any learning situation is influenced by the four factors: the learners, the learning activities, the criterial tasks, and the materials. The SRE framework, shown in Figure 24.1, takes these four factors and illustrates how teachers can vary them as they engage students in successfully reading, comprehending, and learning from a text. In the SRE model, Jenkins "learners" are the students, his "materials" are the reading selections, his "criterial tasks" are the purposes of the reading, and his "learning activities" are the prereading, during-reading, and postreading activities.

While Jenkins's model was the impetus for the SRE approach, the construct most directly underlying the approach is that of scaffolding, first articulated by Wood, Bruner, and Ross (1976). A *scaffold* has typically been defined as a temporary and adjustable support that enables a learner to accomplish a task that he or she would not be able to accomplish without the support of the scaffold. Considering the task of reading and the purpose of SREs, I would add that in addition to helping a reader understand a text he or she could not otherwise understand, a scaffold can help a reader better and more fully understand what he or she is reading and come away from the experience with a more positive attitude toward the text and his or her ability to deal with it.

Another central concept underlying the approach is schema theory, according to which knowledge is packaged in organized structures termed *schemata*. As described by Rumelhart (1980), schemata constitute our knowledge about "objects, situations, events, sequences of events, actions, and sequences of actions." We interpret our experiences—whether those experiences are direct encounters with the world or vicarious experiences gained through reading—by comparing and in most cases matching those experiences to an existing schema. In other words, we make sense of what we read and of our experiences more generally by a tacit process that in essence tells us "Ah ha. This is an instance of such and such."

Closely related to the concept of schema theory is that of the interactive model of reading. While schema theory emphasizes the importance of the reader's prior knowledge, the interactive model serves as a reminder that both the reader and the text play vital roles in reading. In arriving at the meaning of a text, Rumelhart (1977) has explained, readers use both their schemata and the letters, words, phrases, sentences, and longer units in a text. Good readers need to rely appropriately on the texts they are reading and their background knowledge to arrive at meaning, and teachers need to provide them with the sorts of texts and tasks that promote their doing so.

The final construct underlying the SRE model I discuss here is the critical importance of success. As both research and theory have repeatedly verified (Brophy, 1986; National Research Council, 1999; Stripek, 2002; Wentzel & Wigfield, 2009; Guthrie & McPeake,

2013), if students are going to learn to read effectively, they need to succeed at the vast majority of reading tasks they undertake. Moreover, if students are going to become not only proficient readers but also avid readers—children and later adults who voluntarily seek out reading as a road to information, enjoyment, and personal fulfillment—then successful reading experiences are even more important.

There are a variety of ways in which reading experiences can be successful. Several of them are particularly important. First, and most important, a successful reading experience is one in which the reader understands what he or she has read. Of course, understanding may take more than one reading, may require your assistance or that of other students, and may sometimes require the reader to actively manipulate the ideas in the text—summarize them, discuss them with classmates, or compare them to other ideas. Second, a successful reading experience is one that the reader finds enjoyable, entertaining, informative, or thought provoking. To be sure, not every reading experience yields all of these benefits, but every experience should yield at least one of them. Finally, a successful reading experience is one that prepares the student to complete whatever task follows the reading.

To a great extent, children's success in reading is directly under teachers' control. Teachers can select and allow students to select materials that they can read. Teachers can control the extent to which the material students read presents challenges. Teachers can provide support before, during, and after students read that will enable them to meet those challenges. Additionally, teachers can select and help students select postreading activities at which they can succeed.

In concluding this discussion of success, I want to stress an extremely important qualification. Saying students should succeed at the reading tasks they are presented with and that teachers should do everything possible to ensure success does not mean spoonfeeding them. As Smith (1971) forcefully argued when he presented his psycholinguistic analysis of reading, unless readers undertake some challenging tasks and are willing to take some risks and make some attempts they are not certain of and get feedback on their efforts, there is little room for learning to take place. Moreover, as Csikszentmihalyi (1990/2008) has discovered in decades of research, facing significant challenges and meeting them is one of the most fulfilling and rewarding experiences a person can have. In order to develop as readers, students need to be given some challenges. However, it is vitally important for teachers to arrange and scaffold reading activities so that students can meet these challenges.

In the next section of the chapter, I provide two detailed examples of SREs. Before doing so, however, I should point out that this chapter has included several elements of SREs. The chapter opening describing Postman's characterization of the printed word as out of date, Hogan's damnation of that position, and the suggestion that you might identify a contemporary luminary in the chapter to whom Hogan's sentiments might apply were designed to build motivation. The section on the potential of the CCSS was designed to activate background knowledge. The overview of the chapter was designed to build text-specific knowledge. And the "Three General Criticisms" and "Perfect Storm" sections were designed to build background knowledge. The upcoming examples also include elements of SREs. Each includes an Introduction that provides background knowledge; a figure showing the SRE at a glance, which provides text-specific knowledge; and extensive use of headings that serve as a sort of guided reading.

AN SRE TO SUPPORT CLOSE READING OF A SEGMENT FROM A COMPELLING HISTORICAL BIOGRAPHY

Introduction

Good historical biography invites us to imagine people, places, and perspectives in times past—to explore individual strengths and frailties, hopes and apprehensions, and dreams and disappointments as they intersect with the broader historical context. It makes that which seems distant both accessible and comprehensible. In closely reading this excerpt from Doris Kearns Goodwin's *No Ordinary Time* (1994), students witness some of the seeds of the Civil Rights Movement, and in doing so have an opportunity to understand the state of civil rights before World War II, the differing perspectives of the key players in the episode described, and the complexity of the process of social change.

Selection

Goodwin's *No Ordinary Time* is a penetrating and revealing account of the personal and public lives of Eleanor and Franklin Roosevelt during World II (see Figure 24.3). The work, which earned Goodwin the Pulitzer Prize in history for 1995, reveals in rich detail the human stories behind the events that are too often presented as a dull parade of facts in high school history texts. One of the many events described by Goodwin is President Roosevelt's order to end discriminatory hiring practices in the defense industry, perhaps the first precursor to affirmative action in U.S. history. The decision was a difficult and thought-provoking one for Roosevelt. In an eight-page excerpt (pp. 246–253), Goodwin describes the drama surrounding the signing of the executive order Roosevelt issued, Executive Order 8802. The SRE built around this excerpt shows how teachers might use the SRE approach to develop students' reading comprehension and historical understanding.

Prereading	During reading	Postreading
Day 1		
• Motivating • Activating and building background knowledge • Relating the reading to students' lives	• Direction setting • Guided reading	
Day 2		
		• Discussion • Questioning • Writing • Drama • Application and outreach activities

FIGURE 24.3. The SRE for *No Ordinary Time* at a glance.

Students

Supported by the SRE that surrounds it, this selection is appropriate for high school students with various levels of reading proficiency and background knowledge.

Objectives

- To understand the status of civil rights in the United States shortly before World War II.
- To recognize the differing perspectives of key players involved in the decision on Executive Order 8802, and the fact that such differing perspectives are present in most political decisions.
- To recognize the challenges of bringing about social change.

Description of Activities for Day 1: Prereading

Motivating, Activating, and Building Background Knowledge, and Relating the Reading to Students' Lives

- Project the following three classified ads on a screen and ask students what comments they might make about them, what about them would be considered illegal and disturbing today, and when and where they are likely to have been published.

HELP WANTED

Boy—Colored; as porter in drug store. Box C311.

Experienced colored cook, female. Apply Hilltop Cabins.

Hotel Maids. Bath maids and cleaners. Young married women; White, now unemployed; for full or part-time; experience. Call in person at Stevens Hotel, 725 S. Wabash Avenue.

- After taking some student responses, reveal that the advertisements were published in the *St. Louis Post-Dispatch* (6/22/41), the *Atlanta Journal & Constitution* (6/16/41), and the *Chicago Tribune* (6/22/41), discuss students' responses and concerns, and ask whether such advertisements could appear in newspapers today.
- Lead a brief discussion of contemporary prejudice and the possibility of such ads today and note that the excerpt students will be reading describes one of the events that accounts for this change in policy. Then set the scene by explaining the following: The first step toward ending discrimination in hiring was limited to the defense industry. The time is the summer of 1941; although the United States had not entered World War II at this point, the country was providing arms to Britain. Explain further that President Franklin Roosevelt had declared that the United States should become an "arsenal of democracy" for the Allies, thus promoting a massive production of weapons. The growth of the defense industry meant employment for many Americans, but African Americans were often excluded from all but the most menial jobs. African Americans, led by Asa Philip Randolph, were prepared to march in Washington, D.C. to protest job discrimination in the defense industry.

Description of Activities for Day 1: During Reading

Direction Setting and Guided Reading

- Tell students to keep these factors in mind and complete the data matrix shown in Figure 24.4 as they carefully and silently read the selection. (The matrix gives students a purpose for reading and focuses their attention on three central characters in the drama surrounding the establishment of the Fair Employment Practices Commission: Asa Philip Randolph, Eleanor Roosevelt, and Franklin Delano Roosevelt.)
- Note that students should complete the reading at home if they do not complete it in class.

Description of Activities for Day 2: Postreading

Discussion Followed by Students Choosing between an Artistic Activity, Outreach Activity, or a Dramatic Activity

- Engage students in a discussion based on the data matrix. Questions to explore in the discussion might include the following:
  - What were the goals of the three individuals and to what degree did these goals conflict?
  - How did their primary concerns and values differ?
  - In what political strategies did each engage?
  - Was Randolph justified in threatening a demonstration when the United States was embroiled in controversy abroad?
- Ask students to choose one of the following three options, each of which is designed to help them understand the complexity of social change:
  - Examine various perspectives on Executive Order 8802 and the social change it was designed to foster by examining editorials and commentaries published in the summer of 1941 in major newspapers and magazines such as *The New York Times, Crisis, The Chicago Tribune, The Atlanta Journal and Constitution, Ebony, Time* and *Newsweek*. Then arrange the editorials in a display with appropriate analytical comments. Questions you might consider include: To what degree do the writers

	Goals	Concerns	Values	Political Strategies
Asa Phillip Randolph				
Franklin D. Roosevelt				
Eleanor Roosevelt				

FIGURE 24.4. Data matrix for *No Ordinary Time*.

support Randolph's action? To what degree do they support Roosevelt's Executive Order? What concerns are expressed?
- Interview three or more individuals in the community in their late 60s and 70s about the changes they have seen in the workplace with regard to employment and equal opportunity. Topics to explore include the impact of both minorities and women in workplaces previously reserved for White males and any other aspects of social change you see as pertinent. Write up the results of your interviews in a brief summary paper.
- Research the lives of the three principal figures in this episode—Asa Philip Randolph, Eleanor Roosevelt, and Franklin Roosevelt—each of whom was a leader of remarkable foresight, vision, and integrity. Then create and enact a dramatization of a conversation among the three of them, set either in 1941 or in the present day.

Description of Activities for Day 3: Postreading

Presentations of Artistic, Outreach, and Dramatic Activities

- Have groups share and discuss their displays of newspaper clippings and their responses to the questions, present and perhaps elaborate on the summary of their interviews, and present their dramatization of a conversation between Randolph and the two Roosevelts.

AN SRE TO SUPPORT SERIOUS CONSIDERATION OF A SIMPLY WRITTEN BUT THOUGHT-PROVOKING SHORT STORY

Introduction

What does it mean to pledge allegiance to the flag of the United States of America? Why is the recitation to the flag such a controversial topic? What does it mean to stand up for what you believe? Do you have the courage to stand up for convictions even in the face of extreme pressure from peers, teachers, and parents? Has an adult that you admired, perhaps even a parent, ever let you down? These are among the many issues that surface in Abraham Rodriguez's (1999) short story, "The Boy Without a Flag." This interdisciplinary SRE (see Figure 24.5) can be used in language arts, social studies, or humanities classes. It is designed to encourage students to analyze current events and develop their own positions on a controversial issue.

Selection

"The Boy Without a Flag" is a short story by the contemporary Latino writer, Abraham Rodriguez, Jr. Although written in very accessible language and a simple story on the surface, the story give students an opportunity to consider some important and timely issues. The story's protagonist is a young Puerto Rican boy who refuses to join his class in the recitation of the Pledge of Allegiance, because he believes his father does not want him to. When the boy is sent to the principal's office, he is surprised to learn that his father is ashamed rather than proud of his defiance. This leaves the boy feeling as if he is caught between the culture of school and the culture of home. He is, indeed, a "boy without a flag."

Prereading	During reading	Postreading
Day 1		
• Providing test-specific knowledge • Relating the reading to students' lives • Motivating • Writing • Activating background knowledge		
Day 2		
• Relating the reading to students' lives • Motivating • Writing	• Guided reading	
Day 3		
		• Discussion • Questioning

FIGURE 24.5. The SRE for "The Boy Without a Flag" at a glance.

Students

This short story and the activities in this SRE are appropriate for students in grades 9–12. It could be used in either language arts or social studies classes. It is particularly appropriate in diverse classrooms that will reveal various points of view.

Objectives

- To understand the conflict of values presented in the story.
- To understand the dynamics of the parent–child relationship presented in the story.
- To apply current events to the conflicts presented in the story.
- To analyze the issues undergirding themes of citizenship and democracy.

Description of Activities for Day 1: Prereading

Providing Text-Specific Knowledge, Relating the Reading to Students' Lives, Motivating, Writing, and Activating Background Knowledge

- Tell the students that they will be reading a story about a boy who refuses to stand for the Pledge of Allegiance. Ask them what they remember about reciting the pledge in elementary school. Discuss debates about the Pledge at both the national and the local level.
- Have students complete a close reading of the Pledge of Allegiance in groups.

- Break students into groups of three or four. Distribute the pledge handout (Figure 24.6). Ask students to paraphrase the pledge and respond to the questions on it. Then have the same groups write a new pledge that they think most present-day Americans would feel comfortable with. Circulate around the room, providing explanation and support as necessary, as students are working on their pledges.
- Have a spokesperson from each group recite the group's pledge. Ask them to explain how and why their pledge takes into account something the original doesn't. Some students may have chosen to retain the pledge in the original form, and those who did should explain why.

Description of Day 2 Activities: Prereading

Relating the Reading to Students' Lives, Motivating, and Writing

- Have students create strip poems: Pass out strips of paper. Tell students that the story they will be reading is called "The Boy Without a Flag." Ask them to write, "I am the [girl/boy] without a _____."
- Collect the strips and read them aloud as a poem.
- Have students rush-write a word picture depicting what they remember about the atmosphere of their elementary school. Ask students to close their eyes and try to think back to what their fifth- or sixth-grade classroom was like. Then ask them to try to

---

I pledge allegiance to the flag of the United States of America and to the republic for which it stands, one nation under God, indivisible, with liberty and justice for all.

In groups of three or four, read or recite the Pledge, either together or individually.

Restate the Pledge in your own words. Use your normal everyday language.

Who might not be able to recite the pledge comfortably as it is written?

With a partner or with your table group, pretend you are a member of a new set of Congressional lawmakers. Your goal is to write a pledge that most U.S. citizens would feel comfortable reciting—and one that would survive over time. Think about the purpose of your Pledge, as well as concepts and key words.

Write your pledge here.

FIGURE 24.6. Pledge handout.

remember any schoolwide programs in the auditorium. Give students index cards and ask them to write two or three words they thought of. Pick two recorders and have them write the words on the board as students volunteer them. Discuss the overall impressions made by the words. Are they positive or negative?

Description of Day 2 Activities: During Reading

Guided Reading

- Read the first five pages aloud to students.
- Pass out the story map, going over the directions if that seems appropriate.
- Have students in pairs or trios finish reading the story and completing the story map (see Figure 24.7). Make certain that at least one student in each group is a capable oral reader.
- Note that if any groups did not finish the story or complete the story map, students should do so individually, before class the next day.

Description of Day 3 Activities: Postreading

Discussion and Questioning

- Lead a whole-class discussion/recap of the story. Have students rejoin their reading partners from Day 2. Ask members of each group to underline or highlight what they believe is the most important sentence of the story. Then ask members of each group to read their chosen sentence. Discuss the elements of the story that were highlighted or underscored.
- Ask whether the father should have supported the son in his decision not to recite the pledge. Have students line up in the front of the room, with those who strongly believe the father should have supported his son on one end, those who strongly believe that the father did the right thing by acquiescing to school officials on the other, and those who feel neutral about the issue in the middle. Ask students representing each position to defend their stance.
- Hand out the discussion web (Figure 24.8), which focuses on the question of whether students should be required to recite the Pledge, and have students complete it in small groups. Stress that it is important to follow the directions, which are on the handout, closely. If it seems that students have fully discussed the pledge, create a discussion web on another, perhaps broader topic, such as whether parents should always support their children or whether obedience is necessarily a virtue?
- Conclude consideration of "The Boy Without a Flag" with a whole-class discussion centered on students' responses to the web.

So there you have it, two very different SREs. They are different because the two texts are different, the purpose for reading each text is different, and the students for whom each SRE is intended are different. Yet, as different as they are, they represent only an extremely small sample of the myriad SREs possible, a small sample of the myriad ways to scaffold student's efforts to succeed in the reading they undertake.

"The Boy Without a Flag"

A story map is a list of questions and things to think about that, when taken all together, provide a guided map through the story. The questions will help you anticipate where you are going, as well as remind you of where you have been. For this story map, it's a good idea to work with one or two others. Also, as you read, make sure to mark your text with questions and comments. For example:

- Annotate the text in the margins of the document.
- Ask questions about the characters, the author, or things you don't understand
- Underline key passages and phrases and write interpretations
- Look for various writing techniques the author uses—note or highlight them
- Write/highlight main points about the story

Read pages 11–17.

1. Who is telling the story? How old do you think he is? What grade do you think he is in?
2. What do you notice about the author's style of writing?
3. What grade school memories does this story make you think of?
4. Since this story really isn't about Miss Colon's love life, why do you think the author included details about it?
5. The story changes settings on p. 16, switching from school to the narrator's thoughts of his father. What do you learn about their relationship?

Read pages 17–23 (end of first paragraph).

6. The setting switches back to the auditorium here. Why did the author insert all that stuff about the father instead of writing the story in a more normal or linear way?
7. Why didn't the boy stand for the Pledge? What is your opinion about this?
8. What is the response of Ms. Colon and Mr. Rios? What examples of conflicts with teachers can you think of? Were they based on principle? When were you sure that you were right and they were wrong?
9. What is respect? Why does Mr. Rios say that the boy doesn't have respect? Do you agree?
10. How do you think the father will react when he learns about the actions of his son? Why?

Read pages 23–30.

11. The narrator has images that "attack him at night." What's causing the anxiety he's feeling?
12. Why is it so important to the adults that the narrator salutes the flag? What's really at stake here?
13. Read the interaction with the principal on p. 26 very carefully. What is the most disturbing thing about it?
14. Why doesn't the father stick up for the son
15. Respond to this quotation on p. 27: "My father, my creator, renouncing his creation, repentant."
16. Who is The Enemy? Who is your enemy?
17. With your partner, underline what you think is the most important sentence in the story.

FIGURE 24.7. Story map for "The Boy Without a Flag."

Directions for Discussion Web

1. With a partner, discuss the pros and cons of requiring students to recite the Pledge of Allegiance. You might want to take into account recent events on local, state, and national levels. Read the news summaries we provided.
2. Jot down reasons for both positions in the yes and no columns. You only need to jot down key word or phrases.
3. Join with another pair of classmates and try to reach a consensus on this issue. Your goal is to come up with a group conclusion, even though some members may disagree with that conclusion.
4. Select a spokesperson to present your group's view to the rest of the class. Have him or her report on the **best** reason for your group's position.

Discussion Web Based on "The Boy Without a Flag"

Reasons

NO — Should students be required to recite the Pledge of Allegiance? — YES

Conclusion

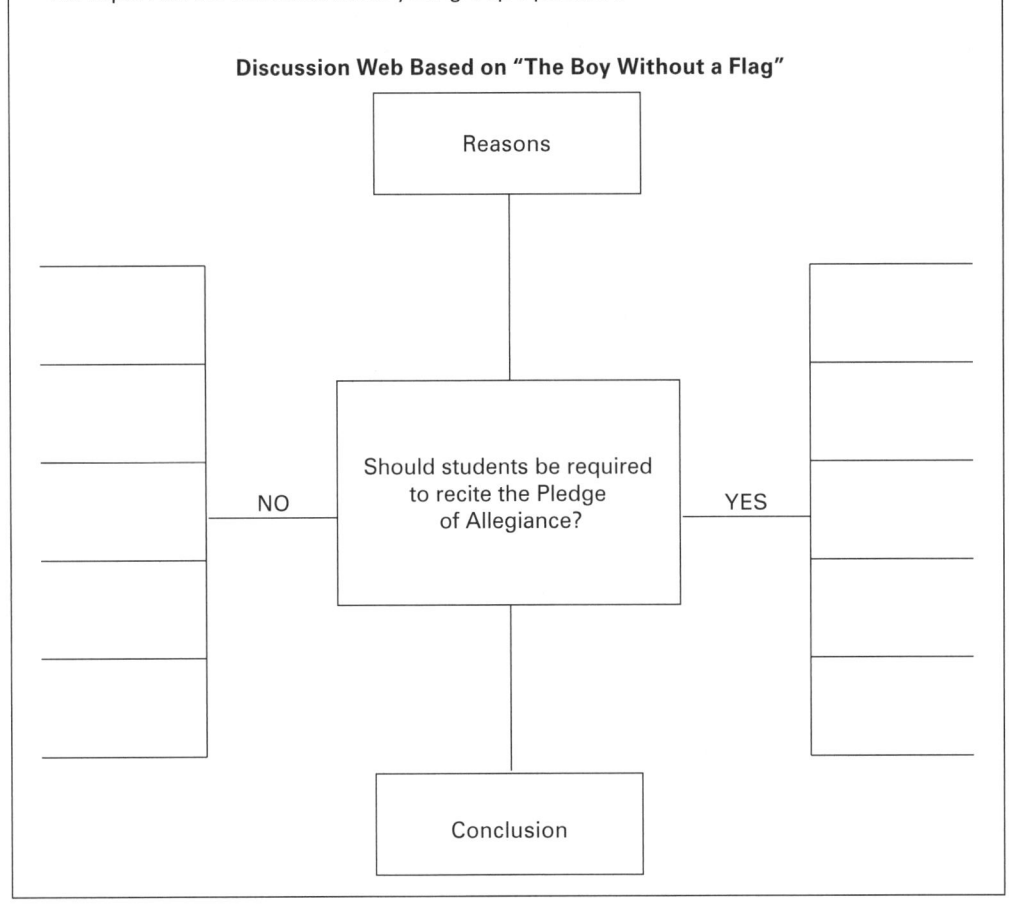

FIGURE 24.8. Discussion web for "The Boy Without a Flag."

CONCLUDING REMARKS

Clearly, both of these SREs are substantial ones. They are substantial because I wanted to provide examples of a number of the possibilities an SRE affords. However, as I have stressed before, this does not mean, and should not imply, that all of or even most reading that students do requires a lot of scaffolding. All students deserve many opportunities to read material that does not require scaffolding, reading that they can do independently. But with the advent of the CCSS and its perfect storm of emphasis on challenging text, advocacy of close reading, and insistence that all students need to repeatedly engage in close reading of challenging text, a great deal of the reading of today's adolescents is likely to require substantial scaffolding. What should determine how much scaffolding students get is the text they are reading, their purposes for doing the reading, and the students themselves. The person who should determine how much scaffolding students get is the one who best knows the students, and their strengths and weaknesses as readers. That person is the students' teacher, not David Coleman or any of the other authors or spokespersons for the CCSS. Of course, teachers need not, and should not, operate in a vacuum. A rich body of theory and research on scaffolding is available (Applebee & Langer, 1983; Appleman & Graves, 2011; Fitzgerald & Graves, 2004, Gibbons, 2015; Graves & Graves, 2003; Langer & Applebee, 2006; Wood et al., 1976), and still more information can be found by simply Googling "research on scaffolding in education."

ACKNOWLEDGMENTS

The SRE for *No Ordinary Times* was modified from an SRE created by Patricia Avery, a social studies educator at the University of Minnesota, that appeared in Graves and Avery (1997). The SRE from "The Boy Without a Flag" was modified from an SRE created by Deborah Appleman, an English educator at Carleton College, that appeared in Appleman and Graves (2011).

REFERENCES

Applebee, A. N., & Langer, J. A. (1983). Instructional scaffolding: Reading and writing as natural language activities. *Language Arts, 60,* 168–175.

Appleman, D. (2010). *Adolescent literacy and the teaching of reading.* Urbana, IL: National Council of Teachers of English.

Appleman, D. (2014). *Critical encounters in secondary English: Teaching literary theory to adolescents* (3rd ed.). New York: Teachers College Press.

Appleman, D., & Graves, M. F. (2011). *Reading better, reading smarter. Designing literature lessons for adolescents.* Portsmouth, NH: Heinemann.

Beck, I. L., McKeown, M. G., & Kucan, L. (2002). *Bringing words to life: Robust vocabulary instruction.* New York: Guilford Press.

Beck, I. L., McKeown, M. G., & Kucan, L. (2013). *Bringing words to life: Robust vocabulary instruction* (2nd ed.). New York: Guilford Press.

Bransford, J. D., Brown, A. L., & Cocking, R. R. (2000). *How people learn: Brain, mind, experience, and school: Expanded edition.* Washington, DC: National Academy Press.

Brophy, J. (1986). Teacher influences on student achievement. *American Psychologist, 41,* 1069–1077.

Buehl, D. (2011). *Developing readers in academic disciplines*. Newark, DE: International Reading Association.

Coleman, D. (2011, April 28). *Bringing the Common Core to life*. Presentation to the New York State Department of Education. Albany, New York. Retrieved from *http://usny.nysed.gov/rttt/resources/bringing-the-common-core-to-life.html*.

Coleman, D. (2013). *Cultivating wonder*. New York: College Board. Retrieved from *cultivating-wonder.org*.

Coleman, D., & Pimentel, S. (2012). *Revised publishers' criteria for the Common Cores State Standards in English Language Arts and Literacy, Grades 3–12*. Retrieved from *www.corestandards.org/assets/publishers_criteria_for_3-12.pdf*.

Conley, D. T. (2014). *The Common Core State Standards: Insight into their development and purpose*. Washington, DC: Council of Chief State School Officers. Retrieved from *www.ccsso.org/resources/publications/the_common_core_state_standards_insight_into_their_development_and_purpose.html*.

Csikszentmihalyi, M. (2008). *Flow: The psychology of optimal experience*. New York: Harper Perennial Modern Classics. (Original work published 1990)

Fitzgerald, J., & Graves, M. F. (2004). *Scaffolding reading experiences for English-language learners*. Norwood, MA: Christopher-Gordon.

Gibbons, P. (2015). *Scaffolding language, scaffolding learning* (2nd ed.). Portsmouth, NH: Heinemann.

Goodwin, D. K. (1995). *No ordinary times: Franklin and Eleanor Roosevelt: The home front in World War II*. New York: Simon & Schuster.

Graves, M. F., & Avery, P. G. (1997). Scaffolding students' reading of history. *The Social Studies, 88*, 134–138.

Graves, M. F., & Graves, B. B. (2003). *Scaffolding reading experiences: Designs for student success* (2nd ed.). Norwood, MA: Christopher-Gordon.

Guthrie, J. T. (2015). Growth of motivations for cognitive processes. In P. D. Pearson & E. H. Hiebert (Eds.), *Grounding Common Core teaching in proven practices* (pp. 107–122). New York: Teachers College Press.

Guthrie, J. T., & McPeake, J. (2013). Literacy engagement. The missing link. In S. B. Neuman & L. B. Gambrell (Eds.), *Quality reading instruction in the age of common core standards* (pp. 162–175). Newark, DE: International Reading Association.

Guthrie, J. T., Wigfield, A., & Klauda, S. L. (2012). *Adolescents' engagement in academic literacy* (Report No. 7). College Park: University of Maryland. Retrieved from *cori.umd.edu/research-publications/2012_adolescents_engagement_ebook.pdf*.

Hefling, K., & Smyth, J. C. (2015, February 15). Computer-based tests bring new era to students as states start Common Core exams week. Retrieved from *www.usnews.com/news/politics/articles/2015/02/16/ear-buds-computers-needed-for-new-standardized-tests*.

Hinchman, K. A., & Sheridan-Thomas, H. K. (2014). *Best practices in adolescent literacy instruction* (2nd ed.). New York: Guilford Press.

Hogan, R. F. (1973). Damn you, Neil Postman. In S. R. Winkeljohann (Ed.), *The politics of reading* (pp. 63–68). Urbana, IL: National Council of Teachers of English.

Jenkins, J. J. (1979). Four points to remember: A tetrahedral model of memory experiments. In L. S. Cermak & F. I. M. Craik (Eds.), *Levels of processing in human memory* (pp. 429–446). Hillsdale, NJ: Erlbaum.

Langer, J. A., & Applebee, A. N. (2006). Reading and writing instruction: Toward a theory of teaching and learning. *Review of Research in Education, 13*, 171–194.

Layton, L. (2014, June 7). How Bill Gates pulled off the swift Common Core revolution. Retrieved from *www.washingtonpost.com/politics/how-bill-gates-pulled-off-the-swift-common-core-revolution/2014/06/07/a830e32e-ec34-11e3-9f5c-9075d5508f0a_story.html*.

Liben, D., Liben, M., & Etienne, R. (2012, August 20). *Common Core State Standards for English Language Arts and Content Literacy: The Key Shifts*. Presentation to the Washoe County School District. Reno, NV. Retrieved from *http://coretaskproject.com/2012/08/21/striving-readers-presentation-materials-from-august-21st*.

Moje, E. B., & Speyer, J. (2014). Reading challenging texts in high school: How teachers can scaffold and build close reading and real purposes in the subject areas. In K. A. Hinchman & H. K. Sheridan-Thomas (Eds.), *Best practices in adolescent literacy* (2nd ed., pp. 207–231). New York: Guilford Press.

Monk, L. R. (2003). *Words we live by: An annotated guide to the Constitution*. New York: Hyperion.

National Governors Association Center for Best Practices & Council of Chief State School Officers (NGA & CCSSO). (2010). *Common Core State Standards for English language arts and literacy in history/social studies, science, and technical subjects*. Washington, DC: Authors.

National Research Council. (1999). *Improving student learning: A strategic plan for educational research and its utilization*. Washington, DC: National Academy Press.

Pearson, P. D. (2013). Research foundations for the Common Core State Standards in English Language Arts. In S. B. Neuman & L. B. Gambrell (Eds.), *Quality reading instruction in the age of Common Cores Standards* (pp. 237–262). Newark, DE: International Reading Association.

Postman, N. (1970). The politics of reading. *Harvard Educational Review, 40*, 244–252.

Ravitch, D. (2013, December 10). Mercedes Schneider explains: Who paid for the Common Core Standards? Retrieved from *www.huffingtonpost.com/diane-ravitch/bill-gates-common-core_b_4079447.html*.

Rodriguez, A. (1999). The boy without a flag. In *The boy without a flag: Tales of the South Bronx*. Minneapolis, MN: Milkweed Editions.

Rumelhart, D. E. (1977). Toward an interactive model of reading. In S. Dornic (Ed.), *Attention and performance: 6th symposium proceedings* (pp. 573–603). Hillsdale, NJ: Erlbaum.

Rumelhart, D. E. (1980). Schemata: The building blocks of cognition. In R. J. Spiro, B. C. Bruce, & W. F. Brewer (Eds.), *Theoretical issues in reading comprehension* (pp. 33–58). Hillsdale, NJ: Erlbaum.

Shanahan, T. (2012, March 20). Part 2: Practical guidance on pre-reading lessons. Retrieved from *www.shanahanonliteracy.com/2012/03/part-2-practical-guidance-on-pre.html*.

Smith, F. (1971). *Understanding reading: A psycholinguistic analysis of reading and learning to read*. New York: Holt, Rinehart & Winston.

Smith, M. W., Appleman, D., & Wilhelm, J. D. (2014). *Uncommon core*. Thousand Oaks, CA: Corwin.

Stripek, D. (2002). *Motivation to learn: Integrating theory and practice* (4th ed.). Boston: Allyn & Bacon.

Wentzel, K. R., & Wigfield, A. (2009). *Handbook of motivation at school*. New York: Taylor & Frances.

Winkeljohann, R. (1973). *The politics of reading*. Urbana, IL: National Council of Teachers of English.

Wood, D. J., Bruner, J. S., & Ross, G. (1976). The role of tutoring in problem-solving. *Journal of Child Psychology and Psychiatry, 17*(2), 89–100.

CHAPTER 25

Teaching Writing to Adolescents
The Use of Evidence-Based Practices

AMY ROUSE and STEVE GRAHAM

As students enter the upper elementary grades and continue to middle and high school, writing becomes an increasingly important academic skill. Teachers use writing to measure students' knowledge and understanding of subject matter in their classrooms (e.g., short-answer questions, essay tests). Also, learning standards and end-of-year assessments typically require some form of writing, regardless of the subject area. Instead of a simple multiple-choice answer or one-word response, assessments often involve questions that require students to defend their answer choice or explain their problem-solving process in writing (Graham, 2008; National Governors Association Center for Best Practices & Council of Chief State School Officers [NGA & CCSSO], 2010).

Adolescents who cannot write well lack not only the skills needed for excelling in class or on writing-heavy assessments but also the skills needed to harness the power of writing as a tool for learning. Writing helps students reflect on, integrate, summarize, and develop deeper understandings of new concepts (Bangert-Drowns, Hurley, & Wilkinson, 2004; Emig, 1977). Writing can also help students learn from what they read (Graham & Hebert, 2010) or explore their feelings and beliefs about a topic (Sedita, 2013).

Adolescents who do not have strong writing skills are further at a disadvantage in their postsecondary lives. College applications typically involve admissions essays, in which students are evaluated on the quality of their writing (Graham, 2006). Employers report that writing is involved, often in multiple forms (e.g., emails, office memos, written reports), in both salaried and hourly jobs. Employers place an even greater emphasis on writing skills for salaried positions, in which salaried employees are screened, hired, and promoted based on their writing skills (National Commission on Writing, 2004).

Given the importance of writing to academic and later success, it is not surprising that the Common Core State Standards (CCSS; NGO & CCSSO, 2010) emphasize writing as necessary for college and career readiness. The College and Career Readiness

Anchor Standards, which span grades K–12, focus on students' abilities to (1) use different writing genres when writing for different purposes; (2) produce clear writing by following the writing process and using technology to publish and/or share writing with others; (3) conduct research to gather information for writing; and (4) write for a range of short- and long-term tasks. The CCSS also address writing more specifically in the content areas (i.e., history, science, and technical subjects) beginning in grade 6. These standards call for students to produce argumentative, informative, and explanatory texts for a variety of discipline-specific purposes (e.g., support scientific claims with evidence, narrate historical events).

Despite writing's importance in adolescent literacy and postsecondary success, a simple database or Internet search for adolescent literacy research reveals a general trend: There is considerably less research on writing compared to reading and many other areas of instruction (Graham & Perin, 2007a). Moreover, teachers repeatedly indicate in national surveys that their teacher preparation programs are not doing a good job of preparing them to teach writing. This is the case for elementary teachers (Gilbert & Graham, 2010), middle school teachers (Graham, Capizzi, Harris, Hebert, & Morphy, 2014) and high school teachers (Kiuhara, Graham, & Hawken, 2009; Gillespie, Graham, Kiuhara, & Hebert, 2014). In these surveys, teachers report receiving little university training to teach writing. Based on these findings, we can understand why these same teachers report assigning few lengthy writing assignments (i.e., more than a paragraph or two) and rarely report assigning writing tasks that require their students to analyze, interpret, or synthesize information.

The emphasis and importance of well-developed writing skills for adolescents stands in stark contrast to the picture that teachers of adolescents paint of their writing knowledge, preparation, and instruction. Thus, our purpose in this chapter is to provide teachers of adolescents, those in grades 4–12, with research-based recommendations for teaching writing to their students. Our recommendations are applicable for teachers of adolescents regardless of their specialization. We believe that writing becomes a shared instructional responsibility in the upper elementary and secondary grades, and that the most effective writing instruction will occur with a joint effort among well-prepared writing teachers across disciplines.

KEY PRINCIPLES OF PRACTICE: RESEARCH-BASED RECOMMENDATIONS

To understand research-based practices for teaching writing to adolescents, we examined three different sources. First, we looked at cognitive models of writing that set the context for much of the instructional research on writing (Flower & Hayes, 1981; Hayes, 1996; Russell, 1997; Zimmerman & Risemberg, 1997). These models tell us about students' progression from novice to competent writers and the multiple demands that writers face as they compose. We also examined recent meta-analyses and literature reviews (Bromley, 2011; Graham, 2008; Graham, Harris, & Hebert, 2011; Graham & Perin, 2007a, 2007b; Graham & Sandmel, 2011; MacArthur, 2006; Rogers & Graham, 2008); these sources provided information about effective methods for teaching writing from scientific studies and from teachers and schools with track records of exceptional writing instruction. We summarized the key practices found across these sources into a list of 25 effective practices for teachers of adolescent writers in grades 4–12. Key principles for effective writing instruction are organized by research-based recommendations for (1) the writing teacher and his or her classroom, (2) writing instruction, and (3) writing assessment. At the end of each section, we provide an example of a classroom teacher putting several of our research suggestions into practice.

The Writing Teacher and Classroom

Before writing instruction begins, the teacher can set up the classroom to provide the support and motivation students need to grow as writers. We also encourage teachers to consider their own motivations and behaviors concerning writing, both of which affect students' willingness and desire to complete writing tasks. Five research-based recommendations (Bromley, 2011; Graham, 2008; Graham & Perin, 2007a, 2007b; Rogers & Graham, 2008) for accomplishing these goals when working with adolescent writers are:

1. Convey enthusiasm for writing. Demonstrate excitement for writing, show students you consider yourself a writer, and share your own writing with the class. To promote student interest and motivation for writing, teachers themselves can be active participants in writing assignments, sharing their own ideas, successes, and struggles with the writing process.

2. Create a positive classroom atmosphere, where writing is highly valued and all attempts at writing are respected. Students, especially those who have had previous struggles with writing, need to feel comfortable persisting when writing tasks become difficult, sharing their writing with others, and receiving feedback from the teacher and peers. One method for achieving this is to directly teach students how to give constructive feedback to each other, with a "golden rule" that the first piece of feedback is always a positive comment about the text. Teachers should also follow this guideline, beginning feedback with positive remarks first.

3. Set high expectations for students' writing and reinforce students throughout the writing process with specific feedback, praise, and/or tangible reinforcements. Teachers should set high expectations for the entire class (e.g., all students are expected to write for a specified amount of time each day or to meet a specific page limit) and regularly check in with students, to adjust expectations as needed based on individual writing progress. Additionally, waiting to provide feedback on a student's writing when the final draft is turned in is too late. Teachers should read their students' writing throughout the process, so that they can praise successes, address and remediate errors, and provide targeted instruction and feedback to shape students' writing along the way.

4. Provide frequent, sustained opportunities for students to write each day for authentic audiences and purposes. Often, the most interesting and motivating writing assignments involve topics and purposes that are personally meaningful to students in and outside of the classroom.

5. Have students use writing across the curriculum. Students should learn that writing is valuable not only in English class, but also has many uses in math, science, and history (not to mention art, music, photography, or any other elective). Teachers who

implement this recommendation create classrooms in which writing is a valued tool that students use throughout the school day for multiple purposes (e.g., to inform, to persuade, to entertain others, to demonstrate knowledge, to reflect on what is known or what was learned, to respond to literature).

Research into Practice

Mr. Fletcher teaches fifth grade. He knows his students will be more motivated to write if they see him express a love of writing and if he shares his own writing experiences with them. So he makes a point to write more, both inside and outside of school. When appropriate, he shares with his students how writing helps him, both personally (e.g., when he wrote instructions for his dogsitter, when he wrote an email to his grandmother who lives across the country, or when he wrote to his city councilman to express the need for speed bumps in his neighborhood) and professionally (e.g., when he had to write a report for the principal about how he would use technology funds, or when he wrote lesson plans for the class). When his students complete informal writing assignments, such as writing in their journals, he writes, too, and often shares what he has written with the class.

As students work on longer written compositions, Mr. Fletcher conducts frequent conferences with them to discuss their progress. Each conference always begins with a positive remark about a student's writing. Throughout the writing process, Mr. Fletcher continues to provide ongoing, formative feedback on his student's compositions, with expectations that each student will respond to his feedback and meet the writing goals they set together (e.g., Add more description to this section; Change overused words, such as *nice* and *good,* to more colorful vocabulary). The fifth-grade students in Mr. Fletcher's class write multiple times a day, not only during their scheduled writing portion of language arts class. Students produce informal writing (e.g., Jot down an answer; Write in a journal to tell how they solved a math problem) throughout the day and across different subject areas. They also work on longer written assignments over the course of several days or weeks.

Writing Instruction

In addition to creating a positive and motivating atmosphere for writing, teachers should also focus on how they teach writing. Fifteen research-based recommendations for delivering writing instruction to adolescents are listed below; the list begins with general principles of effective writing instruction (Flower & Hayes, 1981; Graham, 2008; Graham & Perin, 2007b; Hayes, 1996; Rogers & Graham, 2008; Russell, 1997; Zimmerman & Risemberg, 1997) and continues with more specific instructional techniques for enhancing students' writing skills and writing quality (Bromley, 2011; Graham, 2008; Graham & Perin, 2007a, 2007b; Graham & Sandmel, 2011; MacArthur, 2006; Rogers & Graham, 2008).

1. Teach students how to carry out the writing process (i.e., plan, draft, revise, edit, publish, and share their work) for longer writing assignments. Teachers should model how to plan before writing, show students what a draft looks like (compared to a final copy), and teach students the difference between revising and editing by modeling how to do each before publishing a final copy. Informal writing (e.g., journal writing, quick

writes) may not always involve all steps of the process, but students should be expected to follow the writing process with other, more formal or developed written compositions.

2. Provide explicit writing instruction that includes modeling, explanation, scaffolds, guided practice, and independent practice as students learn new writing skills and writing genres. Explicit instruction can include direct teacher modeling (e.g., composing an outline before writing) and collaborative writing opportunities in which the teacher and students plan, draft, revise, edit, and publish written compositions together. Scaffolds may include supports such as graphic organizers to help students plan or draft their writing or reminders of the steps or stages in a writing process (e.g., when editing, check for CAPS: Capitalization, Agreement, Punctuation, Spelling).

3. Identify students who need additional support. Reteach writing skills through individual or small-group lessons, provide additional scaffolds, and develop modified writing assignments as necessary to meet the needs of these students. Goals and expectations for writing may also need to be revised, based on individual student needs and progress.

4. Introduce reading materials to increase students' knowledge of the characteristics of good writing. Point out the ways in which authors have used specific skills (e.g., imagery, organization, voice) in their texts and ask students to practice applying these same skills in their own writing.

5. Teach students strategies for planning, composing, revising, and editing their written compositions. Include instruction on how students can self-regulate (e.g., set goals, self-monitor, give self-instructions and self-praise) as they write in order to balance the multiple demands involved in skilled writing. With the Self-Regulated Strategy Development model (SRSD; Harris, Graham, Mason, & Friedlander, 2008), students learn writing strategies and learn how to self-regulate their writing efforts. For example, students write (with the goal of later internalizing) self statements to help them think of ideas for their writing, motivate themselves to persist while writing, and remind themselves to check their work after writing. Additionally, they are numerous SRSD writing strategies to teach students how to plan for various genres (e.g., POW + TREE for persuasive writing: Pick my idea, Organize my notes, Write and say more + Topic sentence, Reasons, Explain reasons, Ending) and how to perform various aspects of the writing process (e.g., REVISE for revising a text: Read, Evaluate, Verbalize, Implement, Self-check, End). SRSD involves a series of criterion-based lessons in which students must demonstrate mastery of specific skills or aspects of a writing strategy before moving on to the next phase of instruction (consult Harris et al., 2008, for further information).

6. Explicitly teach students to write summaries of texts. Summary writing instruction can include explicit instruction in strategies, steps, and rules for writing summaries, with the elements of explicit writing instruction outlined in recommendation 2 of this section. Additionally, summary instruction can involve gradual fading of models (i.e., example summaries) as students learn to produce their own well-written summaries. These models should be of high quality and contain all of the essential components of good summaries. As students learn and progress toward writing summaries independently, teachers should remove the model texts and allow students to compose on their own.

7. Encourage students to collaboratively plan, write, revise, and edit their written compositions. Opportunities to work together on writing assignments not only allow students to learn from each other but also create learning situations that are likely more fun and engaging for students who are typically less motivated to complete writing assignments. Teachers can choose which stages of the writing process students complete together and also incorporate assignments in which students complete the entire writing process in pairs or small groups.

8. Set goals for students' writing, including goals for adding more ideas or including elements of specific writing genres. Goals should be individually tailored (based on each student's skills and needs), specific to each student's writing product (e.g., Include three reasons supporting your opinion or belief), and attainable for each student (not so challenging that they are frustrating, but not so easy that students do not have to work hard to achieve them). Depending on a student's readiness, teachers can begin by giving students goals for writing, with gradual movement toward collaborative goal setting between the teacher and each student and eventually to individualized goal setting when appropriate.

9. Allow students to use word processing to compose, edit, revise, and publish their written work. Word processing allows students to produce a legible text; to add, change, move, and delete text easily when revising; to correct errors with style, grammar, and spelling; and to create texts that incorporate multiple modes of representing their ideas (e.g., typed text, pictures, hyperlinks to important information found on the Web). Word processing also removes the task of handwriting, which can slow the writing process for students with fine-motor difficulties. For students to benefit maximally from word processing, teach them how to type efficiently and how to use software capabilities such as spell check. See the Writing Assessment section for more information about word processing for assessment and feedback purposes.

10. Teach students to construct complex sentences. Teach strategies for composing different types of sentences, so that students vary sentence structures within their writing. Also, teach students to combine two or more simple sentences into a single, more sophisticated sentence; this addresses the choppy structure some students tend to use when composing (e.g., *I saw the beautiful sky. The sky was blue and gray. The sky was full of clouds.*) Combining sentences allows students to create compositions of better quality by helping them identify and remediate run-on sentences as well. Teachers can point out sections of a student's writing where sentences can be combined. Alternatively, teachers can provide direct instruction in sentence combining to the whole class or to small groups of students who need more work on this skill. Direct instruction can involve examples with cues about which words to keep in the final, more complex sentence, and which connecting words (e.g., *and, but, or, so*) to use in the final sentence. Alternatively, teachers can use a more open approach in which students combine sentences as they choose, without teacher cues.

11. Teach students to generate and organize their ideas before they begin writing a first draft. Help students use think sheets, graphic organizers (e.g., webs, concept maps, outlines), and other visual representations for planning their writing. The type of visual organization used for planning will likely vary by writing assignment or writing genre

and may vary based on individual student needs and preferences. Also, teach students to research their topic by reading relevant texts to gather ideas for writing.

12. Use inquiry activities in which students examine concrete data. Students then use what they have learned from observing and analyzing the data to produce their written compositions. For example, students could examine unknown objects using a blindfold to write descriptions rich in sensory details from what they discover using senses other than sight.

13. Use the process writing approach. While there is no universally agreed upon definition of the process writing approach (Graham & Perin, 2007b), it is multifaceted and commonly includes having students (a) choose their own writing topics; (b) write for authentic purposes and audiences; (c) engage in cycles of planning, drafting, editing, revising, and publishing their writing; (d) receive ongoing constructive feedback through writing conferences with teachers and peers; and (e) learn writing skills through targeted mini-lessons from the teacher. Sometimes referred to as Writer's or Writing Workshop (Calkins, 1994), this approach to writing combines several of the effective elements of writing instruction (i.e., use of model texts, frequent writing feedback, teaching students to carry out the writing process, writing for meaningful purposes) discussed throughout this chapter. It allows students to have a personal investment and motivation to write with self-selected writing topics, while also providing a structure for completing the writing process and direct instruction in writing skills as needed. When implementing this recommendation, teachers should carefully plan the time (for writing and for instruction), as well as the space necessary for students to write and move around the classroom to conference and work with the teacher and/or peers.

14. Have students study models of good writing. Teach students to emulate features of the well-written texts they analyze, such as genre-specific elements and writing choices made by the author that influenced the reader. These can include models from literature, as described in recommendation 4 of this section. Models can also include teacher-created texts that include specific writing features, as well as peer examples of quality writing. Using peer models of good writing provides an additional way to praise student's writing efforts in a way that benefits the entire classroom of students.

15. Use writing as a tool for improving students' content-area learning. Teachers who implement this recommendation should use a combination of open-ended reflection writing (e.g., Describe how this new science concept relates to the concepts discussed in the last unit of study), as well as writing tasks with a more direct response format (e.g., Write a compare–contrast essay on how the two historical documents described the same event.) Allowing students to use writing to reflect on information in the content areas helps them integrate new information with what they already know, as well as construct new and deeper understandings of subject matter.

Research into Practice

Ms. Francis teaches 10th-grade English and history. In her English class, students compose both narrative and expository texts; most writing assignments last several weeks as students complete cycles of planning, drafting, editing, and revising their work. When new writing genres are introduced, Ms. Francis begins by reading her students examples of the genre in literature. Students consult these literature examples throughout the writing process, using them as model texts for their own writing. Also, Ms. Francis models aspects of the new genre by completing shared writing assignments with her students. As a class (or in small groups, depending on their needs), students identify elements that should be included in a new genre and think about how they will include them in their own writing. Ms. Francis often allows her students to plan collaboratively with their peers, receiving feedback on how they have organized their writing on a prewriting graphic organizer before they begin composing. Students are given some flexibility as they compose; those who appear to understand the new genre typically proceed on their own, while those who need additional support may participate in a few more group writing sessions before beginning to write their own texts.

Although most of the writing process is self-directed, Ms. Francis reviews her students' writing frequently. She arranges teacher and peer conferences for providing feedback to shape students' compositions. Additionally, Ms. Francis delivers targeted mini-lessons to address students' needs as they arise. For example, when Ms. Francis noticed that her several of her students tended to use short, choppy sentences, she provided this group of students a lesson on sentence combining. After the lesson, students created personal goals for combining a specific number of sentences within their own compositions. At subsequent conferences with these students, Ms. Francis checked in to see whether students had met their goals and successfully created more complex and sophisticated sentences in their drafts.

In history class, Ms. Francis often asks her students to demonstrate their understanding of an important historical event by reading several sources and writing an opinion piece from the perspective of a key individual involved in the event. Most of these assignments are completed in small groups, and students have the freedom to research additional sources to support the statements they make in their written texts. Students create multimodal texts, incorporating pictures, soundbytes, and their written opinion pieces, from the perspective of important historical figures. These assignments allow Ms. Francis's students to demonstrate their knowledge of history in ways that are more engaging and require more critical thinking than more traditional ways of assessing history knowledge (i.e., multiple-choice assessments, short-answer recall questions).

Writing Assessment

Using appropriate measures and means of writing assessment is critical for informing a teacher's writing instruction and monitoring students' progress throughout the writing process. Every written product a student produces does not require a formal assessment by the teacher, but teachers should have ongoing ways to evaluate their students' writing strengths and areas of need. We list five recommendations for guiding teachers' use of writing assessment below (Bromley, 2011; Graham, 2008; Graham et al., 2011; MacArthur, 2006):

1. Use a variety of writing assessments, both formative (i.e., ongoing, continuous) and summative (e.g., standardized writing assessments, end-of-year assessments). Writing assessments can include analytic or trait measures, in which teachers rate specific

attributes of writing (e.g., ideas, organization, style, voice), and holistic measures, in which teachers give a single rating to the entire written composition, typically using anchor papers or a rubric. Assessment can also include teacher feedback on specific writing elements (e.g., grammar, word choice), feedback on students' learning and use of a new writing strategy, or curriculum-based measurement (CBM), in which students write for a specified amount of time (usually 3–5 minutes), after which teachers score and graph their individual progress on aspects of writing such as total word written, words spelled correctly, and correct word sequences (see McMaster & Campbell, 2008, for further description of CBM scoring procedures). It is important for teachers to keep students' writing from all stages of the writing process in a portfolio; this provides writing pieces to assess and to demonstrate progress over time.

2. Align the mode of writing assessment with the mode of production with which students are most proficient. That is, if students are proficient at word processing, allow them to take writing tests using a word processor. If students are less experienced or proficient with word processing, allow them to use paper and pencil to complete writing tests.

3. Teach students to monitor and assess their own writing. When students learn to evaluate their own writing, they can better plan to meet writing goals and better decide when to seek help with a writing task that is challenging. Checklists and rubrics can help students decide whether they have included necessary elements in a written product or completed necessary steps in the writing process.

4. Teach students to assess and give feedback on peers' writing. For peer assessment to be meaningful, students should learn how to give constructive feedback on peers' written work, while remaining supportive and positive. Additionally, students need to learn how to listen and respond to peer feedback on their own writing. Many students require direct teacher modeling and guided practice in giving and receiving peer feedback before they can do so independently.

5. Use computer feedback and scoring systems when applicable. Automated essay scoring (AES) software can provide feedback to students throughout the writing process, as well as feedback on final drafts. Programs such as Summary Street (e.g., Franzke, Kintsch, Caccamise, Johnson, & Dooley, 2005), provide not only feedback on the content and organization of students' initial drafts but also scores for final written products (and other useful features; e.g., spell check and graphing of writing performance over time). AES programs also provide a time-saving tool for teachers, because scoring and providing individual feedback on student's writing is a time-consuming task.

Research into Practice

Mrs. Roberts, an eighth-grade English teacher, examines students' scores on the seventh-grade state writing assessment before the school year begins. She also administers a standardized writing assessment recommended to her by the school psychologist and reading specialist within the first month of school. Scores on both assessments give her a general idea of where each student is in relation to his or her peers, and how each student performs in terms of grade-level expectations.

Mrs. Roberts begins the school year with several short units focused on common writing genres (e.g., narrative, persuasive, informational). These units serve as review for the students in Mrs. Roberts's class and allow her to further assess students' writing strengths and areas of need. During these writing units, Mrs. Roberts also gets the opportunity to establish the writing routines and expectations for her classroom and to begin collecting students' writing samples for their writing portfolios. She models for students how to give feedback on each other's writing. She advises her students to use the rubrics she provides them for each genre to score their own writing, before giving it to a peer or the teacher for feedback. She asks peers to use the same rubrics when they are rating each other's written work. The rubrics contain sections for each of the essential components of a given genre, as well as sections for voice/tone, clarity, and mechanics/spelling/punctuation. Students learn to give two positive comments about a peer's writing for each piece of constructive feedback they offer.

WRITING AND NEW LITERACIES

Our list of research-based recommendations for teaching writing to adolescents would be incomplete without summarizing the impact of information and communication technologies (ICTs) on students' writing inside and outside of the classroom (Sweeny, 2010). There is less experimental research on students' use of new modes for composing (e.g., blogging, email, multimodal writing), or new literacies, compared to the amount of experimental research available on more traditional, print-based composing. However, we consulted handbooks, literature reviews, and descriptive studies to outline recommendations for teachers to incorporate multimodal composing and use of the Internet into their classroom writing instruction (Coiro, Knobel, Lankshear, & Leu, 2008; Lenhart, Arafeh, Smith, & Macgill, 2008; Rowsell & Lapp, 2011; Sweeny, 2010).

Although much of the writing adolescents use to communicate outside of school (e.g., Twitter posts, text messages) does not typically conform to the standard English conventions of writing that are assessed in school, we feel it is important to summarize what is known about new literacies and their influences on adolescent writing. This does not mean we expect the assimilation of new literacies into more traditional ways of teaching writing will be seamless. We also find it hard to imagine that standardized writing assessments will adopt technology-influenced writing practices (e.g., multimodal texts) as part of their response structures any time soon. Yet we hope a summary of the types of writing students find motivating or useful in their own lives will help teachers to incorporate these types of writing into the lessons they deliver in their classrooms. After our recommendations for multimodal composing and use of the Internet, we provide an example of how teachers might incorporate new literacies into their classroom writing practices and instruction.

Multimodal Composing

Because adolescents use technology for writing outside of school (e.g., emails, text messages, social media posts) more than ever, even if they do not consider these practices *real* writing (Lenhart et al., 2008), we suggest teachers capitalize on students' skills with digital modes of composing. One way of doing this is to incorporate multiple media for composing in the classroom. When appropriate, teachers can give students the option to produce multimodal texts that include written text, as well as pictures, drawings, hyperlinks, videos, and sound (Snyder & Bulfin, 2008; Sweeny, 2010). Allowing students to use a variety of digital practices for composing may prove more motivating and engaging, particularly for adolescents who are adept at using such practices in their out-of-school lives. As with any good instruction, we recommend teachers assess their students' knowledge and facility with the digital media they allow them to use, providing instruction in how to use digital modes for composing when necessary.

Use of the Internet

The Internet provides not only a valuable source for the research students may do to inform their writing but also an authentic audience for sharing students' writing. Allowing students to post their writing online, on a class webpage, blog, or Wiki, for example, allows them to reach more readers and to consider different audiences when they compose (Roswell & Lapp, 2011; Sweeny, 2010). Students are not limited to posting final drafts of their texts; instead, teachers can encourage their students to utilize the Internet to post ongoing writing drafts and to get feedback from others. Just as we advised teachers should instruct students how to give each other feedback on their writing, teachers should monitor the Internet audience for students' writing carefully to make sure the online feedback students receive from others is constructive and helpful.

Teachers can also use the Internet to help provide motivation and inspiration for their students to write. Students can communicate with other students or authors about their experiences during the writing process. Students can also research their favorite authors and discover how they approach the writing process (Sweeny, 2010). Often, authors have their own websites, where they share information about themselves, their writing, and their sources of writing inspiration. The Library of Congress also has a series of webcasts in which authors discuss their craft (*www.read.gov/webcasts*).

Research into Practice

In Mr. Barry's high school psychology course, comprising mostly juniors and seniors, he assigns students a narrative task in which they write about their childhoods. In previous years, students completed a five-page paper describing key aspects of their childhood experiences (e.g., family relationships, peer relationships, memorable events) and gave a 5-minute presentation to the class to summarize what they wrote.

This year, Mr. Barry decided to expand the list of acceptable media students could use to complete the project. He provided students a rubric with a description of each of the five areas the project must address. Mr. Barry instructed his students to choose any method (e.g., writing, multimodal presentation, music, poetry, art) they liked for completing the assignment as long as (1) they were skilled at using the method(s) they chose, (2) the method allowed them to meet all requirements listed on the rubric, and (3) they could summarize their project in a short presentation to the class. Because Mr. Barry wanted to use writing in his class, he also asked that each student use writing in some way in his or her project.

Mr. Barry encouraged students to begin brainstorming in small groups in class. Students came up with a variety of ways to address the assignment's requirements and bounced their ideas off of each other before beginning to work. Quickly, Mr. Barry learned how skilled most of his students were with digital practices.

Several students decided to use music to summarize their childhood experiences; the lyrics they planned to write would serve as the written portion of their projects. The students who were proficient with music recording and mixing equipment asked the school's music teacher for use of recording equipment and musical mixing software to record their songs. One student decided to make a painting, which included words and phrases, as well as more abstract images. She wrote a description of the elements of her artwork to satisfy the written component of the project.

A large portion of the class decided to complete a traditional essay for the assignment, although many planned to complement their written essays with photographs from childhood events. These photographs would also serve as inspiration for what to include in their essays. The remaining five students chose multimodal compositions for their medium. In the end, these compositions resembled the written essays of the previously described group in many ways. However, embedded within their essays about childhood, students who used multimodal media added hyperlinks to websites describing the cities in which they were born or places where they had memorable childhood experiences. These students also embedded images and photographs throughout their written texts to better illustrate the aspects of their childhoods they wanted to describe to their audience. Several students included sound clips to enhance their writing or recorded their own voices to narrate a particular event or experience from childhood. One student, who was skilled with video editing programs, incorporated short videos his parents had recorded during his childhood to accompany the events he described in his essay.

CONCLUSIONS AND PRACTICAL IMPLICATIONS

The 25 research-based recommendations, coupled with suggestions for incorporating new literacies into classroom writing instruction, provide teachers of students in grades 4–12 an instructional menu of sorts from which to choose items that best suit their instructional preferences and, more importantly, items that best suit their students' needs. Although there is some research supporting effective combinations of the individual writing practices described in this chapter (e.g., MacArthur, Graham, Schwartz, & Schafer, 1995), an optimal combination of effective writing practices will vary for different teachers and for different students. Also, this effective combination of practices will likely change throughout the school year as students' writing skills develop.

We encourage teachers to closely evaluate the effectiveness of the research-based writing practices they implement in their classrooms, monitoring their impact on each student's writing skills and progress. If an effective writing practice is not working, then a teacher should try another effective practice; if an effective writing practice is working, then a teacher should continue to use it as long as it makes sense for his or her students within the context of the writing skills or genres they are learning. With frequent assessment of students' learning of writing skills and genres, teachers can adjust their use of effective writing practices accordingly.

Last, because we know adolescents who do not learn to write well face a host of difficulties, both in and out of school, we remind teachers of the importance of sustained writing instruction throughout the adolescent years. Writing can no longer take a backseat to other subjects. Students need daily opportunities to write for a variety of reasons (across the disciplines), with guidance and support from their teachers, until they can apply new writing skills independently. We believe teachers who begin by conveying enthusiasm for writing and creating a positive, supportive, encouraging classroom atmosphere for writing (see section entitled "The Writing Teacher and Classroom") will be most successful at implementing the other research-based recommendations for writing instruction and assessment described in this chapter. With daily practice, effective instruction, and a supportive classroom environment, we also believe well-prepared writing teachers can change the trajectories of many adolescents who do not have the writing skills necessary for school and postsecondary success. It is a large task, but we hope this chapter will be a good first step for teachers of adolescents across the disciplines.

REFERENCES

Bangert-Drowns, R. L., Hurley, M. M., & Wilkinson, B. (2004). The effects of school-based writing-to-learn interventions on academic achievement: A meta-analysis. *Review of Educational Research, 74*(1), 29–58.

Bromley, K. (2011). Best practices in teaching writing. In L. M. Morrow & L. B. Gambrel (Eds.), *Best practices in literacy instruction, fourth edition* (pp. 295–318). New York: Guilford Press.

Calkins, L. M. (1994). *The art of teaching writing.* Portsmouth, NH: Heinemann.

Coiro, J., Knobel, M., Lankshear, C., & Leu, D. J. (2008). *Handbook of new literacies.* Mahwah, NJ: Erlbaum.

Emig, J. (1977). Writing as a mode of learning. *College Composition and Communication, 28*, 122–128.

Flower, L., & Hayes, J. R. (1981). A cognitive process theory of writing. *College Composition and Communication, 32*(4), 365–387.

Franzke, M., Kintch, E., Caccamise, D., Johnson, N., & Dooley, S. (2005). Summary Street®: Computer support for comprehension and writing. *Journal of Educational Computing Research, 33*, 53–80.

Gilbert, J., & Graham, S. (2010). Teaching writing to elementary students in grades 4–6: A national survey. *Elementary School Journal, 110*(4), 494–518.

Gillespie, A., Graham, S., Kiuhara, S., & Hebert, M. (2014). High school teachers' use of writing to support students' learning: A national survey. *Reading and Writing, 27*(6), 1043–1072.

Graham, S. (2006). Writing. In P. Alexander & P. Winne (Eds.), *Handbook of educational psychology* (pp. 457–478). Mahwah, NJ: Erlbaum.

Graham, S. (2008). Effective writing instruction for all students. Retrieved from *www.renaissance.com/resources/research*.

Graham, S., Capizzi, A., Harris, K. R., Hebert, M., & Morphy, P. (2014). Teaching writing to middle school students: A national survey. *Reading and Writing, 27*, 1015–1042.

Graham, S., Harris, K., & Hebert, M. A. (2011). *Informing writing: The benefits of formative assessment* (A Carnegie Corporation Time to Act Report). Washington, DC: Alliance for Excellent Education.

Graham, S., & Hebert, M. A. (2010). *Writing to read: Evidence for how writing can improve reading* (A Carnegie Time to Act Report). Washington, DC: Alliance for Excellent Education.

Graham, S., & Perin, D. (2007a). *Writing next: Effective strategies to improve writing of adolescents in middle and high schools* (A Report to the Carnegie Corporation of New York). Washington, DC: Alliance for Excellent Education.

Graham, S., & Perin, D. (2007b). What we know, what we still need to know: Teaching adolescents to write. *Scientific Studies in Reading, 11*, 313–336.

Graham, S., & Sandmel, K. (2011). The process writing approach: A meta-analysis. *Journal of Educational Research, 104,* 396–407.

Harris, K. R., Graham, S., Mason, L. H., & Friedlander, B. (2008). *Powerful writing strategies for all students.* Baltimore: Brookes.

Hayes, J. R. (1996). A new framework for understanding cognition and affect in writing. In C. M. Levy & S. Ransdell (Eds.), *The science of writing: Theories, methods, individual differences, and applications* (pp. 1–27). Mahwah, NJ: Erlbaum.

Kiuhara, S. A., Graham, S., & Hawken, L. S. (2009). Teaching writing to high school students: A national survey. *Journal of Educational Psychology, 101*(1), 136–160.

Lenhart, A., Arafeh, S., Smith, A., & Macgill, A. R. (2008). Writing, technology and teens. Retrieved from *www.pewinternet.org/2008/04/24/writing-technology-and-teens*.

MacArthur, C. A. (2006). The effects of new technologies on writing and writing processes. In C. A. MacArthur, S. Graham, & J. Fitzgerald (Eds.), *Handbook of writing research* (pp. 248–262). New York: Guilford Press.

MacArthur, C. A., Graham, S., Schwartz, S. S., & Schafer, W. D. (1995). Evaluation of a writing instruction model that integrated a process approach, strategy instruction, and word processing. *Learning Disability Quarterly, 18*(4), 278–291.

McMaster, K. L., & Campbell, H. (2008). New and existing curriculum-based writing measures: Technical features within and across grades. *School Psychology Review, 37*(4), 550–566.

National Commission on Writing. (2004). Writing: A ticket to work or a ticket out. Retrieved from *www.collegeboard.com*.

National Governors Association Center for Best Practices & Council of Chief State School Officers (NGA & CCSSO). (2010). *Common Core State Standards for English language arts and literacy in history/social studies, science, and technical subjects.* Washington, DC: Authors. Retrieved from *www.corestandards.org/assets/ccssi_ela%20standards.pdf*.

Rogers, L. A., & Graham, S. (2008). A meta-analysis of single subject design writing intervention research. *Journal of Educational Psychology, 100*(4), 879–906.

Rowsell, J., & Lapp, D. (2011). New literacies in literacy instruction. In L. M. Morrow & L. B. Gambrell (Eds.), *Best practices in literacy instruction, fourth edition* (pp. 395–411). New York: Guilford Press.

Russell, D. R. (1997). Rethinking genre in school and society: An activity theory analysis. *Written Communication, 14,* 504–554.

Sedita, J. (2013). Learning to write and writing to learn. In M. C. Hougen (Ed.), *Fundamentals of literacy instruction and assessment: 6–12* (pp. 97–114). Baltimore: Brookes.

Snyder, I., & Bulfin, S. (2008). Using new media in the secondary English classroom. In J. Coiro, M. Knobel, C. Lankshear, & D. Leu (Eds.), *Handbook of new literacies* (pp. 805–837). Mahwah, NJ: Erlbaum.

Sweeny, S. M. (2010). Writing for the instant messaging and text messaging generation: Using new literacies to support writing instruction. *Journal of Adolescent and Adult Literacy, 54*(2), 121–130.

Zimmerman, B., & Risemberg, R. (1997). Becoming a self-regulated writer: A social cognitive perspective. *Contemporary Educational Psychology, 22,* 73–101.

CHAPTER 26

A Close Reading of Close Reading
What Does the Research Tell Us about How to Promote the Thoughtful Interrogation of Text?

AMY KOEHLER CATTERSON and P. DAVID PEARSON

> So what's the deal with close reading anyway? Is it even anything new?
> —A colleague, commenting on this chapter's topic

The practice of close reading has experienced a recent "revival" in adolescent literacy instruction, due to its appearance in the Common Core State Standards for English Language Arts and Literacy in History/Social Studies, Science, and Technical Subjects (CCSS; National Governors Association for Best Practices & Council of Chief State School Officers [NGA & CCSSO], 2010) and the Revised Publishers' Criteria for the Standards (RPC; Coleman & Pimentel, 2012), an influential curriculum development guide. The first anchor standard for reading asks students to "read closely to determine what the text says explicitly and to make logical inferences from it; cite specific textual evidence when writing or speaking to support conclusions drawn from the text" (NGA & CCSSO, 2010, p. 10). *Close reading,* or a synonym of close reading (e.g., careful examination), appears more than 50 times in the RPC.

Upon reading the CCSS and RPC, and considering the broad implications of these documents for classrooms across the United States, many scholars and educators are asking the question our colleague poses in the opening epigraph: What's the deal with close reading? Is it a brand new practice, is it the resurrected ghost of a bygone practice from midcentury New Criticism, or is it a practice that has never really disappeared from classrooms? And how will Common Core era close reading affect adolescent literacy instruction?

Though school districts across the country are now enacting the RPC's vision of close reading instruction, many scholars and practitioners are questioning the theory and research underlying this vision (Applebee, 2013; Pearson, 2013; Smith, Appleman, & Wilhelm, 2014; Snow & O'Connor, 2013). We worry, along with others (e.g., Beers, 2013; Compton-Lilly, 2013), that in an attempt to revive critical engagement with texts in classrooms, the authors of the RPC have swung the pendulum too far away from considerations of the reader's background knowledge and culture, and have marginalized the role of the sociocultural contexts in which texts are written and read. Curriculum developers, school leaders, and instructors who follow the RPC's version of close reading may, we fear, devalue the background knowledge and cultural ways of making meaning that diverse students bring into the classroom and therefore limit what thoughtful textual interrogation can accomplish in adolescents' lives.

Against this backdrop we offer our own vision of adolescent close reading instruction, one that more fully accounts for interactions among the reader, text, activity, and sociocultural context during the reading process (Snow, 2002). To develop this vision, we have traced the history of close reading through key theories taken up by secondary educators in the past 75 years. We have also reviewed empirical work on close reading written from 2000–2015, focusing on studies of, examples of, or critical perspectives on close reading instruction in middle and high school classrooms. In keeping with the theme of this handbook, we have also sought out practice-based methods of adolescent close reading instruction that have been developed by educators over the past 15 years. Our vision of adolescent close reading instruction is also informed by our perspectives as scholars and former teachers and our belief that there is never just one monolithic best "reading." Instead, readers should engage in multiple reading practices and a range of culturally appropriate ways of understanding (Gee, 2007; Heath, 1983; Street, 2003; New London Group, 2000). We hold that prior knowledge and social experiences allow some readers to access and interpret texts within these multiple literacies more competently than others (Bransford & Johnson, 1973; Brown, Collins, & Duguid, 1989; Pearson, Hansen, & Gordon, 1979) and that some reading practices are more valued than others by society (Smagorinsky, 2001).

Keeping our perspectives on language and literacy in balance with the research literature, we propose five principles for adolescent close reading instruction:

1. *Background knowledge.* Learn about students' cultural backgrounds, areas of expertise, and existing literacy practices, and adjust close reading instruction to leverage and build students' content and discursive knowledge.
2. *Authentic reading and writing.* Present students with authentic opportunities to use close reading strategies that mirror the types of reading that happen in the real world, and to draw from these close readings to compose authentic texts.
3. *Metadiscursive awareness.* Promote students' metadiscursive awareness by helping them understand the purposes and structures of texts in different disciplines and genres, and which close reading strategies work for these purposes and structures.
4. *Critical literacy.* Involve students as critics of themselves, texts, and the world as they read closely.
5. *Dialogically organized discussion.* Guide students to ask and answer authentic questions while reading texts closely, and engage them in rich and rigorous conversations about their questions and interpretations.

In the coming pages, we contrast what we are calling a Common Core close reading paradigm with our vision of a 21st-century close reading paradigm for adolescent classrooms. Then, we turn to our five principles of adolescent close reading instruction. In our discussion of each principle, we offer a definition, explain its importance to adolescent literacy, summarize its research base, and describe examples of close reading instructional practices from the research literature that exemplify the principle. For each principle we attend to close reading within both new and digital literacies (Cope & Kalantzis, 2000; Gee, 2010; Knobel & Lankshear, 2014; Kress, 2003; Leu, Kinzer, Coiro, Castek, & Henry, 2013; Mills, 2010) and traditional and print-based literacies, as we argue that close reading instruction must adapt to the "pluralized, hybridized, intertextual, immediate, spontaneous, abbreviated, informal, collaborative, productive, interactive, hyperlinked, dialogic (between author and reader), and linguistically diverse" digital new literacies (Mills, 2010, p. 255), as well as traditional literacies that have been with us for millennia. Finally, given that we have found very few empirical tests of particular approaches to adolescent close reading instruction, we conclude with directions for future research.

A VERSION OF THE OLD, A VISION FOR THE NEW: COMPARING COMMON CORE CLOSE READING WITH A 21ST-CENTURY ADOLESCENT CLOSE READING PARADIGM

Searching for Common Ground: What All Close Reading Shares

Since the premise of this chapter assumes that Common Core "close reading" is different from 21st-century "close reading," here we strive for a simple, ecumenical definition of close reading that can offer common ground for discussing alternative perspectives. In the introduction of Lentricchia and DuBois's (2003) compilation of close reading analyses, DuBois crafts a "common sense" definition of close reading that will serve this purpose well: "Reading with special attention" to a text (p. 2). A reader conducting *any type* of close reading will scrutinize a text; this is the common element across close reading paradigms. Close reading paradigms, however, may differ along many other dimensions. For example, educators may differ in their goals for close reading, ideas about what constitutes a text worthy of close reading, and assumptions about where meaning resides. These beliefs may lead to differences in instructional practice, such as the types of texts chosen, types of questions posed to students, participation frameworks designed, and the overarching curriculum in which close reading is embedded. We argue that the 21st-century close reading paradigm we have imagined differs along these dimensions from the Common Core close reading paradigm in ways that more accurately reflect what we know about the construction of meaning from texts, the needs of a diverse adolescent population, and the demands of literacy in the 21st century.

A Version of the Old: A Common Core Close Reading Paradigm

From our vantage point, the Common Core close reading paradigm, as presented by the CCSS and RPC, resembles a New Critical close reading paradigm that has endured as the dominant mode of textual analysis in English classrooms for much of the 20th century.

The phrase *close reading* originated with the New Criticism, a literary school most active from the 1930s through the 1970s (Gallop, 2007). Though the New Critics did not share a common set of goals for close reading, assumptions about where meaning resides, or notions about what constitutes a text worthy of close reading, they were united in the belief that the text should serve as a touchstone for rigorous interpretive work (Ransom, 1937). Robert Penn Warren and Cleanth Brooks's New Critical close reading paradigm was most influential in secondary classrooms, as their book, *Understanding Poetry* (Brooks & Warren, 1938) was widely used for over 5 decades, with new editions released in 1950, 1960, 1976, and 1978 (Golding, 1995). Within Brooks and Warren's paradigm, close readings could best be accomplished by holding reader bias and consideration of the text's historical context at arm's length: Only then could one appreciate the meaning inherent in the text. As Brooks (1979) put it, "To use a metaphor drawn from the law courts, 'evidence outside the poem' is always secondhand (or even hearsay) evidence as compared with the evidence presented by the text itself" (p. 600).

While populist approaches to textual analysis, such as reader response or critical literacy paradigms, replaced New Critical formalist approaches in research journals by the 1980s, secondary classrooms maintained the status quo of Brooks and Warren-esque close reading (Applebee, 1993; Burroughs & Smagorinsky, 2009; Dressman & Faust, 2014), perhaps because this paradigm was ensconced in advanced placement (AP) English assessment, popular pedagogical resources such as Adler and Doren's (1972) *How to Read a Book,* and instructional methods such as the Junior Great Books program and Paideia Seminars. Since close reading in the New Critical tradition never really gave way to reader response or critical literacy approaches to textual interpretation, many teachers in U.S. classrooms will recognize the Common Core close reading paradigm as reinforcing practices that are all too familiar.

If anything, the Common Core close reading paradigm may be more text-centric than New Criticism. The Common Core close reading paradigm situates meaning entirely within the text, without acknowledging the role of the reader or sociocultural context in interpretation. The authors of the RPC assert that meaning "lies within the four corners of the text" (Coleman & Pimentel, 2012, p. 4), and can therefore be extracted through a process of answering "text-dependent" close reading questions that "do not require information or evidence from outside the text or texts" (p. 6). Such language reveals Coleman and Pimentel's (we believe, problematic) assumption that meaning lies in wait like an archeological artifact to be excavated and placed in a reader's mind, as long as he or she had the appropriate tools to dig it out. We like better Louise Rosenblatt's (1978) metaphor of meaning-as-*poem,* crafted anew each time a reader encounters a text in a specific social, cultural, and historical moment.

The Common Core close reading paradigm is also "old" in its approach to what constitutes a worthy text for close reading. Curriculum designers are asked to provide "short, challenging" texts, as well as "novels, play, and other extended full-length readings," which should all be "worth reading closely and exhibit exceptional craft and thought or provide useful information" (Coleman & Pimentel, 2012, pp. 3–4). We agree with Rabinowitz (1992) that such a limited vision of texts may exclude the analysis of culturally or historically important texts and "privilege figurative writing over the realistic portrayal of material social conditions, deep meaning over surface meaning, form over content, the elite over the popular, and indirect expression over direct" (p. 233). Furthermore, both the CCSS and the RPC demand the close reading of *print* text only (Chandler-Olcott,

2013; Drew, 2012). Multimodal and digital texts are excluded from the reading standards, and the RPC warns that nonprint multimedia such as videos should "[engage] students in absorbing or expressing details of the [print] text rather than becoming a distraction or replacement for engaging with the [print] text" (Coleman & Pimentel, 2012, p. 13).

Finally, the Common Core close reading paradigm is marked by limited goals for close reading: "The criteria make plain that developing students' prowess at drawing knowledge from the text itself is the point of reading; reading well means gaining the maximum insight or knowledge possible from each source" (Coleman & Pimentel, 2012, p. 1). The RPC's emphasis on gaining knowledge from text excludes a wide range of desirable goals for adolescent close reading, such as social action, identity construction, or even pure enjoyment.

We offer an alternative vision of adolescent close reading instruction for the 21st century, one that assumes and asserts that (1) meaning is constructed at the intersection of a unique reader, text, and activity within sociocultural contexts; (2) the term "text" entails print and digital, short and long, carefully crafted and hastily jotted, official and popular; and (3) close reading should build identity, equity, and action, as well as knowledge.

A Vision for Now: A 21st-Century Close Reading Paradigm for Adolescent Classrooms

Our vision of how meaning is made during adolescent close reading draws from the RAND Research Study Group (RRSG), whose members imagine reading as a simultaneous interaction among text, reader, activity, and the encompassing sociocultural context (Snow, 2002, p. 13; Figure 26.1).

As the heuristic suggests, meaning making during close reading is much more complicated than reader-meets-text, reader-extracts-meaning. Instead, textual interpretation is a bit different for every reader, depending on his or her knowledge and motivation to read, the features of the text he or she encounters, and the activity in which reading occurs. Furthermore, the macrocultures of society and the microculture of the classroom

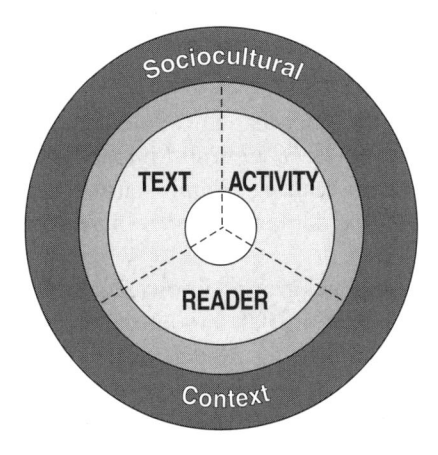

FIGURE 26.1. A heuristic for thinking about reading comprehension. From Snow (2002). Copyright 2002 by RAND. Reprinted by permission.

sanction what readings are acceptable, and the sociocultural backgrounds of the reader and text further shape interpretations (Smagorinsky, 2001). Thus, the power structures, discourses, and cultures in society surround and infuse all other components in the heuristic.

A 21st-century close reading paradigm must also expand the category of texts that are worthy of close reading. It is our belief that close reading instruction that does not incorporate networked digital technology and texts is not 21st-century close reading instruction, since digital literacies and a participatory ethos (Knobel & Lankshear, 2014) have influenced how adolescents read at home (Ito et al., 2010) and how they will someday have to read in college and in careers (Warschauer & Matuchniak, 2010). We also consider popular texts (Alvermann, 2008) and texts from adolescents' peer and home cultures (Lee, 2001) as fair game for close reading instruction.

Our goals for adolescent close reading instruction also move beyond the knowledge-building demanded by the Common Core close reading paradigm. We believe that teachers should aim to engage adolescents' interest in reading and composing (Alvermann, 2002; Guthrie, Klauda, & Ho, 2013), for without engagement, there is no reading, close, distant, or otherwise. We also believe that teachers should guide students to read and write a wide array of texts in different disciplines and genres (Adolescent Literacy Committees and the Adolescent Literacy Task Force of the International Reading Association, 2012), prepare them to be active citizens in a culturally diverse global world (Gutiérrez, 2008; New London Group, 2000), and to help them analyze, critique, and change the cultural ideologies reflected in texts (Freebody & Luke, 1990).

We now turn to our five principles for 21st-century adolescent close reading instruction as a way of illustrating this paradigm at a finer grain of detail for practitioners and researchers alike.

PRINCIPLES OF 21ST-CENTURY ADOLESCENT CLOSE READING INSTRUCTION

Background Knowledge

Learn about students' cultural backgrounds, areas of expertise, and existing literacy practices, and adjust close reading instruction to leverage and build students' content and discursive knowledge.

Researchers converge on the finding that an adolescent reader's content and discursive knowledge (what we refer to as *background knowledge*) has a significant effect on his or her reading practices and reading comprehension (Anderson & Pearson, 1984; Kintsch, 1998; Langer, 1984), particularly as texts increase in complexity (Fisher, Frey, & Lapp, 2012).

The mechanism underlying background knowledge's importance to readers is theorized by the construction–integration (CI) model of reading comprehension (Kintsch, 1988) that arose from the schema theory models of the 1970s and 1980s (Anderson & Pearson, 1984). This theory suggests that in order for readers to *learn* from a text, they must create what Kintsch (1988) terms a *situation model,* or a mental representation of the text that is linked to long-term memory. Prior knowledge is crucial in this phase of the process, since they must have a schema on which to "hang" the ideas they encounter.

Sociocultural researchers tie this background knowledge explicitly to culture; recently, for example, Juzwik (2014) has argued that students raised in Biblical evangelical religious traditions may be better positioned than many of their peers to undertake the type of close reading outlined in the CCSS and RPC. Thus, culture and embodied experience are as much a part of background knowledge as is semantic knowledge.

Implications for Close Reading Instruction

Because of the importance of background knowledge to meaning construction, teachers should learn what content and discourses students already know, and look for opportunities to add to this knowledge as students read with special attention to text. Cultural modeling approaches to close reading instruction (Lee, 2001; Orellana & Reynolds, 2008) are one way to address the gaps between students' existing linguistic and literacy practices and those expected in school settings. Carol Lee (2001), for example, drew on her African American high school English students' knowledge of language play in African American English to build close reading strategies for poetry. Teachers following Lee's approach might learn all they can about their students' cultural and linguistic backgrounds, use discourses from these backgrounds as a launching point for close reading strategy building, and think carefully about how to organize texts such that students are gradually improving their knowledge over the course of the year.

Teachers might also draw on digital technology to scaffold adolescents' background knowledge in the form of multimedia vocabulary hyperlinks, graphics illustrating word meanings, and supplemental multimedia supports such as maps, timelines, and videos (Dalton & Proctor, 2007). Over the course of a curricular unit, teachers might plan which digital technology will build knowledge, practice close textual analysis of digital texts, and gradually release responsibility to students for finding and analyzing new knowledge sources (Boche & Henning, 2015). Teachers may also learn about students' existing digital literacies, and leverage them to teach close reading skills and content, for example, "using Minecraft to design the town of Maycomb may promote [a student's] close reading of *To Kill a Mockingbird*" (Curwood & Fink, 2013, p. 426).

Authentic Reading and Writing

Present students with authentic opportunities to use close reading strategies that mirror the types of reading that happens in the real world, and to draw from these close readings to compose authentic texts.

Too often, when we ask high school students to conduct close readings in English classrooms, we are leading them to craft what Burroughs and Smagorinsky (2009) term *codified discourses,* or those that are valued only in school settings. For adolescent close reading instruction to be authentic, it would have to take into account the "text uses" (Luke & Freebody, 1999) that students will encounter in college, careers, and life, while providing them the instructional support they need along the way.

We borrow Purcell-Gates, Duke, and Martineau's (2007) definition of *authentic literacies*: "(a) reading and writing of textual types, or genres, that occur *outside* of a learning-to-read-and-write context and purpose, and (b) reading and writing those texts for the purposes for which they are read or written outside of a learning-to-read-and-write context and purpose" (p. 14). Theories of situated cognition (Brown et al., 1989), the sociocultural learning of higher mental functions (Vygotsky, 1978), and legitimate peripheral participation (Lave & Wenger, 1991) all suggest that in order to learn in a given domain, learners need to be immersed in the authentic experience of that domain's discourses and culture while guided by more expert others. The theoretical basis for authentic literacy instruction is strong, and the few studies that test the effects of authentic texts and tasks on student outcomes show promise for authentic close reading instruction (see Purcell-Gates, Degener, Jacobson, & Soler, 2002; Purcell-Gates et al., 2007).

Implications for Close Reading Instruction

Andrew Turchon, a middle school social studies teacher, exemplifies an authentic approach to close reading instruction in his unit on map literacy (Dakin, Eatough, & Turchon, 2011). Turchon asked his "student geographers" to read maps closely to discover their purpose: inform, persuade, explain, or compare and contrast. Students drew on their knowledge of maps to provide text-based evidence for their answers—phrases, symbols, or images from the map. Teachers following Turchon's example might think about the reading practices used by experts in the field of study, choose authentic texts that would be read in that community, and lead students through close reading activities designed to make them more aware of the texts' features and purpose.

Digital literacies may offer multiple pathways for students to engage in authentic reading of texts of their own choosing, thus increasing engagement (Alvermann, 2008; Neugebauer, 2013). We can imagine a close reading lesson at the high school level, in which teachers ask students to choose a digital game they play outside of school or a social media platform they frequent, then guide them to develop close reading strategies that would foster new interpretations of these media.

Teachers can also learn much from the authentic close reading that occurs in digital forums, which are heavily intertwined with writing, composing, and creativity. In fan forums, for example, fans share and debate their close readings of television, movies, and books with other fans (Jenkins, 2013). Instruction modeled after online participatory culture might use close reading as an entrée into creative, transformative writing. For instance, teachers testing a Teachers' Strategy Guide for New Media Literacies led students to perform close readings of *Moby Dick* across multiple platforms (e.g., film, song, book), then craft comic strips, plays, music videos, and fanfiction in response (Kelley, Jenkins, Clinton, & McWilliams, 2013).

Metadiscursive Awareness

Promote students' metadiscursive awareness by helping them understand the purposes and structures of texts in different disciplines and genres, and which close reading strategies work for these purposes and structures.

We define *metadiscursive awareness* as knowledge about texts and reading practices (Schoenbach, Greenleaf, & Murphy, 2012). More specifically, the purpose of metadiscursive awareness "should be to identify and explain differences between texts and relate these to the contexts of culture and situation in which they seem to work" (New London Group, 2000, p. 14). In everyday terms, metadiscursive awareness might be construed as how, when, where, and why a learner adapts reading and writing practices to a particular context, such as a discipline (biology vs. literature), a kind of text frame (description vs. argument), or a task (summary vs. critique). As adolescents gain this metadiscursive awareness, it should inform the lenses, purposes, and strategies they choose when closely reading texts in different genres and disciplines. Due to shifts in the CCSS and research that has revealed disciplinary differences in expert reading approaches (Shanahan, Shanahan, & Misischia, 2011), many researchers have asserted that adolescents should be taught to read closely using discipline-specific lenses (e.g., Lee, 2014; Moje, 2008; Shanahan, 2012). In addition to performing these discipline-specific close readings, we want students to be able to approach multimodal and hybrid text genres with a metadiscursive toolkit at their disposal.

One empirical body of work that focuses on developing metadiscursive awareness during adolescent close reading instruction comes from a systemic functional linguistics approach (Halliday, 1978). Working in this tradition, Schleppegrell, Greer, and Taylor (2008) have created and tested close reading instruction that helps students develop a metalanguage for examining the language patterns in history texts. Teachers lead students through a series of questions that help them recognize and interpret what the authors term "reference devices": pronouns, demonstratives, synonyms, verbs, nouns, conjunctions and other features of language. Drawing from these reference devices, students and teachers discuss common processes captured by historical texts (e.g., cause–effect), historical participants and their agendas, and the circumstances in which historical events occur. Above all, students develop a metalanguage for closely reading, discussing, and learning from historical texts. Students whose teachers participated in a summer institute to learn this close reading instructional strategy significantly outperformed comparison group students in all facets of a historical essay aligned with the California State Standards.

Implications for Close Reading Instruction

Functional language analysis presents one instructional model for close reading instruction; multiliteracies pedagogy (Cope & Kalantzis, 2000; New London Group, 2000) provides another. Whereas functional language analysis zeroes in on the implication of grammatical features of text for interpretation, multiliteracies pedagogy seeks to foster a metalanguage about different modes (e.g., visual, linguistic, audio, spatial, gestural). This metalanguage includes understandings of features of genre, such as common patterns of textual organization, as well as understandings of how the verbal, visual, and audial contribute meaning to texts. Cope and Kalantzis (2000) detail how a teacher at William Ross High School organized metadiscursive close reading instruction within a multiliteracies pedagogy using a music video. The teacher first asked students to analyze the song's written lyrics, then she asked what the music, colors, imagery, and editing add to the meaning of the music video. As this example illustrates, multiliteracies pedagogy can develop students' metadiscursive awareness around multimodal text genres, as well as traditional print literacies.

Digital texts are not often bounded and linear; rather, they are interwoven, changeable, and multilinear (Looy & Baetens, 2003). A student may begin to read a webpage about graffiti laws in his or her city and navigate by the end of the session to the Instagram

#graffiti hashtag. Close reading digital texts, then, takes metadiscursive knowledge about how genre features, intertextuality, and multimodality work together to make meaning. Internet reciprocal teaching, in which students teach their classmates about digital text features and reading strategies, may also hold promise as a 21st-century close reading approach (Leu et al., 2013).

Critical Literacy

Involve students as critics of themselves, texts, and the world as they read closely.

Allan Luke (2012) defines *critical literacy* as "use of the technologies of print and other media of communication to analyze, critique and transform the norms, rule systems and practices governing the social fields of everyday life" (p. 5). Teachers designing close reading instruction through a critical literacy lens would demonstrate to their students that texts represent particular points of view and silence others, and that texts can be used as jumping off points for social action (Luke & Freebody, 1999). We believe, with Franzak (2006), that "critical pedagogy that incorporates effective literacy instruction seems to hold the most potential for both improving reading achievement and working toward equitable social arrangements" (p. 221).

One widely cited theoretical framework in the research literature is Hillary Janks's (2000) four dimensions of critical literacy in education: domination, access, diversity, and design. Close reading pedagogy from a domination perspective might focus on how symbolic forms of representation (written language, visuals, sound) reproduce existing power structures. Close reading pedagogy from an access perspective might focus on critiquing and learning dominant genres. Close reading pedagogy from a diversity perspective may call for a wide range of texts to be read and for student's cultural reading practices to be valued. And close reading pedagogy from a design perspective may emphasize that close reading should be but one step on the path to crafting new narratives that effect social change.

In a review of critical literacy interventions at the secondary level, Behrman (2006) claims that while there are many different pedagogical approaches represented in the literature, there are common threads running through studies. Students in critical literacy interventions might read multiple texts, with the goal of highlighting key differences in author perspectives; read from a resistant perspective, with the goal of unmasking power structures represented by texts; produce countertexts, with the goal of lending legitimacy to marginalized voices; conduct student-choice research projects, with the goal of learning about social forces; and take social action, with the goal of engaging literacy for change.

Implications for Close Reading Instruction

We think that instructional frameworks such as Borsheim-Black, Macaluso, and Petrone's (2014) critical literature pedagogy (CLP) hold promise for promoting close reading from a critical literacy standpoint. Teachers using the CLP would lead students through close readings *with* and *against* the text. Close reading *with* a text "includes familiar approaches of comprehending storylines, analyzing literary devices, making personal connections, understanding historical contexts, and developing thematic interpretations" while close reading *against* a text "examine[s] how it is embedded and shaped by ideologies" (Borsheim-Black et al., 2014, p. 124). The authors of the CLP suggest that teachers lead students through interrogating a wide variety of texts, canonical and popular, along five dimensions: canonicity, contexts, literary elements, reader, and assessments. Behrman (2006) argues that close reading for critical literacy is also possible in the content areas. Content-area teachers seeking to promote critical literacy might ask questions such as "How do[es] specific text content, [modes of inquiry, and text genre] gain acceptance and prominence? What counts as 'true' within the discipline, and who makes that determination? Why?" (p. 496).

The proliferation of texts, digital platforms, and tools on the Internet increases the need for critical literacy in close reading instruction (Leu et al., 2013). In 2010, Google CEO Eric Schmidt observed that every 2 days, Internet users create more data than humans created from the dawn of man through 2003 (Siegler, 2010). Partially because the sheer quantity of information on the Internet is staggering, it is necessary to ensure that students develop the tools to recognize that Internet texts and platforms, as literacy objects, are created by authors with agendas (Brandt & Clinton, 2002). Facebook, for example, allows certain types of interaction (e.g., the "like" button), while discouraging others (e.g., making one's profile invisible to advertisers is arduous). This commercial side of the Internet, coupled with the reality that anyone can publish anything, raises the stakes for solid critical reading pedagogy in modern classrooms. Judging the credibility of sources, the validity of arguments, and the subtexts encoded in surface texts are necessary in any close reading context, but especially so in this new digital world of texts.

Though the Digital Age has increased the need for critical literacy in close reading instruction, it has also increased the opportunities for students to engage in close reading. Students can, for example, now analyze multiple versions of texts online (Webb, 2007), remix texts to create alternative narratives (Gainer & Lapp, 2010), and distribute these counternarratives to authentic audiences to promote social change (Avila & Moore, 2012).

Dialogically Organized Discussion

Guide students to ask and answer authentic questions while reading texts closely, and engage them in rich and rigorous conversations about their questions and interpretations.

Dialogue is a medium through which classroom communities can reach collective interpretations of a text (Wells, 2002), students can articulate their thoughts and then reach for those thoughts as new interpretive tools (Smagorinsky, 2001), or students can confront alternative perspectives, therefore moving toward new patterns of reading activity (Engeström, 2015) or belief systems (Bakhtin, 1986). When students are asked to sustain "special attention to a text," often over repeated readings, we think dialogue between teachers and students can drive richer and more nuanced interpretations.

All classroom dialogue is not equal in its effects on student learning, however. In a large-scale study, Nystrand (1997) found that dialogue in the vast majority of studied classrooms was monologically organized, in which the teacher held the discussion floor (and the topic of discussion) far more than did students and adhered to IRE (initiation–response–evaluation) discourse patterns (Cazden, 2001). But in the classrooms in which teachers posed more authentic questions and elaborated on student ideas, students improved their analytic skills to a point where they performed significantly better on standardized writing measures. Nystrand (1997) terms the latter approach "dialogically organized" instruction, drawing on Bakhtin (1986). Dialogically organized instruction typically elicits more student voices and encourages students to build on each other's ideas, incorporates authentic questions to which there is no "right" answer predetermined by the teacher, and scaffolds student offerings with the goal of creating access to more complex ways of reading (Gutiérrez, 1993).

Large-scale empirical studies (Applebee, Langer, Nystrand, & Gamoran, 2003; Murphy, Wilkinson, Soter, Hennessey, & Alexander, 2009) have demonstrated that dialogically organized classroom discussion correlates with positive reading outcomes in adolescent classrooms, with some caveats. Applebee et al. (2003) showed that dialogic instruction, envisionment building, and extended curricular conversation effected better student reading and writing outcomes, but that this type of instruction was rarely present in low-tracked classrooms. In their analysis of the effects of nine dialogically organized discussion approaches for literacy, Murphy et al. (2009) found that increases in levels of student talk did not always correlate with improvements in comprehension, and conclude that talk should be a *means* to an end, and not an end in itself. These studies suggest that teachers of close reading should create opportunities for all of their students to engage in high-quality, rigorous, and authentic discussion about texts. This is especially true for teachers of low-income or low-tracked classes, who are too often pressured to steep students in basic skills instruction at the expense of rich classroom discourse.

Implications for Close Reading Instruction

Smith et al. (2014) offer an alternative to the version of close reading championed in the RPC that allows for dialogically organized discussion. Specifically, they provide a counterlesson responding to Coleman's close reading of Martin Luther King's "Letter from Birmingham Jail" (Engage NY, 2012). Unlike in Coleman's lesson, students in Smith et al.'s imagined classroom would talk about issues in the text before reading, reflecting, for example, about times when they felt weak, strong, or persuasive. As they closely read King's "Letter" and supplementary texts, students would participate in discussion guided by authentic questions, such as "What giants oppose equality and the achievement of civil rights in Dr. King's time and our own?" The authors also provide ideas for participation strategies (e.g., a whole-class brainstorm, jigsaw activity, think-pair shares, role play) to organize the close reading discussion, so that students take up each other's ideas and elaborate on their own. This reimagined lesson better capitalizes on the experiences of all readers in the classroom and frames close reading as a collaborative process that takes place in an interpretive community.

New digital literacies offer more opportunities for dialogically organized close reading pedagogy than ever before. Social media platforms such as Facebook, Instagram, and Snapchat, discussion forums such as Reddit or Stack Exchange, blogs and media platforms such as YouTube, or crowd-sourced informational resources such as Wikipedia all offer pathways for collaboration or discussion on the Web. Chandler-Olcott (2013) envisions an approach to dialogically organized close reading in which students read an online article and its accompanying comments, critically analyze the arguments made, discuss the role of comments in our culture, collaboratively craft class guidelines for comment writing, and author their own comments. Teachers might also introduce digital tools into their classrooms to increase collaboration and discussion as students closely read texts. In a classroom observed by Castek and Beach (2013), seventh-grade students used the annotation app Diigo to highlight key information in a Web text about wind energy, type questions, and respond to their classmates' annotations. While the use of such apps has promise for promoting dialogically organized discussion, teachers should still generate authentic questions, choose motivating topics for discussion, make sure that students have adequate time and knowledge of technology to communicate online, and organize classroom participation frameworks in a way that supports online interactions (Castek & Beach, 2013; Leu et al., 2013).

CONCLUSION

Taking Stock

So now that we have traced the journey of close reading across many decades and offered our personal reading of its virtues and vices, what are we to make of close reading? Does it deserve the close reading we have given it? Is it worthy of our collective and individual attention in classrooms and schools around the world? Will it set comprehension activity, classroom instruction, and conversations about text on a more productive pathway than we have been traversing over the past 40+ years?

Our qualified answer is "Yes . . . maybe . . . under certain conditions." At the risk of being regarded as equivocal on close reading, our statement is as positive an assessment as we can muster in the uncertain state of its implementation in today's schools. Whether close reading represents an advance in our teaching and learning about text *does* depend on which principles and practices get privileged as it is rolled out.

If close reading promotes a "special attention to a text" that requires, as does the RPC, that it stay within the "four corners of the text" (Coleman & Pimentel, 2012), then the answer is "No." Such a stance will promote, at best, reading for *gist* (getting the author's key idea(s) and supporting details) and for *craft* (examining how the author uses language and image to persuade, position, or amuse readers). That's a start, but it falls far short of providing students with a full kit of comprehension tools or a full range of discussion experiences. Likely to be ignored is the all important practice of critical literacy—examining the assumptions and consequences of the text—what we like to call "what is said by silence." And at its worst, such a stance will promote a dogged adherence to literal comprehension practices—in Nystrand's (1997) language, known-answer questions. That would be a setback for both reading comprehension and classroom conversations, because it would deny learners access to the cornerstone of democratic discourse—a skeptical and critical disposition.

But if close reading promotes "special attention to a text" (Lentricchia & DuBois, 2003, p. 2) that acknowledges all reading involves the three other elements in the RAND model (reader, activity, and sociocultural context), then the answer can be "Yes." Just such a model of close reading is what various scholars—including Rosenblatt (1978), Fish (1980), Luke and Freebody (1999), Hinchman and Moore (2013), and Smith et al. (2014) have in mind. This approach begins with the recognition that even the simplest act of close reading—a sentence, a phrase, or even a word—cannot be enacted without acknowledging, either directly or indirectly, the resources and constraints of prior knowledge, activity, and context. For starters, how can a reader monitor his or her reading to determine whether it makes sense without invoking background knowledge? It's impossible! To say that the text makes sense is tantamount to saying that it is consistent with (1) the model of the text base that we, as readers, have constructed to that point in the reading, and (2) the wellspring of knowledge and experience we bring to the act of reading (see Pearson [2013] or Pearson & Cervetti [2015] for a more elaborate version of this argument). So, too, with task: A close reading to determine the gist of the author's position is not the same as a close reading to pinpoint strategic deployment of figurative language designed to shape readers' attitudes toward a character, or a close reading to evaluate the validity of the argument made. And so, too, with context: A close reading of the validity of an argument in anticipation of a test is not the same as a close reading of an argument when researching material for an essay. In taking this position, we also side with one of the most revered proponents of close reading, Mortimer Adler (1941), who, in a classic essay entitled "How to Mark a Book," provided this account of the relationship between a reader and the author of a text:

> And that is exactly what reading a book should be: a conversation between you and the author. Presumably he knows more about the subject than you do; naturally, you'll have the proper humility as you approach him. But don't let anybody tell you that a reader is supposed to be solely on the receiving end. Understanding is a two-way operation. (p. 12)

Adler's account is remarkably similar to the definition of reading in the RAND report as

> the process of simultaneously extracting and constructing meaning through interaction and involvement with written language. We use the words extracting and constructing to emphasize both the importance and the insufficiency of the text as a determinant of reading comprehension. (p. 11)

We rest our case. Close reading is all the closer, all the more accurate, all the more critical, all the more helpful when the text gets a little help from the resources brought to bear from the reader, the activity, and the context.

Research about Close Reading

We would be remiss if we did not close with a plea for more research on the construct of close reading. In part because it was born and bred in the interpretive research traditions of literacy criticism rather than the experimental lens of psycholinguistic studies or the ethnographic lens of critical literacy, there is not much empirical evidence to guide our decisions about what versions of close reading to endorse; we just don't know enough about the consequences of different models. Granted, we have learned a great deal from the work, cited earlier, of Nystrand (1997) and his colleagues and Murphy and her colleagues (2009). But even though we know something about the impact of steady diets of known-answer questions or an emphasis on critique, the findings lack the sort of specificity needed to make precise pedagogical recommendations. So here is our wish list of research issues we'd like to promote in our scholarly community:

- *Text length*. Most of the recommendations for close reading involve short texts—poems, letters, speeches, or excerpts. What does close reading look like when extended over a book or a course of study?
- *Disciplinary literacy*. Is close reading the same phenomenon in science, history, mathematics, and literature? We doubt that it is, but documentation of similarities and differences seems crucial to the future of close reading.
- *Authenticity*. If we can only manage close reading when texts are selected intentionally for the typical sorts of analyses we do in close reading, what does that say about its generalizability? And what about digital texts? Can any text be read closely? Or just some?
- *Relationships to writing*. Most close reading approaches assume that students will be able to draw evidence from their readings that they will then use in their writing. In short, how do ideas from close reading lessons or independent close reading make their way into student compositions?

Close reading will be a better resource for teachers and students when it receives full benefit from the research of the past and the research we can collectively undertake in the future.

ACKNOWLEDGMENTS

This material is based upon work supported by the National Science Foundation Graduate Research Fellowship under Grant No. 1106400. Any opinions, findings, and conclusions or recommendations expressed in this material are those of the author(s) and do not necessarily reflect the views of the National Science Foundation.

REFERENCES

Adler, M. J. (1941, July). How to mark a book. *Saturday Review of Literature,* pp. 11–12.

Adler, M. J., & Doren, C. V. (1972). *How to read a book: The classic guide to intelligent reading.* New York: Touchstone.

Adolescent Literacy Committees and the Adolescent Literacy Task Force of the International Reading Association. (2012). *Adolescent literacy: A position statement of the International Reading Association.* Newark, DE: International Reading Association.

Alvermann, D. E. (2002). Effective literacy instruction for adolescents. *Journal of Literacy Research, 34*(2), 189–208.

Alvermann, D. E. (2008). Why bother theorizing adolescents' online literacies for classroom practice and research? *Journal of Adolescent and Adult Literacy, 52*(1), 8–19.

Anderson, R. C., & Pearson, P. D. (1984). A schema-theoretic view of basic processes in reading comprehension. In P. D. Pearson, M. L. Kamil, R. Barr, & P. Mosenthal (Eds.), *Handbook of reading research* (Vol. 1, pp. 255–291). New York: Routledge.

Applebee, A. (2013). Common Core State Standards: The promise and the peril in a national palimpsest. *English Journal, 103*(1), 25–33.

Applebee, A. N. (1993). *Literature in the secondary school: Studies of curriculum and instruction in the United States.* Urbana, IL: National Council of Teachers of English.

Applebee, A. N., Langer, J. A., Nystrand, M., & Gamoran, A. (2003). Discussion-based approaches to developing understanding: Classroom instruction and student performance in middle and high school English. *American Educational Research Journal, 40*(3), 685–730.

Avila, J., & Moore, M. (2012). Critical literacy, digital literacies, and common core state standards: A workable union? *Theory Into Practice, 51*(1), 27–33.

Bakhtin, M. (1986). *The dialogic imagination: Four essays* (C. Emerson & M. Holquist, Eds., V. W. McGee, Trans.). Austin: University of Texas Press.

Beers, K. (2013). What matters most. *Journal of Adolescent and Adult Literacy, 57*(4), 265–269.

Behrman, E. H. (2006). Teaching about language, power, and text: A review of classroom practices that support critical literacy. *Journal of Adolescent and Adult Literacy, 49*(6), 490–498.

Boche, B., & Henning, M. (2015). Multimodal scaffolding in the secondary English classroom curriculum. *Journal of Adolescent and Adult Literacy, 58*(7), 579–590.

Borsheim-Black, C., Macaluso, M., & Petrone, R. (2014). Critical literature pedagogy. *Journal of Adolescent and Adult Literacy, 58*(2), 123–133.

Brandt, D., & Clinton, K. (2002). Limits of the local: Expanding perspectives on literacy as a social practice. *Journal of Literacy Research, 34*(3), 337–356.

Bransford, J. D., & Johnson, M. K. (1973). Considerations of some problems of comprehension. In W. Chase (Ed.), *Visual information processing* (pp. 383–438). New York: Academic Press.

Brooks, C. (1979). The new criticism. *Sewanee Review, 87*(4), 592–607.

Brooks, C., & Warren, R. (1960). *Understanding poetry.* New York: Holt, Rinehart, & Winston.

Brown, J. S., Collins, A., & Duguid, P. (1989). Situated cognition and the culture of learning. *Educational Researcher, 18*(1), 32–42.

Burroughs, R., & Smagorinsky, P. (2009). The secondary English curriculum and adolescent literacy. In L. Christenbury, R. Bomer, & P. Smagorinsky (Eds.), *Handbook of adolescent literacy research* (pp. 170–183). New York: Guilford Press.

Castek, J., & Beach, R. (2013). Using apps to support disciplinary literacy and science learning. *Journal of Adolescent and Adult Literacy, 56*(7), 554–564.

Cazden, C. B. (2001). *Classroom discourse: The language of teaching and learning* (2nd ed.). Portsmouth, NH: Heinemann.

Chandler-Olcott, K. (2013). Expanding what it means to make evidence-based claims. *Journal of Adolescent and Adult Literacy, 57*(4), 280–288.

Coleman, D., & Pimentel, S. (2012). Revised publisher's criteria for the Common Core State Standards in English Language Arts and Literacy, Grades 3–12. Retrieved from *www.corestandards.org/assets/Publishers_Criteria_for_3-12.pdf.*

Compton-Lilly, C. (2013). Views from the field: The Common Core State Standards and student diversity: Closing the gap. *Wisconsin English Journal, 55*(2), 1–4.

Cope, B., & Kalantzis, M. (2000). *Multiliteracies: Literacy learning and the design of social futures.* New York: Routledge.

Curwood, J. S., & Fink, L. (2013). *The Hunger Games:* Literature, literacy, and online affinity spaces. *Language Arts, 90*(6), 417–427.

Dakin, M. E., Eatough, D. L., & Turchon, A. (2011). A walk on the wilder side. *English Journal, 100*(3), 62–70.

Dalton, B., & Proctor, C. P. (2007). Reading as thinking: Integrating strategy instruction in a universally designed digital literacy environment. In D. S. McNamara (Ed.), *Reading comprehension strategies: Theories, interventions, and technologies* (pp. 423–442). Mahwah, NJ: Erlbaum.

Dressman, M., & Faust, M. (2014). On the teaching of poetry in English Journal, 1912–2005: Does history matter? *Journal of Literacy Research, 46*(1), 39–67.

Drew, S. V. (2012). Open up the ceiling on the Common Core State Standards: Preparing students for 21st century literacy—now. *Journal of Adolescent and Adult Literacy, 56*(4), 321–330.

Engage NY. (Producer). (2012, December 5). Common Core Video Series: Close Reading of a Text: MLK "Letter from Birmingham Jail" [Video file]. Retrieved from *www.engageny.*

org/resource/middle-school-ela-curriculum-video-close-reading-of-a-text-mlk-letter-from-birmingham-jail.

Engeström, Y. (2015). *Learning by expanding: An activity-theoretical approach to developmental research* (2nd ed.). New York: Cambridge University Press.

Fish, S. (1980). *Is there a text in this class?: The authority of interpretive communities.* Cambridge, MA: Harvard University Press.

Fisher, D., Frey, N., & Lapp, D. (2012). *Text complexity: Raising rigor in reading.* Newark, DE: International Reading Association.

Franzak, J. K. (2006). Zoom: A review of the literature on marginalized adolescent readers, literacy theory, and policy implications. *Review of Educational Research, 76*(2), 209–248.

Freebody, P., & Luke, A. (1990). Literacies programs: Debates and demands in cultural context. *Prospect: An Australian Journal of TESOL, 5*(3), 7–16.

Gainer, J. S., & Lapp, D. (2010). Remixing old and new literacies = motivated students. *English Journal, 100*(1), 58–64.

Gallop, J. (2007). The historicization of literary studies and the fate of close reading. *Profession, 2007*(1), 181–186.

Gee, J. P. (2007). *Social linguistics and literacies: Ideology in discourses.* New York: Routledge.

Gee, J. P. (2010). A situated-sociocultural approach to literacy and technology. In E. A. Baker (Ed.), *The new literacies: Multiple perspectives on research and practice* (pp. 165–193). New York: Guilford Press.

Golding, A. (1995). *From outlaw to classic: Canons in American poetry.* Madison: University of Wisconsin Press.

Guthrie, J. T., Klauda, S. L., & Ho, A. N. (2013). Modeling the relationships among reading instruction, motivation, engagement, and achievement for adolescents. *Reading Research Quarterly, 48*(1), 9–26.

Gutiérrez, K. D. (1993). How talk, context, and script shape contexts for learning: A cross-case comparison of journal sharing. *Linguistics and Education, 5*(3), 335–365.

Gutiérrez, K. D. (2008). Developing a sociocritical literacy in the third space. *Reading Research Quarterly, 43*(2), 148–164

Halliday, M. A. K. (1978). *Language as social semiotic.* London: Edward Arnold.

Heath, S. B. (1983). *Ways with words: Language, life, and work in communities and classrooms.* New York: Cambridge University Press.

Hinchman, K. A., & Moore, D. W. (2013). Close reading: A cautionary interpretation. *Journal of Adolescent and Adult Literacy, 56*(6), 441–450.

Ito, M., Baumer, S., Bittanti, M., Boyd, D., Cody, R., Herr-Stephenson, B., et al. (2010). *Hanging out, messing around, and geeking out: Kids living and learning with new media.* Cambridge, MA: MIT Press.

Janks, H. (2000). Domination, access, diversity and design: A synthesis for critical literacy education. *Educational Review, 52*(2), 175–186.

Jenkins, H. (2013). Motives for reading: Fan culture, pop culture, and collaborative reading practices. In H. Jenkins & W. Kelley (Eds.), *Reading in a participatory culture: Remixing* Moby-Dick *in the English classroom* (pp. 81–93). New York: Teachers College Press.

Juzwik, M. M. (2014). American evangelical biblicism as literate practice: A critical review. *Reading Research Quarterly, 49*(3), 335–349.

Kelley, W., Jenkins, H., Clinton, K., & McWilliams, J. (2013). From theory to practice: Building a "community of readers" in your classroom. In H. Jenkins & W. Kelley (Eds.), *Reading in a participatory culture: Remixing* Moby-Dick *in the English classroom* (pp. 25–43). New York: Teachers College Press.

Kintsch, W. (1988). The role of knowledge in discourse comprehension: A construction–integration model. *Psychological Review, 95*(2), 163–182.

Kintsch, W. (1998). *Comprehension: A paradigm for cognition.* New York: Cambridge University Press.

Knobel, M., & Lankshear, C. (2014). Studying new literacies. *Journal of Adolescent and Adult Literacy, 58*(2), 97–101.

Kress, G. R. (2003). *Literacy in the new media age.* London: Routledge.

Langer, J. A. (1984). Examining background knowledge and text comprehension. *Reading Research Quarterly, 19*(4), 468–481.

Lave, J., & Wenger, E. (1991). *Situated learning: Legitimate peripheral participation.* New York: Cambridge University Press.

Lee, C. D. (2001). Is October Brown Chinese?: A cultural modeling activity system for underachieving students. *American Educational Research Journal, 38*(1), 97–141.

Lee, C. D. (2014). The multi-dimensional demands of reading in the disciplines. *Journal of Adolescent and Adult Literacy, 58*(1), 9–15.

Lentricchia, F., & DuBois, A. (2003). *Close reading: The reader.* Durham, NC: Duke University Press.

Leu, D. J., Kinzer, C. K., Coiro, J., Castek, J., & Henry, L. A. (2013). New literacies: A dual level theory of the changing nature of literacy, instruction, and assessment. In D. E. Alvermann, N. J. Unrau, & R. B. Ruddell (Eds.), *Theoretical models and processes of reading* (6th ed., pp. 1150–1181). Newark, DE: International Reading Association.

Looy, J. V., & Baetens, J. (2003). *Close reading new media: Analyzing electronic literature.* Leuven, Belgium: Leuven University Press.

Luke, A. (2012). Critical literacy: Foundational notes. *Theory Into Practice, 51*(1), 4–11.

Luke, A., & Freebody, P. (1999). Further notes on the four resources model. Retrieved from *www.readingonline.org/research/lukefreebody.html.*

Mills, K. A. (2010). A review of the "digital turn" in the new literacy studies. *Review of Educational Research, 80*(2), 246–271.

Moje, E. B. (2008). Foregrounding the disciplines in secondary literacy teaching and learning: A call for change. *Journal of Adolescent and Adult Literacy, 52*(2), 96–107.

Murphy, P. K., Wilkinson, I. A., Soter, A. O., Hennessey, M. N., & Alexander, J. F. (2009). Examining the effects of classroom discussion on students' comprehension of text: A meta-analysis. *Journal of Educational Psychology, 101*(3), 740–764.

National Governors Association for Best Practices & Council of Chief State School Officers (NGA & CCSSO). (2010). *Common Core State Standards for English language arts and literacy in history/social studies, science, and technical subjects.* Washington, DC: Authors.

Neugebauer, S. R. (2013). A daily diary study of reading motivation inside and outside of school: A dynamic approach to motivation to read. *Learning and Individual Differences, 24,* 152–159.

New London Group. (2000). A pedagogy of multiliteracies: Designing social futures. In M. Kalantzis & B. Cope (Eds.), *Multiliteracies: Literacy learning and the design of social futures.* New York: Routledge.

Nystrand, M. (1997). *Opening dialogue: Understanding the dynamics of language and learning in the English classroom.* New York: Teachers College Press.

Orellana, M. F., & Reynolds, J. F. (2008). Cultural modeling: Leveraging bilingual skills for school paraphrasing tasks. *Reading Research Quarterly, 43*(1), 48–65.

Pearson, P. D. (2013). Research foundations for the Common Core State Standards in English language arts. In S. B. Neuman & L. B. Gambrell (Eds.), *Quality reading instruction in the age of Common Core State Standards* (pp. 237–262). Newark, DE: International Reading Association.

Pearson, P. D., & Cervetti, G. N. (2015). Fifty years of reading comprehension theory and practice. In P. D. Pearson & E. H. Hiebert (Eds.), *Research-based practices for teaching Common Core literacy* (pp. 1–25). New York: Teachers College Press.

Pearson, P. D., Hansen, J., & Gordon, C. (1979). The effect of background knowledge on young children's comprehension of explicit and implicit information. *Journal of Literacy Research, 11*(3), 201–209.

Purcell-Gates, V., Degener, S. C., Jacobson, E., & Soler, M. (2002). Impact of authentic adult literacy instruction on adult literacy practices. *Reading Research Quarterly, 37*(1), 70–92.

Purcell-Gates, V., Duke, N. K., & Martineau, J. A. (2007). Learning to read and write genre-specific text: Roles of authentic experience and explicit teaching. *Reading Research Quarterly, 42*(1), 8–45.

Rabinowitz, P. J. (1992). Against close reading. In M. Kecht (Ed.), *Pedagogy is politics: Literary theory and critical teaching* (pp. 230–43). Urbana: University of Illinois Board of Trustees.

Ransom, J. C. (1937). Criticism, Inc. *Virginia Quarterly Review, 13*(4), 586–602.

Rosenblatt, L. M. (1978). *The reader, the text, the poem: The transactional theory of the literary work*. Carbondale: Southern Illinois University Press.

Schleppegrell, M. J., Greer, S., & Taylor, S. (2008). Literacy in history: Language and meaning. *Australian Journal of Language and Literacy, 31*(2), 174–187.

Schoenbach, R., Greenleaf, C., & Murphy, L. (2012). *Reading for understanding: How Reading Apprenticeship improves disciplinary learning in secondary and college classrooms* (2nd ed.). San Francisco: Jossey-Bass.

Shanahan, C., Shanahan, T., & Misischia, C. (2011). Analysis of expert readers in three disciplines: History, mathematics, and chemistry. *Journal of Literacy Research, 43*(4), 393–429.

Shanahan, T. (2012). What is close reading? *Shanahan on Literacy*. Retrieved from *http://contentliteracytraining.pbworks.com/f/shanahan.what%20is%20close%20reading_.6.12.pdf*.

Siegler, M. G. (2010, August 4). Eric Schmidt: Every 2 days we create as much information as we did up to 2003. Retrieved from *http://social.techcrunch.com/2010/08/04/schmidt-data*.

Smagorinsky, P. (2001). If meaning is constructed, what is it made from?: Toward a cultural theory of reading. *Review of Educational Research, 71*(1), 133–169.

Smith, M. W., Appleman, D., & Wilhelm, J. D. (2014). *Uncommon core: Where the authors of the Standards go wrong about instruction-and how you can get it right*. Thousand Oaks, CA: Corwin.

Snow, C., & O'Connor, C. (2013). *Close reading and far-reaching classroom discussion: Fostering a vital connection*. Newark, DE: International Reading Association.

Snow, C. E. (2002). *Reading for understanding: Toward an R&D program in reading comprehension*. Santa Monica, CA: RAND Corporation.

Street, B. (2003). What's "new" in New Literacy Studies?: Critical approaches to literacy in theory and practice. *Current Issues in Comparative Education, 5*(2), 77–91.

Vygotsky, L. S. (1978). *Mind in society: The development of higher psychological processes* (M. Cole, V. John-Steiner, S. Scribner, & E. Souberman, Eds.). Cambridge, MA: Harvard University Press.

Warschauer, M., & Matuchniak, T. (2010). New technology and digital worlds: Analyzing evidence of equity in access, use, and outcomes. *Review of Research in Education, 34*(1), 179–225.

Webb, A. (2007). Digital texts and the new literacies. *English Journal, 97*(1), 83–88.

Wells, G. (2002). The role of dialogue in activity theory. *Mind, Culture, and Activity, 9*(1), 43–66.

Author Index

Note: The letter *f* after a page number indicates figure; *t* indicates table; and *n* indicates note.

Abedin, M., 218, 219
Abrahamsson, N., 361
Abrams, S. S., 304
Achinstein, B., 401
Achugar, M., 333, 337, 368
Adami, E., 300
Adams, C., 242
Adesope, O. O., 276
Adler, M. J., 460, 470
Afflerbach, P., 336
Aguirre-Muñoz, Z., 368
Ajayi, L., 134, 153
Albers, P., 261
Aldana, A., 227
Aldana, U. S., 78, 79, 84
Alexander, J. F., 468
Alexander, K. L., 208
Alexander, P. A., 183
Alexander, R., 139
Alexie, S., 24
Alfaro, C., 84
Alim, H. S., 14, 15, 17, 25, 29, 31
Alirez, B., 280, 281, 284, 287
Allan, A., 43, 45, 49, 53
Allard, E., 86
Allen, D., 25, 31
Allen, Q., 69
Allington, R. L., 176, 313
Allor, J., 96
Altman, I., 225
Alvarez, A., 187
Alvermann, D. E., 11, 17, 22, 23, 64, 65, 183, 186, 240, 279, 299, 313, 363, 402, 462, 464

Amabisca, A., 368
Amanti, C., 30, 64, 152, 277, 368, 412
Amrein-Beardsley, A., 401
Anagnostopoulos, D., 137
Anders, P. L., 279
Anderson, G. L., 402
Anderson, R. C., 462
Anderson, T. H., 246
Anglin, J. L., 220, 221
Anson, C., 305
Anstrom, K., 183
Anzaldua, G., 224
Appel, R., 361
Applebee, A. N., 136, 138, 139, 142, 143, 240, 379, 382, 383, 384, 387, 422, 440, 458, 460, 468
Appleman, D., 130, 137, 184, 187, 305, 382, 421, 426, 428, 440, 458
Arafeh, S., 452
Aragon, M. A., 84
Aristotle, 139
Arlin, M., 310
Armbruster, B. B., 246
Armstrong, M., 412
Aronson, J., 14
Artiles, A. J., 406
Asato, J., 80
Athanases, S. Z., 9, 40, 41, 45, 47, 51, 52, 53
Atkinson, D., 283
Atkinson, E., 38, 39, 43, 45, 53, 55, 57
August, D., 81, 278
Aukerman, M., 226
Autrey, T. M., 405
Avery, P. G., 440

Avila, J., 26, 467
Ayers, W., 152

B

Baartman, L., 223
Baecher, L., 368
Baetens, J., 466
Bailey, T., 337
Bain, R. B., 240
Baker, F. W., 23
Baker, S., 278
Bakhtin, M., 140, 216, 217, 218, 219, 220, 222, 225, 226, 383t, 389, 467, 468
Bakker, A. B., 347
Bal, P. M., 347
Ballenger, C., 7, 203, 402, 405
Bangert-Drowns, R. L., 183, 443
Banister, D., 100
Bardack, S., 71
Barnes, D., 392
Barr, R., 336
Barthes, R., 170
Batchelor, K., 342
Bateman, J., 262, 298
Baugh, J., 25
Bauman, K., 199
Bautista, M., 153
Bazalgette, C., 292, 296, 297
Bazerman, C., 185, 193, 382
Beach, R., 135, 186, 188, 257, 261, 292, 293, 294, 298, 299, 305, 382, 383t, 469
Bean, J. C., 389
Beaumont, G., 223
Beck, I. L., 423
Beck, J., 28
Beck, S. W., 364, 365, 382
Becnel, K., 344
Bednar, M., 43, 48, 51, 52
Beers, K., 458
Behizadeh, N., 139
Behrman, E. H., 466, 467
Belgarde, M. J., 202
Beliveau, L. B., 413
Bell, A., 153
Bell, D. A., 68
Bell, P., 8
Bell, S. E., 153
Bergin, M., 312
Berliner, D., 202
Bernstein, B., 323
Berrill, D. B., 388
Berry, T., 67, 69, 71
Bertrand, M., 408, 409
Bethune, M., 70
Bhagat, V., 312
Bhattacharya, A., 97
Biancarosa, G., 183, 186

Bickerstaff, S., 341
Bicknell, J., 411
Biddulph, M., 153
Biklen, D., 93, 95, 96, 99, 100, 103
Billen, M., 176
Billson, J. M., 71
Bishop, R. S., 23, 46
Bitchener, J., 369
Bitz, M., 312, 316, 318
Black, R. W., 11, 25, 26, 113, 257, 342
Blackburn, M. V., 12, 25, 33, 38, 41, 42, 43, 44, 45, 46, 47, 48, 49, 50, 51, 52, 53, 57, 405
Blackman, L., 97
Blau, S., 223
Blazar, D., 40, 41, 45, 47, 51, 53
Bleich, D., 387, 388
Bleicher, R. E., 219
Blommaert, J., 64, 132
Bloome, D., 138, 186, 240, 379, 379n, 380, 382
Blume, J., 24
Blumenfeld, P., 11
Boatright, M. D., 313
Boche, B., 463
Bode, P., 29
Boerman-Cornell, B., 315, 316, 319
Boesen, M. J., 57
Bogdan, R., 263
Boisvert, P., 100
Boldt, G., 133, 292, 298
Bolz, M., 239
Bomer, R., 63, 152, 207
Boone, R., 102
Booth, C., 341
Borsheim-Black, C., 466, 467
Boscardin, C. K., 368
Botelho, M. J., 46
Botzakis, S., 310, 313, 314, 319
Bourelle, A., 304
Bourelle, T., 304
Bowden, D., 12
Boyd, M. P., 222
Brace, E., 43
Brandt, D., 130, 136, 467
Bransford, J. D., 425, 458
Brass, J. J., 27, 137
Brewster, S., 300
Bricker, L. A., 8
Britton, J., 139, 387, 394
Broaddus, K., 153, 343, 366
Brock, C. H., 279
Broderick, D., 261, 402, 404
Bromley, K., 444, 445, 446, 450
Bronfenbrenner, U., 110, 111, 112, 113, 114, 115, 117, 119, 123
Brooks, C., 383t, 460
Brooks, L., 278
Broomhead, G. P., 185
Brophy, J., 429
Browder, D, M., 98

Brown, A. L., 96, 226, 425
Brown, J. S., 24, 347, 458, 464
Brown, M., 172, 173
Brown, T. M., 409, 410
Bruce, D. L., 262, 305, 342
Brudvik, O. C., 221
Bruner, J. S., 429
Bruning, R. H., 360
Bryan, G., 313
Bucholtz, M., 25
Buckingham, D., 292, 296, 297
Buehl, D., 426
Buescher, E., 379n
Bulfin, S., 453
Bunch, G. C., 84, 86, 87, 365, 367, 368
Burgchardt, C. R., 226
Burke, J., 95, 100, 103, 129, 130
Burkhard, T., 61
Burn, A., 297
Burnett, C., 295
Burnett, R. E, 184
Burns, A., 153
Burns, H., 314
Burridge, P., 410, 411, 412
Burris, M. A., 148
Burroughs, R., 342, 460, 463
Butler, D. L., 405
Butler, J., 38, 39
Butler, O. E., 122
Butterman, O. S., 347
Buzzi, O., 183, 185, 192
Bybee, R. W., 191, 193

C

Caccamise, D., 451
Cahill, C., 408
Calderón, M., 279
Calixte, M., 408
Calkins, L. M., 449
Callahan, M., 262
Callahan, R., 84, 373
Camangian, P., 25, 30
Cammarota, J., 66, 152, 408
Campano, G., 63, 402, 404, 405, 411, 414
Campbell, A., 71
Campbell, H., 451
Canagarajah, A. S., 133, 361
Canagarajah, S., 277, 279, 282, 325
Cancienne, M. B., 411
Capizzi, A., 444
Carbone, P., 88
Carey, C., 137
Carini, P., 400
Carpenter, C., 410
Carrillo, R., 12, 119, 367
Carroll, P. S., 23
Carson, J., 358, 360, 362, 370, 372

Carter, J. B., 261, 310, 311, 317, 318, 319
Carter, S., 382
Cary, S., 313
Castek, J., 292, 293, 294, 459, 469
Castle, K., 405, 407, 408
Castro, E. L., 152
Catalano, R. F., 71
Caton, J., 138, 261
Caton, M., 71
Catterson, A. K., 457
Caughlan, S., 129, 130, 135, 136
Cazden, C. B., 467
Celemencki, J., 408
Cervetti, G. N., 470
Chaiyabhat, S., 71
Chandler-Olcott, K., 93, 99, 113, 119, 460, 468
Chang, B., 63
Chapman, C., 150
Charalampos, G., 152
Charney-Sirott, I., 239, 242
Chávez, V., 302
Cheatham, J., 96
Checkoway, B., 227
Cheng, B. H., 238
Cherednichenko, B., 410
Cheung, A., 278
Chilcoat, G. W., 313
Chin, C., 219
Chion, M., 301
Chiu, C. C., 188
Choudhury, M., 27
Christenbury, L., 152
Christensen, L., 403
Christian, D., 278
Christian, M., 382
Christianakis, M., 262
Chun, C. W., 318
Ciechanowski, K. M., 119
Cihak, D., 98
Cirigliano, M. M., 318
Cisneros, S., 24
Clark, C. T., 12, 41, 43, 45, 46, 48, 49, 53, 57, 170, 174, 405
Clayton, C., 401
Clinton, K., 404, 464, 467
Coats, K., 349
Cochran-Smith, M., 219, 220, 228, 400, 401, 409
Cocking, R. R., 425
Cohen, E. G., 279
Cohen, J., 344
Coiro, J., 192, 452, 459
Colby, G. T., 278
Cole, M., 88, 187, 202, 387
Cole, M. W., 278
Cole, P., 215, 216, 223, 225, 228
Coleman, D., 422, 424, 425, 440, 457, 460, 461, 468, 469
Coleman-Martin, M., 98
Coles, M., 292

Coll, G. C., 112, 120
Collazo, T., 12, 119, 367
Collins, A., 458
Collins, F. M., 173
Collins, K., 94, 95, 103
Collins, S., 343
Colvin, C., 360
Comber, B., 62, 411
Comber, C., 412
Compton-Lilly, C., 110, 122, 458
Condon, D., 153
Cone, J., 402, 403, 404
Conklin, H. G., 159
Conley, D. T., 184, 423
Conley, M. W., 186
Connolly, E. M., 153
Connors, S. P., 311, 313, 318
Contreras, F., 81
Cook-Sather, A., 28, 153, 258
Cooner, D., 412
Cope, B., 186, 459, 465
Copeland, S., 96, 98, 101
Corbin, M., 24
Cormier, R., 24
Costa Saliani, E., 29
Costello, S., 28, 270, 271, 272
Cotanch, H., 293, 294
Coulthard, M., 218
Cowell, L. L., 262
Cox, B. E., 337
Cremin, T., 173, 175, 179
Crenshaw, C., 313, 315, 318
Crenshaw, K. W., 67
Cross, W., 14
Crowe, C., 327
Crowl, M., 192
Crutchfield, R. D., 71
Cruz, B. C., 152
Csikszentmihalyi, M., 430
Cuenca, A., 222
Cumming, A., 357, 358, 362, 363, 371, 372, 373
Cummins, J., 277, 324, 335, 337, 363, 371, 372, 373, 374
Curwood, J. S., 262, 341, 342, 463
Cushman, E., 61, 62, 130
Cushman, K., 153
Cziko, C., 237

D

Dafermos, M., 300
Dakin, M. E., 464
Dallacqua, A. K., 261
Dalton, B., 463
Daniels, C. R., 310
Daniels, H., 347
Danzak, R. L., 261, 318, 364, 366
Daoud, A., 83

Darling-Hammond, L., 401
Davis, J. E., 199, 406
Dawson, C., 135
de Castell, S., 43, 44, 48, 49, 52, 53
de Haan, M., 64
De La Paz, J., 347
De La Paz, S., 97, 183, 242
de Oliveria, L. C., 9
de Ünlüsoy, A., 64
Dean, A., 225
DeCuir-Gunby, J. T., 69
Degener, S. C., 464
DeJaynes, T., 153
del Río, P., 187
Delafield, B., 219
Delgado, R., 200
Deloria, V., 202
Delpit, L. D., 14, 15
DePalma, R., 38, 39, 43, 45, 53, 55, 57
Deshler, D. D., 97, 242
DeStigter, T., 381, 413
Deuker, C., 344
Devitt, A., 192
Dewey, J., 171, 172, 174, 218, 388, 392
Dezuanni, M., 292
Dickar, M., 402
Dickey, K., 405, 407, 408
Diggs, C. A., 98
Dill, B. T., 29
Dixon, J., 137, 140
Dixon, K., 61
Dixon, T., 333
Dockter, J., 342
Doda, N., 153
Doerr-Stevens, C., 296, 299
Dombey, H., 219
Domingo, M., 296, 302
Donnellan, A., 97
Dooley, S., 451
Doren, C. V., 460
Dorner, L., 279
Dover, C., 297
Dowrick, P., 100
Draper, R. J., 184, 185
Draper, S., 24
Dressman, M., 460
Drew, S. V., 461
Dubbels, B., 303
DuBois, A., 459, 469
Dudley-Marling, C., 207
Duffy, M., 93
Duguid, P., 458
Duke, N. K., 463
Duncan, R., 310
Duncan-Andrade, J. M. R., 30, 31, 226
Dunsmore, K., 360
Dunston, P. J., 279
Duran, R., 84
Durran, J., 297

Dutro, E., 414
Dworin, J. E., 207
Dyer, P. A., 240
Dyson, A. H., 264, 313
Dysthe, O., 225

E

Eagleton, T., 382, 383
Early, M., 373
Easton, L., 153
Eatough, D. L., 464
Echevarrìa, J., 367
Eckert, P., 206, 207
Edmiston, B., 104, 224
Edwards, B., 314
Egan-Robertson, A., 186
Eggleston, J., 219
Ehret, C., 298
Ehri, L., 97
Eisner, E. W., 258, 259, 266, 270, 311, 315, 342
Eksner, H. J., 64
El Refaie, E., 294
Elbaum, B. E., 279
Elder, G. H., 111
Elia, J. P., 40
Elkeles, S., 344
Elkins, J., 402
Ellis, L., 119
Elsbree, A. R., 83
Emerson, L., 185
Emig, J., 443
Empson, W., 383t
Engelhard, G., 139
Engeström, Y., 188, 347, 467
Englert, C. S., 360
Enright, K. A., 87, 357, 358, 359, 361, 367, 368, 370
Entwisle, D. R., 208
Enyedy, N., 412
Epstein, D., 40, 42, 48, 51, 53
Erickson, K., 93, 94
Ertl, B., 27
Esposito, J., 152
Esquivel, I., 311
Etienne, R., 424
Evans, K. S., 279
Evans-Winters, V., 71
Everett, S., 137
Ewaida, M., 153

F

Fahenstock, J., 382, 383t
Falter, M., 225
Faltis, C., 85, 86
Fang, Z., 183, 185, 188, 193, 323, 325, 326f, 333, 337

Faulkner, J., 342
Faust, M., 260, 379, 383t, 388, 392, 393, 460
Faux, F., 104
Fecho, B., 215, 216, 225, 226, 227, 403
Felton, M., 242
Felton, M. K., 242
Fergus, E., 65
Ferretti, R. P., 383t, 384
Fine, M., 152, 153, 155, 408
Fink, L., 463
Fish, S., 469
Fish, S. E., 383t
Fisher, D., 178, 179, 240, 261, 304, 313, 314, 315, 336, 462
Fisher, M. T., 200, 257, 412
Fishman, B. J., 238
Fitzgerald, J., 357, 358, 359f, 360, 362, 363, 426, 440
Fleury, A., 193
Flood, J., 336
Flores, N., 89
Flower, L., 183, 444, 446
Fobes, C., 153
Ford, L., 71
Ford, S., 300
Foster, T. C., 383t
Fountas, I. C., 280
Four Arrows, 202
Fowler, J., 183
Fox, M., 153
Francois, C., 344, 345, 347
Frankham, J., 153
Fránquiz, M. E., 153, 367
Fransen, S., 169
Franzak, J. K., 342, 466
Franzke, M., 451
Fredrick, L. D., 98
Fredrick, T., 364
Freebody, P., 462, 463, 466, 469
Freire, P., 15, 56, 67, 72, 216, 217, 218, 222, 225, 226, 404, 405
Frey, N., 261, 313, 314, 315, 462
Friedlander, B., 447
Fritz, A. E., 412
Frost, R., 266
Fry, P. G., 138, 383
Frye, N., 382
Fu, D., 203, 361, 365
Fuke, V., 315
Funnell, K. A., 185

G

Gabriel, R., 176, 177, 179
Gadsden, V., 27, 406
Gadsden, V. L., 259
Gainer, J. S., 467
Gallagher, C. W., 303

Gallagher, K., 174, 221
Gallagher, M. C., 236
Gallego, M. A., 64
Gallo, S., 86
Gallop, J., 460
Gamboa, M., 33
Gamoran, A., 140, 468
Gándara, P. C., 79, 80, 81, 84
Garcia, A., 21, 23, 24, 184
García, O., 78, 79, 80, 82, 85, 86, 277, 278, 361
Gass, S., 279
Gavigan, K., 311, 313, 314
Gay, G., 29, 152
Gaztambibe-Fernández, R., 408
Gee, J., 130, 326, 332, 360
Gee, J. P., 183, 184, 188, 189, 216, 458, 459
Geisler, C., 183, 189
Genesee, F., 278
Genishi, C., 264
George, M., 343
Gershon, W., 302
Gersten, R. M., 278
Ghiso, M. P., 402, 405
Gibbons, P., 324, 440
Giddens, A., 410
Gifford, D., 96
Gilbert, J., 444
Gillespie, A., 444
Gilligan, C., 208
Gilliland, B., 357, 368, 370
Gillis, V., 333
Gillis, V. R., 183
Ginwright, S. A., 65, 66
Giroux, C., 3
Glaus, M., 348
Glaveanu, V., 347
Glenn, W. J., 24, 342
Glover, E. A., 28
Goatley, V. J., 279
Goff, B., 379*n*
Goines, D., 121
Gold, S. J., 153
Golding, A., 460
Gómez, M. C., 80
Gonsoulin, S., 71
Gonzales, J., 43, 45, 46, 48, 50, 53
Gonzales, N. E., 152
Gonzalez, N., 10, 30, 64, 277, 368, 373, 412
Goodman, S., 412
Goodstein-Stolzenberg, A., 29
Goodwin, D. K., 431
Goodwin, M. H., 89
Gordon, C., 458
Gorski, P., 207, 208
Goswami, D., 405, 412
Gotanda, N., 80
Grabe, W., 362, 373
Graff, G., 393
Graff, J. M., 203, 361

Graff, N., 140
Graham, S., 97, 240, 443, 444, 445, 446, 447, 449, 450, 454
Gramsci, A., 411
Graves, B. B., 426, 440
Graves, M., 421
Graves, M. F., 426, 440
Green, C., 11
Greenbaum, V., 40, 45, 48, 51, 53
Greenberg, J., 10
Greene, M., 259, 270
Greenleaf, C., 235, 236, 237, 238, 239, 240, 242, 243, 245, 249, 464
Greer, S., 465
Greever, B., 411
Greytak, E. A., 57
Griffin, P., 202, 387
Griffith, J., 297
Griffith, P. E., 311, 312, 313, 318
Grimes, S., 183
Grinberg, J., 152
Grisham, D. L., 314
Groenke, S. L., 221
Groensteen, T., 311
Grootendorst, R., 389
Grosik, S. A., 358
Grossman, P., 159, 382
Grossman, P. L., 136
Guerrero, C., 408, 409
Guerrero, E., 408
Guerrero, M., 412
Guo, A., 295
Guthrie, J., 178, 179
Guthrie, J. T., 242, 346, 349, 351, 424, 429, 462
Gutiérrez, K. D., 7, 15, 16, 17, 25, 32, 79, 80, 83, 88, 89, 347, 409, 462, 468
Guzzetti, B. J., 33

H

Ha, S. Y., 379*n*
Habermas, J., 390
Haddix, M., 24, 25, 27, 32, 63, 67, 137, 152
Haddix, M. M., 21
Haertel, E. H., 401
Hafiz, 215
Haggerty, K. P., 71
Hakuta, K., 81, 278
Hale, G., 242
Hall, C., 292
Hall, L., 225
Hall, L. A., 5
Hallenbeck, P. N., 313
Halliday, M. A. K., 324, 325*n*, 465
Hallman, H., 135
Hallman, H. L., 222
Halverson, E. R., 40, 47, 48, 49, 52, 53, 299
Hamilton, D., 272

Hamilton, G., 40, 45, 48, 53
Hamilton, M., 64
Haneda, M., 324, 326, 335, 337, 368
Hansen, J., 458
Harklau, L., 357, 358, 361, 362, 371
Harmon, J., 148, 153
Harmon, R., 367
Harper, D., 153
Harper, S. R., 71
Harris, J. D., 386
Harris, K., 444
Harris, K. M., 203
Harris, K. R., 444, 447
Harris, M. L., 97
Harris, T., 103
Harste, J., 261
Hartman, D. K., 240
Hawken, L. S., 240, 444
Hayes, E. R., 188, 189
Hayes, J. R., 183, 360, 444, 446
Hayn, J. A., 341, 342
Heath, S. B., 6, 7, 13, 66, 130, 139, 141, 201, 202, 206, 259, 312, 324, 383, 458
Hebert, M. A., 443, 444
Hedberg, J. G., 221
Hefling, K., 422
Heller, K. W., 98
Helling, K., 27
Helmer, K., 42, 45, 48, 50, 51, 52
Hemingway, E., 390
Hemingway, J., 43
Henderson, M., 305
Henkemans, A. F. S., 389
Hennessey, M. N., 468
Henning, M., 463
Henry, L. A., 459
Hereth, J., 300
Hermans, H., 223, 224
Hermans-Konopka, A., 223, 224
Hernandez, A., 83
Hernnstein, R. J., 200
Heron-Hruby, A., 22, 23
Hertz-Lazarowitz, R., 279
Hibbing, A. N., 153
Hicks, T., 138, 153
Hiebert, E. H., 134
Higgins, K., 102
Hillman, A. M., 192
Hillocks, G., 138
Hillocks, G., Jr., 384, 389
Hinchman, K. A., 65, 186, 426, 469
Hine, T., 23
Hinsdale, B. A., 131, 134, 135, 139
Hinton, S. E., 24, 28, 258
Hirsch, E. D., 15, 16
Hirsch, J., 347
Hirvela, A., 138, 379n, 380
Ho, A. N., 462
Hoa, L., 178

Hobbs, R., 23, 27
Hobson, D., 404
Hobson, S., 405
Hodge, R., 184
Hodges, D., 100
Hoffman, M., 40, 42, 45, 46, 48, 51, 53
Hogan, R. F., 421, 430
Holbrook, M. C., 243
Hollett, T., 298
Hollingsworth, S., 64
Honeyford, M. A., 11, 405
Hong, X., 225
Hood, D., 411
hooks, B., 70, 72
Hopkins, M., 81, 84
Hopkins, R., 71
Hornberger, N. H., 38, 78n
Horschelmann, K., 294
Horsford, S. D., 81
Householder, D. L., 192
Howard, V., 343
Howe, C., 218, 219
Huang, C., 349
Hudicourt-Barnes, J., 7
Hudson, M., 98
Hudson, M. E., 98
Hughes, J. M., 315, 317
Hull, G., 31, 63, 64, 65, 257, 272, 298, 299, 312
Hull, G. A., 16, 87, 88
Hunt, A., 84
Hurley, M. M., 183, 443
Hurwitz, L., 237
Hutchins, R. J., 299
Hyland, F., 369
Hyland, K., 183, 189, 190, 324, 361, 369

I

Ifill, N., 150
Imig, D. G., 159
Imig, S. R., 159
Ingalls, R. L., 12
Irizarry, J. G., 410
Irvine, K., 98
Ito, M., 22, 257, 462
Ivanic, R., 359, 360, 386
Ives, D., 7
Ivey, G., 153, 175, 176, 177, 179, 341, 343, 344, 345, 346, 347, 349, 350, 366
Ivory, G., 279

J

Jacobs, C., 185
Jacobs, D., 310
Jacobson, E., 464
Janik, A., 389

Janks, H., 466
Jansen, H., 192
Jaxon, K. D., 215
Jefferson, T., 72
Jenkins, H., 23, 24, 297, 300, 404, 464
Jenkins, J. J., 429
Jensen, E., 208
Jensen, J. M., 336
Jenson, J., 43, 44, 48, 49, 52, 53
Jetton, T. L., 183, 411
Jewitt, C., 152, 154, 186, 263, 293, 294
Jiménez, R. T., 276, 278, 279
Jocson, K., 23, 26
Jocson, K. M., 262, 412
Johannessen, L .R., 383*t*, 384
Johnson, D., 347
Johnson, E., 32, 33
Johnson, G., 222
Johnson, J., 389
Johnson, M. K., 458
Johnson, N., 451
Johnson, R., 171
Johnson, T. S., 138, 383
Johnston, P. H., 175, 176, 177, 179, 344, 345, 346, 347, 349
Jones, M., 153
Jones, R., 405
Jones, S., 337, 402, 405, 407
Jordan, J., 403
Jorgensen, C., 94, 95, 99, 101, 103, 105
Journell, W., 152
Joy, R., 104
Juzwik, M. M., 129, 140, 221, 463

K

Kachur, R., 140
Kahn, E. A., 383*t*, 384
Kahn, L. H., 261
Kaiser, G., 191, 192
Kajder, S., 202
Kalan, A., 398
Kalantzis, M., 186, 459, 465
Kamil, M. L., 183, 186, 336
Kamler, B., 411, 412
Kanevsky, R., 400
Kanno, Y., 358
Kaplan, J. S., 341
Kaplan, R., 362
Karolides, N. J., 260, 272
Kasa-Hendrickson, C., 95
Kastman-Breuch, L., 305
Katims, D. S., 96
Katz, M. L., 257, 298
Kauffmann, G., 40, 42, 45, 48, 49, 51, 53, 261
Kaufman, P., 153
Kearns, T., 71
Keefe, E., 96, 98, 101
Kellett, M., 153
Kelley, W., 464
Kellner, D., 23
Kellogg, R., 360
Kelly, D. M., 33
Kelly, S., 140, 221
Kemmis, S., 154
Kenney, L. M., 43, 45, 46, 48, 53, 405
Kesler, T., 26, 100
Kett, J. F., 15
Ketter, J., 341
KewalRamani, A., 150
Keyes, C., 276
Keyes, C. S., 279
Khan, S. K., 224
Khurana, S., 312
Kibler, A., 366
Kibler, A. K., 366
Kiili, C., 192
Kim, H., 236
Kim, J., 135
Kim, K., 236
Kim, M.-Y., 379*n*
Kincheloe, J. L., 152
King, A., 315
King, J. M., 262
King, M. L., 425
Kinloch, V., 61, 62, 63, 64, 66, 412
Kinsey, A. C., 210
Kintch, E., 451
Kintsch, W., 360, 462
Kinzer, C. K., 459
Kirkland, D., 65, 130, 413
Kirkland, D. E., 65, 66, 201, 202, 203, 343
Kirsch, I., 173, 349
Kiuhara, S., 444
Kiuhara, S. A., 240, 444
Klauda, S. L., 351, 424, 462
Kleifgen, J. A., 78, 79, 80, 82
Kleijwegt, D., 317
Klein, P. D., 98
Kliewer, C., 93, 95, 96, 97, 99, 103
Klingner, J. K., 81, 84, 279
Kluth, P., 93, 99
Knobel, M., 66, 314, 452, 459, 462
Knowles, J., 344
Knowles, T., 153
Koda, K., 361
Koehler, S., 301
Koenig, A. J., 243
Koppenhaver, D., 93, 94
Kormos, J., 361
Kosciw, J. G., 57
Kramer, K., 119
Kramer, M. A., 405
Krashen, S., 173
Krause, K., 152

Krauss, M. W., 123
Kress, G., 23, 152, 153, 154, 184, 186, 257, 294, 314, 459
Kroll, B., 358
Kruger, T., 410
Kucan, L., 423
Kunjufu, J., 207
Kurth, J., 100
Kyratzis, A., 89

L

Labbo, L., 27
LaCapra, D., 398, 414
Ladson-Billings, G., 29, 72, 112
Laird, J., 150
Lam, W. S. E., 11, 365
Lan, W., 153
Land, R., 367
Landale, N. S., 82
Landry, S. J., 215
Langan, P., 280, 281, 284, 287
Langer, J., 384
Langer, J. A., 131, 138, 379, 383t, 387, 440, 462, 468
Lankshear, C., 66, 314, 452, 459, 462
Lanthier, R., 153
Lapp, D., 178, 179, 336, 452, 453, 462, 467
Larson, J., 7
Larson, L., 333
Latham, G., 342
Lave, J., 183, 189, 244, 464
Lavin, T., 276
Lawrence, C., 68, 69, 70
Lawrence, J. F., 242, 332
Layton, L., 423
Le, C. N., 204
Lea, M., 386
Leander, K., 115, 133, 292, 295, 298
Learned, J. E., 6
Lee, C., 8, 14, 87, 88, 140, 203, 383t, 385, 462, 463, 465
Lee, J. A., 295
Lee, S., 173
Lee, Y. J., 177, 179, 188
Leki, I., 357, 358, 370
Lemke, J., 326, 336
Lenhart, A., 452
Lentricchia, F., 459, 469
Leonard, R. L., 366
Leseman, P. M., 64
Lester, N., 183
Leu, D. J., 452, 459, 466, 467, 469
Levine, A., 159
Levine, S., 8, 17
Levithan, D., 344
Lewis, C., 305, 341, 342, 351, 383t, 412

Lewis, M. A., 24, 341
Lewis, W. E., 383t, 384
Li, Y., 295
Liben, D., 424, 425
Liben, M., 424
Lieberman, A., 215, 406
Lightbown, P. M., 278
Ligorio, M. B., 223
Lin, T.-J., 379n
Lindholm-Leary, K., 278
Link, H., 86
Linney, J. A., 71
Linquanti, R., 81
Litman, C., 239
Livingstone, A., 408, 409
Llosa, L., 364
Lo, J., 245
Looy, J. V., 465
LoRé, R. K., 202
Lovaas, K. E., 40
Love, B., 71
Low, D. E., 310, 314, 319
Lucas, K., 207
Lucas, T., 152
Luhrman, B., 297
Luke, A., 5, 32, 186, 222, 293, 402, 462, 463, 466, 469
Lundberg, I., 96
Lynch, M., 153
Lytle, S. L., 219, 220, 228, 400, 401, 402, 409, 414

M

Macagno, F., 389
Macaluso, K., 129, 143
Macaluso, M., 129, 143, 466
MacArthur, C. A., 444, 446, 450, 454
Macedo, D., 15
Macgill, A. R., 452
MacKay, B. R., 185
MacKay, M. B., 185
Mackey, A., 279
MacLean, J., 105
Magnusson, D., 111
Mahalingappa, L., 371
Mahar, D., 113, 119
Mahiri, J., 63, 66, 131, 402, 409
Majors, R., 71
Mäkinen, M., 192
Manchón, R. M., 357
Manderino, M., 28
Mar, R. A., 347
Marenco, S., 209
Mariage, T. V., 360
Markarian, W. C., 222
Marple, S., 239
Marshall, E., 64

Marshall, J., 140, 379, 383t
Martin, A. C., 400
Martin, C. E., 210
Martin, D., 242
Martin, M., 65
Martineau, J. A., 463
Martinez, A., 184
Martinez, D. C., 78, 87, 89
Martínez, R. A., 88
Martínez-Roldán, C. M., 153
Martinez-Wenzl, M., 84
Martino, W., 42, 45, 48, 53, 209
Marx, R. W., 11, 12, 367
Masny, D., 296
Mason, L. H., 447
Mastergeorge, A., 100
Mates, B. F., 176
Matsuda, P. K., 361
Matuchniak, T., 367, 462
Matusov, E., 216, 225
May, L., 207
May, S., 152
Maya, M., 27, 28
Mayer, A., 84
Mayer, R. E., 295
Mayher, J., 135
Mayikana, L., 412
McAlister, S., 153
McCaffrey, K., 349
McCloskey, E., 103, 105
McCloud, S., 312, 313
McCormick, K., 382
McDevitt, R., 299
McGinnis, T., 29
McGlynn, A., 71
McGlynn-Wright, A., 71
McIntyre, D., 160
McKenny, A. F., 318
McKenzie, C., 129, 130, 134
McKeown, M. G., 423
McKim, K., 115
McKittrick, M., 305
McKnight, P., 242
McKool, S. S., 176, 179
McLaren, P., 152
McLaughlin, M. W., 66
McLean, C. A., 11
McLeod, J., 122
McLeod, S. H., 184
McMaster, K. L., 451
McMillan, T., 122
McPeake, J., 424, 429
McQuillan, J., 173
McRobbie, C. J., 219
McSheehan, M., 95, 99
McTaggart, R., 154
McTavish, M., 66
McVee, M. B., 262
McWilliams, J., 464

Mediratta, K., 153, 155
Mehan, H., 218
Menken, K., 78, 85, 89
Merchant, G., 295
Mesa, M., 279
Meyer, A., 105
Meyer, R., 202
Michaels, S., 324, 405, 411
Michalski, P., 100
Miller, S., 96
Miller, s. j., 25, 209, 413
Miller, S. M., 257, 262
Mills, K. A., 113, 153, 459
Mims, P. J., 98
Mirenda, P., 93, 97
Mirra, N., 184
Misischia, C., 465
Mitchum, C., 305
Moeller, R. A., 313, 344
Moita-Lopes, L. P., 42, 45, 49, 51, 53
Moje, E. B., 3, 5, 7, 9, 10, 11, 12, 14, 17, 32, 66, 68, 113, 115, 119, 120, 152, 183, 184, 186, 193, 236, 240, 242, 312, 336, 342, 343, 348, 350, 351, 367, 384, 385, 402, 424, 465
Moll, L. C., 10, 30, 64, 79, 152, 203, 277, 368, 412
Monk, L. R., 425
Monnin, K., 319
Monobe, G., 368
Monroe, J., 183, 184
Montaño, E., 88
Monte-Sano, C., 242
Moore, D. W., 64, 183, 240, 402, 469
Moore, M., 26, 467
Moorefield-Lang, H., 314
Moorman, M., 174
Morales, P. Z., 84
Moreau, S., 411
Morgan, D., 342
Morgan, W., 223
Morici, P., 200
Morphy, P., 444
Morrell, E., 66, 119, 131, 141, 152, 184, 226, 402, 404, 408, 412
Morris, C., 316
Morris, K., 9, 113, 152, 184, 342
Morris, P., 111
Morrison, A., 97
Morrison, T. G., 313, 316
Mortimer, K., 86
Mosenthal, P., 336
Moshenberg, D., 402
Mosley, M., 405
Moss, B., 63
Mosse, H. L., 310
Mottram, M., 173
Muehling, N., 3
Mueller, F., 237
Muhammad, G., 67
Muhammad, G. E., 25, 32, 33

Mukhopadhyay, T., 97
Muller, C., 84
Muñoz, C., 361
Murakami, K., 219
Murphy, E., 104
Murphy, J. J., 139, 140
Murphy, L., 243, 245, 464
Murphy, P. K., 468, 470
Murphy, S., 169, 180
Murray, C. A., 200, 208
Myers, W. D., 24
Myhill, D., 336, 337

N

Nachtigal, S., 242
Nagy, W., 188, 189
Napoli, M., 64, 295
Naraian, S., 102, 106
Neal Hurston, Z., 143
Neff, D., 30, 64, 277, 412
Negara, G. P. K., 295
Nell, V., 170, 174
Nelson, M. E., 272
Nelson, T. H., 405
Nemeth, E., 62
Nemeth, N. A., 41
Ness, M. K., 240
Neugebauer, S. R., 464
Newell, G., 138
Newell, G. E., 138, 379, 379n, 380, 382, 387
Newman, D., 202
Nichols, J. M., 210
Nicholson, D. W., 259
Nida, E., 278
Nieto, S., 29
Nixon, H., 62
Noguera, P., 65, 66
Noguera, P. A., 71, 152
Nolan, B., 100
Nolan, B. T., 26
Nolen, A., 341
Norris, S. P., 243
Norton, B., 313, 318
Ntelioglou, B. Y., 221
Nystrand, M., 140, 202, 221, 351, 359, 467, 468, 469, 470

O

Oatley, K., 347
O'Brien, D., 105, 115, 117, 182, 183, 186, 188, 190, 240, 257, 261, 272, 294, 303
Ochsner, R., 183
O'Connor, C., 68, 458
O'Connor, I. M., 98
O'Cummings, M., 71

Odelson, D., 314
O'Donnell, R., 211
Ogonowski, M., 7
O'Hallaron, C. L., 86, 326, 336
Olitsky, S., 219
Olson, C. B., 367, 374
Olson, L. S., 208
Oosterbaan, A., 223
Orellana, M. F., 64, 79, 87, 88, 278, 279, 463
Orfield, G., 135
Oropesa, R. S., 82
Orphanides, A., 71
Ort, B. L., 226
Ortega, L., 358, 360, 362, 370, 372
Ortmann, L. L., 182, 190
Ortmeier-Hooper, C., 357, 359, 361, 365
Otaiba, S., 96
Oteíza, T., 333, 368
Otto, S., 382
Overby, M., 9, 113, 152, 184, 342
Owens, D., 153
Oxford, R. L., 278

P

Pacheco, M., 88
Padilla, A. M., 211
Pahl, K., 133, 295
Painter, J., 411
Palincsar, A. S., 96
Palmer, N. A., 57
Palumbo, D., 316
Pantoja, A., 404
Pappalardo, G., 302
Pappas, C. C., 411
Paradis, J., 382
Paris, D., 29, 65, 66, 89, 133, 152, 408
Park, J. Y., 184, 411
Park, J.-A., 368
Parker, J., 27, 28
Parker, W. C., 238, 239, 242, 245
Pasternak, D. L., 135
Patraw, J. M., 43
Patterson, A., 62
Patton, M. Q., 154
Paulus, T., 221
Payne, R. K., 207
Payne, Y., 153
Pea, C., 187
Pearson, P. D., 134, 135, 236, 245, 336, 422, 423, 428, 457, 458, 462, 470
Peek-Brown, D., 11
Peggy, R., 413
Penn, C., 61
Pennycook, A., 133
Penuel, W. R., 238
Perencevich, K. C., 178, 242
Perez, N., 129

Perin, D., 444, 445, 446, 449
Perkins, D. N., 382
Perkins, P., 315
Perreira, K. M., 203
Perry, D. M., 71
Perryman-Clark, S. M., 15
Petrone, R., 24, 341, 466
Petrosky, A. R., 387, 388
Pettigrew, C., 210
Phelan, M., 295
Phelps, S. F., 183
Philips, S. U., 6, 202
Phillips, L. M., 243
Phillips, M., 305
Piliawsky, M., 153
Pimentel, S., 422, 425, 457, 460, 461, 469
Pincus, M., 402, 405
Pinkard, N., 27
Pinnell, G. S., 280
Pinnow, R., 357, 358, 361, 362
Piper, H., 153
Pitcher, S. M., 177, 179
Place, K., 27
Plummer, K., 40
Pointer Mace, D. H., 406
Polat, N., 371
Pole, C., 154
Pomeroy, W. B., 210
Poole, D., 279
Portes, P., 203
Portman, T. A. A., 69
Powell, S., 173
Pratt, M. L., 89, 224
Prendergast, C., 140
Price-Dennis, D., 21, 24, 137
Prins, F., 223
Probst, R. E., 383*t*
Proctor, C. P., 463
Pruzinsky, T., 177, 179
Pugh, K. R., 359
Purcell-Gates, V., 463, 464
Purushotma, R., 404
Purves, A. C., 314
Pustz, M., 310
Puzio, K., 276, 278, 279
Pytash, K., 342

Q

Quintilian, 139, 142

R

Rabinowitz, P. J., 383*t*, 460
Rackley, E. R., 13
Radway, J., 174

Ramage, J. D., 389
Ramey, L. C., 123
Rampton, B., 132
Randolph-Seng, B., 318
Rankin-Erickson, J. L., 153
Rankins-Robertson, S., 304
Ransom, J. C., 460
Rao, K., 100
Raphael, T. E., 279
Ravitch, D., 212, 423
Ray, B., 301
Readence, J. E., 64, 183, 402
Redmond, T., 27, 28
Reed, C., 389
Reese, J., 40, 45, 48, 51, 53
Reich, R., 134
Reichenberg, M., 96
Reisman, A., 240
Renzi, L., 135
Reyes, C. C., 31
Reyes, I., 79, 85
Reynolds, D. W., 364
Reynolds, J., 88, 279
Reynolds, J. F., 278, 463
Reynolds, T., 305
Rice, M., 317, 318
Richardson, L., 406
Richards-Schuster, K., 227
Richards-Tutor, C., 367
Rick, J., 315, 317
Rickelman, R. J., 183
Rieke, R., 389
Riley, K., 402, 405, 406
Risemberg, R., 444, 446
Rish, R., 138
Rish, R. M., 261
Ritchie, S., 404
Roach, A., 28
Robertson, J., 93, 107
Robinson, A. J., 404
Rodriguez, A., 434
Rodriguez, L. F., 409
Roessingh, H., 278
Rogers, J., 412
Rogers, L. A., 444, 445, 446
Rogers, R., 405, 412
Rogers, T., 183
Rogoff, B., 7
Rogow, F., 23
Rolls, A., 183
Ronfeldt, M., 159
Roozen, K., 26
Rorimer, S., 368
Rosa, J., 89
Rosalia, C., 368
Rosario-Ramos, E., 11
Rosas, M., 408
Rose, D., 105

Rose, G., 154
Rosebery, A., 7
Rosenblatt, L. M., 28, 216, 220, 221, 258, 259, 260, 261, 264, 265, 267, 268, 270, 271, 272, 346, 379, 381, 382, 383*t*, 388, 392, 460, 469
Ross, G., 429
Ross-Feldman, L., 279
Roth, G., 310
Roth, W. M., 188
Rothstein, J., 401
Rouse, A. G., 443
Rowe, D., 295
Rowley, S. J., 227
Rowsell, J., 133, 293, 295, 452, 453
Royal, D. P., 319
Rubinstein-Ávila, E., 25, 313
Rudman, M. K., 46
Ruiz, R., 83, 277
Rumbaut, R. G., 82
Rumbold, K., 170, 174
Rumelhart, D. E., 429
Rush, L., 135
Rush, L. S., 135
Russell, D. R., 444, 446
Ryan, C. L., 40, 43, 45, 48, 49, 50, 51, 53
Ryan, M., 222
Rymes, B., 7
Ryndak, D., 97, 99, 100, 101, 102, 103, 105
Ryu, S., 379*n*

S

Saavedra, E., 402
Sabelli, N., 238
Safford, K., 173
Salina, C. S., 367
Sampson, C., 81
San Pedro, T., 66
Sánchez, L., 402, 405
Sanchez, R., 343
Sanders, P. A., 364
Sandmel, K., 444, 446
Sannino, A., 347
Santos, M., 80
Sardone, N. B., 313, 317
Sarigianides, S. T., 24, 341
Sarkar, M., 25, 31
Sarroub, L., 13
Satchwell, C., 386
Saunders, W., 278
Savage, J., 23
Savitz, R., 310
Scarcella, R., 367
Schaap, H., 223
Schafer, W. D., 349, 454
Schall, J., 40, 42, 45, 48, 49, 51, 53
Scharber, C., 188, 261

Scheibe, C., 23
Scherff, L., 135
Schey, R., 38, 46, 48
Schieble, M., 368
Schimier, S., 153
Schleppegrell, M. J., 86, 183, 185, 188, 193, 324, 326, 331, 332, 333, 336, 337, 368, 465
Schmidt, E., 467
Schnakenberg, H. L., 315, 317
Schnellert, L., 405
Schoenbach, R., 237, 242, 243, 245, 247, 249, 464
Schonewise, E. A., 81, 84
Schoonen, R., 361
Schultz, B. D., 153
Schultz, K., 31, 32, 63, 64, 65, 87, 88, 262, 298, 312
Schumaker, J. B., 97, 242
Schumm, J. S., 279
Schwandt, T. A., 264
Schwartz, A., 313
Schwartz, E., 400
Schwartz, S. S., 454
Schwarz, G., 313, 315, 318
Scorza, D., 184
Scott, J., 292, 293, 299
Sealey-Ruiz, Y., 27, 152
Sebba, M., 372
Secor, M., 382, 383*t*
Sedita, J., 443
Segal, J. W., 382
Seglem, R., 23
Semali, L., 186
Semingson, P., 207
Serafini, F., 293, 305
Sewall, G., 185
Seyfried, J., 314
Sfard, A., 192
Shah, S., 153
Shanahan, C., 99, 183, 184, 185, 187, 243, 465
Shanahan, L. E., 257, 262, 301, 302
Shanahan, T., 99, 183, 184, 185, 187, 243, 278, 360, 428, 465
Shapiro, A., 185
Share, J., 23, 27
Shearer, L., 204
Shell, D. F., 360
Sheridan-Thomas, H. K., 426
Sherry, M. B., 140, 221
Shifman, L., 300
Shipka, J., 303
Short, D., 367
Short, J. C., 318
Short, K. G., 261
Shuart-Faris, N., 382
Shultz, S., 12
Shurr, J., 98
Sieben, N., 43, 45, 46
Siegler, M. G., 467

Silva, T., 357
Simeonsson, R. J., 123
Simon, R., 311, 312, 398, 400, 402, 404, 405, 406, 411, 412, 413, 414
Simpson, A., 293
Simpson, L., 411
Simpson, M., 363
Sims, R., 23
Sinclair, J., 218
Sitomer, A. L., 344
Skerrett, A., 13, 63
Skidmore, D., 219
Skinner, M. L., 71
Slavin, R., 278
Slavin, R. E., 279
Slavit, D., 405
Sleeter, C. E., 151, 152
Smagorinsky, P., 138, 140, 152, 199, 202, 203, 207, 208, 220, 261, 342, 383, 458, 460, 462, 463, 467
Smetana, L., 314, 317
Smith, A., 129, 452
Smith, E., 192
Smith, F., 430
Smith, J. M., 42, 43, 46, 48, 52, 405
Smith, M., 140, 310
Smith, M. W., 169, 170, 177, 209, 421, 422, 458, 468, 469
Smitherman, G., 14, 140
Smyth, J. C., 153, 422
Snipper, G. C., 278
Snow, C., 183, 186, 240, 242, 324, 327, 331, 332, 336, 337, 371, 458, 461
Snow-Gerono, J. L., 404, 405
Snyder, I., 453
Soep, E., 302
Soler, M., 464
Solorza, C., 85
Solórzano, D. G., 68
Somers, C., 153
Sommers, C. H., 209
Sommerstein, L., 97
Sonnenmeier, R., 95, 99, 100, 101, 103, 105
Sontag, J. C., 123
Soter, A. O., 468
Soto, G., 24
Soven, M. I., 184
Spangler, S., 305
Speyer, J., 9, 17, 242, 424
Spiegelman, A., 137, 311, 318, 398, 399, 413
Spielberg, S., 303
Springs, R., 190
Spurgeon, T., 311
Spycher, P., 367
Squire, J. R., 336
Srikantaiah, D., 135
Stables, A., 222
Steele, C. M., 14
Stefancic, J., 200

Steinbeck, J., 143
Steinkuehler, C., 342
Stern, D., 68
Stetsenko, A., 347
Stevenson, C., 412
Stewart, M. A., 27
Stewart, R. A., 240, 257
Stewart, T. T., 224
Stillman, P., 405, 412
Stine, R. L., 120
Stith, D., 190
Stockdill, D. B., 9, 236, 351
Stockton, S., 183
Stornaiuolo, A., 16, 272
Stotsky, S., 135, 136, 200
Stoudt, B., 153
Stovall, D., 67, 69, 71
Strasser, T., 344
Strauss, L., 14
Street, B. V., 38, 63, 130, 139, 311, 386, 400, 402, 458
Streng, J. M., 154
Strieb, L., 400
Stripek, D., 424, 429
Strommen, L. T., 176
Sullivan, A., 172, 173
Sumara, D., 170
Sun, Y., 188
Sunderman, G. L., 135
Sung, E., 295
Surabian, M., 102, 106
Sutherland, L. A., 68
Sutherland, L. M., 11
Swain, A. N., 152
Swain, M., 278, 279
Swayhoover, L., 135
Sweeny, S. M., 452, 453
Swiss, T., 298, 299
Sychterz, T., 295
Sylvan, C., 85
Szalacha, L. A., 112, 120

T

Tabachnick, S. E., 319
Tabak, E., 411
Taber-Doughty, T., 98
Tan, A., 143
Tannen, D., 382
Tatalovic, M., 313, 316
Tavin, K., 264, 266, 268
Taxel, J., 207, 208
Taylor, L., 148
Taylor, S. J., 263, 465
Thein, A. H., 57
Thompson, K. D., 81
Thompson, L., 138, 383

Thompson, T., 276, 311, 382
Thornton, S. J., 152
Tierney, J. D., 305
Tinio, P. P. L., 26, 100
Tobin, K. G., 219
Tobin, M., 28
Tocalli-Beller, A., 278
Todorova, M. S., 302
Tonks, S., 178
Toohey, K., 64
Torre, M. E., 153
Toulmin, S. E., 138, 389, 390
Townsend, D., 183, 188, 189, 333, 337
Tracey, C. K., 135
Trefil, J. S., 15
Triliva, S., 300
Trutschel, B. K., 188
Tuck, E., 408
Turchon, A., 464
Turner, M., 174
Tysvaer, N., 9, 113, 152, 184, 342

U

Uccelli, P., 324, 327, 331, 336, 371
Ungerleider, C., 276
Unsworth, L., 297
Unz, R., 80
Uppstrom, A., 46, 48

V

Vadeboncoeur, J. A., 222
Valdés, G., 364
Valencia, S. W., 235, 237, 239, 240, 242, 245, 382
Valenzuela, A., 16
Van den Broek, P., 183
Van der Schaaf, M., 223
van Diepan, A., 344
van Eemeren, F. H., 388–389
van Kruistum, C., 64
Van Leeuwen, T., 154, 184, 186, 294, 296, 314
Van Zee, B. E. H., 192
Vander Zanden, S., 405
VanDerHeide, J., 129, 138, 142, 382
Vargas, L., 203
Varvantakis, C., 300
Vasudevan, L., 28, 32, 33, 63, 66, 67, 115, 117, 153, 258, 262, 298, 402, 404
Vaughn, S., 239, 240, 242, 279
Vega, E. S., 315, 317
Veléz-Ibañéz, E., 10
Veltkamp, M., 347
Vetter, A. M., 40, 41, 45, 46, 49, 50, 53
Villalva, K. E., 359, 364
Voss, J. F., 382

Vossoughi, S., 89
Vygotsky, L. S., 332, 464

W

Waff, D., 402, 403, 405
Wallowitz, L., 43, 45, 46
Walsh, M., 293
Walter, C. C., 383t, 384
Walton, D., 389
Wang, C., 148
Wang, C. C., 153
Warren, B., 7
Warren, R. P., 383t, 460
Warschauer, M., 27, 361, 462
Warshow, R., 318
Waterhouse, M., 296
Watkins, D., 403
Watts, J., 184
Weaver, C., 336
Webb, A., 467
Wei, L., 277, 278
Weigel, M., 404
Wells, G., 467
Wenger, E., 183, 189, 244, 464
Wentzel, K. R., 424, 429
Wertsch, J. V., 187
Weyand, L., 379n
Whelan, D. L., 40, 49, 53
White, C., 242, 332
Whitley, J. J., 215
Wice, B., 400
Wickens, C. M., 28, 341
Wiesel, E., 137
Wiesner, D., 297
Wigfield, A., 178, 242, 346, 351, 424, 429
Wilcox, K. C., 365
Wilder, L., 382, 383t, 385
Wilhelm, J., 177
Wilhelm, J. D., 169, 170, 209, 421, 458
Wilkinson, B., 183, 443
Wilkinson, I. A., 468
Wilkinson, L., 84
Willander, T., 191, 192
Willett, K., 365, 367
Williams, B. J., 14
Williams, B. T., 67, 272
Williams, C. L., 344
Williams, G., 371
Williams, J., 303, 357
Williams, J. D., 278
Williams, J. M., 69
Williams, R., 207
Wilson, A. A., 183, 185, 192
Wilson, E. O., 327
Wilson, S., 403
Wiltse, L., 66

Wineburg, S. S., 191, 242
Winkeljohann, R., 421
Winn, M. T., 66, 71, 402, 408
Winograd, K., 192
Wisenbaker, J. M., 11
Wissinger, D. R., 183
Wissman, K. K., 28, 32, 67, 257, 270, 271, 272
Witek, J., 310, 313, 316
Wixson, K. K., 245
Wojnowski, B., 187
Wolfe, C. R., 183
Wolfe, P., 317
Wolk, S., 200, 318
Womack, E., 71
Wood, D. J., 429, 440
Wood, D. R., 215
Woods, A., 186
Woodson, C. G., 218
Wortham, S., 86
Worthy, J., 174
Wright, B. W., 311
Wright, D. E., 402, 409
Wynhoff Olsen, A., 138, 382

Y

Yagelski, R., 365
Yang, G., 312, 313
Yang, H. C., 25
Yep, G. A., 40
Yi, Y., 32, 365, 368
Yonezawa, S., 153
Yoo, B., 204
Yosso, T. J., 68
You, W., 346
Young, J. P., 11, 402
Yu, F., 365
Yuen, J., 100

Z

Zambrana, R. E., 29
Zammit, K., 293
Zancanella, D., 143
Zarate, O., 317
Zeichner, K., 159
Zeller-Berkman, S., 153
Zellermayer, M., 411
Zenkov, K., 148, 153
Zentella, A. C., 361
Zhang, Y., 135
Zhang, Z., 373
Zhu, W., 358, 359
Zimmerman, B., 444, 446
Zollman, A., 192
Zumbrunn, S., 152

Subject Index

Note: The letter *f* after a page number indicates figure; *t* indicates table; and *n* indicates note.

Abstract language, 325–326, 325*t*, 326*f*, 329
Academic English, 83–84, 86–87
Academic language
   developing, 331–336, 334*t*–335*t*
   overview, 323–326, 325*t*, 326*f*, 336–337
   subject-area learning and, 326–336, 327*t*, 328*t*, 334*t*–335*t*
Academic literacy. *See also* Disciplinary literacy
   argumentation and, 384–386
   engaged academic literacy, 243–254
   overview, 182–187, 193–194
Accommodations, 99–101
Activist literacy, 403
Adaptations, 99–101
Adolescent literacy in general, 3–5, 17–18, 406
Adult-initiated texts, 49–50
Advanced Placement (AP), 238
African American English, 15
African American Verbal Traditions (AVT), 14–15
Age, 47–51
Agency
   engagement with LGBTQQ-themed literacy and, 50–51
   heterosexual hegemony and, 56–57
   multimodal digital texts and, 297–300
   out-of-school literacies and, 67
Argumentation
   Argumentative Writing Project's (AWP), 380–382
   disciplinary frame, 383*t*, 384–386
   formalist frame, 382–384, 383*t*
   instruction and, 381–394, 383*t*

   learning and, 381–394, 383*t*
   missing-in-action text and, 241
   overview, 379–380, 393–394
   reader response frame, 383*t*
   social practice frame, 383*t*
Argumentative Writing Project's (AWP), 380–382, 394. *See also* Argumentation
Arts, 258–259
Asexual youth. *See* LGBTQQ (lesbian, gay, bisexual, transgender, queer, questioning) youth
Assessment
   disabilities and, 98
   identity development and, 117–119
   race and, 201–202
   of students' multimodal productions, 303–305
   writing and, 138, 450–452
Assets-based pedagogies, 83–85
Assigned reading, 248–249, 251
Assistive technology (AT), 101–102, 106
Attitudes toward reading. *See* Pleasure in reading
Authentic reading and writing, 458, 463–464, 471
Autonomous model, 64, 202

B

Background knowledge, 16, 458, 462–463
Basic interpersonal communicative skills (BICS), 324. *See also* Academic language
Bilingual Education Act, 79–80

Bilingual students. *See also* Emergent bilingual youth; TRANSLATE (Teaching Reading and New Strategic Language Approaches to English Learners) approach
  collaborative translation and, 279–282, 282t
  focus on, 78–79
  overview, 15, 276–279, 288–289
Biliteracy, 81–82. *See also* Emergent bilingual youth
Bisexual youth. *See* LGBTQQ (lesbian, gay, bisexual, transgender, queer, questioning) youth
Black adolescents. *See* Cultural contexts; Identities; Race
Bronfenbrenner's model, 110–123
Bullying, 209–210

C

Challenging text reading. *See also* Reading; Scaffolded reading experience (SRE)
  criticisms of the standards regarding, 422–424
  overview, 421–422, 440
  recommendations, 424–426
Chronosystems, 110–112, 122–123
Civil Rights Act of 1964, 79–80
Class, 29–33, 69, 205t, 206–208
Classroom dialogue. *See also* Dialogical practices
  close reading and, 467–469
  historical context of, 218–219
  overview, 8, 215–218, 227–228
Classroom practices, 366–368, 369–370, 445–446
Classroom-based inquiry, 402–404
Close reading
  21st-century literacies, 459–469, 461f
  identities and, 9
  overview, 457–459, 469–471
  research studies, 470–471
  scaffolded reading experience and, 431–434, 431f, 433f
Code breaking, 14–15
Code switching, 14–15, 361, 365, 372
Cognitive academic language proficiency (CALP), 324. *See also* Academic language
Cognitive factors, 360, 362
Collaboration, 447, 448
Collaborative design, 404
Collaborative inquiry, 398–415, 399f, 414f
Collaborative meaning making, 251–252. *See also* Meaning making
Collaborative translation. *See also* TRANSLATE (Teaching Reading and New Strategic Language Approaches to English Learners) approach
  evaluating translations, 286–287
  making translations fit the text, 287–288
  oral translation, 282–284
  overview, 279–282, 282t, 288–289
  writing down translations, 284–287, 286f

College and Career Readiness Anchor Standards, 443–444
College-age students, 318
Comics reading
  diverse learners and, 312–313
  identities and, 312
  instruction and, 313–318
  overview, 310–311, 318–319
  research studies, 311–312
Common Core State Standards (CCSS)
  adolescent literacy and, 3–5
  argumentation and, 381
  close reading and, 457–459, 459–461, 465
  collaborative translation and, 281
  criticisms of, 422–424
  disciplinary literacy and, 186–187, 192
  multimodal composition and, 261–262
  overview, 17
  pleasure in reading and, 169, 179
  reading challenging text, 421–422
  recommendations, 424–426
  scaffolded reading experience and, 430, 440
  writing and, 138, 443–444
  young adult literature and, 348–349
Communication, 16–17
Communities, 53, 401–402
Compassion, 56–57
Competence, 31–33
Complex Instruction approach, 366–367
Composition, multimodal. *See* Multimodal composition
Composition studies
  academic literacy and, 183
  English language learners (ELLs) and, 364–366, 369–370, 372, 374
Concept-oriented reading instruction (CORI), 178
Construction of literacies. *See* Literacies, construction of
Content-area instruction. *See also* Instruction; Subject-matter classrooms
  academic language and, 182–187, 326–336, 327t, 328t, 334t–335t
  disciplinary literacy and, 191–193
  English language learners (ELLs) and, 367, 369–370, 373–374
  missing-in-action text and, 238–239
  writing instruction and, 445–446, 449
Contexts, 44–47, 132–135
Contextualizing, 241
Counternarratives, 67–72
Criminal behavior, 71–72
Critical collaborative inquiries, 399. *See also* Collaborative inquiry
Critical feminism theory, 44
Critical literacy
  academic literacy and, 184
  close reading and, 458, 466–467
  dialogical practices and, 225
  identities and, 33
  queer theory and, 43–44

Subject Index

Critical literature pedagogy (CLP), 466–467
Critical media literacy, 23, 27. *See also* 21st-century literacies; Media literacy
Critical race theory, 44, 67–72
Critical youth engagement, 153
Cross-disciplinary collaboration, 185
Cross-site collaborations, 410–413. *See also* Collaborative inquiry
Cultural contexts
   English language learners (ELLs) and, 373
   home and school discourses and, 6–10
   identity development and, 119–122
   intersectional identities and, 52–54
   out-of-school literacies and, 63–67
   overview, 6–15
   in youth media and pop culture, 29–33
Cultural historical activity theory, 188
Curriculum. *See also* English language arts (ELA) curriculum; Instruction
   21st-century literacies and, 21–22
   Argumentative Writing Project's (AWP), 380–382
   collaborative inquiry and, 403–404
   comics and graphic novels, 316–318
   disabilities and, 99–102
   engaged academic literacy and, 245
   English language arts (ELA), 131–135
   English language learners (ELLs) and, 366–368, 370–372, 373–374
   heterosexual hegemony and, 54–55
   identity development and, 117–119
   multimodal composition and, 261–262
   school fit and, 200
   writing instruction and, 445–446
   young adult literature and, 348–350
Curriculum-based measurement (CBM), 451. *See also* Assessment

D

Deficit narratives, 66–67
Demographics, 81–82, 148–149
Design-based implementation research (DBIR), 237–238
Developmental processes, 110–112, 152–153. *See also* Identity development
Dialogical practices. *See also* Classroom dialogue
   close reading and, 458, 467–469
   historical context of, 218–219
   overview, 215–218, 227–228
   research studies, 219–227
Digital literacy. *See also* Media literacy; New literacies
   academic literacy and, 185–186
   collaborative inquiry and, 413
   importance of, 294–295
   multimodal composition and, 270–271
   overview, 23, 26–29, 152–153
   race and, 203
Digital storytelling, 297–300

Digital technologies, 27–29
Disabilities
   general education curriculum and, 99–102
   overview, 93–95, 106–107
   research studies, 95–106
Disciplinary discourse communities, 189–191
Disciplinary literacy. *See also* Academic literacy
   argumentation and, 382, 383*t*, 384–386
   close reading and, 471
   overview, 6–15, 182, 186, 187–194
   policy and, 186–187
Discourses
   academic literacy and, 183
   disciplinary literacy and, 188–191
   home and school, 6–10
   overview, 130–131
   power and, 15–16
   reconstructing literacies and, 141
   rules of, 15–16
Discrimination, 79–81
Dispositions, 249–250. *See also* Students
Domain knowledge, 359*f*, 360
Dropping out of school
   counternarratives and, 71–72
   emergent bilingual youth and, 81–82
   literacy development and, 153
   photovoice projects and, 148–149
   school fit and, 199–200, 199*t*, 210–212
During-reading activities, 427*f*, 428, 433, 437
Dynamic bilingualism, 85–86

E

Ecological systems model, 110–123
Elementary and Secondary Educational Act (ESEA), 79–80
Emergent bilingual youth. *See also* Bilingual students; Biliteracy; English language learners (ELLs); TRANSLATE (Teaching Reading and New Strategic Language Approaches to English Learners) approach
   academic English and, 86–87
   academic language and, 327
   demographics of, 81–82
   dynamic bilingualism and, 85–86
   focus on, 78–79
   identity development and, 113
   leveraging and, 87–89
   missing-in-action text and, 236
   overview, 89–90, 276–279
   photovoice projects and, 148–149
   policy and, 79–81
   research studies, 82–85
Engaged academic literacy
   instruction and, 247–252
   missing-in-action text and, 243–244
   overview, 253–254
   routines to support, 244–252

Engagement. *See* Engaged academic literacy; School engagement
English language arts (ELA) curriculum. *See also* Curriculum; Instruction
   argumentation and, 381–394, 383*t*
   Argumentative Writing Project's (AWP), 380–382
   comics and graphic novels, 317–318
   construction of literacies within, 136–141, 143
   multimodal composition and, 261–262
   overview, 131–135
   reconstructing literacies and, 141–143
   "Through Students' Eyes" (TSE) project and, 153
English language learners (ELLs). *See also* Emergent bilingual youth
   academic language and, 327
   collaborative inquiry and, 411–412
   composition and, 358–362, 359*f*
   future research regarding, 370–374
   missing-in-action text and, 236
   overview, 276–279, 357–358
   research studies, 362–374
   theory and, 370–374
Enjoying reading. *See* Pleasure in reading
Essential identity model, 41
Everyday language, 324, 325–326, 325*t*, 326*f*, 329
Exosystems, 110–112, 117–119
Explanation, 447
Explicit instruction, 96–97. *See also* Instruction

F

Family, 119–122
Fanfiction, 12, 26, 113
Formalist frame, 382–384, 383*t*
Formative assessments, 450–451. *See also* Assessment
Framing, 382–383
Friends, 114–116, 279, 312
Functional analysis, 333, 335–336, 335*t*
Functional language analysis (FLA), 188–189
Functional linguistics, 188–189
Funds of knowledge, 10–13, 203

G

Gangs, 114–116
Gay youth. *See* LGBTQQ (lesbian, gay, bisexual, transgender, queer, questioning) youth
Gender, 29–33, 208–210, 407. *See also* Gender expression
Gender expression. *See also* Heterosexual hegemony; Identities; LGBTQQ (lesbian, gay, bisexual, transgender, queer, questioning) youth; Sexual identities
   age and, 47–51
   curricular and pedagogical implications of, 54–57
   engagement with LGBTQQ-themed literacy and, 47–51
   heterosexual hegemony and, 45–46, 51–54, 57–58
   intersectional identities and, 52–54
   overview, 38–39
   research studies, 40–44
   TRANSLATE approach and, 279
Graphic novel reading
   diverse learners and, 312–313
   identities and, 312
   instruction and, 313–318
   overview, 310–311, 318–319
   research studies, 311–312
Guided practice, 447
Guided reading, 280–281

H

Heterosexual hegemony. *See also* Gender expression; LGBTQQ (lesbian, gay, bisexual, transgender, queer, questioning) youth; Sexual identities
   age and, 47–51
   collaborative inquiry and, 405
   contextual characteristics, 44–47
   curricular and pedagogical implications of, 54–57
   identities and, 51–54
   intersectional identities and, 52–54
   overview, 38–39, 57–58
   research studies, 40–44
   school fit and, 209–210
Hip-hop, 24–25, 31–32
Historical language, 330. *See also* Academic language
Home factors, 6–15, 119–122
Homework, 238, 248–249

I

Identities. *See also* Sexual identities
   age and, 47–51
   collaborative inquiry and, 403
   comics reading and, 312
   engagement with LGBTQQ-themed literacy and, 47–51
   English language learners (ELLs), 361
   heterosexual hegemony and, 39–44, 51–54, 57–58
   intersectional, 52–54
   multimodal digital texts and, 297–300
   out-of-school literacies and, 31–33, 63–67
   overview, 5–6
   popular culture and, 33–34
   reading identities, 5–6
   writing and, 152
   in youth media and pop culture, 29–34

Identity development. *See also* Developmental processes
  Bronfenbrenner's model of, 110–112
  dialogical practices and, 222–223
  English language learners (ELLs) and, 365–366, 369–370, 373
  overview, 110–111, 123
  research studies, 112–123
  "Through Students' Eyes" (TSE) project and, 157
Ideological perspectives, 38, 63–64
Ill-literacies, 31–32
Independent practice, 447
Individualized education programs, 99–101
Information and communication technologies (ICTs), 452. *See also* New literacies
Initiation–response–evaluation (IRE), 218–219, 467–468
Initiation–response–feedback (IRF), 218–219
Instruction. *See also* Content-area instruction; Curriculum; English language arts (ELA) curriculum; Writing instruction
  argumentation and, 380–382, 381–394, 383t
  close reading and, 459–469, 461f
  collaborative translation and, 279–282, 282t
  dialogical practices and, 215–218
  disabilities and, 95–106, 104–106
  disciplinary literacy and, 194
  emergent bilingual youth and, 84–86
  engaged academic literacy and, 243–254
  English language learners (ELLs) and, 366–368, 370–372, 373–374
  graphic novels and, 313–318
  heterosexual hegemony in school contexts and, 45–46
  instructional design, 9–10, 244–247, 278, 404
  multimodal digital texts and, 295–306
  pleasure in reading and, 178–180
  scaffolded reading experience and, 431f, 433f, 435f, 436f, 438f, 439f
  school fit and, 200
  writing instruction and, 443–444
  young adult literature and, 348–350
Internet use, 453
Intersectional identities, 52–54. *See also* Identities
Intersex youth. *See* LGBTQQ (lesbian, gay, bisexual, transgender, queer, questioning) youth

J

Juvenile detention center confinement, 71–72

L

Language diversity, 132–133
Language learning, 26
Language status, 361, 362
Language-based tasks, 332–335, 334t–335t
Latin@ youth. *See* Cultural contexts; Emergent bilingual youth; Identities; Race
Lau v. Nichols (1974), 80
Learning
  academic language and, 326–336, 327t, 328t, 334t–335t
  argumentation and, 381–394, 383t
  engaged academic literacy and, 245, 248–249
  missing-in-action text and, 241
  purposeful learning, 248–249
Lesbian youth. *See* LGBTQQ (lesbian, gay, bisexual, transgender, queer, questioning) youth
Leveraging, 87–89
LGBTQQ (lesbian, gay, bisexual, transgender, queer, questioning) youth. *See also* Gender expression; Heterosexual hegemony; Identities; Sexual identities
  collaborative inquiry and, 405
  curricular and pedagogical implications of, 54–57
  engagement with LGBTQQ-themed literacy and, 47–51
  funds of knowledge and, 12
  heterosexual hegemony and, 45–46, 51–54
  out-of-school reading and writing and, 33
  queer theory and, 42–44
  research studies, 40–44
  school fit and, 209–210
  in youth media and pop culture, 29–33
Limited English proficient (LEP) students. *See* Emergent bilingual youth
Linear development model, 41–42
Linguistics, 188–189
Literacies, construction of
  English language arts (ELA) curriculum and, 132–143
  overview, 129–132, 143
  photovoice projects and, 155–159
  reconstructing literacies and, 141–143
Literary argumentation. *See* Argumentation
Literature, 136–137
Literature-related argumentative writing, 381. *See also* Argumentation

M

Macrosystems, 110–112, 119–122
Meaning making, 251–252, 259–261, 367
Media literacy. *See also* 21st-century literacies; Critical media literacy; Digital literacy
  fanfiction and, 26
  identities and, 29–33
  overview, 23, 26–29
  production of literacy and, 25–26
Mesosystems, 110–112, 114–116
Metacognitive conversations, 249–250
Metadiscursive awareness, 458, 464–466

Metaknowledge, 359f, 360
Metaphoric language, 325–326, 325t, 326f
Microsystems, 110–112, 113–114
Missing-in-action text
  discovering, 236–237
  engaged academic literacy and, 243–254
  overview, 253–254
  problem of, 237–240
  subject-matter classrooms and, 240–243
Modeling, 447, 449
Modifications, 99–101
Multicultural texts, 24
Multimodal composition. See also 21st-century literacies; Multimodal digital texts
  comics and graphic novels, 315–316
  examples of, 264–270
  overview, 257–262, 270–272
  research studies, 262–270
  writing instruction and, 452–453
Multimodal digital texts. See also Multimodal composition
  academic literacy and, 185–186
  assessment of, 303–305
  collaborative inquiry and, 413
  creating, 295–303
  disciplinary literacy and, 188, 190
  English language arts (ELA) curriculum and, 133–134
  importance of, 294–295
  overview, 292, 305–306
  responding to, 292–295
Multiple literacies, 203

N

National Writing Project (NWP), 406–407
Navigation of power structures/relations, 15–17
Needs of students. See Students
Neighborhood, 401, 402
Networks, 15–17
New literacies, 64–67, 152–153, 294–295, 452–454. See also 21st-century literacies; Media literacy
New Literacy studies, 129–131
Next Generation Science Standards (NGSS), 3–4, 187, 191
No Child Left Behind (NCLB), 81, 186–187, 261–262
Nominalizations, 329

O

Out-of-school literacies
  counternarratives and, 67–72
  critical race theory and, 67–72
  English language learners (ELLs) and, 361, 368
  heterosexual hegemony and, 46–47
  importance of focusing on, 72–73
  overview, 61–67
  reading and writing groups and, 11
  youth media and pop culture and, 31–33

P

Participatory culture, 23
Participatory photography. See Photovoice projects
Pedagogy
  collaborative inquiry and, 403–404, 411, 414–415
  disabilities and, 102–106
  emergent bilingual youth and, 83–85
  heterosexual hegemony and, 55–56
  photovoice projects and, 155–159
  school fit and, 211–212
Peer feedback, 451
Peer relationships, 114–116, 279, 312
Peer-mediated approaches, 278–279
Photovoice projects
  cultural and literacy gaps and, 150–151
  literacies and pedagogies, 155–159
  overview, 148–150, 163–165
  preservice teachers, 159–163
  "Through Students' Eyes" (TSE) project, 148–150, 152–155
Pleasure in reading
  cultivating, 174–178
  importance of, 172–173
  neglect of, 173–174
  overview, 169–172, 178–180
Pluralistic stance, 130–131, 132–134, 141, 143
Poetry Inside Out (PIO) project, 411–412
Policy, 186–187, 191, 203–204, 211–212
Popular culture. See also 21st-century literacies
  graphic novels and, 313–314
  identities and, 29–33
  identity development and, 119–120
  overview, 21–26, 33–34
  production of literacy and, 25–26
Popularity, 312. See also Peer relationships
Positive Youth Development (PYD) program, 409
Postreading activities, 427f, 428, 433–434, 437
Poverty, 205t, 206–208. See also Socioeconomic status
Power, 15–17, 405
Prereading activities, 426–428, 427f, 432, 435–437, 436f
Preservice teachers, 159–164
Procedural knowledge, 359f, 360
Process writing approach, 449. See also Writing
Process–person–context–time (PPCT) model, 111
Professional development, 193–194, 242, 370
Proficiency, 194
Project-based learning, 237–238
Proyecto Latin@ project, 409–410

Purposeful learning, 248–249. *See also* Learning

Q

Queer theory, 42–44
Queer youth. *See* LGBTQQ (lesbian, gay, bisexual, transgender, queer, questioning) youth
Questioning youth. *See* LGBTQQ (lesbian, gay, bisexual, transgender, queer, questioning) youth

R

Race. *See also* Cultural contexts; Racism
  collaborative inquiry and, 405
  counternarratives and, 68–70
  home and school discourses and, 7
  identity development and, 119–122
  intersectional identities and, 52–54
  school fit and, 200–204, 205t, 208
  social class and, 208
  young adult literature and, 24
  in youth media and pop culture, 29–33
Racism, 63, 65–67, 68–70, 72. *See also* Race
RAND Research Study Group (RRSG), 461–462, 461f, 469–470
Reader-response frame, 382, 383t, 387–388
Reading, 136–137, 143, 259–261. *See also* Challenging text reading; Pleasure in reading
Reading comprehension, 240
Reading enjoyment. *See* Pleasure in reading
Reading identities. *See* Identities
Religious communities, 13, 206
Resilience, 67, 119–122
Response to literature
  argumentation and, 387–388
  examples of, 264–270
  overview, 257–262, 270–272
Responsive teaching, 98. *See also* Instruction
Revised Publisher's Criteria for the Standards (RPC), close reading and, 457–459, 460, 469
Risk, 50–51, 56–57

S

Scaffolded reading experience (SRE). *See also* Challenging text reading; Scaffolding
  examples of, 431–437, 431f, 433f, 435f, 436f, 438f, 439f
  overview, 426–430, 427f, 440
  to support close reading, 431f
Scaffolding. *See also* Scaffolded reading experience (SRE)
  disabilities and, 96
  disciplinary literacy and, 188–189
  identities and, 9
  overview, 421–422, 429
  writing instruction and, 447
School contexts, 6–10, 45–46, 366–368, 369–370. *See also* School fit
School engagement. *See also* School fit
  engaged academic literacy, 243–254
  literacy development and, 153
  pleasure in reading and, 173
  young adult literature and, 343, 345–346, 347–348, 351
School fit. *See also* School engagement
  overview, 199–200, 199t, 210–212
  race and, 200–204, 205t
  sex and gender, 208–210
  social class and, 205t, 206–208
School-based literacies, 361, 402–404
Science, technology, engineering, and mathematics (STEM) reform, 187, 191–193
Science learning, 7, 330. *See also* Academic language
Self-Regulated Strategy Development model (SRSD), 447
Sentiments, 359f, 360
Sexual identities. *See also* Heterosexual hegemony; Identities; LGBTQQ (lesbian, gay, bisexual, transgender, queer, questioning) youth
  age and, 47–51
  curricular and pedagogical implications of, 54–57
  engagement with LGBTQQ-themed literacy and, 47–51
  heterosexual hegemony and, 45–46, 51–54, 57–58
  intersectional identities and, 52–54
  overview, 38–39
  research studies, 40–44
  school fit and, 208–210
Sexuality, 29–33. *See also* Sexual identities
Sheltered instruction observation protocol (SIOP) model, 367–368, 374
Sign systems, 261–262
Social class. *See* Class
Social construction, 187–188, 388
Social contexts, 63–67, 405
Social factors, 29–33, 188–189, 293–294, 361
Social justice, 33. *See also* Identities
Social networking literacy practices, 12–13, 27, 28, 300. *See also* 21st-century literacies; Media literacy
Social systems, 410
Social-efficiency approach, 192
Social-practice frame, 382, 383t, 388–393
Sociocritical literacies, 89
Sociocultural approach
  close reading and, 461–462, 461f
  dialogical practices and, 225–227
  disciplinary literacy and, 187–188
  emergent bilingual youth and, 84, 88
  English language learners (ELLs), 359–360

Socioeconomic status, 7, 205t, 206–208
  English language arts (ELA) curriculum and, 135
Sociopolitical questioning, 225–227
Speaking, 139–141, 142
Stance, 400–401. *See also* Collaborative inquiry
Standardization, 134–135, 143
Standardized testing, 27
Standards. *See also* Common Core State Standards (CCSS)
  argumentation and, 381
  close reading and, 457–459
  criticisms of, 422–424
  disciplinary literacy and, 186–187
  English language arts (ELA) curriculum and, 132–135
  missing-in-action text and, 242
  overview, 17
  reading challenging text, 421–422
  recommendations, 424–426
  reconstructing literacies and, 141
  writing and, 138
  young adult literature and, 348–349
STEM reform. *See* Science, technology, engineering, and mathematics (STEM) reform
Storytelling, 297–300
Structuration theory, 410
Struggling learners, 66–67
Students
  engaged academic literacy and, 245, 249–250
  overview, 199–200, 199t
  race and, 200–204, 205t
Students' Right to Their Own Language resolution, 14–15
Subject-matter classrooms. *See also* Content-area instruction
  conditions of, 240–243
  engaged academic literacy and, 243–254
  missing-in-action text and, 236–237
  overview, 235–236, 253–254
Summary writing, 447–448
Supported teacher collaborative inquiry, 405. *See also* Collaborative inquiry
Surveillance, 117–119, 227
Systematic Functional Linguistics (SFL) approach, 367, 368–369
Systematic instruction, 96–97. *See also* Instruction

T

Teacher Inquiry Communities (TIC) Network, 406–407
Teachers
  argumentation and, 381
  collaborative inquiry and, 404–408, 414–415
  dialogical practices and, 215–218
  heterosexual hegemony and, 56
  heterosexual hegemony in school contexts and, 45
  photovoice projects and, 159–164
  writing instruction and, 445–446
Teaching to Learn Project, 398–400, 399f, 410–411, 413–414, 414f. *See also* Collaborative inquiry
Testing, 117–119, 201–202, 242
Tetrahedral model of learning, 429
Text features, 359f, 360, 471
Text-based discussions, 249–252
Textbooks, 185–186, 246–247, 253–254
Text–task alignment, 245–246, 248–249
Textual approach, 188–189
Thematic units, 317–318
"Through Students' Eyes" (TSE) project
  literacies and pedagogies, 155–159
  overview, 148–150, 152–155, 163–165
  preservice teachers, 159–163
Time for reading, 176, 178–179
Title VI of the Civil Rights Act in 1964, 79–80
Transactional theories
  dialogical practices and, 221–222
  English language learners (ELLs), 358–359, 359f, 370–371
  multimodal composition and, 270–271
  reading and writing as transaction, 259–261
Transfer of knowledge, 364
Transgender youth. *See* LGBTQQ (lesbian, gay, bisexual, transgender, queer, questioning) youth
Translanguaging, 277, 372
TRANSLATE (Teaching Reading and New Strategic Language Approaches to English Learners) approach. *See also* Bilingual students; Emergent bilingual youth
  collaborative translation and, 279–282, 282t
  evaluating translations, 286–287
  making translations fit the text, 287–288
  oral translation and, 282–284
  overview, 276–279, 288–289
  writing down translations, 284–287, 286f
Translation
  evaluating translations, 286–287
  making translations fit the text, 287–288
  oral translation, 282–284
  overview, 277–278, 288–289
  writing down translations, 284–287, 286f
21st-century literacies. *See also* Digital literacy; Media literacy; Multimodal composition; New literacies; Popular culture
  close reading and, 459–469, 461f
  disabilities and, 104–106
  identities and, 29–33
  overview, 21–22, 26–29, 152–153

V

Visual literacy, 314–315
Vocabulary, academic. *See* Academic language

W

Warranted assertability, 392–393
Writing. *See also* Writing instruction
  academic literacy and, 184
  comics and graphic novels, 315–316
  construction of literacies and, 138–139
  disciplinary literacy and, 190
  identities and, 9
  pleasure in reading and, 176
  reconstructing literacies and, 142–143
  "Through Students' Eyes" (TSE) project and, 152–159
  as transaction, 259–261
Writing across the curriculum (WAC) approach, 184
Writing in the disciplines (WID) approach, 184, 192–193
Writing instruction. *See also* Instruction; Writing
  new literacies and, 452–454
  overview, 454–455
  research studies, 444–452
Written language, 325–326, 325*t*, 326*f*

Y

Young adult literature
  future research regarding, 350–351
  instruction and, 348–350
  overview, 23, 24–25, 341–342, 350–351
  research studies, 342–348
Youth participatory action research (YPAR), 153, 154, 408–410
Youth-initiated texts, 49–50